19**6**5

After initial setbacks, we had Pakistan on the ropes. They were reeling and had no ammunition left, while we could have gone on for another three weeks. India's old failing, the lack of a killer instinct, came to the fore with people at the top giving wrong information and taking horrendous decisions. For those of us who fought, we were robbed of a decisive victory. A definitive account of those dramatic days.

—Air Marshal Philip Rajkumar, VrC

After his earlier bestselling book on the 1962 conflict with China, the author seamlessly shifts gears and takes us to the 1965 war with Pakistan. From the Rann of Kutch to Kashmir, then to the plains of the Punjab, it's a breathtaking narrative of a war that was fought both on the ground and in the air.

—Lieutenant General Ajai Singh
17 Poona Horse / Butur Dograndi

For those of us who fought and saw so many of our comrades die—many of whom remained unsung for half a century—this book is a fitting tribute to their memory. The author's research and understanding of what and how things happened is both excellent and incisive.

—Major General Somprakash Jhingon
8 Garhwal Rifles / Butur Dograndi

We did all the hard work, time and again coming back with all the information we could gather, and yet, tragically, it never permeated down to the fighting troops. Both in 1962 and 1965, there seemed to be a mental block when it came to using air power to achieve our objectives. The author once again lays all the cards, face up, on the table as only he can. Every Indian needs to read this book.

—Wing Commander Jag Mohan Nath, MVC & Bar
No. 106 Squadron

Also by Shiv Kunal Verma

Ocean to Sky: India from the Air
Military World Games
The Northeast Palette
Assam Rifles: 1835 to 2010
The Long Road to Siachen: The Question Why
Northeast Trilogy (East of Kanchendzonga, Brahma's Creation, and Children of the Dawn)
Courage and Conviction: An Autobiography: General V. K. Singh
1962: The War That Wasn't
South India Trilogy (Tamil Nadu and Puducherry)
Life and Culture in Northeast India
Rainbow's End: Welham Boys' School

1965

A WESTERN
SUNRISE

India's War With Pakistan

SHIV KUNAL VERMA

ALEPH

ALEPH

ALEPH BOOK COMPANY
An independent publishing firm
promoted by *Rupa Publications India*

First published in India in 2021
by Aleph Book Company
7/16 Ansari Road, Daryaganj
New Delhi 110 002

ISBN: 978-93-90652-46-4

1 3 5 7 9 10 8 6 4 2

Printed at Thomson Press India Ltd., Faridabad

For my mother, Usha,
and
the rank and file
of the
Indian Army and the Air Force
who
held the line

Yes, makin' mock o' uniforms that guard you while you sleep
Is cheaper than them uniforms, an' they're starvation cheap;
An' hustlin' drunken soldiers when they're goin' large a bit
Is five times better business than paradin' in full kit.

Then it's Tommy this, an' Tommy that, an' "Tommy, 'ow's yer soul?
But it's "Thin red line of 'eroes" when the drums begin to roll,
The drums begin to roll, my boys, the drums begin to roll,
O it's "Thin red line of 'eroes" when the drums begin to roll.

— 'Tommy' by Rudyard Kipling

CONTENTS

MAPS

The following maps have been included in the photo inserts:

India–Pakistan Border
Rann of Kutch: April 1965
Rann of Kutch: Final Pak Assault
Operation Ablaze
Operation Gibraltar: The Master Plan
Operation Gibraltar: Initial Indian Deployment
Capture of Haji Pir
Operation Grand Slam (Chhamb–Jaurian–Akhnoor)
Lahore Sector
Barki (7 Infantry Division)
Khem Karan
Western Sector (11 and 1 Corps)
2nd Battle of Chawinda
26 Infantry Division

FIGHTING FROM THE ROPES

The Hawker Hunters of Flight Lieutenant Alfred Tyrone Cooke and Flying Officer (later Wing Commander) Subodh Chandra Mamgain's had landed in Dum Dum for the second time on the morning of 7 September 1965. They had first become airborne at daybreak, as a combat air patrol (CAP) covering Wing Commander (later Air Chief Marshal) Denis Anthony LaFontaine's four-aircraft formation over East Pakistan and had touched down only after the other aircraft had safely returned. Cooke and Mamgain had been scrambled again and after taking off had orbited at 25,000 feet, 50 miles north of Dum Dum, in response to two bogeys that radar had picked up inside East Pakistan, around the time the Pakistan Air Force's (PAF) F-86 Sabres had first hit Kalaikunda. They returned after the two Pakistani planes went back into East Pakistan. Tired and hungry after two operational sorties, they had just scrounged some tea from an airman while their aircraft were being refuelled, when they were scrambled for the third time.

Once again the two Hunters were asked by 411 SU, the radar unit at Rampurhat, to hold in the same area where the bogeys had reappeared on the East Pakistan side. The radar unit instructed them that the Pakistani aircraft were to be engaged only if they crossed the border. Cooke was convinced that the two aircraft that had reappeared on the radar screens were a decoy and he kept calling the ground controllers asking them if there was anything on 55 SU's radar that would suggest incoming aircraft towards Kalaikunda. As they were orbiting and scanning the skies for visual contact, the voice of a very excited controller came across on the RT. Kalaikunda was indeed under attack again; could the Hunters make it there?

The three Vampire pilots killed on 1 September at Chhamb—Bhagwagar, Joshi, and Bharadwaj—were either course mates or close buddies of Cooke who used to hang around with him in Poona. 'I was seething with anger and had been praying for a chance to get back at the Pakistanis. The youngest of five brothers and four sisters, I had survived with my fists and was also a boxer in school. In the ring, as an eight-year-old, I had fought a thirteen-year-old who thrashed me in round one. My brother, who was my second, asked me during the break what I was going to do about it. In round two, I went after the guy with a vengeance and in round three, he ran away, saying I was a lunatic. My father had given me a piece of advice which kept ringing in my head—pick a fight only if you know that you will be the one to finish it. I had a lot of self-belief; I knew I was one of the best air defence pilots in the air force, if not the best,' Cooke would say later.

'We also knew what had happened earlier in the morning at KKD...and now the Sabres were back. I checked my fuel level, asked Mamgain to check his and then told the controller: "Ok...give us pigeons back to base". He said, "230 degrees 110 miles," and we set course as fast as possible at 0.95 Mach/550 knots, descending all the time. Mamgain was lagging behind and not responding to my calls so I told him I'd get behind him and shoot him down. That threat had the desired affect and he came on the RT and said he was scared. I told him I was equally scared but it was our duty to defend our base. "Just remember this is what we trained for and try not to think of anything else." A few seconds later he was back in position.'[1]

As the two Hunters descended below 5,000 feet, they lost communication with 411 SU. Cooke tried to switch to Kalaikunda, but the air traffic control tower was under attack. By then Cooke and Mamgain were at 500 feet and had deaccelerated to a more manageable 500 knots. They were still 10 miles from Kalaikunda when they could see plumes of black smoke emanating from the airfield, for the Sabres had managed to hit two Canberras on the ground, which were burning fiercely. Cooke called out to Mamgain, 'Look at those bastards shooting up our home. Let's get at them.'

The Hunters were now in visual contact with the Sabres. Cooke initially thought there were six aircraft in a classic ground attack circuit, with three aircraft on the western side of the north–south aligned runway, and three more on the eastern side. In actual fact, the second attacking formation only had four Sabres, with only one aircraft on the eastern side of the runway. After the first attack, Pakistan's Squadron Leader (later Air Marshal, retired as vice chief of the PAF) Shabbir Hussain Syed had dropped out, leaving it to Flight Lieutenants M.A. Haleem, Abdul Basheer, and Tariq Habib Khan and Flying Officer Afzal Khan to deliver the second coup de grace at Kalaikunda. Haleem was leading the formation with Basheer as his wingman, while the other two aircraft made up the other section.

Cooke called out to Mamgain that he would engage the three Sabres on the western side and that he should go after the others. He signed off: 'Good luck, and let's give those buggers hell!' Compared to the Sabres, the Hunters were flying extremely fast. Cooke went after the aircraft that was on a strafing run. 'He must have been warned by the others and broke off from his dive and did a hard right-hand turn to evade me.' With hundreds of airmen watching on the ground, Cooke struggled to get the Sabre in his sights and once he did, fired a short quarter second burst as he went through his line of flight. With his extra speed, Cooke gained some height, keeping the Sabre in sight.

Cooke, though outnumbered, had his teeth in the Sabres and got behind Afzal Khan's aircraft, chasing it so low that trees were flashing past. As the engagement developed into a classic dogfight, 'he jettisoned his long-range drop tanks so I jettisoned mine as well and went after him again. What followed was a series of tight turns where he would out-turn me and then reverse so that I would end up in front of him and I would use the power of my Rolls Royce Avon engine to get out of his line of fire.'

The extra thrust of the Hunter had literally allowed Cooke to stand vertically on his tail. The Sabre would fall off and, to avoid stalling, he had no choice but to dive towards the ground to build up speed again. Cooke, who had been extensively trained in low-level air combat by Squadron Leader (later Wing Commander) Onkar Nath 'Piloo' Kacker, continued to follow the Sabre, both pilots doing their best to cut speed, fall back, turn and get behind the other. 'This manoeuvre is referred to as "scissors" and it continued for quite some time and [often] we would criss-cross so close to one other that we could see each other's face. I always maintained a position above him as one of the lessons drilled into me by Piloo Kacker was: "Always stay above the enemy and stay behind him".'

Finally, after what seemed like an eternity but was probably ninety seconds of high drama, Cooke got himself into a favourable position and started firing at Afzal Khan from a distance of about 450 yards. Khan was desperately diving and trying to do a right-hand turn to break contact with the chasing Hunter, which, in turn, had another Sabre trying to close in. 'At this time, I noticed that he increased his angle of dive to get away from me and I knew instinctively that he would have been warned by one of his comrades who would also [get] behind me. By then we were very close to the ground and I could see him trying to raise his nose to get level. I was closing in very fast and still firing my four Aden cannons. I broke away from him when I was less than 100 yards and directly behind him when his aircraft exploded approximately 30 feet above the ground and was engulfed in a fireball. I was quite shaken as a result and pulled up sharply, immediately taking on the other Sabre and I managed to get behind him as well.'

The second Sabre was flown by Tariq Habib Khan, who pulled up to 4,000 feet with Cooke hard on his tail. Going into a sharp wing-over manoeuvre, the Sabre went into a vertical dive with the Hunter firing at him. 'I had my gunsight on him and I was astonished that I was not hitting him as he continued in the dive. He started pulling out of the dive and I hesitated, still wondering why he was not being hit, when I realized I was going to fly into the ground so I pulled back on the joystick with my finger still on the trigger and, in the process, expended all my remaining ammunition.'

Unknown to Cooke, in what was a huge blunder, his aircraft and Mamgain's had been loaded with practice ball ammunition instead of high explosive (HE) shells as required for combat sorties during war time. This was why Cooke could see his bullets hitting the Sabre but not having the desired impact. As he pulled out of his dive, he was less than 50 feet above the ground and quite shaken by the experience. Tariq had broken contact and escaped with his badly damaged Sabre. 'I got my bearings and equilibrium back quickly and realized I was a mile south of the airfield. I then saw Mamgain doing a leisurely turn to port about 1,000 feet above the airfield with a Sabre closing in on him from 1,500 yards behind. I called out: "Hard turn port there's a Sabre on your tail," and Mamgain did just that.' Cooke was now on the tail of the last remaining Sabre whose pilot realized he was now the one being hunted. Desperate to shake Cooke off, and unaware that the Hunter was without ammunition, the Sabre started doing aerobatics over the airfield. Calling to Mamgain to come and 'shoot the bugger down' Cooke stayed behind the Sabre as he desperately headed east, finally breaking off as the Sabre crossed into East Pakistan.

So intent was Cooke on chasing down the third Sabre that he hadn't noticed the puffs of grey-black exploding anti-aircraft shells around him as the ack-ack (anti-aircraft) guns around Kalaikunda finally opened up. Cooke was not in the mood to take chances with trigger-happy air defence gunners. He climbed to 10,000 feet which immediately gave him radio contact with 411 SU. As he looked around, he saw his left wing tip was shattered and the pilot tube was pointing upwards, which meant he was without an air speed indicator (ASI). He was also critically low on fuel, so he set course for Dum Dum, asking 411 SU to scramble Hunters to shepherd him in as his ASI was damaged.

With 411 SU failing to respond, Cooke decided to land anyway. Asking the Dum Dum tower for permission to land, he was told, 'Negative, there is a Pan Am 707 on long finals'. With no option but to cut in, Cooke just put his nose down and used his air brake to decelerate 'and throttled back before lowering the undercarriage. Three green lights (indicating all three wheels were down and locked for landing) and I lowered full flaps and did a short finals right hard turn onto the runway with the Pan Am 707 still about two miles behind me.' Cooke knew he was coming in too fast and could easily have ballooned up in the air but he deployed his tail parachute and applied full brakes, managing to get the Hunter under control.

As Cooke turned onto the taxi track at the end of the runway, the Pan Am 707 thundered past as it had to go around again. The Hunter flamed out, its engines dying 500 yards short of the dispersal area, and rolled to a stop. It was completely out of fuel. 'The ground crew eventually came to me on the taxi track and were astonished to see that my drop tanks were missing (jettisoned) and my gun ports were blackened from firing.' There was no ladder at the taxi track so Corporal Bhasin, a burly ex-wrestler, asked Cooke to jump and caught him as he dropped to the ground. The flight sergeant in-charge of the ground crew was staring at the port wing, which had not only become damaged when Cooke flew through the debris of the exploding Sabre but seemed to have clipped a tree as well. With leaves and twigs giving him the clues that he needed, the sergeant said to Cooke in all seriousness, 'Sir, I will have to report you to the CO for low flying.'[2]

Mamgain had landed at Kalaikunda even while Cooke was chasing his attacker without ammunition. He claimed to have shot down a Sabre which was verified by Wing Commander R. D. 'Dicky' Law, who was commanding the Kalaikunda base, and therefore the 'kill' was awarded to him. However, subsequent examination of his gun camera footage failed to confirm any hits. Cooke had his gun camera footage developed in Calcutta. It took a few days for the footage to come back. It confirmed that he had, at various stages of the dogfight, fired at all four Sabres. 'If only I had HE ammunition in my guns, I think I would have got three Sabres. The guns were also aligned for practice sorties, as a result I didn't quite have the desired spread which was mandated for aerial combat.' While Flying Officer Afzal Khan's Sabre crashed in the vicinity of the airfield and his decapitated remains were recovered, Tariq Habib Khan was reported to have ejected shortly after the Sabre crashed inside East Pakistan. However, the PAF subsequently claimed the stricken aircraft had made it back to Tejgaon, but admitted it was written off completely.

BOOK I

Reorganization

Chapter 1

HANDS ON THE TILLER

OLD WINE, NEW BOTTLE!

Yashwantrao Balwantrao Chavan, better known as Chavan sahib, became the 'go to' man for Prime Minister Jawaharlal Nehru when things had gone terribly wrong towards the end of 1962. The twin military thrust unleashed by Mao Zedong's People's Liberation Army (PLA) in both Ladakh and NEFA (Northeast Frontier Agency) on 20 October had resulted in the complete collapse of the army as poor tactical decisions combined with incompetent military commanders on the ground hobbled the Indian troops. In the four days of initial fighting, the ill-equipped and scattered troops in Eastern Ladakh—extending from Daulat Beg Oldie to the Galwan Valley, Hot Springs and those deployed at Chip Chap on the Pangong Tso—had been ruthlessly annihilated. In NEFA, Indian soldiers deployed on the Nam Ka Chu had met with a similar fate, while those fighting at Bum La and Kibithu failed to find any support as those behind them were ordered to withdraw instead of coming forward to reinforce them.

The Indian troops that had abandoned Tawang and Kibithu in the east had taken up fresh positions at Se La and Walong, while the Army HQ replaced almost all the senior commanders with fresh faces. In the west, the Kailash Range had been reinforced considerably, with the IAF even airlifting AMX-13 tanks to support the infantry around the Spangur Gap near Chushul. However, the damage had already been done, for when the Chinese launched their second offensive on 17 November, despite stoic fighting by a few units, the commanders once again collapsed in a quivering heap and threw in the towel. The massacre that followed led to a complete and absolute rout, with Se La capitulating, and Dirang Dzong, Bomdila, and Walong being abandoned. To make matters worse, even though not a single Chinese soldier had appeared on the plains, by 19 November, the entire north bank of the Brahmaputra Valley, including Tezpur, were ready to give up. The military and political failure on the Indian side had been absolute!

Chavan had had no role to play in the Indo–China conflict, which ended with the unilateral ceasefire announced by the Chinese on the midnight of 20/21 November. Yet he would become one of the key figures in the aftermath of the debacle, as he not only reorganized the decision-making structure of the army, but also shaped the post-conflict narrative in a manner that ensured that almost everyone responsible for the fiasco was protected and not brought to book. 'Chavan sahib's brief for himself from day one was crystal clear,' says Ram D. Pradhan, who served as his private secretary during that period. 'His loyalty to the prime minister was absolute and though it was perhaps never articulated, he knew he had to ensure that the existing hierarchy had to be shielded from being blamed.'[1]

Chavan was born on 12 March 1913 in Devrashtra, a small village near Satara, in what was once the Bombay Presidency. The son of a humble farmer, he made his way through Rajaram College in Kolhapur and obtained a bachelor's degree in history and political science at the University of Bombay in 1938. Three years later, he got a law degree from the Law College in Pune.

While he was a student, Chavan, like many of his peers, came under the influence of Mohandas Karamchand Gandhi. In 1930, Chavan had his first brush with authority when he was fined for his participation in the civil disobedience campaigns. Two years later, he was arrested and handed an eighteen-month jail term for flying the Indian flag at Satara. When the Quit India movement began to gather momentum a decade later, he became an integral part of the freedom movement. Reputed to be extremely cool under pressure, by the time of Independence he was recognized as a key political figure in the Bombay Presidency.

In 1946, he was elected to the legislative assembly of Bombay Province. As he served as the parliamentary secretary to Home Minister Morarji Desai, the emergence of communist China and deployments in Sinkiang and Tibet would hardly have been on his immediate radar.

Re-elected to the state assembly (known then as the Bombay State) in 1952, Chavan was appointed the minister for civil supplies, social welfare, and forests by Desai, who had graduated to the position of chief minister. At the time, Chavan's main attention was on the equal development of all regions in the bilingual state of Bombay. However, it soon became obvious to him that within the new federal structure that had emerged in independent India, the region would be better off if it were divided along linguistic lines—the Marathi-speaking areas being brought under Maharashtra while the Gujarati-speaking areas to the northwest were clubbed into a separate state of Gujarat. In 1956, once Desai was inducted into the union cabinet, Chavan was his obvious successor. Re-elected for a third time a year later, he was designated chief minister and, under his stewardship, the two new states came into being on 1 May 1960.

By the time the conflict with the Chinese erupted two years later, Chavan had systematically worked towards creating a strong industrial and agricultural base in his own region, laying emphasis on the cooperative approach to production and distribution. A strong advocate of decentralization, he encouraged the role of local government bodies in day-to-day affairs. It was during his tenure that legislation was passed that laid down the limits of agricultural land that could be individually owned.

The first wave of attacks by the Chinese and the disaster on the Nam Ka Chu, Bum La, and Tawang in 1962 had stunned the country. Even from the sketchy reports that were coming through, it was evident that the Indian Army had suffered severe casualties and hundreds of men were missing. This had led to the Opposition demanding the head of Vengalil Krishnan Krishna Menon, who was then the defence minister. At the international level, too, the Americans saw the developments as an opportunity to get rid of Krishna Menon, whose anti-Western and pro-Soviet stance was well known. With India requesting the US and Britain for help on 23 October, the US ambassador in New Delhi, John Kenneth Galbraith, had let it be known that as long as Menon was the defence minister, it would be a 'serious problem standing in the way of military aid to India'.[2] Despite the prime minister's backing, Menon tendered his resignation on 28 October, which Nehru accepted two days later.

However, Menon's resignation was only a cosmetic realigning of responsibility, a sleight of hand on the part of the prime minister to deflect the immediate pressure on himself in the face of growing criticism. In a bizarre twist to the resignation drama, the government instituted a 'department of defence production' and Krishna Menon was appointed the minister in charge. Almost as if to cock a snook at the Opposition benches, Krishna Menon continued to function from his old office even though Prime Minister Nehru had taken charge of the Defence Ministry on 31 October. Even before the government's critics could find their voice to point out the obvious, Krishna Menon had arrogantly announced to the press that nothing had changed.

With Nehru himself temporarily holding the defence portfolio, a replacement had to be found quickly. The prime minister needed someone who had the stature and the ability to stand up not only to international threats but also to increasing domestic pressure. Chavan was part of the National Development Council (NDC) that met in New Delhi on 4 November where the central government came under severe criticism from Bimala Prasad Chaliha, the Congress chief minister of Assam, for its handling of the situation in NEFA. Later in the evening, five chief ministers—Sanjeeva Reddy of Andhra Pradesh, Biju Patnaik of Orissa, Partap Singh Kairon of Punjab, K. Kamaraj of Madras State, and Chavan from Maharashtra, all from the Indian National Congress—met with Nehru in his office. The chief ministers questioned the continued role of Krishna Menon in the cabinet. Kairon was the most vocal, while Chavan was more empathetic towards the beleaguered prime minister.

The successful implementation and handling of the various policies in Bombay State by Chavan had added immensely to his stature, both within and outside the Indian National Congress. The next day, during a break in the NDC meeting, Nehru took Chavan aside; it was obvious he was smarting from Kairon's plain-speak. He confided in Chavan, 'You see, they want Menon's blood. If I agree,

tomorrow they will ask for my blood.'[3] Predictably, at the executive committee
meeting of the Congress party on 6 November, senior members of parliament
reinforced the call for Menon's head. Even though Nehru shouted at them and
threatened to expel them from the party, it was clear that he had to address the
issue. Chavan, who had returned to Bombay, received a call from Nehru, who,
without indicating any particular portfolio, simply asked if Chavan was willing to
move from the state to the national scene at this critical juncture.

Four days later, Nehru asked Chavan to fly down to New Delhi immediately.
At 2130 hrs, he was received by Vimla Sindhi in Teen Murti House. He was then
escorted by Indira Gandhi to the prime minister's study, where Nehru and the
home minister, Lal Bahadur Shastri, were waiting for him. The meeting lasted
nearly an hour. On being asked to take over the Defence Ministry, Chavan said,
'I have absolutely no background of defence. I have no experience of the central
government. I have nothing to offer other than my patriotism and loyalty to
you.' Nehru had replied, 'I understand, but you will get to know things. What is
necessary is that you should provide political leadership now.'[4]

Before taking over as India's defence minister, as chief minister of Maharashtra,
he had to ensure the smooth transition of power to his successor, Marotrao
Shambshio Kannamwar. The formal announcement that Chavan was the defence
minister designate was made on 14 November by Rashtrapati Bhavan, which
further added to the surge of Maratha pride that one of their own had been
chosen to fight the Chinese. Perhaps swayed by this sentiment, in a public meeting
in Pune, Chavan declared that India was determined to go on fighting China's
Red Napoleons until they met their Waterloo in the high Himalayas. Chavan
then commented that he doubted that the Russians would side with India in
the present crisis. He went on to quote a recent Soviet communique that had
stated that while Indians were their allies, the Chinese were their brothers.

Chavan was way out of line, especially since at that point of time there were
serious differences between Chairman Mao's Peoples' Republic of China (PRC) and
the post–Stalin Union of Soviet Socialist Republics (USSR) of Nikita Khrushchev.
Nehru's rebuke to Chavan came within forty-eight hours, as a special courier
delivered a letter from the prime minister that said: 'Whether your opinion or
belief is wholly justified or not, it is certainly unfortunate that you should have
made these statements.' Nehru went on to elaborate on the sensitivity of the issue,
stating that Chavan's comments could well push the Russians into the Chinese
camp. He finished by stating: 'As you are coming here as the Defence Minister
soon, your views on this matter will naturally attract a great deal of attention not
only in India, but outside India. I hope, therefore, that you will be a little careful
in your references to this topic.'[5] The lesson was not lost on Chavan. Subsequently
he became reticent and rarely expressed any views to the press, especially with
regard to matters concerning national security and foreign affairs.

The situation in Ladakh and NEFA, however, had taken a turn for the worse. On 14 November, Nehru's birthday, at the extreme eastern edge of the country, Lieutenant General Brij Mohan 'Bijji' Kaul tried to capture Green Pimple on the heights above Walong. Three days later, the Chinese relaunched the second phase of their offensive against Se La in the Kameng Division of NEFA while simultaneously attacking Indian positions at Rezang La and Gorkha Hill in the Chushul Sector of Ladakh.

The defence minister designate was spared the horror of having to oversee the army's collapse as reports pertaining to the fighting in Chushul, Se La, and Walong reached Army headquarters (HQ). The collapse in the Eastern Sector and the subsequent panic and preparations for abandoning Upper Assam were unbelievable. Indian officials in the embassy in Peking (Beijing), who had been summoned by Zhou Enlai on 19 November and told of the impending unilateral ceasefire effective midnight 20/21 November, failed to communicate the message to New Delhi. Had they done so, perhaps the prime minister would have been spared the embarrassment of writing a desperate letter to American president John F. Kennedy, begging for help in the form of air support and American pilots to fight on India's behalf.

Lieutenant General S. P. P. Thorat had been summoned to Delhi on 19 November by Nehru. In the wake of Chief of Army Staff General Pran Nath Thapar's resignation the previous evening, it was likely that Thorat would be offered the job. At the meeting, Thorat told Nehru that the Chinese lines of communication were stretched thin and that they would, in all probability, pull back from NEFA altogether.

The fact that Chavan and Thorat were Marathas, both from the Satara–Kolhapur region, may have stopped an insecure Nehru from asking Thorat to don his uniform again. Instead, Lieutenant General Jayanto Nath 'Muçchu' Chaudhuri was appointed the 'acting chief' on 20 November. The next morning, India awakened to headlines announcing the Chinese ceasefire. Much to Chavan and the government's chagrin, the Press Trust of India had spread the news even as the message from Peking via the Indian embassy was on its way.

THE TEAM MAN

Chavan's last day in office as the chief minister of Maharashtra on 19 November underlined his greatest strength—his ability to carry people with him. As he bade goodbye to the Maharashtra state assembly, the leader of the Opposition, K. N. Dhulap, moved an unusual resolution: 'This House does place on record its high sense of appreciation of the valuable services of Shri Y. B. Chavan, both as a leader of the House and as the Chief Minister of the State, the zeal, ability, judgement and the profound skill which he brought to bear on the performance of these services and also his devotion and unremitting attention to the welfare of the State and his uniform urbanity, which have rightly earned for him the respect and esteem of the people of this State.'[6] The stage was set for the transformation of a regional leader into a national figure.

The next day, Chavan was given a spectacular send-off from Bombay where people lined the route to the airport, shouting 'Chavan ki jai'. His Indian airlines flight to New Delhi landed at 1900 hrs. The defence minister designate was startled to see Lieutenant General Chaudhuri, the Southern Army commander, along with some Defence Ministry officials waiting for him on the tarmac. He learnt then that General Thapar had resigned and Chaudhuri had been hurriedly summoned from Poona to take over as acting chief the previous day. He was then introduced to Pattadakal Venkanna Raghavendra Rao, who was the new defence secretary designate, scheduled to take over from O. Pulla Reddy the next morning when Chavan too would be sworn in.

These appointments—of the acting chief and the defence secretary—took Chavan by surprise and he 'felt peeved'[7] that the prime minister did not consult him on these two critical posts. However, he decided not to say anything. Instead, shortly after, at Teen Murti Bhavan, the defence minister designate listened in amazement and disbelief as the prime minister briefed him on the latest events in the presence of Shastri. According to Nehru, Bomdila had been 'outflanked'[8] and the Chinese were poised to attack the Tenga Valley. The Chinese were expected to reach the plains of Assam in a few hours.

The failure of the Indian embassy to immediately communicate Zhou Enlai's message of the impending ceasefire had multiple repercussions. Not only did the prime minister shoot off desperate letters to the American president, it is quite possible that he would not have accepted Thapar's resignation, or made the radio broadcast to the people of Assam conceding defeat.[9] That night, on the eve of his swearing-in, Chavan was visited by Biju Patnaik, the Orissa chief minister who had hoped to don the defence minister's mantle after Krishna Menon's ouster. Given his own seniority and stature, Patnaik's comment to Chavan reflected the complete breakdown of leadership: 'Why have you come all the way to Delhi? The Chinese are moving in with such speed that they may even reach Bombay very soon.'[10] Shortly after Patnaik left, Chavan was woken up by a phone call from a journalist who told him that the Chinese had declared a unilateral ceasefire. It was shortly after midnight and, presuming that everyone else already had this information, Chavan went back to sleep.

The next morning, the swearing-in ceremony was held at Rashtrapati Bhavan, where nearly the entire cabinet was present. An hour later, Chavan was ushered into his new office by the prime minister, who asked him to chair the meeting of the Committee of Service Chiefs and Secretaries to review the situation in NEFA and Ladakh. As Chavan found his footing, his immediate problem was to make the Defence Ministry and Army HQ's decision-making coherent. He was formally introduced to the team he would work with by the prime minister; apart from General Chaudhuri, who was the acting chief of army staff (COAS) and Rao, the new defence secretary, there were Air Marshal Aspy Merwan Engineer, the chief of air staff (CAS) and Vice Admiral Bhaskar Sadashiv Soman, the chief of naval staff (CNS), plus a host of others.

Earlier in the morning, it became obvious that no one, neither Nehru, Shastri, nor the Intelligence Bureau chief, Bhola Nath Mullik, were aware of the ceasefire which had already come into effect. It was at this meeting that Foreign Secretary M. J. Desai formally informed those present that there had been a message from the chargé d'affaires in Peking announcing the ceasefire. Not knowing exactly how to react to this news, they decided to carry on with the main agenda of the meeting which, ironically, was to discuss the blowing up of the various oil refineries in Assam to keep them from falling into Chinese hands.

Chavan was a lucky man. The Chinese ceasefire gave him the time he needed to steady his ship. This was sorely needed as all the necessary essentials of decision-making were sadly lacking. There was simply no systematic analysis of information on which decisions could be based. Nehru had tampered with established norms and pushed his own favourites into positions of power; Krishna Menon had polarized the army and ignored inputs and advice that did not suit him; Mullik, instead of gathering information and presenting it for others to act on, had emerged as the de facto decision-maker whose continued interference in matters military had had disastrous results.

Pulla Reddy, the previous defence secretary, had been reduced to a non-entity by Krishna Menon. Most others, including the mercurial Harish Chandra Sarin, the then joint secretary, were seen to be Krishna Menon's men. It was expected that Chavan would show them all the door. Even the appointment of P.V. R. Rao had raised eyebrows, for he was as wet behind the ears when it came to defence matters as Chavan himself.

Rao was of the old school, an ICS officer who had the reputation of being a hard task-master. He had been working as a secretary under Tiruvellore Thattai Krishnamachari, better known as TTK, also a known Nehru favourite. Shortly after the first meeting, Rao walked into Chavan's office and said: 'Sir, I know I have been appointed as Secretary of this ministry without your knowledge and without your approval. At this time, when we are facing a critical situation, I feel the Defence Minister must have a person of his choice as Secretary of this ministry. I would like you to appoint such a person. I am ready to proceed on leave.'[11]

Chavan's response was typical of the man and it set the tone, establishing his grip on the team of people he had to work with. With an amused smile he said, 'PVR, you are my choice, although earlier I had some reservations.'[12] Rao continued as the defence secretary throughout Chavan's tenure.

In the Defence Ministry, the one name that dominated the buzz was that of

Sarin. A Punjabi by ethnicity, he was born on 27 May 1914 in Deoria, Eastern Uttar Pradesh, and his name topped the list of officers who were seen to be Krishna Menon's blue-eyed boys. Having joined the ICS in 1938 he was allotted to the Bihar cadre but early in his career had been seconded to the elite Finance and Commerce pool. This had brought him directly under the control of Liaquat Ali Khan in 1946, who was the finance minister in the post-War interim government of the Congress and Muslim League headed by Nehru as prime minister. He had served as Defence Minister Sardar Baldev Singh's private secretary soon after independence; this was the beginning of Sarin's remarkable career that spanned decades in the Ministry of Defence. Sarin was a joint secretary in the Defence Ministry when Krishna Menon took charge on 17 April 1957.

Krishna Menon was born in Tellicherry (Thalassery) on 3 May 1896 in what was then the Madras Presidency. He was educated at the Presidency and Law College in what is now Chennai before finishing from University College and the London School of Economics. Few men had such a polarizing effect on people—they either loved him or hated him. Unfortunately, the same was also true in reverse, which resulted in Menon playing favourites, a trait that had severe repercussions during his tenure as the defence minister. Soon after taking charge of the defence portfolio, he had developed a strong aversion for the defence secretary, Pulla Reddy, with whom he would barely exchange a word.

Menon brought with him an air of high-strung energy which appealed to Sarin and many other officers in the ministry. Those who disliked Menon expected Chavan to clear out all his favourites, among whom Sarin's name topped the list. Even though there had been a change of guard, Sarin remained steadfastly loyal to Menon, who he believed had taken major steps towards 'building India's defence production so that India would not be subject to big power politics in defence supplies' and also done the ground work 'to provide an intellectual underpinning to India's defence effort by establishing the National Defence College.'[13]

Chavan's main task, to protect Prime Minister Jawaharlal Nehru from the public backlash that would come the moment the details of what had actually happened became known, depended on the minimal rocking of the existing boat. This meant ensuring that that none of the bureaucrats were brought to book for their role in the Chinese debacle. It would seem the defence minister was quite happy to extend the same courtesy to the army as well. General Thapar's ouster had happened before Chavan took over, while the appointment of Lieutenant General Chaudhuri as acting chief indicated the prime minister was still quite favourably inclined towards Lieutenant General Bijji Kaul and could well rehabilitate him. If Chaudhuri did not have to exorcise his own perceived competition, it is quite likely that the 1962 Sino–Indian War would have completely disappeared from the political consciousness of the country.

THE GOOD, THE BAD, AND THE UGLY—MUCCHU CHAUDHURI

Jayanto Nath Chaudhuri was born in 1908. His paternal grandmother was Rabindranath Tagore's sister and his mother was the daughter of Womesh Chandra Bonnerjee, the first president of the Indian National Congress. He studied at St. Xavier's College in Calcutta before proceeding to Highgate School in London from where he went on to the Royal Military College, Sandhurst. Six feet tall and quite fair, Chaudhuri was the antithesis of a Bengali babu.[14] Returning to India in 1928, he initially served with the 1st Battalion, North Staffordshire Regiment, before joining the 7th Light Cavalry. When World War II broke out, he joined the 5th Infantry Division that fought in Sudan, Eritrea, Abyssinia, and the desert of West Africa. During this period, he was Mentioned in Despatches thrice and was awarded the Order of the British Empire for distinguished service in 1943. After a stint as a senior instructor at the Command and Staff College in Quetta he was transferred to the 16th Light Cavalry. He commanded the regiment in Burma and was twice more Mentioned in Despatches, which surely must be a record of sorts. After the Japanese surrender, he served in French Indochina and Indonesia before returning to India in 1946 with the temporary rank of brigadier.

In 1947, he was selected for the prestigious Imperial Defence College's course after which he returned to Army HQ in New Delhi in 1948 where he was given the pivotal task of coordinating the initial war effort for the Jammu and Kashmir Operations as director of Military Operations & Intelligence.[15] In May that year, he was promoted to the rank of major general and given command of the Secunderabad-based 1st Armoured Division. In September 1948, he was the military commander of the police action against the princely state of Hyderabad (Operation Polo). Here, after some brief fighting, Chaudhuri accepted the surrender of the Hyderabad State Forces from Major General Syed Ahmed El Edroos, who advised the nizam of Hyderabad, Osman Ali Khan, not to fight any further. Chaudhuri was appointed the military governor of Hyderabad State.[16] In January 1952, he was appointed the adjutant general and a year later he took over as the chief of the general staff (CGS). In December 1955, he was promoted to the rank of lieutenant general and was given command of the Jalandhar-based 11 Corps. In May 1959 he had taken over as GOC-in-C[17] Southern Command, from where he was expected to retire. Fate, however, had other plans for him.

Though he himself wrote regularly for *The Statesman*, no one else had a good understanding of the officer. Considering that he had been at the centre of the Goanese liberation (Operation Vijay), became the acting chief on the eve of the Chinese ceasefire, and was the COAS during the 1965 conflict with Pakistan, his views on events are indeed most interesting. Most commentaries about him are fairly cautious, except where they are downright negative. 'Mucchu Chaudhuri was a particular type of well-born, urban, bicultural Bengali, suave, quick-witted, and articulate. One of his obvious traits was his affection of anglicised modes and mannerisms, something which, if over-indulged, often generates a sense of racial inadequacy,' says Major General D. K. Palit, a high-brow Bengali himself.[18]

Sarin had dismissed him 'as being a pretty irresponsible person, more of a showman who knew how to talk and impress people. Anyone who wasn't familiar with the nitty gritty of a situation was usually quite impressed by his briefings, but a lot that he propagated would not necessarily stand scrutiny.'[19] Echoing that sentiment Palit, who was the director of Military Operations (DMO) during the initial years says, 'Despite his glamorous personality, Mucchu's outstanding characteristic was his insecurity, which he attempted to dissemble under an exterior of flippant drollery and a constant striving to be brilliant.'[20]

'What choice did Chavan have?' asked Pradhan, who had been Chavan's private secretary and later served as the governor of Arunachal Pradesh. 'One of the biggest criticisms of Krishna Menon was that he bypassed the chain of command. Chavan had to back the acting COAS, though, pretty early on, he realized that General Chaudhuri had a double personality. He was all smiles and amiable when it came to dealing with his superiors, but he was not so pleasant with people under his command who did not go along with him.'[21]

Chaudhuri had once before been appointed acting chief in August 1961, when Thapar and his then CGS, Bijji Kaul, were away in the UK, attending Exercise Unison. As GOC-in-C Southern Command, this suited him very well at the time. It allowed him to issue directives to himself for the handling of Goa's liberation. Considering the conduct of operations against Pakistan in 1965, especially the Rann of Kutch affair, it is worth examining the state of affairs in Army HQ at that time.

In his book *War in High Himalaya*, Palit dubs this a 'comic opera'. In fact, in his description of the events, he is even more acerbic. 'Mucchu was sensitive to the fact that as Southern Army commander he was not directly concerned in the operational aspects of the western and northern borders, and Bijji had kept him as uninformed on these subjects as hierarchical propriety allowed. Mucchu was now obviously only too eager to seize the opportunity of putting his imprimatur on the Goa operation, not only for the sake of one-upmanship with Kaul but also, perhaps, to sanction for himself, as the army commander who would be responsible for any military task in Goa, greater latitude and resources than Army HQ might normally have conceded....[22]

Shortly after Chavan's first meeting that had been conducted by Cabinet Secretary Sucha Singh Khera, where the blowing up of oil refineries was discussed, an operational order was required to be issued to all formations in the east that Indian troops were not to operate forward of the plains. During the course of the morning, the staff at Military Operations had time to study the constraints and conditions attached to the ceasefire. According to the communiqué, the Chinese in NEFA would withdraw to positions 20 km behind the line as it existed in

November 1959. It was perplexing that Chaudhuri did not give the order to reoccupy the territory vacated by the Chinese.

'I had already come to the conclusion that Mucchu Chaudhuri's great concern at the time was not, as it should have been, to take a firm grip on the army and rebuild its shattered morale, but to avoid taking any operational step that might provoke the enemy and stir up trouble for himself. Having witnessed his predecessor virtually sacked in an operational crisis, and having seen that crisis miraculously abate, he was not going to take any risk that might recreate it and jeopardise his confirmation as Army Chief. His insecurity was never very far from the surface.'[23]

Chaudhuri's hesitation to reoccupy territory vacated by the Chinese may have also stemmed from Nehru's response to Sam Manekshaw in Tezpur. During Manekshaw's briefing, after the newly appointed 4 Corps' commander had spelt out his plans to reoccupy positions, Nehru had said that he did not want the death toll to rise, advising him to desist from reoccupying areas vacated by the Chinese. Chaudhuri, taking his cue from the prime minister, promptly spoke up, telling Nehru that he would reverse Manekshaw's orders. The 4 Corps' commander was enraged and told Chaudhuri he could either let him command his corps the way he wanted to or send him back to Wellington. Indira Gandhi, who was also present, then entered the argument, taking Manekshaw's side, telling Nehru 'that it was shameful that they had a commander who wanted to fight but his hands were being tied'.[24] Nehru tried to reason with his daughter, who, despite not holding an official position in the government, was fairly influential when it came to policy matters. On his return to Delhi, Chaudhuri made sure orders for the reoccupation of territory did not go out.

The appointment of Chaudhuri as the acting chief had taken Chavan by surprise, for as the defence minister designate, the prime minister ought to have consulted him. In the past, whenever General Pran Thapar was away, Chaudhuri had officiated for him and many felt that was all it was to be. For one, Thapar had not really expected Nehru to accept his resignation. And, second, General Thorat had been asked to be in Delhi to meet with Nehru. Third, there was a considerable lobby against Chaudhuri's appointment, both in Army HQ and in the ministries, because his conduct during and after the Goa operation had raised eyebrows. Home Minister Shastri had also been looking into his performance as the military governor of Hyderabad after the takeover of the state in 1948. Finally, it was on Mullik's recommendation that Chaudhuri had been decided on, with the caveat that he would be an 'acting chief' and would function in his present rank of an army commander.[25]

Chaudhuri, who always had his ear to the ground, would have been well aware of all these factors. He was extremely wary of the Nehru–Kaul faction, which had just a month ago seen General Harbakhsh Singh come and go as the 4 Corps' commander in less than a week. The Chinese ceasefire had taken the immediate pressure off Nehru and it was quite possible that once the dust had settled, Kaul could be elevated to chief and Chaudhuri asked to go home. Though Chavan had backed Chaudhuri from day one, the fact that the new defence minister had not been consulted on the new chief's appointment indicated that he had been brought in by the prime minister to handle the internal political crisis that was brewing at the time.[26]

Chavan was indeed under pressure to protect not just Kaul but Thapar as well. In the month since the ceasefire, apart from the knee-jerk resignation of Thapar, not one head had rolled. On 17 December, Chaudhuri decided to take matters into his own hands. He appointed Lieutenant General Thomas Bryan Henderson-Brooks, general officer commanding (GOC) 11 Corps, as chairman of an Operations Review Committee. He was to be assisted by Brigadier Premindra Singh Bhagat, an engineer officer who had won the Victoria Cross in Sudan during World War II and was at the time the commandant of the Indian Military Academy (IMA) in Dehradun. The report was meant to document the events of October–November 1962 in NEFA but its mandate was eventually limited to commenting on the military reasons for the newly raised 4 Corps' defeat. That the Henderson-Brooks Report was confined to 4 Corps is suggestive that as far as Chaudhuri was concerned, the only target of the exercise was Bijji Kaul, his bête noire!

Meanwhile, to rebuild morale, Chaudhuri visited as many formations as he could, telling the men repeatedly 'that there was a big black mark on their faces, which water alone won't wash out and there was only one thing that could wash it out—blood'.[27] He did not know it then, but, under his leadership, within a couple of years, that opportunity would present itself.

Chapter 2

THE FAULT LINES

The British Raj was extremely possessive about the Indian Army on whose shoulders it had built and legitimized an empire. From the earliest days, when the first East India Company ships had made landfall off the coast of Surat in 1612, they, along with the Portuguese, Dutch, and French had been involved in mass murder, loot, and conquest on an unprecedented scale. The European ability to recruit Indian sepoys and hone them into a potent fighting force first became obvious in the Battle of Adyar in 1746 when the French defeated the much larger army of the nawab of Arcot. Ever since then, the history of the subcontinent became awash in blood as the British first defeated their white competitors, before systematically sorting out the 'blackies'.

The Carnatic Wars, Plassey, Seringapatam, the Maratha Wars, Bharatpur, Burma, Afghanistan, China, Bhutan, the Gorkha Wars, Sikh Wars.... The carnage was endless and the British Indian Army was the colonizer's biggest asset. The uprising in 1857 saw the exit of the Company Bahadur and brought in the Crown, which systematically created more divides between Hindu, Muslim, Sikh, and Gorkha troops for its own protection. 'Martial' classes were created, those who had stood by the white man's colours were rewarded, and others ruthlessly strapped to the mouths of cannons and blown to bits or hunted down in the countryside and hanged. The infantry, artillery, and cavalry—the three major arms of the army—were exclusively led by British officers and Kipling's 'East is East, and West is West, and never the twain shall meet' became much more than just a ballad. The very thought of having Indian officers to lead Indian troops was unthinkable.

As the demand for Indianization from the Congress became louder, in 1921, the British cautiously agreed to 'experiment' with Indian officers. The system put in place was but a tilt of the hat to satisfy political demand, for out of the first 83 cadets sent to Sandhurst, only 30 made the grade, which was hardly surprising since selection was entirely by patronage. The Prince of Wales Royal Indian Military College was then set up in Dehradun to help refine the selection process but, by 1939, only 452 cadets had made it to the officer grade. These were the king's commissioned Indian officers (KCIOs) and they would remain at the helm of affairs till the end of General Paramasiva Prabhakar Kumaramangalam's tenure in June 1969.

In the leadership saga, the next phase was the Indian commissioned officers (ICOs) who were all products of the Indian Military Academy that was set up in Dehradun in 1932. Easily one of the finest institutions set up by the British in the subcontinent, the selection process was extremely tough and, over the years, the IMA has produced successive batches that continue to be of the highest quality. The initial lot were extremely well trained and motivated, and there was a quantum jump in the standard of leadership. However, the numbers were very few, with each course barely producing twenty-five to thirty officers every six months, which was far from adequate.

World War II and the resultant influx of war commissioned officers (WCOs) suddenly changed all that. 'Much of the training for regular officers contains learning about the moral values of leadership: the honour, the welfare and the comfort of the men you command. The WCOs missed that. Independence came very suddenly and found the Indian Army full of veteran sepoys, but a higher command hitherto untried in the roles it was to occupy, and officers to hold up the middle who were only professionally part-trained.'[1]

In 1947, the armed forces of the Indian subcontinent were also split, two-thirds staying with India and one-third transferring to Pakistan. The horror of Partition, traumatic as it was, with 15 million people being displaced, was magnified even further as Sikhs, Hindus, and Muslims turned on each other, leaving more than a million dead. To make matters worse, by mid-October, Pakistan let loose armed tribal lashkars into Jammu and Kashmir (J&K) in a bid to force Maharaja Hari Singh to either accede to Pakistan or flee the state with his family.

The raiders could be classified into three categories: there were the Pathan and Afridi tribesmen who were there with the single purpose of loot and rape. After they had expended themselves and looted Baramulla, just short of Srinagar, they headed back to Muzaffarabad to deposit their booty. The second category was armed locals from Mirpur and Poonch districts, mostly ex-servicemen and volunteer militiamen. Most of these men had been told that they were fighting the maharaja's state forces which would otherwise destroy their homes. However, seeing the mayhem created by the tribals, most of them were only too willing to go back to protect their own homes and families. The third category was the Pakistani regular army officers and other volunteers who were on long leave with full pay and allowances. They were the vital cog in an operation of this type, but their numbers were relatively low. Though all three categories were mutually suspicious of each other, they were bound together by the idea of 'jihad' and the prospect of an easy victory. By the time the Pakistani officers could round them up and get the lashkars to turn around and head for Srinagar again, the maharaja had acceded to India and the first Indian troops were flown in by RIAF Dakotas on 27 October. 'A Pakistani prisoner captured on the outskirts of Srinagar when questioned, complained disgustedly of our unsporting use of aircraft whilst he moved on his flat feet!'[2]

The next fourteen months saw intense fighting across some highly inhospitable terrain. The raiders were replaced by regular Pakistan Army troops but they were slowly pushed back. Naushera, Rajouri, Mirpur, Jhangar, and Poonch saw intense fighting, as did parts of the Kashmir Valley and the Trans-Himalayan region that included Zanskar and Ladakh. Skardu fell after bravely holding out for a time, while in most other places, the Indians gradually gained the upper hand. In 1948, at Mountbatten's prodding, Nehru took the matter to the newly construed United Nations and on 1 January 1949 the ceasefire came into effect. Hopes for a permanent settlement evaporated soon enough, for the UN resolution that stipulated that Pakistan would withdraw its troops after which a plebiscite could be held was ignored. With a sizeable chunk of territory, called Pakistan-occupied Kashmir (POK) by India and Azad Kashmir by Pakistan, plus most of the Northern Areas of Gilgit and Chitral under Pakistani control, troops on either side of the ceasefire line (CFL) consolidated their positions and settled down to an uneasy status quo.

Until this point, the situation on both sides had been much the same. But gradually things began to change. On the Indian side, for those in the infantry and other supporting arms, life was extremely tough, especially for those manning the posts strung out all along the CFL. Many of the areas were unmapped. The few maps that were available of the hazardous, remote, and often snow-bound areas were inadequate and inaccurate. Lines of communication had to be surveyed and then trails and tracks cut across extremely difficult terrain. Added to all this was the bitterly cold Kashmir winter which virtually sealed off the Valley and the Ladakh region from the rest of the world.

'Living areas were created out of local resources, which excluded the cutting of fresh timber by explicit and emphatic order, so that the engineer-supplied ballies,[3] strictly accountable, had to be toted everywhere. The resultant stone-built structures, euphemistically called bunkers, were often such that fine snow could blow in through the walls by high winds. And if because of that they were dug low down into the ground, they were often covered by several feet of snow.'[4]

Right from the start, India's senior military leadership failed miserably in standing up for their men, rather philosophically adopting the 'we will fight with what we have' line. In New Delhi, the ramifications of the evolving tussle for control in the civil–military equation were being felt at various levels. The Indian political leadership, which had no experience or idea of geopolitics, and considered the armed forces something of a burden, was intent on playing down the status of the armed forces, even keeping the pay scales down. In 1953, to limit the army's growth, the Government of India ordered a 2 per cent retrenchment. At that time, none of the senior officers protested, even though the Chinese threat had been recognized as being a real one.[5]

In such a scenario, with the military hierarchy looking the other way, the Indian babus 'came into their own. If you put up a case for an extra pair of socks, they insisted on being told how you had managed so far. If a man was killed by lightning, they said it was an act of God and not attributable to military service, so his dependents got no pension, regardless that the man had to remain at a place, and by the very nature of his duties, exposed to lightning. Frost bite and death by exposure were declared non-attributable by these financial caretakers, and their idiocy wasn't challenged. If a man fell down a hill on a dark night and broke limbs which could not be healed in time for him to resume duties within 60 days, he was put on half pay.'[6]

The junior officers' plight was perhaps even worse. Living with the men in these remote pickets, they were not entitled to free rations or even winter clothing and, in the early 1950s and 60s, their pay was just above subsistence level. They were also increasingly responsible for everything, from personally leading patrols, conducting training, accounting for each and every round of ammunition, supervising firing points during training, initialling each and every ledger and hoping like hell nothing went wrong, for there was no senior officer to turn to. Despite this, young men kept reporting at the Service Selection Boards across the country and those that made the grade made it to the IMA which 'sent trained regular officers of a very high standard straight to the regiments. Through the values taught to them, they began to rebuild the regimental spirit. Where this is properly imbued, it fashions a bond stronger than a charm, which runs up and down, through, round and about every officer, like an invisible thread. It is compounded of dangers, deprivations and discomforts shared with men and the intense joy of seeing results achieved because somehow the officers have led the men to it.'[7] This factor, combined with the Indian soldier's ability to tolerate extreme hardships and yet revel in the pride of his little group, company or battalion became the driving force of the Indian Army.

In 1962, it was not the junior leadership that had failed. The problem was with the senior and mid-level commanders who fell apart when the Chinese attacked. In the aftermath of the war, a dispassionate analysis of what went wrong was the desperate need of the hour. But apart from the Henderson–Brooks Report, there was no attempt to hold individuals responsible. Even those senior and mid-level officers who had been stripped of their authority during the conflict were reinstated. So while new raisings were drilled by competent company and platoon commanders, the same senior officers who had not particularly distinguished themselves found themselves in command of larger formations preparing to fight a completely different enemy.

On the Pakistani side, the plight of the men was much the same, perhaps only slightly less hard, for their lines of communication were far more established, with roads leading up to most of their posts. The difference, which became more acute over a period of time, lay in the officer cadre and in the generous availability of modern weapons and munitions. The Pakistani government ensured that their officers were among the best paid public servants, which was good for not just their morale but also their self-esteem.

Along the CFL in J&K, by and large, the Indians were quite passive, dutifully recording and reporting all cross-border violations to the United Nations' observers. The Pakistanis, on the other hand, didn't seem to care. Perhaps it was their idea of area domination, for whenever they felt like—which was quite often—they would infiltrate, sabotage, raid, and even place anti-personnel mines to keep the Indians perennially on the hop. Firing a few bursts from their bunkers and shelling Indian positions was almost second nature to them. Often, they would stand on their bunkers and hurl abuse while exposing themselves lewdly, telling the Indians to get 'permission from Delhi' to fire back. Like all bullies, they enjoyed these little games, but in sectors where the odd Indian commander authorized his men to fire back, they behaved themselves.

In May 1954, Pakistan signed the Mutual Defense Assistance Agreement with the United States. Later that year, it became a member of SEATO along with the US, UK, and five other countries. A year later, it joined the Baghdad Pact, another mutual defence organization, with the UK, Turkey, Iran, and Iraq. The US had not joined this organization, but remained closely associated with it since its inception. In 1958, when Iraq left this pact, it was renamed CENTO (Central Treaty Organization); it continued to comprise Turkey, Iran, and Pakistan as its regional members. Early in 1959, Pakistan signed a bilateral Agreement of Cooperation with the US (as did Turkey and Iran), which was designed to reinforce the defensive purposes of CENTO. Thus Pakistan was associated with the US through four mutual security arrangements and was termed 'America's most allied ally in Asia'. It was the only Asian country which was a member both of SEATO and CENTO.

This led to Pakistan becoming flush with weapon systems and unlimited ammunition. Despite the fine print inserted into the various agreements by the Americans that these weapons could not be used against India, Pakistan gleefully towed the heavy guns to the CFL and started conducting gunnery training for its artillery. Until then, the only armoured division 'East of the Suez' existed in India, but 'then suddenly there was another armoured division on the sub-continental map, equipped with modern tanks and the Pakistanis were talking about blitzkrieging Delhi. While they got away with their antics in J&K and their braggadocio and bluster otherwise increased,'[8] the gap between their officers and men continued to widen.

In 1965, General Mohammad Musa Khan's 'new doctrine' reflected this thinking, where the soldier was relegated to a secondary role. The new Pakistan Army relied on weapon systems, firepower, and bombast to achieve their objectives. Where this failed to work, the soldiers didn't quite know what to do, for the officers were often not there to guide them.

NO FREE LUNCH—THE PRICE OF DEFEAT

Prime Minister Nehru's two panic-stricken letters written to President Kennedy on 20 November 1962 had created a big problem. That they existed at all was the topic of much debate within India, for those in the know were a small circle of men, none of whom were likely to go public with the matter. Hand-delivered to the American president by the Indian ambassador to the US, B. K. Nehru, their content, had it become known, would have been a major embarrassment at that time.

Nehru's earlier appeal to leaders of various countries when the Chinese had attacked across the Nam Ka Chu and in Ladakh had not elicited many favourable responses. In fact, almost all the African and Asian countries who were part of the non-aligned movement, with the exception of Egypt, who Nehru thought would openly side with India, had been non-committal in their response. This was also the case with the USSR, who though not censorious, had held back delivery of the promised MiG-21s which would have considerably strengthened India's air capability. The October flare-up had also coincided with the Cuban Missile Crisis and, as usual, the Americans were on an anti-communist high, a state they had been in since the end of World War II. Having been drawn into Korea, they were at the time getting sucked into Vietnam as well, where communist China was the enemy. The US therefore responded spontaneously to Nehru's call for help and the fact that they did so would have most certainly influenced Mao's handling of the situation, especially the unilateral ceasefire.

On the other hand, the British were rather patronizing to their erstwhile colony, liberally offering unsought advice to New Delhi, especially in matters relating to its relations with Pakistan. Unfortunately for Nehru, during the Cold War, the Americans and the British were on the same side. Both countries despatched high-powered missions to Delhi within a few days of the second Chinese offensive in November: Kennedy sent Averell Harriman, the former governor of New York who was then the assistant secretary of state for East Asian and Pacific Affairs, and General Paul DeWitt Adams, a veteran of the Korean War who was commander-in-chief of the US Strike Command, a unified combatant organization designed to respond to any global crisis. Harold Macmillan, the British prime minister, sent General (later Field Marshal) Richard Hull who was the chief of the general staff and Duncan Sandys, the secretary of state for Commonwealth Relations (Sir Winston Churchill's son-in-law).

Duncan Sandys had been Macmillan's defence minister between 1957 and 1959 and then the aviation minister until 1960. Considered to be a 'hatchet' man, he was extremely heavy-handed in his dealings with people and 'was known as being opinionated…with little underlying realisation of the strategical needs….'[9]

Sandys met Nehru on 24 November and spelt out the British position, telling the prime minister that his country (as well as the US) was committed to help

India fight the Chinese but, for that to continue, India had to immediately resolve the Kashmir problem that had been festering for the last fourteen years. Even as India had braced itself for the second round of fighting with the Chinese barely ten days earlier, the president of POK, Khurshid Hasan Khurshid, who had been Muhammad Ali Jinnah's private secretary, had called for the 'war of liberation' in the Valley to be stepped up. On 16 November, President Ayub Khan himself had been at the forefront of a nationwide protest against British and American aid to India. The Pakistani commander-in-chief, General Mohammad Musa Khan, had been proclaiming that the conflict between India and China was a mere border incident and that Nehru was exaggerating reports so as to get 'arms at a massive'[10] scale from the West so that he could attack Pakistan later. It was a different matter that until then Britain had supplied India with 2,000 automatic rifles and 3 million rounds of ammunition that amounted to aid worth £150,000, which was woefully small.

Sandy's arrival also coincided with Kenneth Galbraith telling Nehru, until then considered a hardliner on Kashmir, that Kennedy would be able to obtain Congressional approval for aid to India more easily if negotiations were started with President Ayub Khan and a quick settlement of the Kashmir problem arrived at. There was talk of raising fifty Indian divisions with the help of the US in the next three years and even throwing the Chinese out of Tibet, something that would redeem not only Nehru's but India's honour as well.

These developments brought into play Foreign Secretary Yezdezard 'Yezdi' Dinshaw Gundevia. A Parsi, he was born in 1908 and educated at Wilson College, Bombay, from where he graduated in 1929. A year later he joined the ICS and was allotted to the United Provinces where he served in various districts. At the time of Independence, he was on an assignment in Rangoon, after which he was posted to the External Affairs Ministry in 1948 as a joint secretary. He had a string of foreign postings, during which time he served in Moscow, Geneva, London, and Colombo, before returning to New Delhi in 1961, where he was promoted to the rank of secretary and given the charge of Commonwealth Affairs. He would later take over from M. J. Desai as the foreign secretary on 5 December 1963 and would play a key role in the build-up to the war with Pakistan.

Through most of December 1962, Duncan Sandys was flitting between Delhi and Islamabad trying to get the two sides to agree on Kashmir. According to Gundevia, Nehru had never been as vulnerable as he had been during this period and the arrival of Mountbatten further complicated the issue.

Mountbatten, who was then the UK's chief of the defence staff, was compulsively drawn towards the affairs of India, especially in matters related to defence, even though he was snubbed by Krishna Menon. He regularly corresponded with Nehru on a variety of matters. By the end of the 1950s, Mountbatten had convinced himself that the only real workable solution was an independent and demilitarized

Kashmir Valley. In 1961 he had first broached the subject with Ayub Khan who had given the former viceroy 'cautious encouragement'.[11] Knowing Nehru's stance on Kashmir, Mountbatten had bided his time, waiting for an opportune moment to broach the subject. With Sandys and the Americans pushing for a settlement with Pakistan, Mountbatten told Nehru he was 'one of the very few Englishmen who really recognized that Kashmir had legally become a part of India'. He argued that if even he felt that the promised plebiscite was overdue, then India's critics would have a much harsher view on it.

Despite being told by various senior Indian leaders that Nehru would be thrown out if he agreed to the proposal, Mountbatten made his pitch for the Independence of the Kashmir Valley, 'a gratuitous piece of advice that was quickly picked up by Bakshi Ghulam Mohammed, Chief Minister of Kashmir, who proposed "internationalisation" (as if it were significantly different).'[12]

Nehru was being told by both the British and the Americans that any formula that was worked out would necessitate India giving a large share of concessions to Pakistan. The logic being put forward was that while Nehru had the charisma to carry India with him, Ayub would have a hard time convincing his people as to why Pakistan was giving up on its claim on parts of J&K.

On 31 December 1962, Gundevia along with Major General D. K. Palit, India's director of Military Operations, started working out possible scenarios. Previously, the CFL between India and Pakistan had been drawn up on an 'as-is where-is' basis as it reflected the actual troop deployment on 31 December 1948. As a result, there was neither geographical nor tactical logic applied on its imposition. Gundevia's brief was to give more to Pakistan wherever possible, but the Valley and Dogra areas were not to be touched. Five alternate sets of lines were drawn up over the next three days, so that there would be enough scope for bargaining, but 'the one with the "maximum give-away" ran as follows: from the north-east (north of Zojila) to Tithwal the border would run along the Kishanganga river; thence southward, cross country so to speak, over the Kazinag range to the top of the Jhelum gorge just west of Baramulla; southwards from there the line kept west of Gulmarg but gave away the valuable villages of Poonch, Mendhar and Jhangar. The line conceded to Pakistan some 3,500 sq km of territory more than they held under the ceasefire agreement.'[13]

For reasons of security, Gundevia insisted nothing be written on the proposed alignment of the maps, which were then put away in a safe in the Military Operations directorate. The briefing for the acting COAS General Chaudhuri was to be entirely verbal. There is no record to show that either Gundevia or Palit discussed the proposed realignment with the prime minister or any other member of the cabinet. The marked maps were next taken out of the safe only when Sardar Swaran Singh, the minister for railways who had earlier headed talks on other territorial disputes with Pakistan, was appointed to head the ministerial delegation to discuss the formal partition of Kashmir.

When Swaran Singh went over the maps showing the proposed demarcation lines, he asked Palit if some more concessions could be made to Pakistan, especially in the Valley. The DMO told the minister that it would become that much harder to defend the Valley militarily if India was to allow Pakistan a toehold there. Swaran Singh said in his avuncular manner: 'We are talking about drawing an international line through Kashmir and not another ceasefire line. There is a difference in hazard between the defence of an international boundary and the defence of a temporary battle line. Once we accept an Indo-Pak boundary through Kashmir, international law will come into play, with all its inhibitions.'[14]

The new marked maps were to accompany a joint US–UK proposal to India and Pakistan in April 1963 entitled 'Elements of a Settlement'. It envisaged the partition of Kashmir on the basis that each must have 'a substantial position in the Vale'. About the only document on the talks in this volume is Pakistan's Foreign Secretary Aziz Ahmed's reaction to a draft communique presented to him by the British High Commissioner Maurice James on 8 August 1963. He not only objected to the principle that both sides must have 'a substantial position' in the Valley but insisted that military aid to India, after the war with China in 1962, must be linked to a Kashmir settlement. Aziz Ahmed was very close to Bhutto. In 1963 Nehru, reversing his position, agreed to the appointment of a mediator. Bhutto's intransigence killed this move.[15]

KASHMIR, THE LOW-HANGING FRUIT

The Chinese ceasefire that came into effect on the night of 20/21 November 1962 had saved the Indian leadership further embarrassment, but the bungling chaos was to continue, this time adversely affecting the western border. The UK and US had spontaneously come out on India's side during the Chinese conflict, but the quantum of actual aid received from the British was negligible. Even though the Chinese had pulled back, India's non–aligned status seemed like a distant memory as American army officers were pushing their agenda of fighting a guerrilla war with the Chinese. While on the one hand Chaudhuri was not willing to risk sending troops back into NEFA, the Americans were talking of raising fifty new Indian divisions to kick the Chinese out of Lhasa.

The defeat meted out by China had created complete panic in the Indian leadership (if one can even call it that) which had allowed the likes of Sandys to start dictating terms to Nehru. Even though the Chinese had unilaterally withdrawn, the Indians were being forced to the negotiating table with Pakistan! If the impression in Pakistan at the time was that the Indians were spineless dhotiwallahs, the blame for this fell on India's handling of the situation. No wonder then that Ayub and Musa and every other Pakistani on the street thought Kashmir was available for easy picking.

Many Pakistanis at the time felt Ayub should have delivered the knockout blow to a tottering India, which would have meant Pakistani forces marching into Kashmir. India's 5 and 27 Divisions had been plucked out of Punjab and airlifted to Tezpur, thereby creating a yawning gap in India's defences against Pakistan. The Western Army Command under Lieutenant General Daulet Singh had been so preoccupied with the defence of Leh that it had paid no attention to its western flank extending from Kargil to Zoji La, making the Indians vulnerable in that sector. In the event of Pakistan launching an attack, the only option would have been to pull out 25 Division from the Poonch–Rajouri–Naushera axis and try and plug the gap. Towards that end, Chaudhuri, for his part, welcomed the talks with Pakistan, for he desperately needed time to realign his own resources. The longer the talks lasted, the fewer were the chances of Pakistani military adventurism.

The Indian contingent, headed by Sardar Swaran Singh, also included G. Parthasarathi, who had been recently appointed India's high commissioner to Pakistan. Parthasarathi, or GP, a former Oxford blue in both hockey and cricket, and who had also represented India in test matches, had until then been holding charge in Peking. In addition, there were also Gundevia, Palit, Shankar Prasad, the secretary for Kashmir, R. Chopra, and B. L. Sharma, all of whom were from the External Affairs Ministry.

Through December 1962, Pakistan had watched in smug satisfaction as India came a cropper against the Chinese, but after the ceasefire Ayub was worried. The Chinese had not only asserted their military superiority over India, they had surprised the world by withdrawing unilaterally. Though the pullback of the PLA in NEFA had been to positions originally held by both sides in November 1959, no such stipulation existed in Ladakh. On the contrary, the Chinese, who had pushed as far forward as per their claim lines, had made it clear that this would be the new boundary between India and the PRC. This effectively meant that the Aksai Chin region was now firmly under Chinese occupation and control.

Smugness turned to worry as it became obvious to the Pakistani leadership that the PRC now needed control of the Shaksgam Valley that sat like a crown on the northernmost part of J&K. One thing the world had learnt about Mao: if Mao wanted something, he simply took it! Pakistan could either fight the Chinese or simply give up. Ayub chose the latter option.

There had been a hint that all might not be well with Pakistan when some of their diplomats in New Delhi sent out feelers to their Indian counterparts asking if India might be interested in reviving Ayub's earlier offer (before the Chinese attack) of joint defence. The matter had gone right up to the COAS who had dismissed it as a gimmick, saying the Pakistanis would never ever 'take sides with India against the Chinese'.[16]

Swaran Singh's delegation had arrived in Rawalpindi on 27 December where it was received with palpable disdain by the Minister for Industries, Zulfikar Ali

Bhutto, and his team of officials, which included the Calcutta-born Saidulla Khan Dehlavi, a second-generation career diplomat who was Pakistan's foreign secretary. That the Pakistanis intended to squeeze the 'defeated Indians' and take Kashmir diplomatically was quite evident from their body language. Shortly after their arrival, Swaran Singh met President Khan who cordially received the Indian minister.

Until Radio Pakistan came on with its evening news bulletin on 27 December, the Pakistanis were holding all the cards. The lead news item was that 'the Chinese and Pakistan governments had signed an agreement in principle about their common border. According to the agreement a tract of Kashmiri territory to the northwest of Hunza had been given away to China.'[17] The Shaksgam Valley in its entirety was now under the control of the PRC, who had taken it from Pakistan without firing a shot!

◆

Despite having egged on both Bhutto and Ayub from the sidelines to make a grab for Kashmir, Pakistan's 'friend from the north' was too preoccupied with Tibet, where its position was much too insecure for it to have intervened in Kashmir. After a tour through Tibet in 1962, the Panchen Lama had written a 70,000-character petition addressed to Zhou Enlai denouncing China's abusive policies. The lama then met with the Chinese prime minister to discuss the petition he had written; at first, there was a positive response from the communist leadership, but by the end of the year (and after the 1962 clash with India), Mao called the petition '...a poisoned arrow shot at the Party by reactionary feudal overlords'.[18] A few years later, in 1964, the twenty-six-year-old Panchen Lama was publicly humiliated at Politburo meetings, dismissed from all posts of authority, and declared 'an enemy of the Tibetan people'. The Cultural Revolution began soon after.

According to the French-born military historian Claude Arpi, 'Great administrative changes were taking place in Tibet in September 1965. The Tibetan Autonomous Region (TAR) was formed and the local Communist Party changed from a Work Committee to a full-fledged communist party organization. Gen Zhang Guohua was named 1st Party Secretary while the previous Chinese commander General Zhang Jingwu left Tibet for good. China was much too preoccupied with these administrative changes to have been able to "help" Pakistan.'[19]

Chapter 3

THE EYES OF AYUB

AN ARABIAN TALE

Zulfikar Ali Bhutto was born in 1928 near Larkana in what was Sindh, British India. His father, Sir Shah Nawaz Bhutto, was the diwan of the princely state of Junagadh. Zulfikar's early years and schooling were in Bombay. First married at the age of fifteen, in his later teens, he became actively involved in the Pakistan Movement. Unlike most people from the subcontinent who went to Europe for higher education, in 1947, Zulfikar Bhutto enrolled at the University of Southern California in the US to study political science. In 1949 he transferred to the University of Berkeley from where he graduated in 1950. During his time in Berkeley, Zulfikar Bhutto delivered a series of lectures on socialism and its feasibility in Islamic countries.

The years around Independence in Junagadh were extremely volatile. Zulfikar's father staged a palace coup and acceded Junagadh to Pakistan, a situation that was not acceptable to India. The accession was reversed by India's military intervention which included the three amphibious landings in the Kathiawar region in October 1947. Later that same month, Pakistan unleashed its armed lashkars into Kashmir in an attempt to force Maharaja Hari Singh's hand, as we've seen. After the Instrument of Accession was signed between the maharaja and India, Indian troops were flown into the Valley.

Bhutto moved to England in 1950 and married his second wife, Nusrat Ispahani, a year later. The Iranian-Kurdish Ispahani would bear him four children, the eldest being Benazir. He did further studies in law and political science at Christ Church, Oxford and, after a stint in teaching, returned to Pakistan where he joined President Iskander Mirza's cabinet. In 1957, he became the youngest member of Pakistan's delegation to the United Nations, where he made what would be the first of many demagogic speeches about India's aggression. With the advent of military rule in 1958, Bhutto seamlessly switched his loyalties to Ayub Khan.

On 16 April 1965, the Central Intelligence Agency put out a top secret note titled 'Pakistan's Foreign Policy Under Ayub and Bhutto' for the powers that be in Washington DC. The main focus of the study was the rise of the mercurial Zulfikar Ali Bhutto as the brightest star in Pakistan. He seemed to have a near hypnotic grip on not just the president, Field Marshal Ayub Khan, but also on the rest of the country. His growing role in policymaking could be traced to his negotiating the Indus Waters Treaty with India in 1960 and a $30-million oil exploration assistance agreement with the Soviets, which was noted as his 'most dramatic success' as commerce minister. Ever since, Ayub seemed to regard Bhutto as a special protégé and had given him wide discretion when he began to take an interest in foreign affairs.

The document noted that Bhutto was made the foreign minister in 1963 at the height of reaction in Pakistan to the US decision to give military aid to India following the attack by China on India's Himalayan border. Since then, Ayub had come to depend heavily on Bhutto for conceiving and carrying out new foreign policy initiatives.

A brilliant orator with the ability to ooze conviction, Bhutto's ideology was a complicated mix of socialism and Islam. After the horrors of Partition, sensing that the people of Pakistan needed a distinct identity from the other people of the subcontinent, Bhutto started to claim that the country was an extension of the Arab world. This was not surprising, considering the fact that Sind, until the British takeover, was ruled by Arabs for centuries. But getting a large number of compatriots to accept this speaks to Bhutto's considerable persuasive ability. Even more so when one realizes that more than half the population of Pakistan at that time was located in the eastern wing (today's Bangladesh) that bordered Southeast Asia.

Being persuasive is one thing, but being able to walk the geopolitical tightrope with consummate ease requires yet another skill set. As the man driving Pakistan's foreign policy, Bhutto succeeded in doing just that; despite Pakistan's hitherto pro-West policy, he managed to carve out a special relationship with China. Though the Americans were wary of this growing closeness, he managed to convince them that Pakistan was pivotal to both the SEATO and CENTO. He repeatedly asserted that Pakistan was non-aligned, making it an important member of non-aligned organizations. He made a lot of noise about pan-Arabic unity and finally convinced countries like Indonesia, that had been close to India, that their interests lay with Pakistan.

In many ways, even though they came across as being diametrically opposite, Zulfikar Bhutto was Pakistan's Krishna Menon. Both men had a near hypnotic hold over the leaders who mattered—Ayub and Nehru. Both held strong socialist views which allowed their countries to reduce their reliance on the West. In the final analysis, just as Bhutto succeeded in hyphenating Pakistan–China, the initial approach to the USSR by India was entirely due to Menon. However, while Menon went about it in a manner that earned him the sobriquet 'India's Rasputin',[1] Bhutto managed to become the bridge between the US and China. The biggest difference, however, was that while India showed Menon the door after the Chinese debacle in 1962, Bhutto survived disaster after disaster, always deftly managing to shift the blame elsewhere.

At a time when communist China was ostracized by the 'free world', Bhutto met Mao during the lead-up to the Sino–Indian clash with the greatest show of respect, almost bordering on the submissive. China, at the time, was fine-tuning its plans to militarily seal its dominance on the Aksai Chin. To divert attention from themselves, it suited Zhou Enlai to sound out an enthusiastic Bhutto about Pakistan attacking India from the west at the same time and taking the rest of Kashmir.

However, for once, Ayub did not let Bhutto bully him into the proposed alliance. The Pakistani president was extremely wary of Chinese designs and, to Bhutto's chagrin, he offered a joint defence union to Nehru (who famously responded with 'against whom?'). For Bhutto, who was breathing fire at every possible forum about Kashmir and using the military interventions in Hyderabad, Junagadh, and Goa to paint India in the worst shades possible, it was a huge lost opportunity.

With India's dismal performance in Ladakh and NEFA, most of Pakistan started believing that 'Hindu India' didn't stand a chance against Pakistan, especially since, as a part of the Western alliances, Pakistan was bristling with US weapon systems that supposedly gave it an edge over India both on land and in the air.

Nehru appealing to the US and Western countries for help the moment the Chinese attacked on 20 October 1962 created an immediate problem for Pakistan. The Americans, obsessed with containing 'the menace of communism', responded immediately. After World War II, the British were in no position to act any differently, so they too followed suit. The few weapons promised to India by the US created an uproar, for the general belief in Pakistan was that India was playing victim in what was just a minor border tussle and using it to arm herself against Pakistan.

With Ayub himself leading the protests against US weapons for India, the Americans were concerned, for Pakistan was a key American ally, in its fight against communism, despite Bhutto and Ayub now cosying up to the Chinese. Assurances were given to Pakistan that Western aid would be given to India with the caveat that she had to resolve the Kashmir problem. No surprise then that three days after the Chinese ceasefire, Duncan Sandys was in New Delhi. However, at that stage, Ayub realized that China meant business and would take the Shaksgam Valley, a critical link between Sinkiang (Xinjiang) and Tibet, with or without Pakistan's involvement.

Apart from negotiating trade and military agreements with China, Bhutto had ensured that despite Pakistan's membership of anti-communist Western alliances, China had never criticized Pakistan. So Bhutto hardly hesitated before giving China what it wanted—the Shaksgam Valley. The Sino–Pakistan Boundary Agreement that transferred 75,000 sq km of Kashmir to China was a stunning development in global geopolitics. It not only helped Pakistan to lessen its dependence on the US, it effectively cocked a snook at the Indians who had been forced to the negotiating table.

Bhutto had not held back his punches during Ayub Khan's presidential election in December 1964 where he was quite the star campaigner. He had lambasted Fatima Jinnah, denouncing Mohammad Ali Jinnah's sister as a CIA agent. He had repeatedly claimed in his election speeches that once Ayub was brought back to power, the government would sort out the unresolved issue of Kashmir, even if it meant using force.

FAULT LINES

Nearly three-quarters of a century after Independence and Partition, there is enough irrefutable evidence to underline the fact that the 'Kashmir problem' was created almost entirely by the British. In 1964, a year and a half after the Swaran Singh-led talks had failed to gain traction thanks to the timing of the Shaksgam Valley announcement, British frustration was mounting, especially since it seemed to be a case of so near yet so far! To understand why successive British governments (Harold Wilson was the prime minister then) were so invested in J&K even after Independence, one needs to briefly look into developments until that point.

When the first British warships arrived off Surat in 1612, the Portuguese, French, and Dutch had already reached the subcontinent 114 years earlier. The flourishing markets of the Malabar coast where the Hindu zamorins of Calicut ruled and commanded the seas with their 'Muhammadan' Kunjali admirals made the Europeans look like barbarians despite all their fancy uniforms and gaudy trappings that were designed to create a sense of awe among the 'natives'. Even after the British arrived, for another century and a half, none of these so-called European powers could establish a foothold in the subcontinent until, as has so often has been the case in India's history, the gates were opened from within at Plassey. This single act of treachery on a faraway battlefield in the dusty Gangetic belt led to the rest of the subcontinent being colonized for the next 200 years. No one escaped the yoke—be they be Christians, Zoroastrians, Jews, Sikhs, Buddhists, Jains, Hindus, Muslims, or Tamils, Biharis, Gujaratis, or Kashmiris.

While most Indians at the time had an extremely narrow world view that was confined to their own region and community, the British invariably looked at India as a whole. Even though the Indic identity existed long before the British colonized the subcontinent, the physical boundaries of the empires of yore were only historical lines that had little meaning in ground reality before the arrival of the British. The concept of modern day 'frontiers' was introduced for the first time by Lord Curzon when he was the viceroy of India between 1898 and 1905 and, in keeping with this thinking, various expeditions were launched, such as the ones undertaken by Captains Morshead and Bailey which, in 1914, became the basis of delineating the boundary between India and Tibet.

At the end of World War I, most Indian troops that had fought 'for king and the empire' in Europe, expected the grant of Home Rule (not Independence) in recognition for their services. Worried that Home Rule would subsequently lead to heightened calls for Independence, the British government's India Office, in conjunction with the Colonial Office (the forbears of MI6) and the Admiralty, was tasked with the preparing of a plan that would protect British strategic interests in the subcontinent. The main emphasis was on retaining control of the oil fields in Persia (Iran) and the Middle East, especially Bahrain. Working on a strategy that took into consideration an 1857-like scenario where a massive uprising would force the British to leave the subcontinent, the plan was prepared wherein India would be partitioned into three—Hindustan, Pakistan, and Princestan.

Though not particularly serious about creating a separate Princestan, it had been included as a bargaining chip to counter any opposition from the Congress party, so as to make the creation of Pakistan a reality. The proposal was then submitted to the House of Commons, but it was officially rejected. In the meantime, on 13 April 1919 the Jallianwala Bagh massacre took place, and the British evoked the Rowlatt Act and talk of Home Rule fizzled out. However, the blueprint for the creation of Pakistan primarily to serve British interests in West Asia and to counter the Russian threat from the direction of the Pamir Mountains had been created, and it became the unofficial document that influenced events thereafter.

The fate of India—and that of Kashmir—had been sealed back in 1919. The concept of a Muslim state was first advocated by Muhammad Iqbal, writer, philosopher, and politician, in 1930. The very word—Pakistan—only came into play three years later, when it was first mentioned by Rahmat Ali (who is known as the originator of the Pakistan Movement) in 1933. Confident that they could play the communal card at will and that Pakistan would remain dependent on British support, the British plan to divide the subcontinent was also influenced by the Great Game—the political and diplomatic rivalry between the British Empire and Russia over Afghanistan, Central and South Asia—that obsessed British military thought at that time. Kashmir's remoteness had so far hidden its strategic importance from the eyes of most Indian leaders who, in any case, had far more immediate problems to deal with than delve into geopolitics.

The famed overland trading route, the Silk Road, was to Kashmir's north. Linking Central Asia with China by way of Tibet, this route was well known to successive caravans and conquering armies, some of whom included the Kashmir Valley in their grand designs. The state of J&K was the largest and one of the most populous of the 562 principalities which dotted the map of India prior to Partition in 1947. It comprised an area of 84,471 sq miles. Like most of the princely states, Kashmir was characterized by absolute autocracy in its internal affairs and a predominantly agrarian economy with a high concentration of land ownership. It had a constitutional status, encompassed in the doctrine of paramountcy, which acknowledged British suzerainty in all matters pertaining to defence, foreign affairs, and communications, in exchange for a large measure of internal autonomy.

The India Office's plan of 1919, despite being officially discarded, had a natural supporter in one of the greatest champions of colonialism, and, ironically, the man at the helm of affairs when the British empire finally began to unravel—Winston Churchill. In October 1929, when Lord Irwin, the viceroy, suggested Dominion Status for India, Churchill led protests in London, calling the idea 'not only fantastic in itself but criminally mischievous in its effects' and asked his countrymen to marshal 'the sober and resolute forces of the British Empire'[1] against the granting of self-government to India. Over the next two years, Churchill delivered dozens of speeches where he worked up, in the most immoderate form, forces hostile to the winning of political independence by people with brown or black skin.

Lest we dismiss Churchill's outburst as that of an out-of-office politician's, it is worth recalling some of his other utterances about Indians in general. During the war years, Leopold Charles Amery, a contemporary of Churchill from Harrow, was the secretary of state for India. Despite the fact that the fate of the subcontinent had been a keen issue of dispute between Churchill and Amery for many years, the Amery diaries underline the British premier's stance on India in no uncertain terms. In March 1941, when Amery expressed his anxiety about the growing cleavage between Muslims and Hindus in India, Churchill at once said: 'Oh, but that is all to the good' because it would help the British stay a while longer. Further, in September 1942, quoting Churchill, the Amery diary reads: 'I hate Indians. They are a beastly people with a beastly religion.'[2] A year later, when the question of grain being sent to the victims of the Bengal famine came up in a Cabinet meeting, Churchill intervened with a 'flourish on Indians breeding like rabbits and being paid a million a day by us for doing nothing by us about the war'.[3]

The National Archives of Pakistan brought out the first series of Jinnah papers comprising two volumes in three parts. Dr I. H. Qureshi, sometime professor of history at St Stephens, New Delhi, and later vice chancellor, Karachi University, confirms that Winston Churchill was closely in touch with Jinnah since the early 1930s and had done the initial spadework to accept the Partition plan. Historians had wondered who Elizabeth Gilliatt was whom Jinnah was writing to on a fairly regular basis. For long it was thought that it was a fictitious name that Churchill had adopted. However, Elizabeth Gilliatt was Churchill's secretary. As Churchill's rival and then prime minister Clement Attlee sought to hurriedly transfer power, Churchill was playing counsellor to Jinnah privately. He advised Jinnah that they should not be seen together in public and all correspondence should be addressed to 'Miss E. A. Gilliatt, 6 Westminster Gardens, London.'

The 'moth-eaten Pakistan' that Jinnah eventually got (the reference chiefly being to not having the entire state of J&K under Pakistan's control after Independence) suggests that larger plans and promises had been made. When Jinnah adopted dilatory tactics in accepting the Partition plan as he was opposed to the partition of Punjab and Bengal, Churchill had sent him a message which Mountbatten conveyed: that all British troops would be removed from India if Jinnah didn't accept the Partition plan. Churchill had added, 'By God, Jinnah is the only man who can't do without British help.'[4]

It's a well-known fact that Churchill was extremely peeved with Mountbatten for his handling of Partition. Had the original Radcliffe Line, drawn up in 1919, been implemented, as expected, then India would never have had any chance of intervening in J&K, accession by Maharaja Hari Singh notwithstanding. By allowing Nehru to push the line to the west in the Gurdaspur region, Churchill felt Mountbatten had spoilt the carefully laid plan wherein Kashmir would have been a part of Pakistan and the Indians would not even have noticed.

Not surprising then that in the immediate aftermath of the 1962 Chinese debacle, Mountbatten should visit India on at least a couple of occasions. Talking about the visits, Chavan's secretary, Pradhan, would say, 'For a man who had once been the Viceroy of India, his visiting India seemed odd, especially since most ministers—especially External Affairs Minister Shastri and Defence Minister Chavan—barely acknowledged his presence.'[5] Mountbatten had first encouraged Nehru to make concessions towards Pakistan, but after the failure of the talks, the former viceroy started pushing Nehru to show his statesmanship by releasing Sheikh Mohammad Abdullah from jail and using the 'Lion of Kashmir' to solve the dispute which, he repeatedly reminded the prime minister, was a black mark on his image.

What choice did Nehru have? The Congress party had willy-nilly inherited the legacy of 'non-violence' from Mahatma Gandhi. Nehru, the first nominated prime minister of Independent India (the first general elections were only held in 1951), despite initially making some woolly-headed remarks about not needing an army, had soon realized the hard truth: unless you carried a big enough stick, you were going to be vulnerable. The amphibious landings in Kathiawar to isolate Junagadh followed immediately by the fighting that erupted in J&K in October 1947, the Hyderabad 'police action' in September 1948, the Naga armed insurgency in 1956, the annexation of Goa in 1961, and then the humiliation at the hands of the Chinese in 1962 had severely dented the image of the peace-loving global statesman that Nehru so desperately wanted to be. After India used military force to drive the Portuguese out of Goa, President Kennedy had wryly remarked that Nehru's decision was 'akin to finding a priest in a whorehouse!' None of this would have escaped Nehru's attention, and with India's defence budget going up exponentially in 1963–64, it perhaps made him even more susceptible to pressure from 'his friend' Lord Mountbatten to settle the unfinished agenda of Partition!

On 24 May 1964, Sheikh Abdullah, until recently a prisoner accused of conspiracy and collusion with Pakistan, flew to Rawalpindi wearing the hat of a mediator. He was welcomed with open arms by President Ayub Khan and, in the words of the *New York Times*, had arrived in Pakistan 'in the hope of achieving what the United Nations and the great powers of the West had failed to achieve: a friendly settlement of differences between India and Pakistan, chiefly the Kashmir issue.' Quoting Nehru, the *NYT* said 'that if Sheikh Abdullah could help in bringing about "closer and more intimate relations between India and Pakistan" he would have done "great service to both countries".'[6]

At the time, Nehru was holding his cards extremely close to his chest and it is unlikely if anyone apart from his daughter, Indira, really knew what had been discussed with Abdullah. It was speculated that there were three options that would be presented to Ayub Khan. (1) A condominium by which India and Pakistan would exercise joint sovereignty over the disputed state of J&K; (2) A subcontinental confederation that would join India, Pakistan, and Kashmir into a loose union—a solution that would effectively include the condominium idea because the two big powers would have to provide for Kashmir's defence, diplomatic relations, and economic welfare; or (3) A United Nations trusteeship over Kashmir to end ten years hence with a self-determination plebiscite. It was also believed that though Abdullah had Nehru's blessings to discuss the options, should Ayub Khan acquiesce to any of them, it would only create the platform for further dialogue.

On 27 May 1964, having returned from Dehradun the previous evening, Nehru collapsed, and his death was announced in the Lok Sabha at 2 p.m. He had left no clear political heir and, in the days that followed, Lal Bahadur Shastri emerged as the front runner—he had the support of Congress President K. Kamaraj and others who were desperate to keep the conservative right-wing Morarji Desai in check. Once sworn in on 9 June, Shastri decided to retain most of Nehru's council of ministers, which meant Chavan kept his job as defence minister. Swaran Singh replaced Shastri in External Affairs while Indira Gandhi was brought in as the Information and Broadcasting minister. Gulzarilal Nanda, who had officiated as the prime minister in the interim, continued to have charge of the Home Ministry.

Nehru's death, just as the ceding of the Shaksgam Valley had done earlier, derailed any possibility of a settlement with Pakistan. On the contrary, the outwardly frail and small physical appearance of Shastri resulted in further feeding Pakistani machismo. Shastri and Khan were to meet in October 1964, and the dhoti-clad Shastri over whom Ayub Khan towered, did not impress the Pakistani field marshal cum president.

Among all the mid-level ranking Indian officers who had served in the Fourteenth Army in Burma during World War II, Ayub Khan had the least impressive record. Ayub and the Indian army chief, General Chaudhuri, had both graduated in 1928 from Sandhurst. While the latter joined the cavalry, Ayub was commissioned into the 1st Battalion 14 Punjab Regiment, the unit he was to briefly take charge of in 1945, before being removed from command and suspended without pay for visible cowardice. Opting for Pakistan during Partition, he was promoted to the rank of an acting major general and given command of the 14th Infantry Division in Dacca, East Pakistan, in 1948. Decorated with Pakistan's second highest gallantry award, the coveted Hilal-i-Jur'at for non-combatant duties, he was brought back to Pakistan where he served as the adjutant general.

In 1951, when Sir Douglas Gracey relinquished the post of commander-in-chief of the Pakistan Army, the names of four 'native' major generals were forwarded to the government, and Major General Iftikhar Khan was selected to assume command. Unfortunately, the general was killed in an air crash before he could take over, and once again the search for a name began. The relatively junior Ayub Khan, whose name was not on the original nomination list, was strongly recommended by Iskander Mirza, the then defence secretary. The clinching argument in Ayub's favour at that time was that he was the least ambitious of all the generals. Prime Minister Liaquat Ali Khan then promoted Ayub to the rank of lieutenant general and appointed him the commander-in-chief. The rest, as they say, is history!

BOOK II

Pakistan Flexes its Muscles

Chapter 4

SLIPPING AND SLIDING

THE RANN OF KUTCH...OR OF SINDH?

In February 2016, half a century after Indian and Pakistani forces had clashed in the Rann of Kutch, I flew into Ahmedabad with the intention of seeing the ground for myself. The army formation there made a brief presentation that covered the fighting in the Rann, after which I covered the 330 km to Bhuj. Accompanied by Captain James Joseph from 16 Madras, we crossed the 'India Bridge' into the Rann early in the morning, after which we followed a single-track metal road to Vigokot, a distance of 180 km. For most of the journey, the road ran along a slightly elevated bund, with miles and miles of desolate, barren, dry marshland on either side. Apart from the odd covey of grey partridge and shrikes that scurried across the road, we saw no signs of life whatsoever. Despite the near perfect road conditions, it had taken me close to ten hours from Ahmedabad to our destination, which was a massive illuminated fence that ran along the entire length of the International Border (IB).

'In 1965 the nearest Indian formation, 31 Infantry Brigade Group, was stationed at Ahmedabad,' Captain Joseph explained. 'During the wet season this is a nightmare. Virtually the entire area is submerged and you must remember there were only rough tracks existing in those days.' The discussion had centred on the nature of the dispute. 'The problem is, the Pakistanis say this is a dead seabed and therefore the laws of maritime demarcation should exist. We don't buy that theory and, since historic times, this area was a part of the Kutch Kingdom that bordered the Emirate of Sindh. Sometimes, though, I wish we would agree with Pakistan and let them have half of this gigantic swamp. In two months, they'll be begging us to take it back,' he laughed.

After a quick lunch at the Border Security Force (BSF) post at Vigokot, we drove along the IB. For the most part there was shallow water on either side of the fence, with a plethora of aquatic birds, including flamingos and pelicans. Finally, we arrived at Sardar Post where a solitary pillar bore the names of the men who had fallen while defending Indian territory against the initial Pakistani advance.

The Great Rann is hard to describe, and needs to be experienced to get a real sense of it. Lying to the east and south of the Indus delta, when it isn't inundated by brackish water between June and October, it is a massive salt waste that resembles a giant dried-up lake with the occasional raised land mass known locally as 'bet'. It covers an area of 23,310 sq km and the northern part, the Great Rann, separates Kutch from Sindh, the boundary running from the south-western border of Rajasthan to the Arabian Sea. Further to the south, the Little Rann acts as the boundary separating Radhanpur from Kathiawar. The area is more or less uninhabited except for the odd hamlet on some of the larger bets and, during the dry season, the coarse grass allows wild asses and nilgai to mingle with domestic camels and herds of cattle that are brought there to graze. The salinity levels of the brackish water are extremely high and, when combined with the extreme weather conditions of oppressive heat and swirling dust, make it one of the most inhospitable regions for humans in the world.

There is evidence to suggest that when Alexander the Great was in Sindh, it wasn't entirely a salt desert, but an inland sea fed by a 'lost river' and the Puran River. The western part of the Rann, extending from the town of Ali Bandar to the Kori creek, was fertile, and there was free movement of people between Sindh and Kutch, without having to negotiate the desert barrier.[1]

At the time of Independence, there was a road that linked Bhuj with Banni and Khavda in Kutch, terminating just before one entered the Rann. From Khavda, a camel trail that could allow vehicles extended northward to Diplo in Sindh. Wet marsh-like conditions up to Mori Bet made the going difficult, but after that, the terrain firmed up, allowing for easier and speedier movement. The total distance was 67 km.

From the Sindh side, the northern portion of the Rann was easily accessible. During the dry months, a motorable road on the Pakistani side also ran along the border, while a track linked Luna, on the northern end of Kutch, across the Rann with the town of Rahim Ki Bazar. This route passed through Karim Shahi, Vigokot, and Kanjarkot. Two other tracks linked Nagarparkar on the Sindh side with the Bela tehsil, one going to Bela and the other to Lodrani.

In contrast to the salt water waste on its eastern flank, Sindh is low, flat country with the exception of limestone and sandstone formations on its western boundary that naturally demarcate it from Balochistan. There are other rocky formations around which the major cities and towns are built. Sindh gets its name from the great Indus River that fertilizes the region and is known in Sanskrit as the Sindhu—the sea or a great body of water. However, according to Sindhi folklore, the region was so called after Sindh, the brother of Hind, the son of Nuh or Noah, whose descendants ruled that country for many generations.

In ancient times, Sindh was believed to be ruled by a powerful Hindu dynasty that had its capital at Alor near Rohri, on the banks of the Mehran (Indus). One of the kings of this dynasty, Rai Sahiras II, was killed in battle while fighting the king of Nimroz, who was on a marauding excursion to Kutch and Mehran in search of loot and female slaves in the seventh century CE. In 712 CE, Sindh and the entire Condominium Indus valley was captured by Muhammad ibn Qasim of the Umayyad caliphate. After that, Sindh remained under various Muslim dynasties.

In 1783, the Talpur dynasty, that traced its descent from Mir Hamza and claimed to be Balochis of Arab origin, established their rule over Sindh. Originating with Fateh Ali Khan, the family split into various branches, each headed by a 'mir', of which the mir of Hyderabad in Sindh was considered to be the most powerful. The East India Company had started making inroads into the region and, given the importance of Karachi, it was only a matter of time before the British moved to annexe Sindh. After the withdrawal of British forces from Afghanistan in 1842, Sir Charles Napier arrived with a large military force under his command. After a series of battles, Sindh was annexed in 1843.

However, even before the British took charge of Sindh, in 1838, the kingdom of the mirs and Kutch were in a dispute about the boundary, with the mirs laying claim to half the Rann. When the British took over five years later, it necessitated the determination of the boundary—they agreed that the boundary between Sindh and Kutch would be the western limit of the Greater Rann. However, there was no urgency to demarcate the boundary. The subsequent Partition of the subcontinent in 1947 saw the erstwhile Emirate of Sindh, since 1936 called the Sindh Province of British India, take its Muslim majority to the Pakistan side. Bhuj, by virtue of its Hindu majority, stayed with India. Almost immediately, as relations between India and Pakistan turned sour, the latter, on 14 July 1948, wrote to India saying that the Sindh–Kutch boundary was still in dispute and must be settled.

In 1949, India dismissed Pakistani claims, saying there was no dispute about what was historically a well-defined boundary. Shortly thereafter, reports from the Kutch administration were received that suggested Pakistan was regularly conducting military exercises next to the border and its patrols were frequently entering the Rann. To contain this and to keep a watch on Pakistani movements, the authorities wanted Indian patrols to be strengthened. Reports of Pakistani activity in the region continued to filter in; by the end of 1955, they had built a new motorable track leading to Gulmamad Talavadi while a couple of contingents of the Sindh Reserve Police had set up posts at Vingi and Baliari opposite the Chhad Bet area. Pakistani graziers who brought their cattle into the Rann were allowed in by paying a small fee. Pakistan's Sindh Reserve Police personnel had considerably stepped up their patrolling and started instigating the graziers not to pay the fee. This led to a formal protest note by India to the Pakistani government, dated 12 January 1956. The note was ignored and on 17 February, an Indian police patrol found the Sindh Reserve Police deployed at Gulmamad Talavadi. A few shots were fired—the first in the Rann of Kutch—which forced the Indian police party to withdraw.

112 Infantry Brigade was headquartered at Dhrangadhra, roughly a third of the way between Ahmedabad and Bhuj. One of its battalions, the camel-mounted 7 Grenadiers commanded by Lieutenant Colonel Rewant Singh, was stationed at

Khavda, approximately 70 km from Chhad Bet. This unique battalion, perhaps the only one of its kind in the world, could trace its origins back to the Jadeja Rajput clans who were descendants of the Kutch rulers. All the peripheral states in the vicinity of the Rann and Thar Desert had their own camel-based forces that were used for fighting when they had resisted the Arab invasions from the direction of Sindh between 1540 and 1760 CE. The British started taking control of the Gujarat region from 1815 onwards and placed the kingdoms of Kutch, Saurashtra, Baria, Rajpipla, Lunawada, Idar, and their state forces under the overall control of the governor of Bombay. All the camel-borne units were subsequently brought together and in 1951 the battalion was given the status of an Indian army grenadier battalion.[2]

One squadron of 7 Grenadiers set out on the 18th on 'a routine patrol'[3] from Khavda and reached their objective by noon the next day. Whether they were aware of the earlier incident or not is open to conjecture, but the Pakistanis in well dug-in positions allowed the Indians to get close before opening fire with light machine guns (LMGs). Two of the men, Grenadiers Prema Ram and Hardial Singh, got hit by bursts. In the ensuing firefight, Havildar Murli Ram managed to drag the two wounded men to cover, in the process getting hit in the chest himself. Murli Ram was subsequently awarded the Shaurya Chakra for his act of bravery.[4] In addition, three Indian camels lost their lives, the first battle casualties in the Rann of Kutch.

Angry diplomatic protests were exchanged between the two countries. Even though the intelligence network on the Indian side was rather poor, reports were coming in that suggested that Pakistanis equipped with medium machine guns (MMGs) and 2-inch mortars were digging in at Chhad Bet. On 22 February orders were given to 112 Infantry Brigade to move to Khavda from Dhrangadhra, a distance of 280 km. Two days later, as the brigade (less 5 Rajputana Rifles) concentrated at Khavda, 7 Grenadiers established a firm base at Bedia Bet, while India once again lodged a protest saying that Chhad Bet was its territory. On 25 February, Lieutenant General (later General) Kodandera Subayya Thimayya,[5] the Southern Army commander, visited the area. 7 Grenadiers put in a dawn attack at Chhad Bet only to find that the Pakistanis had hurriedly pulled out of the Rann into their own territory, leaving a few weapons behind.

With no further activity on the Pakistani side, it appeared that the matter was settled, but a month later, Pakistan decided to rake up the issue yet again. In a note dated 9 April 1956, it claimed: 'It has been emphasised that the Rann is a dead sea. According to the international practice seas are divided equally between states situated on either side of it. The same principle seems to have been followed while settling the dispute over the Little Rann between the two states of Morvi and Kutch. The Pakistani claim to the northern portion of the Rann up to Dharamsala is, therefore, supported not only by possession and exercise of authority, but also by international practice and precedent.'[6] To further strengthen their case, the Pakistanis attached some British maps and documents that supposedly showed the area had always been under dispute.

The 1956 Chhad Bet incident succeeded in doing two things: first, it brought attention to the Rann as a hot spot, for until then the emphasis had been on fighting Pakistan in J&K; and, second, it underlined the vulnerability of the Indian position. The logistical limitations imposed by the terrain on the Indian side were only too obvious. On the Pakistani side, Badin, which had an airstrip and a rail link, was just 32 km from the Rann, and Karachi 200 km away. Based on suggestions put forward by General Satyawant Mallanna Shrinagesh, the chief of army staff, it was decided that certain immediate steps had to be taken. 7 Grenadiers, which had been earmarked to be disbanded, would continue to operate from Khavda, its men deployed in penny packets in support of the Central Reserve Police Force (CRPF) and State Reserve Police that would man the forward posts. The battalion was to reluctantly bid adieu to its beloved camels and function as a regular infantry battalion henceforth. Three fair weather airfields were to be constructed in the Rann itself—Chhad Bet, which could be serviced by Auster AOP.9s, Khavda, and Kotda, the latter with the capacity to handle the larger Dakota DC-3s. The Bhuj airfield was also to be upgraded, so it could handle fighter operations.

In addition, roads were to be built linking Khavda with Chhad Bet and Lakhpat; Mavsari–Tharad–Dhanera–Panthawada–Dantiwada; Varahi–Morwada–Suigan; Bhabhar–Suigan; Radhanpur–Morwada; and Dholavira–Godada–Lodrani–Mosana–Santalpur. Fresh water was a major problem in the highly saline region and a plant was to be set up near Chhad Bet to ensure an adequate supply.

THE BUILD-UP

The ruins of a fort at Kanjarkot just south of the northwestern border of the Rann with Sindh broke the monotony of an otherwise featureless area—flat country with large patches of water. On the Pakistani side, running parallel to the border, were a string of sand dunes that gave the West Pakistan Indus Rangers deployed there an unobstructed view of the Indian side. There were frequent instances of trespass in the area, but these were generally ignored, with rumours of Indian policemen even visiting sex workers on the other side. However, on 13 May 1964, the Gujarat Special Reserve Police (SRP) arrested three Pakistani nationals in the area. They were let off after a while but, once again, the region was in the limelight.

Almost like an encore of 1956, the police posts on the Indian side started sending reports around the second week of January 1965 of a significant build-up on the Pakistani side. To make matters worse, the SRP claimed that the Pakistanis had built a track/road that linked Surai with Ding that passed south of Kanjarkot across Indian territory so it could avoid the sand dunes. According to them, one company of Indus Rangers had been deployed at Kanjarkot to guard the road—

one platoon near the ruins of the fort during the day that used to pull back at night, leaving a listening post, and two other platoons on the sand dune to the north, were dug in with 3-inch mortars and MMGs.

The reports were taken seriously by the Government of India and the district magistrate of Kutch was sent to investigate and report back.[7] By mid-February, Imad Ali, the inspector general of police, Gujarat, confirmed that there were 400 Indus Rangers at Rahim Ki Bazar and an entire wing of Rangers deployed along the border. Two other battalions were being held in reserve at Hyderabad and Chhor, capable of moving at high speed to reinforce any part of the border in a matter of hours.

Protest notes pertaining to Pakistani intrusions in the area were having no effect, with Pakistan either ignoring them or simply filing its own protest. On the Indian side, there were five SRP companies distributed between Vigokot, Karim Shahi, and Chhad Bet. On its own, this force was not capable of enforcing Indian sovereignty at Kanjarkot, but its men had intensified patrolling around the fort towards the end of January.

There was an accepted procedure that was (and still is) followed if either side wished to initiate a flag meeting. The first few attempts by the Indians were ignored by the Pakistani Rangers. On 5 February, four Indian jeeps were intercepted by the Pakistanis who asked them to return to Chhad Bet, which they did. The next day, another Indian patrol moving towards Kanjarkot was blocked by a large number of Indus Rangers. With tension mounting on the ground, finally, on 15 February, a flag meeting between the deputy inspector general, Rajkot Range, and the commandant of the Indus Rangers was held, but it ended inconclusively with both sides reiterating their claim over the disputed area.

Three days later, India sent yet another diplomatic note to Pakistan suggesting that survey teams be sent to demarcate the boundary. On 19 February, G. Parthasarathi, the Indian high commissioner, met Zulfikar Bhutto, then the foreign minister of Pakistan, and repeated the suggestion. Bhutto refused to be drawn into a worthwhile discussion, instead making allegations of air violations in the region by India.

Both governments then almost simultaneously issued operational orders to their respective army headquarters. On 21 February, the first formal order as a part of Operation Kabaddi was issued by Major General P. C. Gupta, GOC of the Maharashtra and Gujarat Area, to Brigadier S. S. M. Pahalajani, commander of 31 Infantry Brigade. The orders stated in no uncertain terms that Kanjarkot had to be captured and, if in the process, the IB needed to be crossed, the brigade could do so.

31 Infantry Brigade consisted of three infantry battalions—17 Rajputana Rifles (Raj Rif) commanded by Lieutenant Colonel Bhartendra Singh, 2 Sikh Light Infantry (LI) under Lieutenant Colonel H. J. Hawes, and 1 Mahar with Lieutenant Colonel Krishnaswamy 'Sundarji' Sundararajan[8] as its commanding officer (CO)—

and 11 Field Artillery Regiment. As it was, the move from Dhrangadhra to Bhuj took almost a week and even then the logistical nightmare of moving into the Rann's unforgiving terrain was just beginning.

The operational order issued by Maharashtra and Gujarat Area was drafted and issued by Southern Command, which at the time was being commanded by Lieutenant General L. P. 'Bogey' Sen. To mobilize the brigade and deploy it in the Rann was one thing, but to order it to capture Kanjarkot and evict the Pakistanis from their positions on firm ground was questionable and, in many ways, reflected the initial Indian attitude at Nam Ka Chu barely two and a half years previously where the Sen–Kaul combine had deployed 7 Brigade in a similar manner. On the face of it, given the difference in terrain, comparing Kanjarkot and Nam Ka Chu may seem far-fetched, but the situation was much the same, if not worse: the enemy occupied the high ground, had access to superior artillery (and armour) support, and was far better equipped. Indian Army units deployed against Pakistan that had been moved from NEFA had to return the self-loading 7.62 rifles and go back to using the bolt-action .303 Enfield rifle. In Nam Ka Chu the commanders had had options which they chose to ignore. At Kanjarkot, had the brigade group decided to launch a frontal attack on the Pakistani positions, the terrain did not offer the Indians any tactical advantages they could build on.

Commenting on the reliability of intelligence in the Rann, General Chaudhuri later acknowledged that he had received adequate information on the southward movement and deployment of Pakistani formations. Whether that information was correctly analysed is subject to debate.

Even though work on roads and tracks had been sanctioned after the clash in 1956, the situation on the Indian side was pitiful. The road between Bhuj and Khavda was unreliable, as the track passed through a causeway that was prone to flooding. Most of the 'roads' marked on the maps were just wooden pegs buried in the ground by the various SRP units operating in the area. Very few hazards were marked on the map and everything looked like caked white salt. The moment vehicles, even jeeps, went over it, the crust would give way and they would sink into the water underneath.[9]

Almost all post-war analyses, both Indian and Pakistani, claim that President Ayub gave the green signal to General Tikka Khan to deploy 8 Division as a consequence of the Indian order to mobilize its 31 Infantry Brigade. Tikka Khan in turn issued his orders to the Indus Rangers to reinforce the Kanjarkot position on 22 February, which though chronologically comes after the issuance of the Indian operational order, was probably taken independently. Tikka Khan also simultaneously asked Brigadier K. M. Azhar, commanding 51 Brigade, to immediately move his tactical headquarters (TAC HQ) to Badin.

Besides Brigadier Azhar's formation, Tikka Khan also had 6 (Independent) Brigade with three infantry battalions and 52 Brigade with two. In addition, his divisional artillery consisted of four regiments—14 and 25 Field with 105 mm howitzers; 38 Field with 25-pounders, and 12 Medium which had 5.5-inch guns. Two mortar batteries were also at his disposal, both equipped with 120 mm French mortars.

On the Indian side, progress in deploying the brigade was extremely slow and frustrating. The biggest problem was availability of fresh water for the troops as the only tube well was in Khavda and it had to provide for the requirements of not just the brigade but also the police forces deployed ahead. There were no bowsers or water tankers with the army and the units improvised by creating large canvas holds on trucks. The stored water had to be moved forward, where the road conditions were such that almost half the stinking but precious load would spill. To keep moving and hasten the deployment, metal perforated steel planking (PSP) sheets were laid out to get past marshy patches.

In the absence of Brigadier Pahalajani, Lieutenant Colonel Sundarji was the officiating brigade commander. By 26 February, 31 Brigade, with all its elements, had only managed to concentrate at Bhuj, during which time political debates were raging in New Delhi. The remote ruins of the Kanjarkot and the recently discovered Pakistani 'road' had catapulted the Indians back in time and depressing comparisons were being drawn with China's Highway G-219 that had been discovered cutting across the Aksai Chin only after the Chinese announced its completion in 1959. As public opinion demanding immediate action began to gather momentum, Prime Minister Shastri gave Home Minister Gulzarilal Nanda the nod to move seven CRPF companies to the Rann immediately while Defence Minister Chavan was asked to put a parachute battalion on standby should it be required to deploy.

On 3 March, Sardar Swaran Singh, India's foreign minister, had to get up in Parliament and assure the members of the Lok Sabha that it was not quite appropriate to draw parallels between the situation at Kanjarkot and the incidents on the India–China front where proper roads had been built by PLA engineers. He explained that the so-called road in the Rann was nothing but the tracks that had been created by the passage of Pakistani vehicles as they ingressed into Indian territory for a relatively short distance. Angry members of the Opposition were not satisfied with the answer and they accused the Government of India of cowardice, demanding that more troops should be sent at once to clear the area of Pakistani intruders.

By 6 March, as the Indian Army struggled to get men and equipment across the Rann to the border, Pakistan's 51 Brigade had already moved 8 Frontier Force (FF), under the command of Lieutenant Colonel Mustafa Janjua, to Khadan and reinforced the defences at Kanjarkot and Rahim Ki Bazar with additional MMGs and mortars. Indian intelligence reports were also suggesting that the Pakistan Army had a couple of tanks, a battery of 25-pounder guns, some armoured fighting vehicles, and a sufficient number of troops at Badin. Twelve Pakistan Air Force fighters had also reportedly been moved to Badin. A parallel build-up was also being reported at Ali Bandar where a military camp had been established with at least four tanks, seven armoured personnel carriers (APCs), and a large number of men who could reinforce their defences at Pabuhar, northwest of Diplo.

Simultaneously, the West Indus Rangers headquarters had been shifted from Diplo to Rahim Ki Bazar and had a reported strength of 400 men. Smaller detachments of 100 men each were known to be dug in at Kulri, Surai, Vingi, Jattalai, Vingi–Jatur, and Kanjarkot. Three days later, General Tikka Khan moved Brigadier Azhar's TAC HQ to a location south of Diplo, at a point roughly halfway between Vingi and Kanjarkot. The Pakistanis were now waiting for the Indians to step in and launch their assault at Kanjarkot.

Apart from eagerly wanting to test out their Patton tanks and other newly acquired equipment from the West, the Pakistan Army was keen to put into practice its 'New Concept of Defence', which was the brain-child of General Musa. Aware that the Indians had more troops available in case of a prolonged conflict, the new doctrine envisaged holding ground by firepower and mobility rather than by manpower. The Pakistani high command felt that an infantry division in a defensive posture with armour integrated into it could hold the same frontage with just about a third of the previous strength. This meant that the balance two-thirds could be utilized for potent counter-attacks. On the flip side, this meant that there would be larger gaps between the defences and subunits would be operating in isolation. To counter this, it was vital that aggressive patrols be sent out and the communication set-up and coordination on the ground between the units be excellent. Should this succeed, General Musa believed that he could cut down on the number of infantry battalions in each division, reducing the number to seven as against the existing nine.

31 Brigade was finally in contact with Kanjarkot by the end of the second week of March, by which time the CRPF companies had also reached the area. Sundarji, who was still officiating and had personally reconnoitred the area opposite Kanjarkot wearing the uniform of the Gujarat SRP, was gung-ho and wanted to immediately launch an offensive to dislodge the Indus Rangers from the Kanjarkot Fort and the sand dunes overlooking it, as had been stipulated in the initial operational order for Operation Kabaddi.[10]

This was overruled by Brigadier Pahalajani, who, having returned, had resumed command of his brigade. In his assessment of the situation, and as the commander on the ground, Pahalajani felt his force levels were not adequate to take on the well-entrenched Pakistani troops. Instead, he asked his battalions to assume a defensive posture and build defences in the areas around Vigokot, Gullu Talao, Vigni, and Kanjarkot. These trenches and shelters were to be reinforced with metal sheets wherever possible. Sundarji, in particular, had to be reined in by Pahalajani from being overly aggressive while patrolling.

Many Indian commentators have talked disparagingly of Pahalajani's 'negative approach', some even calling it 'disobedience of orders'[11] but, in hindsight, he was probably correct in his appreciation of the situation. Had the Indians attacked and even captured Kanjarkot, the waiting Pakistanis would have decimated them on their own ground.

The CRPF companies, though technically under the operational command of 31 Brigade Group, were reporting directly to the Home Ministry and were ordered to take over Sardar Post, which lay 4.5 km southwest of Kanjarkot. The army felt this was not a tactically sound position, but nevertheless four CRPF companies commanded by Major Karnail Singh replaced the SRP on 13 March. One company was deployed at Tac (Tactical) Post, a small one-room structure around which the men dug themselves in. A second company established the Adm (Administrative) Post that was 2 km behind, while two other protective positions on the bets to the west were established. 1 Mahar reinforced these positions by sending Major Sharma, four junior commissioned officers (JCOs), and fifteen non-commissioned officers (NCOs) to assist the CRPF.

Despite having red-flagged the proposed upgradation of the airfield at Bhuj for fighter operations in 1956, IAF Vampires and other fighters were still operating from Jamnagar. Acutely aware of the imbalance that existed between the two sides in the Rann of Kutch, Southern Command initiated a joint exercise with the Indian Navy, codenamed Exercise Arrow Head.

Alarm bells started ringing in Pakistan when the Indian Navy's aircraft carrier, INS *Vikrant*, with its complement of escort ships, Sea Hawks, and Alizes appeared in the Gulf of Kutch on 26 March. Having positioned herself between Mandvi and Dwarka, *Vikrant's* complement of naval fighters began screaming across the Rann skies in what was supposedly a familiarization exercise for Indian troops on the ground. Though in most Indian records the joint Army–Navy exercise is but a footnote, from the Pakistani perspective it would have signalled serious intent. Eighteen years previously, HMIS[12] *Kistna*, *Cauvery*, and *Jamuna*, along with accompanying minesweepers and landing craft had appeared off the coast of Kathiawar and conducted three separate amphibious landings at Porbandar, Jafarabad, and Mangrol after the nawab of Junagadh, instigated by his prime minister, had acceded his predominantly Hindu state to Pakistan. The fact that the then prime minister of Junagadh was Diwan Sir Shah Nawaz Bhutto, the father of Zulfikar, the foreign minister of Pakistan, and one of the key players on the Pakistan side in the Kanjarkot stand-off, may have further underlined the feeling of apprehension.

Pakistani records state that *Vikrant* was accompanied by seven destroyers, some frigates, and the fleet tanker. 'The land and carrier-based aircraft carried out extensive reconnaissance and simulated air attacks over the Rann, frequently violating Pakistan's air space. The main purpose of the exercise, so close to Pakistan, was probably to confound and provoke Pakistan's armed forces, particularly the

Pakistan Navy and the Air Force, or, perhaps to intimidate Pakistan by a show of formidable force.'[13] The reports go on to say that Indian ships worked their way close to the Rann and discharged their guns, perhaps fine-tuning and ranging their ship-borne weapon systems. Also, owing to the acute shortage of clean drinking water, ship boilers were used to distil sea water and attempts were made to get it to the troops by using landing crafts. This proved to be impractical, however and the naval task force withdrew from the area on 30 March.[14]

On the ground, the cat-and-mouse game of one-upmanship had started in right earnest. The presence of the CRPF supported by the MMGs of 1 Mahar created a problem for Pakistani patrols heading out from Kanjarkot. Consequently, in the beginning of April, they positioned a platoon at Ding, which lay to the northeast of Sardar Post. This now interfered with the Indian patrols, so they in turn set up yet another post north of Sardar Post, 1.5 km towards Ding, on 5 April.

By 8 April, regular Pakistani troops started to deploy behind the West Indus Rangers in the Sand Dune Area at Kanjarkot. Another battalion was moved to Pabuhar to act as a reserve and protect the flanks in case of an Indian attack from an unexpected quarter. An entire regiment of artillery—Pakistan's 38 Field with 25-pounders commanded by Lieutenant Colonel A. H. Tamton, along with four tanks and seven APCs—was deployed in the sand dunes at Pabuhar. In addition, two squadrons of F-86 Sabres also arrived at Badin by the end of the day.

Both sides were inching towards each other, each waiting for the other to blink. Something had to give sooner or later.

DESERT HAWK I

The withdrawal of INS *Vikrant* and all other naval ships from the waters off Kathiawar on 30 March allowed Pakistan to regroup. The possibility of an Indian amphibious thrust combined with the dropping of a para brigade into Sindh aimed at capturing Badin would certainly have occurred to both Musa and Ayub. From a purely theoretical point of view, it was a lost opportunity for the Indians. Unfortunately, despite India's unique geographical positioning, with the subcontinent jutting out into the Indian Ocean and a coastline that extends from Kathiawar to the Sundarbans, India has never quite developed a maritime bent of mind. The naval chief was Admiral Bhaskar Sadashiv Soman and ever since 1962 (Sea Hawks and Alizes had been moved to Gorakhpur but air power in an offensive role was unfortunately not contemplated) the navy had been eager to see action. Chaudhuri, who had been the Southern Army commander, was known for his war room brilliance and a naval attack may not have been as far-fetched as it seems at first glance. If the recapture of Kanjarkot had indeed been the clear-cut objective, an amphibious landing would have placed the Indians behind Tikka Khan's 8 Division, going for his home base while he was deployed facing 31 Brigade Group in the Rann.

Ayub and the Pakistan military leadership were extremely concerned at first and then relieved. On the ground around Kanjarkot, the Indians were not showing any signs of belligerence and the Pakistanis sitting on the dunes were getting impatient. Egged on by an aggressive Bhutto and the army, which was keen to test out its new equipment and tactics, and even though it would mean crossing the border into Indian territory, Ayub made up his mind.

By late afternoon on 6 April, Ayub had given the nod to General Musa for a pre-emptive assault on the Indian positions in the vicinity of Kanjarkot. Tikka Khan's 8 Division was given the task of capturing Sardar Post by last light on 9 April and it was codenamed Operation Desert Hawk. On the morning of 7 April, Brigadier Azhar went over the ground with his battalion commanders and finalized 51 Brigade's assault plan. 18 Punjab commanded by Lieutenant Colonel Mumtaz Ali, 6 Baluch under Lieutenant Colonel S. Z. H. Zaidi, and 8 FF under Janjua were tasked with capturing Sardar Post, where one company of CRPF was deployed with two more on the flank and one in depth.

Azhar wanted to launch the attack the same night but it had to be postponed to the early hours of 9 April due to the delay in moving the three battalions to their required locations. Mumtaz Ali's Punjabis from the left and Janjua's FF battalion were tasked with the capture of Sardar Post while Zaidi's Baluchis were to capture the two flanking posts which the Pakistanis had named Shalimar and Jungle. At 0145 hrs, 18 Punjab and 8 FF, despite a fair deal of confusion still prevailing, started moving from their respective FUPs (forming-up areas) and managed to get into attacking positions without being detected by Indian patrols. Shortly thereafter, the 105 mm howitzers of 14 Field, commanded by Lieutenant Colonel Mohammad Iqbal, lit up the night sky as they began pounding the Indian positions. 88 Mortar Battery, under the command of Major Salim Malik, also joined the fray with their French-made 120 mm tubes raining fire on the hapless CRPF posts.

The intense bombardment was lifted at 0300 hrs as Pakistani infantry began its assault on the Indian positions. The flanking post of Shalimar had been vacated by the Indians and it was occupied by 6 Baluch, but the defenders at Sardar Post, supported by the MMGs of 1 Mahar, tenaciously fought back. Captain M. K. Bansal and Havildar Gopinath Bhingardive[15] in particular played a stellar role in keeping the defenders organized. In the darkness, confusion continued to prevail on the Pakistani side, with the leading Punjab elements going for the FF's objectives. Karnail Singh had deployed his sections in a triangular manner, and his own section got involved in a hand-to-hand fight with 18 Punjab. Eventually, Karnail Singh and the bulk of this section was overpowered, but the other two positions continued to hold out.

Both Pakistani and Indian commentators agree that the Pakistan attack on Sardar Post failed despite the fighting continuing for almost fourteen hours. After daybreak, the Pakistani artillery bombardment picked up again as the infantry was not making any headway. At around 1600 hrs the totally exhausted CRPF troops finally decided to fall back 2 km. Brigadier Pahalajani also ordered the 1 Mahar troops to fall back. However, Azhar, fearing an Indian counter-attack, simultaneously decided to break contact and ordered his three battalions to start withdrawing to their start position. As a result, he failed to realize that Sardar Post was now unoccupied.

Today, at the spot where the handful of CRPF men faced the onslaught of an entire Pakistani brigade,[16] there is a small pillar that serves as a memorial for Lance Naiks Kishore Singh and Ganpath Ram and Sepoys Shamsher Singh, Gyan Singh, Hari Ram, and Sidhveer Singh Pradhan who lost their lives. The plaque that briefly describes the fighting puts the Pakistani dead at thirty-four. It also acknowledges that nineteen CRPF men were captured. That figure included the CO, Major Karnail Singh, and a JCO, Jemadar Baldev Singh, plus eight non-combatants. Sundarji, who was otherwise fairly critical of the SRP and the CRPF deployments, reached Sardar Post with a patrol from 2 Sikh LI later in the evening on 9 April to see if the Pakistanis had occupied the position and acknowledged that there were Pakistani dead lying all over the place. 51 Brigade had not only failed to dislodge the CRPF, but had committed the cardinal sin of leaving their own dead behind.

Pahalajani also visited Sardar Post before last light, but the DIG of police at Vigokot was convinced that the Pakistanis would resume their offensive under cover of darkness. Much to the horror of 31 Brigade, the DIG ordered the CRPF companies to fall back from Vigokot. This created a yawning gap in the defences that could have had disastrous consequences. 17 Raj Rif that was being held in reserve was then ordered to rush its Charlie Company to Vigokot post-haste.

2 Sikh LI reinforced its patrol and reoccupied Sardar Post during the night. Orders were issued to 11 Field to locate its headquarters at Dharamsala while one battery was asked to move at night and was positioned at Vigokot by the next morning. However, the number of Sikh LI men holding Sardar Post through the next day was miniscule and Pahalajani spent a nervous day hoping the Pakistanis would not launch a second attack. Fortunately for him, Pakistan's 51 Brigade sat tight, allowing Pahalajani to thin his defences at Vigokot the next day and move a Sikh LI company there as well. On 12 April, 1 Mahar had been ordered to take over the defence of Sardar Post and Sikh LI were moved back to their position at Vigokot on 14 April. A patrol sent out to Kanjarkot returned with the news that the Pakistanis with two companies continued to hold their positions with the addition of at least one jeep-mounted RCL gun.[17] All this reshuffling of troops and moving men between Sardar Post and Vigokot, mostly under Pakistani observation, further convinced Azhar that Indian reinforcements had arrived to support the CRPF. By any standard, Operation Desert Hawk had been a failure, an unmitigated disaster.

The attack had not gone according to plan for Pakistan. The fighting had underlined that a well-entrenched defensive force that was willing to fight and not get intimidated by the bluster of 'superior weapon systems' could give as good as it got. Though the Indians who had fought at the Sardar Post were primarily CRPF with a handful of regular army in support, it should have been obvious to Pakistan right at that stage that it was a victim of its own propaganda. Unfortunately for them, the failure of Desert Hawk was brushed under the carpet, and though it was the end of the road for Azhar, it only increased the belief that once Pakistan fielded its armour, things would then go their way.

The official report put out by the Ministry of Defence in India quotes Sundarji extensively and is perhaps echoing his views when it criticizes Pahalajani for his 'inept handling' of the Sardar Post incident. Given the conditions in the Rann, especially the lack of water and a road communication network, 31 Brigade did a commendable job. Left to Sundarji, since he was also the officiating commander for a considerable length of time, Indian troops would most likely have rushed into Kanjarkot where they would have in all probability been decimated by the Pakistanis who were on firm ground. The Indian performance also suggested that defensive battles could be fought on ground that was not of Pakistan's choosing. Pahalajani may not have been a flamboyant and dashing commander, but he certainly succeeded in holding his ground despite the existing extreme negative conditions.

KILO FORCE VS 8 DIVISION

Even as the Sardar Post battle was being fought, the advance elements of 50 Parachute Brigade under Brigadier A. M. M. Nambiar were arriving in Bhuj. The brigade embarked from the Idgah Railway Station in Agra and the metre gauge trains moved on 'white hot priority' to Ahmedabad with no stops en route. 2 Para was being commanded by Lieutenant Colonel Ram Singh Yadav, 3 Para was under Lieutenant Colonel Bakhshish Singh, 4 Para was under Lieutenant Colonel E. E. D. Rozario, while 17 Para Field with its 75 mm pack howitzers was being commanded by Lieutenant Colonel Romesh Chandra Butalia. The decision to move the para brigade had to have been taken earlier, perhaps in the first week of April itself, so it stands to reason that the build-up on either side after the Sardar Post battle was not linked to the Pakistani offensive per se. The new brigade was to reinforce the Rann along with 31 Brigade Group and on 10 April orders were issued spelling out a new ORBAT[18] which placed the new formation, initially designated as 'Kilo Force' under the command of Major General (later Lieutenant General) Patrick Oscar Dunn[19]. This effectively meant the Indian force level would now stand at two brigades, which, if they adopted a defensive posture, would be adequate to meet the threat from Pakistan's 8 Division that comprised three brigades.

The command of Kilo Force was no longer with Southern Command but orders were being issued directly from Army HQ in New Delhi. This effectively meant that the decisions were being taken by the COAS himself.

Pakistan, however, after the botched attack on 9 April, perhaps aware of the arrival of the para brigade in Bhuj that same evening, now feared an Indian retaliatory offensive, which, given the existing conditions on the Indian side at that time, was a gross misreading of the situation. Nevertheless, by then, Pakistan's general headquarters (GHQ) had decided to reinforce 8 Division with an additional brigade reserve force. In addition, 12 Cavalry (one squadron of Chaffees and one squadron of M48 Patton tanks) was delinked from 1 Armoured Division based at Kharian and 24 Cavalry from Lahore was given to Tikka Khan. By the morning of 12 April, the armour had arrived in the Rahim Ki Bazar area in support of 51 Brigade.

The arrival of the tanks was a game changer and it was obvious by then that the situation was escalating rapidly. Even though the scars of Partition and the subsequent savage fighting in 1947–48 was fresh in the minds of many, there were individuals on either side of the fence who were watching the growing military escalation with increasing alarm.

One of the voices of restraint was that of the Pakistani air chief. Mohammad Asghar Khan Afridi, the second son of Brigadier Thakur Rehmatullah Khan, was born in Jammu in 1921. At that time, his father was serving in the J&K Rifles, a state force. Sent to the Prince of Wales Royal Indian Military College in 1934, Afridi was earmarked for the army and sent to the IMA from where he was commissioned into the Royal Deccan Horse in 1940.

A year later, Lieutenant Afridi was attached to the RIAF (Royal Indian Air Force) as its military adviser and in 1942 his application to be transferred to the air force was accepted. Earning his wings thereafter, he returned to Chittagong two years later and flew numerous sorties with the newly raised No. 9 Squadron on the Hawker Hurricane, mainly in support of ground troops. Both Afridi and Air Marshal Arjan Singh, his counterpart, the IAF chief, were among the first few Indian officers who got to command their various squadrons in the second phase of the Burma campaign. After the war, Afridi moved to Ambala where he was posted at the Flying Instructors School as an instructor. In 1947 he, along with his family, opted for Pakistan.

In the fledgling Pakistan Air Force, Afridi was the most senior 'native' officer. Like Nehru, Jinnah too had initially decided to retain British officers to run the three arms of their armed forces. It would take almost a decade before Afridi would be appointed the first Pakistani to head the country's air force, and even then he was barely thirty-six years old.

Afridi, even in his later years, was known to be an honourable man, with a reputation for straight talking. His personal rapport with the Indian chief of air staff (CAS) had remained good ever since their Burma days. However, in light of the developing situation and the escalating tensions, it came as a surprise to Arjan Singh when his staff officer told him his Pakistani counterpart was on the line wanting to speak with him.

Two and a half decades later, while researching the IAF's history, we had gone over this surprising turn of events.[20] Air Chief Marshal Arjan Singh (he had not at that point of time been made the marshal of the air force) had his log book and his diary with him, and he frequently double-checked dates in them as we discussed various theatres he had served in. When we came around to talking of the Rann of Kutch incident, he once again double-checked the date, which was 12 April 1965. There in his own hand he had written: 'Asghar Khan, on the telephone from Peshawar, said that we should ensure that there is no incident which may commit the air forces into the battle. I entirely agreed with the sentiment.'[21] However, Arjan Singh went on to add, during the conversation, he had pointed out that Pakistan was regularly flying AOP[22] sorties in the area. Afridi had replied that these flights were controlled by the army and not the PAF, but he said he would take care of the problem. Arjan Singh made no commitment and in fact added that even if the two air forces were not to take on offensive roles, the IAF transport aircraft and helicopters would continue to support Indian ground troops if required.

Sentiments apart, the call was perplexing. Arjan Singh immediately informed the defence minister, who was also aware that Pakistan was moving an armoured regiment into the Rahim Ki Bazar area. It was not clear at that point of time if the call was made by Afridi in his personal capacity or as the chief of the Pakistan Air Force. It didn't take long for the mystery to solve itself. On 17 April, the Pakistani air attaché in New Delhi gave Arjan Singh a note as a follow-up to the telephonic conversation. Arjan Singh said: 'I was horrified to see that in the proposal which Asghar had sent, he had mentioned that IAF aircraft should not fly within 10 miles of 24 degrees latitude. This was the first time they had revealed their intentions. I flatly refused to accept such a proposal.'[23]

The 24-degree latitude line bisected the Rann of Kutch and, should the Pakistanis launch a second offensive with armoured support, any such agreement would have given them a huge advantage. Subsequently, Afridi was to claim that in his conversation with Arjan Singh 'he had threatened retaliation against IAF bases in the Punjab if IAF planes attacked Pakistani ground troops. Khan believed that the PAF was at a disadvantage in Kutch and failed to consult either the Pakistan Army or Ayub Khan before communicating with Singh. Facing severe criticism for this omission, [Afridi] defended himself by attributing the non-participation of the IAF in the clashes to his not-so-veiled threats to Arjan Singh.'[24]

Following the deployment of tanks, during the next week Tikka Khan had moved his own divisional TAC HQ from Hyderabad to Badin. 51 Brigade with its component of artillery guns and mortars continued to hold its position at Rahim Ki Bazar while 6 (Independent) Brigade under Brigadier Iftikar Janjua was deployed around Diplo. The Brigade HQ was 8 km from Diplo, opposite Chhad Bet and the formation had three infantry battalions under its command—15 Punjab, 6 Punjab, and 2 FF—with 25 Field Regiment providing the necessary artillery support.

Facing the two Pakistani brigades, both brimming with their relatively large artillery component and supporting armour, General Dunn's Kilo Force, redesignated the 'Kilo Sector' on 20 April, consisted of 31 and 50 Para Brigades. On the western extreme, 1 Mahar was dug in at Sardar Post with 2 Sikh LI at Vigokot. 17 Raj Rif was holding Sarbela Bet and had a company at Chhad Bet. Dharamsala was defended by 2 and 3 Para, while 4 Para occupied the area southeast of it near Mori Bet, which in turn was directly north of Khavda. General Dunn's artillery component until then was limited to one field regiment and the three batteries of 17 Para Field.

The dice was heavily loaded in favour of the Pakistanis. After the failed Sardar Post attack, they had resorted to heavy shelling on a regular basis, their harassing fire making movement during daylight hours nearly impossible. 'The water situation which was bad earlier, had now become even more terrible with two brigades sharing the meagre resources. Transporting water was the biggest problem, given the constant shelling.'[25] Despite Afridi's assurance that he would stop the AOP flights, the Pakistani gunners were constantly being guided by these spotter and observation aircraft.

Amar Jit 'Tiger' Behl from 17 Para Field who, at the time, was a captain further recollects, 'Official records say there were artillery duels, which is actually a bit of a misnomer. Our 75 mm guns had a range of 9,500 yards which put most Pakistani targets out of range. We had to improvise, so we towed them out to positions selected in the morning, engaged targets, then towed the guns back through the swampy terrain, all under the cover of darkness. This continued for a few nights, each time a new location had to be selected, but this had to stop once the Pakistanis moved some RCL mounted jeeps and MMGs into the area.'[26]

General Dunn repeatedly pleaded with Army HQ for more artillery support and also requested armour support. On 20 April, 71 Medium Regiment along with two engineer companies, 70 and 78 Field Companies, reached Khavda. Armour there was none, though some PT-76 tanks that were supposed to have amphibious capabilities were later brought in for trials, but the terrain made it impossible for them to operate. On the other hand, the Pakistanis could deploy tanks as their bases were on hard ground. Even if the Indians could somehow get armour to the border, the supply lines required for their operation made it an impossibility.

On the night of 20/21 April, the shelling had an even higher degree of intensity. As the earth around them erupted, the few remaining SRP posts that were holding their ground at Chhad Bet and Biar Bet abandoned their positions. Operation Desert Hawk II had begun.

Chapter 5

ENTER THE PATTONS

DESERT HAWK II & III: MAKE THE DHOTIWALLAHS RUN!

Brigadier Iftikar Khan Janjua[1], commander of Pakistan's 6 (Independent) Brigade, had been chosen by General Tikka Khan to deliver the knockout punch and the operation was code-named Desert Hawk II. It is hard to understand the military aim behind further escalation in the Rann of Kutch because the capture and occupation of territory was not Pakistan's objective. Pakistan was looking for a swift operation which, with the help of its superior firepower and favourable terrain, would decimate the Indians. In their opinion, Desert Hawk I hadn't worked because armour had not been integrated into the attack. Desert Hawk II seems to have been a test case to see how soon Indian troops would break when confronted with Pakistani infantry supported by the superior fire power of M48 Patton tanks.

After the Sardar Post fiasco, Janjua had plenty of time to formulate his own plan which he discussed with Tikka Khan on 16 April. Based on that, 8 Division issued a four-part operational order at 0400 hrs on 17 April stating that (1) 8 Division would occupy the general area south of Vingoor–Jatrai up to line 9 Northing, while denying Kanjarkot–Ding to the enemy; (2) 8 Division would be prepared to launch an offensive aimed at Gullu Talao–Chhad Bet and Vigokot–Karim Shahi with a view to destroying the enemy deployed in these sectors; (3) The no-man's land in area Ding–Kanjarkot had to be dominated by strong raids and offensive patrolling; and (4) Kanjarkot and Ding, being prestigious positions, would be defended at all costs.

Until the night of 20/21 April, most of Pakistan's artillery fire had been directed at Sardar Post and Indian positions around Vigokot. A Pakistani company-strength patrol from 6 Punjab had probed the area east of Sera Bet (Point 84) the previous night but had not made contact with the Indians. Field guns now joined the fray and heavy fire was directed at these forward screen positions. Accompanied by a forward observation officer (FOO), Captain Mohammad Yaqub, a raiding party from 6 Punjab under the command of Lieutenant Raja Nadir Pervez Khan managed to get inside the Indian defences. The two Pakistani officers accompanied by twenty other ranks killed eight Indian soldiers, blew up their tents, destroyed the water tanks, and set fire to the ammunition dump. The FOO called for covering fire and the raiding party made good their escape with one captured LMG and six rifles. For this spectacular and extremely successful operation, Pakistan decorated Lieutenant Khan with the Sitara-e-Jurat[2] while Captain Yaqub was awarded the Imtiazi Sanad[3].

Another raiding party, this time from 15 Punjab, following similar tactics, went into Gullu Talao on 21 April, only to find the post empty as the SRP personnel had withdrawn the previous day after being subjected to intensive artillery fire.

General Dunn's immediate reaction to the 6 Punjab raid was to despatch a patrol to assess the damage. A few hours later, 3 Para's Bravo Company under Major P. P. Singh along with a battery from 17 Para Field was manning the defences, repairing the damage done by the raiding party during the early hours of the day. Apart from deploying 75 mm guns and MMGs, a couple of RCL guns were also made available for the defence of the post.

Dunn had limited options available to him with Army HQ telling him to make do with what he had! So far, only the forward posts were reporting the sound of Pakistani armour, but no tanks had actually been seen. The commando-type raid was a cause for concern as a mobile enemy striking at different locations from different directions while his defensive formations were pinned down by artillery fire would be nearly impossible to fight. Dunn's only hope was that the Pakistanis would stay with the conventional form of fighting and attack his positions head-on.

Fortunately for Dunn, Brigadier Janjua seemed to have been extremely wary of the Rann's terrain. While discussing his offensive plans for Desert Hawk II, Janjua had told Tikka Khan on 16 April that certain areas were 'not suitable for occupation'. The high ground that was Chhad Bet, which was more or less contiguous with Sindh, was where he had proposed to aim his main thrust. Having decided to use his armour at the pace of the infantry rather than the other way around, the Pakistanis had given the Indian defenders a chance.

The attack on Sardar Post a fortnight earlier by 51 Brigade had seen a lot of confusion among the Pakistani units as they failed to get to their allocated positions on time. Throughout 22 April, Indian posts picked up a lot of noise as the infantry units, tanks, and APCs were on the move. General Tikka Khan and Brigadier Janjua were also busy through the day, getting familiar with the terrain. However, in spite of the reports reaching them, Army HQ in Delhi was sceptical about the deployment of Pakistani armour. By then it had also been decided to keep the air force and naval aircraft out as India did not want to be sucked into a large-scale confrontation in terrain that did not suit it. Army HQ seemed to believe that the Pakistanis were taking up a defensive position opposite Chhad Bet.

Right from the start, General Musa had been hoping the Indians would take the initiative and allow him to fight a defensive battle that would validate his pet doctrine—the much-vaunted 'New Concept of Defence'. The trap had been set at Kanjarkot and though at first it seemed the Indians would rush in, Brigadier Pahalajani had not risen to the bait. The attack on Sardar Post had not yielded any dividends because, GHQ Pakistan reasoned, Azhar's 51 Brigade was devoid of armour. Musa's operational order to GOC 8 Division clearly revealed this line of thinking.

GHQ Pakistan was, in effect, ordering an entire brigade, this time also supported by armour, to launch an attack on Biar Bet which was nothing but a screen position. The operational order issued to 8 Division on 23 April read: '6 Brigade Group will be established in [the] area south of Jatrai upto Biar Bet not later than 1800 hrs today. Enemy post at Biar Bet will be dislodged at the earliest opportunity. Position will be dug and mined and prepared for all round defence. Enemy will be enticed to attack this position and maximum casualties will be inflicted on him. There will be no withdrawal from this position without permission from GHQ. There will be no attack on Chhad Bet.'

GHQ Pakistan, which seemed to have very little belief in the attacking capability of its own army, had decided to shift yet another squadron of armour along with a regiment of artillery from 51 Brigade to 6 (Independent) Brigade's location.

Capturing a screen position that had no major significance on the ground and then enticing the Indians to try and recapture it after all the armour had been strategically positioned to slaughter them was a meaningless plan—if a junior officer had put up such a naive plan, he would have been mocked. Tikka Khan and Janjua had wanted to strike deeper into the Rann, attacking and destroying Chhad Bet–Dharamsala–Vigokot–Karim Shahi and, for this, Tikka Khan wanted the PAF to fly in ground support. Just as he was labelling his plan Desert Hawk III, the last line in GHQ's signal poured cold water on it.

Pakistani artillery fire once again lit up the night sky opposite the 3 Para location (Pt 84 or Sera Bet) at around 0300 hrs. The bombardment lasted for about an hour, after which there was an eerie silence as the alert paratroopers, roughly seventy of them, peered into the darkness, hoping to detect signs of movement. Nothing happened. Major P. P. Singh, the Bravo Company commander had sent Second Lieutenant Sharma with a small patrol party towards Jat Talai the previous evening to ascertain the strength of the Pakistanis. Sharma had not returned. P. P. Singh now had with him Captain Bakshish Singh Gill, the Arty OP[4]. Second Lieutenant S. N. Guptan, the gun position officer (GPO), was deployed approximately 3 km behind Pt 84. 17 Para Field had three batteries, of which 52 Battery was under the command of Major Naresh Kumar Chadha, who was at the Battalion HQ at Dharamsala. Each battery was further divided into two troops, of which Echo Troop, consisting of four guns, had been deployed to support Pt 84. Each gun was towed by a Dodge 15 CWT that had behind it a trailer which was then linked to the gun itself.

At 0600 hrs, Pakistani infantry, about a battalion in strength, could be seen advancing towards Pt 84 from the northwest. The Pakistanis, about 1100 metres away, were well within range of Guptan's 75 mm howitzers. Gill started sending out the firing coordinates and the four guns, from their positions behind Pt 84, opened up. As the artillery shells began to fall, 3 Para's 3-inch mortars and MMGs added to the volume of fire. The Pakistani advance seemed to have been halted. At 0715 hrs, for the first time, Pakistani Patton tanks were seen by the Indians as a squadron plus appeared about half a kilometre behind the infantry. It was the moment of truth, and Gill immediately started giving out fresh coordinates targeting the armour, which was then promptly engaged by Guptan's guns.

The two RCL guns of 3 Para, that had a range of around 2,100 yards, were also firing, as were the Pakistani tanks. Three Pattons seemed to have been hit, but in the smoke and swirling dust, it was hard to be certain. The Pakistanis seemed more intent at firing at the earlier temporary gun position that had been created by 17 Para Field and the trenches that were ahead of the actual post. There were a couple of direct hits on the tanks, but more armour seemed to join the fray as the tanks now adopted a fire and move tactic, getting to within 700 metres of the Indian post. P. P. Singh realized that his men would not stand a chance at close quarters against the numbers advancing against them and so, under the cover of the howitzers that were firing furiously, he started pulling his men out. The defenders had got off amazingly lightly—one soldier had been killed and a handful wounded. Second Lieutenant Sharma and his party were reported missing. Sharma's patrol of four men had walked into a Pakistani patrol. They were overpowered and made POWs without a shot being fired. The paratroopers claimed three tanks and over a hundred Pakistani dead/wounded.

Despite Pakistan's losses, 6 (Independent) Brigade had taken Pt 84. Phase I of Desert Hawk III had been successfully completed. Brigadier Janjua now turned his attention towards the other screen position of 50 Para Brigade at Biar Bet, 13 km to the southwest, where Charlie Company of 3 Para under Major Inder Jit Kumar, with its section of RCL guns and another troop of 17 Para Field in support, were waiting for them.

Second Lieutenant Dinesh Mathur was the GPO with the Alpha Troop of 49 Battery which was also deployed 3 km behind Biar Post on the Biar Bet–Dharamsala axis. Second Lieutenant Arjun Singh Khanna was at 'Arjun Tree' as the Arty OP. At 1630 hrs a probing patrol mounted on three APCs approached Biar Bet and was immediately engaged by the RCL guns and MMGs, forcing it to turn back. An hour later, APCs supported by twelve Patton tanks tried to outflank Biar Bet. They too were fired upon by the RCL guns, after which it was too dark to track their movement. Later in the night, in anticipation of an early morning attack on Biar Bet, another section of RCLs and some additional jeeps along with Major P. P. Singh joined Inder Jit Kumar.

Pakistani artillery started shelling Biar Post intermittently from 0500 hrs on 26 April. Pakistani infantry mounted on APCs supported by thirteen tanks then started advancing on the post from the north-northeast direction while some tanks and

APCs were also seen on the north–northwest side. Pakistani guns then switched to down laying a smokescreen about 700 yards from the post. The Pakistanis also started to shell the Arjun Tree location where the Arty OP was trying to pinpoint the APCs and tanks. Adding to the noise and din, an Indian army Air OP Oscar that had taken off from Khavda and was being flown by Major Sushil Kumar Mathur[5] was keeping tabs on the Pakistani movements below.

Three Pakistani tanks were hit and could be seen burning, but the Pakistanis had two squadrons moving towards the objective. The Indian RCL guns were firing furiously but it was obvious the Pakistanis could not be stopped. Dinesh Mathur at his gun position was asked to provide covering fire as Inder Jit Kumar ordered his men to take the dead and wounded[6] and pull out in sections and fall back on Dharamsala. One RCL section kept firing and was eventually overrun and the gun captured, but most of the men managed to extricate themselves. The last elements, No. 7 Platoon under Lance Havildar Narain Singh, left Biar Bet just as the leading tanks reached the now abandoned battalion defences.

While the jeeps roared past, the 75 mm howitzers were still firing away as the GPO had not received any orders from his CO. At the Chhad Bet–Biar Bet–Dharamsala trijunction, a platoon was positioned to form a light screen. Meanwhile, with no orders from either his battery commander or commanding officer to withdraw, Mathur was still in position. An Oscar circling above him realized what was happening and he brought his plane down over the command post where he dropped a message bag which contained a scribbled message: 'Tanks coming your way!'[7]

Mathur needed no further prompting. His men quickly hitched the guns onto their Dodge 15 CWT trucks and raced off towards their battalion's fall-back position at Mori Bet, just behind Dharamsala. As they approached the trijunction, the troop came under heavy friendly fire from the screen position that mistook the Dodge vehicles for Pakistani APCs and tanks. Naik Siddharthan was hit on the right eye and forehead while Gunner Ramakrishnan was hit by splinters on both legs. Though they were evacuated, both soldiers from 49 Battery later died from their injuries, a tragic case where friendly fire also wrote off a couple of guns.

Despite the accident, the platoon continued to hold its position. It was engaged by the Pakistanis at mid-day but continued to hold out till it was ordered to fall back to Dharamsala at 2230 hrs.

The Pakistanis had successfully captured Pt 84 and Biar Bet in less than forty-eight hours. Though they lost at least six tanks and suffered heavily in terms of casualties, their belief that Indian infantry would not be able to hold out against concentrated armour was vindicated. After the war, a Pakistani commentator noted that if the Indian posts at Pt 84 and Biar Bet had held their fire until the advancing Pakistanis were closer, they would have been a lot more effective and would not have given their positions away so soon. The observation, though valid, overlooks the fact that screen positions are not supposed to dig in and fight to the last man. Their job is to engage the enemy and fall back, which they seem to have done in fair order. Between 17 Para Field and 3 Para, one solitary RCL gun mounted on a jeep was lost.

Though it was known that Pakistani armour was deployed on the Sindh side of the border, it was only on 25 April that Patton tanks had appeared in the Rann of Kutch and were physically seen by the Indians for the first time. Earlier reports had been received with some scepticism, with Army HQ insisting till the morning of the 25th that the build-up on the Pakistan side was defensive in nature.

'I had to take a call,' Arjan Singh said later. 'The defence minister, Mr Chavan, wanted physical confirmation of Pakistani armour deployed against our defences. We discussed the possibility of sending a [photo reconnaissance] aircraft into the area. Given the proximity of Badin and the fact that they had radar and the capability of shooting down an aircraft, it was a bit of a risk. If they brought down an IAF aircraft, the Pakistanis would get a lot of mileage from it.'[8]

Chavan had approved the call and the next morning, even as 3 Para were withdrawing from Biar Bet, two Vampires from 101 Fighter Reconnaissance (FR) Squadron flown by Flying Officer (later Wing Commander) Utpal Barbara and Flight Lieutenant (later Squadron Leader) Joy Prakash Chhetry took off from Jamnagar. Barbara was flying the two-seater T55 version and he had with him Flying Officer (later Squadron Leader) Ashok Vinayak Moghe as his co-pilot, while Chhetry in the single-seater Mk.52 was the wingman clearing his tail. Both aircraft were armed, but they had strict instructions not to use their guns unless they were attacked by enemy fighters. Under no circumstances were they to take any offensive measures on their own, even if they were fired upon by ground forces.

As they took off from Jamnagar, they climbed to 1,000 feet over the Gulf of Kutch. Hugging the coastline while maintaining a tactical formation, the aircraft dropped down to below 100 feet once they entered the Rann. Pakistan had a powerful radar at Badin where F-86 Sabres and the supersonic F-104 Starfighters equipped with Sidewinder air-to-air missiles were known to be present. On the Indian side there was no radar cover and, after leaving Jamnagar air traffic control, there was also total radio silence so the Vampires were entirely on their own. Flying at 300 knots, they soon flew into a dust haze where the visibility was barely 2 kms, and reducing rapidly. Barbara was at 50 feet, while Chhetry was slightly higher, maintaining 70 to 80 feet, constantly switching sides as he kept a lookout for hostile elements.

The barren landscape below them was soon devoid of any landmarks and, at low altitude, navigation required tremendous concentration. There was also the added danger of flying into a flock of large birds like flamingos, pelicans, or ducks that thrived in the large marshy pockets that dotted the area.

The formation overflew Dinesh Mathur's new gun position. 'They were coming in from behind us at ground level and it was terrifying. I realized they were ours, so I screamed at the men not to open fire. Maybe some still did. When the two aircraft flashed past, we saw the Indian markings.'[9] Barbara was still short of Biar Bet when he saw the churned-up mud, which he knew had to be tank tracks. 'Immediately after, I could see ahead of us some sort of flashes, thick smoke blending with the dust and then suddenly spots of fire scattered on the dusty terrain below... I realized then that the flashes were of enemy guns and the fires and smoke were in fact burning vehicles—our vehicles blown up and set ablaze by the enemy.'[10]

Biar Bet was still a few nautical miles away, so Barbara knew the burning vehicles were well inside Indian territory. Suddenly he saw an entire armoured column in front of him with their 'flashing guns which were accompanied by troops on machine-gun mounted jeeps on the sides. I immediately dove on the column taking photographs and taking stock of the situation. I could see the enemy taking evasive action and troops jumping and scattering. They obviously thought it was an air strike.' With limited time over target, combined with poor visibility, the formation made five or six runs over the area, taking close-ups of the tanks in particular. 'I also spotted some troop carriers at the rear of the column and what looked like small field artillery and mortars. There were also more wrecked vehicles lying about but I could not make out if they were ours or were of the enemy. On subsequent runs I saw the enemy firing at us with small arms but fortunately they failed to score any hit.' After spending roughly five minutes criss-crossing the area, the two-aircraft formation then set course for home, still keeping low so as to evade radar detection. It was incredible flying by any standard.

The cameras on board the Vampire had done their job perfectly; in fact, the black and white images were quite amazing. Two hours after landing in Jamnagar, Barbara took off again, this time in the single-seater Vampire Mk.52 with the developed photographs in a packet on his lap. 'At Palam airport, instead of the rickety air crew van, a staff car was waiting, which took me straight to Army HQ for a detailed debrief in front of the chief of the army staff. The staff at Army HQ confirmed that the tanks in question were in fact Pattons. My job was done.'[11]

Images of the Patton tanks were then released to the Press Trust of India. The front page of the newspapers, apart from carrying images of the Pattons, also reported on the defence minister's statement in Parliament announcing that the armed forces had been put on alert following the general mobilization in Pakistan. All India Radio, at the time the only mass communication medium in the country, reported not only on the fighting in the Rann but the voices of Surajit Sen, Barun Haldar, and Pamela Singh also announced to a stunned country that all leave had been cancelled and all army/air force/navy personnel were to report to their respective units forthwith.

Utpal Barbara's photographs were also transmitted to newspapers across the world. This showed that US-supplied equipment to Pakistan, ostensibly meant to fight communism, was in fact being used against India in the Rann of Kutch.

For quite some time, the Indians had been stating that Pakistan was using American tanks and other equipment against India, which was a violation of their terms of use. Pakistan would counter every allegation by making similar charges against India. When more and more evidence was produced and shown to the US, Pakistan had come up with 'an ingenious plea that American military equipment was only "deployed" and not "employed" against India'.[12] Even when the proof by way of Barbara's photos were put out, Pakistan, not surprisingly, suggested that the photographs had been doctored by the Indians.

The two Vampires in the vicinity of Biar Bet and Pt 84 had also succeeded in creating panic on the ground. Fearing an imminent air attack by the Indians, there were frantic signals being sent to the PAF through GHQ to mount an immediate combat air patrol (CAP) over the area. To reassure their ground troops, two Starfighters were sent long after Barbara had left the area. The PAF also ordered two B-57 Canberras to get airborne but these were recalled once they realized that reports of an IAF offensive were incorrect.[13]

With Biar Bet occupied by 0800 hrs, the next task for Tikka Khan was to deploy his troops in a defensive manner. On 27 April, the Patton tanks of 24 Cavalry (minus the squadron with Janjua) were concentrated at Jitrai in case of an Indian counter-attack on Biar Bet, which was now being held by four companies—two each from 15 Punjab and 2 FF. Janjua's Brigade HQ was established at Biar Bet while two artillery regiments—25 Field Regiment and two batteries of 12 Medium Regiment—were brought forward from their earlier positions at Jitrai and Rahim Ki Bazar. In addition, one battery of 38 Field Regiment and 88 Mortar Battery was deployed to cover possible Indian approaches. 'B' Company of 15 FF (Recce & Support), occupied the gun position that had been abandoned by Alpha Troop of 17 Para Field to provide early warning in case of an attack.

On the Indian side, after the withdrawal and loss of both Pt 84 and Biar Bet, Brigadier Nambiar, commander of 50 Para Brigade, had pulled back 3 Para into a defensive position at Dharamsala. On the overall front, General Dunn had, on 24 April, withdrawn the bulk of Brigadier Pahalajani's 31 Brigade which had taken up a defensive position on the Dharamsala–Karim Shahi track, 8 km west of Dharamsala. Both Vigokot and Sardar Post had been heavily mined using the World War II clock ray method. Pioneer platoons under the supervision of the engineers had placed them within 1,000 yards of the forward positions, which was well within the range of the covering MMGs. 2 Sikh LI was manning the defences at both places while also generating a lot of wireless traffic that was aimed at simulating the brigade's presence there. 4 Para, which arrived on 24 April, was told to hold at Pt 183 which was just south of the causeway. This battalion would be the reserve. 2 Para with its component of 17 Para Field and 71 Field Regiment continued to hold the area around Chhad Bet.

Through the next two days, 27 and 28 April, Pakistani Air Op pilots kept constant vigil, the Bird Dogs in the sky guiding the massive barrage of artillery fire that was directed at possible Indian approaches. According to official records, the Pakistani artillery and mortars fired upwards of 2,000 rounds from their medium guns, and 325 mortar bombs. Indian guns, outnumbered yet spiritedly active, killed two Pakistani soldiers and wounded three in a duel with 88 Mortar Battery.[14]

On the night of 27/28 April, a supply convoy consisting of seven 3-ton vehicles lost its way in the darkness and was intercepted by the Pakistanis around Biar Bet. 'Navigation at night was always a nightmare in the featureless surroundings'[15] and soon the vehicles were ablaze as Pakistani guns mercilessly ripped into them. All the men in the convoy were killed except for a lone JCO who survived to tell the tale.

With both sides facing each other in what looked like a stand-off, Prime Minister Lal Bahadur Shastri made a statement on 28 April that clearly spelt out the Indian strategy in the event of Pakistan continuing to adopt an aggressive stance in the immediate future. He stated in no uncertain terms that India was quite prepared for a peaceful settlement in the Rann of Kutch provided the status quo was restored. He went on to add: 'If Pakistan discards reason and persists in its aggressive activities, the Indian Army will defend the country and it will decide its own strategy and the employment of its own manpower and equipment in the manner it deems best.'[16]

On the same day, the British prime minister Harold Wilson wrote to both Shastri and Ayub Khan expressing his grave concern at the alarming turn of events in the Rann of Kutch, offering to act as a mediator to resolve the conflict. Shastri, in keeping with his statement in Parliament, welcomed Wilson's initiative, but Ayub Khan did not react immediately, preferring to give the impression that he was allowing General Tikka Khan another couple of days on the ground to exert pressure on the Indians, who were now closed up in a defensive box. Besides, by holding out on the British offer, it added to the widespread perception within Pakistan—among both civilians and the military—that the 'dhotiwallahs' were on the ropes.

Despite his outward belligerent stance, Ayub Khan was unnerved by Shastri's statement and the general mobilization ordered by India in the Punjab, which marked the beginning of Operation Ablaze. As is often the case, though the Wilson offer had grabbed the headlines, there had been feverish diplomatic activity behind the scenes in the preceding days. The British high commissioner to Pakistan, Sir Maurice James, and his newly arrived colleague in New Delhi, John Freeman, had warned Bhutto and Ayub Khan that the mood in India was in favour of escalating the conflict should the Pakistanis launch the next phase of Operation Desert Hawk III (given the code name Operation Arrow Head), which was to attack and eliminate the two Indian brigades. As a result, Ayub had already told Tikka Khan to 'do nothing to aggravate the situation, or in other words to observe a de facto ceasefire'[17] even before the formal offer of mediation was made.

Ayub kept up the charade for the next two days. Pakistan's GHQ, including General Musa, had no idea what the president was thinking, nor were they aware of Ayub's instructions to Tikka Khan. Finally, after the rest of Pakistan was convinced that Pakistan had pulled off a massive military victory in the Rann of Kutch, Ayub seemingly reluctantly agreed to call off hostilities and a ceasefire was declared on 1 May 1965.

For the troops holed up in the Rann, the brief skirmish that placed them on the front pages of the newspapers was over. Even though the limelight had shifted to the British diplomats as they shunted between Rawalpindi and New Delhi to work out the finer points of the agreement, surviving in the Rann was proving to be quite an ordeal. May brought with it the first rains and created havoc. 'On 23 May there was a virtual cloudburst,' recalls Behl. 'It was impossible to tell [the difference between the Rann and the sea], except for the bets which resembled isolated troopships as men and equipment were shifted onto them. Our guns, ammunition, everything. To add to our woes, a large number of scorpions also had the same idea and there were a lot of scorpion stings which resulted in a few men dying as well.'

There were many acts of heroism but one event was to remain etched in the memories of those who were present there. On 15 June, Major Rajendra Kumar Bali from 2 Sikh LI was notified by his troops that two Pakistani soldiers had wandered into the Indian minefield and were grievously wounded. Both men were alive but would die unless they were rescued and rushed to the nearest medical unit. Ordering his men to stay where they were, Bali unhesitatingly made his way inch by agonizing inch through the minefield, miraculously reaching the injured men without getting blown up himself. The two Pakistani soldiers were then successfully evacuated. 'They gave him a VrC for what he did,' says Behl, his sense of awe still evident after all these years. 'Laying your life on the line for your own men is expected of every officer...but to do so for the enemy who from the looks of it were dying anyway...what can one say?'

The diplomatic back and forth would continue for two months, but there were indications that trouble could well be brewing elsewhere. 'I was a war book officer at that time,' recounted Ambassador Rasgotra. 'An American embassy officer rang me up in the morning and asked for an urgent meeting. He said to me, "Why are people sending forces to Kutch? This is a sham attack to divert your attention from the north. Pakistan Army has been painting the war paint on its tanks. This is a diversionary tactic and a bigger attack is planned in the north." I wrote up a note and sent it to the concerned authorities who took it seriously since I had known that this source was authentic. I think the Americans were warning us. We took this threat seriously.'[18]

Unknown to the Indians, the Pakistanis has been planning Operation Gibraltar in May. Intent on milking whatever they could from the 'victory' in the Rann, the Pakistanis seemed to have completely misread the situation. The 'long-held views of military superiority which had racist undertones'[19] had ingrained itself into the Pakistani psyche, as had the belief that a conflict in Kashmir would also force Western arbitration as was happening in the case of the Rann. Finally, on 30 June, the leaders of India and Pakistan green-flagged international arbitration and the Kutch Agreement was inked on 1 July. Harold Wilson publicly thanked Maurice James for his role in de-escalating the situation.

Accordingly, a tribunal was to be formed to demarcate the boundary between the two countries. Pakistan nominated the former Iranian foreign minister, Nasrollah Entezam, while India opted for Aleš Bebler, a senior Yugoslavian jurist. The third member was to be nominated by U Thant, the UN secretary general.[20] However, by then, fast moving events all but relegated the Rann of Kutch incident to a mere footnote in history.

Chapter 6

OPERATION ABLAZE

EXPANDING THE CONFLICT ZONE

On 29 April, Prime Minister Lal Bahadur Shastri had given his approval for retaliatory strikes against Pakistan outside of the J&K Theatre of Operations.

The brief flurry of punches delivered by Pakistan in the Rann of Kutch where overwhelming artillery, tanks, armoured personnel carriers, and infantry attacked two flanking positions of an infantry battalion had lessons for both sides. While the military leadership in Pakistan treated it and projected the 'fighting' in the Rann as a great military victory which validated their New Concept of Defence, the Indian high command also seemed to be affected by the Pakistani drum-beating. This would have a tremendous impact on the upcoming events of the next few months.

General Chaudhuri, using the pen name 'Mucchu', wrote on various conflicts across the globe, where he often commented on leadership. He would have been acutely aware that he was living in a glass house and was perceived by many as being a 'defensive' general. For a cavalry officer, who is expected to be dashing and aggressive by the very nature of his service, it was an image that was bound to sit heavily on the man. Hyderabad and Goa notwithstanding, General Chaudhuri was not on firm ground where his own image was at stake.

Even Chavan, Chaudhuri's strongest supporter, had reservations about him. 'With his ability to present ideas in a clear, precise and well-structured language, he was respected in the Defence Ministry as an educated general. In fact, he was so good on paper that Chavan often wondered how good he would be in warfare.' Yet the defence minister would never waver in his support of the army chief. 'I remembered a talk with Krishna Menon. He told me I depended too much on Chaudhuri and he is a general who will never fight. I told him that I disagreed with him. He was going by his personal dislikes. I have told him that from what I have seen of Chaudhuri in the last three years, I am sure if it comes to vindicate the honour of the Indian Army, Chaudhuri will fight.'[1]

General Chaudhuri's briefings were spectacular affairs, with the chief mesmerizing his audience with his apparent depth of knowledge. Rarely, if ever, did he need or want to refer to his staff officers, a tendency that his staff had learnt to live with. Throughout the Rann of Kutch episode, Chaudhuri had advocated restraint, not wanting to get sucked into a military brawl with Pakistan on territory and conditions that suited them. Even if the fighting hadn't stopped in anticipation of a ceasefire, it was obvious that with the onset of the monsoons it would have been a dead sector in any case. Perhaps aware of the 'defensive' tag attached to him, the army chief, in his discussions with Chavan and Shastri, started to advocate the need to take an aggressive stance in the Punjab.

In a couple of sessions with the prime minister, Chaudhuri recommended that 'India should, if required, use maximum force in an offensive against Pakistan's Punjab, the strategic core area of Pakistan. Such a course would not only force Pakistan on the defensive but offer India the advantages of initiative and profitable gains of territory for bargaining while giving added security to the Indian Punjab. It would tie down large forces of Pakistan, reducing her potential of mischief in J&K, Pakistan's cherished prize. Any operation in Punjab would directly influence operations in J&K and vice versa due to the proximity of the two areas.'[2] Shastri accepted Chaudhuri's professional advice and on 28 April made his 'when and where' statement in Parliament.

However, despite Chaudhuri's flamboyance and big talk, Operation Ablaze was a knee-jerk reaction, which if viewed objectively (with the benefit of hindsight, one must admit) underlines the muddled thinking on the Indian side. The Indian stance against Pakistan post 1962 was not only defensive, it was completely reactive. While Chaudhuri's instincts were defensive, the Western Army commander, Lieutenant General Harbakhsh Singh, was inclined to be aggressive, sometimes with little regard to actual ground realities. Given that the chemistry between them was not good, Chaudhuri and Harbakhsh were like a pair of terrible twins who had got mixed up at birth. Chaudhuri, armoured corps, cautious and defensive by nature; Harbakhsh Singh, infantry, far more aggressive, at times bordering on the reckless! Following Prime Minister Shastri's statement about choosing the place and time, India deployed for war in the Punjab, only to quickly realize it was holding a feather duster rather than a stick.

Despite India's uneasy relationship with Pakistan, the expansion and reorganization of the Indian Army after 1962 was oriented entirely towards China. While the focus was on raising new mountain divisions, General Chaudhuri did nothing to improve the offensive capabilities of the army in the west, being quite content to maintain the defensive posture not only all along the CFL, but across the entire IB that extended from Punjab to Rajasthan and Gujarat. The limited skirmish in the Rann of Kutch was to abruptly change the equation. With Prime Minister Shastri making it clear that he had the political will to expand the conflict zone, the army now had to keep pace. If Operation Ablaze was supposed to scare the Pakistanis, once the reality unfolded on the ground for Indian commanders, the situation was quite the opposite.

The years of neglect since Independence had created an imbalance in virtually every arm of the fighting forces. Unlike Kashmir, where the terrain primarily placed the emphasis on the infantry, the area around and south of the Chenab was tank country, where armour was expected to play a dominant role. In 1947, as per the 2:1 ratio adopted for the division of the armed forces, India had twelve armoured regiments while Pakistan had six. Operation Ablaze suddenly hammered home the reality that India's fifteen cavalry regiments (one was still being raised) were up against Pakistan's eighteen. To make matters infinitely worse, it wasn't just the numerical imbalance that was causing the Indian commanders some apprehension—even qualitatively, Pakistan had the upper hand.

Four of India's armoured regiments were equipped with 1945-vintage British-manufactured 52-ton Centurion tanks. The other eight were equipped with the World War II American Sherman IV which in 1965 had an upgraded gun. Subsequently, in the mid-1950s, when nine M47 and M48 Pattons and three Chaffees were added to the six existing Sherman regiments, India had opted for two regiments of the French AMX-13. Later, when Soviet equipment became an option, Chaudhuri's China-centric outlook resulted in India opting for the amphibious PT-76, which was mainly suited to fighting in Assam's paddy fields should the Chinese come a-calling again.

Pakistan's edge in armour unfortunately did not end there. The Indian Sherman IVs had been fitted with a gun that was 'a complete flop'[3] and was not only inferior to the Patton but also to Pakistan's tank destroyer armament. The communication systems fitted in the Indian tanks were also outdated. Pakistan also had a large number of APCs which meant their attacking infantry were fully mechanized, to say nothing of the fact that the APCs themselves added considerably to their firepower by virtue of a mounted 50-inch machine gun. If Indian infantry had to follow their tanks, they either had to walk behind or follow in 3-ton vehicles, which were usually not capable of going off tracks. Pakistan's armoured division had three perfectly balanced armoured brigades, which allowed the formation commanders to use an available reserve to exploit any developing situation.

India's 1 Armoured Division's organization, in comparison, was hopelessly out of date. 'It had only one armoured brigade and the division's infantry was still carried in 3-ton lorries. It had no hope of keeping up with tanks in a mobile battle. It had no medium self-propelled artillery and its anti-aircraft guns were antiquated 40 mm Bofors on a motorised platform. Lack of organic reconnaissance resources at regimental as well as formation level was a handicap.'[4]

There were two areas where the Indian armoured units had an edge. One, the Patton gun only fired the armour-piercing, ballistic cap, tank defeating ammunition, which was not as good as the armour-piercing discarding sabot rounds fired by the Centurions. Two, unlike the rest of the Indian Army, where rapid expansion had resulted in a large number of officers, JCOs, and NCOs moving to new raisings, the armoured units had not been diluted, simply because there had been hardly any expansion or induction of new equipment. As a result, the tank crews were not only very familiar with their machines, most of them were extremely proficient, especially in the gunnery department.

The firepower of a Pakistani infantry division was also superior as, at the formation level, their units had more RCL guns, mortars, MMGs, and LMGs. Though Indian divisions had a larger number of battalions, nine as against seven in a Pakistani division, a large percentage were new raisings. In addition, each Pakistani infantry division had an integrated armoured regiment, which further added to their 'shock and awe' capability. This meant a minimum number of troops would be committed to holding ground so as to retain the ability to counter-attack or go into a local offensive posture.

Pakistan's main strength on the ground was in their artillery. Though fewer in number than their Indian counterparts, their guns were more modern with superior mobility, heavier ordnance, and longer range. Pakistani field regiments were equipped with 105 mm guns while the medium regiments had 155 mm howitzers. Their locating devices and spotter aircraft that made up the Air Op were far superior. Each infantry and armoured division had a medium artillery regiment integral to it, apart from which both its 1 and 4 Corps had corps artillery brigades.

◆

'Doab' is a Persian term that describes the tract of land that lies between two convergent rivers. There are four major doabs in Pakistan: the Sindh Sagar Doab between the Indus and the Jhelum; the Chaj Doab between the Jhelum and the Chenab; the Rachna Doab between the Ravi and the Chenab; and the Bari Doab that is bounded by the Ravi in the north and west, the Sutlej to the south, and the Beas to the east. Given the communication systems and the situation that existed at the time, it was obvious that the strategic core area and centre of operations would be the Bari Doab area.

The geography of the Bari Doab, therefore, needs to be understood. Lying adjacent to Pathankot, Madhopur is considered to be the northern gateway to Punjab. The bridge over the Ravi at the time was the only road link between J&K and the rest of the country. The IB runs along the Ravi from Madhopur towards the southwest for 80 km before the river enters Pakistan at Ranian. The IB then continues southwards towards Ferozepur and is no longer based on any recognizable geographical features, the landscape being completely flat and dotted with villages that offer no natural defensive barriers on either side. The Ravi then flows inside Pakistan and the zig-zagging IB creates quite a few enclaves on either side. The city of Lahore is on the Ravi's eastern bank, with Amritsar further to the east across the border in India.

The Grand Trunk (GT) Road bisects the middle sector of the Bari Doab, entering the region by crossing the Beas Bridge and then runs east to west connecting Amritsar, crosses the IB at Wagah, touches the Ravi at the Shahdara Bridge, then takes a u-turn without crossing the river into Lahore. Apart from the central GT Road, the entire region is criss-crossed by a network of roads with canals and their various irrigation networks, mainly running from the northeast to the southwest of the Bari Doab. These water channels act as man-made obstacles for any east-west thrust, restricting any motorized move to the few existing bridges.

Pakistan had developed the Bambawali–Ravi–Bedian (BRB) Canal, also known as the Ichhogil Canal, as an obstacle against any Indian offensive towards the city of Lahore from the east. Running more or less parallel to the IB, keeping approximately 2 to 8 km within Pakistani territory, the canal links the Upper Chenab Canal—passing underneath the Ravi River—from Ichhogil Uttar to the Sutlej-fed Dipalpur Canal near Ganda Singh Wala. Though most of the canal network was constructed during the British Raj, the Ichhogil had been built immediately after Partition. As part of its design, it had been fortified with concrete pillboxes on either bank with gun emplacements and ramps for armour on the western side. On the face of it, the Pakistani deployment seemed to be entirely defensive and, as per the Indian understanding at that time, it appeared that the Pakistan Army would only engage to delay on the eastern bank, preferring to fight from behind the water obstacle.

This meant the city of Lahore was flanked by the Ravi behind it and the Ichhogil Canal in front. From the Indian perspective, there were three approaches to the city: the northernmost axis was along the GT Road from the direction of Amritsar, which meant breaking through the forward defences held by screening infantry battalions, crossing the Ichhogil Canal at Dograi Kalan/Jallo More and then entering Batapur, which was the eastern suburb of the city; the second approach was along the Barki–Lahore axis, from the direction of the Amritsar–Bhikkiwind crossroads; while the third was from the direction of Khem Karan–Kasur. On the other hand, should Pakistan go on the offensive and with its armour spearheading their thrust, Amritsar would be extremely vulnerable. The most dangerous axis in this case would be the Kasur–Khem Karan alignment, for that had the least number of obstacles. Should the Pakistanis break through, they could cut off the Beas Bridge and isolate 11 Corps as well as the city of Amritsar.

Lieutenant Colonel (later Major General) Lachhman Singh Lehl, then the GSO-1 (general staff officer-1) in the Military Operations Directorate, says about the Indian appreciation and plans: 'Coming face to face with the reality of war during "Op Ablaze", Indian High Command veered around to undertaking a limited offensive in the Bari Doab. Until then, 11 Corps with 1 Armoured Division was responsible for the defence of Punjab. During the various discussions between General Chaudhuri, Lieutenant General Harbakhsh Singh, and other senior commanders, the idea of securing the eastern bank of the Ichhogil Canal appeared attractive. It was felt that a defensive line along the east bank of the canal with the northern and southern flanks secured at DBN (Dera Baba Nanak), Hussainiwala, and Sulemanke offered distinct advantages for such a defence line would be based on major water obstacles. The mere presence of Indian troops on the canal, opposite Lahore, would tie down considerable Pakistani forces there, thus reducing reserves and availability of troops for them to undertake offensive tasks in other areas. India, on the other hand, could economize on troops by basing its defences on the east bank of the canal. If India could secure important bridges and establish a bridgehead opposite Lahore, Pakistan would be forced to contain and eliminate it, thus facing considerable attrition to her comparatively smaller army on the grounds of India's choice. By basing her defence on the enemy canal, India would confine the war to Pak territory in addition to the acquisition of a big slice of land. This was possible only if India took the initiative to cross the international boundary. The success, of course, would depend on the degree of surprise which was an essential pre-requisite.'[5]

Under the circumstances, the plan for a limited offensive was extremely bold. When compared to the Ravi or the Jhelum, the Ichhogil as a defensive barrier was not necessarily an insurmountable obstacle. However, it was a major asset for the defender, and by pushing up to its east bank and forcing Pakistan to blow the bridges over it, it would confine the space available to Pakistani armour. It would also catch the Pakistani ruling elite off guard, for they believed that Pakistan had a qualitative and quantitative superiority vis-à-vis India in her tank forces, the Islamic soldier was to the Hindu as a fighter, they had superior firepower on all fronts, and a better equipped air force. They could 'not imagine the Indian Army undertaking an offensive in tank country against Pakistan's tank forces'.[6]

On the other hand, surprise was a factor, but to actually hold ground with troops who were relatively poorly equipped with substantially less supporting firepower was another. A large number of battalions were newly raised and were not battle inoculated. Taking on the set defences of the Ichhogil required special fighting skills for which the men needed to be trained, but at the time of Operation Ablaze only a handful of commanders on the ground who were a part of 11 Corps had even heard of the Ichhogil Canal, or had any idea of how the Pakistani defences were laid out.

1 CORPS & THE RACHNA DOAB

Finally breaking from his China obsession, Chaudhuri had decided to raise 1 Corps and two other divisions. This substantially increased the scope of the offensive, at least on paper. 11 Corps HQ, based in Jalandhar, was being commanded by Lieutenant General Joginder 'Jogi' Singh Dhillon who had Brigadier T. K. Theogaraj's 2 (Independent) Armoured Brigade and three divisions under his command. Major General Niranjan Prasad was commanding the Amritsar-based 15 Infantry Division, which in turn had 38 and 54 Infantry Brigades based in

Ferozepur, 7 Infantry Division was being commanded by Major General (later Lieutenant General) Har Krishen Sibal with 48 and 65 Infantry Brigades; while 4 Mountain Division was under the command of Major General Gurbaksh Singh who had 7 and 62 Mountain Brigades under him.

Being raised in Jhansi, 1 Corps was placed under the command of Lieutenant General Patrick Oscar Dunn, who had been promoted and moved to the new raising immediately after the fighting had ended in the Rann of Kutch. Dunn had served with General Chaudhuri as his chief of staff during Operation Vijay in Goa, and the chief had been impressed by his organizational abilities. Recalled from leave pending retirement, he had been given command of the ad hoc force put together in the Rann, but the fighting had ended almost as soon as it had begun. In the chief's scheme of things, the newly raised 1 Corps was to be his strongest corps where an armoured division would be the prima donna with two infantry divisions in support. Though Dunn had neither served in any armoured formation nor seen any active fighting since World War II, Chaudhuri convinced the government that he was the best man for the job. Dunn's appointment involved multiple supersessions, but with the chief convinced he was the man for the job, the government acquiesced to his request.

The Corps HQ had only come into being in mid-May and was beset with teething troubles. Both the divisions allotted to it were also in a state of flux. The Bareilly-based 6 Mountain Division had come into being in March 1963 and it was being commanded by Major General S. K. Kolra who had 69 and 99 Mountain Brigades under his command. 14 Infantry Division under Major General R. K. Ranjit Singh, then based in Saugor (better known as Sagar in Madhya Pradesh) was still under raising. It had two infantry brigades, 35 and 58, which were deployed on the Tibet border in Uttar Pradesh. In addition, 1 Armoured Division, under the command of Major General Rajinder Singh 'Sparrow' was also allotted to 1 Corps. General Sparrow was one of the officers who had been superseded, but with war looming he agreed to serve under Dunn. However, for most of Operation Ablaze's existence, 1 Corps added teeth to the Indian side only on paper, as frantic efforts were being made to get it to its operational area.

As the plans for the limited offensive in the Bari Doab were being finalized, General Chaudhuri wanted 1 Corps to adopt much the same stratagem immediately to the north in the Rachna Doab. Dunn was to simultaneously thrust forward from the direction of Samba towards the Marala Ravi Link Canal (MRLC) and make that his axis to threaten Sialkot. By adopting this stance, not only Amritsar but Jammu and Pathankot would also be secure. 'Having secured the home bank of the Ichhogil and MRLC, India hoped to squeeze the Pakistanis in the Lahore sector from both front and rear after cutting the National Highway in the Gujranwala–Wazirabad area.'[7]

Harbakhsh, while endorsing Chaudhuri's plan for Dhillon's 11 Corps, felt that Dunn should also be deployed in the Bari Doab. He advocated the launching of 1 Corps through the Indian enclaves of Narot and Nainakot that were on the western side of the Ravi, after 11 Corps had secured the eastern bank of the Ichhogil Canal. Dunn could then proceed towards the Sambrial Bridge along the Sialkot–Wazirabad Road, keeping the MRLC to his left. Harbakhsh felt that the concentration of 1 Corps into a bridgehead across the Ravi into the above Indian enclaves would pose no problem. He argued that this would threaten not only Sialkot, but also Shakargarh and, as the attack developed, it would threaten Pakistan's rear and would necessitate a change of front from north to east.

In Harbakhsh Singh's appreciation, he believed the Pakistani commanders would try and launch their armour-cum-infantry thrust in the Khem Karan–Bhikkiwind sector. Should the occupation of the east bank of the Ichhogil fail to contain the Pakistanis to the western side of the canal, he further argued that his plan would keep both 11 and 1 Corps within mutual supporting range of each other, which would allow for any unforeseen situation and give him a chance to exploit any sudden opportunity that may present itself. By deploying on either side of the Ravi, he felt he would not have that flexibility. Also, until it was decided to raise 1 Corps, 1 Armoured Division along with 50 (Independent) Para and 67 Infantry Brigades had been designated corps reserves. India's 1 Armoured Division being shifted further north meant that the Western Army commander would have no armoured reserves whatsoever for the defence of Punjab.

The proposed Pakistani plan for an offensive in the Punjab was unknown to Western Command. Pakistan's 1 Armoured Division was positioned at Kasur and ready to launch an offensive towards the bridges at Harike and Beas, and thereby threaten Amritsar, Jalandhar, and even Delhi. Its latest Patton tanks were matched only by the Indian Centurion Mk VII. In addition, the Patton had night capability, which was not available to the Indians. The Centurion Mk VII at best had the provision for a night march on a given heading.

Pakistan's 1 Armoured Division had on its ORBAT 3, 4, and 5 Armoured Brigades (24 and 4 Cavalry, 6 and 19 Lancers, and 5 Horse) one Sherman and four Patton Regiments with 12 Cavalry in support as a Recce Regiment. The plan was to launch the armoured division through a bridgehead established by 11 Infantry Division (once again, the Indians had no idea that this division existed) in Khem Karan. After the success of Phase I, the armoured division was to break out on three axes: 4 Armoured Brigade along the Valtoha–Fatehabad axis, with the intention of capturing the bridge on the Beas; 3 Armoured Brigade along Khem Karan–Bhikkiwind–Tarn Taran axis, to capture Jandiala Guru, and cut off Grand Trunk Road; and 5 Armoured Brigade on an axis west of Kasur–Khem Karan–Bhikkiwind.

During Operation Ablaze, the discussions around the deployment of 1 Corps were more or less theoretical for, at the time, these formations were being hastily pushed forward to their new locations. Even then, it was obvious that General Chaudhuri was inclined to earmark the entire 1 Corps for operations in the Rachna Doab or the Sialkot Sector. This effectively left Jogi Dhillon's 11 Corps with an armour element of 9 Horse (Shermans), 1 Horse (Sherman Vs and a squadron of PT-76s), 14 Horse (Shermans), 2 (Independent) Armoured Brigade consisting of 8 Cavalry (AMX-13s), and 3 Cavalry (Centurions).

Interestingly, General Musa, the Pakistani army chief, seemed to be extremely concerned about the Sialkot Sector where he expected the Jammu-based 26 Infantry Division along with India's 1 Armoured Division to frontally attack Sialkot and then break south to try and get behind Lahore. To cope with the Indian threat which would be mainly aimed at West Punjab, the Pakistanis decided to 'deploy the bulk of the army (two armoured divisions, three infantry divisions, including 11 ad hoc divisions and three independent infantry brigades) in the Punjab, where [they] expected the main battles would be fought'.[8]

North of the Ravi in the Rachna Doab, the Pakistani mindset was entirely defensive. It was fairly obvious to both sides that neither had the capability to launch major offensive operations in more than one sector. Musa, therefore, positioned his defences in the Sialkot Sector with the intention of losing as little territory as possible, while he would go for the kill in the Amritsar Sector. Unlike the Ichhogil Canal which was quite close to the IB in the Bari Doab, the MRLC was further inland, leaving unprotected a large swathe of the Rachna Doab that included the towns of Sialkot, Badiana, and Pasrur unprotected. It was therefore vital for the Pakistani forces to keep the MRLC as a last-ditch defensive line while it deployed further east to protect not only Sialkot but also Chawinda and Narowal to minimize territorial losses.

Sialkot was therefore the pivot around which 15 Pak Division's four infantry brigades were deployed along the lines of the New Concept, where they would employ the doctrine of maximum fire and manoeuvre to cause maximum attrition to the attacking Indian forces. The composition of the four Pakistani brigades varied depending on the appreciation of the Indian threat and the importance of the defended area which, owing to the vast distances involved, could not support each other. The line of defence was to roughly stretch from Jassar–Narowal– Chawinda–Sialkot with the Chawinda–Badiana–Pasrur triangle being central to the defence structure.

Pakistan's 101 Infantry Brigade that consisted of two infantry and two armoured regiments (Shermans) was known to be deployed in the Sialkot Sector; 24 Infantry Brigade with two infantry battalions and one armoured regiment (25 Cavalry equipped with Pattons) was in the Chawinda Sector; 115 Infantry Brigade also with two infantry battalions and one armoured regiment (Shermans) was in the Jassar–Narowal Sector; and 104 Infantry Brigade with one infantry battalion and one armoured regiment (Shermans) was being held in reserve behind Sialkot. In addition, 6 Armoured Division, which was still under raising, was based in the Daska area as a GHQ reserve. In the event of hostilities breaking out, Musa planned on moving the armoured division from its forward concentration area near Gujranwala to Pasrur. To keep their powder dry, the Pakistani army initially did not want to commit to battle any of their armoured divisions, being quite content to deploy at least four armoured regiments on the frontline under the immediate control of the infantry divisions that had been raised by reorganizing their armour.

The plan, extensively discussed in Pakistan's Staff College, was to keep both the armoured divisions in their strategic concentration areas—6 Armoured Division at Gujranwala/Pasrur in the Rachna Doab and 1 Armoured Division at its forward concentration area near Kasur in the Bari Doab poised for a counter-offensive as and when needed. General Musa believed this would allow Pakistani armour to blunt any Indian armoured offensive regardless of whether it was launched from East Punjab or from the Jammu side in the Sialkot Sector.

This clearly indicated Pakistan wanted to hold 'the two extremities at Jassar and Sialkot close to the border using the defence potential of the Ravi and the built-up area respectively, while her defences in the centre were further back from the border. Pak had, of course, planned to maintain her presence in the Central Sector along the border with Charwa and Maharajke acting as strong points. Pakistan had located Rangers, Mujahids, and armed ex-servicemen in these villages, each reinforced by about an infantry company with elements of the R&S (Recce and Support) battalion as the Indian threat became imminent.'[9] From the Pakistani point of view, this would have helped threaten the flanks of any Indian move should the Indians attempt to move southwards through the gap between these two places.

As in the case of the formations deployed east of the Ichhogil Canal, in the Rachna Doab too, the Pakistani forward positions were deployed with the intention of getting early reliable information about the direction and strength of any Indian thrust, with the additional responsibility of delaying them as long as they could. The reconnaissance and support battalion was jeep-borne and armed with anti-tank RCL rifles and small arms and was highly mobile. These units were expected to play an important role—they were to not only carry out long-range reconnaissance that would serve as early warnings, but also protect the flanks of the defending forces once they needed to fall back.

On the Indian side, yet again, there was a difference of opinion between General Chaudhuri who preferred an offensive along the Samba–Ramgarh axis and Harbakhsh Singh, who advocated going into the Sialkot Sector through the Indian enclaves of Nainakot and Narot that involved a crossing of the Ravi. Harbakhsh argued that the initial crossing of the Ravi would not face a serious problem as the enclaves would be ideal bridgeheads. He felt it was highly unlikely that Pakistan would pre-empt the move by occupying these enclaves as they were anxious to confine the fighting to the Jammu and Kashmir territory. Second, an offensive on this axis would assault the Pakistanis in the Sialkot Sector from a flank and also threaten the rear of the enemy forces facing Jammu. Third, the chances of surprise were better as a build-up of troops in the Gurdaspur area would be construed as a build-up of forces aimed at the Lahore Sector. A build-up of troops in Samba, on the other hand, was almost certainly going to be picked up as the road running from Madhopur to Samba was constantly under Pakistani observation. Not only would it take longer to ferry troops and armour on the limited number of tank transporters, the element of surprise would almost certainly be lost, giving the Pakistanis enough time to face an attack from this direction. Fourth, the logistics would be easier to handle in Gurdaspur as the administrative set-up already existed to handle the concentration of troops who could be marshalled relatively easily due to rail and road connectivity and the shorter distances involved.

Harbakhsh then came back to his original argument, wherein he had advocated using 1 Corps in Punjab against the Lahore Sector. An offensive from Samba would not permit mutual support between Jogi Dhillon's 11 and Dunn's 1 Corps as the Ravi would not permit the quick switching of forces in the event of any serious reverses. While the Indians would be operating on exterior lines on either side of the Ravi, the Pakistanis could switch forces by using the existing rail and road networks.

Chaudhuri felt that crossing the Ravi during the monsoon period was fraught with risk as there were no bridges spanning the river that linked the two Indian enclaves on the other side. Apart from the initial crossing, the advance would be against the grain of the country and would mean crossing various other smaller streams with sandy river beds. He also believed that the terrain in the Sialkot Sector was ideal country for armour operations so long as he stayed with the grain of the country. The chief felt that an offensive in this sector right from the start would be hard for the Pakistanis to contain, as the Indian 1 Armoured Division would have a wide front in which to manoeuvre as there were no natural or man-made obstacles until the MRLC.

Three other factors needed to be considered by the chief. At this stage, expanding the conflict across the IB was being considered in response to the aggressive stance adopted by Pakistan in the Rann of Kutch. However, since the ceasefire in 1949 had drawn the CFL across J&K, there were regular violations that made the border from Akhnoor to Ladakh extremely volatile. If, at the end of an offensive, India had to have strategic gains, it needed to secure its somewhat fragile lines of communication that existed between J&K and the rest of India. Territorial gains along the Samba–Sialkot axis would then give added depth and security to the vital lifeline linking Pathankot with Jammu, Srinagar, and Ladakh.

Second, a major thrust aimed at the Sialkot Sector would have an immediate and direct impact on the neighbouring sectors of Akhnoor and Naushera. With the Pakistanis in the Bari Doab simultaneously fighting to keep the Indians out of Lahore, the only reinforcements they could then draw on would be by depleting their existing deployment against J&K, thereby reducing their capability to go on the offensive in the north. And, finally, 26 Infantry Division with its considerable assets that was holding the line from Jammu, would also come into play, thereby augmenting India's military offensive capability manifold.

Operation Ablaze clearly underlined the fact that the Indians in May/June were in no position whatsoever to contemplate a thrust across the IB into West Pakistan. This was abundantly obvious to both General Chaudhuri and Harbakhsh Singh. The deployment, however, gave the two apex Indian military commanders a dry run to hone their plans.

The two different perspectives are worth a comment at this stage for the simple reason that the war gaming done during Operation Ablaze set the tone for the subsequent fighting in September. General Chaudhuri's decision, eventually taken only in August, to go with Samba as the launch point for the 1 Armoured Division-led offensive of 1 Corps, meant India had dispersed her own forces even before the actual fighting started. To decisively break through Pakistani defences, or any defences for that matter, logic dictates an attacking army has to bring to bear overwhelming force. Towards that end, Harbakhsh Singh's suggestion that 1 Corps also operate south of the Ravi in the Bari Doab, leaving 26 Division to tackle the Sialkot Sector, would have given the Indians their best chance for an outright and decisive victory. Having taken the decision to split the forces in an attempt to disperse the Pakistanis, both Army HQ and Western Command would later constantly harp on the fact that neither Lahore or Sialkot were ever the objective. This muddled thinking was perhaps the direct result of India's defence mindset—instead of waging all-out war, an offensive stance is always relatively muted. Even in Western Command, Harbakhsh Singh's philosophy was defensive-offence—a mindset that guided the rank and file, evident from the subsequent slow pace of operations, and the old failing that was so evident in 1962—the timidity of brigade commanders and ranks above.

Two other factors need to be pointed out at this stage. First, even though General Chaudhuri had more or less firmed up his battle plan for the Punjab, once Operation Ablaze was called off, he did nothing to mentally prepare his subordinate commanders. When 1 Armoured Division was finally rushed post-haste by train from Jalandhar to Samba just before hostilities broke out in September, none of the officers were familiar with the terrain in the Rachna Doab. Even in the Lahore Sector, despite the fact that Jogi Dhillon was a sapper officer, the Ichhogil Canal was just a name that was mentioned in hushed whispers to a few commanding officers. No one had the faintest idea of what the terrain across the border looked like.

Second, in the entire planning of operations in both the Lahore and Sialkot Sectors, the use of air power seems to have hardly figured. This seemed to be quite the pattern at the time, when the COAS considered himself to be the sole authority who would plan and guide operations, asking the other services only to step in if and when they were called upon to do so. General Chaudhuri was senior to Air Marshal Arjan Singh, the CAS, by ten years, which, in the armed forces, set them apart by a generation. As the chairman of the Chiefs of Staff Committee, 'General Chaudhuri looked upon the Air Force and everyone in it including the air chief as rather young and inexperienced—fit for his avuncular interest but not to be taken seriously. The ability of the IAF to play a useful part in the event of a war was not taken seriously either.'[10]

This tendency of Chaudhuri's had been evident from the moment he took over as the acting army chief in 1962. His writing a column for a newspaper, his fluent handling of briefings, his overall personality seemed to have given him the air of an authoritarian general who 'frequently took spot decisions without consulting his staff. It is unlikely that he opened his professional heart to Air Marshal Arjan Singh who by rank, years of service and age was a generation apart.'[11] Very early in their relationship, Chavan had wryly noted that the army chief put forth a completely different face to his superiors, while being fairly dismissive to his subordinates. 'The present chief is a good man,' the defence minister had said to R. D. Pradhan, 'but he is ambitious and often behaves like a politician.'[12]

General Chaudhuri's self-centric attitude was not necessarily confined to the air force or the navy. Arjan Singh's successor, Air Chief Marshal Pratap Chandra Lal, made no bones about it. 'He [Chaudhuri] discussed the pros and cons with the prime minister and the defence minister and sometime later, the air chief was also informed of what was going on. This was done through informal meetings from which the naval chief was excluded. To ensure security, the general applied the "need to know" yardstick so thoroughly that the Chiefs of Staff Committee and the joint intelligence and planning staffs were completely bypassed. No contingency plans were drafted, nor were the three services asked to define the parts that they would have to play in the event of a war.... He treated the whole business as his personal affair or at any rate that of the army's alone, with the air force as a passive spectator and the navy out of it altogether.'[13]

With General Chaudhuri functioning in splendid isolation, most of the lessons learnt (if any) during Operation Ablaze stayed with him and failed to permeate down to the rest of the army. Subsequently, so obsessed was General Chaudhuri with security that even his principal staff officers (PSOs) were not informed about the date and time of attack until just a few hours before hostilities were to begin. 'This attitude led to an ugly scene in the daily Operation Room conference a few days later when one of the PSOs accused him to his face of fighting the war in his personal interest rather than that of the nation or the army.'[14]

During Operation Ablaze, this failing was also seen on the Pakistani side, which was strange because in the American doctrines that they had adopted, air power was an integral part as was quite evident from the ongoing fighting in Vietnam and Cambodia. In the mid-50s, the Pakistan Air Force had started its modernization under the US Mutual Aid Programme. The first batch of training jet aircraft were given to Pakistan in early 1955, in the wake of which arrived the F-86 Sabres three years later. B-57 Canberra bombers were inducted in 1959 while the supersonic F-104 fighters arrived in 1961. Asghar Khan had taken over as the first home-bred Pakistani air chief from Air Vice Marshal Arthur McDonald in 1957, and though the Pakistanis initially continued to follow the RAF doctrines, the USAF started to train the pilots and technicians in the latest methods and techniques of air warfare. As part of the American influx of equipment, the PAF constructed US standard airfields with hard cover blast pens while modern radars and communication systems were put in place.

As part of the American policy of giving military aid to its front line allies, Pakistan had received approximately 120 Sabres, thirty Canberras, and twenty Starfighters, apart from jet trainers, C-130 transport aircraft, and a squadron worth of reconnaissance planes. During Asghar Khan's eight-year tenure, the transformation of the PAF into a well-honed fighting machine on the US pattern had been completed. During Operation Ablaze, the PAF was at the peak of its operational efficiency. With a dozen squadrons deployed in West Pakistan (one F-86 Sabre squadron was in Dacca), they had a well-planned network of main and secondary air bases, linked by state-of-the-art radar and communication networks.

The pride of the PAF was the F-104 squadron. Not only were the Starfighters supersonic, they, along with some Sabre, were equipped with Sidewinder air-to-air missiles while the bulk of the IAF's aircraft were transonic and only equipped with conventional 30 mm guns. Pakistan's main radar at Sakesar near Sargodha was pivotal, linking all three major air bases—Sargodha, Peshawar, and Badin. In addition, they had constructed a network of satellite airfields around the main airfields, including Karachi.

However, like General Chaudhuri and the IAF, General Musa had not been very successful in evolving integrated fighting techniques with the PAF. In the case of Pakistan, the avuncular hat was worn by the PAF chief. General Musa was to wryly comment later: 'Air Marshal Asghar Khan told us that the main role of his force was to fight the air battle and direct support could be provided after achieving its primary role. Even the army's main counter offensive was planned without any close air support.'[15] Nur Khan, who took over from Asghar Khan as the air chief after Operation Gibraltar was launched (in August 1965), would change that policy.

Under the prevailing system, the two armies made their operational plans in isolation, expecting to fight the land battle entirely on their own. The obvious drawback in adopting this approach was that it was presumed that the other side's air force would also remain passive and, apart from fighting for air superiority, would not interfere with developments on the ground until they had achieved air superiority. Senior army officers on both sides had been brought up in an environment where air support was considered a bonus. This was indeed ironic, for towards the end of World War II in Burma, RIAF squadrons had provided tactical air support to land forces. Operation Ablaze had not only underlined their own shortcomings to the Indian side, it had also established that if and when there was a clash, it would be of a short duration. As the chief of the Indian side, Chaudhuri should have realized he needed to bring every resource at his disposal to try and capture as much territory as he could. His failure to analyse the potential of air power and use it judiciously was undoubtedly a major failing. While Nur Khan would partially rectify the situation on the Pakistani side, the Indians continued to ignore this vital factor.

While General Chaudhuri and Harbakhsh Singh, the Western Army commander, weighed their somewhat slim options in the beginning of May to take the fight into West Pakistan, the gloves were about to come off in a totally different theatre of operations. Kargil had seen some fighting in 1947–48 during the J&K Operations, but in 1965 it was a relatively unknown town on the CFL north of the Kashmir Valley across the Zoji La. From the barren Rann of Kutch and the Punjab, the focus would briefly shift to the high-altitude region of the trans-Himalayas, which would play itself out as a sideshow during Operation Ablaze where nothing much was actually happening on the ground.

Chapter 7

PRELUDE TO WAR: KARGIL

THE DARK SIDE OF THE MOON

Intelligence reports had been received that suggested that Pakistan, buoyed by its success in the Rann of Kutch, was looking to shift its offensive to J&K where it was planning to do something big. These reports were vague and speculative at best. In any case, since early January, there had been constant shelling from across the CFL with a sharp increase in the number of cross-border violations. Reports had also been coming in that indicated that various Frontier Corps formations that included the Khyber Rifles, Kurram Militia, Zhob Militia, Tochi Scouts, South Waziristan Scouts, and Bajaur Scouts were being shifted to POK from the Northwest Frontier Province where they had been earlier deployed. There was also mass hysteria building up across the border where youth were being called upon in large numbers to join the razakars who claimed the time had come to liberate Kashmir from India.

Lieutenant General Harbakhsh Singh, the Western Army commander, apart from the Punjab, was responsible for J&K that was under 15 Corps. 'A tall, soldierly and inspiring figure, wherever he went Harbakhsh was a picture of resolve who went about his business purposefully.'[1] Born on 1 October 1913 in Badrukhan near Sangrur in Punjab, he joined the IMA in 1933. He saw action in the Northwest Frontier Province with a British battalion during the Mohmand Campaign before he joined the 5th battalion 11 Sikh Regiment. At the outbreak of hostilities against the Japanese, he was seriously wounded in an ambush, after which he was a POW once Singapore fell. Three years later, having survived starvation and the brutality meted out by the Japanese, he was repatriated to India in 1945.

Harbakhsh Singh, who had played a key role in the fighting in Kashmir in 1947–48, was pitchforked into NEFA fifteen years later to take command of the situation after Tawang had fallen. 'His mere presence used to electrify the troops and straighten their backs,'[2] an officer who was with him at Se La in 1962 would write of him. Unfortunately, he was given command of 4 Corps only too briefly, and was sent to 33 Corps once Bijji Kaul returned from his temporary absence in NEFA. Many in the army believed that had Harbakhsh Singh remained the corps commander, the fighting with the Chinese would have panned out quite differently.

In the aftermath of the Chinese conflict, as we've seen, General Chaudhuri was most unexpectedly elevated to the position of the army chief. Time and again, Chaudhuri proved to be outwardly flamboyant but inwardly extremely cautious. His performance against the considerably weak Portuguese Army in Goa notwithstanding, he was seen by most as being 'brilliant in the ops room' but shaky on the ground. Even the defence minister, Chavan, whose unqualified support he had throughout his tenure as the chief felt 'on several occasions, when he found that Chaudhuri was unsure of himself, he asked him to visit the Front and get first-hand assessment of the situation. Those visits proved useful for General Chaudhuri, although on two such visits, he had acrimonious and heated exchanges with Lieutenant General Harbakhsh Singh, the Western Area Army Commander.'[3]

Generals Chaudhuri and Harbakhsh represented two different schools of thought. Chaudhuri was the last of the KCIOs, most of whom seemed out of their depth as senior officers, almost fogeyish in their outlook, while Harbakhsh represented the vanguard of those trained in India with a greater commitment to professionalism. In a hierarchical system like the army, these undercurrents may not be so visible under the social graces that govern behaviour, but they are a reality. Most mid-ranking officers of that time were aware of the fact that the army chief and the Western Army commander did not always see eye to eye.

Sitting in Simla and removed from the fighting, Harbakhsh Singh had his own views about the conduct of the Rann of Kutch episode. Major General Dunn had been Chaudhuri's chief of staff during the Goa Operations and Harbakhsh viewed him as 'Chaudhuri's man'. He felt Dunn (and by extension Chaudhuri) had not been aggressive enough. Not one to let a chance go by, he decided to address a letter to all his formation commanders in which he reviewed the sequence of events in the Rann, implying that the Indian side had failed miserably for lack of a backbone (which was the view shared by Ayub and Bhutto). Signing off with a dramatic flourish, the army commander asked: 'Has the martial blood in the veins of Indian Army soldiers dried up?'[4]

Reading the letter aloud on 12 May 1965 was Brigadier Vijay Kumar Ghai, commanding the 121 (Independent) Infantry Brigade Group in Kargil. Present at the conference at Brigade HQ were Lieutenant Colonel Sudershan Singh, the CO of 4 Rajput, two of his company commanders—Majors Baljit Singh Randhawa and Dayal Parshad Nayar (later brigadier)—and the CO of 85 Light Regiment, Lieutenant Colonel Kuldip Singh Bajwa.[5]

Ghai, who prior to picking up his rank and moving up to Kargil had been General Harbakhsh's GSO-1 in Simla, paused for effect, then addressing the gathered officers, he continued dramatically: 'reading between the lines of the Army Commander's DO letter I know what he expects from me. Gentlemen, 4 Rajput will attack and capture Point 13620 and Black Rocks on the night of 13th/14th May 1965.'[6] The brigade commander then unfolded his plan for the attack on the two features. It was fairly straightforward, conforming to the usual Indian Army assault pattern of those days—the attacking troops would move through their own forward defended localities (FDLs), stealthily enter the Valley that separated the enemy from the Indian positions, and then launch an uphill attack.

After he finished, Sudershan Singh and Randhawa said in English and Punjabi respectively, much the same thing: 'No problem, sir...it'll be done.' Nayar, however, after politely beating around the bush, said: 'With the approval of my commanding officer and without meaning any reservations or questioning feasibility of success as per existing plan of attack, can we be provided greater information of the configuration of the ground behind the enemy FDLs and more accurate details of his deployments since what is known to us is what we can see directly.' Before Ghai could enquire if the young officer had been weaned off his mother's milk, Nayar continued: 'I volunteer to lead a patrol behind enemy lines to obtain the necessary information regarding the ground and if possible the layout of the enemy's defences.' This led to a brief discussion, after which it was decided that the battalion had twenty-four hours to obtain the information required, and that 16 May would be D-Day.

Brigadier Ghai was taking a huge risk and perhaps stretching his brief. 4 Rajput, one of the battalions that had suffered severe casualties in NEFA in November 1962, had just seen a change of command as Sudershan Singh had taken over the battalion barely a fortnight earlier. Along with elements of 1 JAK Militia, the Rajputs[7] by themselves made up the Brigade Group. The entire frontage that extended from the area north of Zoji La up to Batalik was ostensibly the area of responsibility of the brigade, which in addition to the infantry battalions also had 85 Light Regiment in support of its troops.

Kargil was quite the forgotten sector. Apart from the main highway which only opened in mid-May once Border Roads could clear the snow and ice across Zoji La, there were no roads, just a few footpaths and rough tracks that ran across the precipitous cliffs that made up the bleak and desolate landscape. Situated across the Great Himalayan Range, Kargil was on the leeward side where the effect of the resultant rain shadow was most noticeable. Most of the posts situated on the surrounding heights were a logistical nightmare mainly maintained by pack animals or by virtue of physically carrying the loads up on the backs of porters. Though Kargil itself rarely got snowbound, most of the heights were constantly battling terrible conditions with temperatures plunging to record lows.

Apart from the fact that Ghai's proposed attack plan was a straightforward frontal assault, the other problem was that the Kargil Sector itself had no Pakistani activity whatsoever. On 24 April, HQ 121 Brigade had received a signal from HQ 15 Corps in Srinagar warning all units in the sector of increased Pakistani aggressive moves and impending danger.[8] Pakistani posts situated in the Kargil Sector, especially Pt 13620,[9] Saddle, and Black Rocks, looked down upon and dominated the Srinagar–Leh Highway and also the town of Kargil itself. This theoretically allowed the Pakistani artillery and heavy weapons from across the border to open fire every time there was any movement on the highway or otherwise.

With CFL infringements and shelling a daily occurrence everywhere else, creating a paper trail of random acts of firing by the Pakistanis was not a problem, especially since the UN observers rarely ever came this far north. Had it been later in the year—mid-June/July/August—Pakistani activity in the sector would have made sense. However, at that time of year, survival would have been the primary concern for them as their posts were at such great heights and lines of communication poor. Even for their guns to regularly shell Kargil would have required a major logistical exercise.

At that time, very little information was available as to the layout of the Pakistani defences at the top of the two features, which from down below seemed almost impregnable. The maps available with 121 Brigade were ¼ inch to a mile and there were no aerial photographs available. The next day after the conference, to get detailed information about the objectives, the designated assault company commanders, Major Nayar of Alpha Company and Major Randhawa of Bravo Company, led patrols to their respective objectives. Having successfully infiltrated the area held by the Pakistanis, Randhawa, to his utter amazement, found that Pt 13620 consisted of three prominent heights with supporting defences situated on them, with approximately 50 yards of flat ground in between. Apart from the main feature, the other two heights were named Conical 1 and Conical 2.

Nayar's patrol was carrying a camera to document the terrain while reconnoitring the Black Rocks feature. It too found the objective to consist of three parts which were named and marked as Peak 1, Peak 2, and Black Rocks on the map. A sub-patrol, led by Captain S. N. Bhatnagar, then got to a designated point from where Bhatnagar fired a single shot from his rifle into the air. The Pakistanis, much to the delight of Nayar and his hidden team, promptly went into a 'stand-to' mode, which served as a demonstration that gave away not only their strengths, but also the position of their main weapons, which included 3-inch mortars and MMGs.

The reconnaissance complete, the battalion started to prepare for the attack. Ghai postponed D-Day by twenty-four hours, which didn't make sense tactically, for the next night was a full moon. Years later, when the official history of the 1965 war was put out, quoting from official records, it was recorded that the 'Pakistanis attacked one of the Indian posts in strength. Though the attack was repulsed, the danger persisted.' Other write-ups identify the post as No. 8 Picket.[10] This was a fabrication, for the attacking companies were congregating at that very position for the next day's operation. Commanded by Second Lieutenant A. K. Chattopadhaya, the men had spent the entire night preparing and marking the approaches for the impending attack. Not a shot had been fired in the area.

Ghai was obviously under a time pressure, which could only have come from the army commander. Given the quantum of force available with virtually no reserves, it is highly doubtful if Army HQ had even the slightest idea about the developments taking place in Kargil. To make matters worse, as the night chosen for the attack was a full moon night, attacking troops moving through patches of snow were lit up by a lunar glow.

The attack was planned in two phases: H-hour was to be 0200 hrs on 17 May and Randhawa's Bravo Company was to capture Pt 13620 after which Nayar was to assault the Black Rocks feature. The southern approach to Pt 13620 was considered almost impossible and the Pakistanis had, therefore, focussed their entire attention on the central gully that was heavily mined and hemmed in by razor-sharp ridges that were emanating from the main feature. Once Pt 13620 was captured, the plan was for Charlie Company to take Saddle, after which Nayar would go for Black Rocks, approaching it from the northeast. Complete secrecy was to be observed; as a result, no civilian porters or pack animals could be used. All preparatory work was done in the hours of darkness, with ammunition loads being ferried to the two designated FUPs, which were less than 100 metres from the forward Pakistani bunkers. The area was so narrow that the men had to move in single file and only one platoon could launch an attack at a time.

It was freezing cold, with sub-zero temperatures and patches of snow almost a foot and a half deep. The conditions actually suited the Rajputs, for they were the ones on the move. They started from No. 8 Picket at 2000 hrs; the going was extremely difficult and slow because of the heavy weapons they had to carry. Kalu, the picket's pet dog, decided to move with the men and continued to do so despite all attempts to make him go back. Bravo Company, moving through a re-entrant, made it to the FUP undetected and, as per plan, at H-hour, Captain Ranbir Singh led the forward platoon towards the objective. 'The leading troops crossed the start line. The enemy post and the perimeter wall were clearly visible in the moon light. It was unbelievable that they had not seen us. There was no fire and the men ploughed through the snow and rocky area for 150 metres. Then hell was let loose on the attacking men. The volume of fire was so heavy and intense that the troops took to ground. The sudden and effective enemy fire suggested that they had come to know of our presence and had held their fire, waiting for us to close the gap. We were up against seasoned and well-trained troops.'[11] The last few yards were a virtual cliff face from where a Pakistani LMG was firing. Wounded in the initial burst, Ranbir Singh ordered Havildar Girdhari Lal to silence the Pakistanis. Even though the NCO was hit, he continued to inch his way forward using every scrap of cover provided by the rugged ground.[12] He was joined by Budh Singh, and they continued to inch forward until they were close enough to hurl two grenades into the LMG post, killing the occupants. Girdhari Lal died too but, miraculously, Budh Singh had survived.

Pakistani small arm fire was supported by medium machine guns, 2-inch and 3-inch mortars. Having reached the perimeter, the Rajputs were engaged in a grim hand-to-hand fight. Dead and wounded soldiers were lying everywhere. Ranbir Singh was also wounded, blood oozing from his head. Major Randhawa then rushed forward, urging the determined troops to keep moving. The company commander led them from bunker to bunker, until he came face to face with a Pakistani JCO. They fired simultaneously and both were killed.

Randhawa's final rush had cost him his life,[13] but it created the foothold on Pt 13620 that the Rajputs desperately needed. With his company commander killed and the other officer wounded, the CO along with Major Bikram Singh Chetri, Second Lieutenants Vijay Kumar Aggarwal[14] and Bhagrawat Singh,[15] and Charlie Company, which was in reserve, arrived at Pt 13620 to find the men still engaged in a hand-to-hand fight with the defenders. Finding that Conical 2 was still holding out, Sudershan Singh grabbed a LMG from a fallen soldier and along with a handful of men, rushed and captured the objective. With 13620 taken, Chetri with his Charlie Company captured Saddle, which had been abandoned by the demoralized surviving defenders.

After the reconnaissance, there had been a complete change of plan. Nayar's Alpha Company had decided to assault Black Rocks from behind and they were to launch their attack once Phase I (the capture of Pt 13620) was completed. They had just reached their concentration area at 0200 hrs when the firing on the other feature started. Recalls Nayar, 'I realized that surprise was lost, for now the enemy would be at their stand-to positions, so I decided to push forward straight away. I directed Second Lieutenant Harbhagwant Singh to take his platoon and capture Peak 1 while Subedar Ranjit Singh was to rush Peak 2. However, the going over boulders and through patches of snow was indeed tough and the enemy started firing with rifles and LMGs at the two advancing platoons.'

Despite heavy fire directed at them, both platoons kept advancing, dashing from boulder to boulder, firing their weapons from the hip. Naik Sapater Singh, one of the section commanders in Harbhagwant's platoon, successfully silenced a LMG position. This demoralized the others, who abandoned the two flanking peaks and fled, rolling down the reverse side. This left Nayar, who had Captain Bhatnagar's third platoon with him, the task of capturing the main feature of Black Rocks, which was dead ahead. With Peak 1 and Peak 2 secured, two sections of Ranjit Singh's platoon also joined the company commander and together they started to advance through the bowl which was covered with snow. They had gone 15 yards when Nayar realized the snow was waist deep and if they stayed there, the men would be picked off one by one. He immediately told Bhatnagar to move with his platoon and try and capture the feature from the northeast. Meanwhile, both Harbhagwant and Ranjit were trying to provide covering fire, but the intensity of enemy fire was increasing by the second.

Black Rocks was proving to be a different kettle of fish with the Pakistanis too well entrenched to be easily dislodged from their defences. Nayar asked the accompanying FOO, Captain N. Darkunde, to call in mortar support from 85 Light Regiment. Since the attack on Pt 13620 was a silent one, Bajwa's gunners, who were equipped with the ML 4.2-inch mortars[16] had to register their targets by graph paper surveys and then wait for fire on call. The men and officers of 853 Light Battery had to carry their equipment and the complement of 600 rounds allocated for the attack up to the mortar positions on their backs, a climb of some 1,000 feet. Since no porters could be used, some Border Roads personnel were inducted to help with the loads.

Owing to the closeness of the opposing forces, the request for fire support was denied. However, with daylight lighting up the peaks, Nayar once again called for supporting fire. Despite the risk of hitting their own troops, the Indian gunners and heavy mortars opened up, allowing the Rajput forward positions to close the gap further. The fire was so accurate that not a single Rajput soldier was hit despite the targets being just a dozen meters ahead of them. The Pakistanis manning Black Rocks fought tenaciously but, eventually, the quantum and accuracy of fire and Bhatnagar closing on them from a flank was too much for them. The survivors finally broke contact and withdrew, leaving behind the bodies of two officers and fourteen other ranks.

By daybreak, Pt 13620, Black Rocks, and Saddle were in Indian hands. In addition to posthumous awards for Baljit Randhawa and Girdhari Lal, Captain Ranbir Singh and Sepoy Budh Singh were awarded Vir Chakras, the commanding officer a VSM, while Nayar, Chetri, Bhatnagar, Subedar Rajender Nath, and Narain Singh were Mentioned in Despatches. 4 Rajput paid a heavy price, losing one officer, two JCOs, and nine men. In addition, two officers, one JCO, and fifty other ranks were wounded. However, the battalion, which captured a large number of weapons, ammunition and rations, had pulled off an incredible operation.

Ghai's, and by extension, Harbakhsh Singh's, little gamble had paid off. From the Rann of Kutch, which from an Indian perspective, was a defensive battle with little to cheer about, the spotlight was now on GOC-in-C Western Command and a remote part of J&K which, at that time, no one outside of the army knew about. The action in Kargil had all the elements that any state thrives on—guts and glory. Provided with a 'victory', the political leadership of the country, the army chief, General Chaudhuri, and Army HQ all fell in line to bask in the glory of this offensive action. General Harbakhsh had also subtly reminded everyone that he was indeed *the* army commander in the west. In many ways, it was symptomatic of the existing leadership which was expected to provide the higher direction of war to fail to realize the true implications of what had happened.

Since January 1965, it should have been obvious that there was a serious problem in J&K. Instead of tackling the issue, matters had been allowed to drift.

Rann of Kutch was just one example, where a local incident involving police patrols kept getting escalated despite neither side having any clear reason to get involved in an armed clash. Meanwhile, in the Kashmir Valley the government and civil administration had little popular support. There had been a definite spurt in cross-border incidents since the beginning of the year. Every incident that took place where there was collateral damage, had a predictable fallout—the local government would blow the incident out of proportion with two aims: 1) to establish it was on account of the army that they were losing popular support and 2) to ensure heavy compensation to regain lost ground.

General Harbakhsh had to be fully aware of the existing ground situation in Kashmir so his green-flagging Ghai's operation to infuse an aggressive spirit in the troops was rather chancy! So far, Kargil had been a dormant sector, but had 4 Rajput's attack failed to dislodge the enemy, what would have happened? There were no reserves whatsoever, so, at best, the battalion, after suffering heavily, would have had to fall back on its defended localities. Troops would have had to be rushed in to reinforce the positions, for the Pakistanis, once provoked, would have most certainly gone on the offensive. It spoke extremely poorly of the senior leadership in both government and the army to let the onus of the decision fall on the brigade commander if things had indeed gone wrong. Besides, if local formations start taking decisions that can result in an all-out war, then there is something seriously wrong somewhere.

However, nothing succeeds like success. Lost in the pages of history is the fact that in less than twenty-four hours, there was another feature called Black Rock Fort that was captured by the Indians. Towards the northeast of Kargil was the town of Leh, separated from the Nubra Valley by the Ladakh Range. To cross over, the road had to negotiate the Khardung La (17582 ft) and then drop down into the valley that was drained by the Shyok River that flowed east to west. Directly to the north lay the then unexplored Siachen Glacier which was the source of the Nubra River. Siachen itself was contiguous with the Shaksgam Valley, while to its immediate east was Daulat Beg Oldi and the Karakash region of the Aksai Chin where the Indians were facing the Chinese.

Near the confluence of the Nubra and the Shyok was situated Partapur, where a small garrison of the Nubra Guard comprising of local Ladakhi troops was stationed under the command of the sector commander, Colonel Kapoor. As a part of their aggressive stance all along the CFL, the Pakistanis had been shelling the village of Bogdang (halfway between Thoise and Chalunka on the southern bank of the Shyok) from their position at Black Rock Fort. Kapoor was working closely with Captain Chewang Rinchin[17] to amalgamate the Nubra Guards and the JAK Militia into a new force that was to be called the Ladakh Scouts.[18] On 16 May the plan to neutralize Black Rock Fort using a company of Nubra Guards under Captain Gill was cleared by Major General G. A. S. Singh, GOC 3 Infantry

Division. Accordingly, the attack was launched on the night of 17/18 May and the Ladakhi troops captured Black Rock Fort. This was followed by the capture of Sabzkot as well which then considerably altered the situation in the Shyok Valley. There were no further raids or attacks by the Pakistanis in this sector.

HELL HATH NO FURY

Brigadier Ghai and his fellow Indian commanders all along the CFL could hardly afford to let their guard down, for the Pakistanis expectedly reacted to the loss of their posts in Kargil like a swarm of angry bees. In the next forty-eight hours they not only launched counter-attacks to reclaim their lost picket, they also put in two separate night attacks on Indian positions next to Kargil town. These were all systematically beaten back through well-coordinated defensive fire.

On the night of 18 May, the Pakistanis unsuccessfully attacked on Dalla, an Indian post southwest of Chhamb. Simultaneously, 25 Division under Major General Amreek Singh that was looking after the area between Poonch and Naushera reported multiple violations of the CFL, with the Pakistanis even engaging in a battalion-strength attack on a post southwest of Mendhar during the early hours of 19 May. Pakistani troops had also ingressed into the area immediately south of Tithwal, but none of the raids had paid any dividends.

The road beyond Zoji La as it made its way to Drass and Kargil through extremely forbidding terrain was extremely vulnerable. To secure each and every height in the region was an impossible task and, given the vastness of the area, a determined group of men could easily occupy a high feature and from there call in harassing artillery fire to interdict the highway below. All attempts to recapture their lost positions in the immediate vicinity of Kargil having failed, the Pakistanis established themselves on Op Hill and Kala Pahar, which overlooked the main highway approximately 16 km short of the town. Even though the Pakistanis had dug themselves in on a feature that was set back from the road, their presence was detected by a 1 JAK Militia patrol on 29 May. It was reported that there were close to 200 men occupying the Kala Pahar feature, which had a nearly 3-km-long ridge tapering down to the highway.

To deal with the increased Pakistani activity in the area, 1 Guards that was under 3 Infantry Division and stationed in Karu, had been moved to Mulbekh and placed under Brigadier Ghai's command on 21 May. 1 Guards had been tasked to ensure the security of the road between Bimbat and Bodh Kharbu, a stretch extending 128 km east of Kargil towards Leh. On 31 May the battalion, led by Major (later Major General) Manjapura Chandra Shekar Menon, the officiating CO, was ordered to move to Kargil.

1 Guards was formerly 2 Punjab, one of the oldest battalions in the Indian Army. Along with two other battalions, it had been converted and brought into the Brigade of the Guards in 1949. A pet project of General (later Field Marshal)

Kodandera Madappa Cariappa, the commander-in-chief at the time, the Guards were the first regiment that had broken away from the class composition followed by the British. In other words, these units had an all-India recruitment pattern. Ghai asked Menon to take a small party with him and move to Picket No. 17 occupied by a platoon of JAK Militia, from where the initial reports of Pakistani ingress had originated.

At 2200 hrs on 31 May, three officers—Captain (later Colonel) Ravinder Singh Saharawat, the CO of Alpha Company, Second Lieutenant M. K. Chengappa, the battalion's intelligence officer (IO), and Second Lieutenant (later Commandant, BSF) Manjit Singh Chimni, the No. 2 Platoon commander—along with Jemadars Khazan Singh, Balwant Ram, and Naik Sansar Singh, set off to reconnoitre the approach towards Op Ridge. Moving in pitch-dark conditions, they cautiously climbed up to within a couple of hundred yards of the objective, after which, prior to first light, they concealed themselves among the rocks, literally under the nose of the newly constructed Pakistani sangars (fortifications).

Throughout the day, the hidden patrol observed the Pakistani troops. It was soon clear that the initial estimate of the enemy's strength as reported by the JAK Militia was accurate, and the Pakistanis were deployed with rifles and LMGs on two other interlinked features—Small Bump and Kala Pahar. The party also concluded that an attack along the route taken by it would be suicidal, for it was not only extremely steep and open, it was probably bracketed by MMGs and supporting artillery guns. The patrol however noticed that there was a fourth feature, which they marked on their maps as Right Ridge, that seemed unoccupied.

Saharawat's patrol fell back under the cover of darkness. Another probing patrol under the command of Second Lieutenant (later Brigadier) Chandra Mohan Mehta also confirmed that the approaches to the Right Ridge were unguarded. On the morning of 2 June, when Major Menon reached Ghai's headquarters, it was obvious that this battle would have to be fought very differently. The Guardsmen were up against a well dug-in force made up of elements of the South Waziristan, Northern, and Karakoram Scouts. These men were accustomed to the rugged terrain, and the altitude and the weather had improved considerably during the last fortnight. To assault this formidable position, 1 Guards would have to attack not from the direction of Picket No. 17 but Right Ridge, and they would require considerable heavy mortar support as well. 114 Light Battery from 32 Light Regiment was moved from 3 Division and grouped with 85 Light Regiment under Bajwa. By the evening of 2 June, 1 Guards began to concentrate at Hardus, a small village near the Harka Bahadur Bridge at the base of Right Ridge. Even as the men started moving into the village, intermittent harassing bombardment of Pakistani positions had begun.

Menon's plan was to capture Kala Pahar and Op Ridge from the northern side, for which he needed to establish a firm base on Right Ridge. Saharawat with his Alpha Company once again set off under the cover of darkness. Right Ridge was located at 11,800 feet, a hazardous 4,000 feet above the launching-off point at the Harka Bahadur Bridge. At 0800 hrs on 3 June, after a brief skirmish with a Pakistani protective patrol in which Lance Naik Mohinder Singh took a bullet to the thigh, Saharawat's company had occupied Right Ridge. However, by then, the Pakistanis were aware of their presence, so they started to shell the area while simultaneously trying to get to a feature known as Three Bumps from where they could dominate Right Ridge.

Saharawat, with a section, broke cover and made his way through the exploding shells towards Three Bumps, successfully denying it to the enemy. Within a few minutes of securing Right Ridge, the battalion had established a communication line and shortly thereafter Menon also arrived to take stock of the situation. Despite their failure to establish themselves on Three Bumps, the Pakistanis kept up a steady barrage of mortar and MMG fire throughout the day and the next night. However, despite the entire approach being subject to fire, the rest of the battalion had reached Right Ridge by 0800 hrs on 4 June. At 1400 hrs, Menon telephonically discussed his plan of attack with Ghai. The Pakistanis had set up their defences on five features: Kala Pahar, which had a platoon plus; Small Bump was being held by a section; Saddle and Red Bump were being held by two sections; and both Op Ridge and Left Ridge had a platoon each. Menon proposed to attack in three phases: Kala Pahar would be assaulted by Charlie Company commanded by Major (later Brigadier) Vijay Narayan Channa as phase 1; Small Bump, Red Saddle, and Left Ridge would then be captured by Delta Company under Major (later Major General) R. P. Singh; and in phase three Op Ridge would be captured by Bravo Company under Captain (later Colonel) Ranjit Singh Grewal. With Ghai approving the plan, H-hour was set for 0230 hrs on 5 June.

The action around Three Bumps was not yet over. The area selected to be the FUP from where the attacks would be launched later that night was under the observation and range of a MMG positioned at Bunker Hill. It was imperative for the artillery to register the target, so Chimni's section was ordered to fall back on Right Ridge at 1600 hrs. Twenty minutes later when the Guardsmen started moving back to reoccupy Three Bumps, to their shock, they found the Pakistanis already occupying it. This new development jeopardized the entire attack plan, so Chimni was ordered by Menon to re-take the post at all costs. Under the covering fire of his platoon, the officer along with two men crawled towards the enemy position, getting to within 25 yards of Three Bumps from where they lobbed grenades at the enemy. The Pakistani patrol fought tooth and nail but eventually, after a hand-to-hand fight, they were forced to vacate the position at 1800 hrs. This was a clear indication that the Pakistanis dug in on the various features around Kala Pahar were going to put up a determined fight.

The entire build-up on the Right Ridge had taken place in full view of the Pakistanis who were also being supported by their artillery. Menon's biggest problem was to get his three assaulting companies to the FUP without incurring severe casualties. He therefore ordered Saharawat to take one platoon from Alpha Company to move between Bunker Hill and the FUP by last light. As per the plan, at 0130 hrs on 5 June, the leading elements of the battalion started to move from the Right Ridge towards the FUP.

Almost immediately, the night sky was lit up with illuminating flares while Pakistani mortars opened up along with small arms. Even as the men went to ground, Second Lieutenant S. N. Tripathi was hit by a splinter in the leg. Charlie Company, which had been under near non-stop fire ever since it had moved up from Hardus to Right Ridge the previous day, went to ground. Naik (later Subedar Major/Honorary Captain) Jagan Nath who was the company commander's runner, pushed Channa to his feet. Seeing their officer move forward under fire, Charlie Company responded and began to push forward again.

As per the plan, at 0215 hrs, 85 Light Regiment started firing at the Pakistani positions. Fifteen minutes later, 1 Guards crossed the designated start line as per schedule, with Charlie Company determinedly closing the gap between themselves and the Pakistani soldiers who were manning the defences on Kala Pahar. As the artillery fire lifted, the Pakistanis brought to bear LMG and rifle fire while the MMG on Bunker Hill, ignoring Saharawat's section, kept up a steady stream of intense fire. Charlie Company, using every bit of cover that was available in the rocky, windswept heights, kept inching forward and, by 0500 hrs had reached the crest of Kala Pahar.

Daylight brought with it other problems. An LMG post supported by a section that was extremely well dug-in to the right of Kala Pahar, halted the momentum of the attack with its accurate fire. Subedar Surat Singh with one platoon tried to neutralize the position, but instead got pinned down 50 yards from the enemy by their small arms fire. Second Lieutenant (later Major) Rajendra Singh, along with Naik Jagan Nath, then started making their way towards the LMG under the covering fire from Surat Singh's men. The grenade lobbed by the officer succeeded in wounding him as well. Seeing Rajendra Singh go down, Jagan Nath rushed the Pakistani bunkers. Despite being shot in the arm, he continued to throw grenades until all the men in the bunker were killed.

It was obvious by this point that the Pakistani positions on Kala Pahar were going to be very hard to overcome. The men had physically hauled a 57 mm RCL gun along with its ammunition up the steep slopes and these now came in handy. Menon, desperate to silence the forward Pakistani positions on Red Bump, ordered Havildar Karam Singh of the Anti-Tank Platoon to engage the enemy bunkers. In a direct firing role, the RCL is a devastating weapon, and soon four bunkers were reduced to smoking ruins. To keep the momentum of the attack going, Menon ordered Delta Company forward, but the MMG on Bunker Hill was ready and waiting for them. In the initial burst of fire, the No. 12 Platoon commander, Second Lieutenant C. V. Tahilramani was wounded while the rest of the company was pinned down by an LMG located on the left side of Kala Pahar.

Advancing without the cover of darkness seemed an impossibility but Menon had no choice but to keep the assault going. The Delta Company commander, R. P. Singh, took it upon himself to crawl towards the LMG post despite fire coming at him from two directions. Seeing R. P. move up, Guardsman Raghbir Singh followed, shouting to the others that he would not let the officer go forward alone. Getting within throwing range, the two engaged the LMG with grenades, but Raghbir had been mortally wounded. He died shortly after his last grenade killed the Pakistani LMG crew.

With the Pakistanis distracted by R. P. and Raghbir, Second Lieutenant S. K. Nanda, with his platoon in tow, made a determined dash towards Small Bump. The platoon immediately came under intense small arms fire from three directions as the defenders on the Red and Right Bumps desperately opened up. Nanda was hit in the thigh but despite going down, he kept crawling forward, engaging the enemy to give his men the required covering fire. The company's Havildar Major, Nand Singh, took immediate charge and though he too was shot in the arm and stomach, he kept the momentum of the attack going. Though a dozen men had been hit and the platoon was severely depleted, the rest of Delta Company charged forward and captured the Three Bumps from the extremely determined but by now exhausted enemy.

Sensing his opportunity, Menon ordered Delta Company to keep moving towards Op Ridge. As per the original plan, Ranjit Singh Grewal's Bravo Company was to have gone through Delta Company and launched the final assault as Phase III on Op Ridge. 'It was a flowing battle with little time to think,' recalls Grewal, 'I was just below the objective and I saw Delta Company forming up and charging. As per the plan it was supposed to be my objective. Without waiting to be told, we followed and headed for Left Spur. I saw Nand Singh sitting there, holding his guts that were spilling out. He asked me for water, so I unclipped my water bottle and gave it to him literally on the run. The Pakistanis by then seemed to have had enough. They were abandoning Left Spur and rolling down the other side.'[19]

Finally, at 0830 hrs, both Op Ridge and Left Spur had been taken. The capture of Kala Pahar, with the fighting raging continuously over a period of six hours, was the first battle fought by the erstwhile 2 Punjab in its new avatar of 1 Guards. The battalion, as the attacking force against a well-entrenched enemy, had eight killed and forty-five wounded, of which four were officers. Nand Singh and many others who were seriously wounded survived mainly because of timely evacuation that was extremely well handled by the regimental medical officer (RMO), Captain R. K. Udayashankar, and two unit officers, Second Lieutenants P. K. Vij and M. M. L. Bhatia. Together they carried the casualties across the steep and rugged terrain to the battalion's Advanced Dressing Station at the Harka Bahadur Bridge, a distance of 7 miles. Sixteen Pakistani dead were recovered from Kala Pahar while another fifty stretcher cases were seen being carried across the CFL by the tenacious men who had eventually been pushed off the feature by 1 Guards.

ALL FOR NOTHING! OP ABLAZE CALLED OFF!

Even though the fighting had come to a halt in the Rann of Kutch towards the end of April in anticipation of a ceasefire, the deployment of the Indian Army all along the IB had sent the alarm bells ringing across the globe. 'This necessitated certain moves plus stoppage of leave and recall of personnel on leave.'[20] Pakistan promptly retaliated, placing all their formations, including the air force and the navy, at twelve hours' notice. Pakistan railways were also put on alert and both 21 and 52 Brigade Group were ordered to move from Quetta to Hyderabad in Sindh in order to reinforce 8 Division. General Tikka Khan, in order to meet any new Indian initiative in the Rann of Kutch, created a counter-attack force comprising a squadron from 12 Cavalry and some infantry. In keeping with the Pakistani fondness for dramatic names, it was code-named 'Changez Force' and deployed at Vingoor.

Despite the mobilization of India's army during Operation Ablaze, the only fighting that actually took place was far away from the plains of Punjab, in the remote windswept heights of Kargil. Brigadier Ghai's 121 Infantry Brigade had started the ball rolling on 17 May when 4 Rajput had attacked and captured Pt 13620 and Black Rocks, and nearly three weeks later 1 Guards had successfully ended the fighting in that sector by evicting the Pakistanis from Kala Pahar.

Throughout Operation Ablaze, General Chaudhuri was fully aware of the ceasefire negotiations that were ongoing. The UK's prime minister, Harold Wilson, had taken the initiative and, on 28 April 1965, written to both Lal Bahadur Shastri and Ayub Khan expressing grave concern over the fighting in the Rann of Kutch. The British suggestion was to call for an immediate ceasefire followed by a troop withdrawal, with both sides reverting to the status quo as on 1 January 1965. This suited Ayub Khan, for it would be a tacit admission on the part of India that the Rann of Kutch was indeed a disputed area. Shastri, on the other hand, had already given his go-ahead to deploy the army in the Punjab (Operation Ablaze); nevertheless, instructions were issued on 1 May to all units in the Rann by HQ Kilo Sector that no offensive action was to be taken. Though truce prevailed, both sides continued to patrol along the area that they were holding. On 23 June, Dunn's Kilo Sector ceased to exist, as responsibility for the Kutch–Sindh border was handed over to Major General (later Lieutenant General) Naveen C. Rawlley, MC[21].

The fine print for the ceasefire agreement continued to be honed and, finally, on 30 June, Harold Wilson's efforts to bring the two Commonwealth countries to a negotiated settlement bore fruit. The ceasefire was to take effect from 0600 hrs IST on 1 July and though the main focus was on the Gujarat–West Pakistan border, the very first clause, stipulating that the two countries would revert to the positions they held on 1 January, meant the Indians would have to abandon the features captured in the Kargil Sector.

In the Rann of Kutch, over the next seven days, Pakistan withdrew its troops and the Gujarat State Police reoccupied Chhad Bet in the same strength as on 31 December 1964. Both India and Pakistan started patrolling the tracks that existed then, the frequency and intensity also being restricted to the terms of the ceasefire. It was also stipulated that the two governments should meet within thirty days and agree upon the determination and demarcation of the border, keeping in mind their respective claim lines. Should no agreement be reached, the matter was to be referred to a three-man tribunal, which would be constituted within four months of the ceasefire. Apart from the Indian and Pakistani representatives, the chairman of the tribunal was to be from a neutral country selected jointly by the two governments. Should both sides fail to agree on a mutual choice, it was then left to the United Nations Secretary General U Thant to nominate someone. The subsequent decision of the tribunal would be binding on both governments and there would be no room for any appeals.

As per the ceasefire agreement, apart from the police personnel manning the Sindh border, regular Indian troops were pulled back to Khavda, keeping south of the causeway from where the Rann effectively starts. 'A total of 417 mines (13 anti-tank and 404 anti-personnel) mainly in the Sardar Post area, could not be removed but the fields were suitably marked and cordoned off. Two CRP battalions were placed under the operational control of Southern Command to establish posts at Suigam, Bela, Lodhrani, Navsari and Chhad Bet. A post at Karim Shahi was also to be established depending upon the feasibility of its maintenance during the monsoon.'[22]

Pakistan, however, had interpreted the outcome of the Rann of Kutch conflict as a sign of encouragement for its future designs on Kashmir. Ironically, Ayub too did not want to escalate the war, because the 'probing in Kutch' had completed a trial run to launch a full-scale attack on India now, having tested the will of India which had 'agreed to settle'. As Altaf Gauhar, author of the biography on Ayub Khan and his minister for Information and Broadcasting recounts: 'For all his realism and prudence, Ayub's judgement did get impaired by the Rann of Kutch in one respect: his old prejudice that "the Hindu has no stomach for a fight" turned to belief, if not a military doctrine, which had the decisive effect on the course of events.'[23]

The Rann of Kutch ceasefire also meant Operation Ablaze was formally called off and the formations that had moved up had to return to their peacetime locations. U Thant took the opportunity to appeal to the Indians that the withdrawal of troops be extended to the Kargil Sector as well.

The withdrawal from the captured features had an adverse effect on the morale of 4 Rajput and 1 Guards. Before the attack was launched on Black Rocks and Pt 13620, the Rajput officers had asked the brigade commander if the United Nations would intervene and insist that the captured features had to be vacated and returned to Pakistan, what then? Brigadier Ghai had categorically stated that there was no question of returning these vital positions, and should the matter come up, it would 'be over my dead body'.[24]

For the men, the returning of the features they had captured where their comrades and a company commander had been killed was a huge betrayal. An angry Sudershan Singh made his feelings known, after which it was decided to shift 4 Rajput immediately to Karu as part of 163 Brigade. Little did the men realize then that Kargil was to be a precursor to Tashkent.

General Chaudhuri should have questioned the withdrawal from the positions in Kargil. As chairman of the chief of staff's committee, he needed to dig in or, if he had not been consulted, make an issue of it. The COAS chose to do nothing.

With Operation Ablaze proving to be all smoke and no fire, both India and Pakistan agreed to revert to their pre-Rann positions. However, neither side was willing to completely lower its guard—Pakistan decided to keep its 1 Armoured Division in the Changa Manga forest near Kasur while India kept its 1 Armoured Division in Jalandhar. Though General Chaudhuri wanted to give the Pakistanis the impression that 1 Armoured Division would remain a part of 11 Corps, there was nothing to stop the chief from asking the officers and senior JCOs of the various regiments in the division from familiarizing themselves with the terrain in the Rachna Doab. In the immediate aftermath of the ceasefire, with the induction of infiltrators into J&K, it was fairly obvious to all that an all-out war with Pakistan was imminent. Despite that, 'a war-like atmosphere did not prevail in the various echelons of the Indian Army. Work continued at a peace time pace with routine postings of officers, leave, raising schedules and annual turnover of units. The only major forward move ordered by Indian Army was to concentrate 6 Mountain Division in the Ambala area by the middle of August.'[25]

Apart from the lack of coordination between General Chaudhuri and the Indian Air Force, Air Marshal Arjan Singh too seemed to have misread the situation. Though the pilots were extremely keen and full of enthusiasm, Air HQ did not seem to seriously believe it would have to take on the Pakistan Air Force. 'Part of this belief may have lain in the assurances that the US gave India after the China War in 1962 that India could withdraw troops and aircraft from the Punjab and Kashmir fronts without fear of Pakistani attack. Be that as it may, it was only after the Rann of Kutch incident that the possibility of war even occurred to the IAF. Till then it was a glorious flying club, with everyone having a lot of fun. After the Kutch incident, for the first time, elementary precautions like camouflage netting for aircraft began to be taken.'[26]

With a 2.3 to 1 ratio in his favour, the numbers looked good for the IAF. Arjan Singh also had the advantage of reserve aircraft that were deployed against China, but at no stage did the air chief think of bringing that factor into play. This despite the fact that the IAF post-1962 was in a state of great flux where 'squadrons had been ruthlessly bled of experienced personnel for the expansion, and the entire organisation was under strain as it added transport, helicopter, missile and fighter units, enlarged existing bases and added new ones.'[27]

On the other hand, the PAF was not at all lackadaisical, even though they were secure in the belief that the Indians were on the back foot in Kashmir and that the fighting would never expand beyond the state's borders. Air Marshal Asghar Khan's retirement raised eyebrows, for it more or less coincided with the launch of Operation Gibraltar. His post-retirement comments that highlighted his Kashmir connection and suggested that 'because of his devotion to the cause of Kashmiris and his attitude towards the war, Asghar would give the operation a "positive and decisive complexion", if he was associated with it'[28] added further fuel to the fire.

According to General Musa, the decision to retire Asghar Khan had been taken months earlier as his extended term of office ended in July 1965. 'Asghar was not associated with the planning of Operation Gibraltar because the proposed clandestine raids did not require any air support except some supply drops which his successor organised at short notice. It was not due to any ulterior motive.' Musa went on to say that the developing situation was there for all to see and in the case of any escalation in the fighting, it was not for GHQ 'to tell the PAF to get ready for war at that particular juncture'.[29] Asghar Khan, like his Indian counterpart, Arjan Singh, was thinking purely in terms of winning the air battle. Air Marshal Nur Khan's entry on the scene meant a fresh perspective. One of Nur Khan's first steps was to add a second objective to the PAF's avowed aim of keeping the IAF out of Pakistani airspace; he added ground attack missions, which he believed would help keep the Indian ground troops off Pakistani backs.

BOOK III

Marauders from the West

Chapter 8

OPERATION GIBRALTAR

WOLVES IN SHEEP'S CLOTHING

Zulfikar Bhutto's obsessive need to do something in Kashmir was about to become a reality. Despite his varied talents and abilities, Bhutto was not a military man and though he had been extremely hawkish about Kashmir, military intervention by Pakistan had not seemed feasible. However, ever since the Kashmir Cell had been created in the Foreign Ministry under his charge, he had been exuberantly 'talking of physical assistance he could obtain from China in the event of a war with India'.[1] Bhutto also let no opportunity pass without impressing on service officers the need for a proactive stance in Kashmir. Taking the cue from the minister, Major General Akhtar Hussain Malik, the GOC of Pakistan's 12 Division that was headquartered at Murree, began to work out a blueprint for a deep penetration force that would meet the requirement.

Since 1948, there had been plenty of analysis as to why the tribal lashkars who had been sent into J&K had failed. One of the reasons suggested was that apart from a few regular officers at the helm, the lashkar columns lacked a worthwhile military structure. If the core of each column had had regular soldiers embedded into it, the invading forces would not have made the mistakes they did. By the mid-1950s, there was intermittent talk about plans to create a force that could create havoc inside IHK (Indian-held Kashmir). However, the two decision-makers, President Field Marshal Ayub Khan and General Mohammad Musa, were not quite ready to endorse any such idea.

Around that time, Lieutenant Colonel Aboobaker Osman Mitha arrived on the scene. He was born in Bombay in 1923 where he grew up in the luxurious environs of Malabar Hill. Deciding to join the army, he passed out of the IMA in 1942 and was commissioned into the 2nd Battalion 4th Bombay Grenadiers. He soon volunteered for the Parachute Regiment and was dropped behind Japanese lines where he carried out quite a few daring assignments. During Partition, he opted for Pakistan and, in 1956, as a lieutenant colonel, became the 'conceptual founder'[2] of the Special Services Group (SSG).

The 7th Battalion 10th Baluch was amalgamated with 312 Garrison Company and was renamed 19 Baluch. For it to be converted into a special operation force, its initial training was with the US Special Forces. Mitha had been asked by GHQ if the SSG could mount an operation similar to the tribal invasion of 1947 and take Kashmir by force. The answer had always been a categorical 'no' and on all previous occasions Ayub Khan and Musa had endorsed his stand. Mitha was to move on in 1962 and his successor, Colonel Syed Ghaffar Mehdi, continued to hone the SSG's fighting skills, which were more suited to developing special skills within the framework of conventional warfare.

Sometime in the beginning of May of 1965, the vice chief of the general staff, Major General Abid Bilgrami instructed Colonel Mehdi to report to Major General Akhtar Malik in Murree. The GOC, considered to be one of Pakistan's finest generals, spelt out 'his plan' that revolved around the SSG boys training a group of 'mujahideen' that would comprise regular army soldiers and volunteers, which would infiltrate Kashmir and create a general uprising 'that would bring India to the conference table without provoking general war'. When Malik added that the mujahideen needed to be sent in by end July the same year, Mehdi was stunned. 'The plan was so childish, so bizarre as to be unacceptable to logical, competent, professionally sound military persons anywhere in the world.'[3]

Mehdi further states: 'I frankly told General Akhtar Malik that the operation was a nonstarter and that I would render the same advice to the Chief and Vice Chief of General Staff. He insisted that I depute some of my [SSG] officers for immediate training of his "Mujahedeen". I had taken three of my officers with me for the briefing; I decided to leave them behind with General Malik and tasked them to do their best in the remaining four to six weeks.'[4]

It was obvious there had been a change in the thinking of Ayub Khan after the Rann of Kutch affair and no one in the chain of command was willing to go against the grain. Musa claims he continued to oppose guerrilla-type operations in the Kashmir Valley but he had neither the courage nor the conviction to stand up to the 'supreme commander'. So when Ayub Khan agreed that deep raids could indeed be launched in Kashmir and asked for a fresh plan and an appreciation of likely scenarios, Musa 'directed Commander 12 Division, Major General Akhtar Husain Malik,'[5] to prepare a draft plan for the operation, code-named "GIBRALTAR", in consultation with GHQ and within the broad concept we had specified. GHQ approved it after making certain changes in it.'

What made Ayub Khan change his mind on 13 May 1965? To point to the 'success' in the Rann of Kutch as the sole reason for going into Kashmir is to insult the man's intelligence, for the fighting in the Rann was hardly a military operation and, as a former chief, regardless of his public posturing, he would have been fully aware of it. Ayub Khan's 'first response to any plan put to him concerning an operation in Occupied Kashmir was to question if the operation was likely to lead to open war. If the answer was yes, he would not approve the plan.'[6] The Indian Prime Minister Lal Bahadur Shastri had already made it clear on 28 April that if Pakistan 'persisted in its aggressive activities' the Indians would be free to choose the where and when of striking back.

According to US sources, the Kashmir Cell had first presented the plan to Ayub in February 1965, and 'he had flatly rejected the idea. "Who authorized the Foreign Office and the ISI (Inter-Services Intelligence Directorate) to draw up such a plan? All I asked them was to keep the situation in Kashmir under review. They can't force a campaign of military action on the government,"'[7] was his response. Bhutto and his team, however, had not given up, for they believed the time was ripe for Pakistan to strike. The army and air force had been strengthened considerably over the last decade with the infusion of US military aid and training, which led them to believe it more than made up for the disadvantage of numbers. Bhutto also repeatedly argued that it was only a matter of time before India's larger economic base would come into play. In May, in a note to Ayub Khan where he once again advocated armed intervention in Kashmir, Bhutto said, 'the current relative superiority of the military forces of Pakistan in terms of quality and equipment was in danger of being overtaken as India's defence build-up progressed'.[8]

In a scenario where decision-making was highly personalized, once Bhutto gave Ayub Khan the assurance that India would confine the fighting to Kashmir, he gave it the go-ahead. The question then arises: who gave Bhutto the guarantee that, come what may, the Indians would be constrained to fight only in J&K? The answer probably lies with China or, more precisely, with Mao Zedong and Zhou Enlai, both of whom had shared their wisdom with Pakistani leaders on how to deal with India, especially with regard to Kashmir. In a subsequent meeting, Chairman Mao spelt it out: 'Look, there are ten fingers, and if you stamp on all ten, they will be hurt, but they will become functional in a few minutes. However, if you were to simply cut one finger off, everyone will know and see the loss. In the future, concentrate on a particular point of India's weakness and launch your attack to completely destroy that formation. You will soon find the rest of the Indian Army on the run, just as it ran before the Chinese Army in 1962.'[9]

The two Chinese leaders along with Bhutto's PLA handlers were not only egging him on, but also assuring him that if India looked to retaliate elsewhere, the Chinese would let it be known that they would open a second front against the Indians. The relationship between China and Pakistan was initially India-centric. The 1962 clash with India in Ladakh and NEFA underlined the obvious advantages of a strategic partnership between the two and this had led to China and Pakistan quickly resolving their own outstanding border issues in a matter of days. The difficulty around accessing documents pertaining to the China–Pakistan axis during that period is partly due to the fact that 'it is the only relationship in Chinese foreign policy that is essentially led by the PLA, with the significant additional involvement of Chinese intelligence services.'[10] However, there are enough discreet remarks that make the truth clear: 'Tell the President,' Zhou said to Ayub's son, 'Pakistan has to take Kashmir. China is ready to support Pakistan. We have troops on the north of Kashmir who are ready and could be used. Do not fire the first shot, and if you require troops for Kashmir, make a request in writing.'

Ayub Khan, after having had a change of heart, wasn't willing to listen to his own military commanders, preferring to go with the appreciation from the Foreign Ministry's Kashmir Cell. So entwined were the Chinese with Pakistani plans that Ayub Khan was even willing to discuss with the Chinese premier Zhou Enlai the strategic methodology and tactics he wished to adopt in case of war with India. General Musa admits rather ruefully: 'I was asked to give my views on these matters, as the President wished to discuss them with Mr Chou En-lai during his impending visit to Pakistan.'[11]

The decision having been taken to go ahead, Pakistan put its faith in one of its boldest generals to give shape to a plan that was based on 'Kashmiriyo mein aazadi ki lagan paida ki jai' (stoke the fire of independence in the Kashmiri people). General Akhtar Hussain Malik and four of his sector commanders got to work on the blueprint for the setting up of a 'clandestine force' that would infiltrate Kashmir and enlist the help of the local people to wrest the state away from India once and for all.

Unlike most of the other senior officers of the time, who came from well-to-do families, Akhtar Hussain Malik was the son of a headmaster in Pindori, Punjab. The lack of decent educational facilities in his village meant he had to walk for miles every day to attend a nearby school, after which his father insisted he graduate from college as well. Jobs being hard to come by, Akhtar Hussain joined the British Indian Army as a sepoy. However, his leadership qualities were evident and Malik was sent to IMA from where he was commissioned in June 1941 into the 7th Battalion 16 Punjab Regiment.

During World War II he served with his battalion in Burma and Malaya, finishing the war as a major, commanding Alpha Company of his battalion. In 1947, like most Muslim officers, he too opted for the new state of Pakistan. Considered to be an outspoken officer, by the time he was commanding 12 Division as a major general, he was not averse to dealing directly with the foreign minister and his bureaucrats from the Ministry of External Affairs, who, with the creation of the Kashmir Cell, had free licence to come and go from Murree. This parallel link bypassed the existing chain of command within the army and was most distressing for General Musa. 'The atmosphere in which the so-called discussions were held compelled me to bring the matter to the notice of the President. As the Army Commander, responsible for the land battles, I felt it was inadvisable for my subordinates to remain exposed to a kind of brainwashing.... The President agreed that such interference in an explosive matter of that kind was undesirable. He assured me he would ask the Foreign Minister not to covertly meet anyone associated with military planning.'[12]

On 15 May, two days after Ayub gave the green light in principle, he arrived in Murree with General Musa. They were accompanied by the chief of the general staff, Major General Malik Sher Bahadur, the director of Military Operations, Brigadier (later Lieutenant General) Gul Hassan Khan, and the director of Military Intelligence, Brigadier (later Lieutenant General) Irshad Ahmed Khan. No member of the Kashmir Cell had been invited for, from that moment onwards, it was to be the army's show.

As has been noted earlier, the code name chosen was 'Operation Gibraltar', perhaps a nod to Bhutto's desire to identify Pakistanis with Arabs. The legendary Arab commander Abdur Rahman Tariq had landed an Islamic army at Jabal Tariq (Gibraltar) and ordered his men to burn the boats they had come on, for Spain and Gibraltar were to be occupied by them and there would be no way for them to go back. Kashmir was to be similarly 'liberated' and there would be no stepping back from the stated objective.

Unfortunately, there are very few Pakistani records available that delve into the details pertaining to the infiltration of Kashmir. In fact, the nearest thing to Pakistan's official record is Shaukat Riza's *The Pakistan Army War of 1965*, but this book does not have any mention of Operation Gibraltar. On the Indian side, B. C. Chakravorty's *History of the Indo-Pakistan War—1965*[13] bases its estimates of the size and composition of the various raider columns on the interrogation of captured razakars and Azad Kashmir soldiers who were taken prisoner. Chakravorty places the strength of the infiltrators at 30,000 and though most Indian historians seem to accept the figure, it seems to be a gross miscalculation.

Considering Malik's 12 Division was known to have eighteen Azad Kashmir battalions, apart from the three regular battalions[14] that were partly milked to create this force, 30,000 men would have been almost double the strength of regular and para-military troops in POK. To house, train, and equip those numbers in absolute secrecy would have been impossible. Therefore, it's more likely that the force consisted of 8,000 to 10,000 men. Earlier, in August 1962, the Pakistan government had given the nod to raise a force of razakars that had already received some training in the handling of light weapons and hit and run tactics. Based in small villages close to the CFL, most of the camps were in the districts of Mirpur, Kotli, and Poonch in remote villages like Nikial, Khuiratta, Kalar Gala, Tarkundi, Pir Kalanjara, and Hajira. None of the people from this part of POK were conversant with the Kashmiri language. In addition, it would seem most of these men were not volunteers, but had been forcibly recruited under the orders of the civil authorities.[15] The activities of the razakars had been limited until then, but they were to now form the nucleus of Malik's secret force. The rest were to include mujahids who had been recruited more recently, elements of the Northern Light Infantry, and a few specialists and officers from the regular Pakistan Army.

In June/July 1965 when Malik was ordered to raise the force, he already had the basic infrastructure in place and all he had to do was amalgamate the existing Rangers and mujahid organizations with 19 Baluch (SSG) and other elements selected from his Azad Kashmir units. Akhtar Malik's first step was to attach instructors in 'irregular warfare'[16] from 19 Baluch, then stationed at Attock, to various Azad Kashmir battalions that were part of 12 Division in POK. Some razakars and mujahids were then brought to these units where they were trained with the regular troops. By June they were shifted to guerrilla warfare schools inside Pakistan located at Shinkiari (Khyber Pakhtunkhwa), Dungi, and Sakesar (both in Punjab), while a fourth camp was at Mang Bajri in POK where they received six weeks of intensive training to further toughen them up and teach them the basics of unarmed combat. In addition, they were specifically taught how to lay ambushes, disrupt lines of communication by blowing up bridges, and assault military camps and supply depots.

The men were then distributed among ten different 'forces', most of them named after inspirational Islamic warriors. The main thrust was to be provided by Salahuddin Force[17] that was to go for Srinagar; Tariq Force was to take on the area to the north, being responsible for Sonamarg, Zoji La, Drass, and Kargil; Jacob Force to ingress the Minimarg region; Murtaza Force to go for the Kel area; Qasim Force was allotted Kupwara, Gurez, and the Bandipora area; Khalid Force to operate in the Trehgaon, Chowkibal, Nangaon, and Tithwal area; Nusrat Force the Tithwal region; Ghaznavi Force to infiltrate Mendhar, Rajouri, and Naushera areas; Babar Force the Kalidhar Range and the Chhamb region; and Sikandar Force and other specialist groups to sabotage communication networks between Jammu and Pathankot.

The numbers probably varied from force to force, but they were all under the overall command of a major from the Pakistan Army. The larger groups like Salahuddin and Ghaznavi consisted of units and companies. A captain commanded each unit and companies operated with an additional officer and a small complement of one or two JCOs while the number of other ranks was unlikely to exceed hundred. The composition of the other forces had to be smaller, but the core element of each company was built around the SSG and men from commando platoons drawn from the Azad Kashmir battalions. The SSG men were to handle explosives, while the razakars and Mujahids made up the rest. Each man was issued civilian clothing and jungle boots and was armed with weapons from which all Pakistani markings were erased. The larger forces had the equipment and firepower that normally would be associated with a regular infantry battalion. This included an AN/GRC-9 wireless set that could be carried by mules, while each company was equipped with Belgian anti-tank RL-83 mm Blindicide rockets and LMGs in addition to 2-inch and 3-inch mortars. Each man was issued a generous amount of ammunition—200 rounds per rifle, 200 to 500 rounds if he was carrying a sten[18] or 750 rounds for every LMG plus four grenades.

Operation Gibraltar was one of the best-kept secrets in Pakistan despite the large number of men involved. Though the security around the operation was flawless, there was an element of clumsiness in its execution. As we have seen, Pakistan had once before used 'non-state actors'[19] to further its military objectives in 1947–48, all the time stoutly denying that it had any role to play in the fighting that followed. Then, too, the plan had failed miserably because despite army officers leading the lashkars, the rest were a fairly ragtag lot who were good at creating mayhem but not particularly capable of fighting against a trained army. In many ways, Operation Gibraltar seemed to be a repeat of the tactics employed eighteen years earlier.

Ever since the India–Pakistan Agreement post the Rann of Kutch incident[20] that had been signed in New Delhi on 1 July 1965, Ayub Khan had been effusively holding forth on the manner in which the two sides had settled the dispute and had been expressing the hope that the two countries would henceforth 'live as good neighbours and direct their resources for developing their economies in peace'. His pious sentiments proved to be a smokescreen for what Pakistan was about to let loose. With the manpower in place, the final touches were being given to Operation Gibraltar when on 1 August it was Akhtar Malik's turn to brief the unit and company commanders who had assembled at Kotli. He impressed upon them the importance of their mission, telling them that it was their last chance to liberate Kashmir. That very night, the first wave of infiltrators started crossing the CFL into Indian territory, from Jammu in the south to Kargil in the north—across what is perhaps some of the most difficult of terrains to defend.

CAUGHT OFF BALANCE

On paper, no one could have been better qualified to take on the Pakistani infiltrators than Lieutenant General Kashmir Singh Katoch who was the GOC of 15 Corps. Born in Srinagar in 1915, he was the son of Major General Janak Singh Katoch who had served as Maharaja Hari Singh's prime minister between 10 August and 15 October in 1947, a turbulent period in the history of the state. Janak Singh had been brought out of retirement as a replacement for Ram Chandra Kak whom the maharaja had sacked as he was suspected of leaning towards Pakistan. During this period, Janak Singh steered the Standstill Agreement that Hari Singh wanted to sign with both India and Pakistan. While Pakistan had agreed, and India was still debating the finer points, the tribal lashkars had begun to threaten Kashmir. As the crisis loomed, Janak Singh asked to be relieved and made way for Mehr Chand Mahajan.

During Janak Singh's tenure, on 13 September 1947, Hari Singh had requested the Government of India for the loan of Lieutenant Colonel Kashmir Singh Katoch as the state wished to terminate the services of Major General H. L.

Scott[21] who was the head of the State Forces. Katoch, who had passed out of IMA Dehradun in 1936, had been commissioned into the 6th Royal Battalion Scinde 13th Frontier Force Rifles. While commanding its Dogra Company as a captain, he had fought in Italy in the Battle of Monte Cassino during World War II and was awarded the Military Cross for his role.[22] However, after arriving in Srinagar, Katoch felt he was too junior to handle the state's army that was coming under increasing pressure from the Pakistan-supported tribal groups. Hari Singh then gave the responsibility to Brigadier Rajinder Singh and Katoch became the military adviser to the maharaja. Rajinder Singh, however, was killed in Uri on the night of 26/27 October. With the state's accession to India, the State Forces then came under the overall command of the Indian Army and Kashmir Singh Katoch officiated as its CO.

In the immediate aftermath of the conflict with China, Katoch had taken over as the adjutant general in Army HQ and later moved to Udhampur from where the entire state of Jammu and Kashmir came under his command. Apart from 3 Division that was looking after Ladakh and 121 (Independent) Brigade at Kargil, he had three other divisions deployed in the state. 19 Division under Major General Swarup Singh Kalaan was headquartered in Baramulla and was responsible for the Kashmir Valley; 25 Division based in Poonch was being commanded by Major General Amreek Singh; while 191 Brigade[23] under Brigadier Byram Faroze Master was responsible for Akhnoor and Chhamb. 26 Infantry Division then looked after the Jammu region further to the south.

All the Indian commanders failed to detect the build-up on the Pakistani side and, as a consequence, they were caught off guard. Katoch's immediate boss, the Western Army commander, Lieutenant General Harbakhsh Singh, was just as culpable. 'The news of PAK's elaborate plan for this gigantic venture came to us as a surprise—our intelligence set up had only vague inklings of what was happening on the "other side of the hill"; of the actual scale and scope of the massive campaign that was to follow, we had no information.'[24] Apart from the intelligence failure, they had also failed to read other tell tale signs on the ground.

Like Katoch, as a younger officer, Harbakhsh Singh had played a critical role in the Kashmir Valley during the 1947–48 tribal invasion. After Maharaja Hari Singh acceded to India, the first RIAF Dakota DC-3 aircraft had lifted the leading elements of 1 Sikh into Srinagar on 27 October 1947. The same evening, the CO of the battalion, Lieutenant Colonel Dewan Ranjit Rai, was killed near Baramulla. Harbakhsh Singh offered to assume command of the battalion, but he was posted as the deputy commander of 161 Brigade. On 7 November, 1 Sikh and 4 Kumaon annihilated the main raider column that was advancing on Srinagar at Shelatang, an action that was to prove decisive. A month later, as the fighting progressed, 1 Sikh suffered severe casualties in Uri. As a result, Harbakhsh Singh voluntarily dropped a rank and took over the truncated battalion that he then led against regular Pakistani troops who had crossed the snow-clad Pharikian ki Gali and captured Handwara.

In May 1948, Harbakhsh was given command of 163 Brigade that effectively cleared the Tithwal area of the infiltrators. He was awarded the Vir Chakra for his performance. Now in overall command of Kashmir and Punjab, reports that started coming in on 5 August from various sectors of armed ingress from across the CFL would have given him a feeling of déjà vu.

Towards the second half of July, there had been a few intelligence reports about the training of a large body of men. However, operatives can only report what they see, then it's up to the commanders to put together the various bits of information and plot for themselves the larger picture. 'That something serious was brewing up across the border, I had no doubt whatsoever,' Harbakhsh was to admit later, 'but for want of accurate information, I could not definitely put my finger on it.' Army HQ and the COAS, General Chaudhuri, were aware of a report filed by an Indian diplomat, Krishna Rasgotra. The Americans had warned him that the action in the Kutch was a diversion and that the bigger attack was planned in the north (i.e. Kashmir).

Though there was an independent brigade and two Indian divisions deployed on the Line of Control (LoC) extending from Akhnoor to Sonamarg, none of them detected such a massive influx of infiltrators. This was surprising because even though the Rann of Kutch ceasefire had been in place for a while, the situation along J&K had not let up as Pakistani artillery had been active through the year.

In Akhtar Hussain Malik, the aggressive Zulfikar Bhutto had found his alter ego. Even though Ayub technically had the last say in flagging off Operation Gibraltar, there were agencies in Pakistan that were quite capable of waging their own private war. Ayub's rebuff of the plan in January was seen as a temporary bump, which Bhutto believed he could overturn at the appropriate time. The incidents recorded by the United Nations Military Observer Group in India and Pakistan (UNMOGIP) pertaining to CFL violations in Jammu and Kashmir told their own story. The UNMOGIP's function was to observe and report, but since the situation was so volatile, the UN secretary general, U Thant, decided not to release the figures, for in his opinion it completely damned Pakistan and he did not want it to appear as if the UN was taking sides. But the numbers were indeed alarming and Harbakhsh would have known this. Since January 1965, there had been a quantum jump in hostile acts especially in the 19 and 25 Division sectors.

While incidents of bombing, arson, and sabotage usually grabbed the headlines, the majority of violations were in the form of concentrated doses of artillery fire from across the border at any target that presented itself to Pakistani forward observers, military or civilian. Poonch was particularly vulnerable as Pakistani positions dominated the town and any movement on the Indian side was visible to the Pakistanis.

The mindset of India and Pakistan becomes obvious if we look at the deployment on either side of the border. The Indians were purely on the defensive, their two main divisions trying to plug the gaps while Pakistan's lone division was deployed based on the assumption that there would be no fighting on the POK side. 'It must be remembered that between the years 1956 and 1965, though we had offensive plans of some sort, the bias was primarily on the defensive. This induced in the majority of commanders an unconscious attitude of defence-mindedness.'[25]

This allowed the Pakistanis, especially an aggressive commander like General Akhtar Hussain Malik, to run riot. Between January and the end of July 1965, there were a staggering 1,800 incidents of cross-border violations and Operation Gibraltar had not even begun. The continuous pounding of Indian positions by the artillery also indicated that the Pakistanis had an unlimited supply of ordnance and weapon systems.

The formal announcement of the ceasefire in the Rann of Kutch and Ayub's subsequent statements may have lulled New Delhi and the senior commanders into believing that all was well, but at the divisional, brigade, and various battalion HQs, there should have been no such illusions. The month of June had seen a steady escalation of violence, which intensified in July, with almost six or seven firing incidents being reported daily. On 30 June, Poonch had multiple fires break out that gutted quite a few houses and shops. Three days later, Brigadier B. C. Chauhan's 104 Infantry Brigade, which was responsible for the Tithwal Sector, had accounted for six hostile acts in its area. Naushera was targeted next as mortars and MMGs pounded Indian positions thrice in two hours on 4 July. Time bombs were being found in public places and state transport buses, with the obvious intent of creating a feeling of angst against the local authorities. On 8 July, it was Srinagar's turn to burn, as incidents of arson swept through the city once again.

Baramulla was where 19 Division was headquartered. The GOC was the highly decorated Major General Kalaan, MC, MVC, who had four infantry and one artillery brigade under his command. All four brigades were deployed guarding the entry points into the Kashmir Valley from the west. As the CFL was not based on any geographical logic, the troops were stationed in pockets that did not necessarily strategically dominate the surrounding area. That the gaps between these positions existed was a well-known fact, but, since 1949, the deployment on the ground had more or less remained unchanged. This left the Indians with no reserves whatsoever and, to make matters worse, there were hardly any troops in Srinagar or the Valley itself to deal with any contingency that might arise deeper inside Indian territory.

The Western Army commander had earlier pointed this out to the COAS and both Chavan, the defence minister, and Gulzarilal Nanda, the home minister, had been briefed about this shortcoming.[26] Accordingly, General Chaudhuri from

New Delhi, Harbakhsh Singh from Simla, and Kashmir Katoch from Udhampur had reached Srinagar on 1 August to discuss the redeployment of not just the army formations but also the police and the home guards with the civil authorities. But it was already too late. Around the time the generals had arrived at a plan that was to be discussed again the next day, Pakistan's Akhtar Hussain Malik was giving his final speech to the guerrilla commanders at Kotli and, by nightfall, the advance guard of the infiltrating columns had begun to slip into Indian territory.

Back in 19 Division headquarters, Kalaan's GSO-1 was Lieutenant Colonel (later Major General) Hardev Singh Kler, a Signals officer who had the reputation of being outspoken to a fault. Kalaan, unable to get along with Kler, had requested Army HQ to replace him with an officer of his choice, a request which the Military Secretary's (MS) Branch[27] had agreed to. Kler's record of service, however, was excellent, and much to Kalaan's chagrin, Kler's new posting was as a directing staff to the Defence Services Staff College, a prize posting.

The GSO-1 of a division is the hub around whom divisional formations usually function. Kler was to hand over to the officer who was relieving him when news came in that 1 Sikh had apprehended a suspect who was part of the advance guard that had infiltrated across the border. The man was on his way to look up relatives when he was caught by the Sikhs. Apprehensive that he would be shot immediately, he was sharing all the information he had. He claimed to be the intelligence havildar of one of the six main task forces assigned to create mayhem in the Valley. His specific job had been to mark the maps for the various groups. The details he was blurting out were so fantastic that no one was willing to believe him. The only exception was Kler.[28]

Kler immediately put out a general warning to all units and police stations. Lieutenant Colonel Kler, as fate would have it, would stay on and play a major role in the fighting.

THE DOGS OF WAR

Kashmir Katoch, the corps commander, was born under a lucky star, as were his two divisional GOCs, Kalaan and Amreek Singh. Even though the Indian troops deployed around the CFL had completely missed the ingress of raiders between 1 and 4 August, fortune was still being kind to them. On 5 August, two men dressed in identical green salwar kameezes appeared near Sher Bag (also referred to as Dara Kassi), a small village in Baramulla District. They approached Mohammad Din who was tending his cattle and offered him ₹400 for information on the surrounding area. Their accent and manner of talking made Mohammad Din suspicious, so on the pretext of complying with their request, he dashed across to the Tangmarg Police Station some 14 km away. The police promptly informed the army, which immediately sent a patrol into the area to investigate. Seeing soldiers coming towards them, the infiltrators dispersed into the forested area but one of them was caught. He revealed that a large number of raiders had come in from Bugina and were camped around Domari Gali in the Tithwal Sector.

Eighty kilometres, as the crow flies, to the south of Tangmarg, a similar scenario was unfolding close to Rajouri, which was part of 25 Division's Mendhar Sector. Wazir Mohammad stumbled onto a group of armed men who were similarly attired in green salwar kameez near Galuthi. These men too offered money for information. Once again, under the pretext of getting help, Wazir Mohammad went to HQ 120 Infantry Brigade where Brigadier Bharat Singh immediately ordered Captain Chander Narain Singh from 2 Garhwal Rifles to put together an ad hoc patrol of platoon strength and investigate the veracity of the report. Moving quickly with Wazir Mohammad as their guide, the patrol closed in on the infiltrators. Despite being badly outnumbered, Chander Narain Singh decided to attack the party which was bunched up. In the ensuing battle, Chander Narain Singh[29] and three of his men were killed, but the raider column disintegrated and fled back towards the CFL, leaving their dead and a large quantity of arms and ammunition behind. Later that night, 3 Dogra at Gulpur was taken by surprise as rockets and machine-gun fire rained down on them from the surrounding hills for almost two hours.

Earlier in the evening, another civilian source had reported the ingress of a large party north of Kupwara through Atham Gali. At first light on 6 August, strong patrols were sent out to locate this group, which would have threatened the Kupwara–Tithwal road. On 6 August, near Bandipora, the rear headquarters of 3 JAK Rifles was fired upon, while another post of 6 Guards at Kalaroos, north of Kupwara, also came under attack. By the evening, 68 Brigade under Brigadier (later Lieutenant General) Zorawar 'Zoru' Chand Bakshi[30] with 6 Dogra commanded by Lieutenant Colonel Sarmukh Singh Khokar was moved to Tangmarg and given charge of the area around Gulmarg that included Chorpanjal, Devar Gali, and Jamian Wali on the Pir Panjal.[31] In addition, all units along the LoC were issued a general alert asking them to send out patrols looking for any suspicious groups. During the next forty-eight hours, reports started coming in of large-scale movement on the POK side as well. 25 Division reported the presence of around 100 raiders in the Tatapani–Balnoi area and smaller groups to the south between Mirpur and Dharamsala.

At that time the Indian Army followed a fairly predictable rotational system—in August/September approximately one-third of the units were relieved and sent to family stations. As night set in on 7 August, one such changeover was taking place. For the outgoing battalion, it was time to celebrate the end of its tenure. What made it even more special was that the incoming battalion was its sister battalion from the same regiment.

KHOYA KHOYA CHAAND...

In the Tithwal Sector, one of the major infiltration routes was through the Pharkian Gali which necessitated the presence of a battalion at Trehgam. 4 Kumaon under

Lieutenant Colonel (later Brigadier) Nasim Arthur Salick had completed its J&K tenure and was in the process of moving to Belgaum. 8 Kumaon, which was being commanded by Lieutenant Colonel M. V. Gore, had reached Trehgam on 1 August and the final taking over formalities were nearly over. By the evening, all heavy weapons and major equipment had been handed over to the relieving battalion and the rest of the baggage was loaded onto vehicles which were to move for Srinagar via Kupwara at first light the next morning.

Until then no one was aware that Khalid Force had moved into the forested area of the Shamshabari Range above Trehgam and was biding its time. Though general alerts had been passed down from 19 Division to all units, in the hustle and bustle of the impending move, no one expected trouble at Trehgam. The area was known as the 'Foxtrot' Sector and 4 Kumaon operated directly under Divisional HQ. Around mid-day, Gore received orders to deploy a section of troops to guard the Kralpora Bridge on the Trehgam–Kupwara road. The two COs discussed the matter and, to save time, decided to deploy a section of 4 Kumaon instead. The next morning, their replacements would move with the convoy and the switch would take place on the bridge after which the vehicles would move on.

Jemadar[32] Umrao Singh moved with one section from 4 Kumaon's Alpha Company. After dropping down from Trehgam to the Kohmil River, the JCO made a huge blunder. Forgetting the time-honoured dictum of occupying the high ground, he got his men to pitch a tent on the northern side of the bridge. He then posted a sentry at either end and settled down for the night.

Salick was feeling uneasy. As a precautionary measure, he decided to send a platoon to Chowkibal where the brigade's rear dump of ammunition was stored. He then ordered two of his subalterns, Second Lieutenants (later Captains) Jagdamba Prasad Joshi and Pushkar Singh, to take out two patrols for the protection of the battalion's location at Trehgam. By 1900 hrs, Joshi, with a platoon also from Alpha Company, had positioned himself on dominating ground above the camp while Pushkar and his platoon was deployed at the rifle range further to the west.

Khalid Force had three targets designated for the night. Split into three groups, they were to attack the Trehgam camp, blow up the bridge at Kralpora, and capture and destroy the ammunition dump at Chowkibal.

At 2000, some shots were fired from the high ground and Joshi came on the wireless and informed the adjutant, Major (later Major General) Deo Pal Singh Raghuvanshi, that he had seen some men in salwar kameez. When challenged, they had fired a few rounds and melted into the darkness. Raghuvanshi telephoned the neighbouring brigade to check if any friendly patrols were operating in the Trehgam area after which he dashed across to the Officers' Mess where 4 Kumaon was being given a farewell party by its sister battalion. Major (later Lieutenant Colonel) Yeshwant Singh Bisht, the Delta Company commander had just finished rendering a soulful performance of a Hindi film song 'Khoya khoya chaand…' and was being cheered and applauded when the rat-tat-tat of a Browning Machine Gun (BMG) shattered the celebratory din.

From Joshi's position, the tracer rounds seemed to arc through the darkness as they went over the tin roof of the mess, fortunately failing to hit their target during the initial burst. His platoon, already on high alert from their earlier brush with the infiltrators, immediately fired at the clearly visible gun flashes. Taken by surprise by this unexpected turn of events, the BMG swung in Joshi's direction and opened fire, accompanied by other weapons. Unable to gauge the strength of Joshi's party in the dark, the infiltrators continued to fire, but did not try to close the gap.

Salick immediately ordered Bisht to gather his Delta Company and move to a hill feature that dominated the ammunition dump at Trehgam. Another officer, Captain (later Major General) Surendra Shah[33] was told to put a patrol together and reinforce Joshi's position. By then there was a deadly silence, for the BMG had stopped firing. Salick told one of his officers he had a feeling that something terrible was about to happen.

At 1100 hrs, machine-gun fire swept across the Kralpora Bridge, killing both the sentries. Some of the men huddled in the tent were also killed in the initial bursts of gunfire; others, like Naik Ram Kumar, managed to spill out and engage the enemy with their LMGs. Unable to close the gap, the raiders fired three Blindicide rockets at the piers of the Bailey Bridge, but failed to bring it down. They then took to hurling grenades onto the bridge. In the ensuing confusion, Ram Kumar spotted the badly wounded Jemadar Umrao Singh lying in the open, so he started to drag him to the cover of nearby rocks. In the process, Ram Kumar was also wounded. Taking advantage of the opportunity, the raiders rushed onto the bridge and began placing demolition charges.

One of the charges on the bridge went off prematurely, knocking a heavier explosive into the river. At this point, Ram Kumar rushed onto the bridge and threw a grenade, which killed most of the demolition party. One of them was wounded badly and Ram Kumar grabbed him and started to drag him back across the bridge. The gallant soldier died on the bridge, holding his captive in an unbreakable vice-like grip. Another wounded soldier, Sepoy Prem Prakash, continued to guard the bridge while two of the remaining soldiers who were still standing started back for Trehgam to get reinforcements.

As the desperate fighting on the bridge eased, Trehgam and the ammunition dump came under a fresh attack at 1130 hrs. By this time the Kumaonese were all at their stand-to positions and successfully returned fire. With Joshi and Bisht joining the firefight from either flank, the raiders, after half an hour of intense firing, withdrew. Despite the element of surprise, the timely action taken by Salick in deploying protective patrols saved the battalion from serious damage at Trehgam.

However, the night was far from over. At 0100 hrs, two of the surviving men from the Kralpora Bridge reached the battalion in an exhausted condition. After hearing their account, Salick ordered the Charlie Company commander Major (later Lieutenant Colonel) Gurbax Singh to move on foot immediately with his men to the bridge. This meant thinning out the defences at Trehgam, which could still face another attack. Subedar Nand Kishore, the senior JCO from Alpha Company, said that since the fate of the men at the bridge was not known, there was an urgent need to get to them in a hurry. Though the risk of running into an ambush was high, the JCO offered to drive there in a 3-ton lorry. Salick agreed, at which point Second Lieutenant (later Major) Pudukunnath Yoyakey Poulose, also of Alpha Company, insisted on going along.

The vehicle moved cautiously, navigating the hilly curves of the road by the glow of its parking lights. It soon caught up with the men of Charlie Company who were moving in single file along the road. Just as it was overtaking the leading elements, the infiltrators opened fire with LMGs and rifles. The men deployed quickly and engaged the enemy, while Gurbax Singh sent out a couple of flanking parties. There was some heavy firing from a nearby field above the road after which there was complete silence. The men returned with the body of an infiltrator, and the advance towards the bridge was resumed.

The grey light of dawn was breaking when Charlie Company reached Kralpora Bridge. To their horror, eleven of their comrades were dead,[34] while three were grievously wounded, including Prem Prakash, who was still the lone man guarding the bridge. Ram Kumar, his arms now frozen as rigor mortis had set in, was still holding onto the wounded Pakistani soldier who turned out to be from 19 Azad Kashmir. The explosives fitted on the bridge by the raiders had needed just one spark to set them off, but Naik Ram Kumar[35] had thwarted that even in death.

Back in Trehgam, at dawn, Captain Surendra Shah's patrol had linked up with Joshi's men and started to move further uphill in the hope of catching the infiltrators out in the open. They ran into a small group shortly and after a quick, sharp exchange, successfully captured three prisoners. Simultaneously, Major Bisht's Delta Company was also pushing its way forward towards Zarhama village. Information gleaned from the three prisoners helped zero in on the enemy's other positions. Even though the infiltrators were sniping at the Kumaonese as they withdrew, Havildar Joga Singh set up a .303 Vickers Machine Gun and started firing long bursts that provided the advancing troops cover.

Salick, with the battalion's mortar platoon, was climbing towards Zarhama when his men spotted two groups of men moving on the rocky ridge line of Pharkian and Puthekhan Galis. Salick quickly got on the wireless set and checked with Shah and Bisht if their troops were moving on the ridgeline. They both confirmed they were well clear of the area, after which the 3-inch mortars opened up, which forced the infiltrators to find cover among the rocks. Surendra Shah and his two platoons quickly closed the gap and clashed with the infiltrators, who gave up all pretext of putting up a fight and fled. The bodies of twenty infiltrators were recovered and the survivors were taken prisoner. In addition, huge caches of rations and ammunition along with a staggering 250 haversack packs were recovered. During the entire mopping-up operation, 4 Kumaon had one man injured.[36]

The casualties suffered by 4 Kumaon at the Kralpora Bridge stunned the rank and file of 15 Corps. Even though the initial build-up and mass scale infiltration had escaped detection, the element of surprise which Akhtar Hussain Malik had hoped for had evaporated. The threat was indeed massive and now all depended on how the Indian formations reacted.

Public sentiment was the key. All this while, Pakistan and the Azad Kashmir Radio had kept up a barrage of misinformation. Talk of sweeping discontent among the local population, great victories for the mujahideen, and straight-faced statements by Foreign Minister Zulfikar Bhutto about Pakistan having 'nothing to do with it' dominated the headlines in newspapers like the *Dawn*, to say nothing of the Urdu papers. Fanciful victories where Indian soldiers were running away as fast as they could dominated the airwaves from Azad Kashmir and Pakistan Radio. There was no shortage of wishful scriptwriters across the border.

Nevertheless, the situation on the Indian side was extremely grim, especially since 15 Corps had almost no troops inside the Valley. Four JAK Militia battalions for internal security amounted to nothing since the raider columns could strike at military and civil targets at will. On 5 August, the moment the first two groups were detected, Harbakhsh Singh issued directives to 26 Division in Jammu to immediately move 2/9 Gorkha Rifles to Srinagar. 4 Sikh LI, stationed at Dagshai, north of Chandigarh was also told to move to Ambala and be on standby to be airlifted into the Valley.

TERROR IN THE GUISE OF WARFARE

After the mopping-up operation of the morning, Lieutenant Colonel Salick gave a detailed account of the night's proceedings to the GOC and to the GSO-1 of 19 Division on the telephone. In light of the mass-scale intrusions, Hardev Kler had been asked to stay on in Baramulla. He informed Salick that 4 Kumaon was to stay on in Trehgam while instructions were shortly being issued to CO 8 Kumaon for its deployment.

On a large map in the Operations Room, Kler was making red circles where infiltrators had been seen. Everything that the Pakistani intelligence havildar had blurted out to 1 Sikh a few days ago was turning out to be true. More news from 25 Division was coming in, which led to more red circles on the map. A pattern was beginning to emerge, which seemed to suggest the net was closing in on Srinagar. Approximately 200 men had been seen in the area around Magam, presumably on their way into the city and they had been engaged by one company of 6 Dogra along with a platoon from the Punjab Armed Police (PAP). One Indian soldier had been killed in the exchange of fire in which a raider was killed while five others were apprehended.

25 Division was also reporting a very large column infiltrating through the forested Kopra belt in the Haji Pir Bulge. The route they were following would take them through Nawgam, Jamianwali Gali, Badgam, and Srinagar. A major cause for concern was the line of communication between Poonch and Galuthi, which was an obvious target for the infiltrators. 14 Jat, commanded by Lieutenant Colonel K. Radhakrishnan, had moved in to Bhimber Gali in July. On 7 August, reports were received that a large number of raiders had come in through the jungle trails and were planning an attack to sever the Poonch–Galuthi link. Captain Tarlok Singh Randhawa was told to immediately put together an ad hoc platoon and intercept them. By midday, contact with the raider columns had been established. For the next ten hours, the Jats chased the raiders, who broke up into small parties and escaped through the various thickly wooded trails.

In other incidents in that sector, repeated attacks had been launched on posts held by 7 Sikh near Poonch, while patrols had also clashed with large groups of infiltrators near Balnoi. On the same night, Ghaznavi Force attacked the town of Mandi which lies 20 km to the east of Poonch. The UNMOGIP report tabled before the United Nations by the Secretary General U Thant put the strength of the infiltrators in this area at 1,000.

Equally alarming was a report from Brigadier Byram Faroze Master's 191 Brigade, the southernmost formation guarding the CFL, that 369 Field Company Engineers at Jaurian Camp had been attacked by raiders using 3-inch mortars, MMGs, LMGs, and rockets. The sappers lost five men and five more were severely wounded. Their establishment, including a few vehicles, was seriously damaged, while the raiders seemed to have gotten away fairly lightly.

According to Akhtar Malik's plan, 8 August was a critical day. He had hoped that all infiltrating columns would have reached their respective target areas by then and would be poised to strike. On that day, thousands of people were expected to congregate at Srinagar from the surrounding villages as it was the festival of Pir Dastgir Sahib. The raiders were to keep their weapons hidden and move in batches with the unsuspecting crowd. The next day, 9 August, was the first anniversary of Sheikh Abdullah's arrest and the National Conference had planned a processional demonstration. The raiders, having got into Srinagar unnoticed, were to join the crowds again. At a given signal, they were to draw their weapons and stage an armed revolt, capture the radio station, the airfield, and other vital installations. The columns further south and to the northeast of the Valley were to cut the roads Srinagar–Jammu and Srinagar–Kargil to isolate Srinagar. This done, it was planned to constitute a "Revolutionary Council", proclaim it as a lawful government, and broadcast an appeal for recognition and assistance from all countries, especially Pakistan. This would be the signal for Pakistan to move in for the kill.[37]

By the evening of the 8th, the civil administration in the Valley had had enough indications that something 'big' was being planned for the next day. Azad Kashmir and Pakistan Radio stations had been broadcasting incessantly, calling on the people of the state to rise up, and had been building up the anniversary of Sheikh Abdullah's arrest. State intelligence sources were reporting a major congregation of infiltrators in the vicinity of Qasba Biru from where they planned to advance on the Srinagar airfield. Chief Minister Ghulam Mohammed Sadiq, fearing the worst, had called Prime Minister Shastri and suggested that the army take over the state and declare martial law.[38] An emergency meeting of the Cabinet was immediately convened in New Delhi where the defence minister said the army chief, General Chaudhuri, who was at that moment with his Western Army commander in Jalandhar, had advised otherwise.

Though the situation was extremely volatile, the element of surprise that the Pakistanis were banking on had been negated by the events over the last three days. Also, the people of J&K had, by and large, shown no sign of supporting the infiltrators. Had martial law been declared on the night of 8 August, it may well have played into the hands of Zulfikar Bhutto and Akhtar Hussain Malik. The decision not to do so also had another extremely important connotation—it reaffirmed the union government's faith in the state government and the civil administration, who could not absolve themselves of their responsibilities.

The TAC HQ of 15 Corps had moved up to Srinagar from Udhampur and Lieutenant General Katoch deployed a company of 8 JAK Militia along with two tank troops and a rifle troop of Central India Horse (CIH) for the immediate protection of the airfield. Later in the night, a large group of raiders was reported to have fired at patrols guarding the Bimna Bridge near Tangpur village. Two companies of JAK Militia and three platoons of PAP were immediately sent to engage the infiltrators. By midnight, 2/9 Gorkha Rifles under their officiating CO, Major Roshan Lal, had also reached the Valley and its leading company immediately went in support of the Militia and PAP. The rest of the battalion reached the airfield where it was briefed by Major General Umrao Singh, the former chief of staff of 15 Corps, now designated GOC 5 Sector. Brigadier G. S. Kale, commander of 163 Infantry Brigade, at the time deployed in Ladakh, was also present at the airfield. Roshan Lal was told his area of responsibility was not just the airfield but extended right up to Sonamarg. By the evening, HQ Western Command had decided to airlift 4 Sikh LI from Ambala and orders were passed to 3 Infantry Division in Leh to despatch 163 Infantry Brigade to Srinagar immediately.

Outside of the Valley, in the 25 Division Sector, Pakistan had seriously upped the ante. However, luck was initially on the Indian side. The Narian fuel dump 15 km short of Rajouri on the Naushera road stored large quantities of fuel and essential lubricants. This was fired at, but no serious damage was done. The immediate launching of patrols to search the area for the raiding party paid dividends as two Pakistani officers were apprehended. They were identified as Captains Ghulam Hussain of 8 and Mohammad Sajjad of 18 Azad Kashmir battalions. Acutely aware that war had not been officially declared and therefore the Geneva convention did not apply, the two were more than willing to give information.

That evening, the entire length of the CFL was lit up with gunfire as Pakistan's artillery put on a continuous firepower display that was aimed at unnerving the Indians. At Poonch it was noted that 25-pounders were also firing for the first time at specific targets. Fortunately, a raid on HQ 120 Infantry Brigade at Rajouri was foiled by alert sentries, but as the evening wore on and there was no let-up in the firing, it was obvious something big was in the offing. 26 Infantry Division was ordered to immediately move 52 Mountain Brigade from Jammu to Rajouri.

The two captured Pakistani officers were proving to be a storehouse of information leading to a clearer picture of the magnitude of Operation Gibraltar. Salahuddin Force had entered the Kashmir Valley through the Chor Panjal route, after which it had split into two; one column heading towards Gulmarg while the second took the approach via Khag. Elements of this group had got into Srinagar and their men were in the vicinity of not just Badami Bagh (the cantonment), but also other military depots, the radio station, and the civil secretariat.

As per Akhtar Hussain's plan, Srinagar was to be attacked on 9 August, but the arrival of 2/9 Gorkhas and the securing of the airfield the previous day had ensured the script did not quite unfold the way the Pakistani general wanted it to. Reports continued to come in from both HQ 19 and 25 Divisions of large groups on the move. Baramulla was reporting the presence of a large group of infiltrators around Bedori in the Haji Pir Bulge. Another group was seen moving forward from Sallar towards Gulmarg and another was approaching Zurahom. In the Poonch area, though, a large number of raiders had congregated in the Mandi Valley and at 0930 hrs had attacked the police station, while cutting off the tracks linking the town with Poonch. They had also occupied the main heights in the area.

At the opposite end, Brigadier Ganesh Kale's 163 Infantry Brigade was approaching Kargil with its two battalions, 1 MLI and 6 Rajput. The third unit of the brigade, 1 Guards, had been in Kargil ever since they moved there in May where they had captured Kala Pahar. After the long drive along the Indus River through the stark countryside, the men were looking forward to a bara khana that was being hosted by 4 Rajput, which was moving in the opposite direction towards Kiari. As the leading vehicles of the convoy approached the bridge at Pashkyum, southeast of Kargil, they realized it had been considerably damaged during the night. After a delay they crossed Kargil only to find the bridge at Shamshah, halfway to Drass, in a similar state. The convoy also came under harassing fire from

Pt 13620, Black Rocks, and Saddle. After yet another frustrating delay, the brigade moved on, the vehicles cautiously negotiating the treacherous Zoji La the next day. ⌐ Not at all pleased with the delay, General Harbakhsh Singh telephonically sought permission from the army chief to recapture these three features which had been returned to Pakistan in June. Accordingly, Brigadier Ghai's 121 (Independent) Infantry Brigade was instructed to attack on the night of 14/15 August as these heights also dominated the main route of ingress for the Pakistanis along the Suru River Valley.

On 10 August, 2/9 Gorkhas continued to aggressively go about the business of clearing the area around Srinagar. Tangpur lay on the western outskirts of the city and the road to Sonamarg, also their area of responsibility, ran through the suburb. A large number of infiltrators had gathered there as well, but they soon went on the run as khukri-wielding Gorkha platoons came after them. A large quantity of equipment and ammunition was recovered. Meanwhile, in HQ 19 Division, Klare was scrounging troops to form four ad hoc companies, which congregated at Badami Bagh by midday. Two companies of 4 Sikh LI finally landed at the airfield while the advance party of 163 Infantry Brigade also arrived. GOC 5 Sector, General Umrao Singh, could finally breathe easy, for he now had adequate troops to meet any immediate contingency within Srinagar. In fact, 8 JAK Militia was ordered to move to the Pir Panjal and set up its battalion headquarters at Shopian, 50 km south of Srinagar. This would help intercept any new raider column if it tried to enter the Valley from either Mendhar or Thanamandi.

In the 25 Infantry Division and 191 Infantry Brigade Sectors, the situation was far more critical as it was easier for the infiltrators to merge with the local populace there. The reported presence of a 250-strong group moving from Saranu towards Kandi directly threatened Rajouri from the east, while there was some activity being reported from Sunderbani. Some Indian posts were subject to 81 mm mortar fire, while further to the south, the administrative base of 4/8 GR came under heavy fire which fortunately did not cause any casualties. 80 Infantry Brigade captured a Pakistani captain along with three raiders while in another encounter near Jaurian, one officer was wounded while three of his men were captured by an Indian patrol. There were also reports of considerable increased activity around Chhamb and Dewa. Two infiltrators trying to return to Pakistan were captured along with their rifles.

First light on 11 August saw the convoy transporting 163 Infantry Brigade start from Sonamarg for Srinagar. The airlift of 4 Sikh LI was also completed by midday. It was now felt that there were enough troops under the command of Umrao Singh to delink 19 Infantry Division from counter-insurgency operations and allow them to plan for an offensive action in the Haji Pir and Kishanganga areas. This did not mean that the situation had stabilized; on the contrary, the infiltrators were more likely to offer fewer targets while adopting hit and run tactics in other parts of the Valley. The army commander, Harbakhsh Singh, was pressing for offensive action, for he believed unless the fight were taken to the enemy, it would continue to be a reactive slugfest which could go on endlessly.

During the previous night, there had been shots fired in various parts of the city. Reports had also come in that there were a large number of infiltrators around Magan, which was situated west of Srinagar roughly halfway to Gulmarg. 6 Rajput, minus Charlie Company which stayed on in Srinagar, was asked by HQ Sri Sector to move there immediately. The battalion arrived there just before dark and camped in a school just off the main road.

25 DIVISION

The night of 11/12 August, the Valley was more or less quiet, but there was no let-up on Indian forward positions around Poonch where Pakistani artillery shelled four pickets and HQ 93 Infantry Brigade throughout the night. There was also some firing around Dubey Bridge and in Bhimber Gali. Further south, in the 191 Infantry Brigade sector, an Indian ambush patrol between two posts around Chhamb was detected by the Pakistanis who launched a battalion-strength attack against it. This developed into a major engagement and it was with considerable difficulty that the patrol was extracted from the area.

Shortly after first light, reports came in of a fifty-strong group moving towards Tosh Maidan. This party was fired at by Indian artillery guns, forcing it to scatter, but there was no way to ascertain if any real damage was done. However, a week after the launching of Operation Gibraltar, 93 Infantry Brigade finally met with some success. 1 Madras, commanded by Lieutenant Colonel C. P. Menon, cleared Pt 4007 near Poonch, killing twelve and capturing sixteen infiltrators. 52 Infantry Brigade, commanded by Brigadier (later Major General) R. D. Hira, recaptured Mandi along with the neighbouring heights. This was a significant development for, until now, the raiders in the Poonch–Rajouri–Naushera area had been calling the shots.

Intermittent firing within various parts of Srinagar after dark suggested the infiltrators were changing tactics. Regularly coming out second best whenever they clashed with the army, they adopted hit and run methods instead. Under constant pressure from their handlers across the CFL to show results, the infiltrators were also resorting to arson. However, this was a double-edged weapon, for the destruction of peoples' homes could turn the populace against them. Through the night of 12/13 August, quite a few posts in the 19 Division Sector came in for heavy shelling, with 25-pounder batteries also opening up. This was usually an indication that the infiltrators were likely to strike somewhere in the next few hours in reasonable strength.

In the 25 Division area, the army continued to be under pressure as the lines of communication were more complex and harder to defend. The bridges at Khanetar and Kalai on the Poonch–Surankot axis came under extensive small

arms fire and it seemed they would be captured. However, a quick response by
the division's artillery guns turned the tables. Both these attacks fizzled out and
though there were casualties, the exact extent of damage to the infiltrators could
not be ascertained.

When Lieutenant Colonel Gore was ordered to move with 8 Kumaon to
Naugam from Trehgam on 9 August, the CO of 4 Kumaon was overheard telling
him to stay away from the Dak Bungalow which could be targeted by the infiltrators.
The battalion moved to the forested slopes of the Pir Panjal which was one of
the key infiltration routes through the Tumari Gali towards Baramulla. Naugham
was connected with Baramulla via Drugmulla by a motorable road over a distance
of approximately 50 km.

Disregarding the warning about the Dak Bungalow, Gore set up the TAC
HQ and logistics base of the battalion in the cramped space around the forest
rest house, which was situated in a bowl about 100 by 150 metres in area. To the
west was a river and to the east was a thickly wooded hill which was picketed.
Between 9 and 11 August, there were two patrol clashes with the infiltrators near
the TAC HQ itself, and there were also reports of encounters in depth areas. Apart
from Gore, others present on the fateful morning of 13 August were the second-
in-command, Major Gopal Singh, the adjutant, Captain Arjun Ray, the RMO,
and three other officers. The HQ was guarded by a platoon with a detachment
of the newly acquired .303 Vickers MMGs and a section of 81 mm mortars. The
logistical element also comprised a troop of mules for carrying rations and other
essentials to the forward troops, and a sniffer dog as well.

Recalling the tragic events of that time, Arjun Ray would write: 'At around
0630 hrs, the infiltrators launched an assault on the TAC HQ from the eastern
and southern directions. They encountered no sentries and about 20 of them
were able to reach the rest house. There was a fierce exchange of fire and hand
to hand fighting that left the CO and 15 soldiers dead, Gopal Singh seriously
wounded, and another 20 soldiers injured. The infiltrators withdrew but invested
the TAC HQ from three sides.

'Evacuation of the injured was a challenge. The Field Hospital at Drugmulla
despatched four regular and three makeshift ambulances. The injured started their
rearward journey to Drugmulla at around 1030 hrs. The infiltrators had allowed the
ambulances to enter but ambushed them while they were returning. We suffered
another five or six dead. The casualty evacuation was called off. Sensing the gravity
of the situation, later in the day, the divisional HQ at Baramulla despatched a
troop of Stewart tanks under Captain Sen and a Sikh company as reinforcement.
This broke the cordon set up by the infiltrators and the situation was restored.'[39]

Another unit whose location was tactically unsound was 6 Rajput under the
command of Lieutenant Colonel Mustasad Ahmad that had been located at Magam
since it had arrived in the Valley from Ladakh two days earlier. Brigadier Ganesh

Kale met with Mustasad Ahmad shortly after news of the Naugam attack and the killing of Colonel Gore had been received. Not too happy with the location of 6 Rajput, they were still discussing their options at midday when two 'eminent people' (i.e., local leaders) arrived at the Battalion HQ with information pertaining to a 200-strong group of infiltrators in the forested slopes opposite Khag village. Though Mustasad was suspicious of the 'eminent' person, Ganesh Kale felt he could be trusted.[40] One of them, Ghulam Mohammad Mir Lasjan, offered to act as a guide and since the rest of the battalion was engaged in flag marches elsewhere, Mustasad Ahmad set off with a small protection party.

Lasjan led the party into an open field inside Khag village, where he quietly slipped off. The infiltrators had opened fire by then, killing one of the lookouts immediately. Having fought their way to a nearby building, the IO, Lieutenant Manjit Singh Bhasin, had been constantly exposing himself to engage the enemy. Mustasad had pulled him down by his shirt sleeves and said, 'Don't expose yourself too much.'[41] The young officer had replied that the bullet with his name had not yet been manufactured in Pakistan when he was shot through his right eye, and collapsed into Mustasad's lap. Three more men including Mustasad's driver had been killed by then. With great difficulty, taking their wounded with them but having to leave the dead behind, the party extracted itself and fell back on the neighbouring village of Birwa.

The next morning, 6 Rajput came under fire from some houses as the regrouped battalion approached Khag. The houses, which were isolated and from where the infiltrators dominated the killing area, were taken out by firing STRIM grenades,[42] which resulted in some of the raiders running out, where they were then killed. Finally, Bravo and Charlie Companies went into Khag, where they found their own five dead from the previous evening in the nearby cornfields savagely mutilated. This was the standard practice adopted by the Pakistanis, be they irregulars or regular troops. A fair number of infiltrators were known to still be in the village and the situation was extremely tense. With Mustasad standing between his angry men and the village's population, 6 Rajput withdrew to its harbour area at Magam for the night.

While the Kumaonese and the Rajputs were unlucky, another major disaster was averted in the 25 Division Sector. At the Bhimber Gali Base Camp, Subedar Duli Chand from 14 Jat was at the training ground when gunfire from a distance reached his location. Not wasting any time, the JCO quickly set off with a platoon on the Bhimber Gali–Poonch road. Intermittent gunfire guided the Jats to a spot 3 km from their camp where approximately fifty infiltrators had ambushed three Indian army trucks. The red flags on the vehicles indicated they were carrying ammunition and it seemed the raiders were preparing to blow them up.

Duli Chand charged the raiders without hesitating who, in turn, hurriedly retreated from the vehicles and occupied a dominating adjacent spur. By then the

JCO had realized the drivers were still trapped inside but enemy fire would not let him approach the vehicles. Once again, a flank attack was put in, this time forcing the Pakistani raiders to break contact. This small, sharp action not only saved a few tons of ammunition, it also saved the lives of four wounded men who were found alive inside their cabins.[43]

While 6 Rajput was regrouping at Birwa to go back into Khag to recover their dead, in New Delhi, the loss of 8 Kumaon's CO earlier in the day sat heavy as Chavan, Chaudhuri, and Rao met the prime minister and some other officials at night. It had been eight days since Pakistan had launched Operation Gibraltar and though the situation was more or less under control, the day had perhaps been one of the worst in terms of casualties. After briefing Shastri on the situation, Chaudhuri said that so long as the army continued to fight the infiltrators on our own territory, it would remain a war of attrition. The raiders could hit wherever they wanted and this gave them the advantage of a first strike that could not be contained. He asked for permission to destroy the infiltrators' bases, saying in the fight against the raiders, the army should not be restricted. Even though Shastri was anxious to avoid any extension of the conflict at that time, he immediately gave his approval.

The prime minister's approval to take the fight to Pakistan could not have come at a more appropriate time. On 14 August, the first intelligence report of a troop build-up opposite Moel was received. This was a significant development, for another simultaneous report indicated a squadron of tanks had been moved to Mattewala which was across the IB opposite Chhamb. A third report indicated regular troops were on the move in the Sialkot Sector as well. Until then, all reported movements and troop concentrations had been related to the irregular forces that made up the raider columns. At the same time, expanding the area of operations, the infiltrators attacked the police station at Palanwala. 191 Infantry Brigade ordered Lieutenant Colonel Gurbans Singh Sangha to send two companies of 3 Mahar to chase the raiders and block their entry into the Mandiala heights. The Mahar battalion, which had handed over all its heavy weapons and vehicles to 2 Sikh earlier as they were being relieved, was operating under extremely difficult conditions with the men even going without food. Nevertheless, the spirited troops, in a couple of sharp actions, captured fourteen infiltrators and killed four.

In the Valley, since 8 August, Major General Umrao Singh, chief of staff, 15 Corps, had been functioning as the commander of the ad hoc Sri Force. On 14 August, this arrangement was formalized and the Corps HQ indicated to both Kalaan and Amreek Singh that their respective formations needed to draw up counter-infiltration plans to take the fight to the enemy. The night of 13/14 August had seen Pakistan open up with medium artillery for the first time in the Uri Sector. The UN observers were asked to intervene, but they expressed their inability to do anything about it. Kashmir Singh Katoch then ordered Indian medium guns to retaliate against Chakothi.

The next day was India's Independence Day, 15 August. The order to draw up a counter-infiltration plan had also permeated down to Byram Master whose 191 Infantry Brigade reported directly to 15 Corps. The brigade commander was at Dewa when a Pakistani Bird Dog spotted them and called for artillery fire. A shell hit the ammunition dump within the camp and in the resultant explosion, Master along with Major Balram, Captain R. K. Chahar, Second Lieutenant Narinder Singh, one JCO, and four other ranks were killed. Two other officers and thirty-eight other ranks were wounded, and six guns of 14 Field Regiment were destroyed. All lines of communication between the forward posts of 6 Sikh LI, 3 Mahar, JAK Militia, and PAP were cut off from Akhnoor. As a result, Palanwala had to be abandoned later in the day.

Byram Master's death overshadowed other equally grim events. In the 26 Division sector, Pakistan launched a raid across the IB and slaughtered fifteen civilians in Bajpur near Samba. Reports were coming in of infiltration parties around Udhampur, which resulted in 3 Kumaon launching search patrols around Bhaj Masta, from where some explosives were recovered. So severe was the impact of the disaster, other pickets, with the exception of those between Moel and Burejal, that guarded the flank approaches to Dewa, also had to be abandoned on 16 August.

In Srinagar, arson continued to be the favoured tactic and fires broke out in the Baramulla area. At Magam, some infiltrators in the uniform of JAK Militia did a reconnaissance of the 6 Rajput positions during the day and at midnight launched a full-scale attack with supporting mortars, a splinter killing Subedar Raghunath Singh, the battalion's officiating subedar major. The battalion, in anticipation of an attack, had re-sited its weapons after dark and the infiltrators were taken by surprise, suffering thirty casualties, with whom they managed to retreat into Khag. The civil population was advised to clear the area, after which the artillery pounded the village from where sporadic fire was still coming from some houses. 6 Rajput came under severe criticism from the UN observer group for having 'indulged in excessive firing', refusing to believe that a large number of infiltrators had been present in Khag despite the evidence shown to them.

Chapter 9

BATTLEGROUND KASHMIR

HARBAKHSH SINGH: THE GENERAL IN HIS ELEMENT

In the second half of August, the dynamics of the fighting in J&K were to change quite dramatically. Until then, Operation Gibraltar had been fought entirely on the Indian side of the CFL, with the Pakistani raider columns choosing the targets, the time, and the quantum of force they brought into play. This meant the Indians were constantly at a disadvantage, a situation that simply could not be allowed to continue. Though random shelling across the CFL was a common occurrence, the concentrated and guided bombardment that had resulted in the death of Brigadier Master and a number of others at Dewa in the Kalidhar area was an indication that Pakistan was raising the level even further. Pakistani border troops had occupied ten Indian posts that had been abandoned because of the volume of fire directed at them.

Though initially caught on the wrong foot by the suddenness and scale of Operation Gibraltar, Harbakhsh Singh was quick to regain his equilibrium and had been vociferously demanding that 15 Corps hit out at the infiltration bases and threaten POK itself. The heights captured by 4 Rajput and 1 Guards in the Kargil area in May had been returned to Pakistan as part of the ceasefire agreement. Indian patrols had reported that the Pakistanis occupied these heights during the day in order to harass and interdict the highway, but it was believed they vacated the posts after sundown. The first offensive operation ordered by Harbakhsh Singh was to recapture these posts. The task was given to 17 Punjab, and three attacking columns under the command of Major Balwant Singh were launched against Pt 13620, Saddle, and Black Rocks in the early hours of 14 August. Though all three assaulting prongs were accompanied with artillery FOOs, the silent attacks were carried out without any casualties.

On 17 August, 2 Sikh that had been a part of 26 Infantry Division arrived at Jaurian in the Chhamb Sector and was ordered to recapture the posts that had been lost two days previously. With 19 Infantry Division handing over the responsibility of chasing down the infiltrators to HQ Sri Force, the division was once again available for offensive operations. Accordingly, on 18 August, Harbakhsh Singh issued a spate of formal orders to various formations: 68 Brigade under Brigadier Bakshi was to capture Haji Pir from the direction of Uri, while 93 Brigade commanded by Brigadier Zora Singh was to move from Poonch and link up with the former along the old Poonch–Uri road. In addition, he green-flagged an offensive by 104 Infantry Brigade commanded by Brigadier B. C. Chauhan to simultaneously clear the Kishanganga Bulge, which would effectively seal off all routes of ingress into the Kashmir Valley.

Meanwhile, Harbakhsh wanted all his commanders to go into offensive postures in other sectors as well. 2 Sikh had set up its firm base west of Dewa on 19 August where it continued to be relentlessly shelled by the Pakistanis through the day. Despite being on unfamiliar ground, the batallion put in attacks in the early hours of 20 August and captured its four objectives—Trikone, Anchor, Red Hill, and Green Hill by the afternoon. 'They followed up with attacks on Laliali Banchalan and Uprala Batala, all objectives being secured by the night of 22-23 August. Thus, within three days, moving over unfamiliar ground, the battalion had reoccupied all ten posts.'[1]

While Harbakhsh Singh was intent on taking the battle to the Pakistanis, Kashmir Katoch, perhaps burdened by the operational situation on the ground, was pulling in the opposite direction. On 15 August he sent a signal to Harbakhsh suggesting the dropping of the Haji Pir plan, but the army commander disregarded it completely. However, since 68 Brigade was part of the Baramulla-based 19 Division, and 93 Brigade came under Amreek Singh's Rajouri-based 25 Division, the role of HQ 15 Corps became all the more critical.

On the 22nd, two days before this assault was to be launched, a post of 2 Rajput in the Tithwal Sector came under attack but it was repulsed. Around the same time there was another attack at Chowkibal, where two men were wounded. After a week of relative quiet in the Valley, for the first time since HQ Sri Force had been set up, a High Altitude Warfare School patrol from Gulmarg got into a firefight with infiltrators near Handwara. The next day, a force of 200 men was reported to be near the village of Malud, while in the 25 Division Sector there was an attempt to blow up the bridge on the Galuthi–Rajouri axis. A combination of all these events perhaps added to Kashmir Katoch's misgivings, so he and Amreek Singh decided to trim down the size of the attacking force that was to approach Haji Pir from the south.

The next morning, Harbakhsh landed by helicopter at Rajouri only to learn from Amreek that the attack being planned bordered on the perfunctory as the division could not muster enough troops to take on the posts of Raja and Rani which dominated the road to Kahuta and Haji Pir pass. The livid army commander not only took Amreek to task, but also gave Kashmir Katoch a severe scolding over the phone. It was then decided that owing to the paucity of time, 3 Raj Rif would coordinate with Zoru Bakshi's 68 Brigade, and that the attacks on Raja and Rani would be carried out in the next ten days. Harbakhsh also sternly told Katoch to go ahead with the offensive actions that were planned for both the Tithwal Sector in the Kishanganga Bulge later that evening.

At 2130 hrs, Chauhan launched 1 Sikh less two companies supported by 138 Mountain Battery and 7 Field Regiment with orders to capture and hold the Richmar Ridge. The Sikhs, led by Major Sumesh Kapur, took on the feature that was defended by a platoon from 16 Azad Kashmir Rifles, but after some resistance, the Pakistanis fled from the ridge. The Sikhs stayed on the heels of the withdrawing platoon, which fell back towards its physical training grounds. There the rest of the Pakistani company was attacked, resulting in eight killed and five taken POW, the attacking Sikhs losing just the one man though seven were wounded. At the same time, along the neighbouring axis, a combined fighting patrol from 2 Rajput and 3/8 Gorkhas secured 1 Sikh's southern flank by capturing the Ring Counter just across the CFL. Though there were no Pakistani troops holding this position, their artillery immediately began to shell it once they realized it had been occupied.

Harbakhsh was like a man possessed—from Rajouri he had flown to Akhnoor and, in the evening, reached Srinagar, from where he went straight to Baramulla. There he went over the final plans for the Haji Pir offensive that was scheduled to begin the next day. Though the weather was terrible on 25 August, 1 Sikh pushed on and assaulted Pir Sahiba, from where they could dominate the already destroyed bridge over the Kishanganga (called the Neelam in POK). This attack too was successful, even though two companies of 16 Azad Kashmir put up a stiff fight. This effectively meant the Sikhs were now in a dominant position and could keep an eye on all the routes into (and out of) the Kashmir Valley. Pelting rain south of Uri however, necessitated the postponement of H-hour for the Haji Pir offensive by a day. The army commander had staked his own reputation on the success of the operation. Harbakhsh Singh knew that Zoru Bakshi was the right man for the job.

OPERATION BAKSHI

Zoru Bakshi was born in Gulyana village in Rawalpindi district of the then undivided Punjab. After graduating from Gordon College he arrived at the IMA from where he was commissioned into the infantry in June 1943. After completing the mandatory year with a British battalion, he was posted to 16 Battalion 10 Baluch, which was then in the Arakans as a part of 51 Infantry Brigade.[2] The brigade fought the Battle of Kangaw, considered to be one of the hardest fought battles of the Burma Campaign. Bakshi was Mentioned in Despatches, the first of his many awards. At the time of Independence, Zoru Bakshi was posted to the Punjab Boundary Force and was witness to one of the worst carnages in human history. As a result of Partition, 16/10 Baluch was allotted to Pakistan and Bakshi was transferred to the 5th Gorkha Rifles.

In March 1948, he was posted to 163 Infantry Brigade which, at that time, was fighting in the Kashmir Valley. As the brigade major, he was Brigadier Harbakhsh Singh's right hand. The brigade had been given the task of advancing towards Tithwal.

The brigade was made up of four infantry battalions and a squadron of 7 Cavalry equipped with armoured cars and two batteries. 163 Infantry Brigade commenced operations from Handwara in May 1948 and, after capturing Chowkibal, they advanced on the 10,000-foot-high Nastachun Pass and captured Tithwal. Within five days they had fought their way over 65 km, killed sixty-seven enemies and taken many prisoners. The brigade was poised to advance towards Muzaffarabad which was a mere 30 km away, when operations were halted by Army HQ following the UN resolution. The Pakistanis, stung by the loss of Tithwal, reacted violently, launching various counter-attacks that were supported by artillery. Despite being on the brigade staff, removed from the direct command of troops, Zoru Bakshi was awarded a Vir Chakra for his role in the fighting.

After the ceasefire and the situation along the CFL had settled, Major Bakshi was asked to undertake a special reconnaissance into Tibet after the PRC had overthrown the Kuomintang government. The hush-hush expedition was launched sometime in the second half of 1949. Zoru Bakshi, dressed as a Buddhist monk, slipped into the Chumbi Valley adjoining Sikkim and Bhutan from Nathu La. He then made his way to Gyantse and Lhasa, before heading back, having covered more than 400 km in two and a half months.

After a second tenure as a brigade major with 123 Infantry Brigade, Bakshi served with 2/5 GR, which was deployed at Mahura in the Uri Sector between 1955 and 58. After an instructional stint at the Defence Services Staff College in Wellington as a lieutenant colonel, he was given command of 2/5 GR, which he commanded in the Congo where he was awarded the Vashist Sena Medal. Back in India, in August 1963, he was posted in the DMO and in 1964 he was the officiating DMO when the Rann of Kutch engagement began.

A few days before Akhtar Hussain Malik launched Operation Gibraltar, Bakshi was promoted to the rank of brigadier and given command of the newly raised 68 Infantry Brigade. Though the brigade was to be a part of 3 Infantry Division based in Leh, for the time being, it was to remain in the Valley. At that time, Bakshi had only one infantry battalion, 6 Dogra, under his command. This battalion was also newly raised and had been one of the first to respond when the infiltrators had been detected on 5 August.

It was not surprising then that Bakshi should be Harbakhsh Singh's chosen man for launching an offensive to capture Haji Pir on nearly the same ground where they had fought together seventeen years earlier. Given to Pakistan after the ceasefire in 1948, the Pakistan Army had been exploiting the peculiar configuration of the CFL in the Haji Pir Bulge, using it to launch the main influx of infiltrators into the Valley. In addition to using these areas for entering Indian territory, there were huge stockpiles of arms and equipment at several places for the resupply of the raider columns. The Haji Pir operation would not only seal off these routes, it would also knock out the logistical foundation of Operation Gibraltar.

On the morning of 13 August, accompanied by GOC 19 Division, Harbakhsh had visited Zoru Bakshi's headquarters at Tangmarg where they discussed the plan to capture Haji Pir. 68 Infantry Brigade, the 15 Corps' reserve, was being specially allotted to 19 Infantry Division for the planned offensive. Apart from 6 Dogra, the other three battalions earmarked were 1 Para, 19 Punjab, and 4 Rajput. 1 Para and 19 Punjab were at that time under the command of 161 Brigade. The paratroopers were manning nine pickets from Seb, opposite Uri, to Kaman on the Jhelum. They were to hand over their AOR to 4 Sikh LI and concentrate on Seb as part of 68 Brigade. 19 Punjab similarly were to be relieved by 6 JAK Rifles. 4 Rajput had only just arrived at Kiari from Kargil, some 130 km upstream on the Indus from Leh. Fresh orders were being issued for the Rajputs to return to the Valley. Bakshi planned to concentrate his brigade at Uri by the third week of August. 68 Infantry Brigade also had 164 Field Regiment with 25-pounder field guns, 144 Mountain Battery, and a troop of medium guns from 39 Medium Regiment.

The Haji Pir pass was at a height of 8,652 feet and it sat astride the Poonch–Uri road. Seen from the direction of Uri, the Hyderabad Nullah comes steeply down from the pass and debouches into the Jhelum below the Uri Plateau. The 20-km road to Haji Pir was dominated by the steep Bedori feature (12,336 feet) towards the east while the western side was flanked by Sank (9,498 feet) and Lediwali Gali (10,302 feet). On the other side, the road then followed the Betar Nullah for 36 km down towards Kahuta and Poonch. Bakshi's plan was to launch a two-pronged attack from the north to be conducted in three phases. 1 Para, commanded by Lieutenant Colonel Prabhjinder Singh, would start the proceedings by attacking from the right and capturing Sank Ridge, Sawan Pathri, and Ledwali Gali by 0500 hrs on 25 August while 19 Punjab under Lieutenant Colonel (later Brigadier) Sampuran Singh would simultaneously attack from the left with the aim of neutralizing Ring Contour and Pathra by 0100 hrs on the same night. In the second phase, 19 Punjab was to capture Pt 10330 and Pt 11107, two key features on the left axis of Haji Pir by 0600 hrs. Finally, 4 Rajput was to deliver the coup de grace and capture the pass and the right axis by 1430 hrs the same day.

There was to be no change in the role assigned to 6 Dogra, which continued to chase down the infiltrators in and around Gulmarg. For his plan to succeed, Bakshi needed more artillery support, at least one infantry battalion in reserve and, most importantly, updated maps and information about Pakistani deployments on the other side. What was known was that the well-prepared posts on the other side were held by three and a half infantry battalions including 20 Punjab and 6 Azad Kashmir, and that the Pakistanis had a reasonable amount of artillery support. Speed and surprise would be the keys to success.

Harbakhsh Singh now dropped a bombshell. There was to be no untoward activity in the sector before the attack was launched, he commanded. 68 Infantry Brigade would have to make do with the existing maps as not much would have changed in the Haji Pir Bulge since 1948. There would be no reconnaissance done in areas held by 161 Infantry Brigade through which the attacking battalions would have to pass. Artillery, the army commander stressed, would have to be used in a judicious manner, since ammunition would be restricted. The field guns had five first line scales, and the medium guns just four first lines. First line means the amount of ammunition carried along with the guns. This also effectively meant the artillery regiments had to make do with what existed with them in their forward areas as no second line replenishment from the rear would be possible.

The army commander believed that there was a tendency among infantry commanders to resort to artillery fire as an automatic solution to all enemy opposition. Apart from not wanting an obvious build-up of guns on the Indian side, which would be reported to the commanders in Pakistan, Harbakhsh believed that when fighting in the hills, during the last stages of an assault, when all types of supporting fire had been lifted, the only way to close in on a determined enemy was through the use of fire from weapons organic to the concerned infantry battalion and company.

Amazingly, Harbakhsh Singh chose not to tell Bakshi that the attack being planned by his 68 Infantry Brigade was one half of a pincer attack and that a similar assault by 93 Infantry Brigade from the south along the road from Poonch was being worked out by 25 Division. The army commander then told Major General Kalaan that he would make available 6 JAK Rifles from 161 Infantry Brigade to Bakshi which would be his reserve and that 19 Infantry Division would simultaneously launch multiple diversionary attacks all along the CFL to keep the Pakistanis guessing. He then 'reminded' Kalaan that he wanted a similar offensive action planned by 104 Infantry Brigade in the Tithwal Sector.

As Harbakhsh got up to leave the briefing, he turned to the commander of 68 Infantry Brigade and told him to give the Haji Pir plan the code name Operation Bakshi. This was going to be the Indian Army's moment of truth. Harbakhsh Singh then said he would set D-Day shortly and inform Kalaan and Bakshi accordingly.

Later that same day, Harbakhsh Singh met GOC 15 Corps in Srinagar. News was coming in of the disastrous attack on the dak bungalow in Naugam where the CO of 8 Kumaon had been killed and the second-in-command wounded, after which the convoy evacuating the casualties had also come under fire, killing yet another five men. There had been another incident at Magam where the CO of 6 Rajput had barely escaped an ambush and an officer and four other ranks had been killed. Harbakhsh suggested to Katoch that 4 Sikh LI be moved immediately from the airfield area in Srinagar to Baramulla, from where it could be moved yet again to relieve 1 Para which was being earmarked for the attack on Haji Pir.

General Katoch expressed his reservations about the Haji Pir offensive, for it committed his corps' reserve while he was still fighting a defensive battle against the infiltrators in the Valley. Though the situation in Srinagar was relatively stable, there were hundreds of infiltrators waiting to hit at any target that presented itself in the Valley. There were also reports of major activity in the 25 Division sector, where the situation was even more precarious owing to the nature of the terrain. However, Harbakhsh Singh was determined to take the fight to the Pakistanis on their turf. His biggest problem at the moment was that Kashmir Katoch, the 15 Corps commander, was not averse to bypassing the chain of command and talking directly to the COAS. Katoch constantly suggested to Chaudhuri that he intervene and get the army commander to drop the idea. Ignoring Katoch's obvious reluctance and after going over the situation in both the 25 and 19 Division sectors, Harbakhsh Singh set 24 August as D-Day for the Haji Pir offensive.

Bakshi finally met the COs of the three designated infantry battalions and the artillery regiment for the first time on 23 August at his headquarters in Uri and went over his plan with them. As their brigade commander leading them and their battalions into battle, Bakshi was acutely aware that he knew nothing about them. In a profession where so much depends on an individual's personal leadership qualities, this was something he just had to live with at that point of time. Amazingly, even at this stage, Bakshi was still unaware of the simultaneous thrust to be launched from the direction of Poonch by 93 Infantry Brigade.

OF MICE AND MEN

The best laid plans can so easily go haywire. On 23 August, 6 JAK Rifles successfully relieved 19 Punjab during the early hours, but dark swirling clouds greeted the day with pouring rain. 4 Sikh LI, caught in the downpour, could not replace 1 Para who were supposed to make their way to the concentration area. H-hour was to be 2150 hrs on 24 September but had to be postponed by twenty-four hours. With the rain continuing through the day, the streams were flooded, which also resulted in 4 Rajput getting stranded at Lagma village. The Rajputs were to follow behind 4 Sikh LI en route to Uri, after which they were to concentrate behind 1 Para in the Sank Ridge area. However, since there was a likelihood of their movement being reported to the Pakistanis, Bakshi decided to divert them towards the 19 Punjab position instead. In the revised plan, the converging arms of the pincer were to still meet at Haji Pir, but now the left column comprising 19 Punjab with 4 Rajput following were to advance along the Ring Counter (Pt 8336)–Pt 10944–Bedori–Kuthnar di Gali axis while 1 Para was to follow the Uri–Sank–Ledwali Gali route to Haji Pir.

The two leading battalions, 1 Para and 19 Punjab, had been waiting at their concentration area. Wet and miserable, they had sat out the twenty-four-hour delay but the rain continued. Finally, at 1400 hrs on 25 August, HQ 68 Infantry Brigade gave the go-ahead for 19 Punjab to start moving forward towards its FUP. Overloaded with their equipment, rations, ammunition, and 3-inch mortar bombs, the men pushed on till they reached the Hathlanga Nullah, a tributary of the Haji Pir Nullah, which was in spate. On the map, the Hathlanga had been of little consequence, but the leading elements were reporting back to Lieutenant Colonel Sampuran Singh that it was a major obstacle. The CO made his way forward to see the nullah for himself and, after taking precautionary measures, he ordered his men to get across. The force of this insignificant stream was enough to cause the first casualties as three men were washed away.

Despite this setback, 19 Punjab had reached the FUP by midnight and launched its assault on the Ring Counter, which was marked on the map as Pathra. This position was relatively lightly held with a few observation posts to give early warning of any developing threat to the main defences on Bedori. By 0200 hrs, Pathra had been captured. Without pausing to consolidate, 19 Punjab advanced at a quick pace, covering the 2,000 yards to the base of the massive Bedori feature. The Pakistani troops had sufficient warning of the impending attack and they waited for Charlie and Delta Companies to reach their designated FUP before they opened fire with heavy machine guns. Pinned down by accurate fire, Sampuran Singh kept trying to rally his troops but it was impossible to advance along the narrow knife-like ridge which was heavily mined and had a steep drop on either side. Soon it was daylight and the Pakistani gunners could go after individual targets. Hoping for a miraculous lucky break, Sampuran Singh hung in there till 1000 hrs, but it was obvious that Pakistan had all the advantage.

At 1000 hrs, 19 Punjab was asked to abort the attack and pull back. The exhausted and disappointed men made their way back to Pathra.

On the Sank axis, 1 Para had started their move forward at 2000 hrs. Major (later Lieutenant General) Ranjit Singh Dyal[3] was the battalion's second-in-command (and the designated overall force commander) and was leading Alpha Company. As per the plan, Charlie Company, commanded by Major (later Colonel) J. C. M. Rao was in the lead and they were to secure the FUP, which they did by 2130 hrs. Alpha and Bravo companies, the two assault companies, were following and they were being guided by Havildar Major Mithu Ram. At the FUP, they were to pass through Charlie Company and take on the defences on Sank. Though the battalion was familiar with the terrain, having been deployed there for a few months, the guide got disoriented and led the assaulting companies away from the FUP. At 2150 hrs, Indian artillery started shelling suspected enemy positions that had to be captured before the main assault on the Sank feature could be launched.

At first light, Ranjit Dyal and the Bravo Company commander, Major H. A. Patil found themselves below and ahead of the FUP. Dyal now had to take a call, for the attack had been delayed by almost seven hours. Hoping to still achieve surprise, he boldly decided to go for the objective. With Alpha Company leading, the paratroopers started climbing towards the Pakistani positions on Sank but, at sunrise, they were still short of the objective. The Pakistanis spotted them and opened fire. The men of Alpha Company immediately went to ground, seeking whatever cover they could find, desperately firing back at the Pakistani positions with their personal weapons. As a result of the wild, uncontrolled firing before the officers could bring in any semblance of order, most of Alpha Company's ammunition was expended.

The pugnacious Ranjit Singh Dyal, furious with his men for their poor fire control, ordered Alpha Company to fix bayonets and charge the well-entrenched enemy. It was a miracle of sorts that the paratroopers were not massacred as they closed the gap and got to the Pakistani forward positions, which were protected by plenty of barbed wire. With the men unable to break through and the space behind them not being wide enough to push others through, Dyal ordered the forward elements to break contact and fall back while the men at the rear provided covering fire. Thirteen men were wounded and, of these, Sepoys Lal Singh and Sadhu Singh had to be left behind. With great difficulty, under the cover of artillery fire, the two companies were extricated from below Sank.

With both his attacks having failed, Bakshi was in a dilemma. To add to his discomfiture, while he was still weighing his options, he received a 'personal for' message from the Army Commander expressing dissatisfaction at the heavy expenditure of artillery ammunition which 'was not commensurate with the results'. Bakshi had already made up his mind to let 1 Para attack Sank again later in the night and was in fact formulating a detailed fire plan for the artillery with the battery commander Major Keshri Singh of 1642 Battery and the commanding officer of 1 Para, Prabhjinder Singh. They were acutely aware that the Pakistanis on Sank were very much alive to the possibility of a second attack on their position and that they would be waiting for them.

'To make certain of the success with minimum casualties to my troops, it was incumbent upon me, as the commander, to make the task of my troops easier by softening up the enemy entrenched in bunkers with a heavy dose of artillery fire especially after the previous night's setback. I knew if the attack failed this time also, I would be sacked in any case. On the other hand, in case of success, the morale and confidence of my troops would be high for future battles and I, as a successful commander, would be better placed to face the higher ups.'[4] Zoru Bakshi decided to ignore the message from Harbakhsh Singh.

Accordingly, 164 Field Regiment opened up, firing their 25-pounders to a coordinated fire plan. Once again Rao's Charlie Company and 1 Para's Mortar Platoon had secured the FUP by 2130 hrs. The assaulting companies this time were to be Patil's Bravo Company and Major Arvinder Singh Baicher's Delta Company, under the overall command of Dyal. This time, everything went like clockwork and the leading elements got to the wired perimeter only to find that the Pakistanis had abandoned the post under the pressure of Keshri Singh's relentless shelling. The two wounded paratroopers who had been left behind earlier in the morning were both found dead—Sadhu Singh had been shot at close range and his body was lying next to the command bunker, while Lal Singh's eyes had been gouged out.

With Sank in the bag, Prabhjinder Singh ordered Dyal to take Sar, which was the next objective about 1,000 yards along the ridge. Alpha Company, despite the casualties suffered by it during the earlier attack, was already on its way to join the rest of the unit at Sank. At 0630 hrs, Baicher started for Sar with Delta Company which he occupied after a forty-five minute sharp exchange with a platoon-strength rearguard. The bodies of two Pakistanis were found en route, probably too badly wounded in the shelling and unable to go on while pulling back from Sank.

With the Pakistanis falling back, the next target was Ledwali Gali, another 1,800 yards along the ridge. As the paratroopers moved in, the defenders once again ran away and by 1030 hrs on 27 August, this position too was in Indian hands. Two more features to the east of Sank, Sawan Pathri and Agiwas, appeared to be occupied by Pakistani troops. Dyal sent the second in command of Delta Company, Captain M. M. P. S. Dhillon, with one platoon to secure the two features that were 800 and 1,800 yards from Sank. Dhillon found Sawan Pathri deserted, but he had to put in a short, sharp attack to drive the few men holding Agiwas off it. Just short of midday, Lieutenant Colonel Prabhjinder Singh had also moved up with the battalion's TAC HQ to join Ranjit Dyal.

The two officers trained their field glasses on Haji Pir, which was just 3.5 km as the crow flies to the east of Sank. The rain had eased up slightly but swirling clouds and mist were partly obstructing the view. However, it seemed there were no defences on Haji Pir. The Pakistanis obviously did not expect the Indians to penetrate that far. Though 1 Para had been on the move for three days, Dyal felt his men had it in them to go for Haji Pir. Prabhjinder agreed with Dyal for, once the Pakistanis rushed in troops to defend the pass, it would take a lot of effort both in terms of men and material to capture the feature.

The trouble was that the Sank Ridge was separated from Haji Pir by the Hyderabad Nullah, which meant a sharp descent, the crossing of the stream, and then a vertical 2,100 feet climb to get to Haji Pir. Prabhjinder Singh told Dyal to get his men ready while he radioed Bakshi to get clearance. While Dyal was eager to move forward, it seemed HQ 68 Infantry Brigade had gone to sleep—there was no answer.

CHAMAK GHARA

The euphoria around 1 Para's amazing run was tempered by an unfolding disaster on the other axis. After pulling back from the base of the Bedori feature, Bakshi had requested 19 Division to assign the task of capturing it to Brigadier M. K. Balachandran's 161 Infantry Brigade. At 2000 hrs, Hardev Kler from HQ 19 Division called up Bakshi to give him the good news that Bedori had been taken by 6 Bihar. Bakshi was extremely sceptical as none of his observation posts sitting at

Pathra had reported any activity or even heard battle noises in the area. Kler, miffed at Bakshi's unbelieving attitude, told him he would connect him to Balachandran. The commander 161 Infantry Brigade confirmed what Kler had said, signing off with a 'What's the problem?'

But there was a problem and no one was able to put his finger on it. 7 Bihar was with 161 Infantry Brigade, while its sister battalion, 6 Bihar, deployed next to it, was part of 41 Mountain Brigade commanded by Brigadier M. R. Rajwade. With battalions having been pushed up in an ad hoc manner and commanders barely familiar with their own COs, there was plenty of scope for confusion.

Having switched 4 Rajput to the western pincer earlier, Bakshi now ordered them to go through 19 Punjab at first light and advance towards Pt 11107 and then Kuthnar Di Gali, skirting Bedori, which they believed was in Indian hands. They were to then make the final push for the Haji Pir pass itself. Accordingly, Alpha Company under Major (later Lieutenant General) Mohan Anand Gurbaxani, moving along the northwestern slope of Bedori, reached the slopes around Pt 11107 by 0730 hrs.

The silence of the morning was abruptly broken by the chattering sound of an MMG and the Rajputs came under fire. Thinking that 6 Bihar was firing at them, Gurbaxani's men made frantic attempts to stop the firing, but more weapons opened up and 4 Rajput continued taking casualties. Realizing Bedori was still in Pakistani hands, the FOO asked for artillery fire. The ranging shell had just landed near the MMG post when the Regimental HQ of 164 Field Regiment, still under the belief that 6 Bihar was holding Bedori, refused further fire support.

The CO, Lieutenant Colonel Sudershan Singh, had by then joined Gurbaxani at the head of the assaulting column. He ordered Alpha Company to charge the slope in short rushes. Four men were killed and Gurbaxani wounded, but a substantial part of the northwestern slope was now captured. The Pakistanis on Bedori top and Pt 11107 reacted angrily at the loss of their forward positions and directed massive fire at the Rajputs, who were pinned down. This situation continued till 1400 hrs when HQ 19 Division finally came on the radio to HQ 68 Infantry Brigade and said Bedori was indeed still with the Pakistanis.

A livid Zoru Bakshi now ordered 4 Rajput to pull back, but almost all routes leading out of the area were under observation and bracketed by Pakistani weapons. Fortunately, the rain had stopped around midday and the resultant low clouds that formed in the valley were a blessing from the heavens. Thanks to the reduced visibility, Sudershan Singh extricated his men from the lower slopes of Bedori one section at a time, taking their dead and wounded with them.

Unknown to the paratroopers, another grim battle was being waged between commander 68 Infantry Brigade and the GOC 19 Infantry Division. Kalaan told Bakshi that since Bedori was still under Pakistani control, 68 Infantry Brigade needed to change its plan and concentrate on capturing this feature instead. Zoru

Bakshi could hardly believe his ears. He remonstrated that the diversion of troops from the Sank axis just when 1 Para was going for the pass itself was ridiculous, for not only would it take time, it would allow the Pakistanis to strengthen the defences at Haji Pir. Kalaan, while sympathizing with Zoru Bakshi, said there was no choice in the matter because AIR had already announced the capture of Bedori on 26 August. Bedori had to be taken and Haji Pir would have to wait. Bakshi then took a momentous decision. He decided he would go for Haji Pir nevertheless.

It was now 1450 hrs, almost four and a half hours since Prabhjinder Singh had asked for permission to go for Haji Pir. After deliberating over his conversation with Kalaan, Zoru Bakshi spoke to the CO of 1 Para and asked who was going to be leading the troops. He then asked to speak with Ranjit Singh Dyal and said to him in Punjabi, 'Agar te jit liya Haji Pir toh tu hero ban jayega, ne toh meinu wah kaid kar lenge' (If you succeed in winning Haji Pir, you will become a hero, but if you fail, I will be arrested.)[5] Within minutes, with Major V. K. Vaswani as his second-in-command, Second Lieutenant J. S. Talwar from 164 Field Regiment as his FOO, Dyal with two platoons of Delta Company and a depleted Alpha Company set off for Haji Pir. The moment the paratroopers set off from Sank, it had started to rain again and the steep descent covered with monsoon vegetation became a slippery nightmare.

Shortly after Dyal's party had begun to move down, despite the inclement weather, they were spotted by an alert lookout on the Haji Pir ridge who engaged them with an 81 mm mortar and an MMG. Another party of razakars that was withdrawing from Sawan Pathri and Agiwas also started shooting at the strung-out paratroopers with LMGs and rifles from a point east of Ledwali Gali. The fire was not particularly effective, but it was a nuisance with the added danger that it would constantly give their position away. Dyal ordered Vaswani to delink No. 11 Platoon under Subedar Arjun Singh from the main column, move onto a flank and engage the razakars. Once they had been dealt with, No. 11 Platoon would rejoin the main column at the Hyderabad Nullah. Should the task take longer than anticipated, then the platoon was to rejoin the rest of the battalion that was moving from Sank to Ledwali Gali.

By 1700 hrs, Delta Company was in the valley and they crossed the Hyderabad Nullah without incident. While Alpha Company of 1 Para was made up of Sikh troops, Delta Company were Ahirs, each group determined to outdo the other in physical endurance. Burdened with their equipment, ammunition, and cumbersome radio sets, the column started moving upstream towards the point from where the climb to Haji Pir would begin in darkness. Daylight was fading fast and the mist and the rain, which had hidden them from the enemy, was not making the going any easier. Dyal was leading with the Sikh troops behind him when he suddenly held up his hand and the entire column came to a silent halt, their weapons ready.

Dyal could smell wood smoke and as he squinted into the shadows he could make out the silhouette of a hut just ahead of him. After quietly surrounding the hut, taking one section with him, Dyal kicked open the door, to find twenty-two soldiers from 6 Azad Kashmir warming themselves around a fire. This was in all likelihood the party that had murdered the two wounded paratroopers earlier. Expecting the same treatment from the Indians, the Pakistanis were more than willing to cooperate in any way to stay alive. Dyal decided that the prisoners, if used as porters, would help reduce the load on his men who, after the gruelling night climb, would be in a better position to take on the defenders at Haji Pir.

Even with the help of the 'volunteer porters', it took eleven hours for the men to painstakingly negotiate the near vertical ascent. At 0800 hrs, amidst the fog and mist, Ranjit Dyal started deploying the remaining platoon of Vaswani's Delta Company just below the pass to give covering fire. The FOO, Lieutenant Talwar, worked out his fire grid in the event that fire support was needed. Dyal then took the remaining men from Alpha Company and led them up the right shoulder of the pass. With fixed bayonets, the paratroopers approached the defences, which, to their delight, had been abandoned. After securing the pass at 1000 hrs on 28 August, Major Ranjit Singh Dyal, 1 Para, radioed the code word 'Chamak Ghara' back to Prabhjinder Singh. Haji Pir was ours!

BEDORI, HAJI PIR, AND THE TRICOLOUR!
Since Bakshi had refused to abort his dash for Haji Pir and focus on Bedori, Major General Kalaan had ordered 161 Infantry Brigade to launch 7 Bihar in a bid to dislodge the well-entrenched soldiers of 6 Azad Kashmir. The impossible terrain combined with the resolute performance of the Pakistanis had successfully foiled this attempt as well. On the morning of the 28 August, just around the time Dyal was cautiously approaching the Haji Pir pass, Lieutenant Colonel Sampuran Singh, still smarting from 19 Punjab's failure to capture Bedori on the night of 25/26 August, now stepped up. He begged Bakshi to give his battalion another crack at the objective. Bakshi gave Sampuran Singh the go-ahead to launch an attack on Bedori from the left flank and rear, while 4 Rajput would keep up the pressure on the defenders from the north and northwest in a bid to attract maximum attention and fire on themselves.

Having seen the Bedori defences up close, Sampuran Singh knew he had to do something different if his men were to succeed later that night. Artillery fire against the Pakistani fortifications (sangars) had proved ineffective so far, mainly because they were carved into the cliff face. He discussed the problem with the artillery officer, Major Oberoi, who was the supporting battery commander. They decided to bring a single 3.7-inch mountain gun forward from the gun position at the rear and, instead of adopting the usual high trajectory of fire, use it in a direct firing role, almost like an RCL. Willing hands lifted the howitzer across the narrow trails and, before last light, the gun crew was at work, firing systematically and with deadly accuracy into the frontal opening of the sangar. This had a devastating effect for the rounds either exploded inside the rocky sangar or just outside, giving the men inside no chance whatsoever.

The blasting of the sangars by a single weapon proved more effective than any fire plan that could be laid out by an entire battery. At 0330 hrs, 19 Punjab's Delta Company led by Major Verma secured the FUP. As the attacking Charlie Company passed through, Sampuran Singh told Major Parminder Singh, the company commander, 'Jatta da puttar hai, chad jan autte!' (You're a Jat Sikh, climb to the top).[6] The first few sangars that would have dominated the 600-foot ascent of the Punjabis had been effectively silenced. However, the upper part of the Bedori feature had sangars that were out of the gunners's line of sight and were still fighting. Parminder Singh's men, Dogras from Jammu and the Kangra region followed the officer and the company JCO, Subedar Damodar Singh, a World War II veteran who had fought in Burma, from trench to trench, sangar to sangar. At 0600 hrs, the emotionally charged Charlie Company commander told Sampuran Singh on the radio, 'Fateh kar litta!' (We have captured it!)[7]

Bedori had been a tough nut to crack. The capture of Haji Pir, on the other hand, was a classic case of bold leadership and a tribute to the endurance displayed by the men of 1 Para. From the Pakistani point of view, it reflected extremely poorly on Major General Akhtar Hussain Malik, GOC 12 Division, who had blundered in not holding either the Sank axis or the Haji Pir pass in strength. Even Bedori was held by a handful of men and there had been ample time to reinforce their position once the Indian intentions were obvious post 25 August. Akhtar Hussain's grandstanding while planning Operation Gibraltar with little or no attention to detail had created this uncomfortable situation for Pakistan. Since the major infiltration routes were through the Haji Pir Bulge, to leave it virtually unguarded was pure stupidity.

Around the time Bakshi was getting the news that Bedori had been captured, 1 Para's No. 11 platoon under Subedar Arjun Singh was reaching Haji Pir. The previous evening, having found a flock of goats near the pass, the exhausted and hungry paratroopers had slaughtered them and devoured the half-cooked meat, having had very little to eat since 25 August. The rest of the day had been spent re-siting the defences, for Ranjit Dyal knew the Pakistani counter-attack would come sooner or later, especially since the surrounding heights were still under their control. An added bonus was that, as darkness started to creep in, a Pakistani column comprising one officer, a JCO, and eight men that was on its way to the Valley had walked straight into the pass. The JCO had tried to make a run for it and was shot dead, after which Captain Maqbool Bhatt[8] and the rest of his men joined the other twenty-two ad hoc porters cum prisoners.

Most uncharacteristically, the Pakistanis did not launch a counter-attack on

Bedori. The entire feature seemed to have been held by a platoon but the defences were designed for two companies that could be supported by at least five MMGs. Just why the Pakistanis were so thin on the ground here will always remain a mystery, for Bedori had been attacked thrice before on the three previous nights. The loss of both Haji Pir and Bedori in quick succession seemed to have left them dazed. There were at least three infantry battalions in the area that were available to the sector commander, yet he did nothing of major significance. Rain combined with poor visibility did not allow Indian helicopters to operate on 29 August. From the Pakistani point of view, every passing hour would allow the Indians not only to consolidate their defences on Haji Pir but also try and get more troops in.

The gaps were closing, for 19 Punjab had advanced beyond Bedori and occupied Kuthnar Di Gali, the defenders having fled yet again. 7 Bihar, which had earlier captured Mehndi Gali now took Jarni Gali, further consolidating the Indian position. By midday, though 1 Para's battalion TAC HQ along with the main body of men was still at Ledwali Gali, Arvinder Singh Baicher with the third platoon of Delta Company had also reached Haji Pir.

By the afternoon, the Pakistanis had started pushing troops up to a feature 1,500 yards to the southwest of Haji Pir. Though low clouds were still hampering observation, the information was relayed to Bakshi, who immediately ordered Dyal to dislodge the enemy before it could build up sufficient strength to counter-attack the pass. At last light, Dyal sent No. 12 Platoon under the command of Subedar Siri Chand to reconnoitre the Pakistani position. It returned in the early hours with the news that the Pakistanis were present in strength and were preparing their defences on the Ring Counter. The JCO also said that there was considerable movement in the valley below, which indicated the position may be further reinforced. Dyal had to take a call. He could wait for the rest of his battalion to come up, or take the initiative once again and assault the Pakistani position with the few men that he had. Given Dyal's nature, the first option may not even have occurred to him.

At 0730 hrs on 30 August, the paratroopers set off once again. The forest provided Subedar Arjun Singh's No. 11 Platoon cover as it climbed the right shoulder of the pass, moving as fast as it could along the narrow ridge towards the Pakistani position, where two platoons of 20 Punjab (Pakistan) were in the process of digging in. With Arvinder Baicher and Ranjit Dyal in the lead, the Ahir troops, shouting their war cries, were inside the defended perimeter before the startled Pakistanis realized what was happening. In the ensuing melee, both the Indian officers were hit and brought down. While Arvinder Singh had been hit in the leg and was unable to move, Dyal had his guardian angels looking out for him. The burst of fire directed at him had hit his carbine and the bullets had ricocheted off his equipment. Other than being momentarily stunned by the impact, Dyal was miraculously unhurt.

The ferociousness of the attack had resulted in complete panic among the Pakistani soldiers, who, despite their superior numbers, abandoned their defences and started to flee. Their officers, however, managed to stop the shaken men who shamefacedly regrouped at a distance. The assault, however, had taken a heavy toll on the paratroopers as quite a few men, including Subedar Arjun Singh, had been wounded. However, the newly constructed Pakistani defences now became the bulwark behind which even the profusely bleeding Major Arvind Baicher was manning a LMG and the Intelligence NCO, Naik Jai Singh, also wounded, was playing the role of the FOO and calling in defensive fire. Having regained their composure and realizing they were up against just a handful of men, the Pakistanis put in repeated attacks, but they were unable to regain the ground they had lost.

At 1030 hrs when No. 2 Platoon of Alpha Company arrived to reinforce Ranjit Dyal's position, there were just nine men left standing. By midday No. 10 Platoon of Delta Company had also joined in. The Pakistanis spiritedly kept up their attacks till 1600 hrs, after which they kept engaging the paratroopers with artillery and mortar fire until it became too dark to see. Convinced that the Pakistanis would launch a major assault early in the morning, Ranjit Dyal spent the night of 30/31 August reorganizing the defences while the wounded were evacuated. Though the rain finally looked like it was lifting, there could be no guarantee of a helicopter evacuation the next morning, so Arvind Baicher was taken down on a mule while the others were carried on stretchers by the porter cum prisoner party of 'volunteers'.

As expected, the Pakistanis had built up their numbers during the night and launched a two-company attack at first light on 31 August. This was beaten back. For the first time since 24 August the weather began to clear, which allowed an IAF Chetak flown by Flying Officer (later Wing Commander) Jehangir Jail Master to touch down in the pass. Over the noise of the rotors, the pilot asked Ranjit Dyal if the men had adequate rations. Dyal told him not to worry about the food as the Pakistanis had left some rations for them to survive on. He added that though there was tons of captured ammunition, it was of no use, for it wasn't compatible with his weapons and he could not use it. Master flew back to Srinagar and two Mi-4 helicopters were despatched shortly thereafter with the much needed ammunition. The next day, 19 Punjab reached Haji Pir via the Kiran feature, while 1 Para's Charlie Company under Major Rao also arrived to consolidate their position. Pakistan's 20 Punjab was still occupying a small feature from where it was harassing the Para defences on the Ring Counter. Ranjit Dyal ordered Charlie Company to launch an attack and clear them out, which it did at the cost of two killed and eight wounded. Haji Pir was now secure.

OPERATION FAULAD (POONCH)

After the capture of Haji Pir (and the loss of key positions in the Kishanganga Bulge), the Pakistanis were in a state of shock, never having believed that the Indians would cross the CFL. The consternation was set aside and the focus had switched to Operation Grand Slam when Pakistan had launched its attack in the Chhamb–Jaurian Sector with the aim of cutting off Akhnoor. However, even as the fighting in and around Haji Pir would continue, Sri Division in Srinagar was also getting more and more aggressive as it sought to take the battle to the raiders.

Ever since it reached the Valley from Jammu on the night of 8/9 August, 2/9 GR had played a stellar role in keeping the infiltrators around Srinagar at bay. Lieutenant Colonel (later Major General) Nand Lal Jamwal had rejoined the unit while it was still deployed around the airfield. Aggressive patrolling by the Gorkhas, who used their limited manpower to good effect, had not allowed the infiltrators a foothold in the Sonamarg area, which was the gateway to Zoji La. On 1 September, Delta Company was moving in a convoy of seven vehicles from Ganderbal to Sonamarg when it was ambushed at Gund. The soft skin sides of the trucks did not offer any protection against a classic ambush and the LMGs and small arms fire killed one soldier and wounded a few others.

After the initial confusion, Major Roshan Lal and the men leapt out of the trucks and charged the enemy. The blood-curdling war cries and the glint of khukris had the desired effect, for the infiltrators abandoned their positions and ran uphill through the forested slopes towards a 7,000-foot dominating feature. The determined Gorkhas chased down all twenty-nine infiltrators, and chopped off their heads. One officer, a Pakistani captain, was captured alive after he slipped and fell. Once the party returned to Battalion HQ, Jamwal on the radio told General Umrao Singh that his men had killed a large number of the enemy. The general said he did not believe it. He might have meant it figuratively, nevertheless, Jamwal had all twenty-nine bodies and the Pakistani captain taken to Srinagar and dumped outside the general's door.

Umrao Singh was furious and he ordered Jamwal to take away the bloody mess. 'Sorry,' said the equally angry CO who was still seething, 'find someone else to do it.'[9] Naib Subedar (later Honorary Captain) Damar Bahadur Khattri and Rifleman Ghan Bahadur Sahi were awarded Vir Chakras while Roshan Lal was Mentioned in Despatches. The Gund encounter was perhaps the last major incident in the Valley after which life in Srinagar more or less returned to normal.

The fighting around Haji Pir would continue for another week, as would operations in the Valley and other sectors that came under the purview of 25 Division. In accordance with Harbakhsh's orders to Amreek Singh on 24 August, preparations were on for the advance to Haji Pir Pass where 1 Para and 4 Rajput, who had since moved up, were waiting for the southern pincer to finally move up. Given the strategic position of Poonch, Zora Singh's 93 Brigade had almost three times the number of troops under command, which was roughly equivalent to the strength of an infantry division. Six battalions—7 Sikh, 2 and 3 Dogra, 14 Kumaon, 3/11 and 4/8 GR—were manning the pickets on the CFL, while 7 Madras was deployed around the airfield. 3 Raj Rif was the brigade reserve, while a newly created commando group called 'Meghdoot Force' under the command of Major Megh Singh[10] was made up of troops from 3 Rajput and some men from 3 Raj Rif.

Ever since the army commander, Lieutenant General Harbakhsh Singh, had decided to counter Operation Gibraltar by going on the offensive, he had wanted the twin thrust against Haji Pir by Bakshi's 68 Mountain Brigade and Zora Singh's brigade to be given the highest priority. However, as we have seen, the corps commander, Lieutenant General Kashmir Katoch, felt that 93 Mountain Brigade did not have adequate troops to undertake an offensive action from Poonch. Katoch was also grappling with the various invader columns across the entire state extending from Akhnoor in the south to Kargil in the north, and his reluctance to launch the southern thrust to link up with Bakshi's men was interpreted by Harbakhsh Singh as a case of the corps commander dragging his feet.

Given the geographical scale of Operation Gibraltar, 15 Corps had no reserves despite additional units having been moved into Jammu and Kashmir. The only battalion that was officially available for offensive action was 2 Sikh, which was deployed in the Chhamb Sector. However, infiltration had been across the board and 191 Brigade had been continuously in action for close to two weeks. Katoch was therefore loath to move the Sikhs to Poonch, but with Harbakhsh Singh refusing to give up on his offensive plans, the corps commander had no option.

The plan was for Zora Singh to advance along a series of dominating features that included Raja and Rani and link up with Bakshi on the Poonch–Kahuta–Haji Pir–Uri axis. Even to get to Raja and Rani, the two major Pakistani positions, it was necessary to neutralize smaller pickets that were also reasonably well defended. It was felt this would effectively tie down the Pakistanis on the southern side of the Haji Pir Bulge, allowing Bakshi to capture the pass. Once these positions had been captured, in Phase II the brigades were to link up with each other.

The delay in moving 2 Sikh meant that on the night of 25/26 August, to coordinate with 68 Brigade's thrust, only a truncated plan aiming at the capture of two screen positions could be launched. Accordingly, two companies of 3 Raj Rif were quickly scrambled to capture Thund and Par posts in the valley below Post 406. These two posts were then held by 3 Raj Rif until the night of 29/30 August when they switched places with 3 Dogra who until then were deployed on the CFL. During this period, Brigadier Rocky Hira's 52 Mountain Brigade had also arrived and assumed the responsibility of the southern sub-sector of Poonch. 14 Kumaon and 3/11 GR were temporarily placed under Hira, leaving Zora Singh free to push forward with 2 Sikh and 3 Dogra.

Raja was 1.5 km to the north of the Indian post that was known by its number, Post 405. The distance between these two positions was barely 1,000 yards. Rani was situated another kilometre further to the northwest of Raja. After the capture of Haji Pir, the entire focus was now on the capture of these two posts that were being held by at least two companies supported by a pair of 3.7-inch howitzers, a 25-pounder medium gun, and a couple of 81 mm mortars. The approaches to both the posts were heavily mined and were known to be defended by at least eight 30 BMGs. Both posts were well stocked with ammunition and rations.

The attack was to be in two phases. 3 Dogra with 2 Sikh in reserve was to capture Raja during the night of 2 September, after which the roles would be reversed and 2 Sikh with 3 Dogra plus one company of 3 Raj Rif in reserve would capture Rani and another feature called Sur Tekri to the north of it. The 25-pounders from 42 Field Regiment and 3.7-inch pack howitzers from 74 (Patiala) Mountain Battery were to soften up the targets along with a battery of 120 mm mortars. A section of 5.5-inch medium guns was also allocated to engage known Pakistani gun positions.

Commanded by Lieutenant Colonel R. B. Nair, 3 Dogra set off for its assembly area on the lower reverse slopes of Post 405. The local guide provided to the battalion deliberately led the Dogras astray. However, despite losing a fair amount of time, they were eventually in position and were shortly followed by 2 Sikh, who also made it to their designated assembly area. Even as the two battalions hunkered down to wait out the daylight hours, the Pakistani observation posts picked up their movement and brought down harassing fire which, by and large, was not very effective. Nair and Lieutenant Colonel Narindra Nath Khanna, CO 2 Sikh, attended the last-minute meeting with the brigade commander, after which they reached their respective battalions by noon.

After last light, 3 Dogra and 2 Sikh moved forward and were at their respective forward assembly areas by midnight. At 0430 hrs on 2 September, the two leading companies of 3 Dogra, under the command of Majors Greesh Chandra Verma and Gurdev Singh Bawa, stepped over the start line and, half an hour later, their battle cries were heard as they engaged the Pakistani defences. At 0515 hrs, a green Very light arched upwards, the success signal 2 Sikh was waiting for. Strangely though, just as the Sikhs were about to move forward, they came under artillery fire that continued for the next thirty minutes. Not quite sure what to make of it, Khanna ordered Captain Anup Dharni commanding Charlie Company and Captain Surjit Singh with his Delta Company to move forward to the northern slope of Raja which was to be the 2 Sikh FUP. At 0600 hrs, in the grey pre-dawn light, both the companies came under machine-gun fire from the direction of Raja.

Unable to comprehend what was happening, Khanna sent his adjutant, Major Sukhinder Singh to the 3 Dogra assembly area. To Sukhinder Singh's shock and horror, he found the Dogra second-in-command giving a fictitious running

India-Pakistan Border

Not to scale: This map has been prepared in adherence to the 'Guidelines for acquiring and producing Geospatial Data and Geospatial Data Services including Maps' published vide DST F.No.SM/25/02/2020 (Part-I) dated 15th February, 2021.

Prime Minister Jawaharlal Nehru (died 27 May 1964); Prime Minister Lal Bahadur Shastri; Defence Minister Y. B. Chavan; COAS Gen J. N. Chaudhuri; CAS Air Marshal Arjan Singh; Western Army Cdr Lt Gen Harbakhsh Singh; Southern Army Cdr Lt Gen Moti Sagar; C-in-C WAC AVM Ramaswami Rajaram; Sec Gen UN U Thant; Nehru and Mountbatten.

President Field Marshal Ayub Khan; Foreign Minister Zulfikar Ali Bhutto; Gen Muhammad Musa; AM Asghar Khan; AM M. Nur Khan; Lt Gen Bakhtiar Rana, GOC 1 Corps; Maj Gen Tikka Khan, GOC 8 Div; Maj Gen Abrar Hussain, GOC 6 Armd Div; Maj Gen Sahabzada Yakub Khan, armour adviser to Rana; Bhutto with Chairman Mao Zedong, the brains behind Op Gibraltar.

Rann of Kutch
April 1965

The coat of arms of the erstwhile princely state of Bhuj; CO 7 Grenadiers, Lt Col Rewant Singh, astride his charger. Before Independence, peripheral states had their own camel-mounted forces; the Royal family of Kutch; the plaque at Sardar Post that marks the spot where half a dozen CRPF men were killed.

सरदार पोस्ट

इसी स्थान पर दिनांक 09 अप्रैल, 1965 को सुबह 03:00 बजे पाकिस्तान की एक पूरी ब्रिगेड जिसकी नफरी 3500 की थी, ने अपनी पूरी ताकत के साथ सरदार और टॉक पोस्ट पर हमला कर दिया जिसकी सुरक्षा के लिए C.R.P.F. की द्वितीय बटालियन की कम्पनी तैनात थी। C.R.P.F. के वीर बहादुर जवानों ने पाकिस्तानी सेना की ब्रिगेड के हमले को 15 घंटे तक बहादुरी के साथ लड़ते हुए दुश्मनों को पराजीत किया। इस युद्ध में पाकिस्तानी सेना के 34 जवान मारे गए थे और 4 को जीवित पकड़ लिया गया। इस कार्रवाई में C.R.P.F. के 6 जवान शहीद हुए और 19 पाकिस्तानी सेना द्वारा बंधक बनाए गए। बल के जवानों की अभूतपूर्व वीरता और साहस की सभी ओर प्रशंसा होने लगी। दुनिया के इतिहास में यह पहली घटना थी जब किसी अर्द्ध सैनिक बल की छोटी सी टुकडी ने पूरी एक ब्रिगेड का ना सिर्फ सामना किया बल्कि दुश्मनों का भारी जान माल का नुकसान भी किया और उन्हें मुंह के बल वापिस लौटने पर विवश किया। इस असमान युद्ध में वीरगती को प्राप्त हुए शहीद जवान इस प्रकार है।

लान्स नायक किशोर सिंह, लान्स नायक गणपत राम,
सिपाही शमशेर सिंह, सिपाही ज्ञान सिंह, सिपाही हरि राम
एवं सिपाही सिद्धवीर सिंह प्रधान।

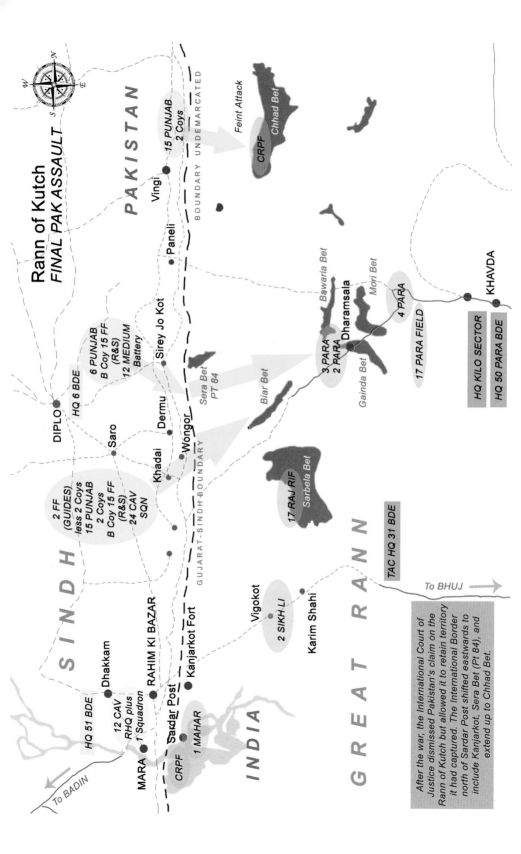

Rann of Kutch
FINAL PAK ASSAULT

PAKISTAN

SINDH

INDIA

GREAT RANN

Feint Attack

CRPF — Chhad Bet

15 PUNJAB 2 Coys

Vingi

Paneli

BOUNDARY UNDEMARCATED

Sirey Jo Kot

6 PUNJAB
B Coy 15 FF (R&S)
12 MEDIUM Battery

HQ 6 BDE

DIPLO

Saro

Dermu

Khadai

Wongor

2 FF (GUIDES)
less 2 Coys
15 PUNJAB
B Coy 15 FF (R&S)
24 CAV SQN

GUJARAT-SINDH-BOUNDARY

Bawaria Bet

Mori Bet

Dharamsala

3 PARA
2 PARA

Gainda Bet

4 PARA

17 PARA FIELD

HQ KILO SECTOR

HQ 50 PARA BDE

KHAVDA

Sera Bet
PT 84

Biar Bet

Sarbela Bet

17 RAJ RIF

TAC HQ 31 BDE

Vigokot

2 SIKH LI

Karim Shahi

To BHUJ →

HQ 51 BDE

12 CAV
RHQ plus
1 Squadron

Dhakkam

MARA

RAHIM KI BAZAR

Sardar Post

Kanjarkot Fort

CRPF

1 MAHAR

To BADIN

After the war, the International Court of Justice dismissed Pakistan's claim on the Rann of Kutch but allowed it to retain territory it had captured. The International Border north of Sardar Post shifted eastwards to include Kanjarkot, Sera Bet (Pt 84), and extend up to Chhad Bet.

An artist's impression of the Vampire photo recce sortie; Photographic evidence of Pattons deployed in the Rann; Fg Offr Utpal Barbara; An Mi-8 helicopter at Khavda; Maj Gen O. P. Dunn (black cap) is received by Brig S. S. M. Pahalajani, Cdr 31 Bde Group.

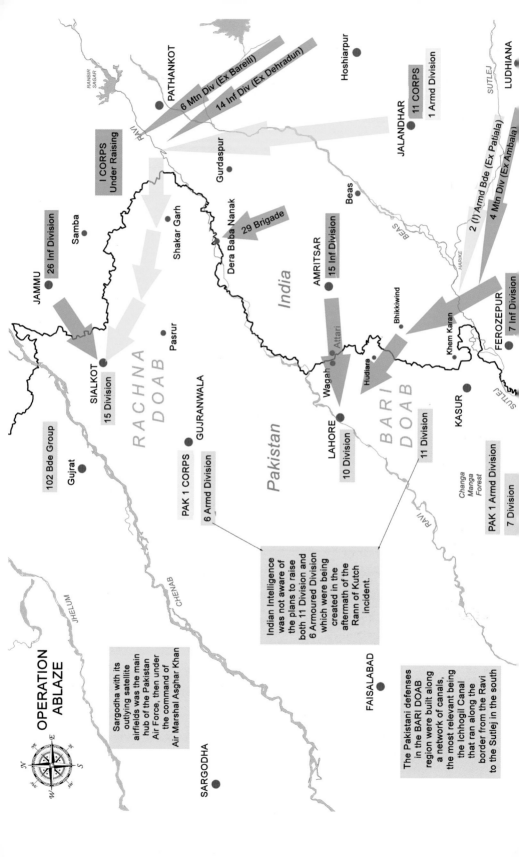

OPERATION ABLAZE

Sargodha with its outlying satellite airfields was the main hub of the Pakistan Air Force, then under the command of Air Marshal Asghar Khan

Indian Intelligence was not aware of the plans to raise both 11 Division and 6 Armoured Division which were being created in the aftermath of the Rann of Kutch incident.

The Pakistani defenses in the BARI DOAB region were built along a network of canals, the most relevant being the Ichhogil Canal that ran along the border from the Ravi to the Sutlej in the south

PATHANKOT

6 Mtn Div (Ex Bareilly)

14 Inf Div (Ex Dehradun)

Hoshiarpur

11 CORPS

JALANDHAR

1 Armd Division

LUDHIANA

SUTLEJ

I CORPS
Under Raising

Gurdaspur

Beas

2 (I) Armd Bde (Ex Patiala)

4 Mtn Div (Ex Ambala)

RANBIR SAGAR

RAVI

26 Inf Division

Samba

JAMMU

Shakar Garh

Dera Baba Nanak

29 Brigade

India

AMRITSAR

15 Inf Division

BEAS

HARIKE

7 Inf Division

FEROZEPUR

Bhikkiwind

Khem Karan

SIALKOT

15 Division

Pasrur

RACHNA DOAB

Wagah   Attari   Hudiara

LAHORE

10 Division

BARI DOAB

11 Division

KASUR

102 Bde Group

Gujrat

GUJRANWALA

PAK 1 CORPS

6 Armd Division

Pakistan

Changa Manga Forest

PAK 1 Armd Division

7 Division

RAVI

CHENAB

JHELUM

FAISALABAD

SARGODHA

Lt Gen J. S. 'Jogi' Dhillon; Lt Gen Patrick Oscar Dunn, GOC 1 Corps; Lt Gen (then Maj Gen) M. L. Thapan, GOC 26 Inf Div; Maj Gen R. K. Ranjit Singh, GOC 14 Inf Div; Maj Gen Rajinder Singh 'Sparrow', GOC 1 Armd Div; Maj Gen S. K. Korla, GOC 6 Mtn Div; Maj Gen Niranjan Prasad, GOC 15 Inf Div; Maj Gen H. K. Sibal, GOC 7 Inf Div; Maj Gen Gurbaksh Singh, GOC 4 Mtn Div.

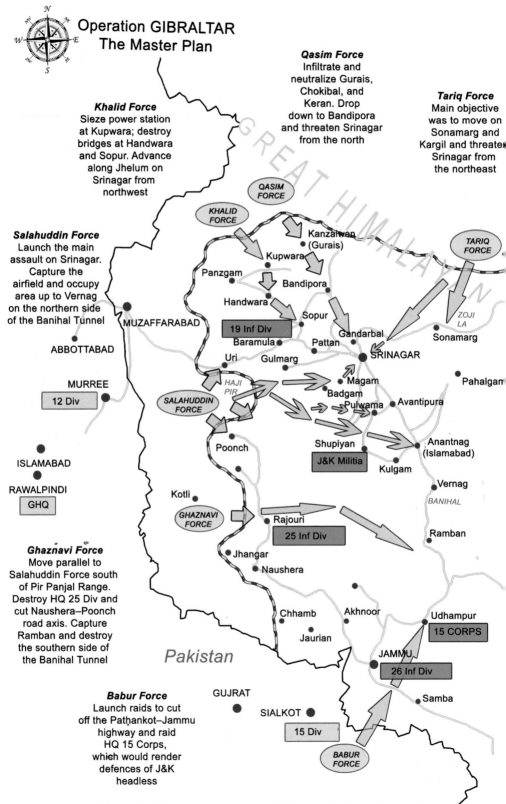

Operation GIBRALTAR
The Master Plan

Khalid Force
Sieze power station
at Kupwara; destroy
bridges at Handwara
and Sopur. Advance
along Jhelum on
Srinagar from
northwest

Qasim Force
Infiltrate and
neutralize Gurais,
Chokibal, and
Keran. Drop
down to Bandipora
and threaten Srinagar
from the north

Tariq Force
Main objective
was to move on
Sonamarg and
Kargil and threaten
Srinagar from
the northeast

Salahuddin Force
Launch the main
assault on Srinagar.
Capture the
airfield and occupy
area up to Vernag
on the northern side
of the Banihal Tunnel

GREAT HIMALAYAN

QASIM FORCE

KHALID FORCE

TARIQ FORCE

Kanzalwan (Gurais)

Kupwara

Panzgam

Bandipora

Handwara

ZOJI LA

MUZAFFARABAD

Sopur

Gandarbal

Sonamarg

19 Inf Div

Baramula

Pattan

ABBOTTABAD

Uri

Gulmarg

SRINAGAR

MURREE

HAJI PIR

Magam

Pahalgam

12 Div

SALAHUDDIN FORCE

Badgam

Pulwama

Avantipura

ISLAMABAD

Poonch

Shupiyan

Anantnag (Islamabad)

RAWALPINDI

J&K Militia

Kulgam

GHQ

Kotli

Vernag

GHAZNAVI FORCE

Rajouri

BANIHAL

25 Inf Div

Ramban

Ghaznavi Force
Move parallel to
Salahuddin Force south
of Pir Panjal Range.
Destroy HQ 25 Div and
cut Naushera–Poonch
road axis. Capture
Ramban and destroy
the southern side of
the Banihal Tunnel

Jhangar

Naushera

Chhamb

Akhnoor

Udhampur

15 CORPS

Jaurian

Pakistan

JAMMU

26 Inf Div

Babur Force
Launch raids to cut
off the Pathankot–Jammu
highway and raid
HQ 15 Corps,
which would render
defences of J&K
headless

GUJRAT

Samba

SIALKOT

15 Div

BABUR FORCE

Not to scale: This map has been prepared in adherence to the 'Guidelines for acquiring and producing Geospatial Data and Geospatial Data Services including Maps' published vide DST F.No.SM/25/02/2020 (Part-I) dated 15th February, 2021.

BrigV. K. Ghai, Cdr 121 (I) Bde; 4 Rajput with captured weapons from Pt 13620; *(below)* Gen Musa conferring the Sitara-e-Jurat on Maj Gen Akhtar Hussain Malik, GOC 12 Div; tribals armed and equipped by the Pakistan Army, a repeat of the tactics adopted in 1947.

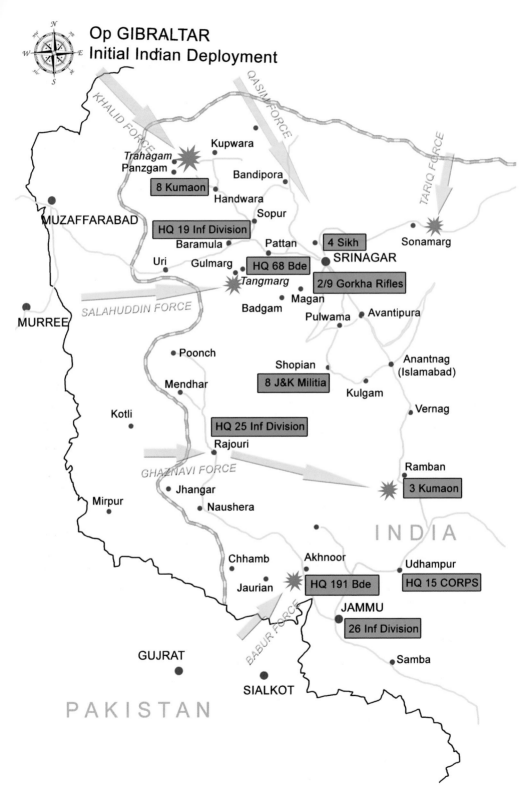

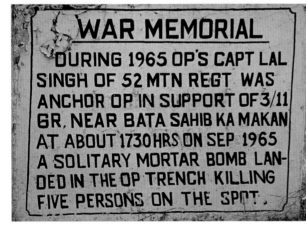

Lt Gen Kashmir Katoch, GOC 15 Corps; Maj Gen S. S. Kalaan, GOC 19 Inf Div; Maj Gen Amreek Singh, GOC 25 Inf Div; Maj Gen Umrao Singh, GOC Siri Force that was set up on 14 August with its HQ in Srinagar; Pakistani irregulars being rounded up; heavy artillery and mortar support from across the Line of Control claimed a lot of lives; Brig A. J. R. Dyer, commanding 31 Comn Z Sub Area, along with HQ J&K Militia under the control of Siri Force took charge of internal duties in the Valley, allowing Lt Gen Harbakhsh Singh to free 19 Inf Div to take on an aggressive stance resulting in the capture of the Haji Pir Bulge.

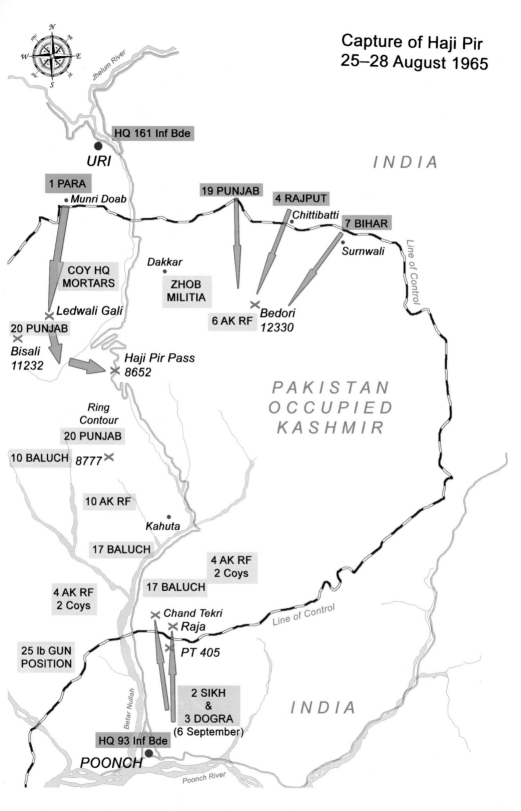

Capture of Haji Pir
25–28 August 1965

Colonel Arul Raj's depiction of the attack on Haji Pir; Brig Zorawar 'Zoru' Bakshi, Cdr 68 Inf Bde; Lt Col Sampuran Singh, CO 19 Punjab; Maj Ranjit Singh Dyal, 1 Para who led the assault; the Defence Minister, Y. B. Chavan at Haji Pir escorted by Sampuran Singh meeting the troops on the pass.

Artist's depiction of the attack on Raja–Rani; MVCs all—Lt Col N. N. Khanna (Posthumous), CO 2 Sikh; Lt Col Sant Sikh, CO 5 Sikh LI; Capt C. N. Singh (P), 2 Garh Rif; Capt Gautam Mubayi (P), 2 Dogra; Sub T. B. Thapa, 4/8 GR; Nk Darshan Singh (P), 5 Sikh LI.

commentary of the 'battle' to Brigade HQ and others on a listening watch with absolutely no idea as to what was happening up ahead. Even as this information was being relayed back to Khanna, the two Dogra companies came falling back. Fortunately, the two Sikh companies kept their composure and the line steadied, but by then it was apparent the attack had failed and both battalions were asked to fall back to their assembly areas from where they were ordered back to Poonch.

In the debriefing that followed, the senior Dogra company commander, Greesh Verma, said the defences of Raja were almost impregnable and with additional covering fire from the Rani side exposing his flanks, he had no option but to pull back. Though Zora Singh was not willing to accept the Dogra explanation for the failure, Amreek Singh, GOC 25 Infantry Division, took a more sympathetic view. As the post mortem of the failed attack gave way to a discussion of the way forward, Khanna set the tone, saying quietly to Zora Singh, 'Give it to me, sir. 2 Sikh will give you Raja.'[11]

Khanna requested the commanders to give him a minimum of two days, so he could probe the defences and plan his subsequent attack. This was agreed upon, but the scheduled date of 7 September would be advanced by twenty-four hours after only one reconnaissance had been done. The roles had now been reversed, with 3 Dogra tasked with the capture of Rani after which it was to attack and capture Sur Tekri. 2 Sikh was to capture Raja. 75 Patiala Mountain Battery was to support 2 Sikh while the Dogras were to be supported by the Heavy Mortar Battery. 42 Field Regiment was to be used only for counter-bombardment. Flank support was to be provided by Meghdoot Force that was also to capture Lambi Tekri in the process.

By mid-morning on 5 September both battalions were at their forward assembly areas and the men were shown the objectives from Pt 405, which in turn was connected to Raja by a ridge.[12] In the early hours of 6 September, both battalions had set off for their respective FUPs and at 0505 hrs, both assaulting units had crossed their start lines simultaneously. Rani, which was being held by a company of 4 Azad Kashmir supported by a platoon of 5 Zhob Militia were taken completely by surprise. 3 Dogra, despite the loss of both their leading COs—Major G. C. Verma and Captain G. S. Bawa—and a JCO, Subedar Bansi Lal, along with fourteen other ranks, pressed home their uphill attack and captured Rani.[13] Three officers, two JCOs, and sixty men had been wounded. The Pakistanis had fought courageously, the thirty-nine bodies strewn across the defences being testimony to the fact.

On the face of it, the Raja defences seemed impregnable and it was not surprising that 3 Dogra had failed earlier. 2 Sikh, even as they crossed the start line, came under very heavy fire. One of the company commanders, Major Kailash C. Kalley, was incapacitated almost immediately, having been shot in the knee. The Patiala Mountain Battery's 3.7-inch howitzers and the RCL guns that had been manhandled onto Pt 405 proved ineffective as most of the shells fell short of Raja's defences. Almost immediately, 2 Sikh started taking casualties and it became obvious that the Pakistanis were fully prepared to take on the advancing troops. With the light improving all the time, the situation was getting desperate. Holding it all together was the CO, who in turn had the battery commander, the soft-spoken Major (later Lieutenant General) Jagdish Singh Virk, with him. Khanna's fearless leadership inspired the battalion to keep the pressure on the Pakistanis even though it seemed like a hopeless situation. To make matters worse, the orders for Virk were not to call in the medium artillery unless it was to engage enemy artillery.

Khanna was like a man possessed. Dashing forward, calling his men to follow him, he yanked down a picket holding the barbed wire that marked the minefield. Miraculously, he then got through the mines—among the men following him, two were not so lucky and had their feet blown off—and was close enough to take on the forward bunker. As he hurled a grenade at it, he was hit, for the first time, on the arm.

Though the Sikhs had successfully closed the gap with the forward bunkers, they were still in a hopeless position, as the quantum of fire (accompanied by the choicest abuse from both sides) had them pinned down. Khanna then slithered down a crawl trench that took him back to the edge of the minefield where he asked Virk to call in the medium guns while he radioed his adjutant, Major Sukhinder Singh, to send the reserve company forward. Just then, the gallant CO was hit by a machine-gun burst in the side of his stomach. It had been a miracle that he hadn't been brought down earlier. His last order before he lost consciousness was that the men must not know he had fallen.

In the battle of attrition that followed, the men were being led by the junior officers. Major Virk too had been shot through the shoulder, but he continued to control fire support. The arrival of Charlie Company, the battalion reserve, under Captain Anup Singh, began to tilt the balance in favour of the Indians. Captain Jai Singh, commanding Alpha Company, then took charge and, along with Captain Surjit Singh, commanding Delta Company, 2 Sikh continued to fight on from the toehold created by Khanna, who died as he was being evacuated. Finally, at 0710 hrs, in what would be one of the bloodiest battles of the war, the success signal was flashed from the top of Raja. 2 Sikh had besides its CO, lost two JCOs—Subedars Balwant Singh and Gurbax Singh—and another thirty-seven men. In addition, three officers, three JCOs and ninety-six other ranks had been wounded. Major Balwant Singh, the second-in-command, then reached Raja from Battalion HQ and took over the battalion. Shortly thereafter, two companies of 3 Raj Rif, the brigade reserve, also reached Raja. Since Rani had already been captured by the Dogras, all that the Pakistanis could do was to subject Raja to intense bombardment, which claimed two more lives.

The leadership displayed by Khanna was of the highest order, and though his citation for a Param Vir Chakra was downgraded to a Maha Vir Chakra, the men who fought under him paid tribute in just four words—'Raja liya, Raja diya!' (We captured Raja, but sacrificed our king!).[14] 93 Brigade then consolidated by capturing Chand Tekri and fighting many smaller operations, as it cleared the way for Meghdoot Force to advance on Kahuta and close the southern pincer by linking up with 68 Brigade subsequently.

The entire Kashmir border had been the responsibility of 12 Division under Akhtar Hussain Malik and things had gone horribly wrong for him ever since he had initiated Operation Gibraltar in the first week of August. General Musa was to write later, 'During the third week of August...we received another Presidential directive...our limited counter offensive in the Chhamb valley was planned after receipt of this clearance.'[15] Even at that stage, the Pakistanis could not accept that the Indians might react and their failure to hold the Haji Pir Bulge was now costing them dearly. So obsessed was the Pakistan high command with the use of armour, it had chosen to focus on the narrow strip of 'tank country' rather than bringing all its resources into play to recapture the pass.

However, blunders were not necessarily confined to the Pakistani side. Even before the attack on Raja and Rani by 93 Brigade, Zoru Bakshi had wanted to push on to Kahuta from the northern side, which would have sealed the escape route of the Pakistanis defending the formidable posts facing Poonch. This was discussed on 2 September with General Kalaan, shortly after the first assault from the southern side had failed to dislodge the Pakistanis. However, GOC 19 Infantry Division seemed fixated on capturing Bisali (Pt 11229) which was the highest feature on the western side of the Haji Pir–Uri road. Lieutenant Colonel Sudershan Singh promptly volunteered the services of 4 Rajput to capture the formidable feature.

As the fighting raged further to the south at Akhnoor, there was a comparative lull over the next two days, even though the Pakistanis continued to pound the Haji Pir pass with artillery. This resulted in 1 Para suffering seven casualties even as they were being relieved on the pass by 6 Dogra. Zoru Bakshi, still not happy with what he considered to be an unnecessary diversion from the main task which was the link-up with 93 Brigade, allotted two companies of 6 JAK Rif under Sudershan Singh's command. At 2200 hrs on 4 September, under the cover of artillery fire, 4 Rajput moved up the slopes and, despite stiff resistance put up by the defending Pakistanis, flashed the success signal at 0330 hrs on 5 September.

Tragically, in the dark, the Rajputs mistook a false crest for the actual top of Bisali. After the gruelling fighting climb, the men were exhausted and had failed to reorganize themselves. At daybreak, led by Lieutenant Colonel Fazle Hamid, four Pakistani companies—one each from 6 and 10 Azad Kashmir Rif, 17 Baluch, and 20 Punjab—counter-attacked the hapless troops strung out on the elongated feature. In a fight that became a virtual carnage, 4 Rajput lost two officers and sixty-three other ranks, while four officers and forty-seven other ranks were wounded. For the Pakistanis, it was a major shot in the arm for, apart from capturing most of the battalion's weapons, they also bagged a large number of prisoners. 4 Rajput, for the second time in three years, had temporarily ceased to exist.[12]

On 5 September, Kalaan and Bakshi met again. Bisali had been an unmitigated disaster and the upbeat troops of 20 Punjab now occupied the Ring Counter south of Pt 8786 as well as Pt 8777. Behind them, the delay in the advance of 68 Brigade meant the Pakistanis had an additional four days to strengthen the defences of Kahuta. Accordingly, at 2300 hrs on 7 September, under the overall command of the by then nationally famous Ranjit Singh Dyal, Bravo and Charlie companies of 1 Para, with artillery on call, began a silent advance in the pelting rain towards the Ring Contour. They had gotten to within 75 yards of their objective when three MMGs opened up from the cliffs of Pt 8786. The leading sections of Bravo Company, led by Major H. A. Patil tried to scale the cliffs thrice, but were unsuccessful. Patil himself was wounded. Major J. C. M. Rao then moved up with his Charlie Company and, despite heroic efforts, the paratroopers failed to make headway despite accurate artillery support.

It was almost inevitable that Rao too would get hit, and at 0830 hrs, Ranjit Dayal was forced to commit Delta Company under Captain T. B. Gurung. With individual firefights raging all around, the Pakistanis managed to break into 1 Para's radio network and got the battalion's mortars to shell their own positions. Gurung, while forming up his company, was killed when a Pakistani artillery shell exploded next to him. After some extremely hard fighting, Pt 8786 was finally taken at 1700 hrs on 8 September. The Ring Counter on the western side of the ridge, however, remained in Pakistani hands as did Pt 8777 that had simultaneously been attacked by 19 Punjab. Bakshi then decided to switch his advance to the eastern side of the ridge, something he had wanted to do all along but for Kalaan's insistence. On 8 September he launched 6 Dogra against Pt 7720 while 19 Punjab were asked to capture Pt 9270, which both units did by first light on 9 September; they then continued to press south. By 1600 hrs the momentum of the advance saw 19 Punjab secure Ziarat, while the Dogras captured Halan Janubi by midday on 10 September. Almost a week behind schedule, a platoon from Major Megh Singh's Meghdoot Force coming up from Poonch linked up with 19 Punjab at Ziarat. On the night of 11 September, 19 Punjab began its assault on Kahuta and, by the next morning, the town was in Indian hands.

By this time, the attention of the world had shifted to the fighting raging in the Khem Karan and Sialkot Sectors. Even though Kahuta had fallen and the link-up between the two brigades had been established, severe fighting continued in the sector. The Pakistanis were still holding the Ring Counter and Pt 8777, as well as strong positions around Gitian, from where they could harass any movement on the Uri–Poonch road. Pt 8777 was 2 km south of the Haji Pir pass and Gitian 1 km.

On 20 September, Zoru Bakshi ordered 6 Dogra commanded by Lieutenant Colonel S. S. Khokkar to assault and capture Pakistani positions a kilometre to the south of Gitian (Pt 7720), while 1 Para was to simulate an attack on Pt 8777 and one company of 19 Punjab was to engage the Ring Contour to divert the enemy's attention. Majors B. K. Mehta, the second-in-command, H. S. Sachdev, and Darshan Singh Lalli led the battalion assault with Alpha and Bravo Company going for Hut Hill and Tree Hill respectively. Left Knoll, the third objective was to be captured later. As the slug fest developed, 6 Dogra came under accurate artillery fire. Darshan Singh Lalli was killed and, with casualties mounting, Bakshi had to commit the reserve company from 19 Punjab into the fray. Even though Gitian was eventually cleared, 19 Punjab lost Major Ranbir and the FOO from 164 Field Regiment. Apart from the three officers, one JCO, and thirty-two other ranks were killed while five more officers, three JCOs, and eighty men were wounded. It was one of the toughest battles fought in the Haji Pir Bulge with neither side giving any quarter.

Though 1 Para was to launch another abortive attack against Pt 8777 on 22 September, the fighting around Gitian underlined the importance of having captured the Haji Pir Bulge. In statistical terms alone, between 68 and 93 Brigades, this would be the largest tract of territory that had been liberated since 1948 and, tactically, it put paid to the easy access Pakistan had to infiltrate into the Kashmir Valley. Fighting in the Kishanganga Bulge had also successfully blocked infiltration routes from the north. On the night of 3/4 September, 3/8 GR had captured Sunjoi after a bloody hand to hand fight. After fighting off repeated counter-attacks, the Gorkhas then consolidated around the Mirpur Bridge that had been demolished by the Pakistanis. 4 Kumaon then assaulted Pt 9013 on 21 September, taking on two 23 Azad Kashmir companies entrenched behind a minefield. It took the Kumaonese three hours but, at the end of it, they had captured the Jura Bridge on the Kishanganga, which was still intact. As a result, by the time the ceasefire came into effect, Chauhan's 104 Brigade completely dominated the sector.

As we now go back to Akhnoor where Operation Grand Slam had unfolded, we must also put on hold the narrative of the fighting further south in the vicinity of Mendhar, better known as the Battle for Chhu-i-Nar or the Battle for Op Hill. Since this was fought after the ceasefire, we shall return to the 25 Division Sector subsequently.

Chapter 10

OPERATION GRAND SLAM

IGNORING THE SIGNS

On 20 August, HQ 10 Infantry Division, then being raised in Bangalore and Belgaum, was ordered to move immediately to Naushera where it would assume operational responsibility of 191 and 80 Brigade Sectors by 15 September. Major General Dharam Bir Chopra, along with his GSO-1, Lieutenant Colonel (later Colonel) Krishna Pillai Padmanabhan Nair and other staff officers reported to Udhampur on 25 August. Harbakhsh Singh and Kashmir Katoch were both present and the army commander spelt out his appreciation of the situation. He believed that Pakistan would launch its main offensive across the CFL with large-scale infiltration using irregular forces. This would then be followed up with a full-scale attack in the Chhamb Sector. 'Lieutenant General Harbakhsh Singh expected an offensive in strength against Akhnoor-Naushera for snapping our...line of communication...towards Rajouri-Poonch.'[1]

Harbakhsh Singh believed that Akhnoor would not be Pakistan's objective. This despite the fact that GOC 26 Infantry Division, Major General (later Lieutenant General) Mohan Lal Thapan, had provided fairly reliable and authentic intelligence about a heavy concentration of troops including tanks across the border. The report also said there was a build-up of regular Pakistani troops at Moel. Taking his cue from the army commander, Katoch told Chopra 'Brigadier Manmohan Singh, commander 191 Infantry Brigade Group is totally new to the sector and the operational developments, having assumed command on 16 August. He is inclined to be "jittery" and tends to "cry wolf". On the basis of a few reports rendered by forward troops of heavy Pakistani infantry and armour concentration opposite his sector, the brigade commander has been voicing his apprehension of an imminent Pakistani attack in strength in his sector.'[2] Chopra was cautioned to ignore 'this tendency' as there was no threat to this sector and the infiltration had already been contained. The corps had no plans to prepare defensive positions east of the Manawar Tawi. The intention was clear—10 Infantry Division would fight the enemy on the CFL.

While it was true that Manmohan Singh had taken over 191 (Independent) Infantry Brigade Group less than a fortnight ago after Byram Master was killed by Pakistani shelling, he had been commanding 162 Infantry Brigade that was a part of the neighbouring Jammu-based 26 Infantry Division. In the beginning of August, at the time Operation Gibraltar was launched, 191 Infantry Brigade was responsible for a total of sixty-six posts. The total frontage that Byram Master was responsible for was 83 km along the IB, which was mainly manned by the PAP and another 32 km along the CFL, which was manned by 3 JAK Militia and backed by 3 Mahar and 9 Punjab, the brigade's two infantry battalions. When Manmohan Singh took charge on 16 August, ten of these posts had been abandoned due to excessive Pakistani artillery fire. By 24 August, the new brigade commander had recovered these posts.

On 26 August, one day after having rubbished reports of a Pakistani build-up in the area, HQ 15 Corps ordered Chopra to set up his Divisional HQ at Akhnoor by 29 August with the skeletal staff he had. 6 Rajput, commanded by Lieutenant Colonel Mustasad Ahmad, was also ordered to move in the early hours of 28 August to Akhnoor, to defend the new divisional location. By 29 August, HQ 10 Infantry Division had been physically established.

The next day, Chopra drove across to HQ 191 (Independent) Infantry Brigade Group that was located at the Mandiala crossing. The units under its command were 15 Kumaon, which was deployed around the Brigade HQ at Mandiala itself; 6 Sikh LI was deployed along the CFL extending from Burejal to Pir Jamal; 3 Mahar with elements of 3 JAK Militia were north of Pir Jamal; and 6/5 GR were defending the general area of Kalidhar. 9 Punjab was on a flank, holding a compact defensive position on the Kalidhar Range. In addition, Manmohan Singh had Charlie Squadron of 20 Lancers deployed west of Mandiala, while 14 Field Regiment had its guns deployed in Chhamb with one battery at Dhok Baniyar. One troop of medium battery was in the area east of Chhamb. 'During his discussion with the commander, General Chopra expressed his concern over the linear nature of the defences that had no depth whatsoever. He pointed out to Brigadier Manmohan Singh that although orders expressly stipulated that no withdrawal from the post along the CFL would be permitted, some of these positions had already been abandoned due to heavy shelling and attacks and would have to be recaptured or reoccupied.'[3]

Though as per 15 Corps directives, Manmohan Singh would only come under the operational command of 10 Division, Chopra suggested that the brigade commander 'consider having properly prepared defences to the east of the Manawar Tawi...the line Kalit-Troti-Jaurian would be suitable for the main defences while delaying positions could be to the west of the river. The hill feature Buchoha Mandi provided excellent command over the area west of the river. This would serve as a firm base for dealing with infiltrators to the north and a defensive position on the line Troti-Jaurian.'[4] Even though both men were new to the area, this made sense.

However, Manmohan Singh's hands were tied. He wearily read out the signal received from 15 Corps forty-eight hours earlier in which Katoch had put down his appreciation of the threat to his sector. 'It is not considered that Pakistani build-up is significant to launch any major offensive against this sector. The main threat in the future is therefore, likely to consist of:

1. Continued attempts by irregulars to infiltrate into the interior and raid headquarters, maintenance routes and administrative areas, and
2. Shelling of forward posts, troop and vehicle concentrations and own gun areas within their artillery range.'[5]

Shortly after General Chopra's departure, the CO of 6 Rajput arrived at the Brigade HQ. The battalion had reached Akhnoor a short while ago. While Mustasad Ahmad was with Major Rusty Dey of 2 Lancers who was the brigade major, he was privy to a revealing conversation between him and 15 Corps HQ. 'Rusty was talking to them in context of some track marks, which he maintained were of tanks. The other end would not have it. Finally exasperated, Rusty burst out. "Damn it, don't tell me that I, an armoured corps officer, don't recognize track marks."'[6]

While 15 Corps was determined not to believe the multiple reports coming in of Pakistani armour concentrations, finally, in Simla, Harbakhsh Singh was willing to concede he may have been mistaken in his earlier appreciation. 191 Infantry Brigade reports revealed the presence of one squadron of tanks in the Mattewala area and heavy vehicular movement all along the IB to opposite the Chhamb area; a concentration of troops was reported in the area Moel. This was the first indication of any regular troop movement opposite the Chhamb sector. But even at this stage, Harbakhsh Singh was only willing to concede that there might be a single squadron of tanks. This would hardly change his threat perception of the area.

While all this was happening on the ground, around the same time, General Chaudhuri and his DMO, Brigadier (later Major General) Narindar Singh, arrived in Srinagar to review the overall situation with Kashmir Katoch. Ever since Operation Bakshi had been launched, the tenor of the fighting had taken on a different complexion. With Haji Pir captured, it was a major psychological blow to Akhtar Hussain Malik's Operation Gibraltar. Though the Indians were not quite out of danger in the Valley, the bold action had paid tremendous dividends. Having not put up much of a fight on the strategic pass and along the bulge, it was felt the Pakistanis would strike back soon. The question then was: where would they strike? Significantly, Harbakhsh Singh was not asked to attend the meeting that was held on 31 August.

The whole of the next day, the chief and the corps commander went over possible scenarios and it is indeed most surprising that both the 15 Corps and Western Army HQ were still oblivious of the Pakistani build-up opposite Chhamb.

Not only could the forward posts of 3 Mahar, 6 Sikh LI, and the squadron of 20 Lancers deployed west of the Manawar Tawi hear the armour from across the border, UN observers also repeatedly warned the Indians that a large number of Patton tanks were congregating opposite their position. Even at this point, the three men that mattered—Chaudhuri, Harbakhsh Singh, and Katoch—continued to be in denial. 'It gives a fair idea of how things were at higher headquarters. ...Nobody wanted to even listen, leave alone accord credibility to anything, no matter how consequential or important it might be, if it did not fit into their pattern of thinking.'[7]

In the review meeting, the chief set the tone: 'Pakistan has not so far officially associated herself with the infiltrators, but if she decides to do so she is likely to attack in Chhamb or in Jhangar-Naushera.... It is difficult to say whether Pak dispositions were purely defensive or were for offensive purposes but, in any case, an offensive by Pak was unlikely to get very far.'[8] It was accepted that Pakistan would now try to do something different—the question was what, when, and where.

After the chief, it was Katoch's turn to articulate his views: 'Pak is bound to react to our taking of Haji Pir and would either go for Jhangar, Naushera or attack in the Chhamb area.'[9] The muddled thinking and the near compulsive need to move troops around is underlined by the fact that Katoch had, instead of strengthening the Chhamb Sector, pulled 2 Sikh and two medium artillery regiments out of 191 Infantry Brigade and sent them off to Poonch four days earlier. This when Brigadier Manmohan Singh was desperately short of manpower and the most obvious thing to have done was deploy troops on Troti Heights.

While 15 Corps continued to play out its absurd drama, the main point of interest to the commanders on the ground was whether Pakistani armour would enter Indian territory across the CFL or cross over a little to the south across the IB, which would have very different implications. It wasn't long before they had an answer to that question.

DAVID VS GOLIATH

Bhaskar Roy was born in Kanpur, United Provinces, in 1936. He did his Senior Cambridge in 1951 at the Doon School before moving to Clement Town, also in Dehradun, where the Joint Services Wing was then located. He was dead keen on becoming a fighter pilot, but his eyesight was a problem so he took yet another short step from there to the IMA. He then passed out with the 18th Regular Course in December 1956 and was commissioned into the Armoured Corps.

With nine years of service under his belt, Major Bhaskar Roy was the Charlie Squadron commander of 20 Lancers with a complement of fourteen AMX-13 tanks that were a part of 191 Infantry Brigade.[10] The ultra-light French-built tanks weighed a mere 13 tonnes, had armour that was 40 mm thick, and had a 75 mm gun which had an effective range of 500 yards. The Pakistanis' M-48 Patton tanks, on the other hand, weighed 45 tonnes, had armour protection that was 120 mm thick, and fired a 90 mm gun which was effective up to 1,500 yards.

At 0330 hrs on 1 September, at the southernmost tip of the CFL and parts of the IB, night turned into day as the flash of artillery guns and mortars lit up the entire horizon. Pakistan's artillery, one of their most potent weapons, was putting on a deadly display. Most troops manning the CFL were battle-inoculated and fairly accustomed to shelling. However, the concentrated and relentless fire was tearing their bunkers and comrades apart. With casualties mounting, those who could began to extricate and abandon their positions. The bombardment continued for two and a quarter hours, after which the awesome sight of Patton tanks advancing in formation could be seen.

The defences on the CFL and the IB in the Chhamb Sector had ceased to exist. The few hapless survivors were either gunned down or bayoneted by the advancing Pakistani infantry. Bhaskar Roy, standing on his seat, the upper half of his body outside the cupola of the well-camouflaged AMX-13, looked at the advancing dust trails and realized he was up against an initial squadron of Patton tanks. He could quite easily give the order to withdraw against such overwhelming odds. But that was not an option.

Bhaskar Roy's squadron had been moved to what was referred to as the Chhamb–Jaurian Sector in April 1965 after the initial clashes had taken place in the Rann of Kutch. At first the tanks were located west of the Chenab River as the bridge was not designed to take their weight, but after Operation Gibraltar started, they were ferried across and positioned closer to the border at Sakrana where 6 Sikh LI, commanded by Lieutenant Colonel Pagadala Kuppuswamy Nandagopal, was located nearby.

Working on the assumption that the Pakistan Army would launch an armoured thrust through his sector, Roy spent the next few days carrying out an extensive reconnaissance of the strip of land between the Chenab and the CFL, a frontage of approximately 20 km. The first thing was to identify the possible routes the enemy would take and decide how best to deploy his own resources to meet the threat.

The Chhamb Sector is sandwiched between the west to east Kalidhar Range and the fast-flowing Chenab River, the eastern edge of the Jech/Chaj Doab (between the Chenab and the Jhelum rivers). The Kalidhar Range rises from the plains to moderate heights ranging between 3,000 and 4,000 feet. The lower reaches of the Kalidhar are densely vegetated with brush and the higher areas with pine. The slopes are ragged and steep, with hundreds of dry water channels that are prone to flash floods in the monsoons. Two perennial rivers, the Poonch and the Manawar Tawi, flow through this region and drain into the Jhelum and the Chenab respectively. The plains area too is a mix of ravines and high ground, divided by the Manawar Tawi into two halves. There were limited spots where armour could ford the river, as a result of which 'the south bank of the river would have to be secured before tanks could cross and exploit further'.[11] In many ways, even with the limited capability of the AMX-13, the terrain was quite suited to fight a defensive battle, especially as one moved closer towards Akhnoor where the gap between the river and the Kalidhar got narrower and narrower.

Both Manmohan Singh and Rusty Dey, his brigade major, agreed with Roy that if and when Pakistani armour attacked their sector, the advance would come from the IB side rather than across the CFL as the ground was more suited for tank movement on that side. The next few days were spent in making plans and identifying suitable places where the AMX-13s could be hidden, engage the enemy, move to another prepared position and repeat the fire and move routine yet again. Not wanting enemy observers to see what they were up to, Bhaskar and his men used other vehicles to practise these movements during day and night hours, working out in minute detail how they would react to various contingencies.

'Ganga Singh, an NCO of the time, recalls that Bhaskar casually remarked at around 0300 on 1 September that the sky felt like shells were about to come raining down. A relentlessly mind-numbing, ear-splitting barrage of artillery fire began precisely at 0330 and lasted until 0500.'[12] As the artillery barrage started, Roy immediately got on the field telephone with Dey seeking permission to occupy the prepared positions the moment the shelling stopped. This was granted. 'Luckily 'C' Squadron was so hunkered down—or as Kushal Singh, the eighteen-year-old 'baby of the regiment' dismissively said, the Pakistani gunners were so bad!—that no immediate casualties were suffered or direct damage taken.'[13]

Watching the artillery at work from the other side with a sense of satisfaction was Pakistan's GOC 12 Division. Malik had moved with his TAC HQ to Kharian on 28 August, from where he had been giving finishing touches to Operation Grand Slam. With the overwhelming firepower at his disposal, the plan was to be executed in three phases—destruction of all Indian troops on the western side of the Manawar Tawi in Laleal, Dewa, Sakrana, and Chhamb by 1000 hrs; capture of Akhnoor and the bridge over the Chenab by midday; and then before the stunned Indians could realize what had happened, the four attacking brigades under his command were to be reinforced by GHQ's strike force, Major General Yahya Khan's 7 Division, and together they were to sweep northwards and take Rajouri by 2 September. Nusrat Force, active in the area as a part of Operation Gibraltar, was to step up its activities around Naushera, Jhangar, and Rajouri.

The fire support that was made available for Operation Grand Slam was unprecedented in the subcontinent's history. A total of ten field, seven medium, and two heavy batteries, adding up to 110 guns[14] that were supporting four assaulting brigades. Two of these—No. 4 Sector Brigade and 102 Brigade—were from Malik's 12 Division, while Yahya Khan's 10 Brigade and 25 Infantry Brigade had been placed under his command as well. Two of Pakistan's oldest armoured regiments, 11 Prince Albert Victor's Own Cavalry and 13 Duke of Connaught's

Own Lancers, were to spearhead the assault at H-hour 0500 hrs on 1 September. As the artillery barrage started, the Sherman Mk II tanks of 13 Cavalry in support of 102 Brigade surged forward, attacking 6 Sikh LI positions in the Rehana and Moel area, while 102 Brigade under the command of Brigadier Zafar Ali Khan supported by Bravo Squadron of 11 Cavalry with M-48 Pattons attacked two companies of 3 JAK Militia.

Nandagopal had been on leave in Kolar when he received orders asking him to rejoin his battalion, 6 Sikh LI. One of the newly raised battalions, the bulk of 6 Sikh LI's troops had no combat experience. Nandagopal had reached the Brigade HQ at Akhnoor on 15 August shortly after news had come in that the TAC HQ at Dewa had been shelled, Byram Master killed, and all communication lines disrupted. Since 6 Sikh LI was manning the defences along the CFL in the area, Nandagopal had rushed to his Battalion HQ at Sakrana only to find that none of the battalion posts at Moel, Paur, Burejal, and Dalla, located at the junction of the IB and the CFL, had been attacked. Brigade HQ had suggested 6 Sikh LI pull back to the high ground at Troti but Nandagopal felt that would give the wrong signal not just to the Pakistanis, but to our own troops as well. When Manmohan Singh took over 191 Infantry Brigade a few hours later, he fully endorsed Nandagopal's decision.

A fortnight later, when the Pakistani guns opened up, the earth seemed to shake and the tremors could be felt even in far-off Jammu. At Burejal, just ahead of Roy's AMX-13 tanks, and at their other locations, the Sikh LI platoons were hugging the bottom of their trenches, waiting for the terrifying fire to lift. Then amidst the deafening roar of the shelling, they heard a different sound, as the tanks closed in from the direction of the IB and CFL under the umbrella of the artillery barrage. At 0500 hrs, the shelling stopped, and almost instantly the Sikh LI RCL guns positioned at Burejal and Dalla engaged the leading Pakistani tanks. The RCL gun crews hardly stood a chance, for the moment they fired and exposed their position, there were enough tanks to zero in on them and knock them out.

Bhaskar Roy's men were holding their fire. Indian counter-bombardment was non-existent, the gun positions having taken their own share of pounding. There were no anti-tank mines, because 15 Corps had refused to accept that Pakistani armour would be committed in that sector. 6 Sikh LI, led by Captain Ravi Kumar, was fighting desperately ahead of them, but the infantry troops were deployed in penny pockets and some of the tanks had already got past the Sikh LI positions. Now between the Pattons and the thin red line being held by Charlie Squadron of 20 Lancers, the gap was rapidly narrowing.

Outgunned almost 6 to 1, Roy prepared as best he could by splitting his squadron into troops of three tanks each, spacing them over a considerable distance to counter the massive spread of the advancing Pattons. He had an insane plan: use the smaller AMX's greater manoeuvrability and wait until an enemy tank was just within firing distance; fire once and move to another position to fire again—a risk-laden effort to make the defence line appear bigger than it was.

Pakistan's impeccably named Operation Grand Slam was designed to cross the Manawar Tawi by 1000 hrs on 1 September and take the strategically crucial bridge across the Chenab at Akhnoor by 1200. 'The goal: snare the only supply route to Kashmir before India could respond. So much for that—six Pattons were destroyed in the very first wave. Propaganda having prepared Pakistani troops for weak defences, the attack was thrown into confusion. By late afternoon, C Squadron had disabled 15 plus Pattons and was still refusing to break, despite being cut in half. Pakistani war despatches note rather blandly, "The enemy resisted stubbornly."[15]

From the very first onslaught, Roy survived on the proverbial wing and prayer, along with countless thermoses of cold coffee and Capstan cigarettes. He agreed to eat a single meal of three or four cashews only late that night after he was ordered—repeatedly—to pull back to Akhnoor. Kushal Singh, who blamed himself for running out of cold coffee (although he doesn't understand the obsession), said he personally saw very little direct action that day—Roy kept telling him to get down because how in God's name would he explain to Kushal's mother that he had got her baby killed?!

Roy lost his first troop leader, the fearless twenty-one-year-old Second Lieutenant Ravi Laroia, very early. Volunteering for what Roy knew would be a calamitous mission, Laroia raced to occupy the strategic heights of the Mandiala Ridge to prevent the Pattons from reaching there first. Bhaskar watched them crest the ridge successfully, only to look on helplessly as Laroia's tank, crew, and Ravi himself were obliterated by the murderous accuracy of incoming firepower. For his selfless bravery, Ravi was posthumously awarded the Sena Medal. This was apparently when Roy decided to move his commanding tank to the very front. The oil painting in the regimental mess shows him standing in full enemy view, commander's pennant flying high, recklessly directing fire visually rather than from the safety of the commander's turret.

Stories abound. Ganga Singh plunged back into the Manawar Tawi after the retreat was ordered. 'Hamari ma ka mandir reh gaya hai' (Our mother's temple has been left behind). He hauled the regimental Chamunda mandir back across the river, dry and safe atop his head.

By late evening, Roy had had four tanks blown out from under him. On the third, a devastatingly well-aimed Pakistani shell killed his driver, decapitated the gunner, then ricocheted to slash past his legs and set his pants on fire. The story goes that he jumped off, stripped down and beat the fire out. A man on the ground shouted, 'Sir, you need pants more than I do,' and gave Roy his own. Roy donned the man's pants and bellowed for someone, anyone, for God's sake, to get him another tank.

Under the circumstances, 191 Infantry Brigade had displayed tremendous grit and determination in standing up to the overwhelming onslaught, starting with 6 Sikh LI, which stubbornly held onto its defences as its posts were surrounded one by one. By 0730 hrs the post at Paur had been surrounded by tanks after which the isolated post was assaulted by the infantry. At Burejal, Ravi Kumar held on gamely till 1100 hrs, when his position was finally overrun. Communication had broken down as the various positions were overrun and, by 1800 hrs, those who had managed to break contact had started arriving at the battalion's headquarters near Chhamb. The losses had been tremendous—one JCO and twenty-five other ranks were confirmed killed, two officers, three JCOs, and thirty-eight other ranks were wounded. Eight officers, nine JCOs, and 428 other ranks were missing. With half the battalion wiped out, at 1900 hrs, Manmohan Singh ordered Nandagopal to fall back on Akhnoor, which he did, maintaining good order.

Gurbans Singh Sangha's 3 Mahar was the other battalion holding the forward defences along the CFL. It was one of the units that had been cut off on 15 August when Byram Master was killed in the Pakistani shelling of Dewa, after which it had furiously chased down infiltrators in the Mandiala Heights and blocked any movement towards Jaurian. Though an additional company of 3 JAK Militia had been placed under Sangha, even a fortnight later, the battalion was still without any heavy weapons whatsoever. Under heavy artillery and mortar fire since 0330 hrs, the Mahar and JAK Militia positions were in the area around Lallialli.

As soon as the artillery barrage lifted, the JAK Militia company commander reported that he was under fire from the advancing Pakistani armour that was engaging his defences. Communication snapped a few minutes later, around which time 3 Mahar's Charlie Company came under heavy tank fire. Sangha, with no anti-tank mines, RCLs, shoulder-fired rocket launchers or anything to fight the enemy armour with, had deployed his men on high ground where tanks could not actually get to them in order to crush them under their tracks. Armed with just their rifles and a few machine guns, the battalion continued to hold ground. HQ 191 Infantry Brigade told Sangha to hang on to his position; artillery, armour, and air support would be made available soon.

VAMPIRES OVER CHHAMB

In Srinagar, the army chief General Chaudhuri, Katoch, and the DMO knew that Pakistan had breached the IB to launch its tanks; they were being kept up to date on the developing situation in the Chhamb–Jaurian sector. Amazingly, in Army HQ, the adjutant general, Lieutenant General Kumaramangalam, had absolutely no idea that Pakistan had launched its offensive earlier that morning. In the absence of the chief, Kumaramangalam conducted the morning briefing at 1000 hrs for Defence Minister Chavan and, based on the previous evening's appreciation forwarded by 15 Corps, confidently predicted that it would take Pakistan a minimum of sixteen days to move troops from their existing positions to the CFL to launch an attack anywhere in Jammu and Kashmir. After the briefing, Chavan left to visit a hospital when there was an urgent phone call for him. The defence secretary, P. V. R. Rao, informed the defence minister at 1100 hrs that Pakistan had launched an attack in the Chhamb Sector with armour support.

At that very moment, his positions falling one by one despite fighting fiercely, Brigadier Manmohan Singh was putting out a desperate plea to his immediate higher headquarters, 15 Corps, asking for air support. This message reached Srinagar while Chaudhuri was still there. The decision to use the air force was not for the COAS to take, for it needed the nod of the Government of India. By then, General Chaudhuri was fully aware of what was happening on the ground and he accordingly briefed Prime Minister Shastri on the telephone.[16] Since the request for air support had already been communicated to the army chief, it is perhaps fair to presume that this was also communicated to Shastri. It is not known if the need to create another front in the Punjab and Rajasthan was also mentioned. Though Chaudhuri was scheduled to meet with Harbakhsh Singh in Srinagar later in the day, the chief, after his conversation with the prime minister, immediately departed from Srinagar, ostensibly for New Delhi, which would have taken three-and-a-half hours at best.

Having boarded the special IAF Dakota DC-3 in Srinagar, Chaudhuri instructed the pilots to take a detour via the Pathankot air base.[17] The unscheduled and unheralded arrival of the army chief at the air force base took the station commander, Group Captain (later Air Commodore) Roshan Lal Suri, completely by surprise. Chaudhuri was in Pathankot for approximately two and a half hours, meeting with the Vampire and Mystère COs. Astonishingly, not once did he mention the situation in Chhamb. Chaudhuri discussed the use of Vampires against the raider columns should the need arise, and asked the station commander to have armed aircraft standing by. The chief finally landed at Palam in New Delhi at 1600 hrs, from where he rushed straight from the aircraft to the defence minister's office while his DMO, Narendra Kumar, went to his office in South Block to execute the orders he had dictated to him on the flight from Pathankot to Delhi.

Chaudhuri's little detour to Pathankot finds mention in the defence secretary's version of events as well. The army chief had squandered two and a half precious hours. His attitude that the air force was a subordinate service has been criticized by Air Marshal P. C. Lal as well. What is even harder to believe is that he said nothing about Chhamb to the Pathankot station commander, preferring to just 'chat with the pilots' about ground support strikes in the Valley.[18] This was not the first instance where the generals did not want to disclose the actual target to the IAF.

At 1300 hrs Chavan had returned to his office from the hospital and since then everyone had been waiting anxiously for the army chief. By the time Chaudhuri reached Chavan's office, it was 1630 hrs. By this time, the situation had become desperate. The first thing Chaudhuri did was to take Arjan Singh aside and the two discussed the situation in Chhamb. Five hours had elapsed since Brigadier Manmohan Singh had asked 15 Corps for air support and even though the battered Indian positions were holding out, it was only a matter of time before Pakistani armour would break through. After taking off from Srinagar, General Chaudhuri had no opportunity to receive any further updates. Launching the air force was one thing, but Chaudhuri now also wanted permission to authorize immediate counter-attacks across the CFL to relieve the pressure on 191 Infantry Brigade. Both the COAS and the CAS were aware that as per the existing norms, the Emergency Coordination Committee (ECC) needed to give the defence minister the go-ahead to involve the air force, for this could escalate into all-out war.

The COAS and the CAS then entered the defence minister's inner office, where Chavan and Rao were waiting, and Chaudhuri formally asked for permission to launch the aircraft and retaliate across the CFL. Chaudhuri said he was coming from Pathankot and the aircraft were ready to go. Arjan Singh pointed out that there was a real risk of hitting our own positions during the air strikes, for there was no way of knowing friend from foe. Surprisingly, Chavan did not make any move to pick up the phone to speak to the prime minister. Then in the next few seconds, two of the most crucial decisions were taken by Yashwantrao Balwantrao Chavan, the fourth defence minister of India. There was no time to go to the ECC or even place a call to Prime Minister Shastri. He just said, 'Go ahead!'[19] It was 1650 hrs.

VAMPIRES INTO THE SETTING SUN

The decision to move 45 Squadron, commanded by Squadron Leader (later Wing Commander) Sudesh Kumar 'Marshal' Dahar[20] to Pathankot from Pune was taken by Air HQ in the third week of August. By 1965, the de Havilland Vampire Mk.52 was not only considered to be obsolete, it was a death trap as this version did not even have an ejection seat. The twin-tailed single-engine fighter's egg-shaped fuselage was made of moulded plywood while the rest of the tail was aluminium. 'Its first flight was during Second World War; at that time, even the propeller-driven Tempest had a higher rate of climb than the Vampire. By 1965, it was hopelessly out of place.'[21]

In 1948 when the UN-sponsored ceasefire came into effect, as per the terms laid down, fighter aircraft could not be stationed in the state of Jammu and Kashmir, a clause that applied to both India and Pakistan. Now that the IAF was being called in for ground support, Arjan Singh believed the Vampire would be better suited for the task.[22] Two things influenced his thinking. As a Hurricane pilot who commanded No. 1 Squadron in the Imphal Valley in 1945, he had been the first to spot and confirm the presence of Japanese troops near Palel. He believed the Vampire was better suited for operations against small bands of raiders than any of the other much faster jets in the IAF's inventory. Second, in the Rann of Kutch, Flying Officer Barbara's successful sortie where he had evaded all the ground fire to manoeuvre himself into a position where he could easily have taken out the Pattons instead of photographing them, had further reinforced his faith in the slower aircraft.

The third factor that was worrying the air chief was target identification. Ever since Pakistan had launched Operation Gibraltar, he was acutely aware that when the IAF was called in, his pilots would be flying blind. The troops on the ground too would not know an Indian aircraft from a Pakistani fighter and the pilots would have both sides firing at them. Even in the defence minister's office, Arjan Singh had told both Chavan and Chaudhuri that there was a huge risk the fighters might hit our own positions.

Twenty-nine minutes after Chavan's go-ahead, the first formation of four Vampires was airborne from Pathankot and they were followed at ten-minute intervals by two more waves. Marshal Dahar, accompanied by Flight Lieutenants Sahay, Inder Parkash Ahuja, and S.V. Pathak, set course in a north-westerly direction for Chhamb, where the surviving soldiers of 3 Mahar, 6 Sikh LI, and 15 Kumaon with a handful of AMX tanks were still keeping the Pakistanis at bay. The setting sun was directly in the pilots' eyes as they overflew Jammu, the foothills seemingly rising out of the ground. Dahar could see the glistening waters of the Manawar Tawi and the pall of smoke that hung like a canopy above Chhamb.

Just then Dahar spotted another aircraft in the sky. He promptly peeled off to investigate while the other three lined up to attack ground targets. The number of tanks and other fighting vehicles in the target area was mind-boggling. Not aware of the actual ground situation, it was natural for the leading aircraft to hone in and attack the easternmost targets, assuming that they were the vanguard of the attacking forces. Dahar, in the meantime, had closed in on the other aircraft which he realized was an Indian Twin Otter. Breaking contact, he rejoined the formation.

The forward position of 3 Mahar was still holding out when all eyes turned heavenwards at the sound of the approaching aircraft. Watching from his Brigade HQ, Manmohan Singh recognized the twin-tailed Vampires and heaved a sigh of relief. Seconds later his relief turned to horror as the first two Vampires seemed to attack the area where 3 Mahar and some of the remaining tanks of 20 Lancers were deployed. Suddenly, the aircraft were strafing the Mahar trenches, their cannon fire combined with the roar of the jet engines was terrifying. More chaos followed as the other two Vampires repeatedly went after our own positions.

By then the Vampires had spotted the Pattons, and they turned their attention to them. Almost immediately, a hail of anti-aircraft fire arced into the sky to meet the oncoming planes. One of the Vampires started trailing smoke and, despite the low altitude, Pathak managed to bail out and his aircraft hit the ground in a ball of fire. Having expended their ammunition, and the time allotted to them (time over target), the remaining three Vampires then set course for home.

Mainly due to the last-minute scramble to go to the army's rescue, even the IAF Air Defence Centre at Amritsar, 230 SU, had not been told that the Vampires were being launched in a ground attack role in the vicinity of Chhamb. The first indication came when Wing Commander Krishna Dandapani's Soviet-manufactured P.35 radar scope had shown the four blips heading north from Pathankot. He had then watched as two more blips appeared on his scope, as F-86 Sabres were scrambled by the PAF. Dandapani's screen was now showing multiple aircraft and, as per the laid down procedure, he called the local sector army commander and warned him of the presence of hostile aircraft. The information, which would have been invaluable for the four men heading into battle, simply could not be passed on.

Squadron Leader Aspi Kekobad Bhagwagar was supposed to lead the third wave, but he had swapped positions with Flight Lieutenant (later Wing Commander) Farokh Jehangir Mehta, who was night qualified as the third wave of Vampires would only be landing after the sun had set. Part of Bhagwagar's formation, that comprised Flight Lieutenants Satish Bharadwaj, Vijay Madhav Joshi, and Wishnu Mitter Sodhi, had been seen by the PAF's Squadron Leader Sarfraz Ahmed Rafique and his wingman, Flight Lieutenant Imtiaz Bhatti.

From the ground, it seemed like a hopeless situation. However, as Rafique went after the leading two Vampires, the two tailing, instead of breaking off and escaping, immediately tried to get behind the vastly superior F-86. In the melee that followed, the two leading Vampires were shot down by Rafique, and Bhatti shot down a third. Bhagwagar, Bharadwaj, and Joshi did not stand a chance. Though Sodhi was also engaged by Bhatti, he managed to dive down into the trees and make good his escape. Their fuel running low, the Sabres then exited the area, shortly after which Mehta's formation, completely oblivious of what had transpired, reached the target area. In the fading light, there was more mayhem, for though the army never actually gave out details of what happened, it is believed the Vampires and the subsequent four waves of Mystères between them shot up three of their own AMX-13s and blew up the trucks carrying much needed ammunition for Bhaskar Roy and his boys.

Even the Mystère IVA, primarily a ground attack aircraft, was no match for the Sabre, but its superior speed allowed it to break contact and avoid getting into a mismatched dogfight. Wing Commander Jimmy Goodman, commanding 31 Squadron, led the first of the four Mystère strikes. The area was lit up by fires caused by the Vampires, and each formation had adequate ordnance and fuel to make as many as six passes over the target area. Quite obviously, for the participating pilots from 31 and 3 Squadron, the fireworks below would have been spectacular. Goodman was to say later 'Our boys were in like a flash and in no time the whole place was ablaze with burning tanks and vehicles...the enemy will never forget the Mystere.'[23]

Tragically, nor would the Indian troops who had also been at the receiving end. Among those who had been hit was Charlie Squadron of 20 Lancers that had, on that fateful first day of Operation Grand Slam, disabled nearly twenty Pattons and significantly stalled the Pakistani advance. Some of these Pakistani tanks, already battle casualties, had also been subject to air attacks, adding to the IAF's overall tally. Flight Lieutenant (later Air Vice Marshal) C. S. Doraiswamy, who was a part of the second wave of Mystères, would ruefully say twenty-seven years later, 'We had very sketchy information. We were told the Pakistanis had overrun the entire area between Jaurian and Akhnoor, so we hit everything we saw. Amidst the glow from burning tanks, we had milliseconds to scan for additional targets.'[24] Interestingly, the PAF, after the initial scramble, did not interfere with the subsequent raids.

Alpha Squadron, led by Second Lieutenant (later General) Shankar 'Chow' Roychowdhury[25] finally broke through to provide relief in the early hours of 2 September. By this time Charlie Squadron was down to three tanks and had suffered severe casualties. Chow recalls smashing through sugarcane fields and seeing Bhaskar Roy's upturned tank smouldering. Convinced Roy was 'finished', he implored his driver to search for bodies. He then saw those familiar, heavy-rimmed glasses peer over the other side of the tank and a hoarse voice say, quite peeved, 'Chow, what took you so long—I need a ride and do you have any bloody cigarettes?'[26]

MAYHEM AT AKHNOOR

At dawn on 2 September, the focus was on the Akhnoor Bridge that spanned the Chenab. As per Malik's original plan, it was to have been captured by 1200 hours the previous day, but due to the stubborn resistance put up by elements of 6 Sikh LI, 3 Mahar, and Charlie Squadron of 20 Lancers, the Pakistanis were still on the other side of the Manawar Tawi. Though the bulk of 191 Infantry Brigade had withdrawn, Manmohan Singh and his Brigade HQ was still 'where [they] had chicken the day before.'[27] 6 Rajput was holding a defensive role around the iron bridge which also had a few anti-aircraft guns deployed around it. Second Lieutenant Govindji Mishra was positioned on the approach to the iron structure and his orders were to not let anyone cross the river so as to keep the bridge clear for reinforcements.

Shell-shocked soldiers, mainly PAP and 3 JAK Militia, were coming in ones and twos, most of them looking more like refugees than soldiers and their numbers swelled through the night. Almost all of them would silently stare at their comrades from 6 Rajput blocking their way, their eyes reflecting the horror of the last twenty-four hours. They had to be marshalled away from the bridge and the road kept clear. However, as their numbers grew, they began to find a voice, and were soon clamouring for help. Neither Mishra or anyone else for that matter could do anything despite the pleas. The Rajput langar then got into the act, the battalion cooks producing hot food for the dazed and starving men.

As the morning progressed, F–86 Sabres attacked the bridge but the anti-aircraft guns kept them at bay. All this while, HQ 15 Corps kept calling on the field telephone line, wanting a minute-by-minute commentary of what was happening. After humouring them for a while, Mustasad Ahmad told the battalion exchange not to put the Corps HQ through. He had other things to do.

The anticipated thrust from the Pakistanis towards Akhnoor did not come that morning. When someone asked Manmohan Singh what they could do, given the paucity of troops to defend Akhnoor, the brigade commander replied, 'Don't worry...they will not attack immediately. They will consolidate.' Seeing the sceptical look on the other officer's face, Manmohan Singh laughed and added, 'They've read the same training manuals as us.'[28]

Having launched Operation Grand Slam with such ferocity, the subsequent developments on the Pakistani side remain a mystery. Three things happened which seemingly knocked the wheels off their grand strategy of running through to Akhnoor on the first day. One, the Indians stubbornly fought back. Perhaps a victim of their own propaganda, Malik seemed to believe that to win the war, all the Pakistanis needed to do was just show up at a designated spot. The fireworks display put on by the massed artillery combined with the advancing Tank Destroyers (M36B2) and Pattons were expected to send the Indians scampering. Two, the Pakistan high command did not expect the IAF to jump into the fray. Unfortunately, the fact that four Vampires hit Indian positions as well before they were shot down has overshadowed their impact on the overall situation. The very fact that three waves of Mystères went in hard on the tail of the Vampires and inflicted serious damage on the exposed Pakistanis also caused the collapse of the Pakistanis' plan. Three, Pakistan's leadership was suddenly seized with a mad desire to play musical chairs.

In the history of warfare, many decisions have been taken which are unorthodox. Some are bold decisions, some are timid; some work brilliantly, some result in complete disaster; but, in almost all cases, there is a chain of thought that is discernible when examined in hindsight. However, what happened on the night of 1 September not only defies logic, various explanations by those who were involved in it have only further muddled the issue: for all practical purposes, Major General Akhtar Hussain Malik, GOC Pakistan's 12 Division, was removed from the command of Operation Grand Slam!

General Mohammad Musa, the Pakistan army chief, later tried to defend the indefensible: 'The change of command in the Chhamb valley was pre-arranged. It was not an after-thought. As commander of our troops in Azad Kashmir Akhtar Malik knew the area and enemy dispositions there, having directed sporadic and minor border skirmishes against them in the region before the guerrilla war was waged. And, as we intended to launch the counter-offensive from within Azad Kashmir and as soon as possible, I felt he should be in command of the initial phase of it (up to Manawar Tawi River). The new commander, not knowing the area as well as he did, might have pleaded for more time than the latter needed, to get himself acquainted with it. Beyond river Tawi, it would have been unsound to allow Akhtar Malik to get involved in the fighting opposite Akhnoor on the extreme right flank of an extensive, hilly area stretching over several hundred miles for which he was responsible. His return to his main headquarters was an imperative operational necessity, and was, therefore, catered for in our plan.'[29]

This makes little sense. More likely, and Pakistan had demonstrated this thinking at Sardar Post and later the attack on Chhad Bet in the Rann of Kutch, if the Indians did not break and run for cover at the sight of the advancing Pakistani tanks, then they did not seem to have an alternate plan.

The question that most people in Pakistan ask is, why did Ayub Khan change commanders halfway, when troops were literally mid-stream across the Tawi? If he had been allowed to stay in command, could Akhtar Hussain Malik, the 'rampaging' GOC of 12 Division, have actually wrung India's neck? There are many opinions expressed on the first question, the most popular being that Malik was Ahmadiyya, which is a sect that is considered to be un-Islamic and that Ayub did not want Malik to grow too big for his boots.

Another theory suggests Ayub never intended to really go for Akhnoor. As had been the case in the Rann of Kutch, it was supposed to be a flurry of punches, after which he expected that India would be all too eager to come to the negotiating table. Ayub was still playing the game by a set of rules that seemed to have been set by the international community and the expected meek response from India. T. C. A. Raghavan, who served as India's high commissioner in Pakistan, felt all the talk of Malik being an Ahmadiyya was of no consequence, for Ayub was too secular in his outlook for that to have even crossed his mind. He too felt that the Rann of Kutch model, jab and then negotiate, would have been Ayub's approach.

As to the second point, if Pakistan had kept the momentum of the first day's fighting going and had not opted for a change of command, could they have got the upper hand? This is also a case of wishful thinking. The Indians were outgunned and outnumbered in Akhnoor, but they had shown resoluteness in defence. Major Bhaskar Roy's MVC was one of the most deserved, for he successfully inspired his squadron of AMX tanks to stand their ground and fight the Pattons. Pakistan's delay in resuming the assault certainly gave the Indians a breather.

The answer in all probability has to do with the Bhutto–Malik equation. At that point in time, Operation Gibraltar was not being seen as a failure despite the fact that the Indians had taken Haji Pir and the surrounding heights, cutting off escape routes. Most of the infiltrator columns were expected to be self-contained and capable of surviving off the land. From Pakistan's perspective, the local Kashmiri population had not as yet risen against India as had been expected, but should Operation Grand Slam succeed, it was reasonable to expect a major upsurge in support.

If Pakistan had pushed beyond Akhnoor, that would have created a monster that Ayub Khan could not possibly control. It is worth remembering that it was, after all, Ayub Khan's suggestion that Malik go for Akhnoor so that Pakistan would have a knife to India's throat. Had the bridge on the Chenab at Akhnoor fallen, Pakistan would have been able to dictate terms. Fighting northwards ran the risk of getting into a battle of attrition with the Indians, a scenario where the Indians usually came out on top.

However, it is unlikely that Ayub was thinking that far ahead. The capture of the Akhnoor Bridge would have catapulted Malik and Bhutto's reputation into a league that would have matched that of Muhammad Ali Jinnah. Ayub had already let the articulate Bhutto shape Pakistan's foreign policy and there was a real danger of the ruthless foreign minister turning on the military government once his purpose had been served. Malik had already put all his eggs in Bhutto's basket. It was too dangerous a combine and something drastic had to be done.

General Musa's claim that Malik was to be in command only for the initial thrust is ridiculous. The Pakistani army chief, who in all probability was not even consulted by Ayub when the decision was taken, could only offer feeble excuses, none of which appear sound. The other excuse put forward by Musa for a change of command was that Malik's communication network was inadequate for him to exercise control over a large frontage.

As the Pakistanis waffled and failed to move on 2 September, the Indians were beginning to feel increasingly optimistic. On the larger front, the infiltrators had been more or less contained in the Valley and though they continued to pose a threat in the Poonch–Rajouri–Naushera sector, with the capture of the Haji Pir Bulge, things seemed to have shifted in India's favour. Both the senior generals believed that the infiltrators in the Kashmir Valley were badly trapped, their main routes of ingress having shut behind them. As far as the Chhamb Sector was concerned, 191 Brigade had fallen back on Akhnoor while 41 Mountain Brigade commanded by Brigadier M. R. Rajwade had used the Pakistani delay to advantage and deployed two battalions—9 Mahar and 1/8 GR—on the Troti high ground to the immediate north of Jaurian. The brigade's sappers also hurriedly laid out a minefield that extended from the Sudan Di Dhok to Chak Bhagwana along the western bank of the Thindewali Khad.

On the morning of 3 September, the Pakistanis finally shook off their inertia and began to move forward from their bridgehead, established on the east bank of the Manawar Tawi short of Palanwala. Pakistan's 10 Brigade commanded by Brigadier Azmat Hayat began to move forward along two prongs with two squadrons of tanks belonging to 13 Lancers, but the ground east of the Tawi was boggy and the tanks found the going difficult. A third squadron was also sent up to expedite the move, but the moment the Pakistanis crossed Palanwala, they came under fire from screen positions set up by Rajwade's 41 Brigade. The Pakistani advance, despite its potent firepower support, was in sharp contrast with the 'shock and awe' tactics that had been adopted by them just two days before against the border posts.

The southern Pakistani prong, which was to have captured Nawa Hamirpur, also took longer than expected and, as a result, Pakistan's 14 Punjab failed to get to Man Chak, the objective that was to the south of Jaurian. Watching the Pakistanis make their way cautiously forward, by the evening of 3 September, Rajwade was confident he could hold out against the attack on Jaurian. By then he had 20 Lancers less a squadron dug into defensive positions along with skilfully sited RCL guns. 161 Field Regiment, the brigade's artillery support, had also been reinforced by a battery of 38 Medium Regiment.

However, it was obvious 41 Mountain Brigade could only delay, and not stop the Pakistani advance, and orders were issued by Harbakhsh Singh for the brigade to fall back on Akhnoor later in the evening on 4 September. The men, who had been on their feet for more than forty-eight hours, were close to exhaustion. Despite that, through the night of 3/4 September, all Pakistani attempts to probe and even bypass the brigade's defences were unsuccessful. In the morning, 6 FF joined 13 Lancers and at 1130 hrs the Pakistanis launched a full-fledged attack on Troti Heights. The Indians defended resolutely, and eventually the attack was called off.

In the meantime, 15 Corps had ordered Brigadier Prithipal Singh's 28 Infantry Brigade to take up a delaying position on the Fatwal Ridge, 6 miles from Akhnoor, by first light on 4 September, the apprehension being that 41 Mountain Brigade might not be able to hold its position at Jaurian. The formation consisted of three infantry battalions—2 Grenadiers, 5/8 GR, and 1/1 GR. Prithipal Singh's brigade had been placed under the newly constituted HQ 10 Infantry Division the previous day, and they were now tasked with covering both the Kalith–Kaink–Akhnoor and the Jaurian–Akhnoor axes with 2 Grenadiers and 5/8 GR. 1/1 GR was deployed further to the north at Chauki-Chaura where, along with 3 JAK Militia, 9 Punjab, and 3 Mahar, it was holding the higher ground. After last light, as 41 Mountain Brigade leapfrogged past the new defences on the Fatwal Ridge, and withdrew to Akhnoor, 20 Lancer's remaining eleven AMX-13 tanks were to take up a supporting position with 28 Infantry Brigade.

Unfortunately, 161 Field Regiment, which was in support of Rajwade's brigade, suddenly came face to face with advancing Pattons and the gunners lost their nerve and the regiment scattered, abandoning their guns and vehicles in the process. When news of the disaster permeated through to the higher headquarters, a furious Harbakhsh Singh ordered GOC 10 Infantry Division, Major General Dharam Bir Chopra, to do everything he could to recover the guns, the loss of which was totally unacceptable.

The shaken battalion, sent back at night, failed miserably and the incident would cast an ugly shadow over the otherwise creditable performance of 41

Mountain Brigade, for Troti Heights and Jaurian finally fell only at 0900 hrs on 5 September.[30]

The focus now shifted to the Fatwal Ridge, the last geographical defensible feature before the Chenab narrowed in at Akhnoor. The Pakistani advance, though dramatically slowed, could not be stopped indefinitely given the quantum of troops available to defend the sector. During the night of 5/6 September, 6 FF and 14 Punjab launched multiple attacks on 28 Brigade's defences, but Prithipal Singh's men tenaciously held on. By the evening of 6 September, Pakistan's 10 Brigade had taken a defensive posture in and around Sauli Chak. By 6 September, the 102 Brigade Group had only reached the western bank of the Mawawali Khad, with 9 Punjab having captured Gopiwala and Jamotian while 8 Baluch had taken Kanger.

India's decision to open the Lahore front on 6 September was shocking to the Pakistani high command. Within a couple of hours, GHQ had issued orders for the immediate withdrawal of Artillery 4 Corps and 11 Cavalry from the Chhamb Sector, to move post-haste to Sialkot. To add to their discomfiture, the Indians quickly went from the defensive to the offensive, launching attacks on the night of 6/7 September on the Troti Heights, and the Kalit–Mandiala and Chhamb crossings. These attacks, that were more to signal intent rather than capture lost ground, were unsuccessful. For Pakistan, Operation Grand Slam that had started with a pyrotechnical display of firepower with the assurance that Akhnoor would fall in a couple of hours had ended as a damp squib. On 7 September, GHQ also withdrew 10 Brigade, leaving just the one brigade and 13 Cavalry to hold the ground that had seen so much blood shed by both sides.

Both sides then more or less settled down where they were on the evening of 6 September. 28 Infantry Brigade with 6/5 and 5/8 GR, and 191 Brigade comprising 6 Rajput and 15 Kumaon—both supported by AMX-13 tanks of 20 Cavalry—on the night of 9/10 September once again tried to dislodge the Pakistanis from the Jaurian Heights, and the Chhamb and Mandiala crossings, but failed to make any headway. On 10 September, Rajwade's 41 Mountain Brigade was pulled out of Akhnoor and handed over to 11 Corps. The ground situation would remain as it was until the ceasefire on 23 September.

BOOK IV

All Out War

Chapter 11

SABRE SLAYERS

THE AIR BATTLE (PART I)

On the morning of 2 September, there was a pall of gloom over Pathankot as the reality of war hit home. Four Vampires having gone down the previous evening, the IAF had got off to a disastrous start. For the fighter pilots, the loss of their comrades notwithstanding, it had to be business as usual. Two Mystères from 31 Squadron, Wing Commander (later Air Commodore) William Macdonald Goodman in the lead with Flight Lieutenant (later Wing Commander) Chandrakant Nijanand Bal as his wingman, got airborne to do a battlefield assessment over Chhamb. Since there were no air defence fighters that morning, four Mystères also got airborne to provide cover. However, two of the Mystères returned to base shortly after take-off.

Goodman set course for Akhnoor and the four aircraft adopted the staggered line abreast formation. The two lead aircraft were flying at low level abreast of each other, with Flight Lieutenants (later Air Marshal) Trilochan 'Tango' Singh and (later Air Vice Marshal) Chandra Sekhar 'Doru' Doraiswamy trailing behind by a kilometre, the gap between the two trailing aircraft being slightly wider. As they reached Akhnoor, Bal spotted four Sabres orbiting the battle area but he kept quiet, for he felt they posed no immediate danger. However, Tango, trailing behind, spotted two more Sabres circling overhead. Four were at low level while two aircraft were above them providing air cover. Tango immediately called out a warning on the radio.

Goodman realized the low flying Mystères would be sitting ducks, and decided to abort the mission before they were spotted by the Pakistanis. They put in a hard turn to the left, and all four aircraft made a beeline back to Pathankot, with Doraiswamy bringing up the rear. 'I don't know about the others, but I was crapping my overalls,' he recalled later. 'As the tail-end Charlie, having to look behind me, the last thing I wanted was to go into the ground.'[1]

Fortunately for the Mystère formation, the Sabres had failed to notice them. The Pathankot station commander, Group Captain Roshan Lal Suri, had next planned a fresh Vampire strike with Mystères as escorts against the Pakistani armoured thrust, but it was called off as it was obvious these missions could not be flown without either Gnat or Hunter escorts to deal with PAF interceptors. Accordingly, Air HQ decided to move two detachments of four Gnats each belonging to 23 Squadron to Pathankot immediately and a third detachment was told to move to Amritsar.

Wing Commander (later Air Marshal) Subramaniam Raghavendran commanded the squadron that was based at Ambala. For months, 23 Squadron had been training its pilots in aerial combat and had evolved the IAF's own Fighter Combat Leader course. Present in Ambala doing a staff job at the time was Squadron Leader (later Air Marshal) Johnny William Greene, who was an old hand on the Gnats and had done the prestigious RAF's Fighter Combat Leader course. Raghavendran asked Greene to move to Pathankot with a detachment consisting of Squadron Leaders Trevor Joseph Keelor and Amarjit Singh 'Kala' Sandhu[2] and Flight Lieutenant (later Group Captain) Mohan 'Manna' Murdeshwar. Raghavendran himself took a second detachment to Amritsar.

A third detachment of 23 Squadron being commanded by Squadron Leader (later Air Marshal) Brijpal Singh 'Siki' Sikand, consisting of Flight Lieutenant (later Group Captain) Virendra Singh 'Pat' Pathania, and Flying Officers Srinivasapuram 'Kicha' Krishnaswamy and Amerjit Singh Gill,[3] was at Halwara and it was ordered to immediately move to Pathankot. Greene's formation followed, getting airborne from Ambala at 1745 hrs. Hugging the ground to avoid radar detection, they landed in Pathankot at last light. Their kit and ground crew was to follow in a transport aircraft. With none of the aircraft showing up on their radar scopes during their move, the PAF was unaware of the arrival of the Gnats at Pathankot.

Though Sikand was senior to Greene, he let the latter take command in deference to his greater experience with fighter combat tactics. With no spare rooms available at the base, the pilots rested on cots in the open. After dinner, they filed into the briefing room where the operations in-charge got straight to the point. 'We want you to shoot down the Sabres. How you do it is your problem, but the Sabres will have to be tackled.'[4] Greene then took over the briefing. It would be a classic baiting mission where a formation of Mystères would get airborne at dawn. They would be followed by the Gnats, who would remain at treetop level. Once the Amritsar SU had detected the incoming Sabres, the Mystères would break away and the Gnats would then engage them.

Throughout the day, unlike the Pakistani ground forces who failed to move forward in the Chhamb Sector on 2 September, the PAF did not sit idle. It flew thirty-six Sabre and five Starfighter sorties as combat air patrols (CAP) in the Jhelum–Muzaffarabad area, launching the F-86 Sabres in pairs, except for one formation of four aircraft that had failed to detect Goodman's formation, thanks mainly to Tango's spotting skills. In addition, Sabres in a ground attack role had attacked various targets in the Chhamb–Jaurian sector, in the process hitting various civilian buildings, including a mosque at Jaurian. A vehicular convoy also got severely hit by the marauding Pakistani aircraft which were more or less unopposed through the day.

At 0700 hrs on 3 September, two Mystères flown by Goodman and Flying

Officer Tajinder Singh Sethi from 31 Squadron got airborne. Imitating the Vampire strike, they flew north as had been the standard practice and headed towards the Akhnoor Bridge at 1,500 feet above ground level (AGL), and then turned left towards Chhamb, all the time staying within Indian airspace. As anticipated, the Mystères were picked up by Pakistani radar, but the low-flying Gnats were not showing on their scopes. Within minutes, 230 SU, the Indian radar at Amritsar, picked up the blips of four Sabres and two Starfighters vectoring on to the Mystères.

The first Gnats led by Greene with Murdeshwar as his wingman were flying in a four-finger formation at approximately 300 feet AGL. Sikand and Pathania made up the other section. Trailing behind them, maintaining an even lower altitude, was Keelor with Krishnaswamy as his wingman, followed by Sandhu and Gill. As they approached Chhamb, the Mystères, having shown themselves, turned hard right and departed the scene, hugging the low hills and setting course for Pathankot. The eight Gnats, however, continued on course, maintaining a speed of 400 knots plus at low level. With the Mystères out of the way, Greene gave the command and pulled back on his stick, pulling the formation up. The voice of Krishna Dandapani came on the air giving a running commentary about the enemy aircraft in the area—'Four Sabres and two Starfighters headed your way.'[5] Dandapani said the Pakistani aircraft were closing in at one o'clock but were still a few miles away.

Johnny Greene led the lead four aircraft into a tight climbing spiral to the starboard as the Pakistani aircraft closed in. Just as Dandapani was talking to the Indian formation, Pakistani radar controllers were vectoring the Sabres and the Starfighters towards the Indians, whom they believed to be either Mystères or Vampires. The first two offensive pairs in a CAP position were picked up by the Pakistani radar and the following defensive four were neglected as they followed 3,000 feet below and 1,500 yards behind in a high-level tactical formation. As a result, the four Sabres and one F-104 with missiles converged from inside the battle circle on to the lead Gnat; one F-86, unable to hold the curve of pursuit, flew into the sandwich between the two formations. It came from above and inside the turn, intent on the lead Gnats and right into the defensive section's ambit.

Krishnaswamy, Trevor's wingman, described the moment: 'We were about to turn when I saw a single F-86, higher and about a kilometre to the right. I reported and Trevor called for jettisoning the tanks, which we did. He went into hard right turn to follow the F-86, which by now was turning right. We had high overtake speed. I could see Trevor's guns blazing suddenly and the F-86 looming large turning right.'[6]

'It was magical,' Trevor would say later, 'there was simply no fear. Dandapani's voice had calmed whatever nerves if any...we were just focussed on what we had trained and trained ourselves to do. At that moment you don't think, you just do.'[7] The F-86 Sabre was dead ahead and Trevor slammed the throttle to close in fast, opening fire with his twin 30 mm cannon at approximately 450 yards, closing in to 200 yards. 'I could see the shells hitting and the Sabre's right wing seemed to disintegrate. It flipped over and seemed to go into an uncontrollable dive.'[8]

Krishnaswamy went on to add, 'I then saw distinctly white smoke emerging from the side of its fuselage. He took off bank a bit. Our overtake speed was high; I used airbrake to control but my leader [Trevor] was pulling away. I steadied and fired a very short burst (7 to 10 rounds) on the target estimated some 300 yards. During this, I asked if I should press on the attack. I did not hear any reply. I could see my leader far to the right in a very tight turn and much lower. I zoomed up to control overtake and saw the F-86 losing height rapidly in a lazy turn descending spiral to the left; I saw my leader far right and low. I decided to join him and cover his tail.'

The first dogfight between the Gnats and the Sabres had other equally dramatic moments. Just as Trevor and Krishnaswamy spotted the lone F-86 Sabre, Sikand, the right lead section in Johnny Greene's four-aircraft formation, spotted the Sabres above him as well. Sikand called out on RT: 'Sabres, one o'clock high, hard right, up', and turned hard right into a climbing turn, bringing him head-on to the Sabres. 'Thereafter, I was involved in a melee with one of them. As I turned, [I initially] thought the rest of the other aircraft would have also pulled along with me but I did not see any other aircraft and found myself alone. The Sabre I was involved with suddenly dived down. I followed him, trying to close onto him. At this point, I called "Pat [my wingman], are you with me?"' There was no answer. I looked around and did not find anybody; I was all alone and realized my RT had packed up. Apparently, no one had heard my calls.'

Pathania had also spotted the Sabres and realized they were trying to put themselves behind Greene's wingman, Murdeshwar. Pathania called out a warning about the incoming Sabre to Murdeshwar. Greene called for a defensive break as the Gnat formation broke into a steep turn to port. Just then the number three pilot, Sikand, broke in the opposite direction and separated from the main formation. Pathania didn't see Sikand go, intent as he was on 'a motherless turn.'[9] He had seen the two Sabres and, though there was an F-104 hanging around above them, decided to go after them. As Pathania closed in on the Sabres, the Starfighter successfully manoeuvred itself to threaten Pathania who was without a wingman and had his tail exposed, thereby thwarting any attempt by the Gnat to fire at the Sabres. Pathania then had to break contact and, with his fuel state at critically low levels, set course for Pathankot.

The other six aircraft regrouped. Murdeshwar also had a problem with his RT for though he could receive incoming transmissions, he could not transmit. He had been in the perfect position to warn Pathania of the incoming Starfighter that eventually broke up his attack, but could not do so. At another point in the dogfight, Krishnaswamy, the youngest pilot in the squadron, had thought his days were numbered when a Starfighter got on his tail. Fortunately, the Pakistani pilot overshot him, presenting a perfect target. Before Krishnaswamy could gather his wits and open fire, the opportunity was gone and the Starfighter slipped away.

Greene's plan to lure the PAF into attacking them was audacious, for the trap set was executed at maximum range. Apart from problems of range, it was believed that the radar coverage beyond Jammu was erratic. The Gnat also had a problem with its guns that frequently jammed. Both the 30 mm cannons were placed on the inlet walls by the side. They were so designed that the links joining the shells together in a belt were deposited in the ammunition box on the other side after firing. 'Instead of falling out into the sky, they travelled across a cross-feed before depositing themselves in the ammo box of the other gun. So when one gun refused to fire, the other gun also stopped firing.'[10]

Greene was aware of these shortcomings, but he knew the Gnats had to show their ascendancy over the PAF and the only way to do that was by taking risks. In the euphoria of Keelor having bagged a Sabre, the fact that Krishnaswamy had fired at the stricken Pakistani aircraft became a footnote in the narrative of the five-minute dogfight. Those five minutes had seen an F-86 Sabre shot down while two others had been outmanoeuvred and forced to flee. The news made headlines all over India and Trevor Keelor became a household name overnight. More importantly, the Pakistanis realized that in spite of their much hyped supersonic aircraft, air-to-air missiles, and state-of-the-art radar systems, they were up against determined, well-trained, and highly motivated pilots of the IAF.

On the ground, their overalls wet with sweat, adrenaline still pumping, the pilots were shepherded towards the briefing room. The excitement was tempered by the loss of Sikand, who it was presumed must have crashed after he got separated from the rest of the formation. Aircraft at the time did not have any radar or navigational aids and pilots had to rely on their maps and a compass to find their way to and from any target. The standard procedure for aircraft operating in and around Chhamb was to complete their mission and then head east. The Pir Panjal range, running west to east was the obvious landmark, after which they followed the river systems and other landmarks to vector back.

Two vampires from 45 Squadron, flown by the CO, Squadron Leader Marshal Dahar, and the flight commander, Flight Lieutenant K. D. Mehra, got airborne to look for Sikand, hunting for the wreckage along the route taken by the Gnats. They were unable to find anything and returned to Pathankot.

Unknown to the Indians, after disengaging with the lone Sabre, a disoriented Sikand started heading east but got further confused when he saw two more Sabres flying in the opposite direction. Alone, lost and running low on fuel, he overflew a river and saw an airfield, where he landed. Within minutes, a Pakistani Rangers jeep pulled up and before he could even think of spiking his aircraft,[11] he was a prisoner of war. Sikand's Gnat was refuelled and flown from Pasrur to Peshawar by Flight Lieutenant Sadd Hatmi of the PAF. He had earlier flown the Gnat in the UK.

BOGEYS IN THE SKY

On 4 September, Pathankot continued to be the hub of all the air activity on the Indian side. With the Pakistan Army renewing its assault against Jaurian, intercepted radio messages indicated that the PAF would be fairly active in a ground support role. After a rain delay in the morning, four Mystères led by Squadron Leader Anthony Louis 'Tony' Mousinho with Flight Lieutenant C. N. Bal as his wingman, Squadron Leader Bhagwan Fatehchand 'Kewal' Kewalramani as the deputy leader with Tango Singh as his wingman got airborne. They were escorted by a pair of Gnats while another six Gnats orbited near Jammu. Four Hunters and two MiG-21s covered Pathankot itself.

The Mystères had a clear run and the formation succeeded in doing considerable damage on the ground. Tony Mousinho shot up a couple of trucks, while Bal fired his rockets at ground troops. The second section followed but, unfortunately, Kewalramani's rocket pod malfunctioned. Tango, flying as number four, then lined up to fire at a tank, but aborted at the last minute. He had seen some tents whose layout indicated it was an important headquarters. He came in again and his rockets found their mark. There were subsequent claims that Pakistani newspapers reported the death of a major general in this air attack, but that seems to be unlikely.

More sorties were flown as the day went by. Four Gnats were engaged by two Sabres and two Starfighters. The Gnat pilots were gaining in confidence as they realized that even with drop tanks, they could fly circles around the F-86 Sabre and, in a clean configuration, could even take on the vastly superior F-104 Starfighter. During this engagement, six Sidewinder missiles were launched against Gill, but none homed in on him. Gill was to later remark they were so close to him as they whizzed past, he could 'literally see the USAF markings on the missiles'.[12]

At 1515 hrs a dozen aircraft got airborne. Four Mystères were escorted by four Gnats led by Keelor, that were followed by four more aircraft led by Greene, the formation consisting of Sandhu, Pathania, and Murdeshwar. As the Mystères, flying at 100 feet AGL, approached Akhnoor with Trevor 1,000 yards behind, they saw the Sabres flying in a circuit, attacking Indian gun positions. Deciding to stay with their own task of seeking out and destroying Pakistani ground targets, Trevor asked Greene's four Gnats to take on the Sabres.

The Sabre formation was closing in fast, and on Greene's signal, the Gnats launched into the Sabre circuit and all four aircraft got behind the Pakistanis who, until then, had not made visual contact. Greene got behind the first Sabre and fired a burst but his angle of attack was too high, so he broke away, leaving the field clear for Murdeshwar, who was coming in behind him. Positioning himself perfectly, Murdeshwar had the Sabre dead centre in his gyro gunsight. He pressed the trigger and his 30 mm guns fired a shell and then jammed! His gun camera, however, functioned perfectly and provided the perfect evidence that the Pakistani pilot was, from that moment onwards, leading a charmed life!

The other Sabres broke out of the pattern and tried to escape. Pathania latched onto the aircraft that went towards Akhnoor, firing three bursts at him before his guns jammed as well. The Sabre, flown by Flying Officer N. M. Butt, started to emit smoke and lose height. The Sabre was also simultaneously being engaged from the ground by Havildar Tata Pothuraja of 127 Air Defence Regiment who was manning a 40 mm L-30 anti-aircraft gun deployed near the Tawi Bridge near Jammu. The burning Sabre crashed near Akhnoor. Butt, according to Pakistani records, ejected, and was later picked up by a Pakistani helicopter.

Back in the air, monitoring Pathania's excited RT natter while closing in on the battle raging below, was Wing Commander (later Air Marshal) Malcom Shirley Dundas 'Mally' Wollen and Squadron Leader (later Group Captain) Arun Kanti 'Mukho' Mukherjee from 28 Squadron who were flying the latest MiG-21 (Type 76) equipped with K-13 missiles. They had been flying an offensive CAP over the same area when Amritsar SU vectored them towards the ongoing dogfight.

Hoping to lock on to a target themselves, the two MiGs dived down into the fray. In a few seconds they had honed in on a couple of aircraft but those turned out to be Mystères. As the MiGs turned away, two Sabres flying abreast of each other passed below and in front of them. Wollen put in a hard right turn, calling out to Mukherjee to follow him. The Sabres seemed to be heading back to base, for they were flying towards the northwest. 'With a good overtake speed, in a slight dive, I released a missile at around 1,200 metres, sighting through the "fixed-ring and bead"; the radar cannot provide information so close to the ground. The missile sped towards the Sabre and exploded below it; perhaps ahead and on the ground.'[13]

In his excitement, Wollen fired his second missile at the Sabre but he was much too close to the ground by then. After release, the K-13 is unguided for half a second, and as the aircraft was too low, the missile went into the ground. The older MiG-21s (Type 74) had cannons, but Type 76s were limited to missiles. Squadron Leader Muniruddin Ahmed, the pilot of the Sabre, was not destined to die that day. Mukherjee had got separated from Wollen when the latter had turned sharply, so he too could not respond to Wollen's call to shoot down Ahmed. A frustrated Wollen then 'engaged reheat, rapidly closed in on the Sabre, was tempted to brush against his fin and passed about 6 metres over the aircraft. Naturally, the PAF pilot was surprised/shaken.'[14]

Ahmed was more than shaken as the sleek MiG-21 glided past him. According to John Fricker in *Battle for Pakistan*, Muniruddin Ahmed called up Ground Control on the RT and stammered, 'B-B-B-B-By G-G-G-G-God, he nearly hit me.'[15]

Later in the evening, Keelor led a four-Gnat formation that escorted another four Mystères who, despite the heavy ack-ack fire, managed to search for targets. A fair number of armoured vehicles and Patton tanks had already been hit by the

Mystères. Yet another four-Gnat offensive sweep led by Greene also failed to find
any Sabres or Starfighters. If it hadn't been for guns jamming and had Wollen and
Mukherjee been flying Type 74s instead of Type 76s, the day's tally could have
been crippling for Pakistan. Equally importantly, Wollen's failure to shoot down
Ahmed held a major lesson for the IAF. 'The shortcomings of K-13 air-to-air
missiles against low flying targets as well as when fired into the sun was well
known, but it was experienced for the first time. This aspect would have to be
borne in mind for future engagements. It was also appreciated that Sidewinders
would have also similar limitations.'[16] More importantly, the mere presence of
MiGs in the sky above the Hunters and Gnats somewhat neutralized the threat
from the far superior Starfighters.

JAGGI NATH DOES AN ENCORE!

Wing Commander Jag Mohan Nath was an unusual man who performed the most
unusual tasks. With direct access to the chief of air staff, Nath was part of No. 106
SPR Squadron that flew the Canberra PR57. The squadron was commanded by
Wing Commander Mukund Ramchandra Agtey but, on most occasions, even he
was not privy to the exact task being undertaken by Nath.

Prior to the 1962 conflict with China, Nath used to regularly fly his unarmed
Canberra configured with photo reconnaissance (PR) cameras from Agra, cross over
the Great Himalayan and Karakoram ranges, the latter around the Karakoram Pass,
then fly up and down the Tsang Po valley photographing the PLA positions. Some of
his sorties extended beyond the Ladakh region to NEFA. Photographs taken by him
pinpointed every Chinese position and these images were regularly made available
to the CGS and the Western Army commander. The fact that the information
made available did not permeate beyond a few select individuals was indeed tragic,
for given the quality and detail of the images that Nath repeatedly obtained, the
Indians should not have been caught napping when the Chinese attacked on
20 October 1962. Despite the failure to effectively use Nath's photographs, the
Government of India had decorated him with a well-deserved Mahavir Chakra.

There was a feeling of déjà vu when, three years later, Nath was once again
required to perform a similar assignment. There was, however, one fundamental
change in the situation, which made the task even more challenging. Not once
during his many sorties into Tibet had the Chinese launched PLAAF aircraft against
Nath, and rarely was he faced with anti-aircraft or even ground fire. The situation
in West Pakistan was entirely different where 'all my missions were done at deck
level during daytime. To avoid being picked up by Pakistani radar one had to be
at treetop level, not more than 30 or 40 feet above the ground. At such extreme
low levels, one's field of vision was limited and navigation was really a question
of timing. When I got to an area I needed to photograph, I would accelerate to
maximum speed and then pull up to 12,000 feet where the cameras would be

switched on. The cameras were loaded with 20 by 36-inch negative film designed for high altitude photography. To avoid blurring due to [high] speed, one had to fly at 120 knots or so, after which one would dive down to treetop level, hoping radar hadn't picked you up. We had started doing these missions shortly after Operation Gibraltar was launched by Pakistan in Kashmir and it became obvious there was a good chance of a conflict.'[17]

On 5 September, Nath was surprised when he was asked to report to Air Commodore Keki Nadirshah Gocal, senior air staff officer, Western Air Command. This was a deviation from the usual procedure where Nath received his orders directly from Arjan Singh. His task was to photograph the Ichhogil Canal and see if there was any Pakistani military build-up in the area around Lahore. Two MiG-21s, flown by Wollen and Squadron Leader (later Air Vice Marshal) Amia Kumar 'Ladoo' Sen[18] were to support Jaggi Nath, but they were to stay on the Indian side of the border, only going to the Canberra's rescue if Pakistani aircraft came up to intercept it. The radar, 230 SU, which was usually Nath's last point of contact before entering Pakistani airspace, was kept out of the loop during this mission.

With Flight Lieutenant (later Group Captain) Gangadhar Ranganath Railkar as his navigator, Nath got airborne from Agra and entered Pakistani airspace near Pathankot at treetop level. Getting to the Ichhogil Canal, he did his usual zoom up to 12,000 feet and began flying in a south-westerly direction, photographing the canal and the area around it. 'We were over Pakistani territory for quite a while when Railkar said we were being tracked by air-to-air radar. We had the "Orange Putter" on the Canberra PR57 which was the air-borne radar tail warning system, and there were four blips showing on it.'[19] Having completed his mission, Nath started doing barrel rolls in case the Pakistani aircraft tried to get a lock on him to fire a Sidewinder. The blips disappeared but as he entered Indian air space, the Orange Putter came on again.

As the Canberra was heading back, Wollen and Sen were critically low on fuel, and had broken off and were preparing to land in Pathankot when Nath called for help. Despite Wollen's low fuel warning flashing, he immediately turned back to investigate. Unaware of Nath's identity, 230 SU had scrambled two Mystères to intercept what it thought was a PAF Canberra heading into Indian airspace. The Mystères were closing in fast and would have opened fire but the confusion was sorted out in the nick of time and 230 SU ordered the Mystères to break off. Wollen then landed in Pathankot with his engine flaming out on touchdown while Nath flew directly to Palam to process his precious film.

Jaggi Nath's sortie was at least forty-eight hours too late. The decision to go into Pakistan was formally taken on 3 September and even the most basic information about what lay on the other side of the border was not available. Army HQ asking for this sortie on 5 September underlines the complete and absolute ignorance displayed by General Chaudhuri in the integration of air assets into his plans. By the time Nath's detailed images were processed and made available, Indian troops were already fully committed, with no prior information available to them, even maps!

Since the COAS was so obsessed with secrecy that even his own army commander and principal staff officers were in the dark as to what he was thinking till the last minute, sending a Canberra to fly all along the Ichhogil Canal a few hours before H-hour bordered on sheer lunacy. Jaggi Nath, the air force, as well as the army were fortunate that Pakistani radar did not pick up Nath's signature on their screens. Or, if they did, they failed to intercept him.

Harbakhsh Singh's noting on PR sorties after the war is telling. 'There was a great need for photographic reconnaissance, especially of enemy troop dispositions of which vertical photo cover was required. Demands were made by all the corps. 1 Corps did not receive the results of their demands. 15 Corps did receive some photographs but only after the conflict was over. In the case of 11 Corps, two demands were met but both of them after a considerable delay.'[20]

Other than Nath's run along the Ichhogil Canal, the IAF had a comparatively quiet day. The weather was bad that morning and even though the situation on the ground in the Chhamb–Jaurian Sector was deteriorating, there were no demands for air strikes by the army. Despite the time lag between 191 Infantry Brigade asking for air support and actually getting it on 1 September, the mechanics of immediate air support continued to remain extremely poor. From the army's perspective, the selection of bomb lines and targets proved to be difficult 'because they were not easy to select on the ground and identify from the air in fast flying aircraft.'[21]

Nevertheless, though CAPs were flown through the day from Ambala, Halwara, and Adampur as well, the only strike formation consisting of four Mystères that got airborne from Pathankot was at 1500 hrs. Led by Jimmy Goodman with Flying Officer (later Air Marshal) Michael 'Mike' McMahon as his wingman, the other section consisted of Flight Lieutenant (later Air Vice Marshal) Vishnu Murti 'Roundy' Raina and Flying Officer Tajinder Singh Sethi. They were escorted by eight Gnats while MiGs provided top cover.

As usual the Mystères were at treetop height, getting to the target area without incident. Down below they spotted a squadron of Pakistani tanks crossing a small rivulet. Roundy Raina, number three in the formation, along with the rest of the Mystères 'pulled up and aimed for the tank with my SNEB rockets. I fired the salvo and, believe me, I got the thrill of my life. I flew over the completely destroyed tank and my aircraft shook due to the blast. The formation got a total of three tanks.'[22] With their rockets expended, the Mystères returned to Pathankot, refuelled and turned around their aircraft and flew one more mission. Later a photo reconnaissance mission was flown over the area by a Canberra that was escorted by four Gnats and two MiG-21s.

Though the IAF played a key role in delaying the Pakistani advance in the

Chhamb–Jaurian Sector, Harbakhsh Singh continued to have a fairly indifferent opinion towards the use of air power. His comments after the war are interesting to note, for this one factor perhaps influenced events more than anything else during the 1965 war. 'The figures given by the Air Force are obviously exaggerated. I feel that even the figures given by our formations are rather optimistic, especially in the case of enemy tanks and guns destroyed or damaged. In arriving at this conclusion, I have in mind the negligible damage caused to our guns and tanks by the Pakistan Air Force which appeared to be comparatively more active.'[23]

In his book, *War Despatches*, Harbakhsh quotes Air Vice Marshal Sondhi who wrote in the *Tribune* on 31 July 1968: 'The manner and circumstances in which the IAF went into action in 1965 to prevent the breakthrough in the Chhamb Sector by Pak infantry thrust, powerfully supported by Patton tanks, are illustrative not only of the political hesitation that delayed the decision on the employment of the air force until it was all but too late, but also exemplified the air force's half-hearted participation before the desperate reaction of the Pak Air Force led to an air war. The outstanding performance of individual pilots, marked as it was by skill, daring and patriotism, and the first-rate technical abilities of the ground crews won the admiration of the nation. But the IAF missed a rare opportunity to demonstrate more fully to the army that it exists otherwise than as a fighting service for its own good—that it has a vital role to play in massive and visible (and not only indirect) support of the army that can be decisive.'[24]

By the end of the day, Radio Pakistan had announced that the Azad Kashmir and Pakistani armed forces had captured Jaurian and it was anticipated that Akhnoor would be taken the next day.

Late in the evening, Keki Gocal had given all station commanders a list of targets for the next day. Almost all the tasks assigned were interdiction targets and 'comprised known and assessed locations of Pakistani formations and units—it can be safely assumed that this target list had been given by Western Command.'[25] By midnight, a flash message was received by all stations confirming that the army would be crossing the IB at 0500 hrs. The message reiterated that none of the Pakistani airfields were to be attacked unless cleared by the government.

A kind of anticipatory hush seemed to descend on all formations. In Pathankot, Adampur and other air bases, most crew rooms were deserted. At various formation headquarters, last-minute preparations were being made. The luminous dials of HMT watches all along the Punjab and Rajasthan borders were laboriously counting down the seconds. Troops were already on their way to their designated FUPs. The 'Shooting War' was about to begin.

Chapter 12

ICHHOGIL CANAL
11 CORPS (PART I)

ALL SYSTEMS GO!

The initial decision to launch the air force was taken by Chavan, India's defence minister, at around 1645 hrs. Permission had been given to cross the IB and launch an attack in the Punjab to relieve the pressure on Akhnoor and Chhamb. While the first part of the defence minister's 'go ahead' that related to the IAF was acted on within minutes, the army needed time to launch the attack.

According to Pradhan: 'It was later in the evening that he [Chavan] informed the ECC of the air strike and got the prime minister's formal authorization on orders given to the COAS to launch an attack on the Punjab front....As a footnote to history it is interesting to recall that at that time there were reports that it was the prime minister who unhesitatingly gave orders to retaliate. Chavan's diary throws light on what actually happened on the late afternoon of 1 September 1965 and his account is corroborated both by the then defence secretary and the chief of army staff.'[1]

This is likely a bit of deft footwork on the part of Pradhan to give Chavan more credit for his 'decisiveness'. General Chaudhuri had spoken with the prime minister on the telephone before taking off from Srinagar and had apprised him of the situation in Chhamb. There is no doubt that Chavan and Shastri had discussed the eventualities before meeting Chaudhuri. The defence minister would have known he had the full backing of his prime minister.

Pradhan then plays it safe. 'During his lifetime, Chavan never contradicted reports that it was Lal Bahadur Shastri who had ordered the retaliation on 1 September 1965. By 1965, Chavan had come closer to Shastri and admired the prime minister for his low key but determined leadership in dealing with Pakistan's venture in the Rann of Kutch. Throughout the conflict and until Shastri's death in Tashkent, the two worked together as a team.'[2] The decisions taken were duly conveyed to both the ECC and the prime minister, who then asked Chaudhuri 'to see him, discussed a few details and further approved the action taken'.[3]

Chaudhuri wanted to simultaneously launch both 1 and 11 Corps across the IB into Pakistan. However, he was so obsessed with secrecy that the date and time of the launch were hidden even from his own officers. 'Surprise was the most important ingredient of the plan and commanders of formations in 11 Corps were informed about D-Day so late that they had to hustle hard to reach their launch points. The underlying idea was to reach the objectives along the Ichhogil and consolidate positions before the Pakistani forces could react in strength against our troops.'[4]

However, despite all the precautions being taken by the COAS, Pakistan's high commissioner to India, Mian Arshad Hussain, sent a message through the Turkish Embassy that India was planning to attack Lahore on 6 September.[5] Until then, Pakistan had gone to great lengths to keep her troops away from the IB, primarily to avoid giving India an excuse to escalate the fighting in J&K into all-out war. However, even though Pakistan's GHQ was at the time focussed on Operation Grand Slam and trying to further build on 12 Division's initial thrust towards Akhnoor, reports had started coming in from 3 September onwards from their forward defences of increased Indian activity all along the Lahore and Kasur Sectors. While Zulfikar Ali Bhutto and the Foreign Office were still insisting that no move should be made without their concurrence, Pakistan's GHQ sent a flash signal at around 2200 hrs on the night of 4 September to all its subordinate units 'to take necessary defensive measures'. 'The ambiguity in the order led to different actions by different formations. Sutlej Rangers were fully alerted on 5 September to be ready against an Indian offensive but the move forward of army formations in Lahore, Kasur and Sialkot Sectors was tardy. A number of units and commanders were not in battle locations when the Indian Army struck across the border on 6 September in the Lahore Sector.'[6]

General Musa tries to give it another twist. 'On the evening of September 4, while working in our control room, my staff and I listened to the news broadcast by All India Radio…saying their prime minister had told the Lok Sabha that afternoon that there were indications that the Pakistan Army were moving forward from Sialkot towards Jammu. Although it came to us as a surprise, because no such move had even been contemplated by us at that time, the blatant lie proved our earlier assessment right and clearly indicated that, with the threat to Akhnoor mounting, Shastri had been persuaded by the top brass to invade Pakistan and that he was preparing the ground for it, internally and internationally. Consequently, I directed the Chief of the General Staff, without consulting the government, to get the army moved to its battle locations.'[7] The reality was very different—not only was Pakistan's military higher command caught completely off guard, so was its political leadership, neither of which had a clear idea about India's thinking.

OPERATION RIDDLE

The plans drawn up during Operation Ablaze for the Bari Doab were code-named 'Operation Riddle'. Lieutenant General Jogi Dhillon's 11 Corps consisted of 15 Infantry Division commanded by Major General Niranjan Prasad, 7 Infantry Division under Major General (later Lieutenant General) Har Krishen Sibal, and 4 Mountain Division commanded by Major General Gurbaksh Singh. Niranjan Prasad was tasked to advance on the Amritsar–Lahore axis along the Grand Trunk (GT) Road so that the main Pakistani defences were confined to the western bank of the Ichhogil Canal. Apart from capturing a large chunk of Pakistani territory in the initial advance, 15 Infantry Division was to capture and then defend three bridges over the Ichhogil; the first on the GT Road axis itself; the second on the Ranian–Ichhogil Road; and the third near Jallo. 7 Infantry Division, operating to the immediate south of 15 Infantry Division, was to advance on the Harike–Khalra–Barki–Lahore axis and capture the bridge over the Ichhogil near Barki, thereby clearing Pakistani defences and holding territory extending south along the canal down to Ferozepur. 4 Mountain Division was positioned immediately south of 7 Infantry Division, with the Khem Karan Sector being its responsibility. It was to get to the Ichhogil Canal and secure the territory on the east bank from Bedian Junction to Lohgarh, and destroy the bridge that linked Kasur to Khem Karan, as it was anticipated that the main Pakistani offensive would develop along the Kasur–Khem Karan–Ganda Singh Wala axis. 4 Mountain Division's primary role was to blunt this offensive.

Two independent brigade groups were also operating under the direct command of HQ 11 Corps. 29 Infantry Brigade under Brigadier Pritam Singh had earlier been a part of Sibal's 7 Infantry Division, but its three battalions—2 Madras, 2 Rajputana Rifles, and 1/5 Gorkha Rifles—had been delinked and given the task of capturing the Jassar Bridge to the northwest of Amritsar in the DBN Sector. On the southern extreme of 11 Corps' AOR, 67 Infantry Brigade Group under Brigadier Bant Singh comprising 14 Punjab, 2 MLI, 3/9 Gorkha Rifles, 4 (Independent) Armoured Squadron (from Mhow), 61 Cavalry, 144 Field Regiment TA, and two Rajasthan Armed Constabulary battalions were to defend Hussainiwala; contain any Pakistani bridgehead that might be established in the Sulemanki area; and stop any Pakistani ingress into the Ganganagar region from this direction.

96 Infantry Brigade under Brigadier V. N. Malhotra comprising 16 Dogra, 6 Kumaon, and 7 Punjab was to be the corps' reserve, as was 2 (Independent) Armoured Brigade under the command of Brigadier T. K. Theogaraj. Consisting of 3, 7, and 8 Cavalry, the brigade also had 1 Dogra, 1 Field Regiment (Self-propelled), and 74 Assault Field Company. Until August, 3 Cavalry had been on the ORBAT of 1 Armoured Division. 2 (Independent) Armoured Brigade until then only had light tanks, but the introduction of 3 Cavalry meant the brigade now had a regiment of Centurions. This proved to be a vital move on the part of the Indian higher command, for the Pakistanis were only expecting the older Shermans and the AMX-13s to oppose their offensive armoured thrust in the Punjab.

Theogaraj's brigade's deployment would depend on how things would unfold, but should it not be pressed into action, it was earmarked to destroy the expected Pakistani armoured thrust from the direction of Kasur. In addition, 11 Corps also had 21 (Independent) Artillery Brigade under the command of Lieutenant Colonel Sucha Singh comprising 60 Heavy Regiment, 40 Medium Regiment; 474 Engineer Brigade under Colonel R. M. Rao; 21 Communications Zone Sub Area with 166 Field Regiment; and, finally, three infantry battalions—19 Rajput, 2 Mahar, and 19 Maratha Light Infantry. 11 Corps TAC HQ moved from Jalandhar to Rayya, about 50 km to the northwest on GT Road.

On the Pakistan side, General Musa planned to defend the Lahore Sector with two divisions. At that time, Indian Intelligence had no idea whatsoever of the existence of 11 Division that was being commanded by Major General (later General) Abdul Hamid Khan[8]. The Indians believed Pakistan's 10 Division, headquartered at Lahore, was being commanded by Major General Sarfraz Ahmad Khan and comprised four brigades. In fact, Sarfraz Khan had only three—two brigades deployed to man the defences while the third brigade was in reserve as a strike formation. Both the divisions deployed in the Lahore Sector were under the direct command of GHQ as Pakistan, at that time, did not have a separate Corps HQ for the command and control of operations in this sector.

114 Brigade under the command of Brigadier (later Lieutenant General) Aftab Ahmad Khan[9] consisted of 16 Punjab, 3 Baluch, 11 Baluch along with Alpha Squadron 30 TDU (Tank Destroyer Unit) that was equipped with up-gunned Sherman tanks and Delta Company of 11 FF (R&S). Aftab Ahmad's area of responsibility was the Attari–Wagah axis, which meant defending the Ichhogil Canal from the southern shoulder of the North Siphon to RD 350 near village Dahuri. Artillery support was provided by 12 Field Regiment which was in direct support.

Brigadier Muhammad Asghar's 103 Brigade was holding the ground along the Ichhogil to the south with 12 Punjab, 17 Punjab, Delta Company of 15 Baluch, Bravo Squadron of 30 TDU, and Bravo Company of 11 FF (R&S). Brigadier Asghar's main task was to cover the Khalra–Barki axis. Both 114 and 103 Brigades had deployed the Sutlej Rangers and R&S elements ahead of their infantry to delay any Indian advance. No armour, or for that matter mines, had been deployed east of the Ichhogil Canal.

The reserve formation was 22 Brigade, commanded by Brigadier Qayyum Sher Khan[10] who had at his disposal 18 Baluch, 15 Baluch (less Delta Company), 23 Cavalry (a mix of Patton and Sherman tanks), Alpha Company of 11 FF (R&S), and 22 Field Regiment in direct support. The divisional artillery was being commanded by Brigadier Jamil Akhtar Aziz. One battery of 9X Medium Regiment was allotted to 114 Brigade, and two batteries were in support of the Khalra–Barki axis under 103 Brigade. 30 Heavy Regiment had two batteries supporting the former while one battery was in support of the latter. Both brigades also had one troop each of 91 (Independent) Heavy Mortar Battery.

After the Rann of Kutch conflict, the newly created ad hoc 11 Division had three infantry brigades that were responsible for the Kasur area: 21 Infantry Brigade was under the command of Brigadier Sahib Dad Khan and consisted of 5 FF and 13 Baluch; 52 Infantry Brigade had Brigadier S. R. H. Zaidi who had 2 FF, 7 Punjab, and 12 Baluch; 106 Infantry Brigade was under Brigadier Nawazish Ali who had 7 Baluch and 1 East Bengal Rifles (EBR) under his command; the three armoured regiments were 6 Lancers, 15 Lancers, and 32 TDU; the divisional artillery was under Brigadier S. D. K. Niazi and consisted of 26 and 38 Field Regiments.

Pakistan's GHQ had also allotted part of 1 Corps' reserve artillery to the newly raised 11 Division, which was expected to support 1 Armoured Division when it went on the offensive. As a result, 35 Heavy Regiment, one battery from 30 Heavy Regiment, 8-inch howitzer batteries, 37 Corps Locating Battery with the capability of pinpointing the position of enemy guns, and 3 Engineer Battalion that had three field companies but had no bridging material.

On the Indian side, right from the word go, the spotlight was going to be on 15 Division. The division was a new raising, having come into being in October 1964. Niranjan Prasad, its GOC, had had the dubious distinction of commanding 4 Mountain Division in NEFA when it disintegrated shortly after the Chinese launched an attack on the Indian positions on the Nam Ka Chu.[11] As Harbakhsh Singh also notes Prasad had been removed from command after that but, fortunately for him, the mess made by the higher commanders was such that he could paint himself a victim and appeal to President S. Radhakrishnan to reinstate him with honour.

The lessons from the 1962 skirmish with China had not been learnt. A major portion of the blame for that needs to rest on the shoulders of Defence Minister Chavan, who made it his mission to protect the political and military establishment. Though the president of India is the supreme commander of the armed forces, Radhakrishnan had morally exceeded his brief by supporting the reinstatement of Prasad. Given command of 15 Infantry Division, it was obvious to both his immediate superior officers, Jogi Dhillon and Harbakhsh Singh, that Prasad was not quite the man for the job. As Captain Amarinder Singh (who later became the chief minister of Punjab) notes in *The Monsoon War*, when he was the aide-de-camp to the Western Army commander, a meeting was held at the Ferozepur airfield sometime in July 1965. Generals Chaudhuri, Harbakhsh, and Dhillon discussed Niranjan Prasad's performance. He was then called in for a reprimand. At the end of the meeting, the COAS issued him a formal warning but he remained in command. In a private conversation later that day, the COAS remarked to the army commander that Niranjan Prasad had a great deal of influence amongst the powers that be in Delhi and that he should 'go easy on him'.

Despite the severe talking-to, problems persisted with Niranjan Prasad, who was called by Dhillon to his TAC HQ at Rayya on 4 September to be briefed personally. 'Due to the difference of opinion between the divisional and higher commanders, the finalisation of 15 Division's plan had taken time.'[12] Prasad was now tasked with advancing up to the east bank of the Ichhogil Canal from Bhaini–Malikpur to Jallo and the three bridges at Bhaini–Malikpur, Dograi, and Jallo had to be captured intact by last light on D-Day.

15 Division originally had three brigades, but Dhillon had taken Brigadier Malhotra's 96 Infantry Brigade and placed it directly under Corps HQ as a reserve formation. 54 Infantry Brigade was under the command of Brigadier Maha Singh Rikh[13] who in turn had 15 Dogra, 13 Punjab (Jind), and 3 Jat under him. Brigadier P. W. Pathak was commanding 38 Infantry Brigade, which had 3 Garhwal Rifles, 1/3 Gorkha Rifles, and 1 Jat (Light Infantry), while 14 Scinde Horse (Sherman Vs) was the division's armoured regiment. Direct artillery support was to be provided by 60 Heavy Regiment (7.2-inch howitzers).

THE CALM BEFORE THE STORM

In New Delhi, ever since the decision to go on the offensive across the IB in the Punjab had been taken by the government, all eyes had been on the developing situation on the Akhnoor front and on the attacks and counter-attacks in the air. In his diary, in which he noted events either the same night or the next day, Chavan records: '2 September: I got further details of the air strike in the morning. It has certainly escalated matters. But at the same time stabilized the conflict—perhaps temporarily in the Chhamb Sector; meeting of leaders of Opposition...made a report to them regarding latest development. They were in co-operative spirit; ECC Meeting—U Thant's report to the Security Council Members discussed. I insisted on military advantages being maintained. Those UK proposals look like a trap. Prime Minister appeared to be strong. I hope he maintains this attitude; *COAS came to unburden his mind—looked somewhat depressed.*'

On 3 September he noted the news about the successful air battle in Chhamb. 'COAS came in the evening. *He was in good mood.* He said he was sorry that he was somewhat depressed yesterday. I can understand this. He has to open his mind, pour it out somewhere. It is good he is doing with me; ECC meeting at 9 pm.'

Even as the army chief's morale was oscillating, diplomatic pressure was steadily building to de-escalate the situation. U Thant's message stated: '[There are] alarming reports indicating a steady escalation of the fighting in the air and on ground, involving regular forces on both sides.'[14] Chavan was determined to hold fast so that the Indian Army could execute the task that had been given to it. In what was perhaps the most critical meeting before full-scale war broke out, Shastri defined India's immediate war objectives to his defence minister, army, and air force chiefs: 'To defend against Pakistan's attempts to grab Kashmir by force and to make it abundantly clear that Pakistan would never be allowed to wrest Kashmir from India; To destroy the offensive power of Pakistan's armed forces; *and to occupy only minimum Pakistan territory necessary* to achieve these purposes which would be vacated after the satisfactory conclusion of the war.'[15]

Chavan's diary of 4 September laments the blunder in Chhamb. 'Real fight near Akhnoor bridge will have to be resolutely fought—otherwise it is going to be disaster for the army and the government—all efforts will have to be made to avert it. I propose to concentrate tomorrow on this; COAS came at 8.10 pm. Gave me the resume of the events in Chhamb last night and today. *He was rather depressed.* Discussed with him plans of the next move fixed for tomorrow.'

Chavan then adds: '*I think that is the step that will change the complexion of the entire situation. If we fail there—and I cannot even imagine of it—the Nation fails.*'[16]

On 5 September the thin line at Akhnoor had held. By the night of 5/6 September, all units of 11 Corps were moving forward to their launch points in the Punjab. 15 Infantry Division and 54 Infantry Brigade were being commanded by two men, who just three years previously, had faced the initial Chinese onslaught. While Maha Singh Rikh had held his ground and been injured, Niranjan Prasad had failed miserably. Now fate was giving them another chance!

Rikh had assumed command of 54 Infantry Brigade a year earlier in Amritsar. Like most infantry brigades, he had under his command three infantry units. As a part of the usual turnover of battalions, 3 Jat commanded by Lieutenant Colonel J. S. Mundy arrived from Sikkim to serve out its peacetime tenure as a part of the brigade. 'There wasn't the slightest inkling of a war in the offing when 3 Jat arrived at Khasa on 4 August 1965. The place was typical of the kind used to dump infantry battalions during their so-called peace tenures. The army's hierarchy and Military Engineering Services (MES) were satisfied that six cook houses, joined by a common drain that ran off sullage water to the wide open spaces nearby, and a well arranged complex of latrine seats were all that was basically necessary to make an infantry battalion comfortable.'[17]

Mundy was acutely aware that his battalion, coming down from Sikkim, was not equipped or trained to fight in the plains. Though the situation in Kashmir had flared up, no one seriously believed it would spill over into Punjab. Post Rann of Kutch, Indian officers knew that the American M-47/48 Patton tanks would be a major factor in combat against the Pakistanis especially where infantry soldiers were up against armour. A few commanding officers like Mundy were obsessed with training, pushing their men all the time. Apart from making them fire whenever they could, they pushed their men in an attempt to familiarize them with the weapon systems and night-time fighting conditions. But at the very basic level, the men had to be taught one of the most crucial aspects of warfare...the ability and need to dig, and dig, and dig!

These trenches were going to be the biggest tactical weapon available to each soldier. Pakistan's main strength was its artillery firepower and armour and the only way to survive that onslaught was for the infantry to go underground. This is because it's the splinters from the exploding shells that kill, and the chances of a direct hit on a trench is correspondingly lower. Pattons, all 30 tons of reinforced armour, could reduce infantry soldiers to mangled pulp in a matter of seconds, but a soldier in a slit trench might not only survive, he could emerge behind the tank and take it on with a Molotov cocktail.

'Take whatever ground cover is available, which will deter tanks from getting too close as they will not know how you are armed. Enemy tanks must never feel you can't hit back, keep shooting at them, even with your rifles,'[18] officers like Mundy and his second-in-command, Desmond Hayde, would repeatedly say. For battle inoculation, they would train by making their men huddle as deep down in their trenches as possible while trucks and other tracked vehicles would drive over them. From the moment 3 Jat arrived at Khasa, commanders, down to the section level, were sent out to become familiar with the terrain and other likely obstacles in the immediate front.

Then, of course, there were the RCL guns, the infantry soldier's reply to attacking armour. Getting familiar with these jeep mounted weapons and how to deploy and use them was to be one of the key factors of the war. All these factors would make all the difference. But 3 Jat was an exception, being one of the few rare exceptions where the battalion was in an area much before the outbreak of hostilities. The majority of the units, as we shall see, were rushed forward from their peace time locations and asked to fight in terrain where they had no idea what was in front of them, or for that matter, around them.

THE MOVE FORWARD

The IB opposite 15 Division ran roughly halfway between Attari and Wagah. Immediately after crossing the border on the Pakistan side, GT Road crossed over the out-of-use Upper Bari Doab Canal (UBDC). Six kilometres further in lay the twin villages of Gosal and Dial, 3 km after which, running north to south, was the Ichhogil Canal that was spanned by the Dograi Bridge. Running parallel to the south of GT Road, with the dry UBDC in between, was a railway line. Rikh's 54 Infantry Brigade, with one squadron Scinde Horse (14 Horse) was to capture the bridges at Dograi and Jallo, while 1 Jat with two troops 14 Horse, delinked from Pathak's 38 Infantry Brigade and directly under Niranjan Prasad's command, were to make a dash for the Bhaini–Malikpur Bridge. With 38 Infantry Brigade less 1 Jat and 96 Infantry Brigade designated as divisional and corps reserve, Niranjan Prasad was effectively left with just one brigade and a battalion, plus the antiquated Sherman tanks of 14 Horse.

As per Rikh's plan, 3 Jat was to prepare the ground for the other two battalions, who would move through them and line up on the Ichhogil Canal. The conduct of the operation was to be in three phases: 3 Jat was to cross the border at 0400 hrs to secure a firm base in area Gosal–Dial (Milestone 15) by a cross-country outflanking move north of GT Road. One company of 15 Dogra was to move with 3 Jat to capture intact the bridge over the UBDC near Milestone 16. Simultaneously one company of 13 Punjab led by a commando platoon was to move along the railway line to capture Jallo Bridge. In Phase 2, 15 Dogra with a squadron of 14 Horse was to advance along GT Road at first light to link up with their company on the UBDC bridge and then make a dash to capture the bridge at Dograi. In Phase 3, 13 Punjab was to build up its company at Jallo Bridge.

Warning orders were received on 2 September and immediate preparations were undertaken. Much to Mundy's chagrin, just then he received orders posting him to Laos in Indochina as part of a UN assignment. On 27 August, Mundy received a report about the Ichhogil Canal which was described as brick-lined, 30 feet high, with walls sloping at 45 degrees, and 112 feet wide at the top, water depth normally maintained at 20 feet with a flow of 2 to 3 knots. Hayde would write later, 'The report stated that though constructed consequent upon the Indo-Pak Canal Waters Agreement, it was designed by Pakistan as a tank obstacle—Indian Intelligence had found out that a chain of pillboxes ran along the entire length. The report didn't exactly say where this canal was, except that it was in Pakistan, nor did it give the information a soldier would need, i.e., what did the pillboxes look like (profile), how many of what weapons were used from within, what were their likely localities, and in what manner were they being concealed?'[19] Another message from Divisional HQ said the GOC, Niranjan Prasad, would be visiting the battalion on 30 August.

The state of affairs in 15 Division can be gauged by the conversation that took place between Niranjan Prasad and Mundy. Prasad asked Mundy about the men's morale, enquiring about the training and regimental spirit. Mundy confirmed that the men were in good spirits.[20] Almost as an afterthought, as the GOC was getting into his jeep, he took Mundy aside and asked if the battalion had been properly briefed on its operational role.

Properly briefed or not, all Mundy knew was that 15 Division, as from the date of its positioning at Amritsar, was to threaten Lahore along a number of axes if Pakistan managed to provoke a war. 54 Infantry Brigade—of which 3 Jat was a part—had the Amritsar–Lahore GT Road axis. All command ranks of 3 Jat to the level of havildar had already taken part in a series of 'terrain studies' on the ground and off the map. The departing general at this point was then asked where exactly the Ichhogil Canal was and he looked at a staff officer, who frantically scribbled it down on his note pad. As on 30 August 1965, the infiltrator situation in J&K notwithstanding and with fighting breaking out all around, there was no talk of war on the Lahore front.

Mundy handed over command of 3 Jat to Desmond Eugene Hayde on 5 September. The significance of the moment was lost, as by last light, the whole of

11 Corps was on the move as infantry battalions, artillery, and armoured regiments began to go forward to their designated assembly areas. 3 Jat reached Ratan Khurd by 2130 hrs from where it moved to the firm base by 0345 hrs on 6 September. Fifteen minutes later, as commanders along the IB looked at their synchronized luminous HMT watches, units of the Indian Army stepped across into Pakistan. The 1965 Indo-Pak War had begun in earnest.

ALLAH! INDIANS!!

There were no fireworks lighting up the sky, just columns of soldiers in their olive green uniforms as they set off for their given objectives on Pakistani soil. 3 Jat was moving at a brisk pace...in fact, too brisk a pace! Almost immediately, the battalion's affiliated Signals unit with their heavy wireless sets for rearward communication with TAC HQ 54 Infantry Brigade was lost, as were the accompanying FOOs and their artillery detachments with their communication sets that were to liaison with the supporting gun positions still in India. This was to have very serious consequences.

Preceding the battalion by fifteen minutes, Naib Subedar Kirori Mal's platoon had surrounded the Pakistani border post at Narayanpura. Should the Pakistani Rangers realize something was up, they were to be silenced with bayonets.

While the soldiers at the post didn't realize that a 'whole battalion trudged through the night a few hundred yards away',[21] a man tending his fields nearby heard them and, swinging a lantern, came to investigate. The orders were not to kill anybody if it could be avoided, least of all a civilian. When the lantern was close enough, Kirori Mal walked up to the man and said conversationally: 'Itthe fauji hilna chalna ho riha hai, tu ja apna kam kar.' (Military movement is happening here, you go mind your own business). The man went away.

The battalion had hardly progressed a few kilometres down GT Road when some distant firing from the direction of Wagah spooked it. The battalion of as yet green soldiers went to ground and the sound of weapons being cocked shattered the stillness of the night. However, before anyone could press the trigger, the voices of JCOs and NCOs bellowed out 'Mat fire karo!' (Don't fire). It was a close call for the Jats, for a volley of gunfire would have alerted the Pakistanis in the vicinity that something was up. It can only be imagined what might have happened if the command has been: 'Fire mat karo'. Given the state of nerves, the first word itself could have resulted in chaos.

An hour later, at 0500 hrs, it was still pitch dark when 3 Jat once again converged on GT Road. Everything was going smoothly, and both Alpha and Bravo Companies were abreast of their objective. Lieutenant Colonel Mundy, destined to sit the war out, had put in place a fairly unorthodox decision which was to serve 3 Jat extremely well. The battalion had just a couple of senior officers who had a few years' service, while the others were young officers (YOs), most of them fresh out of the IMA. Mundy had also appointed senior JCOs who he believed had the sagacity and experience as company commanders and kept the exuberant but inexperienced YOs where they were needed most, commanding platoons. It was Subedar Khazan Singh, commanding Bravo Company, who raised his voice a little and asked the NCO commanding No. 4 Platoon, 'Panch ke sath thara milap sai?' (Are you in contact with No. 5 Platoon?)[22]

Whoever wrote the script for 3 Jat certainly had an eye for drama laced with ironic coincidences. Islamuddin was born in British India in a village in the one-time fiefdom of Bijnor. With the outbreak of World War II, Islamuddin volunteered and was sent by the recruitment office to Bareilly where he was classified by the British as a 'Hindustani Mussalman'. After his initial training he was put on the rolls of 3 Jat and sent to Ranchi to join the battalion which until then had been fighting against German armour. Half the battalion consisted of Muslims from Punjab, Delhi, and the United Provinces, while the other half were Hindu Jats. To Islamuddin and all the other soldiers, it mattered little as to who was Hindu or Muslim...they were quite simply 3 Jat.

Shortly after the battalion moved to the Arakan and Islamuddin was shifted to the Intelligence section of the battalion where his constant companion was a Jat, Rattan Lal. Islamuddin finished the war as a havildar. Having chosen Pakistan in the Partition, he lost both his home and his regiment. Reassigned to the Pakistan Army's 2 Punjab, his by now formidable reputation as an 'Intelligence wallah' followed him wherever he went. In the intervening years he was either attached to a brigade or a divisional headquarters, and by 1965 he had become a senior subedar gathering intelligence for the Lahore-based 10 Division. His beat extended from the Ravi at one end to Kasur on the other, but then nothing happened in Punjab for many years.

Suddenly in August, Kashmir was in the news. A brigade from 10 Division was rushed to the north and the fighting extended south to Chhamb and Akhnoor. All Intelligence units in Punjab were put on high alert, but nothing was happening there. There was an Indian brigade at Amritsar but it rarely came towards the border. As usual, the Punjab Sector was dormant. However, on 5 September, Islamuddin found out that the brigade that had moved was back and 1 Armoured Division was moving towards Kasur. Something was going to happen...but what? The Indians across the border were showing no signs of activity.

At Dial, where Islamuddin was stationed, two officers arrived on the evening of 5 September. One was a major from the Baluch Regiment, the other an artillery lieutenant from 23 Field attached to 11 FF (R&S). Lieutenant Abdul Malik had with him a jeep and a radio set, the usual paraphernalia of an FOO. GHQ Pakistan had sounded the general alert, and the officers told Islamuddin that a company of Baluchis would arrive later that night. The JCO nodded off as his radio operator went into a monologue about his marital problems. At 0300 hrs he was awakened and told that the Baluchis had arrived and fell back asleep. An hour later, he jerked awake to the sound of firing, from the direction of Wagah.

The Baluchis were fast asleep but Islamuddin woke up the major and told him what he had heard. The officer said, 'Trigger happy bastards, those Rangers' and went back to sleep. But Islamuddin was wide awake and he awakened the artillery driver who was sleeping by the jeep. He told him to drive him to Wagah but just then Lieutenant Malik arrived. On hearing about the firing, he ordered the driver to get the radio operator and made his report, 'Firing at Wagah! Guns to action. Await further report. Out!'

Islamuddin had moved ahead and heard it first...the tramping of boots! At first he thought it was another Baluchi patrol, but there were too many men. He peered into the darkness, moving cautiously towards the sound. And then a voice rang out, 'Panch ke sath tera milap sai?' Islamuddin's heart jumped. He recognized the language, 'Allah! Jats!!' He ran back to the jeep where Malik was standing with one leg in the vehicle, the radio transmitter in his hand. 'Indians! Crossing the road at Mile 15, bring down fire immediately!'

Malik kept his cool and relayed the order, giving the coordinates for Mile 15 and calling for fire. A voice from the gun end crackled over the radio, 'Indians? What are they doing?'

'Never mind that! Fire, I tell you, fire!'

But it was too late. The Jats were coming down the road. Suddenly a lorry from the direction of Wagah roared past, and Hayde fired a short burst from his carbine. Seeing the Indian troops, the jeep driver bolted off into the darkness, while the radio operator drew his pistol. Hayde took the pistol out of the radio operator's frozen hand and switched off the radio. He then informed Lieutenant Abdul Malik that he was now a prisoner of war.

In the meantime, Major Sri Ram Yadav, the Charlie Company commander had reached Hayde. 'A great excitement overcame the officer (Yadav). "Hands up," he ordered the officer prisoner (Malik) and shoved his bayonet at him, and the two prisoners shoved their hands as high as they could go. But the excitement was still too great and the company commander repeated, "Hands up or I'll shoot" and then discovered that the scabbard was still on his bayonet. He whipped off the scabbard and this time the hands up was of a no-nonsense type, followed rapidly by the order "Quick March". The prisoners were sent back to the Subedar Major in D Company locality.'[23]

Delta Company under Subedar Swarup Singh was deploying at Mile 15, setting up a firm base along with the battalion's mortar platoon. While Yadav's Charlie Company moved to isolate and contain Dial on the northern side of GT Road, Alpha Company under the command of Major Asa Ram Tyagi on the left and Bravo Company on the right under Subedar Khazan Singh had adopted an assault formation and were advancing towards a grove on the southern side. At

0545 hrs, there was a short burst of gunfire. In the grey light of dawn some men stopped and looked around, but the platoon commander brusquely ordered them: 'Age chalo' (Move forward). There was no further sign of activity.

Tyagi's men continued to advance towards the grove. On the high ground at the centre they could make out the outline of a hut with a tube well next to it. Two platoons of 11 FF (R&S) under Major Arif Jan were occupying the defensive position astride GT Road. Then the machine gun fired again, this time forcing Alpha Company to deploy in a defensive position. In the meantime, Bravo Company had closed in on the grove from where the machine gun had just fired at Alpha Company, and to their surprise they found 'the enemy troops were in stand-to as though on a training exercise: men were moving around, an officer was washing his face, and someone might even have been sent to the machine gun to find out why it had fired. But this same gun suddenly swung around and fired at B Company. The gunner seemed to be about the only one who felt there was a war on and his first bullets made a lucky strike.'[24]

Khazan Singh had just opened his mouth to yell 'Charge' when he was hit smack in the middle of the forehead. Seeing the JCO drop, Bravo Company froze, but by then other Pakistani soldiers were firing at them, so they started firing back. Lance Naik Fateh Singh then rushed the machine-gun post and hurled a grenade, scoring a direct hit. Unfortunately, he was hit by a burst of machine-gun fire and killed on the spot. The bullet that had hit Khazan Singh had hit his helmet and momentarily knocked him out. Just then, the 'dead' JCO got up 'to his commanding six feet two and shouted, *"Sab jawan khare honge aur dushman ko marenge. Jat Balwan!!"* (All the soldiers will stand up and kill the enemy. Jat Balwan!)'[25]

Subedar Khazan Singh was not only on his feet, he was charging at the Pakistanis, his carbine blazing away. The Pakistani officer was standing near his trench shooting at Khazan Singh with his pistol when the JCO killed him. 'Some enemy fought back, some ran away and some sat at the bottom of their trenches with their hands up.' Those who managed to escape the Jat onslaught were corralled by Subedar Mohammad Shafi and they fell back on the canal. The grove had been captured at the cost of five Jat soldiers and eight wounded. Twenty-one FF soldiers including Major Arif Jan were dead and seventeen had been taken prisoner along with a jeep-mounted 106 mm (RCL) gun, a communications jeep, an ambulance, and MMG, and quite a few rifles.

While the fighting at the grove was still on, Bravo Company came under additional fire from the direction of the canal bridge further from the south. Hardly pausing in his stride, Khazan Singh with a platoon, charged in that direction. Though the Jat official history says Bravo Company killed another ten Pakistani soldiers and captured two more machine guns, according to Hayde, the Pakistanis at the UBDC Bridge were firing at something else along the railway line and they quickly made off in jeeps. Considering the gap between the grove and the bridge was almost 400 yards, the latter version is probably accurate.

Around the time the first machine-gun fire was being directed at Alpha Company, Yadav's Charlie Company was approaching Dial village. They had just reached a sugar cane field and a water channel when a few shots were fired at the Jats who had to take cover in a ditch facing the village, when 'the civilian population of the village suddenly erupted out of their homes. They rushed straight at C Company and in their scramble towards the Ichhogil Canal unseeingly ran past. There was no chivalry: first came the men and teenagers of whom a few carried babies and toddlers, followed by older girls each holding on to a younger brother or sister and finally there were the mothers, each shepherding along three to four children.'[26]

The terrifying spectre of war, especially for the civilians caught in the crossfire, is perhaps best illustrated by what happened next. Naik Mahabir Singh was repeating to his men, 'Fire nahin karna. Fire nahi karna' (Do not fire. Do not fire) when a distraught mother, dragging her little boy of four or five years, blindly ran straight at him. 'Just as these two reached Mahabir, the boy's shoe slipped off his foot. The little Muslim boy hopefully looked at the big Indian soldier who picked up the shoe and handed it to him. The boy with a shy grin tried to put it back on his foot, but his mother, with a mad scream, blindly rushed ahead, dragging him along. The shoe was left behind.'[27]

After the initial exodus of civilians, a few scattered Pakistani soldiers emerged from the village. The moment they were fired at, the bulk of them broke cover and bolted off to the north. Most got away but three Pakistani soldiers were shot while another seven were captured by the Jats, who themselves had two of their men wounded. Entering Dial, Yadav found that the aged and the debilitated part of the population had been left behind. They were quickly rounded up and sent off in a group on the road towards Lahore. Every now and then a few desultory Rangers retreating from the direction of Wagah would appear, but when asked to surrender, would fire a few shots and disappear into the sarkanda grass that lined the side of the road. A few, including a party that stumbled on to Hayde, were shot dead. A Pakistani truck carrying eight soldiers who were trying to check the telephone line also blundered into the Jats. After a brief firefight where all the eight Pakistani soldiers were wounded, the truck was added to the expanding list of captured Pakistani equipment that also included two RCL guns, a machine gun, and some more rifles recovered from Dial.

By this time, the sun was up. With Gosal–Dial under their control, the Jats had to prepare for a Pakistani armoured thrust that could develop once the Pakistanis got over the initial shock of the Indian advance. 3 Jat had spent the better part of the previous fortnight preparing for this so, to a man, they started digging feverishly. The war had only just begun. They now had to make sure the firm base would be a mini fortress. As per Rikh's plan, they now expected 15 Dogra to pass through the 3 Jat area and press on to the Ichhogil Canal that, according to the sketchy map that they had, lay just ahead of them.

TRIUMPH AND DISASTER

Both 15 Dogra, commanded by Lieutenant Colonel Inderjit Singh, and 13 Punjab (Jind) under Lieutenant Colonel M. Chatterji had been a part of 54 Brigade and a lot was expected of them. In the brigade plan, 15 Dogra was expected to be the spearhead of the brigade that would be poised to threaten Lahore, with 13 Punjab in support while 3 Jat were to be held in reserve.

One company of 15 Dogra under Major Pandit had set off with 3 Jat from their FUP at Ratan Khurd at H-hour, while the rest of the battalion firmed up just short of Wagah at the IB on GT Road. Pandit had caught the Pakistani Rangers unawares at the checkpost, after which 3 Jat had cleared the area between Wagah and Gosal–Dial where they settled down to wait for the rest of the battalion at Mile 16. As per plan, the leading elements of 15 Dogra crossed the IB along with Charlie Squadron of 14 Scinde Horse under the command of Major Bhawan Swaroop and moved into Wagah at 0540 hrs. Dogra soldiers entered the Wagah Customs Building which also housed elements of Pakistani Rangers. Bursting into the CO's room, they found a Pakistani major fast asleep with his two wives, who became hysterical at the sight of camouflaged bayonet-wielding Dogras. The Dogras left 'the two ladies to fend for themselves and marched the major off to captivity in his pyjamas!'[28]

While the Customs Building was being cleared, the rest of the battalion ran into some resistance on the UBDC Bridge some 300 metres inside Pakistani territory. There were no obvious signs of defences set up by the Pakistani Rangers. The Ranger Colony was situated where GT Road crossed the UBDC. The leading platoon was being led by Second Lieutenant Jayendra Singh. In the grey light of dawn, the Ranger sentries heard them coming and opened fire at such close quarters that the officer was killed on the spot and his havildar severely wounded. The Indian troops immediately went to ground and started firing. Inderjit Singh decided he would wait for the light to improve. Seeing the Shermans of 14 Scinde Horse also moving up, the Rangers ran away. Nevertheless, despite the slight delay, the battalion along with the Shermans reached Gosal–Dial at 0615 hrs.

Just before the leading elements of 14 Horse reached Dial, 3 Jat had two unwelcome visitors. Khazan Singh had just got his head bandaged when a lookout shouted 'Jahaz!' (Aircraft!) Two Sabres from the direction of Lahore flew right over the Jat position that was still being prepared as a firm base. Pulling up from their first run, they languidly turned and came back. Most men had flattened themselves into the partly dug trenches, but Khazan Singh, his white bandaged head very visible from the sky, was caught in the open. Machine-gun fire raked the ground on either side of him as he crawled desperately to a tree, and the JCO continued to lead a charmed life. The PAF had delivered their calling card minutes after first light.

Shortly after the aircraft had departed—fortunately without causing any damage to the Jats—the sound of approaching tanks sent the men scurrying into their partly dug trenches yet again. Events were unfolding at such a rapid pace that the battalion's jeep-mounted RCL guns had not even fetched up. The men, as they had been trained to do, had taken out their improvised Molotov cocktails and were waiting with matchboxes and lighters in their hands, not knowing what to expect. The noise got louder and suddenly tanks loomed out of the dust, coming to a halt right next to the Jat position. Out of the tank's cupola, a khaki-clad figure popped out. Fortunately none of the Jats opened fire and the tank commander introduced himself as Naib Risaldar Kishan Singh, a troop leader from 14 Horse. The forward elements of the 15 Dogra/14 Horse column coming in from Wagah had made contact with the Jats.

In the meantime, 13 Punjab, the third battalion in the 54 Brigade grouping, was amazingly still at the start line at Attari. Chatterji, their CO, had sent a company plus the commando platoon ahead at 0400 hrs to capture the Jallo Bridge, where the rest of the battalion was supposed to reach after daybreak. Like the Jats, the Punjab company and the commando platoon lost contact with the signals section. Chatterji was sitting on his hands when Rikh showed up. Chatterji wasted precious time arguing with the brigade commander, saying he did not want to advance until he had established contact with his forward troops. On getting a dressing-down from Rikh, Chatterji gave the requisite order, but the battalion only got as far as the Wagah Railway Station, where Chatterji froze yet again.[29]

The Punjab advance column had in fact gotten to within 600 yards of the Ichhogil Canal but felt they did not have adequate firepower to take on the alert Pakistani defences there. This group eventually re-joined the battalion which was still patiently waiting for them at the Wagah station.

13 Punjab was a classic case of superb troops being commanded by an officer who was found wanting when the hour of reckoning was upon him. Rikh was undoubtedly frustrated with Chatterji, but the worst was yet to come. Rikh had reached Mile 15 around 0800 hrs when he met up with Inderjit Singh, the CO of 15 Dogra, who seemed to be in a state of panic. 'Sir, he cried, I've had casualties, look at this poor young officer's body lying here, dead.... Brigadier Rikh was a gentleman: he didn't ask to be shown the casualties or to be given details. From the volume of firing that had taken place during the early hours, he believed that a battle of some sort had been fought...'[30]

Leaving a distraught Inderjit Singh behind, Rikh drove into the 3 Jat firm base where Hayde met him. Hayde asked: 'Think you can take on (15 Dogra) battalion's task of advancing to the canal?' Rikh said yes.[31] In less than a minute, the brigade's plan had been altered. 15 Dogra was to occupy the firm base at Gosal–Dial and 3 Jat was now to be the sharp end of the stick. For the Jats, the battle was just beginning.

Hayde decided not to waste any time. He quickly worked out his attack plan and gave his orders, instructing Subedar Swarup Singh's Delta Company to lead the way with a troop of Shermans in support. If the Pakistanis were to heavily engage the advancing column from the front, the battalion was to bypass the enemy by circling around from the north. No one was to stop moving, they were to press forward all the time. The rest of the tanks would follow in the wake of the leading troop, clear any obstacle, and get to the Ichhogil Canal–GT Road junction where they would wait until 3 Jat had cleared the flanking Dograi village. Once the Jats had done that, they would fire two green Very lights which would be a signal to the tanks that the built-up area ahead was clear.

Even at this stage, there was obvious confusion on the Pakistani side. While Hayde was huddled together with his officers and JCOs issuing orders for the next phase, two forward lookouts from 3 Jat, Lance Naik Rohtas and Sepoy Maipal could not quite believe their eyes. Trundling along the road from the direction of Lahore was a blue double-decker bus, with civilians occupying the lower deck and Pakistani soldiers on top, perched up at the level of the trees. Neither Rohtas nor Maipal had ever seen anything quite like this. As the senior of the two, Rohtas knew what he had to do, which was to give clear instructions to his subordinate. 'Sepoy Maipal, the row of electric poles from our back to front is the general line of direction. To full left of the general line of direction is the road. On the road a huge tank-like enemy vehicle. Range 450 yards. Fire!'[32]

The bus had advanced quite far by then. As per standard army procedure, Rohtas should have first given Maipal the range. Nevertheless 'the tank-like contraption' stopped as the firing started, the driver slamming on the brakes and ejecting from his side of the vehicle. The civilians dived out into the ditches and tall grass by the side of the road, while the Pakistani soldiers came down with their rifles held correctly and trotted off in the direction from which they had come. There were no casualties. The captured blue double-decker bus was to become quite an attraction on the streets of Chandigarh.

3 Jat had crossed the border earlier that morning without any of its support weapons. The battalion's fighting vehicles, known as the F Echelon, consisted not only of jeeps that were mounted with 106 mm anti-tank RCL guns, but also tracked T-16 carriers that were carrying both small arms ammunition and mortars, and other soft-skinned communication vehicles. 3 Jat's second-in-command, Major N. L. Marwaha, finally linked up with Charlie Company which was still at Dial waiting for 15 Dogra to take over the firm base from them. Since the first morning raid, the Sabres had been buzzing around, but things were unfolding so rapidly, no one in 3 Jat was paying them much attention.

As the convoy reached Dial, Marwaha made a blunder. He failed to give orders to disperse the vehicles, which should have been the normal thing to do. Suddenly, much to everyone's horror, the first of six Sabres was streaking in for the kill. The first two Sabres that had come calling earlier were from Sargodha, and had not seen any vehicles, so they fired at the Jats and went back. The second formation from No. 19 Squadron had taken off from Peshawar at 0850 hrs and was being led by Squadron Leader (later Air Commodore) Sayed Sajad Haider, who had been diverted mid-air from the initial target area which was Jassar in the Sialkot Sector. At first, like the earlier Sabres that had taken off from Sargodha, Sayed did not see any vehicles. Then when he spotted the F Echelon vehicles of 3 Jat, he assumed that the T-16 carriers were Pakistani tanks since they were so close to the Ichhogil Canal. 'We almost left the area, but I decided to go down and give them a salute... I flipped my Sabre over and was 30 or 40 metres above them when I saw the saffron roundel.' Pulling up sharply, Sayed transmitted to the rest of the formation, 'These bastards are Indians...don't let them get away.'[33]

In the mayhem that followed, a major portion of 3 Jat's F Echelon was destroyed and Marwaha was hit in the leg as he desperately tried to salvage the situation. The Pakistani Sabres, that were completely unchallenged either from the ground or the air, had a field day. Subsequent formations shot up not just 3 Jat's vehicles, they attacked and destroyed many of the assembled vehicles of other units that were strung out on the road leading back in the direction of Amritsar. It was a miracle of sorts that the Sabres did not hit any of 14 Horse's Shermans, though the Pakistani pilots claimed to have destroyed a few. Sajad Haider's description of what he took to be a tank points to this. He claimed the 'tank' was loaded with ammunition. After he fired his 5-inch rockets, he had to pull away but his wingman confirmed the target was hit and 'airborne'. The T-16 Carriers were loaded with mortar ammunition.

The damage done by the Sabres notwithstanding, and any thoughts of artillery support still a distant dream, 3 Jat continued to press forward, closing in on Mile 13 and the much talked about Ichhogil Canal. According to the maps available, Dograi was supposed to be a small village straddling the canal to the right of GT Road. However, leading elements of Alpha Company under Subedar Swarup Singh found themselves in a large built-up area instead. To make matters worse, there were some pillboxes flanking the road from where the Pakistanis were shooting at the Jats.

Not wanting to get involved in a street fight within a built-up area, Hayde ordered his men to swing to the north and make for the canal about 1,500 yards upstream of Dograi. Leaving the tanks on GT Road, all four companies of 3 Jat started to move through the gap between Dograi and the village of Lakhanke. Unknown to the Jats, Second Lieutenant Altaf Hussein Gill from Pakistan's 23 Field Regiment was perched on a tree. With orders from HQ 10 Division to stop the Indians at any cost, at 1020 hrs the FOO, Gill, directed 'the first precise concentrations of artillery and mortar shells. They were suddenly bursting all round, not exploding even remotely at a distance from the men but right on them.... Watching whole companies disappear amidst the dust and smoke, the CO (Hayde) said aloud, "They've had it!" But in between salvos, there stood the battalion, almost wholly intact except for a huddle of bodies here and there, though brought to a momentary mute and dumbfounded halt.'[34]

The battalion's junior leadership came to the fore. Subedar Swarup Singh's voice pierced its way into every man's consciousness as he roared, 'Age baro, kuchh nahi hua. Is fire se age nikal jao, tez kadam se.' (Keep moving forward, nothing has happened. Get ahead of this fire, push on with a fast step.) Swarup Singh's order was taken up by other voices and the men were moving again. Shells and bombs continued to rain down, and though some men fell, no one stopped, and the battalion kept moving forward. In the meantime, Major Yadav had zeroed in on the Pakistani FOO in the tree, and a volley of rifle shots killed the gallant soldier who kept directing the fire till the very last moment.

Yadav's Charlie Company, which was on the extreme left, came under fire from a 3 Baluch platoon that was holding the northeastern flank of Dograi. Despite being caught in the open by Pakistani artillery (in addition to the fact that none of the officers and men had previously experienced heavy shelling), 3 Jat continued to move forward and soon Delta Company on the right had reached the eastern bank of the Ichhogil Canal. A few minutes later, Charlie Company had also reached its objective. The Pakistani shelling, which had been relentless until then, abruptly stopped. Medium machine guns were immediately deployed and the Pakistanis on the other bank were engaged.

From his position on the east bank, Hayde observed many Pakistani soldiers running across the bridge, which was downstream of him. Having got behind Dograi, Hayde ordered Charlie Company to cut off the Pakistanis' retreat. While Delta Company created an ad hoc firm base, Charlie Company's platoons, using fire and move tactics, started to leapfrog past each other to get to the southern side of the bridge. By then sporadic mortar fire had again started coming at the Jats from the direction of Batapur, which was on the other side of the canal. By 1120 hrs, the battalion had consolidated its position at the bridge. Second Lieutenant Kanchan Pal Singh[35] then inserted a cartridge into his Very pistol and fired the first of the two green lights to summon the armour forward.

The maps that 3 Jat had were hopelessly out of date. According to them, the area across the Ichhogil should have been an open field extending up to the village of Attoke Awan which was a fair distance away. Instead, there was a huge complex 'the buildings of which towered into the sky, chimneys sweeping upwards for hundreds of feet, and along the sides of the wall was written "Batapur Shoe Factory".'[36] The eastern bank of the Ichhogil, where the Jats were now concentrated, was dominated by this building and, as if to underscore that point, mortar shells and a machine gun started to fire from Attoke Awan.

Pakistani sappers had blown up the central part of the bridge a little while ago, but the gap was narrow enough to jump across. Ordering Alpha Company to head for Attoke Awan, Charlie Company to engage the defenders at the shoe factory, and the others to clear Dograi, Hayde and Alpha Company jumped across the gap on the bridge. The machine-gun fire had intensified, and while the occasional man got hit, the advancing platoons were moving well.

Just then a couple of Pakistani Sherman Mk IVs roared in from the direction of Attoke Awan, their guns blazing away at 3 Jat's Alpha Company, which, for the second time in less than two hours, was caught out in the open. A few men including Hayde ducked by the side of a mosque, while the rest of the men went to ground, ironically in the mosque's burial ground. In the bedlam of intense firing that followed, it was a miracle that only one Jat soldier was killed and eight wounded. The Jats defiantly continued to fire back at the tanks; the Shermans then turned and went behind the shoe factory. The Pakistani machine gun, probably thinking it had been abandoned, also stopped firing and withdrew.

Simultaneously, while Alpha Company was being chewed up by the tanks, a couple of Pakistani machine guns from Batapur started firing at Charlie Company, who engaged them. The arrival of the Pakistani armour had created a problem for Hayde, who was thinking of disengaging and pulling back when three truck-loads of Pakistani infantry arrived. The temporary withdrawal of the Pakistani tanks allowed Charlie Company to dash across the bridge and while one platoon went into the buildings of Batapur, Subedar Phale Ram's platoon positioned itself to engage the latest lorry-borne entrants into the raging battle. 'Of the two leading lorries, one somersaulted and burnt, and the other just piled up; bodies were strewn around like dummies. The third lorry had lagged behind and made a quick turn off the road where the infantry must have debussed and run away. Suddenly, from one of the lanes leading out of Batapur, a few hundred yards from Phale Ram and his men, the Pakistani tanks re-emerged to cross again towards Attoke Awan.'[37]

Dograi was a huge village with a built-up area sprawling on either side of the GT Road extending up to the destroyed bridge on the canal. After seeing the two green Very lights, Charlie Squadron of 14 Horse had started to move forward. Infantry elements told the tank crews that the village streets were littered with high tension cables. The leading two troop leaders, Second Lieutenant (later Major) Brijendra 'Gucchan' Singh (1st Troop) and Kishan Singh (2nd Troop) had dismounted and moved on foot ahead of the tanks in order to guide them through the village. There was no space for tanks to move on to the bank of the canal and the recent monsoon had rendered the surrounding area boggy. Brijendra Singh's troop reached the canal and deployed on the eastern bank from where it started providing prophylactic fire to 3 Jat, which was fighting across the canal.

Kishan's troop was ordered to remain in depth on the axis while the remaining half squadron had deployed in protection of the northern flank against any threat from the direction of Bhasin.

When the two Pakistani Shermans came roaring back into the open, Brijendra's troop was perfectly positioned near the demolished bridge. His gunner, Sowar Lakhu Ram, in a prompt response to his command, traversed the gun and destroyed the two Pakistani tanks at a distance of approximately 1,000 metres from the canal. 'The first was hit while it was still on the tarmac, probably forward of or behind the turret, for it spun round and round. The second was raising a cloud of dust in its effort to make cover, but Indian tank gunnery is good; it was brought to a jarring halt and, after a while, it began to burn.'[38]

With the two tanks knocked out, the third Pakistani lorry now decided to make a run for Lahore. Hayde, closest to Kishan Singh's tank, frantically asked him to open fire, but the JCO just signalled him to be patient. The tank's barrel was simultaneously going up, and the gun fired and no longer was there a lorry at 3,000 yards rushing back to Lahore. Almost immediately, Pakistani artillery guns that had been silent for a while, started firing again.

The time then was 1500 hrs. 3 Jat had seen continuous fighting ever since it first drew fire from Pakistani positions at Dial. Almost every man in the battalion had been strafed by Sabres, bombed and shelled by mortars, and Alpha Company had been assaulted by 23 Cavalry's Sherman tanks. All this while, the battalion had no artillery support, RCL guns, or any other anti-tank weapons, and no chance to rest even for a minute. It had eleven dead, forty-four wounded, some of whom were to die in hospital later. In the normal course of events, another battalion should have followed up in their wake and already reached the Ichhogil Canal and secured the bridgehead that had been established.

3 Jat had been out of communication with HQ 54 Brigade ever since the Signals element got lost in the early hours of the morning. Rikh's brief visit in the morning was the last contact the Jats had had with the senior officers who were apparently unaware of the implications of their own successes. Considering the loss of their anti-tank weapons and inability of 14 Horse to get across the demolished bridge, Hayde had few options but to start pulling back to the eastern side of the canal. The force of the water was threatening to wash away the remaining macadam which would soon widen the gap, leaving Alpha and Charlie Companies stranded on the western side.

Hayde was sending his casualties and dead bodies back with Alpha Company when Brijendra Singh jumped down from his tank, hopped across the damaged bridge and sought out Hayde. It was around 1515 hrs. The young lieutenant told Hayde he had just spoken to his squadron commander, Major Bhawan Swaroop, who had told him to withdraw to Gosal–Dial and tell Hayde to do the same. After a quick last-minute search for the dead and wounded, the commanding

officer was the last man across, after which remnants of the masonry broke away
and sank into the water.

Hayde then spoke to Rikh on Brijendra Singh's radio and, after assessing the
situation, 3 Jat was ordered to fall back with 14 Scinde Horse.[39] The battalion
complied, with Charlie Squadron helping in extricating the battalion and evacuating
the Jat casualties. Hayde was the last to withdraw while mounted on Brijendra
Singh's tank. At 1715 hrs, they went through 15 Dogra's positions at Dial to
where the 54 Infantry Brigade TAC HQ had been set up. Hayde found his IO,
K. P. Singh, still arguing with the brigade commander about his battalion standing
alone at Dograi. Amazingly, even though all the senior officers in the chain of
command had assembled near the Wagah border during the day, they had no idea
that 3 Jat had not only made it to the Ichhogil Canal, but had even crossed it at
the vital GT Road bridge. The Sabres had created panic in Divisional HQ, and
Niranjan Prasad seemed to have lost control of the situation. It didn't help that
wounded Jats, their perspective having been reduced to 'gaping wounds and intense
pain' when asked what was happening answered, 'Paltan ka satyanas ho raha sai'
(The battalion is being destroyed).[40] Harbouring at Gosal–Dial that night, it was
obvious to the front-line officers that an outstanding success and opportunity had
been frittered away.

A FIASCO ON THE ICHHOGIL

Considering that the entire Pakistan Army on the Lahore front was caught napping,
the PAF's almost instantaneous response had been remarkable. Though a lot of
finger-pointing would take place subsequently, the Sabres, like the Vampires and
Mystères at Chhamb just five days earlier, had been the game changers.

The blueprint for the offensive in the Bari Doab had been worked out
months earlier during Operation Ablaze by the army chief and the Western Army
commander, with very few people being privy to the details. Chaudhuri and
Harbakhsh Singh had argued over every detail, but neither had applied his mind
to the execution. To be fair to Niranjan Prasad, GOC 15 Division had been the
only officer in the chain of command to repeatedly stress the need for air cover.
Prasad had time and again also pleaded for reconnaissance flights that would give
him aerial photographs well before the commencement of operations, but he was
ignored. Chaudhuri, who had the ear of the government, Harbakhsh and even Jogi
Dhillon, behaved as if the air element simply did not exist. As a result, even a few
minutes before H-hour, no one had any idea of what the terrain ahead looked like.

The irony of the situation was, General Chaudhuri had, as we already know,
sent Jaggi Nath to photograph the Ichhogil Canal. Nath had not only done this
with tremendous risk to his own life, but this could have alerted the Pakistanis that
something was indeed cooking on the Punjab front. Photographs of the Lahore
and Barki Sectors (now with the author) were not only seen by Chaudhuri, they

were shown to Chavan as well. The chief did not bother to share the images with anyone. This had disastrous consequences, for no one, even at the commanding officer level, despite desperately seeking the requisite intelligence, had a clue about the terrain across the IB.

The same thing had happened three years ago in 1962. Lieutenant General Daulet Singh had not shared Jaggi Nath's meticulous mapping of Chinese positions with his subordinates. While claiming after the war that he had had no information about the activities on the Chinese side, he had written a glowing citation for Nath who was awarded the first of his two MVCs, the second being for his daring work during 1965, especially the sortie that visually charted the Ichhogil Canal.

Amazing as it may sound, even though Arjan Singh was at hand when Chaudhuri and Harbakhsh Singh worked out the master plan for Operation Riddle, the IAF simply was not a part of it. Forget about any ground support or offensive sweeps, the IAF on 6 September had no plans to carry out any CAPs or counter air operations. This was a sacrilegious oversight and both Chaudhuri and Harbakhsh Singh must share the blame for it. Echoing his immediate superiors' attitude, even after the first Sabres appeared over Gosal–Dial at 0700 hrs, at no stage did Jogi Dhillon's 11 Corps call for interceptors. Neither did the IAF base at Amritsar respond, despite the fact that a detachment of Gnats from 23 Squadron continued to be based there. The second Sabre strike came an hour and a half later, when 54 Brigade vehicles took a hammering with no opposition either from the ground or the air.

Since the army was going to attack across the IB, Air HQ had debated the possibility of simultaneously attacking PAF bases but the suggestion failed to find traction because of the government directive not to attack PAF airfields till the Pakistanis attacked Indian airfields. Logically, once the army had crossed the IB and was on its way towards the Ichhogil Canal, it should have been but natural to have CAPs overhead. However, the 'CAS's operative directive of 3 September specifically prohibited such attacks and it was on the same day that the green light to the army was given. The instructions not to attack PAF airfields were reiterated in the signal 'informing the front-line air force stations that the Indian Army was going to cross the International Border.'[41]

The thought process at the highest level becomes even more confusing for it was not as if the IAF was being kept out of the war in the Punjab Sector. IAF plans for 6 September had been drawn up the previous day and conveyed by Western Air Command to the stations under it. The squadrons based at Adampur and Halwara were earmarked for interdiction strikes in support of 11 Corps, while Pathankot was to continue supporting the Chhamb–Jaurian Sector. The PAF, on the other hand, had not only quickly responded to the Indian thrust down GT Road, it had also kept some of the Sabres on standby for air defence tasks. According to Air Marshal Asghar Khan (who had by then relinquished command), Sargodha, which had the largest number of aircraft, had been providing air support to the army defending Lahore. The aircraft that were not being used for ground support were being kept on a defensive alert, without bombs and rockets.

For any offensive plan spread over a large area, dash and courage are just one aspect. Logistics require a tremendous attention to detail which the trio of Chaudhuri, Harbakhsh, and Dhillon had ignored. Sweeping arrows indicating the movement of troops this way and that on maps amounts to nothing more than wishful thinking when even the basics are not in place.

The poor planning that resulted in a complete breakdown of communication was to have multiple ramifications. 13 Punjab had suffered much the same fate as 3 Jat, for despite having pinned down Pakistan's early warning elements at Jallo Bridge in the morning, no follow-up action meant that the company had to withdraw. With the area behind them littered with destroyed vehicles and the dead and wounded, 54 Brigade had completely withdrawn from the Ichhogil Canal after last light on 6 September and no portion of the canal was under Indian control any longer.

On the second day, 15 Infantry Division's objectives remained much the same: move to the Ichhogil Canal and capture the bridges. By that time, Pakistan had hit Indian airfields including Pathankot, destroying quite a few aircraft on the ground, reinforced its defences with an infantry brigade in the Lahore Sector, deployed its supporting artillery in an effective manner and the PAF continued to play havoc amongst defenceless troops in the open. 15 Infantry Division had not only lost the surprise element, it had failed to consolidate on the previous day's gains and its pattern of operations had become evident to the Pakistanis.

Rikh's brigade having failed to consolidate on the Ichhogil Canal, let us turn our attention to Niranjan Prasad's northern flank where 1 Jat LI was operating. The battalion, commanded by Lieutenant Colonel Balbir Singh, was in Dalhousie when it got its warning orders on 2 September. At that point a part of 96 Infantry Brigade, the battalion moved on the morning of 5 September and reached Ram Tirath in the evening. Balbir Singh who had arrived in Amritsar a day earlier was told 1 Jat LI was being placed directly under 11 Corps and it would have under its command two troops (Alpha Squadron and 14 Horse) and a field platoon of engineers. The battalion would also have a battery of 81 Field Regiment and a light battery in direct support. Their task was to capture and secure a bridge over the canal on the Kohali–Ichhogil Uttar axis situated at Bhaini Dhaliwal. For the immediate offensive, the 1 Jat Group was placed under command of 15 Infantry Division.

Going into action immediately, the battalion reached its concentration area at Ranian Bund at 0230 hrs. With Bravo Company under Captain S. S. Kaler on the left and Charlie Company under Lieutenant Jotiba Patil on the right, 1 Jat LI crossed into Pakistan at 0400 hrs. Alpha Company commanded by Subedar Mukhtiar Singh and Delta Company with Captain Pokhar Singh at the helm were following, planning to leapfrog over the two leading companies and take the Ichhogil Uttar Bridge and Ichhogil Hithar respectively.

One platoon of Delta Company, 11 FF (R&S), under Captain Muhammad Fazil delayed the 1 Jat Group briefly before falling back under the cover of darkness towards the Ichhogil Canal in the Bhasin area to the southwest. Kaler's Bravo Company came under fire from the direction of the Ichhogil Hithar police post. In a brief firefight the Jats killed 3 Sutlej Rangers and continued their advance. At around 0500 hrs, some shots were fired at Patil's Charlie Company, but after that the Pakistanis melted away.

In his version of events, Captain Amarinder Singh says that 1 Jat LI had taken the bridge by 0700 hrs, after which they were caught by surprise by Pakistani artillery fire, but the Jat regimental records claim that the leading companies were about 1,000 yards short of the canal when they came under heavy fire from village Bhaini Dhaliwal at 0530 hrs itself. With both Bravo and Charlie companies pinned down, 'no manoeuvre was possible. The ground was open, with no cover from fire or view. Heavy artillery shelling and mortar fire further worsened matters. At this time all wireless communication having failed, artillery support could not be provided. The reserve companies and tanks, which were initially advancing with them, also could not come up in support, due to the heavy shelling.'[42]

Supplementing the defensive artillery barrage, at 0700 hrs, the Sabres also targeted the 1 Jat Group. The adjutant, Captain R. S. Mavi, who had tried to move forward towards the leading companies after the communication sets stopped working, was wounded. Thirteen men had been killed and twenty-eight, including Mavi, wounded. With no artillery available to counter the Pakistani fire, Balbir Singh ordered his men to fall back and, by 1100 hrs, the 1 Jat Group was back at its assembly point at Ranian Bund. As luck would have it, once again Niranjan Prasad was out of communication with this group. The main reason for the communication failure in this case was that the reports were still going back to HQ 96 Infantry Brigade, 1 Jat LI's parent formation, but now 1 Jat LI was part of the corps reserve. HQ 11 Corps in turn failed to keep HQ 15 Division informed despite the battle being fought in Niranjan Prasad's area of responsibility.

7 INFANTRY DIVISION (FEROZEPUR)

Major General Har Krishen Sibal's 7 Infantry Division was permanently located at Ferozepur. It originally had 29 Infantry Brigade as a part of its ORBAT but this brigade had been detached from the division and placed under the command of HQ 11 Corps to be deployed further to the north. Brigadier K. J. S. Shahaney was commanding 48 Infantry Brigade that comprised 5 Guards, 19 Maratha Light Infantry (MLI), and 6/8 Gorkhas while Brigadier Lerb Ferris had 4 Sikh, 16 Punjab, 9 Madras, and 17 Rajput as a part of 65 Infantry Brigade. 21 CIH being commanded by Lieutenant Colonel Satish Chander Joshi was the division's integral armoured regiment.

Unlike most other Indian battalions that had been moved from their peacetime locations and pitched into combat with no time to familiarize themselves with the terrain, the two brigades earmarked for operations in this sector had short distances to cover. Sibal's division was tasked with capturing Barki and mopping up the Pakistanis on the east bank of the Ichhogil Canal. The two infantry brigades and CIH were allocated the task. The terrain in this sector was more or less flat, interspaced with irrigation channels and patches of scrub.

Barki was located on the road that ran from Harike in India to Lahore. The town sat astride the Ichhogil Canal which was 9.5 km from the IB and 24 km from Lahore. The Upper Bhuchar Distributary and the Hudiara Drain were two major obstacles on the way to Barki. The built-up areas of Hudiara, Nurpur, Barka Kalan, and Barka Khurd that lay on approaches to Barki were well defended and had to be cleared. The defences of Barki were formidable—concrete pillboxes, extensive tunnelling, and adequate artillery support had converted it into a virtual fortress. The Pakistanis had deployed one company in Barki village, two companies on the East Bank of the Ichhogil Canal, and a company of the reconnaissance and support battalion ahead of its defences.

Lieutenant Colonel Anant Singh was commanding 4 Sikh. The battalion had moved to Ferozepur in August 1965 after completing its tenure in Walong in NEFA where it had fought against the Chinese three years ago. Looking forward to its peace tenure, the focus of the battalion was on celebrating its annual Saragarhi Day on 12 September in a grand manner. However, the operational orders issued three days earlier resulted in 4 Sikh stepping across the IB on 6 September at 0400 hrs as the vanguard of 65 Infantry Brigade's offensive thrust on the Khalra–Barki axis. Two small villages situated just across the border on the left side of the main road had to be captured by stealth; Alpha Company under Major Shamsher Singh Manhas neutralized Theh Sarja Majra while Bravo Company commanded by Major Dalip Sidhu captured the Ranger post at Rakh Hardit Singh. This allowed Ferris to establish his brigade's firm base right on the border. 16 Punjab (Patiala) commanded by Lieutenant Colonel (later Major General) J. S. Bhullar then entered Pakistani territory at 0530 hrs and headed for the southern flank of the road where it captured the Ghawindi post that was being held by elements of 11 FF (R&S).

While 4 Sikh and 16 Punjab (Patiala) cleared and guarded the flanks, Shahaney's 48 Infantry Brigade concentrated at Sidhwan–Mughal Chak crossed the IB at H-hour and went straight for the Hudiara Drain. Lieutenant Colonel G. A. Nagle commanding 6/8 Gorkha Rifles was leading the Indian advance with Alpha Squadron of CIH under Major Narinder Dogra in support. There was no opposition until the leading elements of 6/8 GR reached the Hudiara Drain where Pakistan's 17 Punjab's Delta Company and 11 FF's (R&S) Bravo Company were dug in on either side of the water channel.

Covering the Khalra axis, Pakistan's 103 Brigade under Brigadier Muhammad Asghar comprised 12 Punjab, 17 Punjab (Haidris), a company each from 18 Baluch and 11 FF (R&S), two companies from 15 Baluch, and an armoured squadron. According to General Musa's new tactical concept, the eastern side of the Ichhogil in this sector was being held in strength by two companies each of 12 and 17 Punjab.

On the Hudiara Drain, the Punjabis were under the command of Major (later Colonel) Shafqat Baloch who had deployed two platoons on the eastern bank and the third on the western side. Flanking 17 Punjab's positions were a platoon each of 11 FF (R&S). Supporting this configuration was a battery of 24 Field Regiment which was in direct support. By 0700 hrs, 48 Infantry Brigade had made contact with the Pakistani defences at Hudiara, and came under fire from Hudiara village, the bridge area, and from the direction of Nurpur village. With Pakistani artillery opening up in direct support, 6/8 GR was hit hard. Nevertheless, Nagle put in a brisk flanking attack supported by Dogra's Sherman tanks, and by 1030 hrs 6/8 GR had secured the east bank of the Hudiara Drain and secured Hudiara Village, but could not progress any further due to continuous Pakistani artillery fire. Captain R. C. Bakshi,[43] Second Lieutenant P. V. Baraokar, Subedar Jordhan Rai, and nine other ranks were killed, while twenty-five were wounded. With 6/8 GR unable to press the momentum of their advance any further, 5 Guards attacked Nurpur by an outflanking manoeuvre, finally forcing the rest of the Pakistanis to withdraw from Hudiara Drain but not before they blew up the 140-foot bridge spanning the canal. Nupur village was finally captured at 1750 hrs.

Shafqat Baloch was shot through the arm, the bullet shattering the bone, but he had opposed the Indian advance valiantly and was later awarded the Sitara-e-Jurrat (Pakistan's third highest military award) for his action. The five NCOs were awarded the Tagma-e-Jurat and yet another, the Imtiazi Sanad for what was a screening action. '[A] screen is supposed to delay, giving adequate warning to the main body to prepare itself and not involve itself in a pitched battle—Major Baloch achieved this.'[44] However, at the end of the day, the Pakistani soldiers did manage to delay the leading elements of 48 Infantry Brigade and unnerve the brigade commander.

His advance delayed, Brigadier Shahaney reported back to Sibal that 48 Infantry Brigade had suffered fairly heavy casualties in the battle for Hudiara Drain. Sibal then sent 65 Infantry Brigade to take over 48 Infantry Brigade's unfinished task of getting to the Ichhogil Bridge at Barki, which was 5.5 km from Hudiara. With the bridge blown up, 65 Infantry Brigade had to cool its heels at Hudiara, enduring a night of sporadic shelling from the Pakistanis who were using the time to reinforce their defences around Barki.

Of the two thrusts towards Lahore, the offensive along the Khalra–Barki axis had relatively more weight behind it. General Chaudhuri's insistence that 11 and

1 Corps be split between the Bari and Rachna Doab had negatively impacted his own position. His plan was to split the Pakistani forces and spread them thin. But this strategy had boomeranged on 6 September, when both 15 Division and 7 Division had failed to establish a foothold anywhere on the Ichhogil Canal.

The offensive thrust towards Barki had been spared air attacks by the PAF who were too busy giving 54 Brigade hell on the GT Road axis, but the danger of Pakistani armour tearing into the flank of 7 Division's offensive thrust was a major worry for Dhillon. With 4 Mountain Division further to the south earmarked to push from the same direction also vulnerable, it was decided to create a small force that would secure the dividing line between the two divisions. For this vital task 17 Rajput, commanded by Lieutenant Colonel Jit Singh Gill, was grouped with armour, artillery, and other essential resources. Accordingly, on 3 September the battalion group under Gill's command received its orders and was tasked with capturing Bedian Bridge and to deploy in a manner so as to prevent Pakistani ingress through this axis. To deceive the Pakistanis that this task force was a major thrust and not just a battalion group, one troop of CIH tanks, two platoons of 93 Field Company (Engineers), one battery of 66 Field Regiment, and 82 Light Field Regiment less a battery were allotted to Gill.

By 1900 hrs on 5 September the 17 Rajput Group minus its armour had concentrated at Mari Kamboke, the assembly area. At midnight the move towards Wan commenced, and by 0445 hrs 17 Rajput Group had reached its FUP on the Indian side of the IB. At 0500 hrs Alpha Company under Second Lieutenant S. K. Chatterjee moved forward to execute the preliminary task of destroying a Pakistani concrete post covering the approach to Bedian Bridge. Thick sarkanda and high grass made the going difficult and Alpha Company was falling behind schedule. The platoon moving with Chatterjee was fired at from the pillbox, the first burst killing Havildar Rajpal and Sepoy Teg Singh on the spot.

The first casualties a battalion incurs in combat invariably stuns the rest of the men as the reality of war hits home; Chatterjee immediately gathered the platoon around him and started to advance when he too got hit. Naib Subedar Rajbir Singh,[45] commanding another platoon, now engaged the Pakistanis, who by then were being backed up by two tanks that were seen advancing towards the Rajputs. Firing STRIM grenades to keep them at bay, the arrival of 106 mm RCL guns forced the tanks to pull back into Bedian. Though Rajbir was wounded, he kept his grip on the situation and the pillbox was destroyed.

The battalion group resumed its advance towards Bedian which was situated at the junction of the Ichhogil and UBDC. The further flow of water into a network of subsidiary channels was also controlled from there. Bedian being strategically important, it had two infantry companies and two troops of armour defending it. Pakistani artillery and the tanks now opened up on the advancing column. Their fire initially bracketed the area where the guns of 82 Light Field were taking the Indian artillery out of the equation for the day. Firing air bursts, they then began to target the 17 Rajput command positions. Second Lieutenant Hardev Singh Gill's[46] mortar platoon fought back, but the Rajput group was taking casualties as the Pakistanis could clearly observe the Indian deployment which was pretty much out in the open. Second Lieutenant (later Brigadier) R. S. Mann was also severely wounded. By 1000 hrs, the battalion had abandoned the idea of pressing home the attack in broad daylight and it was postponed to 2200 hrs at night. Accordingly, the Rajputs firmed up 800 yards to the east of their objective.

Dhillon then ordered Sibal to have the area around Bedian heavily mined to stop any attempt by Pakistan to get into the rear of both 7 and 4 Divisions. Before the night attack could be launched, the Pakistanis launched a severe counter-attack on 17 Rajput's Charlie and Delta Company positions, but the Rajput line held. At one point a Pakistani tank tried to cross the Bedian Bridge but it was engaged by Second Lieutenant S. M. Akhtar with his section of 106 mm RCL guns.

4 MOUNTAIN DIVISION (KHEM KARAN)

4 Mountain Division, also known as the Red Eagles, had moved from Ambala to NEFA, where it had crumbled against the Chinese onslaught in 1962. After the debacle, it had exchanged places with 5 Mountain Division and returned to Ambala with its AOR being the Khem Karan sector. Based on descriptions 'by those who had met and served with Major General Gurbaksh Singh, he comes across as a wizened person in appearance but stoic in character. Behind those melancholic eyes lurked a resolve to never give up.'[47] With Gurbaksh Singh at the helm of affairs, the division consisted of 62 Mountain Brigade commanded by Brigadier (later Major General) H. C. Gahlaut and 7 Mountain Brigade which was being commanded by Brigadier D. S. Sidhu. Brigadier Jhanda Singh Sandhu was the artillery commander, who was a solid and highly competent all-rounder whose advice the GOC often benefited from. HQ 4 Mountain Division by and large had extremely good staff officers led by the GSO-1, Lieutenant Colonel (later Major General) Sukhwant Singh.

In relative terms, the Khem Karan Sector was a complex labyrinth of roads and water channels, where, on the face of it, Pakistan had a distinct advantage should it go on the offensive. Khem Karan and Kasur were virtually twin townships, both roughly 5 km from the IB due to the 1947 alignment of the Radcliffe Line. The Rohi Nullah which was about 150 feet wide, looped around Khem Karan on both sides of the border. While the Pakistanis had built a 30- to 50-foot-high bund on their side and developed it as a major tank obstacle which acted as a delaying position between the IB and the Ichhogil Canal, on the Indian side it was only partially a problem and could be crossed at various places without too much trouble. The Ichhogil in this sector was at an average

2 to 3 km from the border and along with the Rohi Nullah was an obstacle for any offensive towards Kasur.

On the other hand, the Ichhogil in this region was used extensively for irrigation purposes, as a result of which it had a large number of bridges, viaducts, and aqueducts that facilitated the movement of vehicles, including armour, across the canal. The main Kasur–Khem Karan road had a bridge across the Rohi and also a number of secondary crossing points south of the road, after which it was a free run towards Khem Karan even though there were plenty of small water channels for irrigation and the area was densely cultivated with sugarcane, maize, and bajra. Beyond Khem Karan, a Pakistani armoured thrust could isolate 11 Corps altogether if it got to the bridges on GT Road at Harike and Beas.

Apart from cutting off 11 Corps, in such a scenario, the underbelly of both 7 and 15 Infantry Divisions would be exposed, with dire consequences. Should Pakistan then build on the Beas River as a defence line, it could swing northwards and cut the road and rail link to Pathankot, thereby cutting off Jammu and Kashmir from the rest of India. Even limited success for Pakistan in this sector would spell catastrophe, especially since the Indians had virtually no reserves to fall back on.

Acutely aware of this, after Operation Ablaze, General Chaudhuri had decided to give the division and the sector more teeth. Deccan Horse, commanded by Lieutenant Colonel (later General, who went on to become the thirteenth chief) Arunkumar Shridhar Vaidya, equipped with the Sherman IVs with 76 mm guns, had replaced CIH which had 75 mm guns, as 4 Mountain Division's integral armoured regiment. In addition, Brigadier Theogaraj's 2 (Independent) Armoured Brigade, under HQ 11 Corps, was positioned at Bhikkiwind area to counter any Pakistani armoured action in Khem Karan or Khalra areas.

Finally, being a mountain division, 1 Field Regiment was equipped with the nearly obsolete short range 3.7-inch howitzer, along with 40 Medium Regiment that had the 5.5-inch howitzers. These were deployed as far forward as possible so as to increase their ability to hit targets across the IB.

In reality, 'being a mountain division, this formation was inadequately armed for plains warfare, particularly in the field of artillery and recoilless guns. However, the division had to be utilized, as there was no option and ad hoc arrangements made for necessary support.'[48] In addition, the half a dozen battalions that made up the two brigades of 4 Mountain Division had to travel from their locations near Ambala and the Simla hills and would only reach their concentration areas late at night on 5 September. The first real glimpse they would have of the countryside would be at dawn when they were in the middle of a full-fledged war!

Despite all these obvious drawbacks, the task given to 11 Corps in this sector by Western Command was typical of Harbakhsh Singh's thinking—offensive defence. 4 Mountain Division was to (1) secure Pakistani territory up to the east bank of the Ichhogil Canal from Bedian exclusive to Ganda Singh Wala inclusive; (2)

destroy the bridge over the Ichhogil Canal on the Kasur–Khem Karan road; and (3) occupy a divisional defended sector to contain a likely offensive by 1 Pakistan Armoured Division and an infantry division less a brigade, astride the Kasur–Khem Karan and Ganda Singh Wala–Khem Karan axes. The last part of the order clearly indicates that the triumvirate that had been war gaming the offensive expected the Pakistani counter-offensive to be aimed at Khem Karan. At least on paper, 7 Infantry Division appeared to be the logical choice to hold the Khem Karan Sector. Why this was not considered will always remain a mystery.

Towards the end of August, Intelligence reports had started trickling in of a Pakistani armoured division in Wazirabad. When Operation Grand Slam began, the identification of a couple of Pakistani armoured regiments and elements of Pakistan's 7 Division (part of their Strike Force) had led to the assumption that their main offensive forces were opposite Chhamb. As a result, it was assumed that Pakistan's 1 Armoured Division was not in the Kasur area. Reports suggesting a second Pakistani armoured division was in existence were dismissed by the Indian army chief who stated that the minimum time required to raise a new formation and for it to be battle worthy would be a minimum of nine months. Chaudhuri couldn't have been more wrong!

11 Corps' operational instructions were based on the assumption that Pakistan's 10 Division was solely responsible for the defence of the Lahore Sector and 106 Brigade under Brigadier Nawazish Ali on the Kasur–Khem Karan axis was reporting to Major General Sarfraz Khan as the formation's fourth brigade. As per the corps' appreciation, 106 Brigade was covering an extended front of approximately 45 km. It was further presumed that the brigade's deployment would be more or less along the same pattern as in the other two sectors—one infantry battalion east of the Ichhogil Canal and some elements of R&S holding screen positions. Given the thin Pakistani defences, 4 Mountain Division was expected to reach the east bank of the Ichhogil Canal with the minimum of fuss, capture and blow up the bridges, and then deploy in a compact defensive position on the east bank itself before the Pakistanis could react. Unfortunately, the only thing Indian Intelligence had got right was the presence of 106 Brigade, but that too was part of the new grouping as discussed earlier.

Gurbaksh Singh's plan envisaged 62 Mountain Brigade setting up a firm base southwest of Khem Karan, with 1/9 GR from 7 Mountain Brigade covering the Ganda Singh Wala flank. 62 Mountain Brigade was to then advance up to Rohi Nullah while the east bank of the Ichhogil Canal extending from Theh Pannu to Ballanwala would be secured by 7 Mountain Brigade. The east bank of the Ichhogil Canal extending from the bridge on the Khem Karan–Kasur road to Ganda Singh Wala would then be cleared and occupied by 62 Mountain Brigade. H-hour for 4 Mountain Division was 0500 hrs.

Tired and exhausted after having driven through the previous day and in some cases even part of the night all the way from Nahan, 1/9 GR commanded by Lieutenant Colonel S. S. Pathania was in position as per schedule, covering the Ganda Singh Wala axis while 18 Raj Rif with Lieutenant Colonel Raghubir Singh in command positioned itself to cover the rest of the brigade. Both brigades had been grouped with a squadron of tanks belonging to Deccan Horse.

The Pakistani forward positions were alert and 9 JAK Rif commanded by Lieutenant Colonel (later Major) Goverdhan Singh 'G. S.' Jamwal came under machine gun and artillery fire right from the start. However, supported by tanks and counter bombardment, 9 JAK Rif secured the road crossing over the Rohi Nullah. 13 Dogra, commanded by Lieutenant Colonel G. C. Khosla, sent Alpha and Delta Company across the bridge to capture the high ground at Rohiwal. Coming under intense small arms and artillery fire, the Dogras immediately started taking casualties. Though Alpha Company under Captain J. S. Thakur captured the objective, fire from well-concealed positions took a heavy toll on Delta Company. It finally took four hours of fighting before Charlie Company cleared the surrounding areas. While the Dogras were slugging it out around Rohiwal, to the right of the Kasur Road, Charlie Squadron of Deccan Horse under the command of Major (later Major General) Daya Krishan 'D. K.' Mehta was having difficulty crossing the Dode Drain and only five tanks managed to get across to support 4 Grenadier's attack on Theh Pannu.

Lieutenant Colonel Farhat Bhatti was commanding 4 Grenadiers. The battalion's advance party had already gone to the battalion's future location as per the routine rotational programme of the army. While 4 Grenadiers captured its objective, its sister battalion, 7 Grenadiers (which had seen action earlier in the Rann of Kutch as a camel battalion) failed to capture Ballanwala and fell back on the Rohi Nullah near Sankatra. By noon on 6 September, though 4 Mountain Division had got to some of its objectives, it had failed to establish a compact defended area. On the contrary, its battalions were spread extensively. In 62 Mountain Brigade area, 13 Dogra was at Rohiwal after an extended fight, 18 Raj Rif was holding its position as a screen and also the firm base at Khem Karan along with 1/9 GR, and 9 JAK Rif was deployed around the bridge on the Rohi Nullah. 7 Mountain Brigade's two battalions, 7 Grenadiers and 4 Grenadiers, were also spread out over an extended area.

KHEM KARAN—THE WHEELS COME OFF

Even at this stage, no one had any clue what 4 Mountain Division was up against, which with hindsight may have been a blessing in disguise. 'Unknown to the Indians, Pakistan had deployed its newly raised 11 Infantry Division in the Kasur Sector from Bedin to Ganda Singh Wala both inclusive.'[49] The existence of this division would remain unknown till 13 September. Not only was 11 Pak Division under Major General Abdul Hamid Khan poised and ready for its offensive, the entire formation had moved into its battle positions on the night of 4/5 September. Pakistan had also moved its 5 Armoured Brigade on the same day to Kasur and placed it under Hamid Khan's command. The rest of 1 Armoured Division had also deployed in the Kasur area on the night of 5/6 September, a few hours after which India's 4 Mountain Division launched its own 'offensive'.

At 1400 hrs, Hamid issued orders to 52 Brigade to push the Indians back and establish a bridgehead across the Rohi Nullah by first light the next morning. 13 Dogra was the first Indian battalion that took a hit. After having captured Rohiwal, their defensive stores had failed to reach them and the battalion was without any digging tools, mines, or barbed wire. An hour later, a bewildered 13 Dogra, which was moving around trying to improvise defences, was subject to intensive shelling as the combined fire power of 11 Artillery Brigade, the available guns of the division and the corp's artillery brigade targeted Rohiwal. Mainly firing airburst ammunition, the Pakistani guns created mayhem as shrapnel rained down from the sky. According to Pakistan's 52 Brigade war diaries, over 150 Dogras were killed including two officers, Lieutenants Sharma and Padam Nath. The Pakistanis further claimed that fifteen jawans were captured along with Major Milkiat Singh, the battalion's second-in-command. Under cover of the shelling, Pakistani armour and infantry crossed over the Ichhogil and assembled 500 metres south of the road bridge. The appearance of Pattons, combined with the extensive shelling, resulted in 13 Dogra abandoning its defences and falling back towards the IB, where it was brought to order by Khosla and the other surviving officers and JCOs. The shell-shocked men hurriedly prepared new defences and settled in, grateful for the hours of darkness.

Pakistani shelling of Indian positions intensified after last light. The Deccan Horse tanks, which had until then brought in an element of caution among Pakistani armour, had to withdraw to a safe harbour as they did not have night capability. The infantry, spread thin as it was, now had to deal with a sense of isolation as well. Throughout the night, Pakistani tanks and infantry kept up the pressure, probing for gaps to further isolate the Indians. There was also virtually no let-up in the quantum of artillery fire, as the Pakistani gun positions behind the west bank of the Ichhogil had the entire sector bracketed.

The first to break was 13 Dogra, which had already suffered massive casualties. Once the first few men began to slink off into the dark from their new position, others followed. The deserters left behind their commanding officer, subedar major, and a few others. 7 Grenadiers made another attempt to capture Ballanwala, but ran into even more intensive fire. In the process the battalion completely lost cohesion in the dark. 1/9 GR also had to abandon its positions and fall back towards Khem Karan. The six infantry battalions holding the line had been reduced to three and a half.

The day of 6 September had been an unmitigated disaster from the Indian point of view. In all three major sectors where 11 Corps had gone on the offensive, it had drawn a blank, failing to achieve even one of its objectives.

DERA BABA NANAK & FAZILKA

As part of its overall plan, 11 Corps had planned on protecting its two flanks by launching subsidiary offensives around the Dera Baba Nanak (DBN) and Fazilka Enclaves. DBN marked the northern boundary of the 11 Corps AOR, and it was of strategic importance mainly because of the rail-cum-road bridge over the Ravi River. In January 1960, as per the Indo-Pak Agreement,[50] the 1.5-km long bridge had been given to Pakistan while the Hussainiwala Bridge over the Sutlej River went to India. A narrow Pakistani enclave existed on the Indian side of the Ravi while a larger Indian enclave existed on the western side opposite the Jassar township. Jassar's strategic importance is evident—it was connected to Sialkot via Narowal and Pasrur by both rail and road. It was also linked to DBN on the Indian side by the 1,500-metre rail-cum-road bridge. Any Pakistani ingress in the area would then take them from DBN to Batala and Ajnala which would then make the Amritsar–Pathankot Road vulnerable. From the Pakistani point of view, the reverse was equally relevant; an Indian offensive from DBN to Jassar could then seriously threaten the flanking and rear defences of Sialkot.

In the Pakistani Enclave, an observation tower had been constructed, ostensibly to keep a watch on her territory. This tower also helped to track Indian movements, especially the approaches to the bridge. Given the visual sweep available to any observer positioned in the tower, not only was it difficult to mask any movement, but in case of hostilities, it could be used to direct artillery fire with devastating effect.

General Musa and GHQ Pakistan were extremely wary of any thrust developing on the DBN–Jassar axis. Accordingly, Pakistan's 115 Infantry Brigade with two infantry battalions, one squadron of Sherman tanks, and a field battery were deployed for the defence of the Jassar–Narowal area. The 11 Corps commander decided to detach 29 Infantry Brigade from 7 Infantry Division and tasked them with eliminating the Pakistani Enclave on the eastern bank and capturing the DBN Bridge intact. Even before the formation could move from Ambala to its concentration area around DBN on 4 September, the hospitalization of the incumbent brigade commander necessitated a change of command. Brigadier Pritam Singh, who was commanding a brigade in 26 Infantry Division, was asked to move immediately and take over 29 Infantry Brigade. As Pritam Singh's original brigade also had an operational role, the decision was absurd and illogical, for now both the brigades were to go to war with new commanders.

Pritam Singh's 29 Infantry Brigade had three infantry battalions at DBN—2 Madras with Lieutenant Colonel C. V. Donoghue at the helm, 2 Raj Rif being commanded by Lieutenant Colonel Vohra, and 1/5 GR under Lieutenant Colonel S. N. S. Gurung. In addition, the 16th Battalion, Punjab Armed Police (PAP),

Bravo Squadron of CIH, and 5 Field Regiment completed this grouping. At the designated 11 Corps H-hour, 2 Madras and elements of 2 Raj Rif started to clear the Pakistani Enclave which mainly consisted of tall sarkanda grass and was heavily defended by elements of Pakistan's 3 Punjab and a company of Sutlej Rangers, a few artillery guns, and some tanks. The fighting was fierce and by first light 2 Madras had recovered thirty-two bodies and taken ten POWs. However, a part of the enclave held out and, despite engaging the concrete observation tower with 106 mm RCL guns and even tanks, the observation post could not be destroyed. Under the cover of darkness, some Pakistani troops withdrew across the Ravi, giving the impression that Indian troops had landed in the Jassar area, the implications of which sent additional alarm bells ringing in Pakistan's GHQ.

While 2 Madras and 2 Raj Rif had engaged the Enclave, 1/5 GR had occupied the Dhusi Bund that overlooked the bridge's exit from the Indian side. At 1400 hrs, Pakistan's 115 Brigade counter-attacked across the bridge with its 25-pounder guns providing accurate covering fire from across the river under the guidance of its observers on the tower. A troop of Pakistani tanks supported by infantry came across the bridge while the tanks in the Pakistani Enclave around the observation tower also gave covering fire. Two companies of 1/5 GR, which had neither laid anti-tank mines or positioned RCL guns to cover this most unexpected approach, abandoned their defences.

Unnerved by this reverse, Pritam Singh sent a signal to Dhillon saying in case of additional Pakistani pressure, he may not be able to hold the DBN area and sought permission to withdraw to a new defensive location. With a new commander at the helm of affairs, there was considerable confusion in the brigade HQ which had led to the dispatch of the signal. Nevertheless, it was sent and then received by Dhillon who along with Harbakhsh Singh was returning from HQ 15 Division after a meeting with the hapless Prasad. Fortunately, 11 Corps HQ had a fairly accurate picture of the reality on the ground in the DBN Sector by the time Dhillon returned to his TAC HQ. An unambiguous reply was sent to Pritam Singh that stated 'that there would be no withdrawal from DBN under any circumstances'. Pritam Singh was ordered to counter-attack to recapture the lost ground. In a highly unorthodox move, Dhillon sent his chief engineer, Brigadier Bhide and his GSO-1 Lieutenant Colonel Chhajju Ram,[51] an artillery officer, to HQ 29 Infantry Brigade to make sure his orders were carried out.

Having established a bridgehead across the DBN Bridge, the Pakistanis launched a second attack on the 2 Madras and 1/5 GR positions with the intention of enlarging their hold. This attack failed as the Indians resolutely fought back. At 0245 hrs, 2 Raj Rif counter-attacked. The Pakistanis, thinking a major attack was developing, fell back, leaving two of their serviceable tanks behind. Indian defences were then quickly strengthened and anti-tank mines laid to ensure no Pakistani tanks could approach the Indian positions over the bridge again.

On the evening of 7 December, a convoy of vehicles began to move forward with their headlights on to give the Pakistanis the impression that a major attack was being planned to establish a bridgehead on the western side of the bridge. These moves had the desired effect on the Pakistani commanders who were convinced that the main Indian thrust would soon be launched against Jassar.

The situation on the southern flank was a lot more complicated. Defending the Hussainiwala and Sulemanki Sector, a staggering frontage of approximately 570 km, was Brigadier Bant Singh's 67 Independent Infantry Brigade Group. The AOR extended from the Harike headworks and extended south to Anupgarh. The lush irrigated fields with standing crops which were the hallmark of the Punjab gave way to dry open country along the Sutlej, most of which was covered by miles and miles of sand. The Hussainiwala and Sulemanki Sector could be broken into three sub-sectors; the Hussainiwala headworks; the salient protruding to the west from Fazilka; and the Ganganagar region. It was a foregone conclusion that 'the Pakistan Army would try and capture Hussainiwala and its headworks, and try and push the salient opposite Fazilka so as to straighten the line and improve their future position. Unless Pakistan wanted to capture territory purely from a statistical point of view, it was highly unlikely they would be interested in the Ganganagar sub-sector.'[52]

Bant Singh's brigade correspondingly had four battalions of PAP and another two of Rajasthan Armed Constabulary (RAC) that were operationally under his command. The brigade was headquartered in Jodhpur and the army units affiliated to the group were spread out between Mount Abu, Jaipur, and Mhow. 3/9 GR (Chindits) was being commanded by Lieutenant Colonel Kharka Singh Gurung, 2 MLI (Kali Panchwin) under Lieutenant Colonel T. T. A. Nolan, and 14 Punjab (Nabha Akal) under Lieutenant Colonel C. S. Bhullar made up the infantry element of the group. Lieutenant Colonel Thakur Govind Singh[53] was commanding 61 Cavalry, 4 Independent Squadron of Deccan Horse was under Major Khusro Yar Khan, while 144 Field Regiment (TA) was being commanded by Lieutenant Colonel J. S. Bajwa.

Having received their operational orders on 3 September, even though the units had made it to their designated locations, they were 'not yet operationally fit because of deficiencies of essential items…. The field regiment was without its first line ammunition till the morning of 7 September. The brigade was without small arms ammunition for replenishment till then.'[54] To make matters worse, Bant Singh himself had taken over the brigade on 29 August. None of the units under his command knew him or vice versa, or, for that matter, each other. Almost all the battalions and regiments were under strength, as troops on leave were just about getting the news that they were to report back.

The 67 Infantry Brigade Group was the only Indian formation that had a defensive charter. Dhillon had in fact told Bant Singh not to get unnecessarily involved with the Pakistanis, for 11 Corps did not have the resources to reinforce his brigade group. Incredible as it may seem, 61 Cavalry had moved with 450 horses from Jaipur to Ganganagar. Also the army did not have any high expectations from the PAP or RAC, who, at best, were considered boots on the ground that were early warning screens who were unlikely to fight at all. Nevertheless, as per the task given to Bant Singh, he was to (1) hold the Hussainiwala Bridge; (2) prevent the Pakistanis from establishing a bridgehead in the area opposite Sulemanki; (3) deny the two axes to the enemy, namely Hussainiwala–Ferozepur–Twin Rajasthan Canals and Sulemanki–Fazilka–Malout–Sirsa; and (4) destroy all enemy forces that may enter the Ganganagar area.

Pakistan's 105 Independent Infantry Brigade Group was being commanded by Brigadier Muhammad Akbar who was informed of the Indian invasion in the DBN, Lahore, and Kasur Sectors by GHQ Pakistan at around 0700 hrs on 6 September. Akbar's brigade, which reported directly to General Musa in GHQ, had its regular headquarters in Bahawalpur but it been deployed at Sulemanki since 5 May as a result of the clash in the Rann of Kutch. Throughout Operation Ablaze it had stayed close to its operational area even though the brigade had pulled back to Haveli, as a result of which all its commanders were familiar with the terrain. Though its AOR extended from the inter-formation boundary with 11 Division at Kanganpur and extended south till Bahawalnagar, its primary responsibility was to defend the Sulemanki headworks.

Akbar had three infantry battalions—4 Punjab, 10 Punjab, and 1 Baluch. His artillery component included 32 Medium Regiment that had earlier moved from Multan where it was earlier a part of Pakistan's 1 Corps (Arty), plus an artillery mortar battery. 92 Field Company of engineers, three wings of Rangers, and four mujahid companies plus other support units were under his command. Amazingly quick off the blocks by any standards, Muhammad Akbar spoke to the Pakistani army chief and asked for permission to go on the offensive, especially since the Indians opposite him were dormant. Having obtained Musa's approval, the Pakistanis went on the offensive at 1830 hrs.

Pakistan's 10 Punjab, commanded by Lieutenant Colonel Amir Hamza was to capture the Indian border posts at Jhangar and Sadiqia (Pakka). Then 4 Punjab under Lieutenant Colonel Jahanzeb Arbab was to take the village of Pakka that lay to the east of the Sadiqia post and also capture Bhaini Muhamad Ali Chishti and then cut the Haveli–Fazilka Road at Mile 169. The PAP battalion in the area offered no resistance as 'the enemy commenced hostilities with an intense dose of artillery and mortar fire on our brigade positions. The bombardment commenced at 1800 hours 6th September 1965 and lasted for a period of half an hour after which there was intermittent shelling. Under the impact of the shelling and small arms fire the PAP abandoned their posts at Jhangar, Sadiqi and Khokar.'[55]

14 Punjab under C. S. Bhullar was deployed in depth from Gurmukh Khera

to the Asafwala Border Police Post, but there was nothing Bant Singh could do as there was no ammunition available for 144 Field Regiment to fight back with. On the contrary, the security of the guns was a major concern and it was decided to pull them back into Fazilka. Following the dictum that you can only fight with what you have, Bant Singh created an ad hoc mobile force consisting of two companies of 3/9 GR and 4 Independent Tank Squadron of Deccan Horse. By 0300 hrs the two Pakistani battalions had completed the first phase of their offensive. Extending from DBN to GT Road to Kasur to Khem Karan to Fazilka, India's 11 Corps had, through some incredibly poor planning, created a hole for itself! No wonder the COAS was depressed!

Chapter 13

PUNCH & COUNTER PUNCH
AIR BATTLE PART II (6 SEPTEMBER)

11 CORPS FIASCO

Lieutenant General Jogi Dhillon had an imposing personality. Well-built with an impressive physique and an outwardly strong and fearsome mien, he was too compliant a subordinate to say or do anything his superiors may construe as criticism. On the other hand, he appears to have been fairly brusque with his subordinates, often blaming them for his own failures. The complete fiasco of the Indian 'offensive' on day one has been glossed over, partly because the immediate objective of relieving pressure from the Akhnoor/Chhamb Sector was met by this move. However, there is no denying that in almost all sectors where 11 Corps advanced, or tried to advance, it was an unmitigated disaster.

Before we look at some of the behind-the-scenes drama that unfolded on 6 September 1965, it is worth looking at Dhillon's role in the events that led up to the disaster involving 4 Mountain Division and some key personnel in October 1962, who, by a quirk of fate, were now under his command. Chavan's main agenda, after being sworn in as the defence minister of India, had been to protect Prime Minister Nehru from having to take the blame for the NEFA fiasco. With General Chaudhuri having ensured that Lieutenant General Bijji Kaul took the rap, Chavan was also quite happy to leave things as they were; there was no enquiry, no soul searching, nothing whatsoever!

The decision to send 7 Brigade into battle was taken after the Chinese came calling at Dhola Post. At that time, Kaul was on leave in Kashmir and the DMO, Brigadier D. K. Palit, on a naval cruise on INS *Vikrant*. Dhillon was the deputy CGS and was taking all the decisions in Army HQ. Though the gun was fired from the then Defence Minister Krishna Menon's shoulder, the suicidal plan to send 7 Brigade up the Thag La to throw the Chinese out had come about on Dhillon's watch. The absurdity of the plan given the ground situation, the indifference to logistics, and the inability to see the larger picture had cost the country dear. By the time the others returned to Army HQ, events initiated by Dhillon had gained an irreversible traction of their own.

In 1965, Dhillon was the man on the ground right from the beginning and, through Operation Ablaze, had been party to the evolving offensive plans. Given the fact that the Pakistanis were caught completely by surprise, the failure to break through reflects very poorly on the Corps HQ's overall planning. In the Fazilka Sector, where no offensive was planned, and Pakistan took the initiative, there was no ammunition; in the Khem Karan Sector, where it was anticipated that the Pakistanis would counter-attack, Dhillon deployed the lightly equipped 4 Mountain Division when he could have sent 7 Infantry Division; 15 Infantry Division on the Lahore axis had virtually no air cover and even when Pakistan launched its Sabres in a ground attack role, not once did 11 Corps think of asking for air support; and, finally, in DBN, even though 29 Infantry Brigade had a limited role, it was a close call despite the fact that the Pakistani limited offensive was at the eastern end of a 1,500-metre bridge.

Ironically, the man who had to bear the cost of Dhillon's whimsical decisions in 1962 was once again at the receiving end in 1965.

During World War II, Niranjan Prasad had been a captain in the Indian Army when he was sent as the ground liaison officer with No. 7 Squadron during the Battle of Kohat. He was then seconded to the RIAF where, as a flight lieutenant, he earned his pilot wings. Initially, he flew the Lysander with No. 1 Squadron, then the Vultee Vengeance dive bombers. He was promoted to the rank of a squadron leader and went on to command the RIAF's No. 8 Squadron in the Arakan. After the war, he came back to the Indian Army and played a key role with 161 Brigade in Srinagar in coordinating with the air force. After a stint as the commandant of the 5 Gorkha Rifles Regimental Centre, he commanded 50 Parachute Brigade before he was posted as the GOC of the ill-fated 4 Division in NEFA where he was removed from command after the Chinese overran 7 Brigade on the Nam Ka Chu.

Niranjan Prasad's inability to stand up to Kaul, a shortcoming that seemed to affect the entire Indian Army at that time, had been his undoing in NEFA. Given a second chance three years later, his main objection to the task assigned to him was the vulnerability of his brigades to Pakistani air strikes. The more he pleaded for air cover, the more contemptuous Dhillon became, eventually recommending that Prasad be removed from command as 'he did not have a fire in his belly'. The warning issued to Prasad by Chaudhuri in the presence of Generals Harbakhsh Singh and Jogi Dhillon was to stop whining about air cover and get on with the job of capturing the east bank of the Ichhogil Canal.

Now to come back to 6 September 1965. Harbakhsh Singh and Dhillon were at the 11 Corps TAC HQ at Rayya monitoring the situation when at 1230 hrs the GSO-1, Chhajju Ram emerged from the Ops Room and handed over a signal to them. 'Have been hit hard by Pak air(.) F and B Echelon vehicles largely destroyed(.) Request permission to withdraw.'[1]

Harbakhsh Singh immediately asked the GSO-1 to tell Prasad to stay where he was and that he and Dhillon were on their way to his location. Driving the

Jonga himself, with the corps commander beside him and his ADC, Captain Amarinder Singh, in the back seat, they tore along the deserted GT Road, through Amritsar onto the Wagah border, a distance of 77 km in less than an hour. 'At about 1,000 yards beyond the International Border we found hundreds of troops milling about in a mango grove beside the road. This, to our astonishment proved to be the headquarters of 15 Division. I was at once despatched to find the GOC and bring him to the army commander. I found him sitting on a village *manji* (bed). I saluted and said the army commander wished to see him immediately.'[2]

Clearly Prasad was badly rattled by the air strikes which had caused massive destruction of vehicles strung out all along the GT Road. Both 54 and 38 Infantry Brigades were affected. 'The sight of an unshaven major general with the rear of his crumpled shirt hanging out, was altogether too much for General Harbakhsh Singh. After receiving a severe tongue lashing, General Niranjan Prasad…was asked why he had withdrawn without orders when he had been specifically told to stand fast and do nothing till he (GOC-in-C) arrived. General Prasad began to mumble something about "Pak Air" when the corps commander cut him short and suggested that a summary court martial be convened immediately—it would find him guilty and he would be shot. This would send the right message across the Western Army; otherwise he feared a 1962 like situation may develop.'[3]

Fortunately for Prasad, Harbakhsh Singh chose to ignore Dhillon's advice. Unaware of the actual situation ahead of them where 3 Jat had crossed the Ichhogil Canal, Harbakhsh Singh continued to berate the ill-fated Prasad, going over 15 Division's 'failures' across the board. 'The loss in the number of vehicles, in his opinion, was insignificant. What was abundantly clear was that he had withdrawn even before he had requested permission to do so. He would be removed from his command and his replacement would arrive on the following day. In the meantime, he was to carry on with his task of capturing the Ichhogil Canal that night. The second phase of the operation, the capture of Bhasin, could wait.'[4]

By then it was obvious to all present that Prasad no longer had the confidence to regroup his forces. 'His attitude was passively negative and there was the unmistakable air of the defeatist about him. He stated his inability to undertake any further offensive action on the plea that his formation had lost all capacity for operations.'[5] As the army commander, Harbakhsh Singh had no choice but to sack Prasad, whose trials were by no means over. Also, unfortunately, neither Harbakhsh Singh nor Dhillon proceeded further up GT Road to see for themselves the effect of the Pakistani air strikes. Had they done so, they would have reached Gosal–Dial where Maha Singh Rikh's Brigade HQ was located just short of the Ichhogil Canal itself, barely 8 km further up.

Harbakhsh Singh, in his autobiography, *In the Line of Duty*, includes an even more graphic account in which he says Prasad was hiding in a sugarcane field. He also describes how vehicles were burning all along the road, which is at variance with what his own ADC, Amarinder Singh, says. Harbakhsh Singh also noted that Pakistani Sabres overflew them while he was talking to Prasad and describes how Prasad tried to pull him to cover. However, by the afternoon, the PAF had stopped flying offensive sorties, for the aircraft at Sargodha were being prepared for a larger strike against Indian airfields later in the evening. Junior officers who fought in that sector also categorically state that none of the senior officers came to see the situation on the ground.

The only subject where the Indian and Pakistani press were in agreement in the parallel war of words was in accusing Niranjan Prasad of cowardice. Other versions of what actually transpired are not as damning of the man. 'Prasad had learnt in the meantime that 3 Jat had crossed the Ichhogil so he decided to go forward to meet the brigade commander. …Brigadier Rikh told him that 3 Jat were falling back from the Ichhogil. Prasad ordered Rikh to stop the withdrawal but Rikh was not in communication with 3 Jat. Prasad tried to pass a message over the 14 Horse wireless net and learnt that the battalion had already passed through their area. Prasad now ordered 38 Brigade to recapture the Dógrai bridge.'[6] In the meeting with Harbakhsh Singh and Dhillon shortly after this—which would suggest the army commander met Prasad again after 1730 hrs—the corps commander peremptorily countermanded Prasad's orders to 38 Brigade. He ordered Rikh to recapture Dograi and told Brigadier Pathak to proceed to the east bank of the Ichhogil in the Bhasin–Dogaich area. 'Prasad remonstrated against the countermanding of his orders but was firmly told by the army commander to carry out the task as ordered by the corps commander by first light on 7 September.'[7]

PAKISTAN'S MULTIPLE GAMBLES

Was launching Operation Grand Slam against a single infantry brigade in the Chhamb–Jaurian Sector the biggest tactical blunder committed by Pakistan? Very likely, for with that one decision, Field Marshal Ayub Khan and General Mohammad Musa had thrown away the biggest arsenal in their formidable bag—the element of surprise! Instead, five days later, it was the Pakistanis who were caught by surprise, and were clearly thrown off balance with the launching of Operation Riddle in the early hours of 6 September. Luckily for them, as the day wore on, it soon became obvious that things had not quite gone according to the Indian plan either.

The single biggest flaw in the Indian scheme of things had been the complete lack of air cover on 6 September. Ironically, it was Niranjan Prasad's 15 Infantry Division that was most badly affected, with the PAF having a free run of the skies over GT Road. Prasad, who had served with the RIAF, had time and again tried to point out this fatal flaw, but all he got for his 'whining' was a reprimand from the big three! 'During the series of war games held by Headquarters 11 Corps in June/July 1965, I had kept a close watch for any chinks in the mental attitude of various commanders, especially those at the divisional level, to assess their suitability for command of troops in battle.[8] Even if we were to presume that when the plans were made in June/July, air cover was not an option, then the events on 1 September in the Akhnoor Sector should have opened the eyes of Chaudhuri, Harbakhsh, and Dhillon at that stage. Subsequently, Harbakhsh repeatedly downplays this aspect and glibly writes that the destruction of the B and F Echelon vehicles by the PAF at best set the Indian advance back by two hours. In reality, the air attacks exposed Operation Riddle as a half-hearted jab which even an off-balance Pakistan could fend off rather easily.

Until Operation Grand Slam, Pakistan had been calling the shots. But they did not seem to have any understanding of the Indian military thinking. After the initial euphoria of having 'run over the Indians' in the Rann of Kutch, Operation Gibraltar had been launched with the conviction that India would restrict the fighting against the guerrillas to her side of the CFL. The assumption that Operation Grand Slam was launched because India took the fight into POK and captured the Haji Pir pass is probably wrong simply because the timelines suggest otherwise. The movement of armour and even the half-hearted response to the Indian occupation of Haji Pir suggests Operation Grand Slam was going to happen in any case.

Similarly, if one looks at the Pakistani reactions on 6 September, it would seem Operation Grand Slam II was also in the offing. India's moving forward and attacking across the IB, especially in the Lahore Sector, and 3 Jat's amazing run when the battalion leapfrogged across the Ichhogil and got to Batapur queered the pitch for Pakistan. On the evening of 6 September, though the main attention was on Prasad and 15 Infantry Division's inability to consolidate on the Ichhogil Canal, the real danger was in the Khem Karan Sector where Gurbaksh's 4 Mountain Division was in serious danger of crumbling at the next Pakistani thrust.

Earlier in the morning, Chavan had made a statement to the Lok Sabha. He had stated: 'On the afternoon of 5 September Pakistan aircraft had intruded across the international boundary at Wagah near Amritsar and fired rockets at an air force unit. Anti-aircraft action drove them away. This violation was reported but there were further violations over the same border by Pakistan Air Force and it was quite apparent that Pakistan's next move was to attack Punjab across the International Border. The indication that this was going to happen was building up over some time. In order to forestall the opening of another front, our troops in the Punjab moved across the border in Lahore Sector for the protection of the Indian border.'[9]

Ever since the Gliewitz 'False Flag' incident that Adolf Hitler used to justify the German attack on Poland on 1 September 1939, politicians who blame the other side for them resorting to military action has always been seen as pure rhetoric. Chavan's statement got drowned in the euphoric and lusty cheers in the Lok Sabha. Ironically, across the border, news that Pakistan had captured Jaurian was being greeted with equal enthusiasm. However, there was much more to

Chavan's statement in Parliament that fateful morning, for indeed, as subsequent records seem to suggest, a 'Grand Slam II'[10] was indeed on its way. Thanks to 'Grand Slam I' in Chhamb, a somnambulant India had woken up in the nick of time—perhaps purely by accident!

So what exactly was Pakistan up to? Since it never happened, we shall never know for certain. However, one thing is clear—GHQ was planning something big, and if 'Operation Gibraltar' and 'Operation Grand Slam' are any indicators, boldness was not something Pakistani commanders, at least at the planning stage, shied away from. The execution of those plans was, of course, another matter!

The two pivots on which the Pakistani offensive was probably being planned were 1 Armoured Division commanded by Major General Naseer Ahmed and the newly created 11 Division under Abdul Hamid. A decade later, while talking to officers at the Command and Staff College in Quetta, Naseer Ahmed alluded 'to his division's original mission [as having] "a much deeper hook and a much bigger objective" as compared to an offensive through the Ravi-Beas corridor.'[11] Brigadier Moinuddin, who commanded Pakistan's 3 Armoured Brigade in Naseer Ahmed's division, in response to a question about the projected operations categorically stated that they were not looking at the Khem Karan Sector but were training for operations further south in the Sulemanki Sector. As far as Pakistan was concerned, there were no troops worth the name in the Fazilka area and 4 Mountain Division, even in Khem Karan, was nowhere on the horizon until the morning of 6 September.

According to Naseer Ahmed, on 1 September (the day Operation Grand Slam was launched in the north in the Chhamb Sector) he received a signal from GHQ that had been drafted on 31 August 1965 'in which 1 Armoured Division, on orders from General Headquarters, was required to debouch from a bridgehead provided by 11 Division and cut the Grand Trunk Road east of Amritsar in the area Jandiala Guru.' Had the Pakistanis at that stage thrown in even an infantry-battalion-sized attack at Haji Pir to keep the Indians engaged and not triggered off Chhamb, nothing would have stopped Naseer Ahmed. Even a quarter century later, Harbakhsh Singh admitted that 'a Blitzkrieg deep into our territory towards the Grand Trunk Road or the Beas Bridge would have found us in the helpless position of a commander paralysed into inaction for want of readily available reserves while the enemy was inexorably pushing deep into our vitals. It is a nightmarish feeling even when considered in retrospect at this stage.'[12]

The first reports on the Indian invasion across Wagah came not from the Pakistani Rangers manning various posts on the border, but the PAF's Wireless Observer Wing that detected the attack and immediately passed on the information to Air Defence HQ. The officer on duty, Air Commodore Akhtar, informed President Ayub Khan in the early hours, while PAF squadrons were simultaneously put on high alert. Ayub Khan was most surprised, for he had not anticipated the Indian move. Nor, for that matter, had General Musa. As more and more sectors reported

Indian offensives, Musa and GHQ Pakistan watched in alarm, especially the Indian 15 Infantry Division thrust towards Lahore and the 29 Infantry Brigade assault on the DBN Enclave that was being seen as a precursor to an assault on Jassar. 'India invaded Pakistan on 6 September. From then onward, the country's security took precedence over the missions in Kashmir.... I withdrew from Chhamb the additional artillery allocated to the counter-offensive force and an infantry brigade for deployment in Sialkot front. These moves weakened our offensive powers in the Chhamb Valley. Consequently, and after ascertaining the local commander's views on the assault on Akhnoor with a depleted force, we decided to postpone it.' Lieutenant General Yahya Khan 'also showed reluctance in undertaking it in those circumstances.'[13]

Musa's immediate reaction underlines the fact that for the first couple of days or so, GHQ Pakistan was 'in jitters and groping in the dark...'.[14] For Harbakhsh Singh, it was a huge relief. 'The enemy reacted instantly. Within a few hours, the major portion of medium armour, artillery and a brigade of infantry were ordered to pull out of the Chhamb Sector. Pak's ambitious thrust towards Akhnoor Bridge was checkmated just in the nick of time.'[15]

WHERE IS THE BLASTED IAF? THE SKIES ABOVE ON 6 SEPTEMBER

The failure of the Indian commanders to co-opt the air force into their offensive plans on 6 September raises obvious questions about their competency. On the entire frontage, extending from DBN to Khem Karan (in Fazilka the Indians were not on the offensive), the most sensitive point from the Pakistani perspective was always going to be the thrust aimed at Lahore.

In 1992, Arjan Singh had said quite categorically that there existed an agreement between the air force chiefs that they would not attack one another's bases and installations. The agreement, he had said, had been violated by Pakistan when 'they bombed Pathankot and Amritsar on the evening of 6 September', after which he had instructed Western Air Command to strike back. IAF commentators, not wanting to point fingers at the highly respected Arjan Singh, who was elevated to first a four-, then a five-star rank, have also speculated that this restriction could have been imposed by a 'government order'.[16] That would mean it was either Prime Minister Shastri or Defence Minister Chavan who took that decision. While Shastri was not involved in the details of operations, had it been Chavan, he would have mentioned it in his diary. He does not, for example, shy away from taking responsibility when it came to asking the IAF to desist from attacking PAF airfields in East Pakistan even after they had launched similar attacks on Kalaikunda and Bagdogra.

In any event, between the army and air chiefs, they lost a golden opportunity to not only severely damage or even neutralize the PAF on the morning of 6 September itself, their failure to support 11 Corps with air power first limited

the offensive, and then when the PAF started attacking Indian columns on the
GT Road axis, the failure to call for air cover to check the Pakistani air attacks
ensured India's offensive got off to the worst possible start. Sadly, not a single
meaningful sortie was flown on 6 September by the IAF in direct support of the
ground troops in the DBN, GT Road, Barki or Kasur Sectors. Quite obviously,
there was no political restriction either, for the IAF had flown multiple interdiction
sorties, some against targets on the Ichhogil Canal itself.

In the early hours of the morning, Air Commodore Keki Nadirshah Gocal,
the senior air staff officer (SASO) of Western Command reached Adampur and
assigned ground targets to Wing Commander (later Group Captain) Om Prakash
'Omi' Taneja. The offensive had begun and 1 Squadron (Tigers) was to attack a
Pakistani Army formation HQ in the Gujranwala–Wazirabad Sector inside Pakistan.
An incredulous Taneja asked Gocal why they weren't focussing on hitting Pakistani
air bases. The SASO shrugged and gave what was to be the stock reply through
the day: orders from above.

At dawn, even as the Indian Army was crossing over into Pakistan, four
Mystères got airborne and set course for the designated target area. Taneja had
as his wingman Flight Lieutenant Darshan Singh Brar while the other section
comprised Squadron Leader (later Wing Commander) Patrick Russel 'Paddy' Earle
with Flight Lieutenant (later Group Captain) Suresh Shankarrao 'Lofty' Dange as
his number two. Once over the designated target area, it was obvious that there
was no such target at the given coordinates. A disappointed Taneja, not wanting
to abort the mission, decided to look for 'targets of opportunity' in the general
area of Rahwali, the cantonment area of Gujranwala. The Mystères then spotted
a train with some fuel wagons pulling into the Ghakher Railway Station which
they duly attacked. Unlike the Indians who never called for interceptors on the
previous day, the Pakistani system was attentive—Sakesar radar directed two F-104A
Starfighters from 9 Squadron flown by Flight Lieutenants Aftab Alam Khan (later
wing commander) and Amjad Hussain Khan (later air vice marshal) to zero in
on the Mystères.

Once the Pakistani pilots had made visual contact, Aftab Alam asked Hussain
to stay at 15,000 feet while he went after the low-flying Mystères. With the
Starfighter on their tail, the four Mystères immediately dropped even lower to
treetop level and started to make their getaway. Using his afterburners to jockey
himself into position, the Starfighter got a lock on Earle and launched one of
his AIM-9B Sidewinders. The flash of the missile leaving the rails temporarily
blinded Aftab Alam who instinctively pulled on the stick, taking his aircraft into
a steep climb. Unable to visually follow the missile's path, he rejoined Hussain
and made his way back to his base. A Pakistan Army unit had called in to say
that the Starfighter had shot down the Mystère, which had gone down near
Rahwali air base. Earle had, in a last-ditch effort to pull away from the rapidly

closing Starfighter, jettisoned his drop tanks, which had exploded on hitting the ground. The missile had missed him and while the other three aircraft got back to Adampur, Earle had to touch down in Pathankot owing to a shortage of fuel.

Further to the south of Adampur, four Hawker Hunters from 7 Squadron (Battle Axes) armed with T-10 rockets also got airborne from Halwara to strike across the IB. The formation was led by the commanding officer, Wing Commander (later Group Captain) Toric 'Tony' Zachariah, and comprised senior flight commanders, Squadron Leaders Sube Singh 'Chacha' Malik (later group captain), Man Mohan 'Rusty' Sinha (later air marshal) and Ajit Singh Lamba (later air vice marshal). Two Hunters flown by Squadron Leader Ajit Kumar 'Peter' Rawlley and Flight Lieutenant (later Wing Commander) Shiv Kumar 'S. K.' Sharma escorted them. Their brief was to strike targets of opportunity that flanked the Ichhogil Canal. They fired at some vehicles and gun positions but found nothing worthwhile. Eventually spotting an abandoned railway station near Kasur, they decided to fire their rockets at it. This in IAF lore became the infamous 'tonga strike' because the only living creature at the station was a poor terrified horse hitched to its tonga.

7 Squadron flew quite a few sorties, some even along GT Road, which further underlines the fact that there was no restriction on the IAF. Both Harbakhsh Singh and Dhillon were in the Corps HQ at least till midday, toasting the Indian advance with beer. All the plans made through June/July seem to have been restricted to the higher commanders, for there was virtually no coordination on the ground. When they did get the message that PAF air strikes had crippled the Indian advance, they decided to go see for themselves and not one person in 11 Corps HQ thought of putting in a demand for air cover!

Between 0545 hrs and 0630 hrs, 7 Squadron flew a dozen offensive reconnaissance sorties over the Lahore and Kasur Sectors. A two-aircraft sortie led by Flight Lieutenant (later Group Captain) Daya Krishan 'Dice' Dhiman flew along GT Road and, at that time in the morning, not surprisingly, saw nothing. Shortly after Tony Zachariah's formation took off, 27 Squadron (Flaming Arrows) also launched four Hunters led by their senior flight commander, Squadron Leader (later Air Marshal) Dilip Shankar 'Dalip' Jog. Once again, a target had been given by the army, but the Hunters drew a blank. They returned to base without firing a shot.

7 Squadron's third strike, also on the GT Road axis, took off at 1015 hrs. Chacha Malik was the leader, Squadron Leaders Prabhat Kumar 'Joe' Verma (later Air Marshal), Sureshchandra Bhaskar 'Bhagu' Bhagwat, and Lamba made up the formation, and Dice Dhiman and Flight Lieutenant (later Air Commodore) Herbert Moel 'Herbie' David flew as escorts. With no forward air control (FAC) on the ground or any specific information having been relayed by the army, the Hunters, not surprisingly, saw nothing. This formation of Hunters was in the area shortly after the Sabres had done serious damage to Indian vehicles, reiterating that unless there is close cooperation between the ground and air, it is well-nigh impossible

for fast, low-flying aircraft to find targets.

Malik's frustrated formation turned its attention to a clump of trees into which one of the Hunters fired its rockets. This shot in the dark turned out to be a Pakistani artillery gun position. On their way back to Halwara, they saw a F-104 Starfighter as it flashed past them. A few minutes earlier this aircraft had made two passes over Halwara, having been sent by Nur Khan on a reconnaissance flight after he had landed at Sargodha to plan the pre-emptive strike. Starfighters had also similarly overflown Pathankot and Adampur and reported back, confirming both airfields had their full complement of aircraft.

Two Hunters also did an offensive sweep over the Ferozepur–Kasur–Khem Karan Sector between 1420 and 1500 hrs. Finally, the last formation which took off at 1630 hrs and crossed the IB was Zachariah's complement of four aircraft that was looking for targets of opportunity.

PAF PRE-EMPTIVE STRIKES (6 SEPTEMBER NIGHT)

As a precursor to its armoured thrust towards Beas Bridge, the PAF had planned to launch a pre-emptive strike at nine different Indian targets with fifty Sabres and eight Lockheed T-33 Shooting Stars on 6 September, to be followed by further bombing raids by a dozen Martin B-57 Canberras. The strike force was to take off simultaneously from four different airfields (including Dacca in East Pakistan) just before last light and, apart from destroying aircraft on the ground at Pathankot, Halwara, Adampur, Jamnagar, Kalaikunda, and Bagdogra, they were also aiming to take out the radars at Amritsar, Ferozepur, and Porbandar. The only hitch was that the PAF had not expected an Indian offensive across the IB.

Just as the launch of Operation Riddle by the Indians derailed Pakistan's Operation Grand Slam in the Chhamb Sector, 15 Infantry Division's thrust towards Lahore had major implications on the planned pre-emptive aerial strike scheduled by the PAF for the evening of the same day. At 0830 hrs (Pakistan time) an emergency meeting of the joint chief of staffs was convened. Chaired by the president, Field Marshal Ayub Khan, the PAF was given carte blanche to respond as it deemed fit. Air Marshal Nur Khan had replaced Asghar Khan as the air force commander-in-chief just forty-five days ago. Nur Khan said he had already authorized the PAF to launch close ground support and air defence sorties, and he then sought Ayub's acquiescence to implement War Plan No. 6 of June 1965. Ayub agreed, with the rider that Indian airfields in Kalaikunda and Bagdogra be taken off the list of proposed targets since India had not attacked East Pakistan.

However, Asghar Khan, the retired air force commander-in-chief in his book *The First Round* says it was his initiative that resulted in Ayub green-lighting the pre-emptive strikes on 6 September. That now remains of academic interest, but it does underline the fact that the plans for the pre-emptive strike were being worked on and honed since June 1965, which more or less coincides with the plans being made for Operation Gibraltar. Just because the Pakistani leadership did not believe the Indians would expand the fighting outside of Jammu and Kashmir, it does not mean that Pakistan herself would not look at expanding beyond the region.

Nur Khan returned to the Air Defence HQ. However, he now had a problem, for Sargodha, Peshawar, and Mauripur were engaged in providing support to the ground troops, especially on the Amritsar–Lahore–GT Road axis. Since the lead time required to arm the Sabres was eight hours, it was imperative that all ground attacks be called off by 1000 hrs. Nur Khan delayed the decision and finally the flash message to all concerned units was sent at 1200 hrs. Group Captain Masud, the station commander at Sargodha, called up Nur Khan and told him that only twelve aircraft could be launched by sunset. He pleaded for a postponement, but Nur Khan decided he would go ahead with three strikes of four aircraft each to hit Adampur, Halwara, and the Amritsar radar. Peshawar, where the PAF's No. 19 Squadron was operating from, told Nur Khan it could launch eight strike aircraft, plus two escorts. The entire force under Squadron Leader Sayed Sajad Haider was directed to focus on Pathankot.

At 1500 hrs, Ayub gave his final go-ahead and rescinded his earlier stipulation pertaining to Indian airfields in the east. Nur Khan immediately authorized a signal to Dacca green-lighting airstrikes against Kalaikunda at first light the next day.

The P-30 radars at 230 SU at Amritsar picked up Haider's formation almost as soon as it got airborne. No sooner had 'track hostile' flashed, Wing Commander Dandapani had reached for the telephonic hotline to Pathankot asking to be put through to the station commander. His eyes glued to the scope, Dandapani watched as the Pakistani formation climbed to 25,000 feet, heading towards Gujranwala in an obvious attempt to give the impression that Halwara was the target. The formation then dived down to evade further detection, but the radar continued to pick up signs of their real intent. Group Captain Roshan Suri was not available, so Dandapani briefed the OC flying, Wing Commander Kuriyan, that a large number of Sabres from Sargodha were coming his way and that he should scramble fighters to intercept them. He also told Kuriyan that the Pakistani formation had gone off the screens, but one track was clearly visible as that fighter was probably flying ahead, scouting for interceptors.

There are two or three versions of how Kuriyan and Suri reacted, but what is clear is that Dandapani's warning was not heeded. Wing Commander Raghvendran, the 23 Squadron CO, had been badgering Roshan Suri to let him mount a Gnat CAP since 1730 hrs. For some inexplicable reason, Suri kept postponing the decision.

It was normal practice for CAPs to be flying overhead at dawn and dusk when the probability of incoming raids was the highest. The same also applies when aircraft are returning or taking off, for they are at their most vulnerable at that time. Around the same time that Dandapani was relaying the warning, a six-aircraft formation was, in fact, in the process of being recovered. Tango Singh was returning from Chhamb where his four Mystères had been attacking the withdrawing Pakistani armoured and artillery columns. The two escorting Gnats, flown by Murdeshwar and Flight Lieutenant (later Air Marshal) Janak Kapur, had asked to return to base earlier as their flight endurance was limited. However, the number three in the formation, Flying Officer (later Group Captain) Dinkar Shantaram 'Dinky' Jatar had a problem with his undercarriage and Murdeshwar decided to escort him back to Pathankot.

A Fairchild C-140 Packet had arrived from Bareilly earlier in the day and was parked on the tarmac. Two MiG-21s had also returned from a mission and, as per the existing SOP, these were being refuelled outside the blast pens. Tango, Flying Officer (later Wing Commander) Russell Douglas 'Russ' Montes (his number two), and Flight Lieutenant Raina (number four) were still in their cockpits, taxiing towards the blast pens. Murdeshwar and Jatar, their low fuel warning lights blinking in the Gnat and the Mystère, made a simultaneous landing from opposite directions and were just short of their designated blast pens when the Sabres hit Pathankot.

In the ensuing chaos that lasted over a dozen minutes, it is a miracle that no one was killed. Tango, Montes, Raina, Murdeshwar, and Jatar were all caught in their cockpits. As they jumped from their aircraft and ran for the cover of trenches, the rat-tat-tat of the Sabres 'canon' was heard, 'the din infernal and the effect quite devastating! This was punctuated by great "boofs" as aircraft on the ground caught fire and blew up. And suddenly, it was all over! It had lasted 10-12 minutes, but was almost an eternity to those who witnessed it!'[17]

They had lost six Mystères, two MiGs, one Gnat, and one Packet. In addition, two Gnats and a Mystère were damaged and three airmen were injured. In the immediate aftermath of the raid, the ground crew did a tremendous job, taking huge risks as they moved in to contain the fires. Pathankot was an unmitigated disaster. The odd ack-ack gun had fired during the attack, but they opened up only after the Pakistani aircraft were well on their way back.

Pakistan's original plan was to launch eight Sabres against Adampur from Sargodha, but owing to the Indian invasion, this was truncated to a four-aircraft formation. Squadron Leader (later Air Commodore) Muhammad Mahmood Alam was leading the formation that took off fifty minutes after Haider's strike force had got airborne from Peshawar. After crossing the IB, Alam followed the Amritsar–Delhi railway line, but Alam missed the airfield altogether. The Sabre formation was spotted northwest of Phagwara by three Dakotas from 43 Squadron flying from Sarsawa to Amritsar, but fortunately the Sabres failed to see them. By then Alam knew he had overshot Adampur, so he ordered the formation to turn back. Just as they neared Tarn Taran, they were spotted by Peter Rawlley who was the number two in a formation of four Hunters from 7 Squadron who had got airborne from Halwara to attack ground targets in the Lahore Sector.

The formation was being commanded by Zachariah, who failed to hear Rawlley's call. The low-flying Hunters were attacked by the Sabres and a treetop level dogfight ensued. The Hunters were configured with rocket rails which created an enormous amount of drag and Zachariah failed to give the order to jettison tanks. Tragically, as the Hunter formation executed a hard turn to evade the Sabres, Rawlley's aircraft hit the ground. Sinha, Sharma, and Zachariah managed to fire at the Sabres but gun camera footage showed none of them scored any hits. Alam claimed and was awarded two kills in this dogfight. Whether Rawlley was hit by Alam or his aircraft went into the ground was never conclusively established.

The strike against Halwara was to employ eight Sabres from Pakistan's No. 5 Squadron as well, but only four could be made ready. And only three took off ten minutes after Alam's formation had set off for Adampur. Squadron Leader Rafique, who had shot down two Vampires on 1 September, was in the lead with Flight Lieutenants Yunus Hussain and Cecil Chaudhary as numbers two and three respectively. By this time, the light was fading and visibility was dropping fast owing to a haze over Halwara. A few minutes after take-off, Alam warned Rafique on the RT that there were Hunters in the area and that his formation should keep a sharp lookout for them.

Even before Zachariah's remaining three Hunters were due to land at Halwara, two Hunters from No. 7 Squadron flown by Flying Officers Prakash Sadashivrao 'Pingo' Pingale and Adi Rustum 'Adi' Ghandhi (both were later air marshals) had taken off at 1710 hrs to provide air cover. Anticipating a simultaneous incoming air raid, two more Hunters from No. 27 Squadron flown by Flight Lieutenant (later Air Marshal) Dev Nath Rathore and Pilot Officer (later Wing Commander) Vinod Kumar Neb had been scrambled. Pingale and Ghandhi had set up a left-hand CAP over the airfield while Rathore and Neb did the same 180 degrees opposite their position. On the ground, Flight Lieutenant G. S. Thapa was manning a 20 mm aircraft gun being used in an anti-aircraft role and he saw the Sabres pulling up sharply for an attack. He opened fire and the rounds were seen hitting one of the Sabres. In the air, Pingale had just realized the Sabres had arrived when he heard gunfire behind him. 'I looked back and saw a Sabre between me and Adi and belching smoke from all his guns. I tried to turn into him but found my controls had gone into manual and smoke trailed from my left wing. The Sabre started overshooting me, so I tried to reverse onto him. My hydraulic audio warning had come on, with left wing smoking. I got the wings level and ejected.'[18]

Meanwhile, Adi Ghandhi got behind Rafique's Sabre and fired at him, but he himself was hit by the Sabre flown by Chaudhary. His left wing on fire and with his Hunter disintegrating, Ghandhi bailed out over the airfield. However, Pakistan claims Ghandhi missed Rafique's Sabre, which had a gun stoppage. However, with both Pingale and Ghandhi shot down and his three-aircraft formation low on fuel,

Rafique ordered Chaudhary to take the lead and set course for Adampur in the fading light. Rafique was unaware that there were two more Hunters in the sky.

Rathore and Neb had seen the Sabres and they rapidly moved in for the kill. Rathore, closing in on Rafique who was flying behind Chaudhary on the right, ordered Neb to get after the Sabre on the left which was being flown by Yunus Hussain. Rathore, closing in rapidly, opened fire from 600–500 yards, registering some hits, and then with his gunsight on Rafique's cockpit, he fired a second burst. The Sabre banked sharply to the left and hit the ground in a huge ball of fire. Neb had closed in on the second Sabre and he fired a burst from 400 yards. Chaudhary gave a call for a defensive break but Yunus Hussain pulled up, offering Neb the full form of the aircraft to aim at. From 100 yards, he was hardly likely to miss. Chaudhary's was the lone Sabre that made it back to Sargodha from the third strike.

The pre-emptive strike, despite being truncated from a planned fifty-eight aircraft to just fifteen Sabres, had spectacular results for the PAF—thirteen aircraft destroyed or damaged on the ground, three Hunters lost in the air, as against two Sabres shot down near Tarn Taran while returning from Halwara. Unfortunately for the Pakistanis, both Rafique and Yunus Hussain were killed and their bodies were buried the next day in accordance to the last rites of their faith. For the IAF and especially the Battle Axes (7 Squadron), the loss of the soft-spoken and highly regarded Rawlley was a huge blow.

Late at night, a grim Arjan Singh drove to Chavan's residence and informed him about the PAF attacks on Pathankot, Halwara, Adampur, Amritsar, and Jamnagar. Chavan simply told Arjan Singh, 'Don't worry about the past, the future is now more important.'[19] But there was more to come that night.

Through the evening and night, a steady stream of Martin B-57 Canberras launched a series of bombing raids targeting airfields in Punjab and Gujarat from their bases at Peshawar and Mauripur. In most cases, they dropped 4,000-lb bombs in the first pass, and would follow it up with rockets in the second. The first attack targeted Jamnagar around the time Rathore and Neb were shooting down the two Sabres. As it was before last light, the attacking B-57s had an unhindered view of the airfield's layout and all the targets parked there. Apart from the Vampires, which were permanently stationed at Jamnagar, Naval Sea Hawks and IAF Otters were also dispersed around the airfield. Five more raids followed through the night— the first few had the advantage of not only aligning themselves with the Mandvi Light House for the bombing run, they could navigate visually, for Jamnagar was brightly lit. By the time the last raid took place at 0300 hrs, blackout had been enforced and the B-57 flown by Squadron Leader Shabbir Alam Siddiqui with his navigator Squadron Leader Aslam Qureshi were probably hit by ack-ack or got disoriented and crashed just outside of Jamnagar. Four Vampires were damaged in the raids, but these were repaired and made operational again.

Adampur was also targeted by the B-57s on more than one occasion; the first B-57 came calling just after last light when two MiG-21 Type 74s were parked on the operational ready platform (ORP) waiting for the pilots, Squadron Leader Surendra Kumar 'Polly' Mehra[20] and Flight Lieutenant (later Squadron Leader) Purushothama 'Pushy' Dass, who were walking to the aircraft. 'There was a deafening blast and [a] stream of hot air shot away from us. An instant later there was an inferno from where the ORP aircraft was parked, and we realized it had been hit; there was no doubt when we heard the 30 mm shells bursting with the heat.'[21] Both pilots jumped into a nearby septic tank. The second MiG-21 was also damaged slightly. The unknown PAF pilot, aided by the runway lights that were on in anticipation of the MiGs taking off, flew with tremendous skill and earned the sobriquet '8-pass Charlie'. There was no further damage but the constant air raids kept Adampur, Pathankot, and Halwara stations awake all night. Three bombs were dropped on Pathankot and despite the bright light of the moon, only a part of the runway was damaged. The PAF missed Halwara altogether, dropping their bombs outside the air base.

The Halwara Canberra raid may well have been a diversion, for it was immediately followed by a Hercules C-130 that dropped sixty-three paratroopers. Similar drops also took place at Adampur and Pathankot, on or around the airfield. As was the case with the pre-emptive strikes, the original idea to drop commandos belonging to Pakistan's SSG had been initiated by Asghar Khan. Colonel Mehdi, the CO of the battalion whose earlier objections to the tactics being adopted in Operation Gibraltar had been brushed aside, had once again pointed out the absurdity of the plan.

Asghar Khan refused to be drawn into a discussion, preferring to believe in the infallibility of his own ideas. Mehdi was equally emphatic—he pointed out that the chance of success against fully alerted targets was almost nil, and with no mechanisms in place to retrieve his men from amidst a hostile population, the paratroopers would be butchered. With GHQ and Musa mum on the subject, Asghar Khan said it would be left to the discretion of Ayub Khan. The president, whose track record in World War II was abysmal, had been taken in by the glamour of the proposal, and green-lighted it.

As predicted by Mehdi, the three drops from the three C-130s were an unmitigated disaster. Each group consisted of three officers, one JCO, and other ranks who were equipped with automatic weapons, 2-inch mortars, explosives, a wireless set, and other assorted paraphernalia. In the bright moonlight, the chutes were clearly visible, and the base duty officer quickly armed all technical staff with rifles and pistols. In the general excitement, everyone blazed away into the tall sarkanda grass that grew next to the taxi tracks and dispersal areas. The Punjab Police reinforced by muleteers of the Army Supply Corps Transport Company found themselves herding captured Pakistani paratroopers, who were all rounded up over the next couple of days. The commander of the Pakistani contingent, Captain (later Brigadier) Hazur Hasnain, hijacked a jeep and with five men managed to get back to the Pakistani lines. Squadron Leader (later Wing Commander) Shri Krishna Singh who was from the Accounts Branch, was overseeing the entire operation and captured one of the Pakistani officers. He was the first officer from the non-combat arm of the IAF to be awarded the VrC.

In Pathankot, the paratroopers under the command of Major Khalid Gulrez Butt landed outside the airbase but failed to rendezvous. Villagers were quick to inform the sub-area headquarters and a force of 200 men as well as the local populace started rounding them up. The same story played out at Adampur, where the drop took place too far from the airfield. The PAP along with two armoured cars from the local National Cadet Corps formed hunting parties and started flushing out the Pakistani commandos from the fields of standing crop where they were hiding. The Adampur group was under the command of Captain (later Colonel) Saeed Afzal Durrani, a Sword of Honour winner from the Pakistan Military Academy, Kakul. Of the 180 SSG commandos dropped, 136, including Butt, Durrani, and six officers were taken prisoner while twenty-two were killed, mainly by villagers in Adampur. Another fifteen, led by Naib Subedar Muhammad Azam, managed to evade capture and made it back to Pakistan, which was barely 10 km from the Pathankot airfield.

'JAWAAB DENE AYENGE—HINDUSTAN KI KASAM!'

In 1973, Bollywood released its blockbuster film *Hindustan ki Kasam,* starring Raaj Kumar as an IAF pilot who, after Pakistan's unprovoked attack, looks up from the smoking ruins and delivers one of the most famous lines in Hindi cinema during that era: 'Jawaab dene ayenge—Hindustan ki kasam! (We will retaliate—by our motherland!)' Pakistan's pre-emptive strike, bold and innovative on paper, was poorly executed. Given the resources, Nur Khan knew he had to deliver a death blow to the IAF. The Haider-led strike on Pathankot had opened the door, but since Halwara and Adampur were not hit, the opening had slammed shut.

The attack on Pathankot meant the gloves were off. By 1900 hrs, 35 Squadron (Rapiers) based in Poona was ordered to launch a ten-aircraft strike at Mauripur, 4 miles to the northwest of Central Karachi, which was the main base of the Pakistani B-57s. The IAF was equipped with the English Electric B(I)-58 version of the Canberra, which was the original design developed by the British. Wing Commander A. S. Bakshi was to fly the lead Canberra with a marker flare and target marker bomb, after which the remaining aircraft, spaced at intervals of a minute, would zero in and deliver eight 1,000-lb bombs, a total load of 57,000 lbs of TNT. The aircraft were to take off at midnight but, due to various reasons, Bakshi's Canberra finally roared off the runway only at 0300 hrs.

The crew consisted of a pilot who was perched above the navigator who lay on his stomach and looked forward and down from his glass bubble in the nose.

Skirting Bombay, the aircraft had clear skies till Jamnagar, which seemed to be under attack as the pilots could see flashes from explosions in the distance. After overflying Jamnagar, the aircraft started to descend so as to approach Karachi at low level, after which they were to pull up to 7,500 feet, select their targets and drop their load over Mauripur. However, as the aircraft started to descend, they ran into fairly heavy clouding.

Even as the lead aircraft were pulling up for their bombing runs, Bakshi broke radio silence and said he had not been able to drop the marker flares despite having made a couple of attempts due to the intense clouding. He told his squadron he was abandoning more attempts, at which point, one of the pilots asked for instructions. Bakshi was categorical—they were 'not to drop the load unless target was sighted and positively identified'. Flight Lieutenant (later Air Vice Marshal) Dalip Singh Dahiya was bringing up the rear of the formation. After aligning up his bombing run 'he decided to continue on the same course for another 2-3 minutes; thereafter, he descended in a turn. When his aircraft had descended to 1,000 feet and they had been heading towards Jodhpur for about a minute, he and his navigator spotted Mauripur runway. Dahiya put on the full power and started a climbing turn to come in for a bombing run. It was at this moment that the ack-ack opened up. The aircraft was aligned and aiming point was the center of the ack-ack fire. "Bomb doors open" and "bombs gone" calls were made by Sandhu.'[22] Unfortunately, after the aircraft landed at Jodhpur, it was found that the bombs had 'hung' and not released from the aircraft.

Young pilots in their mid-twenties and early thirties, their planes loaded with bombs on the first day of the war, showed tremendous discipline in the air. During the briefing, Bakshi had said Mauripur was the target, and as was the prevailing practice those days, no secondary targets were given. Even as most of the aircraft set course for Jodhpur, they overflew Hyderabad in Sindh which, amazingly, had failed to implement the blackout. The PAF scrambled Sabres to intercept the Canberras, but 'in the process suffered their first casualty of the day. Flying Officer Sikander Azam, who had taken off from Mauripur, crashed near Karachi.'[22] Yet all eighteen pilots and navigators held their fire, mainly to avoid civilian casualties. It was one of the most important events of the 1965 war and, ironically, perhaps one of the least talked about.

On 7 September, a second strike was launched when seven B(I)-58 Canberras took off from Agra at 0000 hrs heading for Sargodha. The aircraft were from the Agra-based 5 Squadron led by Wing Commander (later Air Marshal) Prem Pal Singh, and the Jet Bomber Conversion Unit (JBCU) under Squadron Leader (later Wing Commander) Padmanabha 'Bob' Gautam. However, they failed to get a visual fix on the airfield owing to poor visibility and extremely heavy anti-aircraft fire. However, with blind reckoning, they dropped their bombs in the general vicinity of the airfield.

Chapter 14

THE PUNJAB PLAINS
11 CORPS (PART II)

7 SEPTEMBER

With the advance bogged down along the entire 11 Corps frontage, the morning of 7 September was critical. Pakistani formations had recovered from their initial surprise and kept the pressure up by bombarding Indian positions through incessant shelling through the night. 15 Division, despite being ordered to advance by Harbakhsh Singh and Jogi Dhillon, had pushed 38 Infantry Brigade forward, only for it to firm up around Sadhan Wali, 2 km short of the Ichhogil Canal. After Jogi Dhillon's late-night visit, it was decided that Niranjan Prasad would be replaced as GOC. 'I came to the reluctant conclusion that he had lost all will for battle and that no amount of persuasion would infuse the required spirit into him to continue the offensive. His stay in the division under these circumstances was, I thought, most harmful. I, therefore, decided to relieve him of his command. Major General Mohinder Singh became the new formation commander on [the] night [of] 7th/8th September.'[1]

The unfortunate drama around 15 Infantry Division was far from over. Apart from the partial advance by 38 Infantry Division under Pathak and regular shelling by the Pakistani artillery, there had been no change in the ground situation during the night. Towards the early hours of the morning, 54 Infantry Brigade HQ came under heavy artillery fire and Maha Singh Rikh was lucky to escape with his life as he was hit by a splinter behind the ear. He was evacuated and replaced by the artillery brigade commander, Brigadier Sahib Singh Kalha, who took temporary charge.

During the night, communication between Prasad and Brigade HQ had broken down once again. With nothing much happening during the morning, at around 1530 hrs, Prasad set off to meet Brigadier Pathak at his brigade location. By this time, Prasad knew he was being replaced and he had spent the last few hours drafting his petition to the President of India protesting against his 'wrongful removal'. Prasad, accompanied by his ADC and a small protection party, lost their way and stumbled upon a defensive position occupied by 17 Baluch. Coming under fire, Prasad and his party managed to escape capture by fleeing through sugarcane fields. Realizing that Prasad had left his briefcase in the jeep, the ADC offered to go back for it but Prasad told him to leave it as he was under the impression that the vehicle was on fire. His jeep, with the 15 Division GOC's pennant, star plate and, even more embarrassingly, his briefcase, soon became the property of 17 Baluch. Prasad's draft petition addressed to President Radhakrishnan was gleefully read out again and again on Radio Pakistan.[2]

While Prasad was trying to make contact with 38 Infantry Brigade, Kalha, in accordance with Dhillon's directives, was issuing orders to his three battalions that made up 54 Infantry Brigade. 15 Dogra was to occupy Dograi while Chatterji's 13 Punjab would simultaneously capture the UBDC–Ichhogil area and the railway bridge over the Ichhogil Canal. Hayde's 3 Jat was to create a firm base for 13 Punjab astride the UBDC Canal in the area where the 6th distributary left the main canal on the right side. H-hour was to be 0100 hrs on 8 September and once these objectives were met, Kalha was to issue fresh directives.

Having got over the initial surprise and then watched the Indians implode on the eastern side of the Ichhogil Canal on 6 September, Major General Sarfraz Khan, commanding 10 Division, was honing his own battle plans. As he was responsible for the Lahore Sector, the obvious thing to do was to fight the Indians at Dograi, on the eastern bank of the Ichhogil which, being a built-up area straddling GT Road, would allow him to gain strategic depth as well. Accordingly, Sarfraz Khan ordered Brigadier Abdul Qayyum Sher commanding 22 Brigade to occupy the vacant Dograi on the night of 7/8 September. Pakistan's 23 Cavalry, commanded by Lieutenant Colonel Ghulam Mohammad, was to cross the Ichhogil Canal over the Bhasin Bridge and while one squadron of tanks was to probe the Indian defences to the southeast (38 Infantry Brigade), the main body of tanks with two companies each from 18 Baluch and 15 FF were to move south along the east bank of the Ichhogil and occupy Dograi.

While both sides prepared to occupy Dograi on 8 September, Mohinder Singh, the GOC-designate 15 Infantry Division, reached Western Command's TAC HQ at Ambala in the early evening. Mohinder Singh had been the deputy master general of Ordnance in New Delhi. An artillery officer who had been decorated with the Military Cross during World War II, he had performed creditably during the J&K Ops of 1947-48 but had been sidelined from the command stream and been marking time prior to his retirement. The irony was not lost on Mohinder Singh, who had remarked wryly earlier in the morning, 'I was not fit to command an infantry brigade, let alone a division. Now in war, I am suddenly the most suitable officer to command a division in a crisis.'[3] In Ambala, the chief of staff, Major General Joginder Singh briefed Mohinder and asked him to proceed to the headquarters of 11 Corps at Rayya.

It was 2200 hrs by the time Mohinder met the BGS, Brigadier Prakash Grewal, who painted a grim picture. He then met the corps commander, Dhillon, who let loose a tirade against the people on the ground. 'They were a pack of incompetents, not knowing their job, lacking fighting spirit, devoid of soldierly qualities, lacking professional efficiency and thoroughly disorganised.' Dhillon paused, which allowed Mohinder Singh just enough time to ask the vital question—what was the operational task being given to the division?

Prasad had described the thinking at the higher headquarters in relation to the tasks assigned to him as being 'woolly headed' and 'muddled'. Mohinder Singh listened to Dhillon and then said 'he would carry out the assigned task only after he could evaluate it and re-plan the operation if necessary after due reconnaissance and discussion with his subordinate commanders.'[4] Dhillon expressed his annoyance but there was little he could do. He ended the interview with a brusque: 'In any case you are the divisional commander now, you do whatever you like.'[5] Leaving Rayya behind him, Mohinder Singh reached his divisional TAC HQ near Attari at 2300 hrs. Even as Mohinder Singh started looking at the map in the Ops Room, 54 Infantry Brigade had already started to move to their respective FUPs with H-hour just two hours away. Across the Ichhogil Canal, Pakistan's 10 Division was also on the move.

To the south of 15 Infantry Division, Major General Sibal's 7 Infantry Division remained more or less where it had reached on the night of 6 September. The 17 Rajput group line had held through the night and both sides sat out the daylight hours, eyeing each other warily. By the evening, the Pakistanis created a breach in the UBDC and the water gushed towards the Rajput positions, that were fortunately on high ground. From the Pakistani perspective, by flooding the area, should any Indian armour get across the Bedian Bridge, it could no longer get into the vicinity of Lahore from this axis.

Meanwhile, on the Hudiara Drain, the engineers had succeeded in constructing a Bailey bridge by 1545 hrs and once again the Indians resumed their advance. Sibal, appreciating that 48 Infantry Brigade had suffered fairly heavy casualties in the battle for Hudiara Drain, switched 65 Infantry Brigade Group into the lead with the task of securing the Ichhogil Canal at Barki. Accordingly, 9 Madras under Lieutenant Colonel B. K. Satyan, led the way and captured Barka Kalan by last light where it then dug in for the time being, still short of the east bank of the Ichhogil Canal.

The situation in the 4 Mountain Division Sector was even worse. Dhillon's rant at night about subordinate commanders to Mohinder Singh may have had more to do with the overall situation in his corps' AOR. In the afternoon Dhillon had visited 4 Mountain Division and after returning to his headquarters had just finished writing a handwritten 'top secret' note to Harbakhsh Singh when the designated 15 Division GOC reached Rayya. His note was explosive:

'The strength of six infantry battalions had been reduced to an overall total of about three and a half battalions in 24 hours of action commencing 0400 hrs

6th September. This reduction was partially due to enemy action but mostly due to desertion.'[6] The letter then went on to describe the situation in 13 Dogra, stating that the battalion had broken ranks 'without any enemy pressure except perhaps shelling'. Dhillon then listed the six infantry battalions under the command of 7 and 62 Mountain Division and stated that 'of these, only 4 Grenadiers and 1/9 Gorkha Rifles are intact. I am told by the General Officer Commanding that the Commanding Officer of 9 JAK Rifles left his position, without orders, on the night of 6th/7th September taking a company of infantry with him. 7 Grenadiers are only about two companies strong. 18 Rajputana Rifles has about 10 per cent desertions and the General Officer Commanding thinks that this unit is cracking up. I am further given to understand by the General Officer Commanding that desertions are restricted to infantry units only and no other arm or service in the division is affected.'

Dhillon goes on to lament that not a single task assigned to 4 Mountain Division had been carried out or, for that matter, any bridge on the Ichhogil Canal blown up. 'The morale of the division being what it is, it is my considered view that any defences held by the present units in 4 Mountain Division cannot withstand even slight enemy pressure. This is a most serious situation in the present stage of operations.'

Dhillon then recommended that the tasks assigned to 4 Mountain Division be given to some other formation and, apart from a couple of battalions, the rest be disbanded immediately. Dhillon signed off requesting Harbakhsh to visit the Khem Karan Sector for himself, where he said Gurbaksh Singh was planning to defend the Asal Uttar area which was further east of Khem Karan. It is also obvious from the letter that Dhillon had absolutely no idea of what was happening on the ground, for he still seemed to believe that the bigger crisis was in the 15 Infantry Division where both 38 and 54 Infantry Brigades had failed to make it to the Ichhogil Canal on the second day as well.

11 Corps' entire game plan seemed to hinge on creating a credible threat to Lahore, on the assumption that the Pakistanis would panic and be incapable of thinking of anything else. Dhillon's visit to the Khem Karan Sector had obviously done nothing to improve the situation. On the contrary, he seemed to have missed the implications of the Pakistani build-up altogether. This was even more surprising because in all the initial war games, Dhillon, Harbakhsh, and Chaudhuri had harped about the fact that Pakistan's main armoured thrust would develop in this region.

The Indian plan, worked out by Dhillon and given to Gurbaksh Singh's understrength 4 Mountain Division to execute, was fundamentally flawed. Attacking on a frontage of 30 km, the division was spread out thin. At no point was there a concentration of troops that could have, by the sheer weight of numbers and firepower, punched its way through to the objective, which was the Ichhogil Canal and the bridges. This basic flaw, also applicable to the other sectors in 11 Corps, was further amplified by the fact that none of the commanders on the ground were familiar with the terrain or, for that matter, the objectives. More than half a century after the event, Major Mehta from Deccan Horse recalls, 'It was a joke. No maps, no information, nothing. A few hours before H-hour, I was told to hop on to a milk van in civil clothes, then switch to a Punjab Armed Police jeep and go see the terrain on our side. Even those vehicles broke down. My squadron was in support of 4 Grenadiers. I had no idea who their commanding officer was, who the company commanders were. This was the case across the board.'[7]

The night of 6/7 September had been a nightmare for most Indian commanders strung out short of the Ichhogil Canal. 4 Grenadiers was at the lower east bank of the Ichhogil Canal but had failed to capture or destroy the bridge assigned to it; three companies of 9 J&K were also holding onto the lower bank of the Rohi Nullah with a yawning gap of 12 km between them. A similar gap existed on the left where the 7 Grenadier attack on Ballanwala had also failed and 13 Dogra had been decimated by the intense artillery fire brought upon them by the Pakistani guns. With the bulk of Deccan Horse's Charlie Squadron still stuck in the drain, the few tanks that got across under Major Mehta and Second Lieutenant (later Lieutenant General) Tajinder Singh 'Mao' Shergill did fire at the support structures of the bridges at Waigal, Gil, and Chathanwala, but the damage was only superficial. 'As darkness started to creep in, I ordered Mao to fall back to harbour while I went back to the drain to somehow get the remaining tanks out of there during the night. With the Pakistanis probing most of our positions, I was ordered to abandon the tanks but that was something I had not been trained to do.'[8]

Pakistan's forces in the Khem Karan Sector were poised for an offensive of their own, and they were quick to counter-attack. From the Pakistani point of view, the Indian thrusts in the Kasur Sector—'most probably designed to breakthrough with a view to outflanking Lahore from the south'[9]—having been stalled, GOC 11 Division, Major General Abdul Hamid, was directed to counter-attack, capture Khem Karan and establish a bridgehead in that area for Pakistan's 1 Armoured Division to advance towards Amritsar. For General Musa and the Pakistan high command, at that stage uncertain about the location of India's 1 Armoured Division, there was no option but to go on the offensive themselves.

On the night of 6 September itself, Brigadier Zaidi's 52 Brigade was given the task of establishing a bridgehead across the Rohi Nullah. 2 FF (Guides' Infantry) commanded by Lieutenant Colonel Fateh Khan was to establish a foothold on the eastern side of the Rohi. Just as the Indians were operating blind, Zaidi too had no idea of the Indian disposition. Purely by luck, the place he picked to establish the bridgehead was in the gap that had been created by the retreating troops of 62 Mountain Brigade. By 2300 hrs, two companies had established a horseshoe pattern that was further reinforced by the rest of the battalion.

However, in the dark, 2 FF had failed to fully occupy the bridgehead area in full, which allowed the bulk of 9 J&K to tenaciously hold onto their position despite the withdrawal of the commanding officer and one company. To complicate the issue, the Pakistanis were having serious problems bridging the Rohi behind 2 FF. 5 Armoured Brigade consisting of 6 Lancers (Pattons), a squadron from 15 Lancers and 1 FF had been delinked from Pakistan's 1 Armoured Division and placed under the command of Abdul Hamid to enlarge the bridgehead through which the armoured division would then launch its counter-attack on 11 Corps.

At 2330 hrs, Pakistan's 3 Engineer Battalion began to cut a passage through the high embankment that ran along the western bank of the Rohi Nullah. To economize on time and effort, the point selected was a slight depression in the embankment. However, when the engineers started to lay the floating bridge, they found that the water at that point was not deep enough to sustain it. With the clock ticking, there was no choice but to look at an alternate site slightly to the south, where the entire exercise had to be repeated.

6 Lancers, which was leading 5 Armoured Brigade's advance, started from its assembly area as planned at 0400 hrs. Until then, except for the delay in bridging the Rohi Nullah, things had gone fairly smoothly for the Pakistan Army in the Kasur Sector. However, when it came to going on the offensive, the Pakistan high command proved to be as woolly-headed as their Indian counterparts. Pakistan's 11 Division and 1 Armoured Division were being directly controlled by GHQ and, in the absence of a Corps HQ, they began to fumble. As no one had worked out basic traffic regulations, the obstacle crossing control organization began to falter from the word go. With the bridge not yet ready, the area between the Ichhogil Bridge and the bridge site on the Rohi was soon jammed with tanks and vehicles.

With most of the units in 62 Mountain Brigade having fallen back during the night, at 1000 hrs, Gurbaksh Singh ordered 7 Mountain Brigade to fall back from Theh Pannu to Asal Uttar, northeast of Khem Karan, where he decided to occupy a divisional defended area. All available officers and JCOs then went about collecting the groups of men who had fallen back. Using every means at their disposal including threats, they then led the shell-shocked and shaken troops to their unit-defended areas, where they went to work on their defences.

To defend Asal Uttar, Gurbaksh Singh had to reposition his artillery that had been deployed ahead to support the advance. Most of these gun positions had large stockpiles of ammunition that could not be carried back at short notice. Brigadier J. S. Sandhu, commander 4 Artillery Brigade, ordered 40 Medium and 1 Field (SP) Regiments to bombard Kasur and all likely Pakistani approaches over the Ichhogil Canal. 'The artillery guns went hammer and tongs, firing off all the ammunition they couldn't carry back. This led to breaches in the canal and quite a few underpasses in particular became unusable because of flooding. This added considerably to the confusion on the Pakistani side. I was still struggling to get my tanks out. I ran into Major (later Major General) Ram Nath who immediately dedicated a few guns that blasted the area opposite us which gave us time to get out of our predicament.'[10]

Finally at midday, the bridge over the Rohi Nullah was declared operational and the leading elements of Pakistan's 6 Lancers began to go across, but they still had a problem negotiating the steep climb over the opposite embankment. Around the same time, one of the tanks on the Ichhogil Bridge hit the railing and plunged into the fast-flowing waters of the canal, drowning the crew. Traffic had to be diverted. Meanwhile, on the opposite slope, one of 6 Lancer's tanks stalled, bringing everything to a halt.

At 1600 hrs, Gurbaksh Singh ordered Deccan Horse's Alpha Squadron along with one troop of Bravo Squadron to extricate the three companies of 9 J&K that were stuck next to the Pakistani bridgehead. The Shermans reached the battalion's position and neutralized Pakistani MMG posts that were cutting off 9 J&K's avenues of retreat. Though Pakistani artillery immediately opened up, the tanks started loading the battalion's casualties. Just then a troop of Pakistani Chaffee tanks appeared on the flank and knocked out two Indian Shermans. Risaldar Achhar Singh immediately engaged the Chaffees and two tanks were hit. With the infantry having pulled out by then, the rest of the squadron followed suit. Five tanks of Major Mehta's Charlie Squadron were still stuck in the drain south of Rajoke. Gurbaksh Singh ordered 1 and 4 Troop under Shergill to hold a position east of the Dode drain. Meanwhile, Mehta, having commandeered every available bullock cart, had piled them up on the home side of the drain and hoped to drive the tanks out over them.

This was the situation in 4 Mountain Division when Dhillon visited the formation in the afternoon. Now back in Rayya, completely unaware of just what was coming at him, he had sat down to write his handwritten report to the army commander.

OF COMMAND AND CONTROL

The relationship between General Chaudhury and Harbakhsh Singh had deteriorated to its lowest point. In his autobiography, Harbakhsh Singh says, 'It may be reiterated that despite my regular pleas that any reserve forces to be committed against Sialkot must be launched from the area of Gurdaspur, so that initially they would be available to me as a reserve on the Punjab front, in case something went wrong there, General Chaudhury raised these reserve forces as I Corps, under Pat Dunn, and decided to launch them against Sialkot from Samba area, leaving me without any reserves on the Punjab front.'[11] In a damning critique of the COAS, Harbakhsh adds 'I was not told anything about these plans, nor even invited to the co-ordinating conference at which these plans were made. And yet, before their launching, I Corps was handed over to me for the conduct of the operations!'

'Operation Nepal', the code name given by Chaudhuri to the offensive in the Rachna Doab, was scheduled for the night of 7/8 September. Not only were the Indians unaware of the magnitude of the threat in the Kasur/Khem Karan Sector, having pulled back into Asal Uttar for the night, they had no idea that leading elements of Pakistan's 6 Lancers were already just short of Khem Karan with whatever elements of infantry and tanks that had got across the Rohi Nullah. Meeting with no opposition at all, the Pakistanis hunkered down for the night.

From the information available with Harbakhsh, the situation in 4 Mountain Division was grim and though the Sialkot thrust was to be launched in the early hours of 8 September, he decided to head for Khem Karan in the morning. The Western Army commander's options were limited—the only reserve he had was 2 (Independent) Armoured Brigade, which during the night of 6/7 September, had become reduced in strength in the area south of Amritsar when 8 Light Cavalry was ordered by Dhillon to cover 29 Infantry Brigade at DBN which was reporting a developing armoured thrust across the DBN Bridge.

As a result, on the morning of 7 September, Brigadier Theogaraj, Commander 2 (Independent) Armoured Brigade, was left with 3 Cavalry that was being commanded by Lieutenant Colonel (later Major General) Salim Caleb in the immediate vicinity of Khem Karan. The Regimental HQ was with Charlie Squadron at Bhikkiwind, Alpha Squadron was at Patti while Bravo Squadron was at Chabal Kalam. Salim Caleb had instructions to deploy forward only on the orders of Brigadier Theogaraj but, unfortunately, there was no communication with Brigade HQ. At this stage the deployment of 2 (Independent) Armoured Brigade was still oriented towards 'threats from the Jassar–Dera Baba Nanak–Amritsar, Lahore–Amritsar and Lahore–Barki–Khalra–Bikkiwind. Further on the night of 7 September...8 Cavalry was placed under the command of 15 Infantry Division and deployed north of Amritsar. It is obvious that the XI Corps headquarters had paid little attention to its claimed appreciation that the main enemy thrust would come out of Kasur through Khem Karan; it had deployed only two mountain brigades with 4 Mountain Division towards the main threat and frittered away resources of 2 (Independent) Armoured Brigade towards imaginary threats from other parts of the Corps zone.'[12]

Through the night of 7/8 September, 4 Mountain Division, unaware that Pakistan's 6 Lancers were harboured at a hand-shaking distance from Khem Karan, had worked feverishly to prepare and strengthen the sector defended by the division. Anti-tank mines were laid on likely approaches and Deccan Horse along with the infantry battalions that had been in disarray only a day before, prepared for the Pakistani attack at Asal Uttar. When Harbakhsh Singh reached 4 Mountain Division, he expected the worst based on Jogi Dhillon's missive but was relieved to find 'that although the situation was pretty serious, it did not call for a recourse to the recommendations made by General Officer Commanding XI Corps. In any case, the changeover of the formation was clearly out of the question. We had no reserves available for this purpose, nor was it sound tactics to break contact with the enemy at that stage.'[13]

While Harbakhsh Singh was at 4 Mountain Division, Pakistan's 5 Armoured Brigade carried out a reconnaissance-cum-probing mission in strength with a combined force of Chaffees and Pattons, making a bold attempt to get to the gun areas at 1000 hrs. By then, despite the difficulty in getting across, Pakistan had almost two brigades east of the Rohi Nullah. While 5 Brigade had the whole of 6 Lancers and 1 FF in the bridgehead, during the night, 21 Brigade consisting of 2 and 5 FF, had also got across. 24 Cavalry, ordered to cross the Rohi Nullah at first light, was also moving into the bridgehead. Despite the fact that there were no Indian troops in the area, there had been a few instances of friendly fire among the jittery Pakistani troops.

Brigadier Bashir, commanding 5 Armoured Brigade, had started his advance at 0700 hrs. Uncertain of the Indian deployment, he planned on a two-pronged drive by both his armoured regiments. Code-named Group Ali, 24 Cavalry with one company of 1 FF moved to outflank Khem Karan from the west with the aim of cutting the Khem Karan–Bhikkiwind axis at Chima. Group Gul, consisting of 6 Lancers Alpha Squadron with one company of 1 FF under command started to move on the Khem Karan–Patti axis with the intention of capturing Valtoha. Group Shabbir with a squadron each from 6 and 15 Lancers plus the remaining two companies of 1 FF was to be the brigade reserve, which was to move on orders to capture 4 Mountain Division's headquarters as well as the GOC. Facing the Pakistanis were Major Jimmy Vohra's Alpha Squadron and Bravo Squadron along with the infantry elements of 7 and 62 Mountain Brigade.

Harbakhsh Singh watched the Pakistani thrust develop, but, strangely, gave no orders for the deployment of 2 Independent Armoured Brigade. His focus was entirely on keeping 4 Mountain Division together as a cohesive fighting unit. In a crisis situation, Harbakhsh Singh's cool demeanour certainly had an impact. 'I discussed the situation with the General Officer Commanding 4 Mountain Division and tried to introduce an atmosphere of calm and confidence in what looked like a very chaotic and confused state of affairs. Fortunately, General Officer Commanding 4 Mountain Division's response was reassuring and self-confident. Within a short space of time he gave all the promise of re-establishing his command and control over the situation. I came away with the feeling that thenceforth 4 Mountain Division would not budge from its position.'[14]

The first round was going to be critical, for it would set the tone for the rest of the fighting. Group Gul, with Alpha Squadron of 6 Lancers in the lead, reached the Khem Karan distributary where it got held up at the road crossing. Simultaneously, the recce troop of 6 Lancers and the company of 1 FF moved from the east of Khem Karan. Lieutenant Colonel Sahibzad Gul, commanding 6

Lancers, ordered Charlie Squadron from Group Shabbir to hook left and cut the Khem Karan–Bhikkiwind road at Bhura Kuhna, but this group came under tank and RCL fire and was asked to pull back. Bravo Squadron of 24 Cavalry, which was a part of Group Ali, was asked to advance towards Bhura Karimpur, which they reached at 1000 hrs. 5 and 2 FF then firmed up in the enlarged bridgehead.

Vohra's Alpha Squadron had been tasked to stay in contact with the Pakistanis and halt the advance of the armour. Keeping to the middle of the Bhikkiwind–Khem Karan axis, his tanks had got into position using for cover the trees and the large tracts of sugarcane growing in the fields adjacent to the road. Bravo Squadron had, in the meantime, taken up a position to the south of Asal Uttar, on the Patti–Valtoha axis. As the Pattons advanced, the gap between them and the Deccan Horse Shermans was barely 600 to 800 yards. 'It was a question of who fired first and accurately. Eleven tanks of the enemy were knocked out or damaged while A Squadron lost four tanks, three destroyed and one bogged down.'[15] The order to withdraw was given and the Pakistanis broke contact, pulling back after fairly heavy losses. Vohra's Alpha Squadron had won the first round, but the battle was only just beginning.

As the initial tank skirmishes were taking place in the morning, a stream of retreating civilians was going past 3 Cavalry's positions and the news was not good. There was talk of a massive armoured build-up as more and more Pakistani armoured vehicles were crossing the Rohi Nullah, which had a second bridge constructed by Pakistan's 1 Armoured Division over it. There were still no instructions from Brigadier Theogaraj or from HQ 11 Corps for 3 Cavalry to join battle at Khem Karan. For Salim Caleb, the lack of orders was frustrating. He had used the three months during Operation Ablaze to familiarize his officers with the terrain along the border to the west and southwest of Amritsar. The regiment was deployed at Jandiala Guru, after which it moved back to Nabha. Throughout this period, Caleb was like a man possessed—tank crews were subject to intense gunnery training to the point where even tradesmen could strip and assemble machine guns.

In addition, as 11 Corps reserve, Caleb and Arun Vaidya had war-gamed possible scenarios and, based on the terrain and the probable strength of the Pakistani armour, they believed that the Pakistani thrust would develop on the Bhikkiwind axis through Khem Karan. This would also be along the natural grain of the country and they would not have to overcome any major obstacles, either man-made or natural. The Rohi Nullah, inside their own territory to the west, and the Sutlej to the east, would protect the flanks of the Pakistani offensive forces as they swept through to GT Road and Amritsar. The Indian armoured corps officers believed that this very advantage could be turned into a disadvantage if the Pakistani offensive were met as far forward as possible, which was around Bhikkiwind where the width of the frontage available to the enemy was barely 7 to 8 km. As the Pakistani advance gathered momentum, the terrain would open out to the northeast and it would be well-nigh impossible to contain the Pakistanis given the numerical advantage they had in tanks. With no orders coming from any of the higher HQs, Caleb knew he had to take the initiative. The enemy bridgehead had to be contained in the Asal Uttar–Chima area. With Deccan Horse heavily outnumbered, 3 Cavalry could not afford to let the Pakistani armoured formations get past.

Taking the all-important decision himself, Caleb decided to move 3 Cavalry towards Khem Karan without waiting for orders. Bravo Squadron commanded by Major (later Colonel) Prabhakar Shripad 'Belu' Belvalkar started dashing at full speed towards Asal Uttar while Alpha Squadron commanded by Major (later Brigadier) Surish Chander Vadera moved in a similar fashion to the east on the Valtoha–Patti axis. The Regimental HQ along with Charlie Squadron under the command of Major (later Brigadier) Narinder Singh Sandhu followed hard on the heels of Belvalkar's tanks. 'Having covered a distance of over 20 kilometres from Bhikkiwind in two hours and with contact with the enemy imminent, both squadrons deployed in battle formation. Salim had warned all tank commanders to be careful and to look out for our own tanks—in this case Shermans of Deccan Horse that were operating in support of 4 Mountain Division at Asal Uttar.'[16]

The arrival of the Centurions was a huge morale booster for the beleaguered 4 Mountain Division. Shortly after their arrival, Belvalkar met Vaidya who brought him up to date on the tactical situation. Caleb also reached Vaidya's command post and, between the two commanding officers, they coordinated various details including the exchange of radio frequencies for regimental netting.

With their initial probe having failed to dislodge the Indians, the Pakistanis should have changed tactics, but they seemed determined to assault Chima head-on in the hope that 4 Mountain Division would panic and abandon their defences. Just before Vaidya and Caleb met, the main Pakistani column, Group Ali, led by Bravo Squadron 24 Cavalry, supported by a motor battalion mounted on armoured personal carriers, had started to advance astride the main axis in front of Deccan Horse's depleted Alpha Squadron, while a second column tried to outflank the Chima positions from the west. Major John Hamilton Gardner, commanding the Pakistani column, got to Manawan, from where he wheeled eastwards to advance on Chima. Brigadier Sidhu, commanding 7 Mountain Brigade, was a former commanding officer of Deccan Horse. He had issued orders to his infantry units that they were to dig deep into the ground and not fire at the advancing Pakistani tanks, allowing them to go over their positions. The Deccan Horse tanks would deal with the Pakistani armour, while the infantry would take on the Pakistani infantry following in the wake of their tanks. The men of 7 Mountain Brigade followed the brigade commander's instructions perfectly. The Pakistani tanks, using their anti-aircraft and co-axial guns to spray the area ahead with prophylactic fire, were not engaged by 1/9 Gorkhas and 4 Grenadiers and the tanks went over their trenches, including one that had Sidhu crouching in it. This allowed Indian Shermans of Bravo and Alpha Squadron hidden behind the two battalions in the sugarcane fields to engage the Pakistani tanks effectively.

The Indian infantry, displaying nerves of steel, stayed buried and waited for the Pakistani infantry to close the gap, opening fire only when the APCs were within range. The RCL guns, however, had effectively engaged the advancing Pakistani armour and the leading tank of Bravo Squadron received a fatal hit while another was badly damaged. A third tank ran over a mine and blew out its track.

Despite the heavy volume of fire from the 4 Grenadier positions, the remaining Pakistani tanks swung slightly to the right and reached the Khem Karan–Bhikkiwind road about 800 yards south of Chima, roughly between the area defended by 1/9 Gorkha Rifles and 4 Grenadiers. The commanding officer of 24 Cavalry ordered his Alpha and Charlie Squadrons forward to marry up with Bravo Squadron but, unfortunately for him, the communication systems failed. He accordingly sent Captain Javed Tipu in a jeep from Manawan back towards Khem Karan, but the jeep got stuck and Tipu could not get the instructions across.

However, Alpha Squadron of 24 Cavalry had, on its own initiative, decided to follow Bravo Squadron, but as it came abreast of the 1/9 Gorkha positions, it came under fire from their RCL guns, which opened up in unison with 4 Grenadiers to their right. Instead of following Bravo Squadron, Major Sher Altaf, the commanding officer of Alpha Squadron, also wheeled right and got into a firefight with the Gorkhas. Major Sami, commanding Charlie Squadron, had been told by the commander of 5 Brigade that the other squadrons had already reached the road, so he too, on his own initiative, decided to advance along the Khem Karan–Bhikkiwind road.

1/9 Gorkha Rifles suddenly had tanks in front of them, tanks between them and the position held by 4 Grenadiers on the right, and tanks moving from the south on the road behind them. This assault was too much for the battalion and the men began to abandon their positions at Bura Khuna. The Gorkhas got away unnoticed, for Sami, coming face to face with some of 1/9 Gorkha positions on the road, had swung right and continued to move parallel to the road, ignoring 18 Raj Rif which was to his immediate right. Sami's attention was directly ahead of him, where two troops of Deccan Horse's Bravo Squadron along with other anti-tank guns were deployed facing the west. Behind them, in a direct firing role, were the guns of 4 Mountain Division's Artillery Brigade. Vaidya had moved to the artillery command post and he helped direct the guns against the Pakistani armour while Major Bal acted as the FOO, giving corrections on the radio.

Sami's Charlie Squadron was taking a severe pounding from the Indians, as artillery guns, Deccan Horse tanks, and the 18 Raj Rif RCLs started firing at the Pakistani tanks from the eastern flank. This forced Sami to swing left onto the main road behind the 4 Grenadiers location and take up a defensive position on the Khem Karan–Bhikkiwind road. It was 1430 hrs and for the first time, the Centurions of 3 Cavalry were face to face with the Patton tanks. The first shots were fired by the Pattons as the leading tank commanded by Daffadar Wasan Singh was approaching the village of Chima. 'We were approximately 800 yards from Chima village. As we rounded a slight curve on the road, I felt the tank shake and heard a sound from the right side from the rear. I looked up to see a tank with its gun smoking. I realized immediately that it was an enemy tank and had fired at my tank, grazing it somewhere at the rear.'[17] With Wasan Singh was Acting Lance Daffadar Charan Singh who was the gunner. This was his moment of truth. 'I suddenly saw a strange shape emerge in my gunner sight which I recognized as a Patton tank. The Commander, Dfr Wasan Singh had already started his fire orders and without waiting for him to complete, I laid my gun (aimed) at the center of the Patton and fired. The enemy tank burst into flames.'[18]

Two minutes later a second Patton had been destroyed and by then two leading troops of Centurions were in contact with the Pakistanis. Belvalkar's voice was loud and clear over the radio, 'Press hard and get all the bastards before they turn back and run.' Even as the first tank was burning, Belvalkar pulled out his camera and photographed it. The photograph was later carried on the cover of the *Illustrated Weekly of India*. 'In the next half an hour, four more Pattons and a Chaffee were destroyed by B Squadron. The effort of 24 Cavalry to get around our defences at Chima was defeated and no further attempt was made by them to move forward.'[19]

Significantly, while the battle between the Centurions and the Pattons was raging, Second Lieutenant Prakash Abraham Joseph, Troop Leader 2 Troop, cursed his gunner for firing when he hadn't given him the command to do so. The bang and jolt he had felt was akin to the tank's gun going off, but, in this case, he had taken a hit from a Patton at a range of approximately 800 yards. The armour piercing shell was designed to withstand the shock of punching through armour plating and expected to detonate inside the tank, killing the crew and blowing up the tank. However, the shell fired by the Patton had hit the mantlet of Joseph's tank and lodged itself in the armour.

While 24 Cavalry was engaging the bulk of the 4 Mountain Division defences from the western side, Group Shabbir had reorganized itself and started to advance on the Khem Karan–Valtoha axis at around 1130 hrs. Chaffees of Bravo Squadron 15 Lancers were the vanguard of the attack with a company of 1 FF following. Charlie Squadron of 6 Lancers brought up the rear, being the force's reserve. This group made extremely slow progress, eventually getting to within 1,000 yards of the 18 Raj Rif positions, which was reinforced by a troop from Bravo Squadron Deccan Horse. 18 Raj Rif's RCL guns, along with the solitary troop facing south, opened fire, bringing the Chaffees to a halt. The Pakistanis tried to push their infantry forward, but could not progress beyond the line where the tanks had come to a halt. Despite bringing into play a battery of self-propelled guns, the stalemate with 18 Raj Rif would continue for the next four hours, with the Indians keeping up their volume of defensive fire.

Group Gul, however, had been ordered by Brigadier Bashir to change its thrust line and advance along the Khem Karan–Valtoha railway line, keeping to the southern side so as to bypass the 18 Raj Rif position altogether and capture Valtoha from the south. Sahibzad Gul with Alpha and Bravo Squadron of 6 Lancers advanced without any opposition on the southern side of the railway line. The APCs of 1 FF had failed to materialize, so Gul collected a platoon of infantry, mounted them onto the Pattons and set off. While crossing the relatively smaller Machike Minor Canal, the tanks inadvertently breached the banks but carried on towards Valtoha, reaching the railway station at 1500 hrs.

Having got into the underbelly of 4 Mountain Division, Lieutenant Colonel Gul halted his advance and got on the radio to ask Brigadier Bashir to send his Charlie Squadron along with the infantry and replenishments. But Bashir wanted Gul to push on to Warnala, which would have taken him past the area held by 13 Dogra and 7 Grenadiers onto the Divisional HQ itself. The presence of Group Gul at Valtoha had not been detected by the Indians and had they advanced further, their presence opposite Gharyala may well have determined the outcome of the battle. As it was, Gul was reluctant to carry on and, with darkness creeping in, Bashir ordered his column to return to Khem Karan, where it was to harbour for the night. The return journey began at 2000 hrs, but ran into serious trouble, for the waters from the breached Machike Minor had by then spread up to Valtoha. Three Pattons got bogged down and these were destroyed by Indian tank hunting parties later that night. The Pakistanis had thrown away a tremendous opportunity.

Why Gul didn't move forward is perplexing. Having got past the main defences of 4 Mountain Brigade, with two squadrons of Pattons at his disposal, his insistence on infantry support after he had negotiated the initial difficult part with just a platoon was probably just an excuse. In all likelihood, his force had spotted Alpha Squadron of 3 Cavalry that had been ordered by Caleb to try and outflank the Pakistanis by going through Valtoha onto the eastern flank.

After the engagement on the road near Chima, Belvalkar's Bravo Squadron could not move forward because the destroyed Pattons were blocking the road and the 4 Grenadier and 18 Raj Rif defences were on either flank. Quick to grasp the tactical situation, Caleb had ordered Major Vadera, who was advancing towards Khem Karan further to the east, to go past Valtoha and see if he could move along the railway line axis and trap the Pakistanis in a pincer. Getting to the Bahadur Nagar area, the leading tank got bogged down while two others were also finding it difficult to move. Unaware of the Pakistani presence in the area, Vadera reported back saying the terrain was not suitable for armour and should the Pakistanis try to approach from a flank, they would also get trapped. Leaving the bogged Centurion under the command of Daffadar Raj Singh, Alpha Squadron rejoined the rest of the regiment at Dibbipura.

3 Cavalry's Charlie Squadron under Narinder Sandhu was manoeuvring to threaten the flank of 24 Cavalry from the west. This had put the Pakistanis in a precarious position. The terrain around Mahmudpura–Lakhna had got inundated owing to the breaching of various irrigation channels due to the movement of tanks and almost half the squadron got bogged down, including Sandhu. With just seven tanks still mobile, Second Lieutenant (later Lieutenant) Ram Prakash 'Joe' Joshi used his initiative to get to Bhura Karimpur by last light. Though the Charlie Squadron Centurions did not make contact with the Pakistanis, they would have been observed. Badly mauled by the tanks of Deccan Horse, 3 Cavalry, and the RCL guns of 4 Grenadiers, 1/9 GR, and 18 Raj Rif, the remaining Chaffees and Pattons pulled back towards Bhura Kuhna under cover of darkness. The Pakistani bridgehead had been restricted.

As darkness enveloped the plains of Punjab, tanks from both sides withdrew into harbour. 3 Cavalry's Alpha and Bravo Squadrons pulled back a few kilometres while the tanks with Joshi were harboured in the area around Bhura Karimpur. While the crews of both 3 Cavalry and Deccan Horse worked feverishly though the night, cleaning their gun barrels and replenishing their ammunition, Theogaraj and the two commanding officers knew the day's events had been a precursor to the forthcoming battle that would have to be fought the next day. For Gurbaksh Singh, GOC 4 Mountain Division, the day had finished on a positive note. Even 1/9 Gorkha Rifles, which had abandoned its defences in the face of two prongs of attacking Pattons, was quietly filtering back to its position.

A lot would depend on what the Pakistanis would do, but it was quite likely that having got more tanks across the Rohi Nullah, they would again try to bulldoze their way through the infantry positions and overrun Asal Uttar. Despite the inundation of a fairly large area that restricted movement to the east, it was likely that they would try and outflank the Indian defences from both sides with fresh armoured regiments. As far as the Indians were concerned, 4 Infantry Division had to show the same resolve, while 3 Cavalry's Centurions would try and remain in contact with the enemy, denying them space. This would force the Pakistani tanks to come head-on at 4 Grenadiers and 1/9 Gorkhas, whose RCL guns combined with the Deccan Horse tanks would then take on the Pattons in the area of their own choosing.

Due to the bridging problems, Pakistan's build-up had been delayed and on 8 September, GHQ had decided to limit the offensive to the tanks of 4 and 5 Armoured Brigade that were already across. According to General Musa, 'One of the Canal Masonry bridges was damaged. Major General Abdul Hamid and Commander 1 Armoured Division, Major General [Naseer] Ahmed, requested that they be allowed to build a bridge from their own resources.... I agreed although surprise was lost. The bridge was built…during the night 7/8 September and our remaining armour crossed the canal.'[20] The main offensive had been postponed and would now be launched at 0400 hrs on 9 September.

7 INFANTRY DIVISION—BARKI (8 SEPTEMBER)

Immediately to the north of Khem Karan, 7 Infantry Division continued to hold the flat and open ground that was characteristic of Western Punjab that 48 and 65 Infantry Brigades had captured on 6 and 7 September. On 8 September, having breached the UBDC in the vicinity of Bedian, the Pakistanis had ensured that apart from the odd artillery duel, there would be little activity in the southern part of the sector that was being held by 17 Rajput. Barki, further upstream on the Ichhogil Canal through which the main Bhikkiwind–Lahore highway went, however, remained the main objective for 7 Infantry Division. Towards that end, 4 Sikh was asked to attack and capture Barka Khurd during the day.

54 BRIGADE—AROUND DOGRAI (8 SEPTEMBER)

Around Dograi, there was feverish activity on both sides. Brigadier D. S. Kalha, having taken over from Maha Singh Rikh earlier, under pressure from Harbakhsh Singh had worked out his plans to regain lost ground. During the day on 7 September, he had issued his orders. 3 Jat was to provide a firm base from where 13 Punjab was to secure the canal and railway bridges along the UBDC axis. 15 Dogra with Alpha Squadron of 14 Cavalry was to then approach Dograi at first light from the west of Gosal–Dial and occupy the town that had remained vacant ever since 3 Jat had withdrawn on the evening of 6 September. H-hour was set for 0100 hrs on 8 September. Depending on how matters developed, the brigade commander then planned to use Hayde's 3 Jat to exploit the situation.

On the Pakistani side, GOC 10 Division, Major General Sarfraz Khan, responsible for the Lahore Sector, was also determined to occupy Dograi. Accordingly, he ordered Brigadier Abdul Qayyum Sher, the commander of 22 Brigade, to move into Dograi during the night. The brigade group, consisting of two squadrons of 23 Cavalry commanded by Lieutenant Colonel Ghulam Mohammad and two companies each from 18 Baluch and 15 FF, was to cross the Puldis tributary by the Bhasin Bridge. While one squadron of 23 Cavalry was to head south-eastwards to probe for Indian defences, the rest were to occupy Dograi. With things for the Pakistanis going as per their plan, Delta Company of 18 Baluch was already dug in at Dograi and defending the two bridges when the Indians reached there.

As Alpha and Bravo Companies of 13 Punjab closed in on their objectives, the Pakistanis withdrew from the road bridge. By first light the Punjabis had dug their fire trenches and were engaging the enemy who was still holding onto the railway bridge. Delta company of 13 Punjab was ordered to advance but came under heavy artillery fire. Caught in the open, 13 Punjab came under fire not only from the Baluchis but also from the two tank squadrons of 23 Cavalry who arrived at Dograi and opened up with high explosive shells and their co-axial machine guns. Taking severe casualties, the Punjabis were left with no option but to withdraw, the battalion disengaging and extracting itself through the 3 Jat positions. The Pakistanis were quite content to dig in at Dograi, while 3 Jat remained where they were through the daylight hours of 8 September. At 1900 hrs, Kalha ordered Hayde to pull back and take up a defensive position at Santpura. 3 Jat started to withdraw at 2130 hrs and, by first light on 9 September, were manning their new defences.

Brigadier Pathak's 38 Infantry Brigade had suffered a defeat on 6 and 7 September. Having first captured and then withdrawn from the bridge at Bhaini Dhilwal, 1 Jat had frittered away its gains. Subsequently the withdrawal of 6 Kumaon to Ranian from the bridge after the Pakistanis launched a determined counter-attack on 7 September meant the brigade had made very little headway. Pathak then decided to launch a third attack on the bridge in the early morning hours of 8 September. Combining 6 Kumaon with the remaining troops of 1 Jat, the Indians launched yet another attack. Pakistan's 16 Punjab, supported by armour, successfully thwarted the Indians who, yet again, were pushed back to Ranian.

Success continued to elude 38 Infantry Brigade. On the GT Road axis, Pathak ordered 1/3 GR to capture the bridge on the Bhaini–Malakapur axis. The task, one of the initial stated objectives of the brigade, had been pending for two days. As the Gorkhas began to advance along the northern side of the road at first light, they came under heavy artillery and MMG fire. Yet again, the Indian attack failed to dislodge the Pakistanis from their defences on the east bank of the Ichhogil Canal.

In the DBN Sector, at 0930 hrs on 8 September, Pakistani sappers blew part of the bridge, destroying the span closest to them. After the initial scare on the previous day when Pakistani armour had got across the Ravi, Pritam Singh's 29 Infantry Brigade had achieved its objectives and successfully established a vital fact. It was clear from Pakistan's destruction of the bridge that it had no offensive plans for the DBN Sector. At 1100 hrs the Pakistani observation post and other troops in the Enclave surrendered. Dhillon redeployed 1/5 GR and 2 Madras in other hard-pressed sectors, leaving 2 Raj Rif and 16 PAP to keep an eye on Pakistani movement across the Ravi. At the northern end of 11 Corps, the bridge over the Ravi having been partially blown, Dhillon ordered 29 Brigade to rejoin its parent formation, Major General Sibal's 7 Infantry Division. Leaving one battalion behind to cover DBN, the brigade moved on the night of 8/9 September. The threat of a Pakistani armoured thrust from DBN having evaporated, the AMX-13 tanks of 8 Cavalry also fell back and were in Khem Karan by nightfall on 8 September.

Chapter 15

RETRIBUTION: IAF ON 7 SEPT

EAST PAKISTAN & ALFRED COOKE

East Pakistan was known to have one squadron of Sabres which was based at Tejgaon. While Eastern Air Command, based out of Shillong, was oriented towards the China and Burma borders, Central Air Command (CAC), with its headquarters in Calcutta's Tollygunge, was expected to deal with East Pakistan. A network of airfields, most of them legacies of World War II, gave the CAC under Air Vice Marshal (later Air Marshal) Shivdev Singh plenty of options. Kalaikunda in West Bengal had three types of aircraft—16 Squadron commanded by Wing Commander (later Air Commodore) Peter Maynard Wilson was equipped with Canberra B(I)-58s; 14 Squadron (Bulls) led by Wing Commander Denis Anthony LaFontaine[1] had Hawker Hunters; while Squadron Leader (later Air Marshal) Madhabendra Banerji was commanding 24 Squadron (Hawks) that was flying the Vampire FB.52s. There were two more Hunter squadrons stationed at Jorhat and Chabua and another three squadrons—4, 29, and 47—that were equipped with the French-made Dassault M.D.450 Ouragans.

Radar coverage in the east had severe limitations. The antiquated 55 SU at best provided early warning at Kalaikunda, while 411 SU at Rampurhat could give the pilots in the air only basic information. The operational role for the Hunters in the eastern sector was limited to countering a Chinese threat and 'no offensive role against East Pakistani targets was conceived or planned. The only role planned in case of hostilities against Pakistan was air defence for Indian installations.'[2]

On the evening of 6 September when CAC received a coded signal green-lighting offensive sorties into East Pakistan, plans were hastily prepared to attack Jessore and Chittagong, surprisingly leaving out Tejgaon, which was the main base for the PAF Sabres in Dacca. Shivdev Singh himself dashed across to Kalaikunda in the evening, where he briefed Wilson and ordered him to launch a two-aircraft Canberra strike against Chittagong at first light. LaFontaine was called in next. Shivdev Singh had conflicting intelligence reports that indicated that a detachment of Sabres were at either Comilla or Jessore. Eventually, after a lot of discussion, a six-Hunter formation was to be launched at 0430 hrs.

Meanwhile, Eastern Air Command had also received the same signal and, at 0200 hrs, Squadron Leader (later Group Captain) Mian Naranjan 'M. N.' Singh, who was commanding a detachment of four Hunters from 37 Squadron stationed at Gauhati, was ordered to launch an attack on Kurmitola airfield, which was being constructed in Dacca as its international airport. Permission to attack Tejgaon was categorically refused. The formation was to take off at 0450 hrs.

In addition, 4 Squadron (Fighting Oorials) based at Hasimara, hurriedly planned a four-Ouragan strike led by Squadron Leader (later Air Marshal) Man Mohan Singh against Lal Munir Hat while 24 Squadron was to launch a four-Vampire strike from Barrackpore against Jessore under the command of Madhabendra Banerji. In almost all cases, the number of aircraft chosen for the raids was small and the intelligence given to the pilots was non-existent. M. N. Singh, who was to attack Kurmitola airfield, was shown a black and white photograph of the airfield that was more than fifteen years old.

Aggravating the situation was the bad weather that almost all the planned strikes ran into as the entire region extending from the Meghna River to Chittagong was experiencing pelting rain. Most strikes either failed to spot the objectives or, at best, expended their ammunition on insignificant targets. The two Canberras, flown by Peter Wilson and Squadron Leader Raghunath Kashinath Karve, made their way to Chittagong through treacherous weather. Wilson made three runs and his navigator, Squadron Leader (later Wing Commander) Odayanmadath Shankaran, dropped his bombs on the intersection of the runways. Much to their consternation, the bombs failed to explode, probably due to their vintage. Karve then lined up his aircraft over the target area and his navigator, Flying Officer (later Air Marshal) Govind Chandra Singh Rajwar squarely hit the runway and, fortunately, this time the bombs exploded.

The same bad weather also adversely affected the PAF. A section of Sabres was launched from Tejgaon to intercept the 37 Squadron Hunters that had hit Kurmitola. Flying Officer A. T. M. Aziz reported visual contact with M. N. Singh's three-Hunter formation (one aircraft had failed to start up) and as the Sabre gave chase at low level, it hit the ground and exploded. Wilson and Karve too had a narrow escape, running into two 14 Squadron Hunters who had not been informed about the Canberra strike. Mistaking the Canberras for Pakistani B-57s, Flight Lieutenant Alfred Tyrone Cooke and Flying Officer (later Wing Commander) Subodh Chandra Mamgain closed in for the kill, breaking off in the nick of time as Cooke realized they were the IAF's B-58s.

Once again, the Indians had taken the initiative but the offensive raids had been, in Wilson's description, a fiasco. The failure to target Tejgaon, the main airfield, was not only baffling, it allowed Pakistan's 14 Squadron the liberty to execute its own offensive plan!

During Operation Ablaze, when the Indian Army first deployed in the Punjab and the threat of all-out war became a reality, neither Army HQ nor Air HQ bothered to beef up their ground intelligence. As a result, when the fighting expanded beyond J&K in September, the commanders on the ground had very little information. In the case of the IAF, apart from fifteen-year-old photos of airfields, there was very little information pertaining to the deployment of the PAF's assets. In August, when Operation Gibraltar had been unleashed by Pakistan in J&K, an agitated Cooke had suggested to his commanding officer, LaFontaine, that an IAF officer needed to get on the Indian Airlines flight to Dacca and come back with information pertaining to the dispersal of the Sabres at Tejgaon. LaFontaine had ticked off Cooke, saying what he was suggesting was most ungentlemanly and would amount to spying!

Intelligence units were making wild guesses—there was one report suggesting the Sabres were stationed at Comilla, while another suggested that some of them had been positioned at Jessore. Yet another input suggested the Sabres in East Pakistan were also equipped with the Sidewinder missiles, which would give them a clear advantage in the event of a high-altitude engagement.

While Wilson and Karve were bombing Chittagong and the Vampires from 221 Squadron were attacking Jessore, LaFontaine led a four-aircraft Hunter sweep at 20,000 feet between Jessore and Tejgaon, with the intention of luring the Sabres into air combat. The four Hunters were being trailed by Cooke and Mamgain, who were initially supposed to provide top cover for the Vampire strike at Jessore. Once radar had a fix on the Sabres' location, the Hunters were to return to Dum Dum, arm up with rockets and bombs, and then attack Tejgaon. Adding to the confusion, CAC had decided not to tell LaFontaine about the Canberra raid over Chittagong, which had resulted in Cooke and Mamgain nearly shooting down the returning aircraft.

With Indian aircraft criss-crossing the skies over East Pakistan, Group Captain Ghulam 'Gulli' Haider, the station commander at Tejgaon, was intent on staying alert. Despite the wet weather conditions, reports were coming in of Indian strikes against Chittagong, Jessore, and Kurmitola. A few Sabres were scrambled—the loss of Aziz meant Pakistan's 14 Squadron, commanded by Squadron Leader (later Air Marshal) Shabbir Hussain Syed, was down to eleven Sabres. Haider, along with Syed, was trying to stay focussed on their plan to attack Kalaikunda. They had fine-tuned the details that they had been working on since 2 September when they had received an alert along with dispersal instructions. In the event of a war, Haider was on his own, with the liberty to deploy his assets as he deemed fit.

Surrounded by India on three sides and the Bay of Bengal to the south, Haider was in much a similar position as his air chief in West Pakistan, where the PAF was facing a much larger number of aircraft. A hard-hitting successful strike against India's main airfield and the destruction of as many aircraft as possible would give him an outside chance of delivering a crippling death blow. Thirty-seven years later, Nur Khan, in an article in Pakistan's *Defence Journal* said, 'In spite of the advice from local army soldiers and the Government of East Pakistan not to take any initiative that might provoke the Indians, it was difficult to hold back

Shabbir (Syed) and his squadron from launching an offensive.'[3]

For the Sabres to catch Kalaikunda by surprise, they would have to come in low from the direction of the Bay of Bengal. This circuitous route meant they would have to cover 300 km at low level over the sea, necessitating 'a full load of external fuel in two 120 and two 200-gallon drop tanks, leaving only their 0.5-inch machine guns as weaponry.'[4]

Haider needed to keep some aircraft for air defence. All said and done, it was a bold decision. Five Sabres led by Syed got airborne from Tejgaon at 0600 hrs and headed south towards the open sea. Flight Lieutenants Haleem, Basheer, Tariq Khan, and Flying Officer Afzal Khan completed the strike force. They banked to the right and, skimming over the surface of the sea, set course for Kalaikunda. The aircraft were too low for 55 SU to pick them up on its radar. Once over the Kalaikunda runway, the Sabres pulled up sharply. To their delight, aircraft were neatly lined up on the tarmac. Kalaikunda was virtually undefended as most of the anti-aircraft guns had only arrived the previous day and, except for a couple, had not yet been deployed. Those that had been positioned had their canvas muzzle covers on to protect them from the overnight showers and morning dew.

The Sabres faced no opposition as they formed up in a 'race course pattern' to carry out their attack. The Vampires, which had failed to take off for the strike against Jessore due to bad weather, were lined up on the squadron dispersal area and were shining in the sparkling sunlight, the fuselages having been washed by the overnight rain. Their camouflage nets had been removed and they were fully armed in anticipation of the planned raid that was to have taken off at sunrise. Wilson and Karve's Canberras, having landed minutes ago, were parked across the runway on the blast pen dispersal area and the two crews had just entered the ATC building for their debriefing on the Chittagong raid.

They had just sat down at 0630 hrs, when the sound of low-flying jets and gunfire had them scrambling to the terrace of the ATC to see what was happening. While most started looking around for cover, Wilson stood there majestically and 'gave a running commentary on the relative positioning of the attack patterns of the Sabres and admired their training and motivation. He was remarkably cool and composed.'[5] Within minutes, the four Vampires were ablaze, their exploding ammunition adding to the din and confusion.

The Sabres, limited by the fact that they only had their machine guns to attack with, then turned their attention to the two Canberras that had returned from Chittagong. A few seconds later, these too were blazing infernos. Then, just as suddenly, the Sabres were gone!

The only silver lining for the Indians was that in their excitement at being presented the perfect target, the Sabre pilots had failed to see the Hunters that were also lined up in their dispersal area. While everyone's attention was on the burning aircraft outside, Wilson was calculating the flying time to Tejgaon. He told

Wing Commander R. D. Law, the officer-in-charge, flying, that the Sabres would be back. Having seen the number of aircraft at the airfield, it was too tempting a target for them to give it a miss. Working out the turn around time and their likely approach again from the direction of the sea, Wilson said the second attack would come at 1030 hrs.

In New Delhi, Arjan Singh conveyed the news of the disaster at Kalaikunda to Chavan at 0945 hrs. Coming as this did hard on the heels of the Pathankot raid, the defence minister suggested to the air chief that the IAF stop all further raids into East Pakistan, for the last thing the country needed was China using that as a pretext to enter the conflict. Chavan noted in his diary that Arjan Singh concurred with him.

Wilson was dead right. The return of the four Sabres would lead to one of the most epic dogfights of the war as Cooke took them on almost single-handedly, shooting down two, and damaging a third (see Prologue).

The PAF later claimed a much higher number of aircraft destroyed in the two raids, but the final toll was four Canberras and four Vampires. Pakistan also claimed the second formation was engaged by nine Hunters. Even now, more than half a century later, Cooke chuckles, 'That's a real compliment! The Pakistani pilots reported there were nine Hunters in the sky—it really felt like that?'

TIGERS OVER SARGODHA (7 SEPTEMBER)

The pre-emptive strike by Pakistan on the Indian airfields the previous day had removed all restrictions on the use of offensive air power. Air HQ in New Delhi ordered multiple strikes to be launched against the Sargodha complex that consisted of four airfields and what was the very hub of the PAF. 1, 8, and 32 Squadrons, equipped with the Mystère IVA ground attack fighter, were stationed at Adampur, close to Jalandhar in Punjab. The first attack would be launched by No. 1 Squadron (Tigers). Commanded by Wing Commander Omi Taneja, the Tigers were divided into two flights of eight aircraft each with Squadron Leaders Earle and Denzil 'Denny' Edward Satur (later air vice marshal) as flight commanders. Together they got working on the details.

Since the fateful evening on 1 September over Chhamb–Jaurian, only the Mystère and Gnat squadrons at Pathankot to the north of Adampur had seen action, while the rest waited impatiently. Finally, No. 1 Squadron was sent into action at dawn on 6 September. After the first search and strike mission in the Gujranwala sector, nothing happened for the rest of the morning. At 1300 hrs, the assembled pilots heard on the radio in the crew room Ayub Khan broadcasting to his countrymen on Radio Pakistan that the Indian Army had committed aggression by crossing the IB in the Sialkot, DBN, and Lahore Sectors and that Pakistan had no option but to defend itself. All the keyed-up pilots anxiously waited for orders to go into action but none came.

Around 1700 hrs on 6 September, the news had filtered in that the Pathankot airfield had been raided by the PAF and a number of aircraft had been destroyed. As dusk fell, the pilots were told to go back to their rooms. Flight Lieutenants Vinod Kumar 'Frisky' Verma and Philip Rajkumar (both later became air marshals) had got on to Frisky's Jawa motorbike and set off for the mess when there was a loud explosion at the southern end of the runway and the anti-aircraft guns opened fire. Glowing red balls of tracer shells arced through the fading light and in their glow, Rajkumar picked out the silhouette of a PAF B-57 Canberra bomber go past. He yelled, 'Frisky, B-57 over us!' and they dived from the motorbike into a trench. The Pakistani bomber carried out a second attack and dropped a bomb near the ATC building in the middle of the 3,000-yard runway. After about fifteen minutes the all-clear sounded and the two pilots gingerly rode back to the mess in the pitch dark because blackout had been enforced not only on the base but all over Punjab.

In the mess, pilots from the other two Mystère squadrons on the base and a number of senior flying instructors from Training Command who had been attached to the three squadrons for operational duties were gathered in little knots, talking in hushed tones about yet another PAF raid on Halwara earlier in the evening that had caused considerable damage, but the good news was that two F-86 Sabres of the PAF had been shot down by Hawker Hunters in the process. In the meantime, some more bad news came in—a MiG-21 parked at the end of the runway had been destroyed by the B-57. It was obvious then that the IAF would have to retaliate the next day but no one had any idea of where and when. Earle came to the mess and told all the pilots to have an early dinner and get some sleep. Rajkumar says in his notes that he 'slept fitfully'. When they assembled in the briefing room, they rushed to the board and 'saw the formation details for a twelve aircraft attack on Sargodha'. Rajkumar saw that he was to be the 'tail end Charlie. As enemy aircraft attempting to intercept our formation would have to approach from the rear to bring their forward firing guns to bear on our aircraft, the last man in the formation's job was to warn the others about an impending attack. The job required the keen eyes of a hawk and a rubberneck to keep looking as far back as possible. It was a crucial duty and I had been chosen to do it.'[6] Two senior flying instructors, one of them Squadron Leader Ajammada Boppaya Devayya, were standbys in case any of the first twelve aircraft dropped out.

Taneja started the briefing—the excitement and tension in the room was palpable. The aircraft had to start up and taxi out to the take off point in the correct sequence in total radio silence on unlit taxi tracks. The runway lights would come on only when they were ready to roll. Take off would be in pairs, with each aircraft occupying one half of the runway and the interval between pairs was to be thirty seconds to avoid the jet wake of the aircraft in front. They were to take off at 0528 hrs and fly at 300 feet AGL in darkness for thirty minutes and carry out their attacks at thirty second intervals at 0558 hrs, just as dawn was breaking over the target. The very low altitude was chosen for the inbound leg to avoid radar detection. Navigation would be only by compass and stopwatch as darkness would not permit map reading. Taneja was to lead the first four aircraft armed with eight T-10 rockets each, Satur, the second four armed with two 18 SNEB 68 mm rocket pods each and Squadron Leader (later Air Commodore) Sudarshan Handa the last four with two 1,000-lb bombs each. As the target was at the extreme distance the Mystère could go at a height of 300 feet AGL with a full fuel and armament load, they had to fly at the optimum speed for range which was about 120 mph slower than the preferred tactical speed for manoeuvring at low level. Each of the twelve pilots was given a specific target to attack on the airfield, with preference for aircraft spotted on the airfield.

The pilots synchronized their watches and the briefing ended at 0500 hrs. Some biscuits and tea had been served during the briefing by junior pilots who were not part of the formation. Each pilot had loaded his revolver and stuffed it into his flying suit along with some Pakistani currency. These items were to facilitate escape in case they were shot down. They strapped on their back parachutes, picked up their flying helmets and checked that everything was in order. Dry mouthed, they started walking to the pen where their aircraft were parked, when the air raid siren went off and the anti-aircraft guns started to fire the now familiar red tracer shells. It was a clear starlit sky and Rajkumar picked out a moving pinpoint of light overhead and quickly realized that the gunners were shooting at a passing satellite at a height of a couple of hundred miles! They kept up a barrage for a few minutes. Some of the pilots jumped into a nearby trench and waited for the all-clear to sound when they heard Taneja's aircraft, which was parked close by, start up. It was already 0518 hrs, only ten minutes to go for take-off and the pilots ran towards their aircraft, climbed into the cockpit, started the engines and strapped in while they were revving up. Rajkumar at number twelve caught up with the other eleven aircraft, which were ghostly shapes on the taxi track. Taneja and his four aircraft lined up and took off on time, followed by Satur and his formation of four.

As Handa rolled on to the runway followed by his wingman Flight Lieutenant Darshan Singh Brar, Rajkumar saw the two standby aircraft with their engines running parked to one side of the take-off point. His sub-section leader Flight Lieutenant (later Group Captain) Dil Mohan Singh 'Kay' Kahai took up position behind Handa who started to roll for his take off. 'I suddenly saw one of the standby pilots, Devayya, move on to the runway and begin rolling in front of Kay. The second bomb dropped by the PAF B-57 the previous night had exploded to one side of the runway about 1,500 yards from where we began rolling. A lot of mud was lying on the runway and the jet wake of the preceding aircraft had created a dense dust cloud. As I raised the nose wheel at about 140 mph I entered the dust cloud and lost all visual reference. After about three or four seconds I emerged from the cloud ready to lift off when I saw this enormous Mystère filling my front windshield. Devayya, who had no business to be in the formation as no one had dropped out, had drifted into my half of the runway and I was about to collide with him! Fortunately for me, the Mystère had a characteristic, which I knew about, of yawing to the right if one attempted to get it off the ground before it was ready to fly off on its own. I did exactly that and the heavily laden aircraft yawed and staggered into the air. I quickly raised the wheels to reduce drag and concentrated on staying in the air. The aircraft accelerated slowly and after what seemed an eternity I had things under control but I had lost sight of Kay's aircraft.' Rajkumar headed northwest for the Beas River Bridge in the hope of spotting the formation, but it was an impossible task in the darkness as the aircraft were flying with their navigation lights switched off. He used up the fuel and returned to base with his bombs. About twenty minutes after he landed, the rest of the formation returned. Handa's formation had missed the target due to a navigational error and had returned to base with their bomb loads.

Taneja's section had zeroed in on Sargodha but no one had realized that sunrise at Sargodha was a few minutes later, as it was to the west of Adampur. As a result, the airfield was still under a shroud of darkness. To add to the drama, Pakistani ack-ack guns were quick to respond, laying out a curtain of fire for the incoming Mystères. The formation attacked the technical area, hangers, and circular pens, and though Taneja saw two Sabres and a Starfighter on the ORP, at the end of his attacking run the following aircraft failed to see the targets. Only after they had landed did they realize that Devayya was missing.

MULTIPLE ATTACKS ON SARGODHA

While on the one hand there was hardly any intelligence available, Air HQ, acting on what it considered to be credible information, had tasked 8 Squadron (Pursoots) to simultaneously target Bhagtanwala, which was part of the cluster of airfields used by the PAF some 20-odd kms further to the west of Sargodha. Accordingly, eight Mystères comprising two formations had trailed 1 Squadron's Tigers from Adampur.

From Adampur, direct routing to Sargodha took the aircraft over Amritsar and kept Lahore to the south, after which it was a straight run over miles of cultivated crop, mainly sugarcane and cotton. The first formation consisted of squadron leader (later Wing Commander) Madhukar Shantaram 'Mickey' Jatar, Flight Lieutenants Vinod Kumar 'Jimmy' Bhatia (later air marshal), Pramod Chandra 'Chopi' Chopra (later squadron leader) and Vinod 'Pat' Patney (later air marshal) while the second formation was made up of Squadron Leaders Edwin Godfrey 'Sir Gads' Salins (later air vice marshal), Mohan Vasudeo Kashikar (later wing commander), Flight Lieutenants B. I. Singh and Arun Keshav Sapre (later squadron leader)[7]. To marshal their fuel so as to reach Bhagtanwala, the Mystères had to fly at 300 knots at a height of 300 ft AGL which was rather risky especially with the Tigers ahead of them stirring up the hornet's nest en route.

As the Pursoots approached Amritsar, the second formation started reporting bogeys with alarming frequency. In the early morning light, the exploding black puffs from ack-ack guns deployed around the radar unit were taking on the shape of menacing Sabres and Starfighters. Jatar, who realized what was happening, was quick to transmit a stern 'shut up' and the nervous chatter dried up. A few minutes later, at around 5,000 feet, a lone Sabre was spotted crossing from left to right. However, in the morning haze, the Pakistani aircraft seemed to be oblivious of the low-flying Indian aircraft and the formation decided to ignore him and continue with the task at hand.

Getting to Bhagtanwala unopposed, the Indians were in for a disappointment. What at first glance appeared to be parked aircraft turned out to be decoys. After perfunctorily strafing and bombing the place, the eight Mystères returned to Adampur where they were disappointed to learn that only a few aircraft had gone on to hit Sargodha. The error in timing the sorties combined with poor intelligence was frustrating. Jimmy Bhatia was to say later: 'One wonders what would have happened if we had also gone to Sargodha Main which would have meant a concentrated 20-aircraft strike and the combined haul of enemy aircraft destroyed on ground would have been a befitting reply to the PAF's attack on Pathankot a day earlier.'[8]

The other airfield that was cleared to launch attacks against the Sargodha group of airfields was Halwara. Situated approximately 40 miles south of Adampur to the southwest of Ludhiana, it formed a triangle with both Amritsar and Lahore. As per the overall plan, after the first wave of Tigers and the Pursoots had struck Sargodha and Bhagtanwala, the Hunters from 7 Squadron (Battle Axes) were to be over Sargodha Main at 0610 hrs. Almost simultaneously, coming in five minutes behind, Hunters from 27 Squadron (Flaming Arrows) were to strike against Chhota Sargodha, one of the satellite airfields.

Both squadrons were to go in with similar configurations; the Battle Axes' four-aircraft formation was being led by Zachariah, with Lamba, Sinha, and Sharma. Two escorts in an air combat configuration—Squadron Leader Bhagwat and Flying Officer Jagdev Singh 'Little Ben' Brar were to provide top cover. During the briefing held early in the morning, as a 1958-vintage photograph of Sargodha airfield was being shown to the pilots, a message was received from Adampur asking if the strike by 1 Squadron could be postponed, but the request was denied as additional follow-up strikes had been planned.

The Flaming Arrows were being led by the squadron's senior flight commander, Squadron Leaders Dilip Shankar Jog (later air marshal), Onkar Nath 'Piloo' Kacker (later wing commander), Flight Lieutenants T. A. K. Chaudhri, and Flying Officer P. S. 'Parry' Parihar, with Flight Lieutenants D. N. Rathore and R. K. Dass acting as escorts. As both sets of pilots were about to proceed to their aircraft, the air raid warning sounded at 0445 hrs as a B-57 attacked Halwara just before first light and dropped four 1,000-lb bombs on the northeast and southwest of the airfield. Though these did not cause any damage, it delayed Zachariah's formation by fifty minutes. Jog's formation, however, took off ten minutes earlier. Of the six aircraft, Dass had to drop off due to his aircraft being unserviceable, which meant Rathore was the lone escort.

Proceeding to the target at low level, Jog's formation pulled up for the attack only to find a deserted airfield. Ignoring the heavy ack-ack, all four aircraft vented their frustration and fired off their rockets at any buildings and installations they could see. On the way back, the formation drifted further south than had been planned and suddenly they were over the Chak Jhumra airfield on the outskirts of Faisalabad. Two Sabres could be seen on the ORP and Rathore, trailing the formation, fired a long burst starting from short of the parked aircraft and ending up well beyond them. Jog, in the meantime, led the others into a steep wingover and came in to attack once again and shot at a factory just outside the airfield's perimeter.

A few minutes later, the Hunters were bounced by Sabres—one of them getting behind the fourth aircraft being flown by Chaudhri. Though hit by a couple of cannon shells, the Sabre had to break off the attack as Rathore turned into him, the two aircraft coming within a fraction of colliding. The other Sabres tried to close in on Rathore, but he easily shook them off, though they continued to chase the Hunter formation towards the IB. Somewhere near Kasur disaster struck as Kacker's aircraft suddenly flamed out. Kacker called out, 'My engine has flamed out. I am pulling up to eject. Good luck, boys.' On the ground he was soon surrounded by villagers. Initially he tried to bluff his way out by claiming to be a Pakistani pilot, having gotten rid of the documents and badges on his flying overalls. Fortunately, the police arrived at the scene fairly quickly and took him away to serve as a prisoner of war for the next five months until he was repatriated. Ironically, around the same time in the morning, on the other side of the subcontinent, Kacker's student Cooke was fighting the aerial battle of a lifetime.

The 7 Squadron formation trailing behind was approximately overhead Shaheen Abad, just short of Sargodha when bogeys were reported. However, they turned out to be the Hunters of 27 Squadron heading back a couple of minutes before they attacked on Chak Jhumra. When the Battle Axes formation had finally started up, Sharma's Hunter too had dropped out due to aircraft unserviceability, reducing the strike formation to three aircraft with two escorts. By that time, the skies over Sargodha were swarming with Pakistani aircraft. A few seconds after the contact with Jog's formation, Rusty had called another 'bogey', this time an F-104 at 10 o'clock followed by Sabres which had already jettisoned their drop tanks. To make matters worse, a second F-104 also appeared on the scene.

The Hunters, configured for ground attacks with rocket pods and drop tanks, had no alternative but to get out of the area. Zachariah ordered 'Hard port and disengage' and the formation, including the escorts, turned sharply to the left, firing their rockets into the ground and punching the jettison button for the drop tanks to fall off. Lamba's drop tanks refused to disengage, but he managed to roll out behind Zachariah after completing 180 degrees of the turn. There was no sign of Rusty while Bhagwat and Brar were last seen continuing to turn, presumably to take on the Sabres. Both the aircraft set course for Halwara at treetop height and, in the process, they overflew Chak Jhumra and noticed a number of aircraft. Both the Hunters, short of fuel and minus their rockets, were in no position to put in an attack. As they neared Halwara, much to their relief, they found Rusty's Hunter ahead of them.

Both Bhagwat and 'Little Ben' Brar were shot down and killed between the eastern side of the Chenab River and Sangla Hills by Squadron Leader Alam who, after Rafique, became the second pilot to claim two kills. However, Alam and the PAF, not content with his fairly impressive feat, also claimed three more Hunters. Still not satisfied with having downed five Hunters, Alam claimed to have shot them all down in the space of thirty seconds.

SARGODHA: FATAL ATTRACTION

As the Hunters returned to Halwara, back in Adampur, the debriefing of the first raid on Sargodha was going on. No one knew what had happened to Devayya's Mystère. Taneja said the performance of Handa's formation was unacceptable. He ordered the formation to attack Sargodha in broad daylight at 0945 hrs! This was most unexpected because there would be no cover of darkness for the inbound leg and the alerted defences would give them a hearty reception. There was a high chance of being intercepted by enemy fighters and getting shot down.

After a quick breakfast, Sudarshan Handa went over the briefing once again and Darshan Singh Brar, Kahai, and Rajkumar listened in stony silence. Since the attack would be in daylight, they were given specific targets picked out from an aerial photograph taken by a reconnaissance aircraft some years earlier. They were to carry out a shallow glide bombing attack, releasing the bombs at about 800 feet and pull out by 200 feet AGL. To avoid being damaged by the exploding bombs at such a low height the bombs were fitted with a twenty-second delay fuse to give adequate time for the aircraft to get clear. The return leg was to be flown at tactical speed at as low a height as possible, consistent with safety.

The four-aircraft formation took off at exactly 0945 hrs aiming to be over the target in thirty minutes. The day was sunny and cloudless with unlimited visibility and after take-off they formed up in a low-level tactical formation. Handa was in front, with Kahai about 1,000 yards to his right. Brar and Rajkumar were behind and to the outside of the leaders at a distance of 200 yards. This way

Brar could look to his right to spot any approaching fighters and clear the area behind Rajkumar and Rajkumar could do the same for him by looking left. As they crossed the IB, Rajkumar saw Brar's gun ports winking as he fired a short burst to check that his guns were working. Philip checked his gun sight and did the same as Handa descended to about 100 feet AGL. Rajkumar kept looking behind Brar all the time but did not spot any enemy aircraft.

The formation hit the railway line about 20 miles to the northeast of the target and Handa turned left to follow the railway line to Sargodha. This was the moment to open full power, accelerate to tactical speed, and turn on the armament switches. Two minutes later Handa's call—'pulling up'—came over the radio and all four aircraft eased up to 2,500 feet and rolled into a shallow dive to the left in a south easterly direction. As they settled into the dive, they saw the Sargodha runway for the first time and quickly scanned the skies for Pakistani aircraft. Rajkumar recalls: 'After ensuring that there was no immediate threat to the formation, I tried to identify my target, which was a missile dump to the south of the runway. The four aircraft were now strung out in a line with Handa in front and me at the top of the dive about 1,500 yards behind him. Suddenly I saw a bright orange flash on the ground at the northern end of the runway and Handa yelled, "Aircraft at end of the runway."[9] After dropping his bombs on a bulk petroleum installation to the north of the runway, Handa spotted four aircraft, three F-86 Sabres and one F-104 Starfighter parked on the ORP at the northern end of the runway. He opened fire, and his guns blew up a Sabre with his burst. I shouted "Sir, you got him" and saw black puffs dot the sky in our dive direction. The anti-aircraft guns of Sargodha had opened up. I was meant to drop my bombs on the target at the south of the runway but was not able to point my guns at that juicy target. I released my bombs at the briefed target and fired my guns at what appeared to be aircraft standing on the southern ORP but there was no explosion, indicating they were decoys. During my bombing dive I had lost sight of the other aircraft and as I pulled out of my dive at barely 100 feet AGL, I saw Handa's aircraft on the horizon about 800 yards ahead with Brar to his left. Brar called "Bogey, left 8'o clock high". I looked to my left, saw only black puffs and called out that it was flak.

'With the bombs gone and the drop tanks empty I was now at 500 mph at less than 100 feet AGL when I saw Kay about 500 yards to my left. We were now flying in two pairs in broad frontage with Handa and Brar in front and Kay and I about 800 yards behind....While still deep inside Pakistan my fuel was considerably less than the planned figure. I reported this to Handa and he eased back on the throttle. We were flying really low and fast at this time because I could see the jet wake from Handa's aircraft cutting a swathe over the standing crop in the fields we were flying over. When we were flying to the north of Lahore I saw a glint in the sky above and to the left of the formation. It could only have come from a turning aircraft and I reported "Bogey, left 7 o'clock high" and Handa called out "Buster" which meant opening full power. As we crossed the border my low fuel red warning light came on in the cockpit indicating a fuel reserve of about 10 minutes at the engine power I was using and I reported this to Handa. He replied "You are over India now and you can eject if you have to". I had no intention of doing that and we unintentionally flew over the radar unit at Amritsar. Our own anti-aircraft guns started firing at us and I saw the red tracer shells coming straight at me and then burning out. Fortunately no one was hit and I called out that I was easing up to 6,000 feet AGL to spot Adampur. To my relief I saw the runway from a distance of about 15 miles. I throttled back, descended to traffic pattern height, did a tight pattern and touched down with barely three minutes of fuel left in my tanks.'[10]

Back in the crew room every one clustered around Handa and the others to hear about the results of the raid. When Rajkumar announced that Handa had destroyed a Sabre on the ground, a cheer went up. Kahai had dropped his bombs on the other aircraft at the northern ORP and Brar had dropped his bombs on an aircraft hangar. 'We had no idea what damage our bombs had caused because there was no post raid reconnaissance to assess the damage. Ours was the most successful mission of the entire day because we had returned unscathed from the enemy's lair after destroying an aircraft and some installations on the ground. Handa's formation had redeemed itself in style after the early morning mistakes! I grabbed a cup of tea, sat down and noticed that my hands were shaking. The 90-minute adrenalin rush was over.'

Handa's log book entry for the same sortie records that on the return trip three Sabres chased the formation. So a second wave of Mystères, led by Squadron Leader Earle had got airborne for Sargodha when Handa came on the radio and said his formation was short of fuel and was being chased by the Pakistanis. Earle decided to abort the Sargodha mission and instead cover Handa's formation, with whom they caught up around the IB. The flash that Rajkumar caught and called 'bogey' may have been this formation of Mystères. None of the other three aircraft in Handa's formation saw any Sabres.

The last and final strike against the Sargodha complex was launched at 1500 hrs by the Tigers. Satur along with Flight Lieutenants B. S. 'Bipin' Raje (later group captain), J. P. Singh (later air commodore) and U. B. 'Babul' Guha took off in formation but, almost immediately, Satur had problems with the fuel transfer in his aircraft and returned to Adampur with his wingman, Raje. The other two Mystères continued with the mission, reached Sargodha and dropped their bombs. Almost immediately they were bounced by the waiting Sabres, forcing them to jettison their drop tanks and set course for home, skimming the treetops at high speed. Guha, flying behind J. P., reported two Sabres 1,500 yards behind him. This would be the last communication from Guha, who was shot down by Flight

Lieutenant A. H. Malik with a Sidewinder—the first and only Mystère to be shot down by a missile. According to the PAF, a second Sidewinder was launched at J. P.'s aircraft but it hit the ground instead.

GROUND SUPPORT (7 SEPTEMBER)

To coordinate with the army, the Lahore–Sulemanki Sectors were being coordinated by the army's Western Command and the air force's Advance HQ, Western Air Command. 2 Tactical Air Control had joined 1 Corps on 5 September and, the next day, No. 1 Company Air Support Signal Regiment from Delhi also joined 1 Corps with ten tentacles. Pathankot and Halwara were designated as support airfields for the Chhamb–Sialkot Sector. The GLO Section cover for these airfields was arranged directly by Army HQ. By 7 September, all ACTs and tentacles were in position in the respective formations.

While the main focus of both Adampur and Halwara was on attacking Sargodha, Mystères and Hunters were also assigned ground targets during the day. The targets assigned to 1 Squadron, however, underline the disconnect between the army and the air force. The fighting on the ground on 7 September extended from the Sulemanki Sector to DBN Bridge on the Ravi, the Sialkot Sector not yet having been activated. Yet at 1345 hrs, a two-aircraft formation flown by Earle and K. K. 'Joe' Bakshi was sent off on an armed reconnaissance mission over the Gujrat airfield. The two Mystères flew northwards, keeping Pathankot to their east before darting into Pakistani airspace north of Sialkot. Not surprisingly, they found little of interest other than some vehicles parked next to a camouflaged tented headquarters which they set on fire with their rockets before returning to Adampur.

In the afternoon, 8 Squadron launched Jatar, Bhatia, Chopra, and Patney as the Black Formation followed by Salins, Flying Officers D. K. Patel, Kashikar, and Sapre as the Blue Formation to look for armoured and troop concentrations near the DBN Bridge. The Mystère's armament included two 30 mm DEFA cannons, a full component of 19 SNEB rockets (or a full set of twelve 60-lb rockets) carried either side as two underwing pods, and two 1,000-lb bombs, that earned it the well-deserved sobriquet 'Flying Armoury'. Patney fired at a few armoured vehicles in the vicinity of the bridge, but the formation peeled off and decided to attack the Pasrur airfield instead. Finding nothing there, they strafed the runway before heading back. The Blue Formation, which decided to do three passes over the DBN area, was more successful in its search for targets, returning to base after destroying a number of vehicles including four tanks.

32 Squadron (Thunderbirds), though not fully operational, also launched a four-aircraft strike in support of the army in the Lahore sector with Wing Commander (later Group Captain) Emanuel Raymond Fernandes in the lead with Flight Lieutenant Hamir Singh 'H. S.' Mangat, and Flying Officers Suresh Vishnu 'Jiggi' Ratnaparkhi (later group captain) and Dara Phiroze Chinoy as other

members. They too claimed to have destroyed at least two tanks and a few soft-skinned vehicles, while one of the Mystères was slightly damaged by ground fire.

For the Hunters based at Halwara, the morning raids on Sargodha had been a complete disaster. Sending two back-to-back formations after the Mystères had twice before penetrated the air space around Sargodha was poor tactics, especially since the two squadrons, 7 and 27, were on different radio frequencies and could not communicate with each other. A 30 per cent attrition rate with very little to show in terms of damage inflicted on the Pakistanis was a dampener. In the absence of FACs on the ground and with very little real intelligence pertaining to targets on the ground, the twenty aircraft launched for ground support was almost perfunctory in nature.

Chacha Malik, S. K. Sharma, Dice Dhiman, and Flying Officer (later Air Chief Marshal) Shashindra Pal 'Bundle' Tyagi were ordered to strike near Sulemanki and were given four target coordinates. Most of these locations were thickly wooded areas and the only vehicles that could be seen were 3-tonners, some of which were engaged. At one stage Dhiman looked back to find three, perhaps four, Sabres headed towards him. He turned into them and found one F-104 overshooting him. He successfully managed to disengage from them and return safely to base.

Lamba and Flying Officer T. S. 'Tolly' Dandas carried out an armed reconnaissance mission in the Kasur Sector. They spotted a concentration of armour as it was trying to get into the Khem Karan bridgehead. Though the information was passed on by them during the debrief, the coordination with the army was so poor, that they did not receive this update. Three out of the five formations that flew till last light flew over the Khem Karan/Kasur Sector and, strangely, none of them spotted any major concentration of armour.

Pathankot, having taken the brunt of the Pakistani attack the previous evening, was having a relatively quiet morning. Two Mystères from 31 Squadron flown by Flying Officer 'Daddy Cool' Anukul and Flight Lieutenant Ashok Chandra 'Andy' Sharma (both later group captains) headed towards Sialkot searching the Suchetgarh area for any armour activity in anticipation of 1 Corps' offensive that was to be launched the next morning. Considering the lengths the army had gone to in order to keep its impending offensive the next day a secret, 31 Squadron's probe into Suchetgarh and, later, 1 Squadron's armed reconnaissance mission over the Gujrat airfield were unnecessary. As it was, both these formations had not learnt anything new.

3 Squadron next launched a four-Mystère strike against Chandhar and Rahwali, two satellite airfields near Hafizabad and Gujranwala. The formation was led by Squadron Leader 'Jessi' Jasbeer Singh with Flying Officer Bohman Irani as his wingman, followed by Flight Lieutenants Tango Singh and Doraiswamy as escorts. Almost immediately after take-off, Tango's aircraft became unserviceable as his undercarriage failed to retract and he had to return to Pathankot, leaving Doraiswamy

as the lone escort to take up the number three position. Flying due west in a line abreast formation, the Mystères approached Hafizabad and then pulled up to 4,500 feet. To their utter amazement, the airfield was deserted and very obviously not operational.

The three aircraft then turned 170 degrees and followed the railway line from Hafizabad to Gujranwala, pulling up once again as they reached the outskirts of the city. Down below to the north was the Rahwali cantonment and once again the airfield was deserted. Spotting a rotating radar antenna, Jessi followed by Irani and Doraiswamy fired their rockets at it, creating a huge ball of fire. Just then Jessi reported a 'bogey' but Irani and Doru both told him his tail was clear. Jettisoning their drop tanks, the three aircraft set course for home.

Jessi would give yet another 'bogey' call and once again Irani and Doraiswamy could see nothing, both of them calling 'tail clear'. At extreme low level, the aircraft were barely clearing the ground obstacles by five or ten feet. Once or twice Jessi weaved his aircraft as he seemed to be in visual contact with something. Just as they were approaching Shakargarh, Jessi's wing hit the ground and the aircraft cartwheeled and exploded in a ball of fire. Shaken by the tragic event, Doraiswamy and Irani both eased up and returned to Pathankot.

The loss of Squadron Leader Jasbeer Singh was a big blow. Twenty-seven years after the event, while describing the sortie, Doraiswamy, who had been abreast of Jessi when he hit the ground while Irani was trailing behind as his wingman, felt that the change in the formation's configuration mid-air had perhaps confused Jessi, who may well have mistaken the third Mystère for a Sabre.

Orders for yet another strike based on equally scatty intelligence were also received by 31 Squadron who launched a four-Mystère strike against Pasrur where a squadron of Sabres were supposedly located. Mousinho and Roundy Raina with Chandrashekharan and McMahon as their wingmen put in the attack only to find a herd of cows grazing peacefully on the runway. Nevertheless, seeing what seemed to be a camouflaged area at one end of the airfield, three Mystères fired off their rockets at it—Raina's pods malfunctioned, the rockets refusing to fire.

In addition to the thirty-one sorties flown against the Sargodha complex, the IAF flew multiple daylight strike missions, almost all against airfields in the Rachna Doab region. Nearly all of them drew a blank. The two Mystère raids by 1 Squadron against Sargodha Main were successful not only for the damage they did, but also because they managed to get through the Pakistani defences. However, on almost all the raids, the Mystère was operating at its extreme range, which only allowed the pilots to make a single pass over the airfield and strike at whatever targets were before them. In such a scenario it was also almost impossible to get an accurate report of the damage.

In the Western Theatre, the IAF lost three Hunters and two Mystères while attacking Sargodha, while the Pakistanis admit to the loss of four F-86 Sabres and an F-104 Starfighter. Added to this was the loss of Jessi's Mystère and a Dakota that was destroyed on the ground when, at 1605 hrs, four Sabres attacked the poorly defended Srinagar airfield. There was no prior warning of the incoming attack and w with no radar and just a few anti-aircraft guns, a civil Dakota and a United Nations Caribou were severely damaged, the latter having to be written off. 'At the end of the day, it was evident that the IAF, retaliating against the previous days' strikes by the Pakistanis, had reacted in a knee-jerk manner. Though a few sorties were flown in support of the ground offensive in the Lahore Sector, they were too few to make any palpable difference. The strikes against the airfields at Gujrat, Pasrur, Chandhar, and Rahwali only underlined the complete lack of actionable intelligence on the Indian side. '7 September marked the end of the doctrine of daylight, dusk and dawn raids on airfields by the IAF and the PAF. Neither air force could sustain the attrition they had suffered. Thereafter, no raid took place in the western sector against the airfields of the opposing side.'[11]

Chapter 16

THE SIALKOT SECTOR
1 CORPS (PART I)

8 SEPTEMBER (SAMBA)

Operation Nepal, in which India's 1 Armoured Division was to sweep through the Rachna Doab and threaten Sialkot, was General Chaudhuri's plan in every sense of the word. He had decided to launch the Indian offensive in the Sialkot Sector from Samba, and nothing the Western Army commander, Lieutenant General Harbakhsh Singh, said was going to change his mind. With 11 Corps tying up the Pakistanis around Lahore, Chaudhuri was not in the mood to listen to any contrary views. As a result, he not only kept Harbakhsh Singh out of the loop, he fell back on a combination he was comfortable with—moving Patrick Oscar Dunn from the command of the Rann of Kutch to the new raising that was 1 Corps. Promoting Dunn to a three-star rank meant playing around with the hierarchy. Chaudhuri was willing to risk it, even though Dunn had no experience of armour.

Dunn's appointment meant he had under his command Major General Rajinder 'Sparrow' Singh, GOC 1 Armoured Division, one of the officers he had superseded. Sparrow had commanded 7 Cavalry during the 1947–48 Operations in J&K and had played a pivotal role in the fighting, even pushing his Stewart tanks up onto Zoji La. He had been awarded the MVC and though he was due to retire, with war clouds looming, he had offered to serve under Dunn. In all probability, Chaudhuri, who had high expectations from 1 Corps, had initially planned to keep the formation directly under Army HQ, in order to exercise control himself. However, considering 15 Corps to the north and 11 Corps to the south of 1 Corps' area of operations were under the Western Army commander, he somewhat reluctantly brought Harbakhsh Singh into the loop just before the fighting started.

Chaudhuri had gone to great lengths to catch Pakistan on the wrong foot. The Jammu-based 26 Infantry Division had been delinked from 15 Corps and shifted to Dunn's formation that also consisted of 14 Infantry Division, 6 Mountain Division, and 1 Armoured Division, all of which were based a considerable distance from their operational locations. Despite all of Chaudhuri's war-gaming, these changes created chaos.

Major General Thapan was told he would be part of the newly raised 1 Corps on 2 September, when the situation on his northern flank was extremely grim, with Pakistan making a bold bid to capture Chhamb and Akhnoor. Dunn promptly took away some of 26 Infantry Division's integral armour and artillery, which, for any formation, would be disconcerting. 6 Mountain Division, consisting of 69 and 99 Mountain Brigades, under Major General Kolra, was equipped with weapons and communication systems supplied by the Americans after the 1962 conflict and its artillery consisted of 'obsolescent 3.7-inch howitzers and US aid Brandt mortars. Being a mountain division, it was trained to fight in the high Himalayas. It had no training for a plains role and none in infantry-tank cooperation.'[1] 14 Infantry Division, a new raising under the command of Major General Ranjit Singh, even at this late stage, was scattered all over as its units rushed to their demarcated battle stations. Travelling by road and rail, units had started reaching Pathankot by the evening of 6 September and the division had not assembled in its concentration area on the night of 7/8 September. Even when Dunn issued orders for corps operations, GOC 14 Infantry Division had still not arrived.

Sparrow's division consisted of two brigades—1 Armoured Brigade commanded by Brigadier (later Lieutenant General) Khem Karan Singh and 43 Lorried Infantry Brigade commanded by Brigadier H. S. Dhillon—and was relatively well trained. With 3 Cavalry having been delinked and allotted to 2 (Independent) Armoured Brigade, the division now had only three regiments equipped with Centurions. 'To make up for its reduced punch, the division was allotted 2 Lancers (upgunned) and 62 Cavalry (Sherman IVs with high velocity 76 mm gun). The upgunned regiments (2 Lancers and 18 Cavalry) mounted the super velocity French 75 mm gun of AMX tanks but without necessary modifications in the elevating and traversing gear system. During operations, these tanks had serious problems keeping battle-worthy.'[2] The lorried infantry brigade, as the name implies, had three infantry battalions mounted on 3-ton vehicles and T-16 carriers. Unlike the Pakistan Army, whose mechanized forces were mounted on M113 APCs, the Indians were at a huge disadvantage.

6 Mountain Division had moved primarily by civil vehicles to the Samba area to create a firm base for 1 Corps. Moving by train, the tarpaulin-covered tanks of 1 Armoured Division moved from Jalandhar towards Amritsar during daylight hours on 2 September, but once it got dark, the trains changed direction for Pathankot. Moving on tank transporters from there, the bulk of the armoured division was in Samba by the evening of the next day. To keep Pakistan guessing as to the actual whereabouts of the armoured division, work was started on strengthening bridges leading to Akhnoor.

According to Amarinder Singh and Maun Shergill in *The Monsoon War*, in a meeting between Dunn and Sparrow on 5 September, the latter had argued in favour of launching his division at first light the next morning, which would have

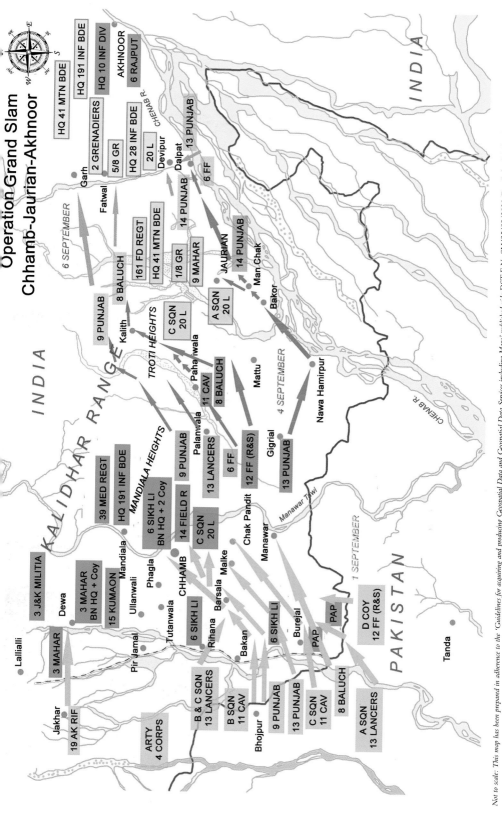

Operation Grand Slam
Chhamb-Jaurian-Akhnoor

C Sqn 20 Lancers with its lightweight AMX-13 tanks commanded by Maj Bhaskar Roy with 6 Sikh LI, 3 Mahar, and 15 Kumaon faced the initial onslaught of Pakistani armour at Chhamb. Maj Gen Chopra's newly raised HQ 10 Inf Div was not in position when Op Grand Slam was launched;

Brig Manmohan Singh, Cdr 191 Inf Bde; Vampires from Pathankot in action in fading light on 1 September; President Ayub Khan in conversation with Maj Gen Yayah Khan while Gen Muhammad Musa looks on; Pakistan's inaction over the next two days allowed the Indians to hastily prepare their defences near Jaurian—6 Sikh LI JCO planting mines.

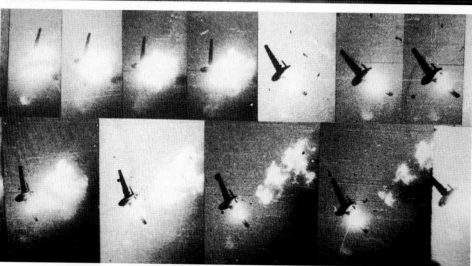

(Facing page) An artist's depiction of Sqn Ldr Trevor Keelor outflying a Sabre; Flt Lt V. S. Pathania; Sqn Ldr Denzil Keelor; Wg Cdr K. Dandapani, 230 SU; Gnat scramble; *(Above)* Depiction of Flt Lt Alfred Cooke shooting down the first of two Sabres over Kalaikunda; Flg Offr V. K. Nebb's gun camera footage; CAS Arjan Singh with Nebb and Flt Lt Rathore at Halwara.

An artist's depiction of the daylight raid on Sargodha that struck at the heart of the PAF *(painting by Gp Capt Deb Gohain)*; pilots from 1 Sqn (Tigers) pose for a group photograph after the war *(standing L to R)* Flt Lts J. P. Singh, A. J. Singh, V. K. 'Frisky' Verma, Sqn Ldr A. Sridharan, Flt Lt D. M. S. Kahai, Sqn Ldr P. R. Earle, Wg Cdr O. P. Taneja, Flg Offr V. K. Sethi, Flt Lt Sudarshan Handa, Fg Offr D. S. Brar, and Flt Lt Philip Rajkumar. *(kneeling L to R)* Sqn Ldr K. K. Bakshi, Fg Offrs A. Rehman, K. S. Cheema, K. Dey, Flt Lts A. K. Brahmawar, and B. S. Raje.

Sqn Ldr J. M. Nath photographed the Ichhogil Canal extending from the Ravi to the Sutlej. Having successfully completed the mission, the developed images were flown to New Delhi and the photographs were handed over to the CAS and the COAS by Nath himself. These photographs were then also laid out for the defence minister to view; the painting by Mrs Priyanka Joshi depicts the low-flying Canberra off Barki. Tragically, none of the officers on the ground, including commanding officers of infantry and armoured units, were shown the images. The lack of intelligence was a major factor that would hamper the progress of the Indian advance.

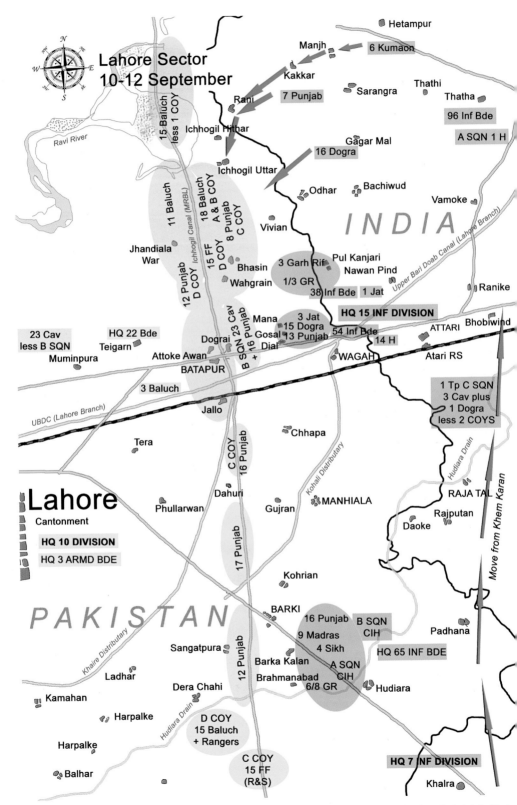

Lahore Sector
10-12 September

Not to scale: This map has been prepared in adherence to the 'Guidelines for acquiring and producing Geospatial Data and Geospatial Data Services including Maps' published vide DST F.No.SM/25/02/2020 (Part-I) dated 15th February, 2021.

Maj Gen Mohinder Singh who took over 15 Inf Div; Brig Niranjan Singh, Cdr 54 Inf Bde who replaced the temporary commander, Brig D. S. Kalha; Lt Col Desmond Hayde, the dynamic commanding officer of 3 Jat; the Jats on the roof of a building looking out for Sabres and Mysteres; 2/ Lt Brijender Singh, 14 Scinde Horse, astride a destroyed Pakistani Patton tank; Indian troops pressing forward on the Ichhogil Canal.

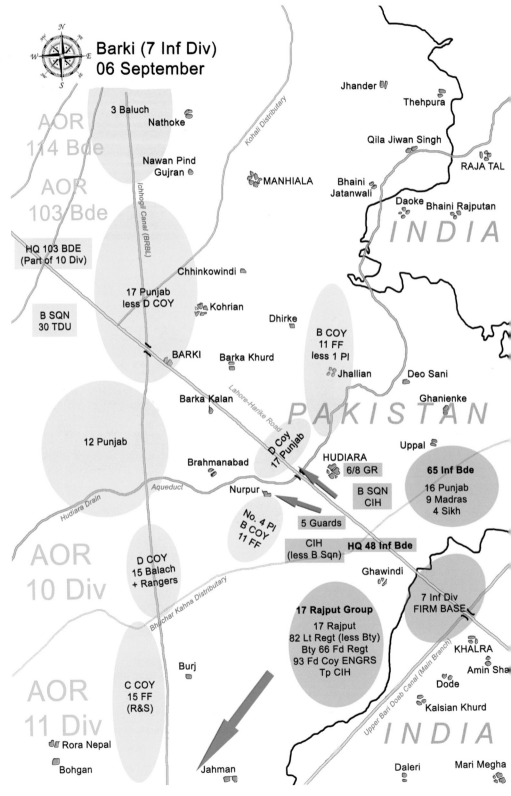

Barki (7 Inf Div)
06 September

AOR
114 Bde

AOR
103 Bde

3 Baluch
Nathoke

Nawan Pind
Gujran

Jhander

Thehpura

Qila Jiwan Singh

RAJA TAL

MANHIALA

Bhaini
Jatanwali

Daoke

Bhaini Rajputan

INDIA

HQ 103 BDE
(Part of 10 Div)

Chhinkowindi

17 Punjab
less D COY

Kohrian

Dhirke

B SQN
30 TDU

BARKI

Barka Khurd

B COY
11 FF
less 1 Pl

Jhallian

Deo Sani

Ghanienke

Barka Kalan

PAKISTAN

12 Punjab

Brahmanabad

D Coy
17 Punjab

Uppal

65 Inf Bde

16 Punjab
9 Madras
4 Sikh

Aqueduct

Nurpur

HUDIARA

6/8 GR

B SQN
CIH

Hudiara Drain

No. 4 Pl
B COY
11 FF

5 Guards

AOR
10 Div

D COY
15 Balach
+ Rangers

CIH
(less B Sqn)

HQ 48 Inf Bde

Ghawindi

7 Inf Div
FIRM BASE

17 Rajput Group

17 Rajput
82 Lt Regt (less Bty)
Bty 66 Fd Regt
93 Fd Coy ENGRS
Tp CIH

KHALRA

Amin Sha

Dode

Kalsian Khurd

AOR
11 Div

Burj

C COY
15 FF
(R&S)

INDIA

Rora Nepal

Daleri

Mari Megha

Bohgan

Jahman

Not to scale: This map has been prepared in adherence to the 'Guidelines for acquiring and producing Geospatial Data and Geospatial Data Services including Maps' published vide DST F.No.SM/25/02/2020 (Part-I) dated 15th February, 2021.

The Ichhogil Canal at Barki. The milestone on the other side of the river reads 'Lahore 14 Miles'; Lt Col Anant Singh, CO 4 Sikh; the Barki Police Station; Pakistani artillery in action, keeping up a relentless barrage; Maj Aziz Bhatti, Nishan-e-Haider, who was killed at Barki.

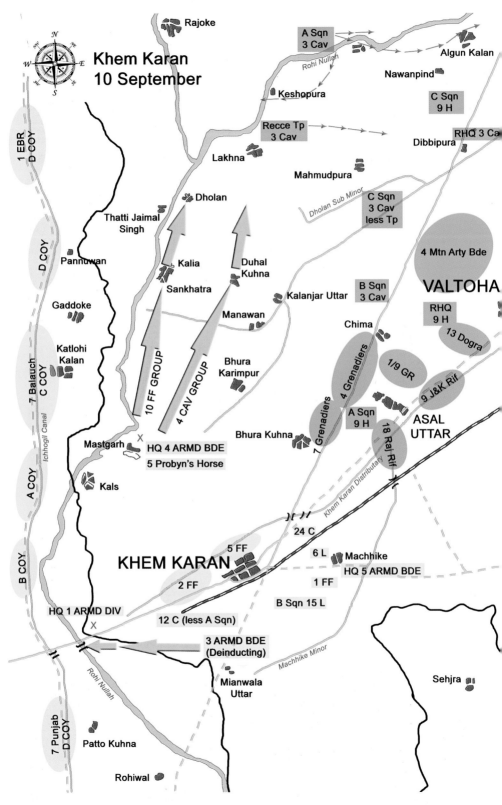

Not to scale: This map has been prepared in adherence to the 'Guidelines for acquiring and producing Geospatial Data and Geospatial Data Services including Maps' published vide DST F.No.SM/25/02/2020 (Part-I) dated 15th February, 2021.

(*Above*) 20 Sqn's strike against Raiwind Railway Station which adversely affected Pakistan's fighting capability in Khem Karan only underlines what could have been had the army-air force coordination been better. While PAF Sabres were invariably at hand to lend ground support, the IAF was restricted mainly to interdiction sorties; (*Below*) fighting a desperate battle on the ground to contain the Pakistani armoured thrust, Lt Cols Arun Vaidya (CO 9 Deccan Horse) and Salim Caleb (CO 3 Cav) confer with Brig T. K. Theogaraj, Cdr 2 (I) Armd Bde.

(*Facing page*) A Sherman tank belonging to 9 Deccan Horse; Lt Col A. S. Vaidya and others with a destroyed Patton; another Patton near Mahmudpura; bogged down tanks of 4 Cav. (*Above*) A RCL jeep in action at Asal Uttar; CQMH Abdul Hamid, PVC (P); Lt A. R. Khan and 2/ Lt V. K. Vaid in front of Pattons at Bhikkiwind; Lt Col Raghubir Singh, CO 18 Raj Rif; Lt Col F. Bhatty with troops of 4 Grenadiers with Abdul Hamid's damaged jeep.

(Above) Twisted metal reduced to junk, remnants of Pakistani armour after they were towed to Bhikkiwind that was given the sobriquet 'Patton Nagar'. The iconic photograph was taken by Lt Col Hari Singh, CO 18 Cav, who carried with him his trusted Franka Schneider camera to record the combined handiwork of 9 Deccan Horse, 3 Cav, and the various infantry battalions of 4 Mtn Div.

The deliberate breaching of canals further accentuated by the movement of tanks helped confine the Pakistani armoured thrust.

coincided with the 11 Corps' advance in the Lahore sector. Sparrow reasoned that this would catch the Pakistanis off balance and even though 14 Infantry Division, which was to capture Zafarwal and protect the eastern flank of the advance, was not yet in a position to do so, he was prepared to do without their support. The additional armoured thrust, combined with the attack by 96 Infantry Brigade at DBN, would divide Pakistan's 15 Infantry Division and 6 Armoured Division that was deployed against 1 Corps. Thapan's division was already deployed for the offensive and could easily launch its own attacks further to the north from Jammu. Dunn seemed to accept Sparrow's suggestion, but later in the day after consulting with Harbakhsh Singh's HQ, orders were issued that the offensive would start on the night of 7/8 September and 1 Armoured Division would debouch into the Rachna Doab at first light.

Dunn's failure to press home the argument with his superiors was a major missed opportunity for the Indians. Unknown to Western Command or any of the subordinate HQs, Pakistan's 6 Armoured Division was still at Nandipur, north of Gujranwala on 6 September. Most of Pakistan's formations were still not in their defensive positions, and the likelihood of the Indian offensive achieving complete surprise was extremely high.

1 Corps launched its offensive two days later, by which time not only had the main element of surprise been lost, but almost all Pakistani units were in their battle positions. H-hour for 6 Mountain Division, with two brigades of 14 Infantry Division that had reached their designated launch-off points under its command, was 2300 hrs. Kolra's primary task was to establish a bridgehead in the Maharajke and Charwa areas. Accordingly, the guns of 1 Artillery Brigade, which had been positioned in support of 6 Mountain Division, opened up on schedule. 69 Mountain Brigade, commanded by Brigadier (later Lieutenant General) Eric Alexander Vas was to capture Maharajke. The brigade had 3 Madras, 4 Madras, and 9 Kumaon and was supported by Alpha Squadron of 62 Cavalry. Simultaneously, 99 Mountain Brigade under Brigadier Dharam Singh, with 4 Raj Rif, 6 Garhwal, and 2/5 Gorkha Rifles along with Bravo Squadron of 62 Cavalry in support, was tasked with capturing Charwa.

26 INFANTRY DIVISION (JAMMU)

The H-hour for Thapan's 26 Infantry (Tiger) Division was 2330 hrs. Its primary task was to contain the Pakistani forces at Sialkot, where both 15 Infantry Division and 101 Brigade headquarters were located. Brigadier Sardar M. Ismail Khan was commanding the Pakistani division while Brigadier Syed Mahmood Hussain was commanding the brigade. India's 162 Infantry Brigade was being commanded by Brigadier R. S. Sheoran. It comprised 6 Jat, 7 Jat, and 1 Sikh LI with Charlie Squadron of 18 Cavalry in support. 1 Sikh LI was tasked with capturing Kundanpur in Phase 1 after which 7 Jat, commanded by Lieutenant Colonel (later Lieutenant

General) Raj Kumar Jasbir Singh was to capture Niwe Wains and then Unche Wains. 6 Jat, commanded by Lieutenant Colonel M. D. Soman, was to be held in reserve.

Thapan, like Sparrow, had advised Dunn to launch the 1 Corps offensive on the night of 5/6 September. In fact, Thapan had visited 7 Jat in anticipation of the impending assault and issued his orders to the battalion. However, when the formal orders were received, the keyed-up battalion was told the offensive had been postponed, first by twenty-four hours, and then again by another day.

1 Sikh LI was the first to move, crossing the IB along the Jammu–Sialkot road at 2330 hrs. The Sikh LI assault was preceded by a heavy concentration of fire provided by the divisional artillery. Within minutes, the area beyond the FUP was illuminated. Owing to Chaudhuri's obsession with security, local formation commanders had not been allowed to recce the area opposite them; as a result, 26 Infantry Division had zero intelligence pertaining to the deployment of the Pakistani forces opposite them.

Ever since 6 September, Syed Mahmood Hussain had been a busy man, working on the defences that covered the Jammu–Sialkot road, also referred to as the Suchetgarh axis by the Indians. Over 10,000 anti-personnel and 464 anti-tank mines had been laid by his 101 Brigade, the task having been completed by the morning of 7 September. Charlie Company of Pakistan's 19 Punjab was manning the advance positions from Unche Wains to Kundanpur while its flanks were covered by Charlie Company of 13 FF (R&S) whose platoons were deployed in the area around Kasire and from the road to the banks of the Aik Nullah. Major Durrani, commanding Bravo Squadron of 20 Lancers, had been given overall command of the forward positions.

1 Sikh LI's attack was met with determined resistance, but after some bitter fighting, they pushed the Pakistanis back. Even though Pakistani tanks started to engage the advancing troops, 1 Sikh LI successfully got to the Jammu–Sialkot railway line. Second Lieutenant Virendra Pratap Singh and his platoon of sixteen men had fought their way along the railway line, getting to the north of Kundanpur, where they found themselves surrounded by the Pakistanis. Despite being in a precarious position, Pratap's platoon managed to survive long enough, forcing the retreating forward elements of both 19 Punjab and 13 FF (R&S) elements to disengage.

Wireless communication between 1 Sikh LI and HQ 162 Infantry Brigade had broken down and Brigadier Sheoran had no idea of the ground situation. 7 Jat had moved into the FUP that had been occupied by 1 Sikh LI and was waiting for the green signal to launch Phase 2. Alpha Company, commanded by Major Kulwant Singh, was to capture the area left of Unche Wains, including the high ground that dominated the objective. Bravo Company, under Major S. S. Malik, was to attack towards the right of Unche Wains. Major Ashok Kumar's Charlie Company was to capture Niwe Wains while Captain Inderjit Singh's Delta Company was to exploit the area west of Unche Wains.

Brigade HQ wanted to know what was happening ahead of the 7 Jat position. Jasbir Singh had moved up to the FUP and was conferring with his company commanders when Pakistani artillery started to bombard the four Jat companies, who were caught in the open without any trenches or natural features to protect them. Havildar Major Balbir Singh and Lance Naik Udai Singh were killed and three other men were wounded. Most communication systems had been severed in the bombardment, except for a lone telephone link. Even though nothing was known of 1 Sikh LI's situation, Jasbir Singh asked Sheoran if he could launch Phase 2 immediately, for had the Jats stayed at the FUP any longer, casualties would rapidly mount. Sheoran agreed and the officers started to round up the scattered companies. Alpha and Bravo Company then crossed the start line in good order. Given the intensity of the Pakistani shelling, 7 Jat had got away with relatively minor casualties.

1 Sikh LI had captured the high ground which allowed 7 Jat to push forward towards its objectives. The assaulting companies brushed aside opposition from 13 FF (R&S) and 19 Punjab, neutralized the defensive pillboxes, and took up defensive positions around Niwe Wains and Unche Wains. Charlie and Delta Companies then went through and started digging in 500 metres ahead of Niwe Wains. By 0145 hrs, the battalion was well entrenched and commenced probing further towards Khane Chak on the Jammu–Sialkot road towards Salia. Contact was also made with 1 Sikh LI which had cleared Kundanpur by then.

There was complete silence in the area now, with no reaction from the Pakistanis. Jasbir Singh reported back to Sheoran and apprised him of the situation. The enemy seemed to have been taken completely by surprise and after the initial resistance by the forward defences, the Sialkot garrison had no plans for an immediate counter-attack. Charlie Squadron of 18 Cavalry, commanded by Major A. K. Poplai was immediately asked to move forward with 6 Jat's Delta Company under Major K. K. Lall. It was still dark when Poplai and Lall went through 7 Jat's companies who were dug in along the Sialkot road with both Niche Wains and Unche Wains barely 200 yards away from them. This force managed to reach a point short of Dhaluwali where the Pakistanis had their ditch-cum-bund (DCB) defences.

The forward companies of 19 Punjab and 13 FF (R&S), despite taking casualties, had fallen back in reasonable order to the main positions of 101 Brigade. Pakistani armour, Bravo Squadron of 20 Lancers, had come up to meet the Indians but had also fallen back in the darkness. 6 Jat and Poplai's tanks engaged the Pakistani defences which were manned by Alpha Company of 19 Punjab at the Patesar–Hir Bandh and Bravo Company of 2 Baluch on the Palkhu Nullah. With Pakistani armour reinforcing the Pakistani defences, a firefight ensued. Charlie Squadron succeeded in destroying one Chaffee, damaged a few others, and lost one of their tanks.

Daylight saw some isolated Pakistani pockets that were still in Niwe Wains come alive. Rather than go into the village looking for the enemy, Jasbir Singh decided to call in medium artillery fire, even though his own positions were precariously close to the target area. Some tanks of 18 Cavalry also arrived and blasted the houses from where fire had been directed at the Jats. Delta Company then went in and mopped up the enemy soldiers. By 0745 hrs, the area around Niwe and Unche Wains was secure. 6 Jat and Charlie Squadron then withdrew from the DCB and pulled back to Salia by 1430 hrs.

Bravo Squadron 18 Cavalry commanded by Major (later Lieutenant General) Jai Dev Singh Khera had, in the meantime, probed along the northern flank of 162 Brigade's offensive. The squadron crossed the Palkhu Nullah at Khane Chak and advanced on the Chaprar–Sialkot track for a short distance, but they were immediately engaged by the Pakistani artillery. Not having any infantry support, Khera decided to pull back to his start point.

To the south, 168 Infantry Brigade, commanded by Brigadier A. K. Luthra, comprising 2/1 GR, 5/4 GR, and 8 JAK Rif with Alpha Squadron of 18 Cavalry, was to capture Anula and Bajragarhi. 168 Field Regiment was in direct support. The area of Bajragarhi had a lone platoon of 13 FF (R&S) that had been under the command of Pakistan's 24 Brigade that had moved to Narowal on 7 September. While 5/4 GR quietly occupied Anula unopposed, at first light, 2/1 GR, and 18 Cavalry began to advance on the Bajragarhi–Sialkot axis. The Pakistani screen positions fell back and, amazingly, failed to report the Indian advance to either 101 Brigade or 15 Division, who first learnt of the Indian advance when Alpha Squadron 18 Cavalry commanded by Major (later Lieutenant General) Gurdev Singh Kler arrived at the Jura Bridge over the Aik River on the outskirts of Sialkot. Luckily for the Pakistanis, the bund flanking the approach to the bridge was being held by a section of Delta Company 19 Punjab.

Kler's tanks had left 2/1 Gorkhas behind and he had no option but to stop short of the bridge and wait for the infantry to capture it. The Pakistanis on the bridge had seen the tanks approaching. At 1100 hrs, the section commander, Havildar Jumma Khan got on the field telephone and told his company commander, Major Mohammad Aslam Khan, that he had seen eight Indian tanks approaching the bridge. The Pakistanis reacted quickly, sending a troop from 31 TDU to reinforce the Punjabis. By the time 2/1 GR reached Kler, the Pakistani tanks had arrived on the other side of the river as well.

Dunn's plan was for his three divisions to push back the Pakistani defences along the IB extending from Suchetgarh to Nakhnal. Even though 14 Infantry Division was unable to deploy as per plan, both 6 Mountain Division and 26 Infantry Division had more or less achieved their modest objectives by the morning of 8 September and the stage was set for a major offensive by Sparrow's 1 Armoured Division. The plan was 'to debouch through the middle of the above sector at first light to launch a deep thrust into the guts of Pak defences.'[3] Pakistan's reaction in the Rachna Doab had been restricted to artillery fire in support of their various screen positions which had fallen back in good order to their main defences. As had been the case with the Lahore offensive, 1 Corps too had no plans that called for air support, even though the PAF had flown a few sorties in support of their ground troops. On the other hand, unlike 11 Corps, none of the battalions had broken ranks due to the intense artillery fire.

On the Pakistani side, however, at the higher level of command, confusion continued to prevail through the night. The DBN axis continued to play heavily on the Pakistani mind. 'In the early hours of 7 September, the enemy again launched an attack, which was obviously a feint, on our troops who were still holding the far end of the railway bridge over the Ravi. But it seems the acting commander of 15 Division gave credence to false reports from unreliable sources and got unnecessarily alarmed. He painted a grim picture of the situation to HQ 1 Corps and GHQ, and managed to obtain clearance for demolishing the bridge, which was blown up at about 8 a.m. on 7 September.'[4]

Rumours of Indian commandos operating behind Sialkot town had further added to the panic, the situation only stabilizing when General Tikka Khan took over as the divisional commander. 'After 7 September, the enemy's diversionary effort in area Jassar petered out, and there were only occasional artillery duels till the end of the war. India did not develop any threat from this direction to the right flank and rear of our forces operating further west in the Pasrur–Chawinda area.'[5] As soon as the Indian attack had started in the Lahore Sector, Pakistan had ordered its 6 Armoured Division to move to Daska. Both its armoured regiments, 11 Cavalry and 13 Lancers, along with 4 Corps Artillery Brigade that were the crux of Pakistan's thrust towards Akhnoor were withdrawn on 6 September after it became obvious that the Indians had extended the fighting across the IB.

With still no information about the whereabouts of India's 1 Armoured Division, GHQ Pakistan continued to react to unconfirmed rumours. Reports of an Indian paradrop in the Wazirabad area during the night of 7/8 September set the alarm bells ringing and GHQ Pakistan promptly sent 6 Armoured Division to deal with the imaginary threat. With India's 6 Mountain Division and 26 Infantry Division launching their offensives, Pakistan's 6 Armoured Division was once again ordered to revert to its role of GHQ Reserve in the Sialkot Sector. The formation returned to the Pasrur area by the night of 9/10 September.

8 SEPTEMBER (1 ARMOURED DIVISION)

1 Armoured Division was supposed to be General Chaudhuri's trump card with which he hoped to threaten Sialkot and secure an early end to the war. Ever since the conflict had started to simmer, Chaudhuri's tactics had been restricted to containing the multiple offensives of Pakistan and putting the pressure back

on them by opening or threatening to open new fronts. Fairly astute and aware about the history of warfare, Chaudhuri knew this was his make or break moment. Having sidelined Harbakhsh from the chain of command, he now had to depend on Sparrow and the two brigades that were under his command.

By splitting his forces between the Bari Doab and the Rachna Doab, Chaudhuri and his senior commanders had created a situation where the Indians had failed to hit hard at Pakistan in the 11 Corps Sector. The Indian approach was baffling, but in many ways it reflected the thinking of the army chief. Having forsaken doing anything on a grand scale, Chaudhuri's approach aimed at creeping 'about the battlefield anxiously taking all security measures against every conceivable enemy move'[6]. Sparrow's plan was to capture both Phillora and Pagowal by last light on 8 September, using K. K. Singh's brigade along the Sabzpir–Phillora axis and Dhillon's lorried brigade along the Mastpur–Kalol–Pagowal axis. Dhillon was to skirt around Maharajke and Charwa so that he did not get entangled with the operations of 6 Mountain Division.

At 0530 hrs, barely thirty minutes before H-hour, 1 Corps HQ sent a message to Sparrow saying that the Maharajke flank had not been fully secured, so he may like to postpone launching his division. Ironically, this was the very reason why Sparrow's earlier plan to launch into the Rachna Doab on 6 September had been turned down. Sparrow told Dunn he was not willing to wait any longer. Forty-eight hours after he had initially wanted to go in, Sparrow's 1 Armoured Division went into battle at 0600 hrs on 8 September, the tanks advancing in the area between Charwa and Nakhnal towards Phillora. 16 Cavalry led the advance along the divisional centre line, advancing along the Rangor–Parel–Pindi Bhago–Chobara–Gadgor–Phillora axis while 17 Horse, commanded by Lieutenant Colonel Adi Tarapore, moved along the Baghiari–Musial–Rangre–Khanpur Saidan–Tharoo road. Charlie Squadron of 62 Cavalry was providing flank protection west of the Degh River.

After the fiasco of the Jassar advance, the Pakistanis needed to be certain that the advancing armour was indeed the famed Indian 1 Armoured Division. Though caught off balance, the Pakistanis finally had a clear idea of what they were up against. Pakistan's 24 Infantry Brigade was immediately ordered to go back to its area of operational responsibility around Phillora–Gadgor while 25 Cavalry was ordered to advance along the Gadgor axis to stop the Indian armour as far north as possible.

16 Cavalry's Bravo Squadron under the command of Major Maurice Ravindran led the Indian advance. The two leading troops were under Second Lieutenant Vinay Kaistha and Risaldar Shanmugan, who were followed by the Regimental HQ which carried the pennant of Lieutenant Colonel Sidhu-Brar. Alpha Squadron under Major M. A. R. Sheikh then followed with Bravo Company of 5/9 GR in troop-carrying vehicles behind them. Charlie Squadron under Major A. C. Khanna brought up the

rear. The column met with no opposition and made excellent time, reaching Chobara by 0745 hrs. While passing Pindi Bhago, 16 Cavalry had come across fresh tank tracks, some abandoned Pakistani concrete bunkers, and communication cables that they cut. Just short of Chobara, the tanks engaged two Pakistani military vehicles and a jeep and destroyed one of them.

At the 1 Armoured Brigade HQ, K. K. Singh was pleased with 16 Cavalry's rapid advance, but was concerned by the relatively slow progress being made by Tarapore's 17 Horse that had only reached Musial. Bravo Squadron under command of Major (later Lieutenant General) Niranjan Singh Cheema had led the advance across the IB but Major D. N. Ghorpade's Alpha Squadron on the left flank had found the going difficult as their route took them through sugarcane fields that restricted visibility. To conform with the advance of 16 Cavalry, Tarapore ordered Cheema to take the lead and Ghorpade to follow, while the rest of the regiment moved in their wake. At approximately 0800 hrs, as the leading tanks of 17 Horse reached Rangre, they came across a platoon of withdrawing Pakistani infantry from 2 Punjab's Delta Company.

'There was a platoon of them huddled around a well. …Cheema stopped his tank and laying his gun on their position, waved out for one of them to come forward. A Havildar[7] came forward with his rifle. On being asked who he was, he answered—"Mussalman hun." Maj Cheema answered he knew that and asked him what unit he belonged to. "Main Pakistan ka sepoy hun," he replied. Maj Cheema then asked him to lay down his rifle and ask all the others with him to come forward and do the same. To this his reply was "As long as I live, I will fight for Pakistan," and turning about he started to run back to join his colleagues.'[8]

Though Cheema fired his .30 Browning machine gun at Fida Hussain and the others, 'Fida scrambled back safely. There was no wireless communication between the company headquarters and the platoons and Fida was again chosen to act as a messenger to inform the platoons that the tanks approaching the company's positions were hostile. Running from one platoon to the other, Fida was picked up by an Indian tank's machine gun and killed.'[9] Though the Pakistani version goes on to say RCL guns opened up, the Indian tanks did not encounter any recoilless rifles at this stage. 2 Punjab's Delta Company, in a hopeless position, broke up into small groups and melted away towards the west. By their own account, they lost twenty men including the brave Havildar Fida Hussain.

As Cheema was talking to Fida Hussain, Sparrow was at the regimental headquarters (RHQ) of 4 Horse (Hodson) that along with 9 Dogra's Delta Company was the divisional reserve dispersed north of Ramgarh. Sparrow was upbeat, telling Lieutenant Colonel (later Brigadier) Madan Mohan Singh Bakshi that K. K. Singh's 1 Armoured Brigade would soon reach the Phillora–Tharoh line. Bakshi was told to get 4 Horse ready to move at short notice, for Sparrow wanted to pass them through the leading regiments with the intention of attacking Pasrur. Sparrow was also aware that in the 26 Infantry Division sector, two squadrons of Lieutenant Colonel (later Brigadier) Hari Singh's 18 Cavalry, Charlie Squadron under Poplai, and Alpha Squadron under the command of Kler had moved forward from the 168 Infantry Brigade bridgehead and had engaged the Sialkot defences in the Patesar–Hir area and the Jura Bridge respectively, the latter reaching the Pasrur–Sialkot railway line at Kishenwali. At this stage Sparrow (and K. K. Singh) was unaware of what was happening with 62 Cavalry's Charlie Squadron, which was tasked with protecting the left flank of the division's advance.

Under the command of Major S. S. Kirtane, the 62 Cavalry tanks were to cross the IB at the same time as 17 Horse. However, even before they could get to the start line, communication with 1 Armoured Brigade had broken down. To make matters worse, five tanks had got bogged down while Charlie Squadron was still within Indian territory. Amazingly, Kirtane decided to stay and recover the bogged tanks and ordered Captain D. P. N. Singh to cross into Pakistan and carry out the operational orders given to the squadron. D. P. N. Singh proceeded to the rendezvous point where an infantry company was supposed to link up with him. With no radio communication and no sign of either the rest of the tanks or the infantry company, D. P. N. Singh proceeded with the task of protecting the brigade's left flank on his own. K. K. Singh had ordered Charlie Squadron to take up a position around Bijapur on the west of the Degh Nadi, but, owing to a misunderstanding, D. P. N. Singh proceeded to Zafarwal instead, where the young captain was surprisingly accorded a warm welcome by the local population.

Sparrow's second brigade, 43 Lorried Brigade, was to have crossed the border simultaneously with 1 Armoured Brigade and captured Pagowal by last light. However, right from the start, the plans had gone haywire. The crossing point over the Aik Nullah that had been selected had become slushy owing to overnight rains. The alternate route of advance selected was through Nakhnal and south of Charwa and Maharajke. When Sparrow met Bakshi at 0800 hrs, 43 Lorried Brigade was still three hours away from crossing the IB.

'Sparrow's plan to advance to Chawinda along two divergent axes had split 1 Armoured Division into two separate groups. The flexibility of the armoured division was reduced, as it was not possible for the two groups to support each other in time and space due to the increasing distance, nature of ground, inadequate tracks and the prevailing air situation. Artillery support was also split as it was not feasible to support both groups from a central location due to range limitations. Without adequate infantry, 1 Armoured Brigade was severely handicapped in protecting a secure firm base, holding captured ground and attacking enemy held villages.'[10]

Despite these limitations on the ground, both 16 Cavalry and 17 Horse continued their advance. Though Pakistani writers have said the Indian advance was supported by the IAF, once again, neither Western Command nor 1 Corps HQ had put up any specific demands for air support, causing the ground troops to lament the absence of the IAF. At 0815 hrs, PAF F-86 Sabres, in a virtual replay of what had happened on GT Road two days previously, attacked the two columns. Using rockets and front guns, the Sabres were unchallenged for close to twenty minutes. 'The tank commanded by Duffadar Guman Singh, of A Squadron, 17 Horse, was strafed and rather than close down, he opted to engage the aircraft with a .30 anti-aircraft Browning machine gun. Guman Singh was injured in the head and later succumbed to his injury. As the PAF aircraft were firing tracer ammunition, it set the inflammable equipment outside the tank on fire; the tank was later recovered. The air-raid caused some confusion but little other damage to tanks, but echelons and soft vehicles at the rear suffered, which led to administrative difficulties later; in the 16 Cavalry group, a rifleman of 5/9 Gorkha Rifles was killed. As the air attack had failed to destroy tanks, there was an upsurge of morale and cryptic remarks like "very poor shooting" reverberated.'[11]

Until then, India's armoured thrust had met with limited opposition, the air attack notwithstanding. 11 Corps' limited push in the DBN area on 6 September where 29 Brigade had taken on the Pakistani salient on the Indian side of the Ravi continued to give Lieutenant General Bakhtiar Rana, the GOC of Pakistan's 1 Corps, and his immediate subordinates, the jitters. Despite blowing up the bridge on the morning of 7 September, Brigadier Ismail Khan, who was now the officiating GOC 15 Infantry Division, and Brigadier Muzaffarudin, commander of 115 Infantry Brigade, kept giving tentative orders to their own formations. In their perception, the Dharam Enclave on the west bank of the river was a major threat, and they expected 1 Armoured Division to use it as a bridgehead to attack Jassar, after which the Indians could swing in either direction to neutralize Lahore or Sialkot or both.

At 1800 hrs, Ismail had called up Brigadier Abdul Ali Malik, the commander of the 24 Brigade Group, and asked him to move immediately to Narowal and counter-attack Jassar where the situation was critical as the Indians had succeeded in establishing a bridgehead on the Pakistani side of the river. Malik had two infantry battalions—2 Punjab and 3 FF—and 25 Cavalry under his command. The brigade group was deployed around Chawinda, Maharajke, Bini Sulehrian, Daryapur, and Nar Singh while the bulk of the armour was concentrated around Dogranwali, with a squadron stretched out along the Maharajke-Kangre track. Malik, however, chose to react with caution. Aware that any move to the south, when the bulk of the Indian armour was probably opposite him on the other side of the border poised to attack, would be foolhardy and dangerous, he chose to move with just his small operations group that included 25 Cavalry's commanding officer, Lieutenant Colonel Nisar Ahmed.

Malik reached Narowal where he was met by Ismail and Muzaffaruddin. The officiating GOC of 15 Division ordered 25 Cavalry to move to Narowal during the night. Earlier in the day Nisar Ahmed had done a recce of the direct route from Dogranwali to Jassar but his jeep had become bogged down in the Degh River. 25 Cavalry's Alpha and Bravo Squadron were equipped with the older M47 Patton tanks while Charlie Squadron had the newer M48s. Nisar Ahmed had moved them towards Narowal via the Pasrur route during daylight hours, and the rest of the regiment now was asked to follow the same axis. However, as the Pattons neared Narowal, at 0200 hrs, the orders were countermanded. An hour later, they were told to fall back on Pasrur where, by first light, all three squadrons were once again ready to move, their fuel tanks replenished.

At 0600 hrs, Malik asked Ahmed to meet him on the Pasrur–Chawinda road. The brigade commander told Ahmed that the Indian attack had begun and they had attacked Maharajke and Charwa and it was likely that 3 FF and the gun area had been overrun. 25 Cavalry was on familiar, reconnoitred terrain. Moving quickly, with his Bravo Squadron in the lead, Ahmed met with no opposition and the Patton M47 tanks with 90 mm guns took up positions beyond Phillora at the crossroad area. Hoping to hold Alpha and Charlie to the west of Phillora to strike at the advancing Indians from the flank, Ahmed asked the recce troop of Alpha Squadron to stay near the bridge on the Phillora–Dugri road.

Reports of the Indian advance were coming in thick and fast. Charlie Squadron's Second Lieutenant Shamshad Kaimkhani, who was following behind Nisar Ahmed, was intercepted by Captain Farrukh Khan, 25 Cavalry's technical officer, who confirmed that the Indian tanks had crossed the border at Charwa. Kaimkhani was told to continue his advance on the Pasrur–Chawinda–Charwa track. Shortly thereafter, Nasir Ahmed appeared in his jeep, and he ordered Kaimkhani to leave the track, move cross-country and deploy to the left of Bravo Squadron.

As the Pakistanis raced into position, the complete absence of the IAF made their job easier. Just then, the first Sabres were beginning to attack Indian armour and though the tanks had gotten away relatively lightly in the first aerial attack, B Echelon vehicles had taken a severe beating. 2 Tactical Air Control had been attached to HQ 1 Corps on 5 September at Kalu Chak and 1 Company Air Support Signal Regiment reported to the newly raised corps headquarters the next day. Ground liaison sections at supporting airfields were also far from adequate, thus allowing the PAF a free run yet again. Despite the earlier confusion, Nasir Ahmed's 25 Cavalry was in position at the crossroads south of Gadgor by 0900 hrs when the leading tanks of Bravo Squadron 16 Cavalry made contact with them.

Seeing the Pattons deployed along the tree line on the road, Second Lieutenant Vinay Kaistha was the first to open fire, and a Patton tank was put out of action. The troop led by Risaldar Shanmugan immediately moved into the standing sugarcane fields to the left of Kaistha's position, while the Pattons moved to their east, where they engaged 16 Cavalry's Centurions advancing between Gadgor and Gillanwali. The sugarcane crop restricted visibility so the Pattons of 25 Cavalry and the Centurions of 16 Cavalry engaged each other from within 50 to 200 yards. The Sabres were intermittently overhead, looking to strafe the Indian tanks the moment they broke cover. Lieutenant Vinay Kaistha was killed when his tank got strafed by a Sabre shortly after the first engagement with the Pakistani tanks. After that his troop lost contact with the rest of the regiment. The commanding officer, Lieutenant Colonel Sidhu-Brar, had to push his own tank into some mud houses and acacia trees to escape the PAF. Shanmugan's tank had also been hit and he reported over the radio that he was severely wounded. Major Ravindran ordered his two remaining troops to move forward and try to engage the Pattons around Gadgor by approaching from a flank.

At 0920 hrs, with the fighting raging ahead of his position, K. K. Singh briefed Sparrow that 16 Cavalry had run into strong opposition at Gadgor. At that point of time, only the two troops—those of Kaistha and Shanmugan—had been in contact with the enemy. 17 Horse, though attacked from the air, had yet to make contact with Pakistani armour as they had just crossed Sabzkot. Sparrow immediately instructed his mobile signal detachment to pass a message to the commandant of 4 Horse, Lieutenant Colonel Bakshi, to immediately move forward and await further instructions at Chobara.

To support Ravindran's Bravo Squadron, Sidhu-Brar ordered his Alpha Squadron, under the command of Major Mohammed Ali Raas Sheikh,[12] to put in a 'left hook' from the east in support of Ravindran's remaining two troops. Sheikh was north of Chobara, and the task allotted to him would take him dangerously close to 17 Horse that was moving southwards towards Tharoh, barely 6 km away. Almost immediately, the Sabres were overhead, which resulted in Sheikh going off the air. Second Lieutenant Arvind Kumar was in the lead as Alpha Squadron laboured through dense sugarcane fields. Though the standing crops made the going extremely difficult, it also provided cover from the Sabres. Proceeding to the east of Gillanwali, the squadron then turned south towards Kamoke in the narrow area between the east Hasri Nullah and a smaller tributary. As his tank was about to emerge from a sugarcane field, Kumar ordered his driver to halt. Barely fifty yards ahead of him, parked under a tree, was a tank, its gun pointing in his direction.

Acutely conscious of the fact that 17 Horse's Centurions were not that far away, Kumar looked through his field glasses and saw the Urdu markings on the side of the turret. He gave precise fire orders and the Patton was destroyed, as was another which in the initial confusion started to approach the tree to see what had happened. Taking advantage of the cover provided by the sugarcane, Kumar's Centurion Mk VII took on a third Patton a short while later and destroyed that too. Hemmed in by a curve in the river, the rest of Alpha Squadron also began to cautiously position themselves around Kumar. Just then, Kumar's tank jerked and 'looking to the rear he found the rubber gun barrel guard had been shot off. In the distance he saw a Centurion tank, its barrel emitting a tell-tale wisp of blue smoke that was peculiar to Centurion APDS ammunition. He waved his beret furiously and fortunately, no more shots came.'[13] While Kumar was extremely fortunate, the initial break to the east had exposed 16 Cavalry's flank to the Pattons and at least three tanks were hit badly.

Sidhu-Brar was getting reports from his recce troop that an additional troop of Pattons had appeared to the west of Gadgor. With both Alpha and Bravo committed and the former out of radio contact, the commandant of 16 Cavalry desperately tried to raise Charlie Squadron, which was still nowhere to be seen. 'The only answer elicited from Major Avinash Khanna, the squadron commander, was that they were coming up. A while later, Major Sheikh,[14] grievously wounded, was evacuated.'[15]

With tanks blazing away at each other in the confined space, Sidhu-Brar gave an exaggerated report to K. K. Singh about the Pakistani strength that his regiment was up against. In response, the brigade commander ordered 16 Cavalry to stop its forward advance and take up a defensive position instead in order to hold the captured ground. With the gap between the East Hasri Nullah and its tributary narrowing, 17 Horse were moving closer and closer to the flank of 16 Cavalry. At 0945 hrs, when the regiment was roughly on the Josar–Tharoh line, PAF F-86 Sabres once again singled out Major Cheema's Centurion, which was forced to take evasive action. Though Pakistani artillery guns had also opened up by then, K. K. Singh ordered 17 Horse to speed up the advance, adding that since 16 Cavalry was heavily engaged at Gadgor, the area ahead of them was likely to be relatively thinly held.

With his Bravo Squadron holding 16 Cavalry and having sent Charlie Squadron forward, Nisar Ahmed had been told by a Pakistani soldier that a few Indian tanks were seen moving towards Mahmudwali, 3 km east of Chawinda. Immediately Ahmed moved with Alpha Squadron under the command of Major Effendi to counter this new threat. Realizing there were no tanks in the area, the Pakistanis had moved towards the Phillora–Dugra crossroads.

At 1030 hrs, 17 Horse's Bravo Squadron made contact with the Pattons that had reached the treeline east of Tharoh. According to Nasir Ahmed, 'as we came out in the open the enemy tanks opened fire from area Dugri-Tharoh... the squadron lost one tank that was destroyed by enemy's direct tank fire...'.[16] Having expected to run into Indian Shermans, the Pakistanis realized they were up against the heavier Centurions. In the exchange of fire, at a range of 800 yards, the first Centurion of 17 Horse commanded by Second Lieutenant (later Major) H. I. S. Dhaliwal was hit and caught fire. Despite suffering burns himself, Dhaliwal successfully pulled out both his gunner and his driver.[17] Over the next one hour, a furious tank battle raged over a 15 km frontage that extended from the southwest of Josun–Wachoke to the area east of Tharoh, with both 16 Cavalry and 17 Horse trying to outflank the Pakistanis. Tarapore ordered Alpha Squadron to face east to protect the flank, while Charlie Squadron was ordered to move up and support Cheema's Bravo Squadron.

By 1220 hrs, with both 16 Cavalry and 17 Horse holding their ground and having sorted out their initial communication issues, the Indian forward squadrons continued to engage the Pakistanis. Madan Bakshi's three squadrons that made up Hodson's Horse had, in the meantime, reached Maranwali, and the Centurions were perfectly poised to go on the offensive on either flank. However, in K. K. Singh's Brigade HQ situated at Kandral behind the IB, there was utter confusion with regard to the location of 62 Cavalry's Charlie Squadron. Some tanks had been seen moving west to east at around 1130 hrs and this had thrown the entire headquarters of 1 Armoured Brigade into a tizzy. There was also still no information about the whereabouts of Khanna's missing squadron that was accompanied by 5/9 GR, while 43 Lorried Brigade had yet to get off the blocks.

By this time, the Pakistanis had a fair idea of the direction of the Indian attack and had redeployed 25 Cavalry's Charlie Squadron along with Alpha Company of 2 Punjab to cover the area between Phillora's crossroads and Gadgor. Watching this move develop were Sidhu-Brar and his Bravo Squadron commander, Ravindran. Still fighting with just two-thirds of his regiment, Sidhu-Brar was acutely aware of his mounting losses. From his position south of Gadgor, it appeared that the Pakistanis were bringing more armour into play. Indian artillery fire at this point was ineffective, mainly because of the poor visibility due to the sugarcane. To complicate matters, the FOO had his arm blown off when his tank got hit, and he had to be evacuated. At this point K. K. Singh asked Sidhu-Brar to get into his Rover and meet him at Maranwali.

K. K. Singh, who had himself commanded 16 Cavalry earlier, conferred with Sidhu-Brar: they felt 16 Cavalry and 17 Horse were up against two regiments of Patton tanks. A short while ago, when 4 Horse's Bravo Squadron under Major Bhupinder Singh had reached Kotli Dhudian, K. K. Singh, in accordance with Sparrow's orders to detach some armour to protect the left flank had already asked the Centurions to deploy facing west along the Nar Singh-Kotli Dhudian axis in the event of any Pakistani Pattons trying to get to Gadgor from that direction. While Sparrow wanted to make doubly sure there was no gap in his flank owing to the communication breakdown with Charlie Squadron of 62 Cavalry, the orders issued to 4 Horse meant K. K. Singh was abandoning the earlier thinking of deploying the reserve regiment in an offensive posture.

The brigade commander ordered Sidhu-Brar to withdraw the two squadrons of 16 Cavalry and redeploy them east of 4 Horse Alpha Squadron at Chobara. As they began to withdraw, Sidhu-Brar, who had got back to his tank, almost came to grief at the hands of Major (later Lieutenant Colonel) K. S. Dhillon's Alpha Squadron. One of the Centurions opened fire on what they thought were advancing Pattons at 1,500 yards. Immediately, a figure popped out of the cupola and, standing on the turret, began to furiously wave what looked like a turban. 'As the tank halted in front of me I was disturbed and shocked to recognize known but haggard and fatigued faces. It was 16 Cavalry Commandant's tank. KS Sidhu-Brar was in the commander's seat, accompanied on the turret by Captain Maurice Ravindran and Lieutenant B. M. Kapur, the Intelligence Officer. I climbed on to the hull and apologised profusely... the CO said "Rab di mehar hai" (God is very kind).'[18]

The seeds of uncertainty were beginning to take root. The initial engagement by Ravindran was with 25 Cavalry's Bravo Squadron equipped with M47s; this was followed by 17 Horse that had clashed with Alpha Squadron which was also using the same type; the arrival of Charlie Squadron's M48s had convinced the Indian commanders that there were almost certainly two Patton regiments in the area opposite them. Incidents of 'friendly fire' continued to compound the problem. Reports were being received by K. K. Singh from his Brigade HQ that enemy tanks had attacked a battery of 71 Medium Regiment at Kangre. The commanding officer of the artillery regiment, Lieutenant Colonel Prithi Pal Singh, confirmed to K. K. Singh that his battery had come under fire from armour. Subsequent analysis leaves little doubt that since there were no Pakistani tanks around Kangre, one of the tanks that had got detached from 62 Cavalry's Charlie Squadron during a Sabre strike had fired on the guns.

The incident at Kangre was the last straw. By 1400 hrs, K. K. Singh had decided to redeploy his brigade in a crescent-shaped defensive block. He ordered Tarapore to withdraw and redeploy in the area Pindi Bhago–Phullar Brahman. Bravo and Charlie Companies of 9 Dogra were allotted to 17 Horse. Madan Bakshi was told to also pull back Hodson's Horse and, with three companies of 5/9 GR, take up a defensive position in the Kotli Dhudian–Nar Singh–Hasri Bridge region. In essence, K. K. Singh had abandoned his offensive, pulled his brigade back and adopted an eastern-facing defensive 'box' to meet the anticipated threat from the direction of Kangre.

According to Maun Shergill, Sparrow was not party to this decision and was only briefed by K. K. Singh after the orders had been issued and the Indians had started to withdraw. To make matters worse, 'the commander, Brig KK Singh, appreciating that his flank was exposed and that we were now faced with two regiments of enemy armour, decided not to give battle frontally and ordered 17 Horse to wheel back and take positions in area Pindi Bhago to protect the left flank of the brigade.'[19] The name—Pindi Bhago—which in Punjabi means 'run home', created havoc as some troops thought it meant they were to get back to the IB.

The Indian withdrawal, especially at a time when the Pakistani armour was fully stretched and making no headway despite the presence of the PAF, led to even more confusion on the Indian side. Support elements that had not seen any action were now suddenly face to face with armour, and were struggling to identify friend from foe. Tank crews manning the newly defined perimeter of the defensive box opened fire at 62 Cavalry moving from east to west. 16 Cavalry was also shot at by 17 Horse while making their way up from the south to the northwestern end of the box.

The chaos and incidents of friendly fire were not restricted only to formations of 1 Armoured Brigade. Dhillon's 43 Lorried Infantry Brigade was finally given an alternate red route to advance by, the green route having been a non-starter after the leading tanks of 2 Lancers got bogged down. Only one company of 8 Garhwal Rifles had managed to proceed on the original axis and get to Ranjitpura. The brigade, stranded at Saidanwali, finally started its move into Pakistan at 1315 hrs, with Alpha and Bravo Squadrons of 2 Lancers leading the way, both with only three troops each. After a few minor engagements with small pockets of Pakistani Rangers, mujahids, and ex-servicemen reinforced with infantry, the tanks under the overall command of Major B. R. Sharan reached the Sabzpir crossroads when they came under fire from a Centurion.

17 Horse's gunnery skills notwithstanding, Second Lieutenant Jai Singh's tank took a hit, wounding one of his crew and setting the camouflage netting on fire. While the fire was being put out, some Shermans returned fire. While radio signals went back and forth ordering the two sides to cease fire, sporadic fire from the Centurions continued. Until then, 43 Lorried Infantry Brigade had no idea that the offensive had been called off and 1 Armoured Brigade had pulled back into a defensive box just ahead of the leading tanks of 2 Lancers. Lieutenant Colonel M. S. Sandhu then tried to move towards 17 Horse's position, but was immediately engaged by yet another Centurion. Looking to find cover, Sandhu and his crew quickly evacuated the tank, but the regiment's IO, Second Lieutenant Tipu Seth, stayed to receive an incoming message. The young officer's luck ran out when the next shot fired by the Centurion found its mark. Three crew members were killed on the spot and Seth was mortally wounded. 2 Lancers was ordered to stop short of the Sabzpir crossroads, at handshaking distance from 1 Armoured Brigade. By then elements of 35 Infantry Brigade had also moved in to the Sabzpir area to secure the defensive box and provide a firm base for the next day's operations. Charlie Squadron of 16 Cavalry never fetched up all that day.

Dhillon had, in the meantime, reached Charwa, where the RHQ and Bravo Squadron of 62 Cavalry had been waiting since the morning. Along with the rest of 8 Garhwal Rifles, 62 Cavalry was ordered at 1445 hrs to proceed to Maharajke. Shortly thereafter, the PAF, which continued to have an unchecked run in the skies, struck again. The Garhwalis would hunker down at Sungial, while 62 Cavalry went into harbour with 69 Brigade at Koloi, just beyond Maharajke at 1850 hrs.

Unaware that the Indians had withdrawn and gone into a defensive huddle, Commander 24 Brigade ordered Ahmed to launch a counter-attack. Charlie Squadron supported by Bravo Squadron of 25 Cavalry under the command of Major Raza Khan supported by 2 Punjab's Alpha Company began to advance on Gadgor at 1700 hrs. Expecting the Indians to open fire at any minute, the

Pakistanis went through Gadgor until they came under fire at Maranwali. The two sides continued to exchange punches till darkness fell, after which Raza Khan was ordered to fall back at the Phillora Road crossing where 25 Cavalry was to camp for the night. Lieutenant Colonel Nasir Ahmed, on going through the captured documents recovered from Indian tanks that had been found in the Gadgor area, realized for the first time that he was up against the highly vaunted 1 Armoured Division and three infantry divisions in the Sialkot Sector.

Commenting on the events of 8 September, Harbakhsh Singh wrote: 'In the melee that followed this encounter, both 16 Cavalry and 17 Horse failed to determine the strength of the opposing armour and displayed little skill in out-manoeuvring it. What is more depressing, the regimental commanders lost control over their units and to make matters worse, the Brigade Commander made the unfortunate decision to withdraw 17 Horse from Tharoh for countering an alleged serious tank threat to the left flank. This was a grave error of judgement as 4 Horse, which by this time had been released to the brigade by General Officer Commanding 1 Armoured Division (Sparrow), could have been used to meet any flank threat posed by the enemy armour. The blunder cost us dearly. We made an advance of only four miles beyond the bridgehead when a much deeper penetration could have been achieved. The fleeting chance, that could have been exploited to gain a striking success, was lost for ever.'[20]

Dhillon's 43 Lorried Infantry Brigade had also been a non-starter. Literally going around in circles, it spent more time fighting the terrain rather than the enemy, and with great difficulty, some elements of the formation had made it to Kaloi, barely 3 km beyond Maharajke. With the light fading fast, the brigade closed ranks to harbour for the night. General Chaudhuri's great hope of a lightning strike by 1 Corps into the interior of Pakistan in the Sialkot Sector had come to nought.

26 Infantry Division had played its part, so too had 6 Mountain Division, despite the logistical nightmare of moving a division to its battle location at the last minute. Despite the troops on the ground standing up well to the concentrated Pakistani artillery fire on day one of the fighting in this sector, the two main reasons for the dismal performance was entirely due to a failure at the higher command level. First, by splitting his two brigades along two divergent axes, Sparrow (and Dunn) had violated the very basic concept of an armoured thrust. Instead of concentrating his force where they could function as an integrated team, 'the diverging axes permitted neither coordination nor cohesion of effort; it was like driving in a wedge from the wrong side.'[21] Harbakhsh's criticism after the event would indicate he wasn't part of the decision-making process. With Dunn also reduced to being a bystander as far as the operations of 1 Armoured Division were concerned, the needle of suspicion points at the army chief himself for having masterminded the tactics. Sparrow was too much of a 'yes man' to have stood up to his army chief.

Second (again the responsibility lies entirely on Chaudhuri's shoulders), the complete lack of coordination with the IAF is mind-boggling. This points to the fact that in all the conferences and sand model exercises conducted between Operation Ablaze and the actual breakout of the fighting in the Punjab, air support was simply not factored in. To cover up for their own shortcomings and tactical failures, the impact of the PAF on the battles fought in the first few days of the war had been dismissed offhand by Harbakhsh.[22] It was easy for the Western Army commander to rip into Niranjan Prasad and make him the scapegoat, but quite honestly, had the 1965 war been fought twenty years earlier with Stalin or Hitler being the supreme commanders, most of these gentlemen would have been shot for incompetence. The generals had failed. It was now up to the men to stand up and salvage the situation.

Chapter 17

A GRAVEYARD FOR PATTONS

11 CORPS (PART III)

4 MOUNTAIN DIVISION—KHEM KARAN (9 SEPTEMBER)

Pakistan's third offensive against 4 Division's defences started at 0230 hrs on 9 September. Once again, the assault developed along the same three axes, the main difference being this was a night attack. 'Using their infra-red driving capability, the Pakistanis expected the onrushing tanks to overwhelm the defending troops.'[1] However, the shock-and-awe tactic did not work as the Indians refused to budge, forcing the Pakistani armour to pull back. Strangely, Pakistani infantry did not join in these assaults. During the night, 4 Mountain Division had also readjusted its positions as 1/9 GR had fallen back. The laying of mines and digging and improving fields of fire would go on throughout the night. 2 Armoured Brigade having been allotted to 4 Mountain Division, the Indian armour was redeployed in a crescent formation covering the area from Sankatra–Dholan–Chima to Valtoha with a strongly held defended sector in the middle astride the Bhikkiwind and Patti roads. Apart from freshly laid mines, the approaches were covered by RCL guns and the Shermans of 9 Horse. The Centurions of 3 Cavalry covered the right and rear of the defended sector, while AMX-13 tanks of 8 Cavalry were expected to neutralize any threat to the left flank. The gun areas in Chima were in a position to bring concentrated fire on the whole front. Most importantly, after the events of the previous day, 4 Mountain Division had begun to believe that it could also destroy Pakistani armour.

Information about what was happening on the Pakistani side was skimpy at best. Pakistan's 1 Armoured Division had managed to get most of its 4 Armoured Brigade across the Rohi Nullah into the confined space of the Khem Karan bridgehead. It now had at least five more armoured regiments confined in the narrow area, with very little space to manoeuvre. All this while, 24 Cavalry and 6 Lancers continued to launch attacks at Asal Uttar, but even as night gave way to day, nothing changed. The tanks with infantry behind them would close in, come under heavy fire from the Indian tanks and RCL guns, and pull back. As the morning ticked away, at no stage did Major General Naseer Ahmed Khan, GOC of Pakistan's 1 Armoured Division, think of making a concentrated attack on 4 Mountain Division.

By the afternoon, under increasing pressure from GHQ to get a move on and capture maximum Indian territory, 4 Armoured Brigade, commanded by Brigadier A. A. 'Tony' Lumb (previously of Royal Deccan Horse), was ordered to move north parallel to the IB along the Rohi Nullah and the Khem Karan Minor Canal, occupy Mastgarh, and then capture Duhal Kuhna and Bhura Karimpur, which would put the attacking force to the west of Chima. At 1300 hrs, two units of the brigade, 5 Horse and 10 FF, set off with 15 (SP) Field, 21 Medium and 35 Heavy Regiments, together carrying a formidable punch in terms of sheer firepower. India's 4 Mountain Division, deployed mainly around Asal Uttar, had no idea whatsoever of this development. Charlie Squadron of 3 Cavalry that had got to Bhura Karimpur and the Khem Karan Minor on the previous day had been withdrawn to Mahmudpura by Brigadier Theogaraj, the commander of 2 (Independent) Armoured Brigade.

However, Naseer Ahmed Khan had made a major blunder. Though there were no Indian troops in the area, the presence of subsoil water made it the softest terrain in the area and the Pakistanis were soon horribly bogged down. Hardly had they extracted themselves from this swamp than they found themselves in another. With darkness creeping in, Lumb requested Ahmed Khan to allow him to camp at Mastgarh, but he was told to keep moving through the night after replenishing his formation. Considering the ground situation, however, Lumb decided to ignore the order and 4 Armoured Brigade harboured for the night at Mastgarh.

At the same time, Brigadier Bashir's 5 Armoured Brigade got into action again after a brief hiatus. After the probing actions had not yielded any results in the morning, Bashir spelt out fresh objectives to his three main attacking groups: Group Ali, consisting of 24 Cavalry and two companies of 5 FF were to attack on the Khem Karan–Bhikkiwind axis; 6 Lancers and two companies of 1 FF that made up Group Gul were to make for Valtoha, the assault being planned along the firm ground between the road and the railway line; and Group Shabbir, consisting of the remainder of 1 FF, was to establish a firm base near Mile 2 on the track to Valtoha.

At 1300 hrs, Group Gul, once again under the command of Sahibzad Gul, started to advance. 6 Squadron's Bravo Squadron, with Captain Khaliq Yar Tiwana, was down to seven tanks as the Pakistanis had not been able to recover any of their tanks from the previous day's fighting. 18 Raj Rif and Deccan Horse's Bravo Squadron, dug in along the Machike Minor and Asal Uttar, knocked out two more Pattons, but Tiwana managed to get past the Indian position with the remaining five. Sahibzad Gul, quick to exploit the situation, ordered Tiwana to push on to Valtoha, and the rest of 6 Lancers was ordered to follow. Even before Alpha Squadron could close the gap with 18 Raj Rif, Sahibzad Gul, standing in the open cupola of his command tank, was hit by a burst of machine-gun fire and killed. By then, Deccan Horse tanks were running short of armour-piercing shells and could not stop Alpha Squadron from going through in the wake of Tiwana. The third squadron, however, was not so successful. Risaldar Risal Singh fired the last armour-piercing shell, destroying a Patton, after which the Shermans switched to high-explosive ammunition. 6 Lancers' Charlie Squadron, though unable to penetrate through the Indian position, kept firing and Major J. S. Bal's tank was badly hit, killing his radio operator on the spot. Shortly thereafter, two more of his crew were killed by machine-gun fire, while Bal himself was wounded when a tank shell hit his foot.

With 18 Raj Rif refusing to yield ground and keeping the mechanized infantry at bay, the Pakistanis broke contact and began to withdraw. After Sahibzad Gul was killed, Group Shabbir was combined with Group Gul, and Lieutenant Colonel Shabbir took over command. This impetuous thrust by Naseer Ahmed Khan and Bashir defies logic. Bravo and Alpha Squadron, separated from the infantry, were engaged by the Indian artillery. With darkness setting in, the much-vaunted infrared capability allowed Tiwana's group to break contact and make their way back to the bridgehead at Khem Karan without further losses.

Group Ali, which was supposed to launch its offensive at 1300 hrs to coincide with Group Gul and Group Shabbir's move, started way behind schedule. While 18 Raj Rif and Bravo Squadron had been fighting Group Gul to their left, 4 and 7 Grenadiers were looking towards Khem Karan, waiting for signs of activity. Finally, at 1600 hrs, the tanks of 24 Cavalry, under the command of Major Sabir Uddin, could be seen approaching the Indian positions on the Khem Karan–Bhikkiwind Road. Deployed in the area between Bhura Kuhna and Asal Uttar, the Grenadier RCL guns and the Shermans from Deccan Horse's Alpha Squadron came into action. The pattern was much the same, with some Patton tanks managing to penetrate the Indian defences, which were not willing to give an inch. In the enveloping darkness, Group Ali also decided to break contact and camp south of Bhura Kuhna. However, once the Indian artillery guns had finished with Tiwana, they turned their attention to Group Ali, which suffered quite a few casualties. Four Pattons had been destroyed by Bravo Squadron and 18 Raj Rif, while Alpha Squadron along with the two Grenadier battalions had accounted for another five.

There was a baffling lack of common sense in the Khem Karan Sector on the part of the Pakistani commanders during the day of 9 September. It is also strange that neither the PAF nor the IAF launched air strikes, especially the latter who would have found a large concentration of Pakistani armour in the bridgehead established by them across the Rohi Nullah. Ahmed Khan's attempt to outflank the Indians by moving his heavy armour through the softest of terrain while launching a three-pronged attack against their established positions only points to the fact that he was unnerved by the presence of 3 Cavalry's Centurions that had arrived at Khem Karan the previous day. The fierce skirmishes with the dug-in tanks of Deccan Horse and the units of 4 Mountain Division had only succeeded in further building the confidence of Major General Gurbaksh Singh's men.

On the ground, the reluctance of Pakistani infantry to follow the tanks even when they got past Indian positions was also becoming quite noticeable. 'To capture enemy territory in the first instance and then abandon it and then withdraw to square one, is bewilderingly irreconcilable… for this to happen on two consecutive days is beyond comprehension.'[2]

7 & 15 INFANTRY DIVISIONS—BARKI & GOSAL-DIAL (9 SEPTEMBER)

Brigadier Lerb Ferris's 65 Infantry Brigade had spent 8 and 9 September getting into position to attack Barki. 4 Sikh having moved into Khurd the previous day, 16 Punjab (Patiala) commanded by Lieutenant Colonel J. S. Bhullar occupied Brahmanabad on 9 September. Heavy artillery fire had kept the men huddled in their shallow trenches through the day and the biggest problem faced by the battalion was thirst. The men, in the absence of food or water, survived by sucking and chewing on the sugarcane that was all around them. With both battalions in a position to advance on Barki, it meant that Barki had lost its outer ring of defences and all that stood on the west bank was a screen of two platoons, one each of 12 and 17 Punjab under Major Aziz Bhatti. However, the Pakistanis, apart from relentlessly subjecting the Indian troops to unending bombardment, had used the last forty-eight hours to reinforce Barki, which they had to defend at all cost.

'The defences in the village were based on concrete pillboxes suitably camouflaged to resemble huts [eleven such pillboxes were counted later]. Each pillbox measured 15 ft square with 3 ft concrete walls. Each was manned by three to four men with automatic weapons and they were well stocked for sustained operations. Extensive tunnelling and communication trenches were built to ensure uninterrupted movement even during severe artillery fire.'[3] In addition to one company of 17 Punjab, there was also a company of R&S and the entire area around the village and surrounding area was bracketed with accurate defensive fire by the Pakistani heavy artillery. To make matters even more complicated, the western bank of the canal was higher than the eastern bank.

In the afternoon, Dhillon held a conference at HQ 7 Infantry Division. Besides Sibal and Ferris, Brigadier K. J. S. Shahaney, commander 48 Infantry Brigade, and Lieutenant Colonel Mehta, CIH, were also present. Dhillon was under tremendous pressure. 4 Mountain Division, despite its initial reverses in Khem Karan, was just about holding the line at Asal Uttar, and it was but a matter of time before the main attack led by Pakistani armour would test the defences again. Throughout the 11 Corps sector, the fighting had been intense and artillery fire had taken a heavy toll on the men. Earlier in the morning, Dhillon had sent a flash signal to Western Command asking for additional troops. '15 Infantry Division has lost during three days of battle the equivalent of four infantry battalions out of a total of nine. The case of 4 Mountain Division is similar where the losses have been two-and-a-half battalions out of a total of six. 7 Infantry Division is a little better and the losses have been equivalent to two battalions out of nine.'[4]

Dhillon now impressed upon Sibal and the other officers present the absolute necessity of not only capturing Barki, but also reaching the Ichhogil Canal. Giving the example of the operation at DBN, Dhillon suggested that they use the CIH tanks at night.

Sibal's 7 Infantry Division had missed a golden opportunity earlier, which was in keeping with the general chaos that had marked most of 11 Corps offensive operations. On 8 September, after 4 Sikh had captured Brahmanabad in a daytime attack that led to four dead and nineteen wounded, the battalion could see what looked like an embankment of a canal approximately 2 km away.

With the village secured, Lieutenant Colonel Anant Singh asked his Alpha Company commander, Major Shamsher Singh Manhas, to send a reconnaissance patrol to the embankment, to see what lay beyond it. Meeting with no opposition, the patrol was taken aback to find itself standing on the much talked about eastern bank of the Ichhogil Canal, with no sign of the Pakistanis. The day being hot and sultry, the boys could not resist a dip in the cool water. The report was passed on to HQ 65 Infantry Brigade, but for some unfathomable reason, Ferris refused to believe 4 Sikh's report that this section of the Ichhogil Canal was not held by the Pakistanis.[5] Had 65 Infantry Brigade acted on this information, it could have secured both banks without a fight and used it as a base for launching a flanking attack on the occupied section of Barki, thus avoiding the subsequent costly operation.

However, Ferris's 65 Infantry Brigade now had little option but to take on Barki frontally. The approach from the left was out of the question because it meant going through flooded paddy fields. Similarly, to send attacking troops from the right meant taking a much longer route from the brigade's FUP that was almost entirely along an unprotected flank. It was also exposed to enemy weapons on the canal bank that ran to the north of the road. The frontal approach, though devoid of cover and bracketed by Pakistani artillery, was the shortest and protected from fire from the high canal bank. Initially, Ferris wanted 16 Punjab to capture Barki but Bhullar was not confident that his troops could capture a built-up area. Ferris then told Anant Singh, CO 4 Sikh, that the attack would take place on the night of 10/11 September. H-hour would be 2000 hrs. Until then, the forward companies would just have to brazen out the artillery fire and survive on stalks of sugarcane.

To the north, 15 Division's 54 Infantry Brigade was establishing itself more securely astride GT Road and the UBDC. 3 Jat had moved to Santpura in the early hours and was having a 'relaxed' morning. '[T]he most basic act of war, which is to send out patrols to bring information about the enemy, was neglected. The villages of Lakhane, Mana and Jhuggian Mian Darswali lay abandoned in no-man's land. 3 Jat was happy for this day of respite and having dug its trenches... every man was comfortably asleep at the bottom before the early morning of 9 September. Major (later Major General) Baldev Raj Varma, the battalion adjutant hastily returning from leave, coming upon this restful scene and with nobody to talk to, said to himself, if this is war, not bad.'[6]

Having lost the RCL guns in the initial air attacks on 6 September, the lack of anti-tank weapons was a cause of worry for 3 Jat. Despite being in the thick of the fighting, Hayde had managed to put in a report to that effect. Fortunately for him and the battalion, the request had been noted and two RCL guns were to reach the battalion at 0400 hrs. However, the officer who reached 3 Jat had with him a total of six rounds, which amounted to three per gun.

Hayde had a lot of faith in the 14 Scinde Horse troop that had been with the battalion ever since the first fateful night at Dograi. In this sector, both sides had Shermans, but the Pakistani tanks had a 90 mm gun while the Scinde Horse tank's main armament was a 75 mm gun. Second Lieutenant Brijendra Singh's experience on 6 September had strengthened his belief that if he engaged the Pakistani tanks from secure hides, be it from behind houses or sugarcane fields, if the range was less than 1,500 yards, the gunnery skills of his crew would prevail. Lieutenant Colonel Raghubir Singh, the commandant of 14 Scinde Horse, had also decided not to shift his tank troops around. As a result, apart from having built a rapport with 3 Jat, Brijendra Singh also had spent the time he had working out firing positions and routes he needed to follow at top speed, to not only keep his tanks out of the Pakistani range but also get from one place to another in the event of having to fight a defensive battle.

Though this was applicable across almost sectors, in the 54 Brigade area, the Pakistanis also had a nearly 5:1 superiority in artillery guns. The brigade was being supported by 'a medium battery which fired 80 pound shells but the effect was indifferent since the ammunition was in short supply.'[7]

Though the Western Army commander was confident 4 Mountain Division along with 2 (Independent) Armoured Brigade would hold the Pakistanis at Asal Uttar, Dhillon was more concerned about Amritsar. On the Attari–Wagah front, the performance of 15 Infantry Division had left him very uneasy. All the war games conducted during Operation Ablaze had not envisioned a scenario where the offensive thrust would fail to get even to the east bank of the Ichhogil Canal. By the afternoon, after the briefing at 7 Infantry Division culminated with the orders to capture Barki, Dhillon made his way back to HQ 11 Corps. His signal in the morning asking for reinforcements had resulted in Western Command issuing orders to 41 Mountain Brigade under Brigadier (later Major General) M. R. Rajwade to move immediately from Akhnoor to the 11 Corps area. Dhillon allotted this additional brigade to 15 Infantry Division that very evening. This was strange because 4 Mountain Division, which was desperately short of troops and had been in regular contact with the Pakistanis since 6 September, only got a hastily organized company from the advance party of 17 Sikh who were scrambled to Asal Uttar mainly due to Harbakhsh Singh's own initiative.

Though Dhillon would subsequently claim that shifting 2 (Independent) Armoured Brigade to Asal Uttar was perhaps the best decision he had taken as the 11 Corps commander, he, in fact had nothing to do with it. On the contrary, with the armour shifting to the south, Dhillon was getting increasingly nervous about holding Amritsar should the Pakistanis suddenly go on the offensive. In a surprising move, Dhillon sent an SOS to 3 Cavalry to detach a troop and despatch them at first light to Attari, a distance of 60 km. The Centurion troop under the command of Captain (later Lieutenant Colonel) Naginder Singh, were to move via road. In what was perhaps one of the most elementary blunders of the war, Dhillon failed to tell his headquarters to inform 15 Infantry Division of this impending move.[8]

If Dhillon was panicking at his 11 Corps HQ, the situation with General Chaudhuri in New Delhi was not very different. The COAS had received Dhillon's letter suggesting the immediate replacing of 4 Mountain Division. Fearing the worst, the COAS met with Defence Minister Chavan, who recorded in his diary: 'Had a very hard day on all fronts—Very fierce counter-attacks mounted and we are required to withdraw in Kasur area.'[9] By Kasur area, Chavan was referring to the fighting at Khem Karan. He goes on to record 'COAS was somewhat uncertain of himself. I suggested to him that he should go in forward areas so that he will be in touch [with the] realities. He said he would go next day.' It is interesting to note the battle front in Khem Karan was causing such anxiety even to the defence minister in Delhi whereas Dhillon not only chose to deploy 41 Mountain Brigade in the Lahore Sector, he even took away a troop of 3 Cavalry on the morning of the expected attack.

Harbakhsh Singh's account of what happened later that night and the next morning has been confirmed by Pradhan, Chavan's private secretary:[10] 'Late that night on 9 September, the Chief of Army Staff rang me up to say that he had read Corps Commander 11 Corps letter sent to me and his advice was to save the whole Army from being cut off by Pakistan's Armour push, I should put back to the line of the River Beas. I was aghast at this suggestion and said that since it was a tactical order, he had to come to the Front with me to give it, or else he had to issue an Operational instruction, as is the custom in the Army.'[11] The COAS had not visited any of the forward formations until then.

Early September in Punjab the nights are reasonably pleasant, the heat of the summer having simmered down with the monsoon rains. Unaware of the backroom drama at the higher levels, divisional, brigade, battalion, company and platoon commanders, jawans drawn from all corners of the subcontinent, gunners, infantrymen, tank crews, and those who were keeping the supply lines open, all settled down for the night, many of them at the bottom of slit trenches, each man wondering what the next day would bring for him. Most of these men had seen their comrades ripped apart by artillery fire and the fear of death would come back with the daylight hours. The story was much the same extending from the DBN Sector, where silence ruled across the width of the Ravi River to Khem Karan and beyond in the Rajasthan Sector. To the immediate north of the partly blown up bridge at Jassar, General Dunn's 1 Corps had also settled down for the night. As the sky began to take on the grey hue of dawn, the occasional clucking of nightjars began to fade…it was just a matter of time before the sinister rumbling of artillery guns would turn on the heat again.

THREE BATTLES THAT TURNED THE TIDE—KHEM KARAN (10 SEPTEMBER)

The COAS arrived at the Ambala airfield the next morning at 1000 hrs. Ironically, while troops in the frontlines were begging for air support, Chaudhuri's aircraft came with a fighter escort. Chaudhuri and Harbakhsh had a heated argument, not realizing that it was an academic discussion, for Pakistan's 1 Armoured Division had already been on the move for over six hours and pitched battles were raging in both the Khem Karan and Gosal–Dial areas. The Indian offensive in the Sialkot Sector had taken Pakistan by surprise for, on the face of it, to avoid splitting her forces, the northernmost point from where the Indians were expected to advance would logically have been Dera Baba Nanak/Jassar. Once it became obvious to Musa that India's 1 Armoured Division was indeed in the Sialkot region and further to the north than he had expected, he decided to pull out his divisional reserve from the Khem Karan bridgehead and move immediately to Lahore where it was placed under 10 Division before being further moved to Sialkot.

Pakistan had already launched its 4 Armoured Brigade on an outflanking move the previous day in a bid to get at the Assal Uttar defences. Brigadier Lumb's formation, having battled with the swampy terrain, was leaguered at Mastgarh. At midnight 9/10 September, GOC Pak 1 Armoured Division, unfolded his master plan for the annihilation of 4 Mountain Division. Though an infantry officer himself, Naseer Ahmed seemed to be ignoring the lessons of the previous two days and determined to win the battle only with his Pattons, with mechanized infantry mounted on APCs following them. With this plan, his options were limited, for 4 Armoured Brigade had already been committed. With his reserve of 3 Armoured Brigade withdrawn, he only had 5 Armoured Brigade to play with.

For the attack on 10 September, Naseer Ahmed decided he would once again push 5 Armoured Brigade along the Khem Karan–Bhikkiwind Road with Chima being the objective. Lumb's 4 Armoured Brigade would then launch a coordinated flank attack from Milestone 32. In order to enhance his artillery firepower, Naseer decided to put 26 Field Regiment of 11 Division on the same wireless net as his own artillery brigade.

At 0350 hrs, 4 Cavalry with Alpha Company of 10 FF (Mechanized) had set off for Milestone 32. However, it was to be a repeat performance as the tanks and the APCs continued to battle the impossible terrain. The dense vegetation, mainly sarkanda, made visibility a problem and neutralized the long range of the Patton's main gun. At 0600 hrs, the thunder of Pakistani artillery from the gun positions within the bridgehead could be heard targeting 4 Mountain Division's defences. Almost three hours after the Pakistani armour had started advancing, the reconnaissance section of 3 Cavalry at Lakhana under Daffadar Mool Singh reported the movement of tanks from the north of Bhura Karimpur towards Dholan. The time was then 0640 hrs; Lieutenant Colonel Salim Caleb immediately adjusted the position of Charlie Squadron 3 Cavalry between Bidhal and Mahmudpura to meet the developing threat.

There had obviously been no scope whatsoever for 4 Mountain Division to play around with its defensive layout in the last few hours. When the men were not facing Pakistani probing attacks, they were continuously trying to improve their defensive layouts and get a few hours of rest. At the end of the day on 9 September, Brigadiers Theogaraj and Caleb were both aware that the Pakistanis had built up considerably within the Khem Karan bridgehead. Mool Singh's warning that Pakistani armour was on the move confirmed their belief that the main Pakistani attack against 4 Mountain Division had begun. Sitting on his charpoy at the regiment's TAC HQ at Dibbipura, Caleb could only hope all the man hours put into the training of his tank crews would pay off.

Until this point Indian communication systems had been notoriously poor, time and again failing commanders and men alike. Partly to offset that liability, at first light Brigadier Theogaraj moved his 2 (Independent) Armoured Brigade TAC HQ to Caleb's location. The two commanding officers of 9 Horse and 8 Cavalry also followed suit. With all orders being issued in person, in addition to reducing response time, it also meant there was no scope for the Pakistanis to listen in and intercept messages.

Arun Vaidya's 9 Deccan Horse with its Shermans continued to occupy centre stage; Alpha Squadron was in the Chima area with the by now fully battle inoculated 7 Mountain Brigade; Bravo Squadron was dug in at Asal Uttar with 62 Mountain Brigade; and Charlie Squadron had two troops at Dibbipura–Nawapind and two more south of the 4 Artillery Brigade's gun area. Supporting the 4 Mountain Division defences in a horseshoe-like manner was Caleb's 3 Cavalry. Alpha Squadron was at Algun Khurd–Maddar with its tanks deployed at the Algun Khurd Bridge and at the Maddar–Rohi Nullah crossing while one troop was north of Dibbipura; Bravo Squadron was deployed around Mile 34 and Charlie Squadron less two troops was on the Khem Karan Minor. The reconnaissance troop had observation posts at Lakhna, Warowal, and Valtoha. 8 Cavalry's AMX tanks were the last line of defence—one squadron at Rasulpur, another at Valtoha deployed along the Khem Karan distributary.

Pakistan's 5 Armoured Brigade had, during the last two days, shown a marked preference for making a late start. Even on 10 September, they would only get active towards the late afternoon, generously leaving the field to Brigadier Lumb's 4 Armoured Brigade, which was cautiously advancing. 'It was almost as if the enemy tanks knew that ahead of them, in concealed positions, awaited the Centurion tanks, and they hoped that the Centurion tanks would give their positions away by premature movement. They underestimated the steadfastness and high standards of training of 3 Cavalry tank crews.'[12]

Apart from the slow pace at which his brigade was moving, Lumb was getting increasingly frustrated as the positions of 4 Armoured Brigade's two columns had got switched. 10 FF (Mechanized) with Bravo Squadron 4 Cavalry were meant to advance on the western side, while the remaining two squadrons of 4 Cavalry were to be on the inside towards the Indian defences at Asal Uttar. This had somehow got mixed up, and though the commander tried to rectify the situation from a helicopter, it was too late. All he could do was exhort Lieutenant Colonel Mohammad Nazir to get a move on.

By then 3 Cavalry had been observing the Pakistanis for almost an hour. At 0830 hrs, Charlie Squadron 3 Cavalry, that was between Lakhana and Dholan, reported tanks closing in. Simultaneously, 4 Grenadiers on the Khem Karan–Bhikkiwind Road was reporting the presence of tanks in front of its position. The Centurion troop let the Pattons get to 1,200 yards before they opened up. The bright flash at the target end indicated a hit and two Pattons came to a grinding halt. In the ensuing firefight, two more Pattons were hit. Seeing the number of Pattons advancing past his position, Major Narinder Sandhu clambered onto the roof of a house in Lakhna. Two of Charlie Squadron's Centurions had also been hit, fortunately with no casualties. From his vantage position, Narinder Sandhu kept up a running commentary for RHQ as Pattons continued to advance past Lakhna towards Maddar. Risaldar Aparbal Singh, leading a troop from Alpha Squadron 3 Cavalry, then got into the action, destroying another Patton and an APC. Charlie Squadron hit seven tanks and destroyed two more APCs.

Lieutenant Colonel Bhatti's 4 Grenadiers, deployed on the Khem Karan–Bhikkiwind Road with 7 Grenadiers to their left and 1/9 GR to their right, had been subject to heavy artillery fire since 0600 hrs. Behind them were 18 Raj Rif, 9 JAK Rif, and 13 Dogra, all the units manning their defences, which were not easily visible in the cotton and sugarcane fields. As the artillery barrage lifted from their position, Charlie Company 4 Grenadiers, could see Pattons from 4 Cavalry in an assault formation heading straight for their position. By then, the RCL detachment of 4 Grenadiers had made quite a name for themselves, especially company quartermaster Havildar Abdul Hamid who, on the two previous days, had twice stopped Pakistani armoured attacks in their tracks with accurate shooting that had destroyed a few tanks and led to the abandonment of others.

Though the Pattons were barely 200 yards away and coming closer, the battalion's mortar officer, Lieutenant (later Lieutenant Colonel) Hari Ram Janu, drew Abdul Hamid's attention to the tanks. At near point-blank range, the 106 RCL had a devastating effect. The hollow charge fired by the RCL set fire to the tank. An hour later, at 0930 hrs, yet another attack developed. Once again, a Patton got close to Charlie Company's No. 9 Platoon that was being commanded by Second Lieutenant (later Brigadier) Vijay Kumar Vaid. Abdul Hamid's RCL detachment was positioned about 150 yards off the road. Even as he brought the RCL to bear on the third tank, the gallant RCL crew was killed by a direct hit. Brigadier Sidhu's TAC HQ was adjacent to the 4 Grenadier defences and one tank of Deccan Horse was positioned there. In all probability, the Pakistani tank was hit by the Sherman as it fired at Abdul Hamid's jeep, for the attack had been stopped yet again. Abdul Hamid, the NCO whose RCL gun was found with a round in the breech, would subsequently be honoured with a posthumous Param Vir Chakra, the country's highest award for exceptional valour in the face of the enemy.

What happened on the Khem Karan–Bhikkiwind road next remains a bit of a mystery. In all probability, with his 4 Armoured Brigade sending frantic messages for replenishment of fuel and ammunition as its losses against the Centurions steadily mounted, Major General Naseer Ahmed was getting desperate for 5 Armoured Brigade to get a move on. At 1430 hrs he had landed in a helicopter at Milestone 38 and was irate that 5 Armoured Brigade had not even started moving. He desperately needed the Khem Karan–Bhikkiwind Road opened so he could move supplies to Lumb's brigade. Incredible as it may sound, even after two days of fighting, the Pakistani commanders had little idea as to how the handful of troops in 4 Mountain Division were deployed. Ahmed ordered Brigadier Ahsan Rashid Shami, the brigadier, artillery, 1 Armoured Division, to drive him and Brigadier Bashir, commander of 5 Armoured Brigade, to the front so they could see for themselves what was going on around Chima. At the last second, Ahmed probably changed his mind and asked the two brigadiers to go without him. Shami was driving the GOC's vehicle. They were followed by the COs of 24 Cavalry and 3 (SP) Field Regiment, as well as Alpha Squadron of 24 Cavalry, which was getting ready to launch its offensive. Taking a troop of tanks with them, the cavalcade of four jeeps entered no-man's land. As they moved forward, they didn't see much apart from the odd burnt out or abandoned tank and RCL jeep. With cotton and sugarcane being the two main crops on either side of the road, visibility was extremely poor.

No. 9 Platoon, Charlie Company of 4 Grenadiers, was sitting astride the Khem Karan–Bhikkiwind Road, its defences virtually invisible from the road. Its fire discipline was extremely good, and since there were both Indian and Pakistani tanks in the area, the men usually held their fire until ordered to engage the target. The leading jeep suddenly found itself next to a trench and stopped. Brigadier Shami, seeing two soldiers in the trench, quickly drew his pistol from its holster and, pointing it at them shouted in Hindustani, 'Hathiyaar phek do; tum ghire huain ho' (Throw down your weapons; you are surrounded).

The two grenadiers in the trench, Shafi and Naushad, overawed by the presence of a senior officer, stood up and gaped at the jeep. Someone then shouted, 'Maro! Goli chalao!' (Kill them! Open fire!). It's one thing to take on charging tanks and infantry across open gun sights in combat, but to press the trigger at point-blank range into a senior officer's face is quite another. The sharp command, plus the fact that 9 Horse tanks had begun firing, snapped Grenadier Shafi out of his paralysis. He pressed the trigger of his automatic weapon and kept it pressed until the entire magazine had emptied. As Brigadier Shami collapsed, the jeep shot forward and overturned, and the other vehicles behind them started to turn to try to get away. The tanks behind them opened up with their machine guns and main guns, firing indiscriminately, forcing 4 Grenadiers to go as low as they could in their trenches. 9 Horse's HE shells and machine-gun fire added to the chaos. A shocked and dazed Bashir, miraculously unhurt, had crawled out of the jeep and disappeared into the nearby sugarcane field.

Shaken, the remaining jeeps and tanks withdrew to Milestone 38. Lieutenant Colonel Ghulam Hussain, commanding 3 (SP) Field Regiment asked the artillery division to lay down a concentrated barrage on the Indian positions while Naib Risaldar Khali-ur Rehman was ordered to rush forward with a full squadron of 24 Cavalry tanks and try and recover the two brigadiers.

The relentless shelling meant no one from 4 Grenadiers had as yet approached the wreckage of the jeep. Soon the rumble of armour could be heard and Pakistani tanks came down the road, firing at everything on their starboard side. Vaid and his men, still huddled in their defences, thought the final Pakistani attack had come. However, much to their surprise, the tanks stopped near the destroyed jeep and, over the din of the gunfire, the Grenadiers could hear a voice shouting, 'General saab, aap kidhar ho?'[13] Then the entire Pakistani column started to withdraw. Unknown to the Indians, Brigadier Bashir had been recovered by the Pakistanis. Also unknown to them at the time, 5 Probyn's Horse, scheduled to launch its attack at 1700 hrs in conjunction with 24 Cavalry, had stood down its plans to capture Chima and Asal Uttar. 4 Mountain Division's defences had held.

Meanwhile, as the morning wore on, Pakistan's 4 Cavalry, egged on by Brigadier Lumb, had no option but to keep moving forward. After the initial contact with Charlie Squadron and Risaldar Aparbal Singh's troop at Maddar, the second squadron of 4 Cavalry turned and advanced towards the east of Lakhana, heading towards Mahmudpura. RHQ was forewarned by Narinder Sandhu about the move, so

Second Lieutenant Joshi, with his No. 2 Troop plus another two tanks, 'waited patiently along the Khem Karan Minor, well camouflaged with the bund of the minor giving their tank hulls protection.'[14]

'I could see approximately 10–12 tanks 2,000 yards away moving northeast towards Mahmudpura. I was sure I had not been detected; so I let them close in.' Salim Caleb's voice on the tank's radio was calm and reassuring, 'Hold fire till they are in certain killing range.' Joshi's gunner was champing at the bit, wanting to open fire immediately. 'I ordered all tank commanders to hold fire until I fired and to ensure all tanks were destroyed, I allocated the enemy tank targets to each of my tanks. The distance had by then closed to 1200 yards. The seconds ticked by…then Joshi gave his fire orders, "Sabot 800, on tank", the APDS rounds were in place… "on" said the gunner… "fire!"' Within a second, Joshi's gunner fired and he saw a flash through his binoculars, which indicated a hit. The operator, Sowar Dharampal Singh, who was also the loader, also saw the Patton being hit and he shouted 'Maara' over the radio.[15]

The three-round technique of the Centurion made it a formidable weapon. Between 1,200 and 600 yards, the flat trajectory of the anti-tank ammunition did not require a range estimation. The gunners had to set a mid-range and blast away, firing off three rounds in less than fifteen seconds. The months of training combined with this method of firing ensured a 90 per cent success rate.

All six Centurions were blazing away, picking up their targets one by one. In the next 15 to 20 minutes, nine Pattons were destroyed along with two RCL jeeps. Adding to the Pakistani discomfiture, the artillery guns opened up from the gun area. The OP officer of 1 Field Regiment (SP) was with Joshi on his tank, directing the fire. In the entire action, the Pakistanis could not get off even a single round in the direction of the Centurions.

The third squadron of 4 Cavalry had not come into contact with Charlie Squadron 3 Cavalry, but their alert commanding officer on the Lakhna rooftop was watching every move of the Pakistanis. Once again, he passed on information in real time about the direction of their movement and Surish Vadera's Alpha Squadron quickly readjusted its position north of Mahmudpura where it waited for the advancing column to come within range. Salim Caleb, once again cool and collected, came over the radio: 'Whoever remains cooler under stress for a longer time will win. Identify, take good aim and shoot. God be with you.'[16]

Naib Risaldar Jagdeo Singh's troop opened fire and soon three Pakistani tanks were destroyed. In the confined area, amidst the smoke and din of the raging battle, it was hard to tell friend from foe. For the Pakistanis, it was a hopeless situation and all they could hope for was the cover of darkness so they could try and regroup. In the fading light, Centurions from both Alpha and Charlie Squadrons continued to hit their targets. Finally, with visibility fading, Caleb ordered all tanks to open fire with their main and machine guns. With the artillery guns joining the party, Pakistani tank crews could be seen abandoning their tanks as they started to burn. Salim Caleb wanted to ensure he broke the remaining fighting spirit of the officers and men of 4 Cavalry. That evening, even though the tanks desperately needed replenishing, Caleb ordered all tanks to stay where they were. 'No one will change position or withdraw.'

Platoons from a company of 1 Dogra attached to 3 Cavalry made their way to the various squadrons to protect them where they were. As exhausted tank crews tried to catch some sleep, other supporting arms, using all forms of transport, both military and civilian, hauled in ammunition and fuel for the tanks that had been in action now for almost seventy-two hours. At the divisional, brigade, and regimental headquarters, no one quite realized the magnitude of what had happened. A Pakistani radio message that was intercepted—'Barra imam mara gaya' (the seniormost officer has been killed)—suggested that the GOC of 1 Armoured Division, Major General Naseer Ahmed, had been killed. For the men at the bottom of their trenches and by the side of their tanks, that was unimportant. They desperately needed to get some sleep before the guns started booming again. As the day had unfolded, three Indian Army units—4 Grenadiers, 9 Deccan Horse, and 3 Cavalry—plus the artillery guns of 4 Artillery Brigade, would put in a combined performance that any combat group would have been proud of. Because of the close area in which the battles were fought, very often the same target was engaged by the infantry, the gunners, and the armour, which was but natural as each would record the battle from their own perspective.

THREE BATTLES THAT TURNED THE TIDE—DIAL/SANTPURA (10 SEPTEMBER)

His head stuck out of the tank's cupola, Captain Naginder Singh was in the lead, his troop speeding in a bid to get to Attari. The 60-km run was kicking up a lot of dust, and the tank crews were also scanning the skies in case the PAF came calling. Around this time, the other troops of Naginder's Charlie Squadron 3 Cavalry were sitting tight in their positions waiting for the Pattons of 4 Cavalry to come into their kill zone. Disappointed at having had to miss the anticipated action at Khem Karan, Naginder felt if indeed an armoured threat was developing in the direction of Amritsar, the presence of his few Centurions would help support the Sherman Vs of 14 Scinde Horse. Seeing the Centurions would scare the Pakistanis.

No one, however, had bothered to tell 15 Infantry Division about Naginder's move, and when they saw the dust kicked up by the Centurions, all the units assumed that Pakistani armour had broken through and was getting in behind them. Waves of apprehension started to sweep across the Indian units deployed inside Pakistan. To make matters worse, at 1000 hrs, Pakistan's heavy and super-heavy artillery opened up as a prelude to an attack on both 54 and 38 Brigade positions.

The Pakistani strike force—22 Brigade with 23 Cavalry in support—assaulted the Indian positions with the intention of driving 15 Infantry Division out of Pakistani territory. The 18 Baluch Group with one squadron of 23 Cavalry was to exert pressure on 38 Infantry Brigade while another infantry group with Bravo Squadron 23 Cavalry less two troops was to take on 54 Infantry Brigade frontally, from the direction of Lakhanke. The remaining two troops were to circle around Dial, clear the area between Mana village and the Pul Distributary, and take 15 Dogra, 13 Punjab, and 3 Jat from behind. Once the Mana gap was clear, the second squadron would make a dash for Gosal, Santpura, and the bridge over the UBDC on GT Road.

The 15 Dogra front trenches took the brunt of the initial shelling. Their CO, who should have been removed from command on the very first day, continued to be a bundle of nerves. 13 Punjab, holding the defences adjacent to them, was also in a similar predicament. 3 Jat was dug in directly behind 15 Dogra at Santpura while Alpha Squadron 14 Scinde Horse was behind them in the area of Dial Grove. As the shelling lifted, Lieutenant Colonel Inderjit Singh could see Pakistani armour advancing menacingly in an assault formation. Completely losing his composure, Inderjit Singh and one of his rear company commanders made a headlong dash for the only T-16 carrier that was positioned near his bunker. Desmond Hayde, who was witness to the unfolding scenario, would write later: 'To say that their departure from the scene of events was precipitate would be a masterly understatement.'[17]

The Pakistani tanks were almost on the 15 Dogra position, when the men, seeing two of their senior officers take to their heels, started to abandon their trenches. Junior officers and JCOs tried to hold the battalion together but the Dogras had been shelled heavily and they 'ran not as cowards but as men who were confused, they remained in their sections and platoons and when they passed through 3 Jat they halted, re-grouped and awaited further orders which were not long in the coming from an extremely irate Brigade Commander.'[18] Brigadier Kalha's own trench was adjacent to the 3 Jat position. He too had stood in disbelief as the L-16 carrier took off in a great hurry. For a moment, it had stopped near the brigade commander and a 'turbanless and dishevelled figure did a lot of shouting and then the carrier roared onwards, sped on its way by the choicest Punjabi invectives hurled by the brigadier.'[19]

Major Sam Doctor, having made it back to the regiment the previous day from Ahmednagar, had taken command of his old Alpha Squadron 14 Scinde Horse. However, he only had a troop of his own and another troop from Charlie Squadron that was under the command of Second Lieutenant Brijendra Singh, who was sitting with him in a grove where the camouflaged tanks were parked. Doctor was giving the junior officer advice on marriage-related subjects when the news came in that the forward positions of 15 Dogra were under attack by Pakistani armour.

There were no Indian defences in Mana village. Even as the men were starting up their combined strength of six tanks, the two officers could see the Pakistani threat developing. Doctor decided to set off towards the Pul Distributary in the Lakhanke–Mana area in a bid to outflank the new threat. Since Brijendra Singh was more familiar with the terrain, he offered to lead.

The ferocity of the attack and the breaking of the 15 Dogra line had created a momentum that carried the Pakistani tanks past the 3 Jat defences. Ahead of them, the six Indian tanks were racing to get into a position where they could take them on. Seeing a wet patch ahead of him, Brijendra Singh swung his three tanks to the right and made for a spot near Talaran where the Pul Distributary turned northwards. Coming a few hundred yards behind him, Doctor decided to skirt the wet patch from the left instead and, almost immediately, one of his tanks got bogged down.

Doctor ordered the tank commander over the radio to bail out and the two other tanks stopped to pick up the crew. By then the tanks had been seen by Risaldar Ghulam Ali's troop, who fired at them. Caught with his broadside exposed, the first round hit the rear of Doctor's tank, destroying the engine. So far everything seemed to be going Pakistan's way. However, Brijendra Singh's troop now reached their position and, looking over his left shoulder, Brijendra Singh could see the Pakistani tanks. His three tanks swung around and opened fire, their salvo destroyed two tanks including that of the Pakistani troop leader, Ghulam Ali, who was killed.

'As the Pakistanis frantically looked around trying to determine where the shots had come from, they came under fire from the last remaining 106 RCL gun of 3 Jat, the other section manned by Lance Naik Daryao Singh having been blown to bits by tank fire. "Ustad, dahine ki taraf se," (From the right, sir) Lance Naik Suraj Bhan called out. The barrel was already turned to the right arc, the sight taken at 400 yards on the sarkanda line and Lance Naik Sheo Narain watched [through his sight...as the tank got nearer and nearer]. It burst through the grass, Sheo Narain pressed the small wheel which lay under his hand, the recoilless gun went off with a big roar and the tank took on a very shot look.'[20]

The first RCL round hit the leading Pakistani Sherman and the HE set it on fire. The other tanks in the troop halted, unsure of where the RCL had fired from. The second tank hesitated momentarily and reversed into a clump of sarkanda when the second RCL round hit where it had been two seconds ago. Sheo Narain's third and last round hit the second Pakistani tank, after which Suraj Bhan and Sheo Narain were not looking anymore, having flattened themselves down in the dirt while streams of machine-gun rounds came in their direction.

Rattled by the loss of three (or four) tanks in a matter of minutes, the remaining troops lost their nerve. Brijendra Singh, having destroyed the two tanks, could see Doctor's tanks standing there, seemingly immobile. There was no response on the radio, so he held up his thumb to indicate he had hit the Pakistani tanks, which had stopped advancing. Just then one of the crew emerged from the cupola and, after dropping to the ground, collapsed near the tank. Brijendra Singh jumped down from his tank and sprinted towards Doctor's tank. There he asked the soldier on the ground 'Major saab kithe hain?' (Where is the Major?) Without waiting for an answer, he clambered up and looked inside and saw some movement in the gunner's seat, but just then the ammunition started exploding. The heat blast forced Brijendra backwards.[21]

Having suffered unexpected casualties, the Pakistanis had convinced themselves that there were far more Indian tanks in the area than they had expected. Reversing at top speed, all tactics forgotten, the surviving tanks stampeded through the 3 Jat defences from back to front. Fortunately for the Pakistanis, none of the battalion's rocket launchers worked, nor did any of the Molotov cocktails find their mark, though they added considerably to the unfolding drama. Pakistani infantry coming up to attack were now in the direct path of the retreating tanks.

Major Dilawar Khan, the squadron commander leading the frontal attack got hit. Hayde claims it was Brijendra Singh's tank that fired (Brijendra Singh did not claim this tank), but it may have been friendly fire or perhaps the last remaining tank that had been with Doctor. The Pakistani officer's brains were splattered inside the tank next to his horrified radio operator who, even as his tank slithered out of control down an embankment, screamed on air 'Dilawar down! Dilawar down!!' Meanwhile, one of the troop leaders had seen Brijendra Singh's troop continuing to fire. 'It looked like a lot of tanks to him and something had already played havoc with his squadron from along the line of the Pul Distributary. So he concluded that Indian armour was now racing to cut off the Pakistani tanks at the bridges over the Ichhogil Canal and let out a scream that was universally taken up. "Enemy regiments getting behind, make for the Ichhogil, make for the Ichhogil."'[22]

The forty-minute action was over as the attack evaporated. Brigadier Kalha, shepherding men from 15 Dogra back towards their trenches, found Desmond Hayde standing and looking at the retreating Pakistanis, the dead the luckier ones among the wounded and mutilated bodies.

'I can give you Dograi tonight...' said Hayde.

'No... not tonight. But certainly after a few nights,' replied Kalha.

Meanwhile, Inderjit Singh's T-16 had been intercepted by Major General Mohinder Singh at the divisional headquarters at Khasa, further down GT Road. 'Who are you and what has happened?' The colonel, wide-eyed with fear babbled that 54 Brigade had been overrun...the commander captured...CO 3 Jat killed, destroyed...massive tank attack, two armoured brigades at least followed by infantry, advancing towards Amritsar...coming right behind me...some Pakistanis saw that I was the CO; they tried to capture me. I wrestled and fought and got away; they fired and nearly killed me.[23]

Messages were flashed to 11 Corps HQ, but fortunately communication with 54 Brigade was re-established. The brigade major flashed a message: 'Attack by some enemy armour at 1000 hrs, 15 Dogra dislodged from its defences, CO absconding. Attack beaten off by Jats and own armour, situation restored, details follow.' GOC 15 Division read the signal and pointed at Inderjit Singh: 'Place him under close arrest.'

On the Pakistani side: 'Brijendra's looping actions had created a dread in the minds of Pakistani commanders that they would be cut off at the Ichhogil Canal. So in their explanations to justify why they had not "destroyed those Indians at Dial", they said they were counter-attacked by two Indian armoured regiments, which were leading the resumed Indian advance towards Lahore. They fought desperately, they claimed, knocked out 10 Indian tanks and halted the advance for the time being. In fact, it was revealed by the later capture of 16 Punjab *War Diary* that the Pakistanis had abandoned all their positions at the Ichhogil Canal and withdrawn to Lahore, to return shame-facedly on 11 September.'[24] Had Brigadier Kalha authorized it, Dograi would have been taken easily that evening. 15 Dogra's command was handed over to the second-in-command, Major A. R. Singh[25] while 13 Punjab was taken over by Lieutenant Colonel E. D. H. Nanawati.

The second Pakistani thrust, aimed at containing 38 Infantry Brigade, had met with greater success as 1 Jat and 6 Kumaon, deployed at Ranian–Kakkar, had been unable to withstand the heavy bombardment followed by a combined infantry and armour attack. With the Indians being pushed back to Lopoke, the Pakistanis seemed to be re-occupying their former defences on the right flank of 15 Infantry Division. The fighting in this sector, combined with the alarming initial reports coming in of the Pakistani attack against 54 Infantry Brigade, had left 11 Corps feeling extremely insecure. At that point of time, the battles were also raging in Khem Karan, and the army chief was at that very moment pressing his Western Army commander to cut his losses and withdraw to the Beas River in order to 'save the Indian Army'.

Amidst this confused and uncertain scenario, fate had yet another bizarre card to play. Shortly after the Pakistanis had withdrawn, the recce troop of 14 Scinde Horse picked up the dust trails of Naginder's Centurions that were reaching the 15 Division area. With no prior information about the movement of Indian tanks, Lieutenant Colonel Raghubir Singh thought it was an outflanking move by the Pakistanis. The regiment's communication system with GOC 15 Division was down, so Raghubir Singh sent a note with a runner saying he was ordering all tanks of 14 Scinde Horse to withdraw to the UBDC Canal where they were to deploy in a hull-down position. This defensive posture, where his tanks were concealed with just the turret and the gun showing, increased the chances of putting up a fight against the vastly superior tanks of the Pakistanis. As a result, 14 Scinde Horse was soon deployed in a heightened state of alert, facing the wrong way.

Dhillon had been pressing Western Command and Army HQ for more troops for the defence of Amritsar, which, with the withdrawal of 38 Infantry Brigade, was becoming even more precarious in his opinion. He had asked for the Centurions mainly because 8 Cavalry had been drawn further south for the battle of Khem Karan and he had let it be known that 14 Scinde Horse was apprehensive about facing the enemy Pattons and the M36B2 Tank Destroyers. By the evening, to counter the possibility of the Pakistanis getting behind 15 Infantry Division, 11 Corps had moved Brigadier Malhotra's 96 Brigade to plug the gap. 50 Parachute Brigade, commanded by Brigadier A. M. M. Nambiar, which was the army headquarters reserve and was being allotted to the corps, was asked to occupy the area vacated by Malhotra's brigade. To cover up for his own lapse, Jogi Dhillon, GOC 11 Corps, allowed Major General Mohinder Singh, GOC 15 Infantry Division, to sack Raghubir Singh.

THREE BATTLES THAT TURNED THE TIDE—BARKI (10 SEPTEMBER)

To the immediate north, in the 7 Infantry Division sector, 4 Sikh had spent a miserable day in the forward trenches battling not just the constant shelling but also severe thirst. By the evening, news was coming in that the Pakistanis had taken a severe hammering in Khem Karan to their immediate south but the magnitude of what had happened was not as yet clear.

As per Anant Singh's plan, Delta Company under Lieutenant Kamalji Singh was to marry up with a squadron of CIH at Mile 16 at 1900 hrs and then the tanks were to advance with full headlights on, using their main and secondary armament up to 400 yards short of Barki. Behind the tanks would be civilian trucks loaded with planks which were to help the armour get across the Barki Drain in case the small bridge was destroyed by the Pakistanis. The trucks too were to keep their lights on, so that the Pakistanis believed a much larger force was on its way as had been the case at DBN. Thereafter, Major Shamsher Singh Manhas's Alpha Company and Subedar Sadhu Singh's Charlie Company were to attack West and East Barki respectively at 2000 hrs, assisted by the tanks. Anant Singh's battalion headquarters and Bravo Company under Major Dalip Sidhu, which was earmarked as reserve, were to follow the lead companies. After the success of this phase, 16 Punjab was to pass through and capture the canal that was another 150 yards beyond Barki.

Much to the battalion's chagrin, as the clock ticked down towards 1700 hrs, there was no sign of the CIH tanks. Repeated frantic messages to HQ 65 Infantry Brigade yielded no response and, to make matters worse, the commander of 7 Artillery Brigade, Brigadier C. V. Advaney, appeared on the scene, stood atop a nearby tube well and started shouting at the top of his voice, 'Stop the attack—the targets have not been registered'.

Anant Singh faced a classic commander's dilemma at this stage. Should he postpone the attack or go ahead without the tanks and artillery support? Any hesitation on his part would have communicated itself to his troops. Even though it meant a complete change of strategy, he told his adjutant, Captain Surinder Sagar Duggal, to inform Brigade HQ that 4 Sikh was going ahead without artillery or armour support. Time and again, the junior leadership made up for the bungling of the higher headquarters.

In the meantime, the battery commander, Major (later Lieutenant Colonel) H. S. Sarao from 165 Field Regiment, suggested that the roof of a three-storey house was being used by the Pakistanis to control their fire and he directed the Indian guns to target it. Under his direction, the guns of 7 Artillery Brigade opened up. However, the Pakistanis, fully alert to the situation, kept up their own barrage that did not allow 9 Madras to move up and secure the firm base which was to be used by 16 Punjab.

Pakistan's 17 Punjab, under the command of Major Aziz Bhatti, was defending the objective. Bhatti had created an observation post for himself and his FOO, Captain Mahmood Anwar Sheikh from Pakistan's 24 Medium Regiment, on the roof of the three-storey building in Barki from where they could control the battle. After having accurately guessed where the fire was being directed from, the next day Sarao found a one inch to the mile 1964 edition Pakistan Survey Map, artillery task tables, maps marked with direction finders and targets, binoculars, a field telephone, and a US Army bayonet. A pool of blood on the roof suggested the counter bombardment had indeed caused a few casualties.

With Alpha Company on the left and Charlie Company on the right leading the advance, 4 Sikh stepped across the start line at 2000 hrs. Both the companies immediately came under effective automatic fire from the entire village front and various defences on the Ichhogil Canal. The Pakistanis illuminated the area with mortars and artillery, and their MMGs began to fire at the lead companies.

Barki straddled the Bhikkiwind–Lahore Road and while the majority of habitation was on the right side, the police station and a few houses were on the left. The Barki Drain ran from right to left, cutting across the road, with the Ichhogil Canal a little distance beyond the drain. Alpha and Charlie Companies were to clear the fortified right side, while, according to the original plan, the armour and Delta Company were to assault and capture the police station and neutralize the Pakistani defences on that side of the road and on the east bank of the Ichhogil.

At 2025 hrs, the two assaulting companies were 400 yards from the outskirts. The casualties were piling up but the CIH tanks had still not fetched up. Step by step, undeterred by the quantum of fire, the two companies closed in. Eventually, only 100 yards separated them from the objective—the proverbial last hundred yards which is the ultimate test of the infantry's skill and guts. Anant Singh and his band of officers and JCOs had fired up their men, who were determined to succeed. Just then, Shamsher Singh had a bullet go through his thigh, but he was in no mood to seek medical attention and continued to command his boys.

However, a well-sighted MMG and fire from different directions held up the advance. With casualties mounting, Alpha and Charlie Companies seemed to be losing their momentum and, for a while, it seemed impossible to tell which pillboxes the fire was coming from. Though bleeding profusely, Shamsher Singh was still very much in charge and called for mortar fire on the well-fortified Pakistani positions. Subedar Ajit Singh and his platoon had, in the meantime, zeroed in on the main MMG that was creating the maximum obstruction. Realizing that if they just stayed there more men would be killed, the JCO stood up and, roaring the Sikh battle cry, charged the pillbox. Despite being hit by a burst on his chest, he managed to lob a grenade, which wiped out the MMG post.

Moments like this so often galvanize everyone else into action and 4 Sikh was like a battalion possessed after that. There were others who sacrificed themselves as well and cleared further obstacles. As the Sikhs let out their blood-curdling war cry 'Bole So Nihal' the Pakistani soldiers were paralysed in their bunkers. Some came out with their hands raised in surrender while others started running from their pillboxes. House by house, pillbox by pillbox, Alpha Company cleared the northwestern portion of the village while Charlie Company tackled the northeastern side. At this point, Delta and Bravo Company following were told to advance and capture the police station on the other side of the road. The time then was 2110 hrs and the tanks had still not arrived at the scene of battle.

4 Sikh's next objective was to secure the eastern bank of the Ichhogil Canal that lay approximately 150 yards from the western edge of Barki, while 16 Punjab was to go through and secure the canal area on the other side of the road. For some time after the capture of Barki, no one seemed to know what was happening due to lack of coordination and the existing communication gaps. Two green Very lights at 2110 hrs fired by 4 Sikh's assaulting companies had signalled the capture of Barki, but in the absence of tanks, 16 Punjab's second phase assault was delayed. If anything, Pakistani artillery had taken the signal as a cue to intensify their firing. So intense was the shelling that the men were forced to go to ground and take positions in an irrigation channel close by. Duggal had had a part of his nose blown off, after which he found his batman lying on top of him as a shield, simply saying 'Sahibji, gola pehalan mere te digu' (The shell will land on me first).

At 2200 hrs, the CIH tanks appeared ahead on the road and started firing into Barki, not realizing it had already been captured. Pakistani artillery fire had been relentless and now casualties from friendly fire compounded the problem. Duggal and the signal officer, Lieutenant B. S. Chahal, sprinted up to the tanks to inform them not to engage the village and instead fire on the canal bank left of the road. 'With the hatches closed it was impossible to get to the tank commanders. Even banging with rifle butts proved to be of no avail. After about

30 minutes, a JCO popped his head out of the hatch. We [the two officers] grabbed hold of him and explained the battle situation. Even then it took him considerable time to obtain permission from his squadron commander to switch fire to the canal bank.'[26]

The leading CIH tank had reached close to the police station when an anti-tank mine went off, damaging the tank's track and effectively blocking the forward movement of other tanks. Lieutenant Colonel Joshi and his squadron commander, Major Tandon, jumped into a 4 Sikh RCL jeep and came up to the destroyed tank. After assessing the situation, the CO ordered the rest of the tanks to move left of the road. On the way back, the jeep with the officers blew up on a mine. Both officers succumbed to their injuries. It would later be discovered that the anti-tank mines that had been laid by the Pakistanis were, in fact, of Indian manufacture. 'Someone acting prematurely had despatched a load of anti-tank mines in a civilian hired truck to be laid after capture of the objective. The truck was either not escorted or was poorly briefed. No one stopped it. The poor civilian driver drove straight into the hands of the enemy, possibly a day before commencement of our attack. The Pakistanis made effective use of our gift against us.'[27]

4 Sikh's assault and successful capture of Barki was a relatively short affair, the actual assault lasting barely ninety minutes. Yet it was one of the most fiercely contested actions where a resolute and determined infantry not only assaulted and defeated a well-entrenched enemy, it also withstood an artillery barrage of an estimated 2,500 shells. In many ways, though CIH tanks were supposed to support the 4 Sikh attack, Barki also underlined the difference between the Indian and Pakistani approach to combat. When it came to offensive actions, Pakistani infantry preferred to hold back, relying on their armoured units, especially those equipped with the Pattons, to overrun the Indian defences. Even among the mechanized infantry, there seemed to be a tendency to wait for the tanks to destroy the enemy completely. Their biggest weapon, which also caused the maximum casualty among Indian troops, was the concentrated fire power of Pakistani artillery guns.

During this period, Major Bhatti was at the canal bank, covering the withdrawal of his heavy weapons and troops from their bunkers on the east bank. 'He was the last to get back across the canal. Once across, two of his wounded men were spotted on the east bank asking to be rescued. Bhatti once again went across in a raft and brought the men back.'[28]

The leadership at the ground level on both sides had been exceptional. Shamsher Singh Manhas agreed to be evacuated along with Duggal only after his immediate objective had been seized. 4 Sikh's JCOs were outstanding, leading by example. Even after capturing Barki, the Pakistani shelling had been relentless, but once the CIH tanks finally arrived, 16 Punjab had started to advance with them. Anant Singh then ordered Alpha Company to send a section under a JCO towards the Ichhogil Canal bank to secure a foothold there. However, an MMG positioned on the elevated west bank spotted the party and the JCO was killed on the spot.

Phase 2 of the attack finally got underway almost an hour after 4 Sikh had fired the green Very lights. As the tanks started moving through Barki village towards Ichhogil Canal, Pakistani artillery switched their fire from the village to the area between Barki and the Ichhogil Canal. Pakistani artillery was using immense amounts of illumination and air-burst ammunition, keeping in sync with American tactics and the large stocks of ammunition provided to them under the Military Aid Programme. Thousands of small arms rounds, tracers, flares, and artillery shells were brought to bear on the advancing Indian troops. At around 2330 hrs, the Pakistanis successfully blew the bridge. On the other side of the road, Alpha and Bravo Companies of 4 Sikh also moved up to the canal bank. At 2345 hrs, the firing from the Pakistani side abruptly stopped. The Battle of Barki was over. Major General Sibal's 7 Infantry Division had formally made it to the Ichhogil Canal.

THE DEAD AND THE LIVING (10/11 SEPTEMBER)

It couldn't have been worse for Pakistan in the Lahore/Khem Karan Sectors on 10 September. General Musa had watched his GOC 1 Armoured Division, Major General Naseer Ahmed, completely bungle the planned offensive that aimed at cutting off the Beas Bridge. For reasons he still didn't understand, the Pakistani attack aimed at recapturing territory on the GT Road axis had failed miserably when a squadron of 23 Cavalry had bolted from the battlefield, taking the Pakistani infantry back with it all the way to Lahore. And Barki had fallen just before midnight. However, in the Sialkot Sector, India's 1 Armoured Division had been strangely inactive after its initial advance on 8 September, but Musa knew it was a matter of time before it would get moving again; when that happened, he also knew it would be very difficult for his existing armoured units and troops there to check the Indian advance deeper into Pakistan.

The fighting at Barki had resulted in Pakistani posts further downstream on the Ichhogil Canal sending panicky messages to HQ 10 Division saying Indian armour was crossing over onto the west bank across the Hudiara–Ichhogil siphon. Without verifying the authenticity of the reports, 103 Brigade HQ situated on the Barki–Lahore Road at Pathanwala fell back to Lahore. On hearing the news, 12 Punjab had also pulled back from the western embankments opposite Barki shortly after the bridge was blown.

This had a cascading effect as 3 Armoured Brigade, which had been loaded onto trains and was moving to Sialkot after having withdrawn from the Khem Karan bridgehead, was stopped in Lahore itself. In addition, the few remaining elements of 22 Brigade still on the eastern side of the Ichhogil Canal were ordered to pull back to Lahore. Had Brigadier Kalha given Lieutenant Colonel Desmond Hayde the nod to attack Dograi that night, they would have found the place unoccupied.

On the Indian side, the reports of the day's events were making their way to various headquarters. In New Delhi, General Chaudhuri got the news that Indian Centurions had been in action almost through the entire day and the Pattons had suffered severe losses. He was also told that 4 Mountain Division and 9 Deccan Horse had held out. Chaudhuri's evening visit to Chavan resulted in the entry: 'COAS met in the evening briefing meeting. His visit to forward areas has done him quite good. He was more certain of himself.'[29]

Chapter 18

A BUFFALO IN A WALLOW
1 CORPS (PART II)

9 SEPTEMBER (BLOODY NOSE?)

After the battle around Gadgor the previous day, the Pakistanis had used the night to strengthen their defences considerably. Lieutenant General Bakhtiar Rana, the GOC of Pakistan's 1 Corps, had initially deployed a single battalion from 24 Brigade in prepared defences at Gadgor, primarily in a delaying role, while the rest of the brigade was dug in at Chawinda. Since 25 Cavalry had stopped the Indian armoured advance temporarily, he decided to give the operational responsibility of the area between the Aik and the Degh rivers to 6 Armoured Division, even though it was not as yet fully operational. However, it had been strengthened by the return of 11 Cavalry to the Sialkot Sector from Akhnoor after the Indians had expanded the conflict into the Punjab on 6 September.

24 Brigade with its headquarters at the Phillora crossroads was reinforced with 14 Baluch and it moved back into its planned defences at the crossroads and at Gadgor. The Baluchis had deployed a company each around Jahr, Josan Kotli, and Wachoke, while 3 FF, which had suffered heavily during the day, deployed its remaining troops on the Rurki Kalan–Saidanwala axis with one company at Saboki. 2 Punjab continued to hold the main defences of Gadgor, with a company on the Gadgor–Chobara track that was to the north of the town, another was deployed to the south while a third was at Kalewali, south of Phillora. Based on Pakistani maps and subsequent write-ups, it is now known that '1 Field Regiment SP was south of Kalewali with 25 Cavalry in leaguer east of it. 9 FF (mechanized/motorized) was deployed at Tharoh. A Squadron 31 TDU was at Gunna Kalan, A Squadron 33 TDU at Phillora, 10 Cavalry (Guides) at Badiana, 22 Cavalry west of Badiana. 14 FF south-west of Badiana and 11 Cavalry at Pasrur. The 1 Armoured Division's assessment of the enemy armour was not correct. There was no enemy armour in Zafarwal, only the battalion headquarters of 13 FF R&S with its D Company deployed forward in platoons. There was indeed a regiment plus along the Chobara-Phillora axis, 25 Cavalry Pattons and A Company 33 TDUs. However, there were three Patton and mixed regiments within forty-five minutes to one hour from Phillora....'[1]

After the fiasco on 8 September, India's 1 Armoured Division seemed to have no clear plan of action. At first light, Hodson Horse's Alpha Squadron had probed forward from the 'box' held by 1 Armoured Brigade in an attempt to draw out the Pakistani armour. Naseer Ahmed's 25 Cavalry had been in its battle position by 0400 hrs and watched the Centurions move towards Gadgor with the artillery engaging the Pakistani positions. However, there was no major engagement though Ahmed claimed three Indian tanks were destroyed. GOC 1 Corps, Lieutenant General Patrick Oscar Dunn, having left the entire conduct of armoured operations to his subordinate, GOC 1 Armoured Division, Rajinder 'Sparrow' Singh, had, in the meantime, ordered 35 Infantry Brigade under the command of Brigadier A. C. Cariappa to consolidate the terrain captured so it could become the firm base for further advance. Cariappa accordingly moved from Arina to the Cross Roads area. 116 Infantry Brigade, under command of Brigadier (later Major General) S. Y. Munshi, moved with two battalions from Pathankot to the general area around Ikhnal, while the third unit, with one squadron from 62 Cavalry, moved to Kangre, all moves being completed by 1200 hrs on 9 September despite repeated strikes by the PAF. Amazingly, even at this stage, the IAF was nowhere to be seen and the Sabres destroyed a number of administrative vehicles.

Also resuming its advance towards Kaloi at first light, 43 Lorried Infantry Brigade made slow progress. Lieutenant Colonel (later Commandant, BSF) B. M. Singh, commanding 62 Cavalry, was apprehensive about Pakistani anti-tank weapons being positioned en route and time was lost as 8 Garhwal Rifles supported by two squadrons of 62 Cavalry and 101 Field Regiment attacked in the Pairo Shian–Kotli Lala area, only to find no enemy present there. By 1400 hrs, Kaloi was finally occupied.

Consequent to the firm base at Sabzpir being consolidated, Major (later Lieutenant General) Hriday Kaul with a squadron of 2 Lancer's tanks was asked to move towards Kangre to link up with 5 Raj Rif. There were clear signs of the previous day's fighting—two Centurions, both casualties of air attacks, and the abandoned artillery guns with the ammunition vehicles were still smouldering.

By midday, the situation opposite the 1 Armoured Division box seemed to have settled down. Though the Pakistanis knew by then that they were up against a vastly superior force, they decided to launch an attack nevertheless. 25 Cavalry was asked to assault Chobara along with 2 Punjab and 3 FF. The moment the Pakistanis deployed and reached the Maranwali–Mandhiala line, Indian artillery and anti-tank weapons opened up, ensuring the attack could not get started. Through the day, the PAF launched four airstrikes against 1 Armoured Division. Though they failed to hit any tanks, they continued to inflict serious damage on soft vehicles. The absence of the IAF was beginning to affect the morale of the ground troops, prompting Sparrow to request Dunn to call for air support, especially over the next three days.

Meanwhile, Korla's 6 Mountain Division was tasked with securing various villages in the occupied area. In a series of minor operations, Thirkarwala, Jarwal, Khanor, Sangial, Joia, Dinga, Tikre, and Saidainial, were cleared by Eric Vas's 69 and Dharam Singh's 99 Mountain Brigades. As was their custom, the withdrawing Pakistan Army had armed a few local residents, who had been firing at the Indian troops. These pockets of resistance were rounded up, disarmed, and set free in Pakistani territory.

In the 26 Infantry Division Suchetgarh Sector, at Unche Wains–Niwe Wains, Sheoran's 162 Infantry Brigade and, at Bajragarhi, Luthra's 168 Infantry Brigade came under counter-attack from a strong Pakistani armoured group consisting of 20 Lancers, the 1 Corps Reconnaissance Regiment equipped with Chaffees, and 31 TDU which had Sherman IIs that were mounted with the 90 mm main gun. Concentrated artillery fire on the Indian positions preceded each attack but the Indians held their ground. Having got a fix on the Pakistani gun positions, the Tiger Division's 26 Artillery Brigade, commanded by Brigadier J. S. Punia, counter-bombarded the Pakistanis.

At 0920 hrs, HQ 1 Corps had told Sparrow that the Pakistani attack was developing to the immediate right of 1 Armoured Brigade's position and it may be an opportune moment for 1 Armoured Division to get behind the Pakistani attacking armour and destroy it. But Sparrow didn't think there was enough time to get his tanks across the Aik River and felt it was not feasible for his division to deplete its strength. 1 Armoured Brigade was out of radio communication with 17 Horse, who could hear the messages from the Brigade HQ but could not transmit messages back. Sparrow was of the opinion that he needed a much larger quantum of armour, as he still believed that he was being opposed by a much larger force.

By the morning of 9 September, it was known that 4 Mountain Division at Khem Karan was up against Pakistan's 1 Armoured Division. As per the assessment on the Indian side, this accounted for five of the seven known Patton regiments. With 18 Cavalry also having run into Pattons to the north around Sialkot, it was communicated to Sparrow he was up against just the one Patton regiment. This assessment was not entirely accurate and the major Pakistani attack on Khem Karan was yet to come.

Sparrow, with his star plates and formation flag in place, accompanied by Brigadier Om Prakash Malhotra[2], commander, 1 Artillery Brigade, proceeded on a reconnaissance between 'Rurki Khurd towards Rurki Kalan. This was the area between West Hasri Nullah and East Hasri Nullah and the area was covered with tall sugarcane and low paddy fields with maize that was 4 to 6 feet high. A number of villages dotted the area on high ground. The distance between the two nullahs seemed to increase after Chobara. If there was rain the terrain was likely to become soft and prove heavy going for a large body of tanks. The reconnaissance group came under observed artillery fire and occasional small arms fire but remained untouched....'[3]

Sparrow's objective was still Chawinda but he hoped to shift the direction of attack on Phillora from east of the Hasri Nullah to the west of the stream. This was easier said than done, because the previous day 17 Horse had not only found the going in the area difficult because of the sugarcane, the ground around Sabzkot had been relatively soft. Not too happy with his options in the corridor between the two streams, Sparrow felt he needed to reconnoitre the terrain further to the east before he took a call on his next line of action. This effectively meant his division and the Indian offensive in the Sialkot Sector would have to await further orders.

As the day drew to a close, HQ 1 Corps placed both 35 and 116 Brigades under the operational command of Sparrow.

10 SEPTEMBER (FRESH PLANS)

In Army HQ in New Delhi, the vice chief of the Indian Army, Lieutenant General Paramasiva Prabhakar Kumaramangalam,[4] walked into the Ops Room where officers were looking at maps, trying to stay abreast of the developments in the Sialkot Sector. It was obvious that the psychological impact of the fighting on 8 September had left its mark on the minds of the commanders in 1 Armoured Division who had overestimated the fighting potential of the Pakistanis. They had spent the last forty-eight hours waiting for a counter-attack that hadn't come. 'Have you ever seen a buffalo in the summer in a pond?' asked the General, 'It does not go forward. It does not go back. It just sits. That is what the Armoured Division is doing.'[5]

Sparrow would have been more than alive to the expectations from him. His two brigades having failed to capitalize on the element of surprise on 8 September, Sparrow needed to find ways to catch the now fully alert and dug-in Pakistani defenders off guard. Having spent the entire previous day and the earlier half of 10 September going over the ground, Sparrow had made up his mind to move 1 Armoured Brigade to the 43 Lorried Infantry Brigade area so that the armoured division could operate as a single entity. The route he chose had its pitfalls and Sparrow was banking on the fact that the Pakistanis would be taken by surprise. Brigadier Malhotra, though an artillery officer, had commanded the 37 Coorg Anti-Tank Regiment and, even more importantly, had been with Sparrow throughout the reconnaissance. He now prepared an elaborate fire programme, which included as a measure of deception, shelling Pakistani positions in the direction of Sabzpir as well.

While Sparrow was fine-tuning his divisional attack on Phillora for 11 September, Pakistan 1 Corps had divided the operational responsibility in the Sialkot Sector between 6 Armoured Division and 15 Infantry Division with effect from midnight 9/10 September. 6 Armoured Division was given the responsibility for the defence of the Gadgor–Phillora–Chawinda–Badiana–Pasrur area while 15 Infantry Division was made responsible for the defence of Sialkot and Jassar areas.

In his book *Defeat into Victory*, Field Marshal William Slim records that when the situation on the front lines was particularly bad, to keep up the morale of all concerned, he always told his staff, 'Well, things could always be worse!' On one such occasion, an officer looked at him and asked him, 'How?' Slim says he could have cheerfully murdered that fellow! 'Well, it could be raining' he had responded! Just before 1 Armoured Brigade was due to begin its move from the defensive box, there were a couple of short sharp showers. HQ 1 Armoured Brigade, in a blatant violation of radio protocol, sent a three-word signal to the divisional headquarters stating, 'It is raining!' The move, originally scheduled for 1700 hrs, was delayed and could only start after last light.

This delay proved to be providential. At 1800 hrs F-86 Sabres put in yet another attack, once again targeting infantry positions as the Centurions had not as yet started moving. The anti-aircraft guns of 29 Air Defence Regiment deployed at Sabzpir opened fire, and the ack-ack brought two of the Sabres down in full view of the troops. Having been strafed repeatedly, the men came out of their trenches and cheered wildly as the aircraft went down. Unfortunately, the IO of 5 Jat, Captain H. C. Gujral, who had moved up to liaison with 5/9 GR, was caught in the open and was decapitated. This brave officer had been awarded a VrC three years previously during the Chinese conflict.

Finally, as darkness began to envelop the plains of Punjab, 1 Artillery Brigade started bombarding the Pakistani positions around Gadgor and Sabzpir. While the troops of 35 Infantry Brigade and the Sherman crews of 2 Lancers watched from the firm base, the three Centurion regiments, the sound of their engines hidden by the gunfire, began to make their way towards Rurki Khurd where they were to harbour—16 Cavalry at Gat; 17 Horse (Poona) at Kaloi and 4 Horse (Hodson) at Kotli Lala. All three regiments were at their respective locations by midnight. 43 Lorried Infantry Brigade, leaving 8 Garhwal Rifles and two squadrons of 62 Cavalry at Gat, was also on the move by 2200 hrs. 5 Jat was leading the advance towards Rurki Kalan, but the rain had made the ground soft and slushy. RCL jeeps and F-Echelon vehicles were stuck in the mud and had to be repeatedly physically pulled out, making the progress painfully slow. 5/9 GR, in the meantime, also reached its designated concentration area at Libbe. 5 Raj Rif, with a squadron each from 62 Cavalry and 2 Lancers, was entrenched at Kangre. Once the three regiments were on their way, the gunners redeployed their guns in the area west of Sabzpir.

While the three Centurion regiments were on their way, news began to trickle in that the Battle of Khem Karan had been fought during the day and 4 Mountain Division had broken the back of Pakistan's 1 Armoured Division.

That the highly-vaunted Pattons had come a cropper against 9 Deccan Horse's Shermans and 3 Cavalry's Centurions had an electrifying effect across the rank and file. 4 Mountain Division had done its job. Now Sparrow's men knew they had to perform.

11 SEPTEMBER (THE BATTLE OF PHILLORA)

In the early hours of 11 September, as per the revised Pakistani deployment, Pakistan's 11 Cavalry commanded by Lieutenant Colonel Abdul Aziz Khan had moved out of its harbour area and deployed. Alpha Squadron was in the Saboki area moving to replace the depleted 25 Cavalry in Gadgor after 24 Brigade had been moved to Pasrur for rest and refit the previous evening; Bravo Squadron was deployed at Kotli Kadam Shah while Charlie Squadron was at Wachoke. Between Wachoke and Phillora, at the rest house, was the RHQ. 10 Cavalry (Guides) was deployed to the immediate east of Badiana, while 22 Cavalry was further to the west. In total, there was one Patton regiment in the immediate vicinity of Phillora, while three (including 25 Cavalry) were close enough to move into Phillora within an hour.

An intense pre-dawn bombardment of Rurki Kalan marked the beginning of the battle for Phillora. 5 Jat and 5/9 GR were the vanguard of 43 Lorried Infantry Brigade. 5 Jat was commanded by Lieutenant Colonel (later Colonel) Raj Singh and it had been ordered to capture Rurki Kalan after which it was to deploy around Nathupur. The battalion began to move forward at 0630 hrs. Charlie Company under Lieutenant G. S. Kahlon was in the lead, followed by Delta Company under Lieutenant R. K. Mazumdar. Raj Singh's Battalion HQ was followed by Alpha and Bravo Companies under Captains M. P. Singh and B. K. Das respectively. Almost immediately, the first PAF air strike of the day engaged the battalion. Once the Sabres had expended their ammunition and flown away, Pakistani artillery firing air bursts opened up. Despite severe casualties that included five killed, 5 Jat resolutely carried on and cleared Rurki Kalan which was to be the new designated firm base for the capture of Phillora. 5 Jat then deployed its companies in the area between Kotli Bagga and Nathupur.

5/9 GR was under the command of Lieutenant Colonel B. S. Grewal and was given the responsibility of capturing Libbe, which was to the right of Nathupur. Major A. K. Bagchi, the Bravo Company commander, was also the battalion's second-in-command.

At first light, the three Centurion regiments had also begun their simultaneous advance, moving from north to south. Lieutenant Colonel Madan Bakshi's 4 Horse with its three squadrons was on the left, moving on the Rurki Kalan–Saboki and Rurki Kalan–Wachoke axes; Adi Tarapore's 17 Horse, also with three squadrons, was moving on the Ingan–Kotli Bagga–Libbe thrust line; while Sidhu-Brar's 16 Light Cavalry was on the right flank following the Kandal–Chahr–Khakhanwali bearing. Major Ravindran was commanding the amalgamated Alpha and Bravo Squadrons, while Squadron Leader Avinash Khanna brought up the rear with the as yet untested Charlie Squadron. Behind the leading squadron of each advancing regiment were the tanks that made up the RHQ. Behind 17 Horse came K. K. Singh's brigade headquarters and behind him, Sparrow's divisional headquarters, both accompanied by their respective communication set-ups.

Sparrow was determined to move all three regiments together, since on 8 September the leading tanks of Bravo Squadron 16 Cavalry had not only run ahead of 17 Horse, but had also lost touch with Khanna's Charlie Squadron. Meeting no opposition en route, by 0730 hrs, Ravindran was at the Y-junction at Khakhanwali where he deployed his squadron covering the western approaches from Sialkot and Badiana. Khanna's Charlie Squadron also deployed in the Chahr area, which allowed him to keep an eye on the Seaol–Pagowal (Bhagowal in Pakistani maps)–Haral axis. Having seen the dust thrown up by 16 Cavalry, Pakistan's 10 Cavalry (Guides) along with the RCL guns immediately moved from their location at Badiana and deployed south of the Chawinda–Sialkot railway line. Ravindran's squadron and the Pakistani armour then got into a long-range firefight which would continue over the next few hours with neither side achieving anything of note. However, the immediate objective of 16 Cavalry had been achieved as they had secured the left flank for the advancing 1 Armoured Brigade.

4 Horse had advanced with 5 Jat towards Rurki Kalan, its Charlie Squadron commanded by Major C. D. Urs helping the Jats occupy the new firm base. The air attack and the subsequent shelling had little effect on the moving armour, though Urs was hit in the face by a splinter. He refused to be evacuated and subsequently lost an eye. Alpha Squadron, which was being commanded by Major M. V. Raju since Major Dhillon had been seriously wounded the previous day, skirted Rurki Kalan from the east while Bravo Squadron under Major Bhupinder Singh went past from the west. Both Alpha and Bravo Squadrons successfully reached their objectives and blocked the Gadgor–Phillora track in the Saboki area and Wachoke respectively.

In the centre, flanked by 4 Horse and 16 Cavalry, Major Verinder Singh's Charlie Squadron 17 Horse with a total of twelve tanks was making good progress. It was ordered to halt just short of Libbe as 5 Jat and 4 Horse had still not cleared Rurki Kalan, the air strike and artillery fire having delayed the schedule. For an hour, 17 Horse sat it out, until it was given the green signal to resume the advance at 0815 hrs. Within minutes, as Verinder Singh's troops reached the Libbe–Nathupur–Saboke line, Charlie Squadron was the first to come under fire, the M36B2 90 mm Tank Destroyers opening up from their hidden positions within the sugarcane from 300 yards. The M36B2 combined the hull of the M10 Tank Destroyer with the Sherman's reliable chassis. It was armed with a massive turret mounting that carried the 90 mm gun M3. In the US Army, tank destroyers were designed to destroy armoured thrusts. During the Korean War, they had been extremely effective against any of the Soviet-designed tanks.

Captain Ajai Singh,[6] Charlie Squadron's second-in-command, was in the centre of the box formation. The leading two troops immediately returned fire and within a few minutes three Pakistani Tank Destroyers had been hit and were on fire. One Centurion under the command of Daffadar Salok Singh had taken a hit, but only the gun barrel and elevating gear had been damaged. As the other two troops of 17 Horse positioned themselves to engage the Pakistani armour, Major Cheema swung his Bravo Squadron to the right and joined what was fast becoming a gruelling tank battle.

Around this time, as the 4 Horse Centurions went past Rurki Kalan, the three tanks that made up the RHQ missed a turning and got separated from the two advancing squadrons. Continuing southwards, the adjutant, Captain (later Brigadier) Jitendra Pal 'J. P.' Singh, also got left behind. The remaining two tanks of Madan Bakshi and the second-in-command, Major K. L. Duggal, then ran smack into the Pattons that were covering the left flank of Phillora near Libbe. In the brief exchange of fire, Madan Bakshi destroyed three Pattons and Duggal hit one, after which he disengaged and headed east to follow Bravo Squadron. Bakshi was not so lucky, for his tank was hit at least twice, setting it on fire. Bailing out with his crew, the commandant of 4 Horse spent the next eight hours hiding in the sugarcane fields until he was picked up by 17 Horse in the evening.

J. P. Singh, trailing behind the two tanks, saw his CO's tank on fire and as he could not raise Duggal on the radio, asked Bhupinder Singh to assume command of 4 Horse. By then, Raju's Alpha Squadron was astride the Gadgor–Phillora track. Pakistan's 11 Cavalry's Alpha Squadron, which had replaced Naseer Ahmed's 25 Cavalry at Gadgor, was in the process of scrambling back towards Phillora. Eight Pattons, four RCL jeeps, and five MMG-mounted jeeps were soon destroyed. 'One of the jeeps belonged to Captain Raza, commanding 11 Cavalry Reccee Troop. Much needed maps were also found from the vehicles.'[7]

Bhupinder's Bravo Squadron reached the Wachoke area where Charlie Squadron of 11 Cavalry was waiting. Using fire and move tactics, Bhupinder skilfully manoeuvred his troops to draw out the Pakistani Pattons that were hidden in the tall sugarcane. Urs having been evacuated after Charlie Squadron had secured Rurki Kalan, the command had passed on to Lieutenant Sonny Nehra. Hearing the firefight develop ahead of him, Nehra moved up with his squadron and deployed on the right of Bhupinder's squadron. All three squadrons of 4 Horse were now positioned in line and the combined firepower of the Centurions was playing havoc with both Alpha and Charlie Squadrons of 11 Cavalry. As the Pattons tried to withdraw towards Phillora and Chawinda, 4 Horse's gunnery skills came into play. 'It was easier to shoot down moving tanks and in the ensuing encounter Pakistan lost twenty-three tanks while 4 Horse lost only one. Amongst others, Pakistan lost commanding officer 1 Field Regiment (SP) who was killed while commanding officer and second-in-command of 11 Cavalry were wounded when an artillery shell burst in their midst. 9 FF had been routed and fell back to Chawinda in driblets.[8]

Focussed on the fighting in front of them, the Centurion crews heard the by now familiar sound of approaching fighters once again. To their utter surprise and delight, the aircraft came in low and opened fire with their cannons and rockets, strafing the Pakistani positions. A huge sigh of relief went up—the IAF had finally arrived and their fireworks were adding to the discomfiture of the Pakistanis. Bravo Squadron of 11 Cavalry, which had been lying low, trying to conceal itself, now began to move, manoeuvring from the south of Phillora towards Kotli Khadim Shah on the Phillora–Bhagowal track. However, Verinder Singh's Charlie Squadron 17 Horse, having lost five Centurions but having destroyed six M36B2s, had already redeployed there and the Pakistanis found their exit route cut off in this direction as well.

With his armoured brigade in contact with what he believed were two Patton regiments, Sparrow decided to push the two squadrons of 62 Cavalry along with 8 Garhwal forward from Kaloi as well. Though the Sherman Mk IV tanks were decidedly inferior to the Pattons, Sparrow wanted 'to keep his thrust line west of 1 Armoured Brigade going. The task given by the GOC to B. M. Singh[9] was, "To secure the important Cross Roads (Area South West of Bhagowal) so as to protect the West flank of 1 Armoured Brigade attack on Phillora."'[10]

Under the circumstances, it was reasonable for Sparrow to assume that most of the Pakistani Pattons would be committed against 1 Armoured Brigade. Accordingly, 62 Cavalry had started to advance along the Kaloi–Haral–Bhagowal track. Getting past Haral at 1110 hrs, the column skirted Bhagowal and was within 1,500 yards of the crossroads when it was engaged by two troops of Pattons hidden in a grove. The Shermans fired back, resulting in the withdrawal of the Pattons behind Bhagowal. Pakistani artillery fire then engaged 62 Cavalry, which deployed its Bravo Squadron commanded by Major (later Major General) Kanwar Maharaj Kumar Singh Barach to the southwest of Haral.

As per the original plan, by 1015 hrs, 43 Lorried Infantry Brigade was ready to launch its assault on Phillora with 5 Jat from Nathupur and 5/9 GR who had also firmed up at Libbe. However, since the armoured clashes were still continuing, K. K. Singh sent a message to HQ 1 Armoured Division, saying that the attack should not be launched until HQ 1 Armoured Brigade gave it the green signal.

The tank battles had continued through the morning, well past mid-day. 4 Horse having severely mauled and then outflanked them to the east, the surviving Pakistani Pattons and M36B2 Tank Destroyers had pulled back and concentrated south of Khakanwali–Phillora. The Jats had been witness to most of the fighting up close, as the tanks from both sides had grappled with each other. In the ensuing confusion, two Pattons had strayed close to the Charlie Company position. Sepoy Sukhbir Singh had crawled up to one of the Pattons and lobbed a grenade into its cupola. The crew was killed and the tank had started to burn, but Sukhbir Singh was also killed before he could return to the safety of his comrades. Sukhbir was subsequently Mentioned in Despatches.

THE CHARGE OF THE GUIDES (BATTLE OF PHILLORA)

Before the guns opened up in the morning, Pakistan's GOC 6 Armoured Division, Major General Abrar Hussain, had reason to feel satisfied. An infantry officer from the Baluch Regiment, he had played a major role in the induction of US equipment into the Pakistan Army. In 1964, promoted to the rank of major general, he had been tasked with converting the 100 (Independent) Armoured Brigade into 6 Armoured Division. With just two armoured regiments and an infantry battalion, he did not even have an integrated brigade headquarters in his division. Furthermore, between him and the GOC 1 Corps in the chain of command, was an armour adviser, the RIMC-educated Major General Sahabzada Yaqub Ali Khan[11], the chief architect of the Pakistani defensive-offensive philosophy. Though Abrar Hussain had two fresh regiments by 11 September—10 Cavalry (Guides) southwest of Badiana and 22 Cavalry west of Badiana, 25 Cavalry that had moved from the defensive position at Gadgor to Pasrur also became part of his command.

Sparrow's tactics had caught the Pakistanis off-balance and with 11 Cavalry suffering heavily at the hands of 4 Hodson's Horse in the early stages of the battle, the situation was extremely grim. The quantum of the attacking forces was as yet not known, and even though some 10 Guides Cavalry tanks were in a shooting match with 16 Light Cavalry since 0730 hrs, at 1045 hrs, Abrar Hussain ordered Lieutenant Colonel (later Brigadier) Amir Gulistan Janjua to launch a counter-attack against the Indian western flank.

Within forty-five minutes of receiving his orders, Janjua lined up his two remaining Alpha and Charlie Squadrons at Baba Bhureshah and the area around the level crossing on the Badiana–Bhagowal road. Alpha Squadron was to attack north-eastwards with Chahr as its objective, while Bravo Squadron was to overrun Libbe. Charlie Squadron, equipped with the M36B2s, was to move to Kot Izzat and cover the withdrawal of 1 (SP) Field, 31 Field, and 8 Medium Regiments all of whom were in danger of being overrun by Indian armour. Giving his final orders over the wireless, the Pattons of Alpha and Bravo Squadrons then lined up along the railway line. At 1130 hrs, in a scene anachronistically reminiscent of a cavalry charge, Janjua gave the one-word order: 'Charge!'

Brave and spectacular as it was, under the circumstances, the Pakistani armour was committing hara-kiri. In the fighting so far, in the entire Punjab Sector, whenever armour had come up against armour, it had been a slugfest. The terrain, mainly due to the sugarcane crop, made it a cat-and-mouse game where troops and squadrons tried to outflank each other and destroy the other with superior gunnery. The Indian advance had moved forward extremely cautiously, its commanders obsessed with protecting their flanks. Pakistan had paid the price of being overconfident in offence at Khem Karan just the previous day. 10 Cavalry Guides was now committing the same mistake.

Thundering forward from the direction of Rakh Bhure Shah–Changrian, the Pattons were an awe-inspiring sight. Ravindran's Bravo Squadron 16 Light Cavalry had been at Khanawali trading gunfire with the Guides for the last four hours, but most of it had been at long range and more or less ineffective. During the charge, the Pattons succeeded in hitting three Centurions but lost six Pattons. Major Avinash Khanna's Charlie Squadron was deployed widely around Chahr and had still not been in contact with Pakistani armour. Khanna also did not have any RCL guns supporting his position. Alpha Squadron of 10 Cavalry Guides came at them full speed, resulting in what Pakistani commentators called a 'drubbing' but they also admit that a fierce tank versus tank battle ensued for over an hour. Charlie Squadron 16 Cavalry did, however, destroy at least two Patton tanks during this period. 10 Cavalry Guides Pattons did get to Chahr and 16 Cavalry's Charlie Squadron fell back, as is evident from the fact that later in the evening 'a squadron of 16 Cavalry with Sidhu and Avinash Khanna in the leading tank approached 62 Cavalry area. They said they were lost and looking for their regiment. Sidhu was removed from the command of 16 Cavalry.'[12]

Khanawali was the dividing line between 16 Cavalry and 17 Poona Horse, which was holding the Khanawali–Gil frontage to the west of Libbe. Bravo Squadron 10 Cavalry Guides commanded by Major Ziauddin Abbasi apart from engaging Ravindran's Centurions, also ran straight into 17 Poona Horse, which was ideally positioned to take on the Pattons. While Bravo Squadron immediately engaged the Guides, Alpha Squadron moved up two troops to protect the left flank. Just then, two troops of M36B2 Tank Destroyers appeared on Charlie Squadron's flank. Adi Tarapore, taken by surprise, ordered Verinder Singh to pull back from Khanawali but since that would have placed a company of 5/9 GR located there at the mercy of the Pakistani tanks, the squadron commander refused. Instead, he turned his Centurions to meet the new threat. 'The ground was open and the only cover was provided by sugarcane fields, hence maximum security was provided by movement, the enemy was continuously engaged and the Centurion 20-pounder gun, stabilized for traverse and elevation did considerable execution. Adi Tarapore also destroyed two enemy tanks. The battle lasted forty-five minutes until whatever was left of the enemy withdrew.'[13] Abbasi and his second-in-command, Lieutenant Hussain Shah, were both killed while on the Indian side Second Lieutenant V. Swarup was wounded. There was only minor damage suffered by a Centurion in this engagement.

CAPTURE OF PHILLORA

Finally, the green signal was given for the advance on Phillora. 5 Jat and 5/9 GR moved to the left and right of the Libbe–Phillora track with Charlie Squadron 17 Horse, down to just seven Centurions, providing flank protection. At 1240 hrs, five Pattons opened fire at 800 yards. The Centurions immediately returned fire, setting three Pattons on fire while a fourth was abandoned by its crew, its engine running and gun loaded. 5/9 GR's Charlie Company under Captain M. Dutta was quick to pounce on the tank. Wachoke was cleared en route. As small arms fire was coming from Khanawali, Grewal mistook it for Phillora and ordered 5/9 GR's Delta Company under Major Ram Prakash Bassi along with Charlie Company to clear it. Wading through waist-deep water, the Gorkhas came under intense fire and two men were killed, two were wounded, and one man went missing. While his two companies were still grappling with Khanawali, Grewal ordered Bagchi to continue advancing with 5 Jat towards the crossroads while he, with Alpha Company, moved to capture a position to the southwest of the crossroads.

Short of the crossroads, the rest house that had been the RHQ of Pakistan's 6 Armoured Division and other formations including 24 Brigade and 11 Cavalry had been abandoned in a great hurry. There were 'maps and other documents, including signal diagrams, authentication sheets, slide equipment, and the telephone exchange captured from the rest house at Phillora…. [O]ther equipment captured included one radio relay station, one engine for lighting, one charging set, six jeeps, one truck one ton, two lorries 5 ton loaded with ammunition and eight trailers loaded with officers' kit. The enemy had obviously been surprised by the sudden appearance of Gorkhas and left in a hurry.'[14]

By this time, both Bravo and Alpha Squadrons of 17 Horse had married up with the advancing column, with the latter moving on the Gil–Kotli Jandran axis. In a grove just beyond Khanawali, Pakistani tanks were lying in wait and they succeeded in destroying a Centurion. In the firefight that followed, Adi Tarapore was hit in the arm by a shell splinter, but he refused to be evacuated. A short while later, when more Pattons appeared, Tarapore destroyed two of them. Resuming the advance, as 5 Jat reached Phillora, it was subjected to a severe dose of artillery fire. For a while it looked like the battalion was going to wilt under the intensity of the shelling. However, Sparrow himself had moved up and he egged the troops on, who then resolutely went through Phillora. Finally, at 1530 hours, the two infantry battalions reached the Phillora–Sabzpir track junction.

Though 43 Lorried Infantry Brigade and 1 Armoured Brigade had reached their immediate objective, 62 Cavalry's Shermans on the extreme western flank of the division now had to deal with Pakistani Pattons that were continuing to probe, looking for any weaknesses that could be exploited.

At the crossroads, 5/9 GR and 5 Jat were digging in, expecting the Pakistanis to launch a counter-attack. Pakistan's 24 Brigade had moved back to Chawinda and three companies of 14 Baluch had occupied the prepared defences at Wazirwali, Kalewali, and Ballowali, the three northern approaches to the town. 2 Punjab and 3 FF were dug in, defending the western and southern approaches. 25 Cavalry, down to twenty tanks comprising two squadrons had also reached Chawinda. The 24 Brigade Pakistani gun positions were around Matteke.

Though 11 Cavalry had been severely mauled, the 10 Cavalry Guides' surviving tanks were still a threat to the two squadrons of 62 Cavalry that had been deployed on either side of Haral. Ever since their brief encounter with Pattons in the grove near Bhagowal, there had been no activity in their area. At 1600 hours, Major Barach reported the movement of armour from the southeast of Bhagowal. Worried that the Pattons were trying to outflank the regiment, Alpha Squadron and the RHQ of 62 Cavalry fell back on the 8 Garhwal defences at Gat. Sparrow was in constant touch with 62 Cavalry, and on being told that the regiment was being outflanked, he immediately despatched his command troop under Captain K. P. S. Sidhu to reinforce Barach's Shermans which were still holding their ground east of Haral.

Barach asked Sparrow for permission to engage the Pattons, but Sparrow asked him not to open fire as 16 Cavalry Centurions were still in the area. At 1630 hours, B. M. Singh had withdrawn further to Kaloi and he again reported that Bravo Squadron was being outflanked and requested permission to pull them back. Sparrow told him that regardless of what happened, 62 Cavalry was to hold its position, even if it meant being 'decimated to the last tank'.[15]

The Pattons, the remnants of Alpha and Bravo Squadrons' 10 Cavalry Guides, continued to close the gap with Barach. His crews pleading with him to open fire, he gave the order when the Pattons were still 1,000 yards from the Shermans. Two Pattons were hit in the opening salvo and caught fire. In the ensuing firefight, the fire power of the Pattons destroyed five Shermans. A chastened Lieutenant Colonel Janjua, having been mauled by 17 Poona Horse a short while ago, decided not to press home the attack. The presence of Sidhu's Centurions, which had by then deployed west of Barach's position, may have also created doubt in Janjua's mind. B. M. Singh asked Barach to fall back on Kaloi, but Bravo Squadron 62 Cavalry only pulled back to Gat where it harboured for the night. Sparrow's gamble to protect his flank had worked, though it cost five Shermans.

Back at the crossroads, the Jats and the Gorkhas were being regularly engaged by the Pakistanis. Sporadic machine-gun fire had wounded five men from 5/9 GR before the battalion's 2-inch mortars silenced it. At 1700 hours, a 5 Jat patrol reported that the Pakistanis were building up for a counter-attack. Das's Bravo Company quickly moved forward and the attack was foiled. However, in the exchange of fire, the company lost both its forward platoon commanders, Naib Subedars Ram Kishan and Hanuwant Singh. Shortly thereafter, at last light, the CO of 9 FF, Lieutenant Colonel Abdul Majid, having left his men at Gadgor to fend for themselves, blundered into the Indian position. Both sides were taken by surprise as 43 Lorried Infantry Brigade had not been informed that there were Pakistani soldiers in Gadgor. 17 Horse and 4 Horse were beginning to pull into harbour when Alpha Company 5 Jat saw a group of three jeeps and five tanks come down the road. Subedar Mukhtiar Singh stopped the leading vehicle and both sides simultaneously realized they were talking to the enemy. Abdul Majid managed to push the startled JCO aside and dashed off into the sugarcane, while the Pattons, probably from 25 Cavalry sent to extricate 9 FF, began firing indiscriminately in all directions in a desperate bid to get away.

With Pakistani armour in the vicinity and the threat of counter-attacks, Major Verinder Singh's Charlie Squadron 17 Horse remained deployed after dark on the Phillora–Chawinda track. At 2015 hours, five Pattons of 25 Cavalry came down from the direction of Gadgor. 17 Horse and the artillery guns immediately engaged these tanks, forcing them to withdraw in the direction of Chawinda, leaving behind one Patton that was claimed by 17 Horse.

Finally, at around 2115 hours, in what was to be the last act of the day, three machine-gun mounted jeeps followed by a few trucks loaded with 9 FF soldiers and some other vehicles came down the road. 5 Jat was fully alert by then and the column was halted as it came under fire from the Indians. Two of Verinder Singh's tanks quickly got into action and started shooting up the vehicles but the Pakistani soldiers had debussed by then and opened fire with all their weapons. For the next hour, it was a free-for-all. At one stage, the Pakistanis seemed to have identified Lieutenant Colonel Raj Singh and they tried to overpower the CO and his protection party. Lieutenant R. K. Mazumdar and a few others quickly went to their CO's rescue and, after hand-to-hand fighting, succeeded in freeing Raj Singh.

The Pakistanis had disintegrated by this point and escaped into the sugarcane fields. They left behind eighteen dead and sixty wounded and three were taken prisoner. The Jats had lost four men, while Lieutenant R. D. Sharma, Subedar Richpal Singh, and ten others were wounded. It was then that they realized that Mazumdar was missing. A week later, on 19 September, a patrol from 5 Jat would find his body tied to a tree in the Josun area. His hands and feet had been bound by rope, his eyes had been gouged out, and his body was covered with bayonet wounds. It was a sad end for the popular young officer.

Phillora had been captured. In fact, the Pakistanis had given up without a fight, abandoning it even as 5/9 GR and 5 Jat reached the rest house. An upbeat General Sparrow sent a signal to HQ 1 Corps for onward transmission to the GOC-in-C Western Army command: 'Personal from GOC to Higher Tiger. Phillora captured 1530 hours. Large number of tanks equipment destroyed and some captured intact. Ask for anything more and it will be delivered by the Black Elephant. Request Higher Tiger to convey this message to the founder of the Black Elephant. Our sabre is still sharp.'[16]

The 'Black Elephant' was the formation sign of 1 Armoured Division and the founder was the COAS, General Chaudhuri, who had been the first Indian GOC of the formation. Higher Tiger, of course, was Harbakhsh himself. Sparrow had good reason to feel upbeat, for his three Centurion regiments had got the better of at least two Patton regiments, which, in his appreciation, was the quantum of Pakistani armour lined up against him. At the time of sending the signal, 62 Cavalry had not yet sent the first of its messages to Sparrow saying Pattons were closing in on their position, nor had 25 Cavalry tanks appeared at the crossroads against 5 Jat.

The Battle of Phillora was remarkable mainly because the Indian armour, despite being the attacking party, had inflicted grievous tank losses on the enemy. Harbakhsh Singh's later estimate put Pakistani Patton and 'Tank Buster' M36B2 losses at around fifty, of which half were physically verified on the ground. He also claimed six Centurions had been lost along with five Shermans. The official Indian record puts the figure even higher: 'As many as 67 enemy tanks were destroyed/ damaged on this day for Indian loss of only six Centurions. This was mainly due to the skillful manoeuver of tanks and gallant leadership of commanders in action. Because of the heavy concentration of armour in this battle, it was considered to be the biggest tank battle since World War II.'[17]

'An accurate assessment of enemy tanks destroyed in a fluid tank versus tank battle is difficult. This is due to multiple engagements, restricted visibility in close terrain of high crops, engagement of tanks already disabled or abandoned, counting merely flashes as "kills"; also as night falls, recovery teams work throughout the night to bring in disabled and damaged tanks so that they can be repaired and brought into line. As of old, the side that holds the battlefield is considered the victor of the spoils of battle and finds it easier to recover its damaged equipment; the Indian 1 Armoured Division held the battlefield at Phillora on 11 September 1965.'[18]

General Sparrow's message to the army chief and the army commander on the afternoon of 11 September is indicative of the pressure on him. Though 4 Hodson's Horse and 17 Poona Horse along with the rest of 1 Armoured Division had performed extremely well and got to their objectives, the reality was that the Indians had not even reached the objectives they had set for themselves on 8 September. The biggest gain was that Pakistan 'had started the war with a cocky confidence in the superiority of the Patton tanks over the tanks in the Indian Army. The destruction of 4 Cavalry on 10 September in the Khem Karan Battle and the loss of 11 Cavalry in the Battle of Phillora on 11 September must have unnerved Pak armour commanders and their High Command.'[19]

SIDE SHOWS AT ZAFARWAL & PAGOWAL

The Indians were not only sitting astride Phillora, 11 Cavalry and 9 FF had been decimated and Chawinda was within Sparrow's grasp. Pakistan's GHQ and GOC 6

Armoured Division, Major General Abrar Hussain, was rushing whatever troops he could lay his hands on into the Chawinda area. On the morning of 12 September, much to Hussain's relief, the Indians, apart from sending out patrols, seemed quite content 'through a policy of steady creep forward, to edge their way up to the line Kalewali by 1700 hours'.[20] The window of opportunity that had been created by the troops on the ground with their resolute performance had been shut when Lieutenant General Dunn, GOC 1 Corps had issued the second of two signals the previous evening.

The first was in response to General Sparrow's message when Indian troops had reached Phillora. 'My congratulations to GOC and all ranks. A Bloody, Bloody, Bloody good show.' The second had to do with the order for regrouping for the next phase of operations. 99 Mountain Brigade, commanded by Brigadier Dharam Singh, was placed under Sparrow and was to relieve 43 Lorried Infantry Brigade which was to fall back to Rurki Kalan during the night of 12/13 September. 2 Lancer less a squadron was placed under the command of Dharam Singh. Cariappa's 35 Infantry Brigade would continue to hold the defended area opposite Gadgor, while 58 Infantry Brigade under the command of Brigadier J. S. Mandher would also shift from 14 Infantry Division to 1 Armoured Division.

In addition, Korla's 6 Mountain Division was ordered to capture Pagowal by 12 September to secure the right flank of the Indian-held territory. Korla planned to use Eric Vas's 69 Mountain Brigade with 62 Cavalry less a squadron to execute the task. On the left flank, Munshi's 116 Brigade was to revert to its parent formation, 14 Infantry Division. 5 Raj Rif would continue to hold Rangre and would be supported by a squadron of Shermans each from 62 Cavalry and 2 Lancers. 5/5 Gorkha Rifles was to capture Zafarwal by establishing a patrol base there by the night of 11/12 September and then build it up to one battalion later in the day. The Op Order made it clear that neither Sparrow nor Dunn had any intention of pressing on to Chawinda. Sparrow had, in fact, asked for additional forces. Since the Battle of Khem Karan had been fought, he wanted 3 Cavalry and 8 Light Cavalry to be returned to him. The request was denied.

So far, the Western Army commander, Lieutenant General Harbakhsh Singh, preoccupied with the fighting in the Khem Karan Sector, had been unable to visit 1 Corps. True to form, in his book *War Despatches*, the junior leadership earns high praise from him, while he is scathingly critical of Dunn and Sparrow: 'The triumph of junior leadership could have been turned into a better achievement by a more mature handling of armour at higher levels. We missed an excellent opportunity to completely cripple the enemy armour potential during this battle.' He went on, 'The Battle of Phillora would always rank high in the annals of armoured warfare—a glowing tribute to skilful junior leadership and astonishingly accurate gunnery.' Though he had been talking to Dunn on the telephone to keep himself abreast of the situation, it is obvious from his remarks that the Western Army commander had been excluded by Chaudhuri in 1 Corps' theatre of operations. Harbakhsh Singh reached the headquarters of 1 Corps in Pathankot on his maiden visit at 0800 hours on 12 September.

5/5 GR, also known as FIVFIV or the Chindits, commanded by Lieutenant Colonel D. C. Katoch, despatched Delta Company under Major S. C. Roy on a probing mission to Zafarwal at 2130 hours. Situated on the eastern side of the Degh Nadi, Zafarwal was an important communication centre that was believed to be lightly held by the Pakistanis. Roy had instructions to move at night and occupy the town if it was not defended. However, the battalion headquarters lost contact with the company soon after its departure due to the failure of its wireless link. Katoch then ordered Charlie Company under the command of Captain Tapan Roy Chaudhary to move at first light by surface transport to Mirzapur, also on the east bank of the Degh Nadi, and make contact with Delta Company as soon as possible. Charlie Company, after encountering minor opposition at Deoli, occupied Mirzapur at 0910 hours.

However, unknown to Katoch or Chaudhary, 5 Raj Rif (Napiers) at Kangre had made contact with Roy who had occupied Zafarwal and asked for another company to be sent to strengthen his position. This message could only be conveyed to Munshi at 1020 hours, who immediately ordered Katoch to move with the rest of his battalion to Zafarwal. Major General Ranjit Singh, GOC 14 Division, concurred with Munshi, and further ordered Bravo Squadron 2 Lancers under the command of Major B. R. Sharan, located with 5 Raj Rif at Kangre, to move immediately in support of the Gorkhas at Zafarwal.

Delta Company having got to Zafarwal, 'with their Mongoloid features, the Gurkha troops of the leading enemy company had no difficulty in convincing the simple folks of Zafarwal that they were Chinese troops come to the aid of Pakistan.'[21] So enthused were the 'simple folk' at the timely arrival of their 'big brother' that they enthusiastically helped the Gorkhas dig trenches and prepare the defences. In the meantime, some civilians made it to Dhamthal where an incredulous Major Ijaz Ahmed, commanding Alpha Company 13 FF (Recce & Support), was told that strange-looking troops had arrived and were digging positions on the southern side of Zafarwal. Although completely unaware of any Indian thrust in the area, Ijaz Ahmed's company headquarters plus a platoon under his command were deployed in a screen position by 115 Brigade that was stationed at Jassar. In addition to a handful of his own men, there was also a troop from 33 TDU Recce Group at Dhamthal.

Taking off in jeeps at break-neck speed, the Pakistanis split themselves into three groups: an RCL group, MMG group, and LMG group. At 1030 hours, about a kilometre short of the reported Gorkha positions, Ijaz Ahmed split his forces and attacked Delta Company from three sides. With no heavy weapons and no sign of any reinforcements or supporting armour, Roy had no option but to fall back on Mirzapur where he linked up with Chaudhary's Charlie Company by 1145 hours. Shortly thereafter, Katoch had also reached with the rest of the battalion. An attempt was made to capture Zafarwal later during the day, but with no supporting firepower, 5/5 GR could make little headway.

Kangre had been under intermittent but heavy shelling since 0800 hours. When Major Sharan was ordered to move Bravo Squadron 2 Lancers in support of 5/5 GR, 'for some unknown reason the squadron took over two hours to refill and did not move out till 1230 hours. En route to Zafarwal the squadron came under enemy artillery fire in area Pindi Mahrasan. After the shelling it made no attempt to push forward to Zafarwal and, having idled away the rest of the day, returned to Kangre at 1850 hours.'[22]

Around the time Harbakhsh arrived at 1 Corps HQ, no one had any clear idea about what was happening in Zafarwal. 'I was briefed by the corps commander as to the situation that morning, and I expressed dissatisfaction not only with the conduct of Zafarwal operations but also on the apathy or the lack of enterprise on the part of 1 Armoured Division. I was assured that the division was then ready to debouch for a dash towards Chawinda.'[23] Having given his views on what needed to be done, General Harbakhsh Singh left for 11 Corps HQ by road at 1300 hours.

With the aggressive army commander having been seen off, Dunn and his staff got busy trying to monitor the situation at Zafarwal while also planning an attack on Pagowal. Dunn first wanted to protect 'the right flank of the projected attack on Chawinda against enemy interference from Sialkot'.[24] It was felt that the Pakistanis could threaten the western flank along Bajragarhi and Pagowal axes. As the Bajragarhi axis was adequately guarded by 26 Division, Dunn decided to task Korla's 6 Mountain Division to capture Pagowal. As per the Indian assessment, Pagowal was occupied by an infantry company. Its capture would not only secure the right flank, once Chawinda was captured, it could also serve as a firm base for the capture of Badiana.

While on the Indian side, the thinking was limited to the two flanks, Zafarwal and Pagowal, General Musa and GHQ were showing 'remarkable decisiveness and flexibility to adjust to the strategic centre of gravity shifting to northern Pakistan Punjab. The Indian Army and particularly Western Command headquarters remained oblivious to this critical shift of strategic balance.'[25] His offensive plans having fallen apart at Khem Karan, Musa knew he could not afford to lose the defensive battle that he knew he had to fight to save Chawinda. During the day, one of his first priorities was to strengthen his artillery. Accordingly, 4 Corps Artillery Brigade was moved post haste to Chawinda to supplement the already existing 6 Armoured Division's integral guns. By nightfall 12 September, Chawinda had one self-propelled field regiment, one field regiment minus a battery, one heavy regiment, and one light anti-aircraft battery to support 24 Brigade.

Despite the mauling 11 Cavalry and the Guides had received the previous day, Pakistan's 6 Armoured Division had kept the defence of Chawinda as its main priority. Its loss would not only have unhinged Pakistan's defences in the Chawinda–Badiana–Pasrur complex, there would then be nothing between the Indians and the Marala Ravi Link Canal (MRLC) from where they could not only get behind Sialkot, but also cut across the national highway in the Gujranwala–Wazirabad area.

In addition, there had been a major re-haul at the command level. Major General Sahabzada Yaqub Ali Khan, until then the armoured advisor to the 1 Corps commander, had taken charge of 1 Armoured Division which had moved to Pasrur with a reconstituted 4 Armoured Brigade that now had 5 Probyn's Horse, 19 Lancer, and 10 FF in its ranks. The area between Pasrur and Chawinda was to be the division's responsibility. 3 Armoured Brigade, having left 7 FF at Lahore, had reached the Ghuuienke area with 19 Lancers and 16 (SP) Field Regiment by 1500 hours. By the evening of 12 September, Pakistan had created a favourable artillery and armour superiority in the Chawinda area. Any chance Dunn and Sparrow had of bludgeoning their way into Chawinda had evaporated. To further complicate matters, though the Indians were aware that the Pakistanis were thinning out from the Khem Karan Sector and reinforcing Sialkot Sector, Harbakhsh Singh refused to listen to Sparrow's repeated entreaties to switch 3 Cavalry and 8 Light Cavalry back to him.

During the night of 12/13 September, the two infantry battalions of 43 Lorried Infantry Brigade, 5 Jat and 5/9 GR, had been pulled back to Libbe and Rurki Kalan, leaving 99 Mountain Brigade with 2 Lancers less a squadron to defend the captured area around Phillora. By then Pakistan had five Patton, one Sherman, and one Chaffee regiment in the Chawinda complex and would soon have the ability to launch a counter-offensive. In addition, the Pakistanis having received a scare in the morning, Zafarwal, by last light, was being defended by a large quantum of troops that were part of 115 Brigade. The battalion headquarters of 13 FF R&S, 4 FF under the command of their new commanding officer, Lieutenant Colonel Mohammad Hayat, and Alpha Squadron of 22 Cavalry under Major Mohammad Masood with their Pattons were deployed around the town.

The next day would see fighting on both the flanks, as 5/5 GR put in a fresh bid to capture Zafarwal on the left while 69 Mountain Brigade would go for Pagowal. Major D. V. Neolekar, leading the Gorkha vanguard from the firm base at Mirzapur, put in a determined attack at 0630 hours on 13 September. 5/5 GR had again been promised armour support but once again Sharan's Bravo Squadron 2 Lancers, coming from Kangre, failed to link up with the battalion. Up against fortified positions supported by RCL guns, MMGs, and tanks, the Gorkhas pulled back. Their regimental records are categorical—the 2 Lancer Shermans never showed up!

The Pakistanis, however, confirm a second attack at 1130 hours when Bravo Squadron's tanks suddenly emerged from the trees on the eastern bank of the

Degh Nadi and attacked 4 FF positions. Shermans versus the M48 Pattons was an unequal contest at best, but the determination of the Indian assault led to Mohammad Masood losing his nerve and ordering the two troops on the left to fall back. Claiming that four Shermans were destroyed mainly by the RCL guns of 4 FF, the Indian tanks also withdrew. 116 Infantry Brigade's attempt to establish itself at Zafarwal was a complete failure. From this point onwards, 116 Brigade supported by Sharan's Shermans were tasked to hold the Ikhnal–Kangre line, which was the eastern flank of 14 Infantry Division.

During the day, throughout the sector, apart from consolidating defences and securing logistics routes, all units were occupied with replenishment and repairs while some readjustments were made on the ground. 35 Brigade still under command of 1 Armoured Division shifted its area of responsibility slightly to the east, realigning itself from the Sabzpir crossroads to the Gadgor area. 99 Mountain Brigade was holding the defences around Phillora, while 1 Armoured Brigade remained deployed between Phillora and Libbe.

Eric Vas was given the task of securing Pagowal. 3 Madras, under Lieutenant Colonel B. K. Bhattacharya had, since the capture of Maharajke on 7/8 September, been involved in some minor operations. Its sister battalion, 4 Madras, also known as the Walajahbadis, had also seen some bitter fighting at the same time and lost their CO, Lieutenant Colonel Harbans Lal Mehta. 3 Madras, with Bravo Company 4 Madras under its command, formed the brigade's vanguard that also included Bravo Squadron 62 Cavalry under Major Barach. Bravo Company 3 Madras, led by Major P. Chowdhary started from their firm base at Kaloi at 0400 hours and reached Haral, north of Pagowal, without meeting any opposition.

At Haral, Barach suggested to Bhattacharya that instead of the direct approach towards Pagowal, it would be better to launch the attack from the left flank via Koga. Bhattacharya did not want to tamper with his plans at the very last minute, but after discussing the matter with Eric Vas, it was decided that the Shermans along with Bravo Company 4 Madras would go in for a left hook while 3 Madras would assault the objective frontally. Seeing the tanks approach Koga, the company-strong Pakistani unit decided to abandon Pagowal. In any case, Eric Vas did not want troops to get embroiled in capturing the town and had instructed Bhattacharya to take up a defensive position at Milestone 8 on the Sialkot Cantt–Phillora road. By 0600 hours, after brushing aside a platoon left behind as a screen position, the Indians had reached their objective and 3 Madras was digging in along the road.

Vas along with 9 Kumaon and his brigade reconnaissance group also reached by 0630 hours and the Kumaonese were asked to deploy adjacent to and south of the 3 Madras position, along the Sialkot City Road. By 0700 hours, the gun positions for the artillery supporting 69 Mountain Brigade were being prepared. Bravo Company 4 Madras and the 62 Cavalry tanks were deployed behind, between Koga and 3 Madras. At 0730 hours two Bird Dogs (turboprop artillery spotter planes) appeared overhead. Minutes later, 69 Mountain Brigade was subject to one of the fiercest concentrations of artillery fire, directed by the Air OP. Close to thousand rounds in a space of two hours bombarded the Indians, killing among a few others, Major Chowdhary. Despite the intense shelling, the brigade held its ground. The Pakistanis then resorted to intermittent shelling through the afternoon.

At 1600 hours, Pakistan's 6 Armoured Division finally woke up from its slumber. PAF F–86 Sabres attacked the entire Indian line extending from Pagowal to Libbe, which was followed by a heavy dose of artillery fire. Ordered by Abrar Hussain to make a show of force between Pagowal and Chawinda, 10 Cavalry Guides sent forth their Bravo Squadron and 22 Cavalry Bravo Squadron advanced against Eric Vas's brigade. The Guides were first observed by 2 Lancers from the 99 Mountain Brigade location at Khanawali, who, despite being woefully understrength, opened up at extreme range. They were supported by Centurions from Charlie Squadron 4 Horse which were also deployed there. A few Pattons seemed to get hit, after which the Pakistanis swung westwards. This afforded 17 Horse, positioned at Libbe between Khanawali and Pagowal, target practice as the Pattons exposed their flanks when they moved from east to west parallel to the Phillora–Pagowal road. The Pakistanis admitted to losing two Pattons while three personnel were killed and three wounded.

Bravo Squadron 22 Cavalry, as yet untested in combat, advanced against Pagowal frontally. It was the turn of the Indian artillery guns to open up. 23 Artillery Brigade, now a part of 1 Corps, plus other artillery units deployed at Pagowal, bombarded not only the Pattons but also the reconnaissance troop that was advancing along the left flank. When the Pattons had closed the gap to 1,500 yards, Barach's Shermans also opened up. Within seventy-two hours, 62 Cavalry was in action against Pattons for a second time. In the din of the gunfire, smoke, and dust, the Pakistani reconnaissance troop was mistaken for Chaffee tanks by the Indians. However, after losing two Pattons and with the light fading, the Pakistanis began to withdraw. Bravo Squadron 22 Cavalry would report back and claim it had destroyed three Centurions. Apart from the claim being unfounded, it is interesting to note that the Pakistanis still had no idea they were up against Shermans. The total casualties suffered by 69 Mountain Brigade, mainly due to the artillery bombardment, included three officers, two JCOs, and eleven jawans killed and four officers, one JCO, and forty-four men wounded.

To ease the pressure and ensure that the Pakistanis did not move troops from the Sialkot region towards Chawinda, Dunn ordered Major General Thapan to keep up the pressure in the 26 Infantry Division area. Both 162 and 168 Infantry Brigades had held off Pakistani counter-attacks since 8 September and had even expanded their respective bridgeheads. Brigadier R. D. 'Rocky' Hira's 52 Mountain Brigade from 15 Corps had joined the Tiger Division on 12 September, which allowed Thapan to have a divisional reserve. 168 Brigade ordered 8 JAK

Rif commanded by Lieutenant Colonel Prem Kumar to capture the dominating high ground of Kalarwanda. Leading the attack, Major Surender Mohan Sharma[26] captured the objective while 2/1 GR occupied Rasulpur by 1000 hours on 13 September, both units supported by a troop of Shermans belonging to 18 Cavalry.

Chapter 19

A VICTORY BUNGLED
11 CORPS (PART IV) 11 TO 13 SEPTEMBER

4 MOUNTAIN DIVISION—KHEM KARAN (11 SEPTEMBER)

In the grey light of the false dawn on 11 September when even the birds had not started to chirp, Naib Risaldar Jagdeo Singh was startled awake. Alpha Squadron 3 Cavalry had spent the night north of Mahmudpura near Khem Karan Minor as per Lieutenant Colonel Salim Caleb's orders issued the previous evening. While the exhausted crews of the tanks slept next to their Centurions, willing hands had physically carried forth ammunition and fuel to replenish the squadron. Now as he looked through his field glasses, Jagdeo thought he was imagining things at first, but he counted nine Patton tanks barely 1,000 yards away in front of him. The tanks were parked in a haphazard manner, their barrels pointing in different directions, which was most unusual.

Major Surish Vadera, the squadron commander, was woken up and even as he moved towards Jagdeo Singh to see for what was going on, the men around him were on the move, clambering into the parked Centurions. Vadera estimated there was probably one squadron of Pattons in front of him. Ordering two of his troops to place themselves on the flank of the Pakistanis to cut off any chance of their getting away, he opened fire with his remaining Centurions.

The Pakistanis were probably asleep when they came under fire. Badly trapped with nowhere to go, most of them started abandoning their tanks and a few of the men were killed. Those who got away dashed into the sugarcane fields. When all resistance had died down, Vadera assembled a reconnaissance party and cautiously approached the Pattons, the two troops of Centurions covering them. In all, there were nine abandoned Pattons, each one in perfect running condition. 'Radio sets in many cases were "on". In some cases, the engines of the Pattons were running; in others the batteries had run down because all the electrical switches were left "on".... A new M113 APC was also captured and from it the 4 Armoured Brigade Operation Order giving the grand plan of Pak 1 Armoured Division was recovered.'[1]

Major General Gurbaksh Singh at HQ 4 Mountain Division had also had the quietest night. He and his two deployed brigades were woken up by the sound of gunfire early in the morning. Cramped from having been in their trenches for seventy-two hours, the men scanned the sugarcane and cotton fields looking for the familiar signs of advancing Pattons, but there was nothing to see. A few hours later, with 4 Mountain Division still at stand-to, a message was received that Alpha Squadron 3 Cavalry had captured nine Pattons and destroyed quite a few others. Unable to believe his ears, the GOC got into his jeep and rushed off to take a look for himself.

The news of the Pakistani defeat at Asal Uttar began to spread like wildfire. The COAS, General Chaudhuri, was in the Ops Room when the 'news of the capture of a squadron worth of abandoned serviceable Pattons was received. He ordered a re-check of the information, and on confirmation bolted out of the room into the corridor like an athlete. Someone in the Operation Room suggested champagne but he was already out in the corridor.'[2]

Meanwhile, back in the sugarcane fields between the Rohi Nullah and Khem Karan Minor, it was decided that one of the Pattons would be driven to Dibbipura. This required 'elaborate plans and precautions to ensure Indian troops did not open fire on this tank. Vadera got into the driver's seat of Patton tank No. BA 077651 and, following the working instructions neatly laid out on plates by the American manufacturers, he started the Patton. Then with the main 90 mm tank gun pointing towards Pakistan and both headlights on, with a white vest serving as a white flag, the tank was driven into the Indian lines'.[3] It was impractical to start recovering all the abandoned tanks which were lying all over the place. To prevent the Pakistanis from coming back and taking these tanks away, they decided to flood the area by breaching Khem Karan Minor. In addition, the main guns were disabled by removing the firing pin assembly and taking away critical electrical parts.

While the tanks were being disabled, Second Lieutenant (later Major) Parminderjit 'PJ' Singh Mehta, who was watching the men at work, thought he saw some movement in the adjoining sugarcane fields. Not really expecting to find any Pakistanis so close to the abandoned tanks, Mehta reported to Caleb who told him to take a section from 1 Dogra and 'check out the area'. Mehta 'went back to my original position with the 18 men under command. I ordered the men to cautiously surround the sugarcane field and placed riflemen and LMG to cover all escape routes. Thereafter, I shouted aloud, ordering those in the field to come out with their hands up and surrender. On hearing my voice some personnel dressed in khaki walked out with their hands up.'[4] Among those whom Mehta bagged were Lieutenant Colonel (later Colonel, was awarded the Sitara-e-Jurrat) Mohammad Nazir, commandant 4 Cavalry, Majors Ayub Khan and Mohammad Anwar, both squadron commanders, Captain (later Colonel) Abdul Aziz Ahsan, and sixteen other ranks.

In the afternoon bulletin, Barun Haldar announced on All India Radio the decimation of 4 Cavalry at Asal Uttar and the capture of a squadron of tanks.

By the evening, the capture of the commandant and the others was also on the air waves.

Lieutenant Generals Harbakhsh Singh and Jogi Dhillon arrived at HQ 4 Mountain Division shortly after 3 Cavalry had rounded up the prisoners. For the army commander, the scale of the victory was exhilarating, especially since Chaudhuri and Dhillon had seemed ready to give up forty-eight hours ago. Not only had his faith in the defensive abilities of 4 Mountain Division been justified, it was also obvious to him that the Pakistani armoured division had withdrawn from Asal Uttar altogether. Earlier in the day, Harbakhsh had also seen a report from the IAF that had noted the movement of a large column of tanks heading towards Lahore. 'The initial interrogation reports from the dazed, disillusioned and peeved prisoners of war indicated demoralisation, lack of fighting spirit and the destruction of their armoured division.'[5]

This was a heady cocktail of information, and Harbakhsh reacted as expected. Forgotten was the fact that on the opening day of the offensive, 6 September, the very same 4 Mountain Division had failed against Pakistani defences and had been pushed back to Asal Uttar, where the roles had been reversed. Pakistan's armour, once committed to assault through the Khem Karan bridgehead had attacked the Indian positions which had a limited infantry component. Also Pakistani tanks had got through to Valtoha twice and they had been pulled back, indicating that the bridgehead was defended by an adequately strong defensively deployed formation. Amazingly, even at this stage, let alone Harbakhsh Singh, no one on the Indian side was even remotely aware of the existence of Pakistan's 11 Division or, for that matter, what the ground situation opposite them actually was.

The quantum of artillery fire that had been brought to bear on Asal Uttar and the surrounding areas indicated that there were at least two artillery brigades deployed around Khem Karan. Also, had Pakistan's 4 and 5 Armoured Brigades linked up as they were supposed to do, there would be a sizeable strength of infantry to occupy the captured ground as the Pattons made a dash for the Beas Bridge. Just because its main armoured thrust had failed, there was no reason to assume that Pakistan would give up Khem Karan that easily. Harbakhsh Singh's presence at HQ 4 Mountain Division and his gung-ho attitude perhaps influenced the others to keep their own counsel.

With Dhillon as his main adviser, Harbakhsh decided to give no respite or time to the Pakistanis to recover. Given Harbakhsh's tendency to sack officers on the spot for 'not having fire in their belly', Gurbaksh Singh watched silently as the army commander hatched his plan to launch an immediate offensive action in order to recapture the lost ground on the first two days of the failed offensive.

The two generals decided between them that the Pakistanis had pulled back from Khem Karan, leaving at best an infantry company, maybe with elements of an R&S company acting as a screen along the Khem Karan Distributary. Their plan was for an infantry battalion to infiltrate the area later that same night and occupy the built-up area behind the Pakistani troops that would be facing in the direction of Asal Uttar. At first light, 7 Mountain Brigade under Brigadier Sidhu would then advance on the Bhikkiwind–Khem Karan Road. The moment they made contact with the Pakistani defences, the battalion behind, which would be hidden in the houses, would open fire. The shock of finding Indian troops behind them would be too much for the hapless Pakistanis, who would run helter-skelter and Khem Karan would be in the bag.

This plan was bizarre in the extreme. Apart from the fact that it was based on too many assumptions, it also reflected the same mindset that had been displayed earlier by Pakistan's GOC 1 Armoured Division, Major General Naseer Ahmed: that the enemy would give up the moment one's own troops appeared. Gurbaksh was asked to nominate a battalion that would take on the task of getting behind Pakistani lines.

By then almost everyone knew how this would go. Harbakhsh was the colonel of the Sikh regiment, something he was very proud of, with good reason. 4 Sikh, which had captured Barki the night before, celebrated Saragarhi Day every year on 12 September. It commemorated the stand made by twenty-one men of what was then the 36th Sikhs. Saragarhi was a small fort between Fort Lockhart and Fort Gulistan in the NWFP that housed a signalling piquet. On 12 September 1897, thousands of Orakzai and Afridi tribesmen surrounded Saragarhi and Havildar Ishar Singh and his twenty men chose to fight to the last man, killing hundreds of Afghans even as they perished one by one. All twenty-one soldiers plus the one safai karamchari (sweeper) were posthumously awarded the Indian Order of Merit First Class, which was then the equivalent of the Victoria Cross. Harbakhsh Singh, who had commanded 4 Sikh, wanted the battalion to celebrate Saragahi Day at Khem Karan.

Gurbaksh Singh said none of his battalions were in a state to take on the task of advancing on either pincer. 2 Mahar at that point of time was the integral infantry battalion of 2 (Independent) Armoured Brigade and was at Kot Kapura and had, as yet, not been through the baptism of fire. Though Lieutenant Colonel (later Colonel) Kanwar Sain Bakshi's battalion did not know the terrain, it was decided that the battalion would lead the advance with Alpha Squadron of 9 Deccan Horse and two troops from Bravo Squadron 3 Cavalry. This was to be the main thrust down the road.

As for the other pincer, even though 29 Brigade's two battalions—1/5 GR and 2 Madras—had been at Bhikkiwind since 9 September, a visibly excited Harbakhsh Singh and Jogi Dhillon jumped into their jeeps and raced off to HQ 7 Infantry Division where Major General Sibal was asked to nominate a battalion for the enveloping action planned for later that night at Khem Karan. Under normal circumstances, of the six infantry battalions available, 4 Sikh would have been the last choice, but nevertheless, Lieutenant Colonel Anant Singh was sent for 'to ask him personally if he would be willing to undertake the arduous task.'[6]

4 Sikh was ordered to move immediately by road to Valtoha while Anant went ahead to meet Gurbaksh Singh at the headquarters of 4 Mountain Division. Reaching there at 1830 hours, Anant listened in disbelief as he was told by the GOC that as soon as his battalion arrived, it had to move to Khem Karan and occupy the town during the night. 'However, like the good soldier that he was, he accepted the challenge without even mentioning that he and his men had no sleep for the two previous nights and in their attack on Barki the battalion had suffered nearly 150 casualties.'[7] By then the Harbakhsh/Jogi Dhillon assessment of the Pakistani strength had assumed epic proportions! They told Anant not to worry about a Pakistani tank threat as there was no Pakistani armour left in the Khem Karan Sector. Anant was told that at best there were some administrative units in the town which could be dealt with easily. In any case, by first light, 7 Mountain Brigade and Indian armour would have trundled down the Bhikkiwind–Khem Karan road. Besides, guides were being provided and once 4 Sikh reached Valtoha they would take them straight to Khem Karan.

Not quite knowing what to do, his battalion already en route from Barki, Anant dashed back to HQ 7 Infantry Division where he sought out his divisional commander. He told Sibal about the near-impossible timeline, the unfamiliar terrain, and that he had no idea where his unit was. Anant Singh was to later say 'GOC of 7 Infantry Division refused to own me by saying, "You are out of my Division; you are 4 Mountain Division's pigeon now."'[8] Anant then called Brigadier Grewal, the BGS at HQ 11 Corps, who told him to talk to Brigadier Sidhu, the commander of 7 Mountain Brigade. Anant went back to HQ 4 Mountain Division and at 2130 hours, asked Sidhu to call up Gurbaksh and request him to postpone the assault—code-named Operation Gaddi—by twenty-four hours. The brigade commander assured Anant he would look into the matter.

An hour later, Sidhu convened a meeting at his brigade headquarters where Bakshi met his new commander for the first time, 2 Mahar having been put under command of 7 Mountain Brigade. Also present were Arun Vaidya, CO 9 Deccan Horse, Lieutenant Colonel Jesus from the artillery and Major Mahipat Singh, the brigade major. Without even introducing himself to Bakshi, Sidhu got straight to the point and said the army commander had decided the enemy had suffered heavy losses and the brigade was being asked to exploit the situation and recapture Khem Karan, the only Indian town under Pakistani occupation.

Like Anant Singh before him, Bakshi was incredulous. He told Sidhu 2 Mahar had hitherto been engaged in protecting tanks in their harbour areas, that the battalion had come from Rajasthan and were equipped with the .303 rifle, LMG, and MMGs with 2-inch and 3-inch mortars. The ammunition they required was completely different from what was being used by mountain divisions. His battalion had no idea what the terrain was like between Chima and Khem Karan, they had no maps, their weapon systems were outdated with only the first line of ammunition, and his radio sets were of the .88 and .31 varieties, which were not on the brigade's net. Bakshi too asked for a postponement of twenty-four hours which would allow him to send out probing patrols to see what and where the Pakistani defences were. With Arun Vaidya also supporting Bakshi, Sidhu finally called up Gurbaksh, who flatly refused to postpone the assault, saying the matter was not in his hands.

WHO NEEDS ENEMIES…KHEM KARAN (12 SEPTEMBER)
Just how badly Harbakhsh Singh had misread the situation can be gauged from the fact that Pakistan, despite most of the remnants of its 1 Armoured Division having pulled out, was holding the Khem Karan bridgehead with four infantry battalions—6 Baluch, 10 FF, 2 FF, and 5 FF—plus at least two depleted armoured regiments, two squadrons of a light regiment, and 3 (SP) Field Regiment. To ensure 'the fire in the belly' did not diminish, Harbakhsh and Dhillon decided to camp for the night at HQ 4 Mountain Division, where they spent most of the night under a huge mango tree.

At 2300 hours 4 Sikh assembled near Valtoha. Anant selected fifty men who were considered fit enough to accompany him from each of the four companies, while those who were still arriving from Barki would follow. There was a feeling of déjà vu as the battalion found itself waiting again, this time for the promised guides who were to lead them to Khem Karan. In the meantime, a signals detachment had arrived with a wireless set that could at least communicate with HQ 4 Mountain Division. Unable to wait for the promised guides, at 2330 hours, Anant set off with 200 men along the railway line towards Khem Karan. The men were on a man-pack basis, and were also physically carrying two RCL guns.

For the already exhausted men, the RCL guns soon became an ordeal, hampering their progress. After struggling for a while with the heavy load, it was decided that the anti-tank guns would be left there and be brought up by the rest of the men who were coming up behind with Major Dalip Sidhu. Unfortunately, the signal detachment also stopped with the guns. After a while, the column left the railway line and followed the Machike Minor Canal that took them to the south of the town. At 0445 hours, Anant thought they must be close to Khem Karan. They had not run into any Pakistani posts or patrols en route, so Anant decided to wait for daylight in a maize field so he could get his bearings.

The Sikhs, who had been navigating by instinct, had blundered into the night harbour of 3 (SP) Field Regiment and Bravo Squadron of 12 Cavalry. Seeing the tanks, Anant presumed they were the squadron of tanks that was supposed to link up with him at Khem Karan. The Pakistanis were also beginning to wake up. Seeing an officer standing on a tank, Anant walked up to him and asked him if he was from Deccan Horse. An equally startled Lieutenant Khizar-Ullah whipped out his pistol and told Anant that this was not the Deccan Horse squadron and that Anant was his prisoner. Some of the men tried to make a break for the sugarcane fields but the artillery troop opened fire, killing an officer, a JCO, and thirteen other men. With Lieutenant Colonel Anant Singh, 5 officers, 7 JCOs, and 113 ranks were taken prisoner.

The few who did manage to escape soon ran into Major Sidhu who was bringing up the rear with the two RCL guns. Sidhu, who wasn't clear about what had happened, decided to head back to Valtoha. Captain Amarinder Singh, the army commander's ADC, saw a Sikh soldier 'wearing a Sikh regimental uniform coming from the direction of Khem Karan. I called him and asked him what he was doing here and he said, "Saab paltan ghere'ch aa gaie" (Sir, the battalion was surrounded). I told him to wait, and went in to tell the Army Commander.'[9] By then Sidhu had also arrived and the story began to emerge. No one knew what had happened to Anant or the other men at that point.

Earlier, at 0430 hours, Lieutenant Colonel Bakshi had given the final orders at Chima to Major Jimmy Vohra, Alpha Squadron 9 Deccan Horse, who had under his command three troops of Sherman Mk IVs, and Captain John Wates, who was commanding the two troops of Centurion Mk VIIs from Bravo Squadron 3 Cavalry. Wates had rejoined the regiment a few hours earlier and was champing at the bit, having missed all the earlier action. Two troops from Major D. K. Mehta's Charlie Squadron 9 Horse under the command of Second Lieutenant T. S. Shergill had been sent as a reserve by Arun Vaidya.

In the prevailing scenario, no one thought it necessary to inform the 2 Mahar Group that 4 Sikh's pincer movement had fallen apart, even though both Harbakhsh Singh and Dhillon were aware of the debacle by 0630 hours. By that time, the 2 Mahar Group had been on the move for almost an hour and a half and had met no opposition up to Bhura Kuhna. In fact, the column had found a number of abandoned vehicles, including jeeps and tanks, plus a large number of weapons and ammunition.

When the 2 Mahar Group was halfway between Bhura Kunha and the Khem Karan Distributary, with 2,000 yards still to go, the Pakistanis opened fire from well-concealed positions on either side of the culvert. A Centurion troop was leading on the left while a Sherman troop was on the right with the leading company of 2 Mahar in between. As MMG, RCL, and artillery fire engaged the 2 Mahar Group, the infantry went to ground. Alpha Squadron 9 Horse and 3 Cavalry also opened fire from either side. A Pakistani RCL jeep was suddenly visible near the culvert and it took a direct hit from Wates' Centurion. Bakshi moved forward to assess the situation. Climbing onto the roof of a hut, by following the line of fire of the Pakistani weapons, he concluded there was at least an infantry battalion and a squadron of armour.

Messages were passed back to HQ 7 Mountain Brigade and Bakshi was told to plan an assault at 1115 hours. Half an hour before that, the Indian artillery would bombard the Pakistani positions, which would also simultaneously be hit by the IAF. Orders were accordingly passed down to all the company commanders and troop leaders. 2 Mahar's Charlie Company commanded by Captain R. K. Kapoor would assault from the left with the Centurions and Bravo Company under Lieutenant Hukum Singh would move with the Shermans on the left. No sooner had the orders been passed than the Pakistanis jammed the Indian radio frequencies.

At 0930 hours, the Pakistani artillery decided to up the ante and, for the next hour and fifteen minutes, the Indian troops were subject to concentrated fire. While there was no sign of the promised air support on the Indian side; the PAF, with its usual formation of four F-86s, added to the fireworks. Casualties were mounting by the minute, but the 2 Mahar Group held on. In fact, despite the shelling and the air attacks, almost all the companies managed to get to their designated FUPs.

From his tank, partly sheltered by a bund, 'Wates had seen Kapoor's company move into position. At 1115 hours, even though the Indian artillery and the IAF had failed to show up, the Indians threw themselves into the attack. The armour surged forward in extended line assault and, with their machine guns and main guns blazing, closed in on the Khem Karan Minor. Wates's tank was hit twice when he was 75 yards short of the canal. With his engine stalled and the tank smouldering, he was forced to "bail out" with his three crew members.

'The enemy, in the meantime, had opened up small arms fire on us and I could feel the bullets whizzing past my head. I expected to be hit at any moment. We ran the first 200 yards diving here and there when a shell landed, but once we came out of the small arms range we took it easy. On my left, I saw two tanks of No. 2 Troop in flames; one was trying to pull back. Here I also saw an infantry company with their bayonets fixed advancing in assault formation. I was scared that they might shoot us. I took off my beret, waved to them encouragingly and shouted, *"Agay jao, kuch nahin hai agay. Shabash!"* (Go ahead, there is nothing in front of you. Well done!)'[10]

But there was plenty in front. Kapoor asked Wates if he could get the tanks to silence some MMGs. The two officers parted company, one moving resolutely forward while the second was looking to commandeer another tank. The PAF was back overhead, strafing the Indian positions. An artillery shell landed next to Wates, wounding him.

Charlie Company gained another 200 yards when Kapoor went down, his body riddled with MMG bullets. On the left, Lieutenant Hukum Singh was also dead. Yet the attack did not waver; despite their .303 Enfield rifles being no match against the automatic weapons of the Pakistanis, the men kept advancing.

Their officers down, platoon commanders took over. Naib Subedars Jagannath Sawakhande and Sitaram Kamble took their place, and when they fell, mortally wounded, others stepped up. Of the six platoon commanders, three were killed and two wounded. The battalion's IO, Second Lieutenant J. P. Gaur had been pulling back the wounded until he got hit by a rocket, his body sliced in two. The adjutant and the subedar major were also wounded.

At 1230 hours, the attack was called off and the 2 Mahar Group was ordered to fall back on Bhura Kuhna. Arun Vaidya then ordered the two reserve troops of Shermans under Shergill to move up to the south of Bhura Kuhna to cover the withdrawal. The cost of this ill-planned exercise had been huge—three officers, two JCOs, and forty-four other ranks of 2 Mahar were killed, while two officers, four JCOs, and eighty-two other ranks had been wounded. 9 Deccan Horse had lost one Sherman while 3 Cavalry had its highest casualties, as four Centurions were destroyed, mainly by anti-tank weapons. Three crew members were missing, one of whom was later confirmed as killed, while one was repatriated with other POWs after the war.

REINFORCING FAILURE...AND SOME LIES (KHEM KARAN)

At 1300 hours, with a steady stream of casualties being brought back, Brigadier Sidhu sent a message to Gurbaksh: 'Advance held up own side of Khem Karan Distributary. I assess enemy has directly opposing us minimum one infantry battalion, a squadron of armour (Pattons) and R&S company. His artillery and air is very active and accurate, heavy casualties in men, tanks and other equipment, two companies infantry mauled up due enemy tank fire, shelling, air action and MMG fire. Own artillery fire ineffective due to damaged wireless equipment and some casualties among forward observation officers; complete armoured regiment, two fresh infantry battalions and continuous air support necessary to hold and sustain operation. I recommend we call off this operation.'[11]

With the abrupt departure of the army commander shortly after receiving the news that 4 Sikh had run into trouble, it was up to Gurbaksh Singh to take action. From his reaction to Sidhu's message, it seems neither Harbakhsh nor Dhillon had bothered to share the information with GOC 4 Mountain Division. Gurbaksh Singh messaged Sidhu back asking him to make one more effort to try and link up with 4 Sikh. One more troop of Centurions was being allotted to 7 Mountain Brigade along with two companies from 9 JAK Rifles under the command of Major Jamwal. These, plus the two reserve troops of 9 Deccan Horse, were to launch a second attack at 1600 hours and make contact with the road block established by 4 Sikh in the enemy's rear.

Sidhu responded that the force being allotted was inadequate to dislodge the Pakistanis at the Khem Karan Distributary. In reply, Gurbaksh Singh sent Sidhu an emotional plea, 'Do it for my sake!'[12]

The second assault was just as disastrous. Once again there was no air or artillery support as two troops of Charlie Squadron 9 Deccan Horse moved towards the Khem Karan Distributary. The Shermans were engaged by RCL jeeps belonging to 10 and 2 FF and, soon, two Shermans from No. 1 Troop were hit by the anti-tank guns. The third tank with Maun Shergill (Sparrow's younger son), got bogged down. No. 4 Troop with just two tanks had got to the Khem Karan Distributary, but 9 JAK Rif failed to keep up with the armour. 9 Deccan Horse lost all three tanks in the evening operation and, at the end of the day, one officer and three other ranks were killed and five badly burnt. Shergill and his crew of three were taken prisoner.

At 1830 hours on 12 September as darkness set in, Harbakhsh Singh's Operation Gaddi lay in a shambles. Khem Karan was still very much with the Pakistanis.

The attempt to capture Khem Karan must rank as one of the most shameful chapters in India's military history. Though the men were magnificent—they fought as hard as they could despite all the odds being stacked against them—their commanders failed them miserably. After the war, Harbakhsh Singh would gloss over his role in the disaster in all his writings, while Dhillon, who had become quite adept at blaming his subordinates, would go on record to say, 'The failure of 4 Sikh operation for the capture of Khem Karan was a failure of leadership of the Commanding Officer. He did not carry the RCL guns and showed utter lack of determination, when having reached Khem Karan before sunrise, did not enter it.'[13]

Captain Amarinder Singh's first person account of what happened earlier that morning places Harbakhsh Singh in the 4 Mountain Division Operations Room at Valtoha.[14] There is nothing ambiguous about the account, it even quotes the Sikh soldier and goes on to name the officers who briefed the army commander. However, so determined was Harbakhsh Singh to distance himself from the disaster that he claims he was not at Valtoha and had returned to his headquarters on 11 September 'late that evening and reached Pathankot the next morning by a special train and was at I Corps Headquarters by 0800 hours'.[15] Taking Amarinder Singh's account as accurate, the only way Harbakhsh Singh could have reached Dunn's location by 0800 hours was by helicopter.

Harbakhsh Singh, like Dhillon, blamed the failure of the 'master plan' to recapture Khem Karan on 12 September on 'unfortunate incidents' (4 Sikh), and the disintegration of 2 Mahar under artillery and air attacks, claiming 'the battalion suffered some casualties and a few of its men broke the line'.[16] His biased description of the combat in which he builds up his own regiment and downplays the Mahar performance is in very poor taste indeed. Having taken control of operations in 4 Mountain Division during the latter half of 11 September, it would have been only fair to take responsibility for his actions. Instead, Brigadier Sidhu, whose 7 Mountain Brigade had so gallantly defended Khem Karan over the last three days, was removed from command.

The animosity that existed between Chaudhuri and Harbakhsh and their perennial game of one-upmanship was assuming alarming proportions because it was directly affecting the performance of the Indian Army along the entire front. Chaudhuri had, on his part, deliberately sidelined Harbakhsh from the 1 Corps theatre of operations and was trying to remotely control the battle in the Sialkot Sector. With Harbakhsh breathing down his neck after the capture of Phillora on the morning of 12 September, Dunn had blurted out the real reason for the slow advance, telling Harbakhsh that Chaudhuri 'did not want him to stick his neck out too much forward'.[17] The defence minister, Chavan, was fully aware of Harbakhsh Singh's tendency to browbeat his way through a crisis, but some of Chaudhuri's wariness of the army commander had rubbed off on him. After the Khem Karan fiasco, which Chavan logged in his diary as a 'stupid incident', Chavan played a big role in keeping the incident out of the press, even though Pakistan Radio was making capital out of the capture of Lieutenant Colonel Anant Singh and his men.[18]

Finally, on 13 September, exactly a week after the Indian offensive had started in the Punjab, it finally dawned on Harbakhsh Singh that Pakistan's 11 Infantry Division had been deployed in the bridgehead against them at Khem Karan all this time.

7 & 15 DIVISION (11–13 SEPTEMBER)

Having captured Barki and occupied the eastern bank of the Ichhogil Canal on the night of 10/11 September, 9 Madras had replaced 4 Sikh which had fallen back to Hudiara to get some rest and tend to the dead and wounded. While 16 Punjab consolidated its positions on the east bank, on the west bank of the Ichhogil, the remaining troops of Pakistan's 17 Punjab under Major Bhatti continued to fly the flag after the others had followed 103 Brigade's rearward deployment. Throughout the day, both sides intermittently shelled the opposite bank. On the morning of 12 September, at around 0900 hours, while Bhatti was sitting on the branch of a tree directing Pakistani artillery fire across the canal, he was hit by splinters from a stray shell. Awarded the War's only Nishan-e-Haider, Pakistan's highest award for bravery, his citation, however, says he was killed by a tank shell.

On 10 September while all eyes had been on Barki, to the south, towards the 4 Mountain Division sector, 48 Infantry Brigade was given the task of capturing and demolishing the bridge on the Ichhogil Canal west of Jahman. The task had been carried out by 5 Guards supported by two troops of CIH, but this operation did not meet with success. The next day a second attack was attempted, using two infantry battalions along with the armour. Despite the divisional artillery throwing in its weight behind the attack, a number of tanks got bogged down and once again the bridge remained in Pakistan's control. The failure of this operation resulted in Brigadier Shahaney being replaced by the highly decorated Brigadier Piara Singh.

By the evening of 11 September, 4 Sikh had left for 4 Mountain Division's location at Valtoha, 32 kilometres away via the Patti–Khem Karan–Kasur Road. With the bridge at Barki having been blown up, there was relative quiet on the 7 Infantry Division front for the next few days.

Even while Harbakhsh Singh was racing between 4 Mountain Division and 7 Infantry Division, Dhillon continued to worry about the 15 Division Sector. Though he had plugged the gap by deploying 96 Infantry Brigade in the area, he was anxious about a Pakistani armoured thrust towards Amritsar. An IAF Canberra, flown by the omnipresent Nath, had also reported the movement of some fifty Pakistani tanks heading towards Lahore.

HQ 11 Corps ordered Brigadier Theogaraj to move the bulk of his 2 (I) Armoured Brigade to the GT Road axis by first light 12 September. 3 Cavalry was to stay on in Khem Karan, the two troops from its Bravo Squadron earmarked to support the 2 Mahar attack in the morning to reclaim Khem Karan from the Pakistani 'administrative units' that were occupying it. However, Alpha Squadron 3 Cavalry, 8 Cavalry less a squadron (AMX-13), and one newly arrived 7 Cavalry squadron of PT-76 tanks moved out at 2030 hours and were in position by first light. However, hardly had 2 (I) Armoured Brigade got to the GT Road area, information was received that Pakistani armour was again building up at Kasur, for perhaps yet another offensive thrust in the Khem Karan area. Dhillon accordingly instructed Theogaraj to take his entire brigade back to Khem Karan. By midnight 12/13 September, the brigade was back to where it had been thirty-six hours ago!

Having created a big scare on 10 September, Captain Naginder Singh's troop of Centurions had been asked by HQ 11 Corps to act as a screen along the GT Road with Bravo Squadron of 14 Scinde Horse. After the fiasco on 10 September at Santpura and Dial, Pakistan had withdrawn its 22 Brigade and replaced it with 114 Brigade, which accordingly took charge of the area extending from Jallo to Attoke Awan. 16 Punjab moved into Dograi, 8 Punjab was responsible for Attoke Awan and the UBDC, 3 Baluch deployed at Batapur, and 12 Punjab, having unstuck from Barki, was positioned on the Ichhogil Canal north of Dograi. On the Indian side, 13 Punjab and 15 Dogra, both with new COs, were dug in astride GT Road between Milestone 13 and Dograi, with 3 Jat holding its position behind them.

On 11 September, a troop of Pakistani Shermans appeared. Naginder's Centurions opened fire and destroyed one of the Pakistani tanks, and the others pulled back. Pakistan's 23 Cavalry had two squadrons of Patton M47s and, the next day, the Pakistanis came down the road once again from the direction of Milestone 13. Once again Naginder's Centurion fired, adopting the time tested three-round method. The Patton, hit twice, was completely destroyed by the armour piercing discarding sabot (APDS). The other tanks, having confirmed for themselves the presence of Centurions in the sector, did an about-turn and were not seen again. By then virtually every other Indian weapon in the area was blazing away at Naginder's Patton, and it would be claimed as a confirmed kill by many.

Having had to send back 2 (I) Armoured Brigade, Dhillon was still not entirely comfortable with the situation on the 15 Infantry Division front. The initial objective of getting to the east bank of the Ichhogil continued to elude both 54 and 38 Infantry Brigades. 96 Infantry Brigade, initially deployed in a defensive role to counter any Pakistani thrust towards Amritsar on the Ranian–Chogawan axis, was to go on the offensive and capture Ichhogil Uttar and Ichhogil Hithar and occupy a stretch on the banks of the UBDC at Kohali. 50 Parachute Brigade, the latest inductee into the Lahore Sector, was to capture Bhasin by first light on 14 September. On the night of 11/12 September, it was deployed at Phul Kanjri.

14 Scinde Horse, despite being equipped with almost obsolete tanks, had performed exceptionally well. The officers and men of this regiment were furious to see their commandant, Lieutenant Colonel Raghubir Singh, be made the scapegoat for what was so obviously the fault of HQ 11 Corps. The devastated Raghubir was replaced by Colonel Bharat Singh, the deputy commander of 2 (I) Armoured Brigade on 11 September. A new formation called 'Bharat Force' was created wherein 14 Scinde Horse was clubbed with 1 Skinner's Horse, commanded by Lieutenant Colonel G. B. S. Sidhu, which was around then disembarking at Amritsar, having come from Varanasi. The two regiments with their Sherman Vs and Sherman IVs were placed under the new formation.

Chapter 20

THE SLUGFEST AT CHAWINDA
RACHNA DOAB (14-23 SEPTEMBER)

THE FAULT LINES

D-Day for the attack on Chawinda was 14 September. Major General Rajinder Singh 'Sparrow' had made a bid for additional armour to be allotted to him, especially 3 Cavalry, but the bulk of the reinforcements had been given to 11 Corps in the Lahore Sector. Meanwhile, the two-day delay in resuming the offensive after the capture of Phillora had given the Pakistanis the time they needed to shift the major portion of their 1 Armoured Division from the Kasur (Khem Karan) Sector to the Sialkot Sector. The Pakistani generals certainly seemed more alive to the overall situation and despite having taken severe blows in both Khem Karan and Phillora just seventy-two hours earlier, Musa and GHQ Pakistan had recovered their equilibrium and considerably strengthened their fighting capability.

The Indians, on the other hand, after the performance of their own armour, now had the psychological edge. They had lost their fear not just of the Patton tanks, but also to a great extent of the PAF which, despite being far more proactive than its Indian counterpart, had failed to decisively impact any battle on the ground. Though at the fighting formation levels the morale was upbeat, the situation at the higher echelons of command were far from satisfactory.

Lieutenant General Harbakhsh Singh's brief and only visit to HQ 1 Corps on the morning of 12 September had cemented the fault lines that already existed. As the army commander departed, he was fully aware that the corps commander had gone through the motions of briefing him but his orders were clearly coming from elsewhere. Though Harbakhsh claims he returned to Khem Karan in his book *War Despatches*,[1] there is no mention of the army commander's presence in 4 Mountain Division later that evening.

In all probability, the army commander went back to his own headquarters in Ambala from where he had a heated discussion with the COAS and 'unpleasant words were exchanged between the two'.[2] Harbakhsh remonstrated with Chaudhuri for interfering with tactical decisions which, as the army commander, was his prerogative. Chaudhuri, on the back foot at that stage after the embarrassing display of nerves earlier, tried to placate Harbakhsh by apologizing to his subordinate.

This cleared the decks for future interaction, which meant now it was entirely up to HQ Western Command (Harbakhsh) as to when and where forces would be allocated.

In New Delhi, there were other factors that were influencing Chaudhuri's thinking. U Thant, the secretary general of the United Nations had arrived on the afternoon of 12 September after having met Ayub Khan and Bhutto in Rawalpindi. Pakistan's all-weather friend, China, seeing India expand the conflict into Punjab and Rajasthan, began to worry that Pakistan had bitten off more than it could chew. China accused U Thant of being an American agent; it also delivered a note to the chargé d'affaires in Peking, accusing India of having violated the Sikkim border on multiple occasions in July and August.

In what was intended to be a clear warning and a major morale booster for Rawalpindi, the Chinese threatened that 'India must bear the responsibility for all consequences arising therefrom'.[3] The timing of the threat was interesting; it was obviously aimed at stampeding India into accepting a ceasefire and bringing the focus back to Kashmir. Contrary to advice from the Chinese, Pakistan had given India the opportunity to escalate matters by launching the Akhnoor offensive.

Though both Prime Minister Shastri and Defence Minister Chavan felt the Chinese were bluffing as they had no major objectives of their own and could hardly afford to antagonize the US by intervening in the Indo-Pakistan conflict, the Chinese would remain a niggling factor in the background throughout the next fortnight. U Thant met Shastri and briefed him about his meeting with the Pakistanis.

Shastri had already shown he was capable of counter-aggression, a character trait not associated with Indians ever since they had adopted Gandhi's non-violent methodology to oust the British. The Chinese feared that the air strike against the Indian airbase at Kalaikunda by the PAF could give Shastri the excuse to initiate an offensive against East Pakistan. Should that happen, the Chinese feared that Pakistan would not only expect but demand that China open a new front.

U Thant told Shastri that Pakistan had admitted having first crossed the IB during the Chhamb–Akhnoor offensive and were now agreeable to a ceasefire with certain conditions. Shastri rejected Pakistan's terms straight away. U Thant then wrote to both Shastri and Ayub on 12/13 September night, urging them to suspend the fighting. A meeting of the Emergency Committee of the Cabinet (ECC) was convened at 0900 hours and then again at 1830 hours where Shastri seemed inclined to accept the proposal for the cessation of hostilities. The next day, 14 September, the *Washington Post* carried a despatch from its New Delhi correspondent, Selig Harrison, which said the ECC was divided on the issue of a ceasefire. The report said Chaudhuri was against accepting any UN proposal for a ceasefire because the Indian Army was poised for a major breakthrough in the plains of the Punjab shortly. It also stated that the defence minister, Chavan, wholeheartedly supported the army chief.

Reports of the fiasco in Khem Karan had taken the sheen off the earlier successes in the Punjab plains and though in the Haji Pir Bulge the two columns from Poonch and Uri had established a link, thereby capturing a large chunk of POK territory, Chavan needed Chaudhuri to get a move on. Even though neither Lahore nor Sialkot were objectives unless they were actually threatened, it was unlikely that Ayub and Bhutto would tone down the war rhetoric especially since the Pakistani public was being fed stories of victories. However, with Harbakhsh asserting himself, Chaudhuri also knew he could not influence the battle without removing the Western Army commander from his position.

Even as Harbakhsh ignored Sparrow's demand for 3 Cavalry to be moved to reinforce 1 Armoured Division, it was obvious that by then there was a disproportionate amount of armour in the 11 Corps sector. It had finally dawned on Harbakhsh Singh that Pakistan's 11 Infantry Division did exist and was in indeed in the Kasur/Khem Karan area, so any fresh offensive in that sector was no longer a possibility. In the 7 Division sector, the bridge over the Ichhogil Canal at Barki had been blown up, so it was unlikely a Pakistani threat could develop from there; the same thing was also applicable to the GT Road and further to the north where the bridges at Dograi and DBN had been destroyed. This effectively only left the bridge over the Ichhogil at Bhasin where 38 Infantry Brigade had since been strengthened with 96 Infantry Brigade and 50 (I) Parachute Brigade.

Even if Harbakhsh left 9 Deccan Horse at Khem Karan, CIH at Barki, and 14 Scinde Horse on the GT Road with 3 Cavalry behind them, he had a surplus of at least three armoured regiments—the newly inducted 1 Skinner's Horse (Sherman IVs), 7 Cavalry (PT-76s), and 8 Light Cavalry (AMX-13s). Alternately, each one of these armoured regiments could have been clubbed with 9 Deccan Horse, CIH, and 14 Scinde Horse, allowing Harbakhsh the liberty to move 3 Cavalry, as Sparrow had requested. Harbakhsh Singh chose to take neither of the two options.

In 54 Infantry Brigade, Brigadier Niranjan Singh had replaced the stopgap commander Brigadier Kalha on 12 September. Dhillon was acutely conscious of the fact that in his area of responsibility, he had failed to recapture Khem Karan, barely managed to establish a toe-hold on the east bank of the Ichhogil Canal at Barki, and made no real progress on the main GT Road–Lahore axis. Even though Niranjan Singh had no time to familiarize himself with his command, Dhillon was leaning on the 15 Division GOC, Major General Mohinder Singh, to 'do something'.

FIRST BATTLE FOR CHAWINDA (14 SEPTEMBER)

Few commanders on either side, Indian or Pakistani, came close to the personal bravery consistently displayed by Sparrow. Following his armoured formations in his jeep, star plates and formation flag in place, he was everywhere during the initial advance on 8 September and then again on 11 September. Constantly under fire during his reconnaissance, he did not ask any of his staff officers to do anything he was not willing to do himself. Apart from his dynamic presence on the battlefield, he was also proving to be generous to a fault.

The first gift that he bestowed the grateful Pakistan high command was the precious gift of time. Not only had the Pakistanis used the two days of virtual inactivity on the part of India's 1 Armoured Division to fortify all approaches to Chawinda, they had also shifted 4 Armoured Brigade from Khem Karan into the Sialkot Sector. The brigade was being commanded by Brigadier Riaz ul Karim who had taken over from Brigadier Lumb on 11 September and had under his command 5 Probyn's Horse, 1 FF, and 15 SP. This added yet another Patton, an infantry, and a self-propelled artillery regiment to the forces that were to assist 6 Armoured Division.

Sparrow's second gift was to attack Chawinda's defences nearly frontally. It is a universally accepted fact that in a set defensive battle, the attacker needs superiority of strength of at least 3:1. On 8 September the Indian advance had achieved complete tactical surprise and though it was challenged by the PAF, it had been stopped by a solitary Patton regiment (25 Cavalry) which had managed to place itself in its path. On 11 September, by sidestepping and advancing, Sparrow had caught 11 Cavalry from a flank, after which 20 Guides Cavalry decided to present Indian armour with easy targets.

Dunn, GOC 1 Corps, issued his orders for the assault on Chawinda on 13 September. The plan was obviously drawn up by Sparrow, who until then 'had overall control not only of 1 Armoured Division but the troops deployed for flank and the rear zone behind his divisional area of operations. Dunn, General Chaudhuri's hand-picked Corps commander, had made little tangible contribution towards influencing the operations of 1 Corps. His influence on the tactical conduct of the offensive operations had been marginal and the results in the first week of operations had fallen far short of what was expected from the strongest Indian corps.'[4]

4 Hodson's Horse was to advance from Chahr to Fatehpur and cut the Badiana–Pasrur Road around Buttar and then swing south-east towards Sarangpur. It was to destroy any Pakistani tanks that may try to escape from or attempt to reinforce Chawinda. 17 Poona Horse was to thrust toward Kalewali–Chawinda and be prepared to support 43 Lorried Infantry Brigade's assault on Kaliwal–Wazirwali and later Chawinda if ordered. 69 Mountain Brigade Group with 16 Light Cavalry under command was to ensure that Pakistani armour was prevented from joining the main battle in the area south of Phillora and Chawinda from the direction of Sialkot. 43 Lorried Brigade with 20 Rajput under command from 35 Infantry Brigade was to advance and attack Chawinda from the firm base near Wazirwali. 1 Artillery Brigade was to have its gun positions in the area around Saboke in support of 1 Armoured Division.

Sparrow's plan for a frontal advance from Phillora to Chawinda had centred around the use of the Centurion regiments as battering rams, with the infantry battalions as also-rans. The tactics he was adopting were akin to what the Pakistanis had done in Khem Karan, where they seemed to believe that all they had to do was to show up in their tanks and the enemy would throw in the towel. In Khem Karan, the Pakistanis were up against a weakened 4 Mountain Division, whereas in Chawinda the Pakistanis not only had parity in armour, their artillery was vastly superior and for reasons that continue to baffle, they still had the PAF on call most of the time.

Sparrow functioning as the de facto corps commander meant HQ 1 Corps was virtually non-existent in the scheme of things. Contrary to what Sparrow and HQ 1 Armoured Division believed, 35 Infantry Brigade was not at Gadgor but had its HQ at Manga with 5 JAK Rifles, commanded by Lieutenant Colonel Sukhdev Singh, deployed at hand-shaking distance of Chawinda at Chak Dea Singh. HQ 35 Infantry Brigade on its part had no clue as to which formation it was to be a part of—1 Armoured Division under Sparrow, Ranjit Singh's 14 Infantry Division, or Korla's 6 Mountain Division! Until Korla met Major (later Major General) Yashwant Deva, the brigade major, and told him 35 Infantry Brigade was under his command and that Brigadier Cariappa was waiting for him at the Alhar Railway Station, it was not at all clear which formation the brigade was under. 20 Rajput had been placed under 43 Lorried Brigade and was to remain at Gadgor, while 5 JAK Rifles had moved forward and occupied Chak Dea Singh on 12 September. Its third battalion, 6 Maratha LI, commanded by Lieutenant Colonel Adappa Mathew Manohar, was at Phillora but no one seemed to know which formation it was reporting to.

Alpha Squadron 4 Hodson's Horse under Major Raju led the Indian advance starting from Libbe. They had a clear run till Jallowali where they ran into Pattons belonging to Charlie Squadron 22 Cavalry. In the initial engagement, two Pattons were destroyed and supporting Indian artillery fire accounted for a third tank. The Pakistani armour pulled back and the dense vegetation around the Manga area made it difficult for the Indians to continue the attack. Lieutenant Colonel Madan Bakshi decided to push Charlie Squadron through the gap between Changarian and Jallowali, bypassing the headquarters of 35 Infantry Brigade. Just north of the Alhar Railway Station, the Centurions clashed with Pattons again, this time from Alpha Squadron 10 Guides Cavalry.

Four Pattons were destroyed in the engagement, including the tank of the Guides' commanding officer, Lieutenant Colonel Jahanzeb Khan. Later this tank was found to be intact but for a single APDS round which had penetrated the turret. For Bakshi and 4 Hodson's Horse, this was the levelling of scores with the Pakistanis who had destroyed the regimental command Centurion on 11 September. Once again, the Pattons pulled back and Alpha Squadron 4 Hodson's Horse was at the railway embankment by 1100 hours while Charlie Squadron headed for the railway station from the direction of Basran. Alhar Railway Station itself was unoccupied but the neighbouring area of Chak Dea Singh was held by 5 JAK Rif.

As a result of the outflanking movements, Pakistani troops from 3 FF holding the defences between Manga and Chawinda's outer ring fell back towards Wazirwali. By 1400 hours, Bravo and Charlie Squadrons of 4 Hodson's Horse were concentrated around the Alhar Railway Station while Alpha Squadron did a U-sweep up to the Hasri Nullah and linked up with 16 Cavalry, which was in the gap between 69 Mountain Brigade and its left flank.

Once 4 Hodson's Horse had reached the Chawinda–Sialkot railway line in the Alhar area, Brigadier K. K. Singh ordered 17 Poona Horse to move forward and capture Wazirwali, beyond which the outer ring of Chawinda's defences lay. Verinder Singh's Charlie Squadron 17 Poona Horse was accompanied by 9 Dogra's Bravo Company commanded by Major (later Major General) Kripal Singh Kohli. Alpha Squadron moved on the eastern flank with the intention of securing Kalewali while Bravo Squadron was on the west in the Kot Izzat area.

Verinder's depleted squadron of ten Centurions, with Bravo Company 9 Dogra riding piggyback, was engaged by the Pakistani screen position holding Wazirwali at 1330 hours. By this time Delta Company 3 FF had fallen back from the Manga area towards Jalalpur Mahr. Though they were expecting 4 Hodson's Horse to assault them from the direction of Alhar–Chak Dea Singh, the Pakistanis were now suddenly confronted with 17 Poona Horse coming towards them from the direction of Phillora. The Pakistani RCL detachments fired at the Centurions but none of them hit the advancing Indian tanks. As the jeeps tried to withdraw, one of them received a direct hit. Lieutenant Colonel Muhammad Siddiq Akbar ordered his two Cobra anti-tank missile detachments to take on the Centurions. In all, five missiles were fired and all of them failed to hit their targets. However, this was the first time anti-tank missiles were fired in this sector.

Wazirwali was captured by 1430 hours by 17 Horse and the Dogras. Though the Pakistanis had lost almost a platoon and a few tanks in the fighting, the Indian advance had come to a halt, with 4 Hodson's Horse remaining at Alhar Railway Station and 17 Poona Horse deployed around Wazirwali. Pakistani artillery fire continued to make life difficult for the Indians. Once again, the PAF had the skies to itself, its F-86 Sabres even destroying Sparrow's jeep and forcing the occupants to dive for cover. Sparrow's ADC, Captain (later Brigadier) Mahesh Kumar Singh Chauhan and another officer were wounded in the air attack.

20 Rajput, commanded by Lieutenant Colonel Saranjit Singh Kanwar, was to be the vanguard battalion earmarked for the capture of Chawinda. Moving from Gadgor to its FUP, a large depression between Kalewali and Wazirwali, Bravo Company under Captain I. K. Chhitwal, and Charlie Company under the command of Major Harish Swami, were in position by 1430 hours and they settled down to await the green signal to attack.

The Rajputs were determined to capture Chawinda. As the battalion waited, it soon became obvious that the information given to them about the Pakistani defences ahead of them was inaccurate, and even their FUP was compromised. At least four MMGs had already started firing at the Rajputs who also came under observed artillery fire and were subject to a massive bombardment of super heavy shells. At 1600 hours, with casualties mounting by the minute, Kanwar told the adjutant, Major Madan Mohan Mathur, to join him in singing 'Watan ki rah mein, watan ke naujawan shaheed hon' (For the sake of the Motherland, may her sons be prepared to die) from the 1965 patriotic film *Shaheed*. The singing helped to steady the troops, but with five dead and twenty-seven wounded, perhaps Mathur could have chosen a different song. At 1700 hours, orders were received to pull back the battalion as the attack had been called off.

By last light, it was obvious the Indian frontal assault by 1 Armoured Brigade had not made much progress with only nominal gains by way of capturing the village of Wazirwali; Alhar having been in the possession of 35 Infantry Brigade all along. Having spent the day tackling what were at best flank attacks by Pakistani armour and screen positions to the main defences of Chawinda, the armoured brigade had failed to create the breach in the defences so that the planned attack could take place.

Subsequently, Harbakhsh Singh would be scathing in his comments claiming that in spite of our superiority in forces, we had failed to capture Chawinda and with that 1 Armoured Division threw away a cheap success and added another failure to its spate of lost opportunities.[5] Though Harbakhsh's comment is valid in terms of the progress, or non-progress, his assertion that the Indians had 'superiority in forces' suggests he was either completely removed from the ground realities or that he had simply made up his mind, as he had in Khem Karan just forty-eight hours earlier, that the Pakistanis had been routed and had lost the will to fight. The former is most likely since he also claimed that 4 Hodson's Horse had 'captured Alhar'.

While 17 Poona Horse and 4 Hodson's Horse had advanced towards Chawinda, on the extreme right flank, Eric Vas's 69 Mountain Brigade with 62 Cavalry continued to hold Pagowal, facing south towards the Chawinda–Sialkot railway line, apparently poised to threaten Badiana. 16 Cavalry occupied the stretch between the West Hasri Nullah tributary and 69 Mountain Brigade, moving forward on the Khakhanwali axis towards the railway line which ran on an embankment. Hardly had the advance begun than it got involved in a tank fight with Pattons from 22 Cavalry which continued all day. PAF's F-86 Sabres and the Pakistani gunners also kept hitting the regiment throughout the day.

At 1630 hours, 16 Cavalry was ordered to make a dash for the railway line and, if possible, threaten Badiana. Even as the Centurions were edging forward, they came under a massive bombardment from the Pakistani artillery, RCL guns, and tanks that were hull–down behind the railway embankment. The engagement continued until darkness enveloped the area. Though 16 Cavalry was not directly involved in the assault on Chawinda, it had successfully bottled up the Pakistani brigade at Badiana.

From the day's fighting, it was obvious to Sparrow that the Pakistani screen positions extended in a crescent shape from the general area of Chak Dea Singh up to Kalewali, which effectively covered all the approaches to Chawinda from the direction of Phillora. In addition, the Pakistanis were making good use of the railway embankment beyond Alhar 'and the built-up area of Wazirwali-Kalewali villages to develop a strong and coordinated defence line. The defences manned by tanks, RCL guns and infantry were well supported by artillery and inflicted heavy losses on our tanks.'[6]

Meanwhile, around Chawinda, even though 17 Poona Horse and Bravo Company 9 Dogra were dug in around Wazirwali for the night, by recalling 20 Rajput, commander 43 Lorried Infantry Brigade, Brigadier Dhillon, had left the area around Kalewali unoccupied.

5 Jat and 5/9 GR had been the vanguard for 43 Lorried Infantry Brigade during the advance to Phillora. Both battalions had been pulled back to give them a breather, but since the Gorkhas had a higher number of casualties, 5 Jat, after milking the Gorkhas of their equipment, were asked to move from Kaloi at 0300 hours early in the morning. 5 Jat was in position by first light at its FUP at Wachoke after which it had to await further orders. Earmarked to follow 20 Rajput into Chawinda as per the original plan, once the attack was cancelled, orders were received that 5 Jat should move forward and capture Kalewali, where a squadron of 17 Horse was deployed.

The Jats moved quickly, but before they could get to the FUP, the Pakistani observation posts picked up their movement even in the fading light and the battalion came under a heavy barrage of artillery fire. The battalion moved with two companies up—Alpha Company under Captain M. P. Singh on the left and Bravo Company under Captain B. K. Das on the right. The Pakistani artillery guns that had been firing at multiple Indian targets through the day from Chawinda continued to be extremely effective. The 4 Corps Artillery Brigade, equipped with the most modern US guns, were superbly led by their commander, Brigadier Amjad Ali Khan Chaudhry, who played a crucial role in limiting the Indian advance.[7]

The Jat advance was supported by the Indian artillery who took on the heavier Pakistani guns. With formations being shifted around, it was not clear which artillery guns were to support which advance. Captain Das's Bravo Company met with stiff opposition, but the Jats determinedly captured Kalewali by 2100 hours. They had lost four men and had twelve wounded. Just as the battalion started to dig in for the night, it was ordered to fall back to Wachoke as HQ 43 Lorried Infantry Brigade felt that Kalewali was way too forward and would become untenable in the event of an infantry counter-attack during the night, or, for that matter, an armoured assault on its positions at first light.

Braving the almost relentless artillery fire that followed them as they withdrew, 5 Jat was back where it had started from.

20 Rajput and 5 Jat's withdrawal from Kalewali was a shocker, for at 0200 hours on 15 September, Sparrow, under the impression that the Pakistanis had withdrawn from their screen positions into Chawinda for the night, ordered Dhillon to re-occupy Kalewali. However, the advance only commenced at midday. Once again Alpha and Bravo Companies, under heavy observed artillery fire from the Pakistani guns, led the way and the battalion occupied Kalewali by 1330 hours. Three jawans were killed, while one JCO and ten other ranks were wounded.

Kalewali was to serve as the firm base for the attack planned for 15/16 September and 20 Rajput went through the Jat position to form up southeast of Wazirwali, with the forward edge of the FUP resting on the Hasri Nullah. 8 Garhwal Rifles, commanded by Lieutenant Colonel Joseph Ephraim Jhirad, moved to the right of the Rajputs while 5 Jat was to be the reserve. H-hour for the attack was to be 2300 hours.

While the infantry battalions were getting into position—20 Rajput suffering another twenty-seven casualties in the process—17 Poona Horse remained in the Wazirwali area through the day, being relentlessly shelled by the Pakistani artillery guns. 4 Hodson's Horse and 16 Cavalry had spent the night north of the railway embankment with the latter guarding the west flank along the West Hasri Nullah. At 1030 hours, six Chaffees put in an appearance in the Chak Bidia area south of Palowal and these had been engaged by Alpha Squadron 62 Cavalry's Shermans.

Later in the day, Pattons had advanced towards Alhar from the direction of Jassoran, west of Chawinda but to the north of the railway embankment. These were engaged by Charlie Squadron 4 Horse and Naib Risaldar Surat Singh destroyed four tanks. He was killed later in the day by an artillery shell. Two more troops of Pakistani armour also put in an appearance from the direction of the Rakh Baba Bhure Shah Reserve Forest, but pulled back after more tanks were destroyed.

By nightfall, it was obvious that while Indian Centurions were always eager to engage Pakistani armour, they were displaying a marked hesitation in closing with the defences of Chawinda. The commanding officers of both 20 Rajput and 8 Garhwal Rifles told Brigadier Dhillon that they had not had adequate time to do a daylight reconnaissance. Dhillon then spoke to Sparrow, requesting him to postpone the attack by twenty-four hours. Sparrow agreed and once again the battalions withdrew from their FUPs.

This decision that led to Sparrow's 'no show' on 14/15 September would have ramifications at various levels. General Chaudhuri, who had been telling the defence minister and members of the Western media that 'there was going to be a spectacular victory', had egg on his face.

Despite having told Chaudhuri to stay out of the strategic conduct of operations, the Western Army commander seemed least interested in this sector; the corps commander, initially having left everything to 1 Armoured Division, had no functional control when Sparrow called up Dunn at the end of the day and told him Chawinda would have to be captured by one of the two 'supporting' infantry divisions, after all. 'The failure of 1 Armoured Division to capture Chawinda ended the pre-eminence of Sparrow in the operational conduct of 1 Corps.'[8]

SOUTH OF THE RAILWAY LINE—JASSORAN (16 SEPTEMBER)

Dunn, Sparrow, and Korla met at 1000 hours on 16 September at Maharajke to review the situation. After Sparrow had thrown up his hands and asked Dunn to ask the infantry divisions to capture Chawinda, Dunn had decided to give the task to 6 Mountain Division, which had been his most successful formation so far, capturing Charwa, Maharajke, and Pagowal with minimal fuss. 14 Infantry Division under Ranjit Singh, on the other hand, had botched up the Zafarwal operation and had, in many ways, foreclosed the option of an attack on Chawinda from the eastern side. Korla had also served with Dunn in 7 Baluch in Burma, and, unlike Ranjit Singh who was an armoured corps officer, he was hard-core infantry, perhaps best suited for the task at hand.

Dunn had also had to weigh the other options before he met with his two divisional commanders. He had the option of switching his main thrust line further to the west aimed at Badiana, which would have also brought his most potent formation, 26 Infantry Division into play. Or he could go back to the Zafarwal axis and bypass the strongly defended Chawinda and go for the MRLC along the original thrust line before Sparrow had moved his advance to the west. Not wanting to deviate from Sparrow's original plan, Dunn had decided to make just the one change—Korla to be responsible for the capture of Chawinda with Sparrow in support!

Major General Korla would retain 99 Mountain Brigade as his divisional reserve while 35 and 58 Infantry Brigades were placed under his command to capture and hold Chawinda on the night of 17/18 September. Once Chawinda was captured, 6 Mountain Division was to exploit towards Pasrur and Dugri Crossroads while 1 Armoured Division was to move west and capture and hold Badiana where it would be joined by 69 Mountain Brigade. 14 Infantry Division was to then get into the act and capture Zafarwal, for which 1 Armoured Division was to send a squadron of Centurions from Badiana.

Ten days into the War, Dunn was still not clear on what needed to be done. Amazingly, GOC 14 Infantry Division was not present, nor were the heads of any of the supporting arms—artillery, sappers, or signals. There was no discussion pertaining to the defences of Chawinda or any talk of coordinating with the IAF that, in any case, had barely put in an appearance. 'A corps plan, on the blink, was made to capture Chawinda, Badiana and Zafarwal—three built up areas of unsure enemy potential, each a difficult nut to crack. 6 Mountain Division, with two borrowed brigades, was given the task of attacking Chawinda.'[9]

Prior to leaving for Maharajke to meet Dunn, Sparrow had issued orders to 1 Armoured Division to push across the railway embankment and achieve local armour superiority in the area by capturing Jassoran, Sodreke, and Butur Dograndi. Sparrow reasoned that this would cut Chawinda off from Pakistani troops at Badiana and Pasur and would also allow 6 Mountain Division to use Jassoran as a firm base for the night attack. Even at this stage, Sparrow seemed either unaware or unwilling to acknowledge 35 Infantry Brigade's presence at Alhar/Chak Dea Singh and the fact that the brigade had prepared its own launch pad for a night attack on Chawinda.

8 Garhwal Rifles, commanded by Lieutenant Colonel Jhirad, had been placed under the command of 1 Armoured Brigade. Having been in the area of Wazirwali for two nights by then, 17 Poona Horse asked the Garhwalis to sweep the village as they suspected jitter parties were still operating from there. Alpha Company commanded by Major (later Major General) Som Prakash Jhingon and Delta Company under Major (later Lieutenant Colonel) Suresh Chander Gupta entered Wazirwali at 0530 hours and cleared the village, during which time, Alpha Squadron 17 Poona Horse tanks moved off towards Alhar for their planned assault.

At 0600 hours, Bravo Squadron crossed the railway embankment and ran into Pattons belonging to 11 Cavalry. In the brief firefight, three tanks were knocked out and the others forced to withdraw. The next immediate objective was Jassoran which was occupied by 0800 hours after which the squadron waited for Kripal Kohli's Bravo Company 9 Dogra to clear Jassoran of any enemy presence. The advance having taken place in broad daylight, the Pakistani artillery opened up, pinning the Centurions and the Dogras in Jassoran. As per the 17 Horse regimental records, 'Never before had enemy shelling been heavier or taken a bigger toll.'[10]

Jassoran and Sodreke both lay on the southern flank of the Chawinda–Badiana Road. 4 Hodson's Horse, advancing to the west of Bravo Squadron Poona Horse, had initially only committed its Bravo Squadron under Major Bhupinder Singh which advanced cautiously towards Sodreke. As had become the pattern by then, Pattons from Alpha Squadron 10 Guides Cavalry appeared on the western flank while the Centurions were still on the northern side of the Chawinda–Badiana Road. In the initial engagement, two Pattons were destroyed while the others fell back. On reaching the road, Bhupinder Singh could see two troops of Pattons from 19 Lancers and RCL guns deployed around Sodreke.

Madan Bakshi told Bhupinder Singh to hold his position and ordered Alpha Squadron to move forward towards Lalewali keeping Bravo Squadron on its right and Jassoran to the left. The Centurions were engaged by a troop each of Pattons and Shermans along with some RCL guns that were deployed to cover the gap between Rakh forest and the Bheloke–Lalewali area. Three tanks were destroyed after which the others withdrew. By 0900 hours both squadrons were deployed astride the Chawinda–Badiana road.

With the Sialkot–Prasur railway line taking a ninety-degree turn at Chawinda, the area south of the embankment extending through Jassoran–Sodreke–Badiana was like a large amphitheatre. The Pakistanis had deployed two of their Patton Regiments in an arc to the south and hoped the Indians would walk into 'the killing zone'. Madan Bakshi, having seen the Pattons, realized he was vulnerable and chose to hunker down short of the Chawinda–Badiana road.

K. K. Singh, meanwhile, was egging Adi Tarapore on, urging him to push on to Butur Dograndi from where he felt the Centurions could dominate and cut the Chawinda–Prasur road link as well. Already, the Pakistani artillery from within Chawinda was turning on the heat, laying down a tremendous barrage that was being supplemented by MMGs and 106 RCL guns that were adding to the discomfort of the Indians. 8 Garhwal Rifles had moved up to Jassoran from Wazirwali and, as per the brigade plan, Jhirad was looking to Tarapore for further instructions. Tarapore, having realized that a frontal attack towards Chawinda from Jassoran was out of the question, decided to attack Butur Dograndi instead. While Jhirad and Tarapore discussed the change in plan, Major Abdul Rafey Khan, the battalion's second-in-command, led the battalion to the designated FUP. He was joined by Jhirad at 1000 hours.

Tarapore felt that by capturing Butur Dograndi he would be able to get behind the Chawinda defences. On the contrary, he would be walking into a dangerous situation as Pakistan's 25 Cavalry Regimental HQ and Alpha Squadron 33 TDU were at Naugaza and the tanks deployed along the railway embankment supporting 3 FF which was to engage any Indian advance. 25 Cavalry's reconnaissance troop was south of Butur Dograndi while the Pattons of Alpha Squadron 19 Lancers were to their west. The main gun positions of the Pakistanis were south of Naugaza.

The Garhwalis, committed to assault Butur Dograndi in broad daylight, started advancing from the FUP at 1130 hours. Charlie Company commanded by Major Bagwan Singh Mall was to the west while Bravo Company under the command of Captain (later Brigadier) J. S. Bhullar was closer to the railway embankment. Charlie Squadron 17 Poona Horse was advancing with the Garhwalis in an assault role while Bravo Squadron continued to give fire support from Jassoran. Having seen the battalion move out of the FUP, Jhirad had a final word with Tarapore and was heading back when his jeep, the only vehicle available with 8 Garhwal Rifles, received a direct hit from an artillery shell. Jhirad,[11] though nearly sliced in half, was miraculously still alive. His driver and radio operator got away with minor injuries, while the IO, Captain Vijay Chandra, was unscathed. The commanding officer of 8 Garhwal Rifles was carried to a 3-ton but died even as he was being evacuated to the ADS[12]. 'He had only once asked for water.'[13]

Command of the battalion passed to Rafey Khan but he was in a hopeless position as the battalion's communication system had been destroyed along with Jhirad's jeep. Positioning himself behind Verinder Singh's tank, he could only hope the two vanguard companies could continue to advance despite the devastating artillery fire that seemed to come down on every Indian movement. Verinder's tank also received a hit from an RCL gun that damaged the Centurion's tracks but the remaining six Centurions somehow managed to edge closer to Butur Dograndi, finally stopping about 2,000 yards short.

The Garhwalis had been advancing under the blazing sun. Bhullar's Bravo Company had its three platoons spread out, when he realized no one was following. The tanks had been about 500 metres behind but Bravo Company had lost track of them. To take stock of the situation Bhullar stopped Bravo Company next to a well, which was partly hidden from enemy observation because of a few trees. 'I swung Sarweshwar Prasad's platoon to another well with a broken down hut and with a scraggly clump a couple hundred yards to my left. There was a sugar cane grove a hundred or so yards to my right and I ordered Gurmukh Bali's platoon to that area. We were about 1500 meters short of Butur Dograndi.'[14]

Coming up from behind, Rafey Khan commandeered Gurmukh Bali's platoon and proceeded towards Butur Dograndi, where he came under intense machine-gun fire, losing seven of the twenty men he had collected. The platoon was pinned down and badly off for water. A rifleman volunteered to go back with the bottles and get some water and it was through him that Bhullar learnt what had happened. 'Before I could get the bottles filled from the well, I saw Gurmukh and some boys trailing back. I gave him hell for not letting me know. He said Rafey had given him no time. Just then I saw Rafey come directly from the front. I was boiling and ready to sail into him but when I saw his face, ashen and soaked with sweat and grime with his shirt caked with mud and wet, I held my peace.'[15]

At 1400 hours, Tarapore asked K. K. Singh to release Alpha Squadron which was still at Wazirwali to reinforce Verinder's Charlie Squadron which continued to be under relentless shelling. The Pakistanis brought up some of their Cobra anti-tank missiles as well. K. K. Singh ordered 2 Lancers to move into Wazirwali, after which Alpha Squadron moved past Alhar and the railway embankment and reached Tarapore's position at Jassoran. The Regimental HQ decided to move with Alpha Squadron and they linked up with Verinder's remaining four Centurions about 1,500 metres short of Butur Dograndi.

There was some machine-gun fire coming from the area forward of the left platoon. Ajai Singh's Centurion had moved up to where Bhullar's Garhwalis were and at their request 'a tall burly Sardar loomed up and holding the .30 Browning casually in both hands, he began to nonchalantly rake the area ahead left to right and near to far.'[16]

At 1530 hours it was decided to pull the tanks back towards Jassoran. Though the Chawinda–Kasrur Road was within the range of their main guns, the railway embankment in between was an obstacle. Taking the Garhwali dead and wounded with them, the Centurions started to withdraw. By then the rest of 8 Garhwal had arrived and Rafey gave precise orders to Charlie and Delta Companies. They were to occupy the area he had vacated earlier after which Jhingon and Bhullar's companies were to pass through their positions and dig in close to Butur Dograndi. Since no radio sets were available, once the Garhwalis had deployed, a green Very light was to be fired.

As the tanks began to withdraw, Pakistani armour decided to pursue them. Tarapore's tank was hit, injuring a crew member. In the midst of the firefight, Tarapore got out of his tank and shifted the wounded man to the adjutant's tank. Two Pattons were hit and the Pakistani armour decided to break contact and call for artillery fire instead. 17 Poona Horse pulled back towards Jassoran. In the confusion, however, Tarapore's tank was left behind. Meanwhile, Charlie Squadron 4 Hodson's Horse was told to move to Jassoran to reinforce 17 Poona Horse, which had taken quite a beating. The Pakistanis, despite being well dug in, had suffered at the hands of the Centurions as well. 25 Cavalry had lost five Patton M48s and 33 TDU had three Shermans destroyed by tank fire, and nine tanks in the action with 4 Hodson's Horse.

Rafey, in the meantime, decided not to hold the village of Butur Dograndi, choosing instead to dig in 8 Garhwal's four companies in the sugarcane fields a few hundred metres to the north. Around last light, the green Very light arched upwards. Just then, Adi Tarapore[17] was dismounting from the adjutant's tank for a much-needed cup of tea. They say the shell that gets you is one that you will not hear. Tarapore was killed on the spot. Captain Jasbir Singh, the regiment's signal officer, the son of a former commandant of 17 Poona Horse, was mortally wounded and Kripal Kohli's radio operator and the company havildar major of 9 Dogra were killed.

A BUNGLED BATON CHANGE

After the meeting at Maharajke, Korla had spoken to the three brigadiers now under his command. Brigadiers Cariappa and Mandher, commanding 35 and 58 Infantry Brigades respectively, and Dharam Singh, who was commanding 99 Mountain Brigade. The plan to capture Chawinda on the night of 17/18 September was simple—Mandher's brigade would launch its assault through the Kalewali–Wazirwali axis, Cariappa would attack using Jassoran as his firm base. 99 Mountain Brigade was to be the reserve formation. In essence, the railway embankment would divide the areas of responsibility.

As far back as 11 September, Korla had told the brigade major of 35 Infantry Brigade that the formation was going to function under him, perhaps under the impression that Chawinda would be captured by the infantry divisions. This obviously did not happen and no orders to this effect had ever been issued in writing and, for all practical purposes, HQ 1 Armoured Division had been functioning as HQ 1 Corps. The new set-up announced on the morning of 16 September meant there was still no real infrastructure on the ground to coordinate between the various formations. HQ 1 Armoured Division, focussed on fighting the Pakistani armour, however, continued to stay with its assessment[18] that Chawinda was defended by just two infantry companies plus at best a squadron of armour, and though, by then, even the Pakistanis knew that HQ 35 Infantry Brigade was at Manga and its battalions in the Chak Dea Singh and Alhar Railway Station area, HQ 1 Armoured Division kept insisting the brigade was still at Gadgor.

At this point, with 6 Mountain Division being given the responsibility to capture Chawinda, it would have been natural for HQ 1 Corps to ensure that a system was in place to maximize battlefield management and that there was adequate coordination, cooperation, and liaison between the formations. On the contrary, Dunn and HQ 1 Corps were conspicuous by their absence; orders were being issued for grouping and regrouping formations without the knowledge of role, organization, strength, weakness, and training of the various constituents. 'The new plan allotted the primary role to 6 Mountain Division with 1 Armoured Division playing a supportive role. Regrettably, in this case, personalities mattered— not the intactness of formations and cohesive support of all arms. There was no team spirit, camaraderie and togetherness; let alone knowledge of neighbouring units and subunits—which was which, with what mission and where located.'[19]

In the evening of 16 September, the Alhar Railway Station was a relatively safe place to be since the Pakistani artillery was entirely focussed on 8 Garhwal Rifles and 17 Poona Horse, who were between Jassoran and Butur Dograndi. Cariappa had met with the commanding officers of 20 Rajput, 5 JAK Rif, and 6 MLI and they were working out the assault plans for the evening of 17/18 September. Though the battalions had some idea of the lay of the land in the Kalewali and Wazirwali area, they were clueless about the approach from Jassoran.

Mandher's 58 Infantry Brigade was in a similar predicament. His two infantry battalions, 4 JAK Rif and 14 Rajput, were both unfamiliar with the Kalewali–Wazirwali area. Both Cariappa and Mandher asked their respective commanding officers to use the morning of 17 September to get familiar with their objectives, for which they would have to aggressively patrol the area and mark out their individual approaches.

The morning was bright and sunny and a deadly stillness hung in the air. Having got a fix on 35 Infantry Brigade's position, it wasn't long before F-86 Sabres and the Pakistani artillery started hitting Manga and the Alhar railway station area, an exercise that would continue throughout the day. To the south, across the railway embankment and south of Jassoran, closer to Butur Dograndi, Alpha Squadron 17 Poona Horse had spent a jittery night with no infantry protection as they still had not linked up with 8 Garhwal Rifles, even though they were deployed close to one another. At 0800 hours, the first Pakistani shells began landing around the Garhwali positions. The initial concentration of fire was on Butur Dograndi itself, and the area was pulverised until Pakistani observers realized the Indians were not there.

Watching from his trench was Joginder Singh Bhullar: 'The shelling became heavy and we began to get plastered. And then I saw what [we had done so many times during exercises] while attacking some objective or the other. In the distance, well spread out was a line of enemy walking towards us slowly but steadily. They were more towards my left and nearest to Gabar's platoon. I yelled orders to hold fire—not waste ammunition—and to make each round count. More so as we were carrying only pouch ammunition, which came to 50 rounds per rifle and 500 per light machine gun. The unit reserve of 40 and 400 rounds respectively was supposed to be in our "F" echelon vehicles but these had not followed us!

When the enemy line was about a hundred plus yards away, we began to fire and the line went to ground i.e. they lay down behind any small bund or whatever cover they could get and began to return our fire. The jokers seemed unwilling to close in and make a fight of it.'[20]

With the two sides having come so close to one another the Pakistani artillery had stopped firing. Some Pakistanis got up and started shouting that they were Jat troops of the Indian Army. As Gabar ordered his platoon to stop firing, reasoning that the olive-green uniforms had turned khaki because of the mud, he caught a machine-gun burst across his chest. 'Suddenly a shiver went through the whole company because coming towards us were two Pattons, one behind the other. I was surprised to see them come rather hesitantly and very very slowly... I got Gulab, with his antitank grenades to my command post. I thought of taking the shot myself but thinking that it would be bad for morale if I missed, I coached Gulab who was pretty jittery and forgot to rest his rifle in the corner of the trench. As he fired, we saw the grenade take a slow curved flight towards the leading tank. For a second I thought that my range estimation had been low. But no, the grenade managed to just reach the tank and it hit and burst on the tank tracks. The tank shuddered and came to a dead stop.

'I told Gulab to duck deep as I expected the tank to swivel its main gun in our general direction and blow us to smithereens and kingdom come. For a second, nothing happened. Then we peeped up and to our astonishment saw the crew of the tank clamber down and run back to the rear tank. This tank then slowly pulled back in reverse. Well nigh the whole company took pot shots. I am ashamed to say that our shooting standard was pathetic as no one hit anything.'[21]

At 1030 hours the Pakistanis put in another attack. By then casualties were mounting, with both Bhullar and Bali having been wounded, but the tenacious Garhwalis held on. The Centurions had also manoeuvred themselves into position to support the dug-in troops. The Pakistanis, on the other hand, were getting extremely frustrated. A company of 3 FF with a troop of 25 Cavalry Pattons had been told to capture Jassoran and the Indians just happened to be sitting in the way. With casualties mounting through the day, it was finally decided to withdraw from Butur Dograndi.

Major Abdul Rafey, having ensured the surviving men were falling back in good order, was loading the Garhwali wounded onto a Centurion with the IO, Vijay Chandra, and the RMO, Captain Sonkar, when a 106 RCL caught Rafey plumb in the middle. Alive, but dismembered so badly that he could not even be lifted, he merely waved to both these officers to leave him and get the others out because they could see the enemy infantry advancing—slowly and cautiously. The doctor was to say later that considering the condition Rafey was in, he could not have lived for more than ten minutes.[22] As for the IO, he had two commanding officers killed on consecutive days while they were right next to him.

By last light, 8 Garhwal Rifles had withdrawn from its position around Butur Dograndi and pulled back through Jassoran. Major Jhingon was now commanding the battalion, which had performed superbly under the circumstances. Evacuating the wounded, many of them cramped inside the Centurions, was a herculean task. One squadron of 17 Poona Horse along with Kripal Kohli's Bravo Company dug in for the night at Jassoran while another squadron fell back to Libbe.

Unable to clear Jassoran because of the Garhwalis, the Pakistanis had turned their attention to recapturing Wazirwali in the latter half of the day. Alpha Company 5 Jat had moved into Wazirwali along with a troop of 2 Lancers that had relieved Major Ghorpade's Alpha Squadron 17 Poona Horse that had then moved up to Butur Dograndi. 5 Jat had then split into two groups—Charlie Company along with Raj Singh's battalion headquarters and other support elements joined Alpha Company, while the second group, Bravo and Delta Companies, occupied Kalewali under the command of Major A. S. Pawar. Hardly had the Jats started to prepare their defences than they were subjected to an intense dose of shelling.

Through the morning of 17 September, while the fighting raged first to the south of Jassoran and then at Wazirwali, Korla was getting extremely concerned.[23] He had briefed the two attacking brigade commanders the previous day but their proposed firm bases for the attack to be launched later that night were the scene of intense fighting. It was almost as if the Pakistanis had guessed Wazirwali and Jassoran were the two areas chosen by the Indians. By mid-morning, Korla had informed Dunn that he was not in a position to launch the assault later that evening.

Though the reconnaissance trips had been limited, it was obvious that the defences of Chawinda were not only formidable, but were being improved by the minute. That the Pakistani sappers were good was obvious from the way their defences had been prepared wherever they had been encountered. They could be seen laying mines and strengthening the Chawinda defences and it was clear there were at least three, if not four, infantry battalions with a dug-in armour unit with artillery guns of various calibres in situ, plus other mobile artillery units of Pakistan's 1 Armoured Division in range. As against this, the total attacking force that Korla had at his command was five infantry units with limited artillery support. At night the armour was not in a position to support 6 Mountain Division.

Around 1000 hours, Korla had spoken to Dunn and told him 6 Mountain Division needed at least a twenty-four-hour postponement before he could even think of launching a night attack. Just around that time, Harbakhsh Singh reached HQ 1 Corps, and Dunn informed him that Korla needed to delay the assault to the night of 18/19 September. In his usual grandiose manner, Harbakhsh records: 'I, however, impressed on General Officer Commanding 1 Corps the urgency for expeditious action and told him that he was far behind schedule from his final objective. In the afternoon I left for Headquarters 11 Corps by road.'[24]

To make matters worse, a report was received towards the late afternoon that the commanding officer of 5 JAK Rif, Lieutenant Colonel Sukhdev Singh, had been wounded while on reconnaissance of the objective, and had since been evacuated. The command of the battalion had passed onto the second-in-command, Major Suraj Singh.

At 1600 hours Brigadier Grewal, BGS HQ 1 Corps, messaged Sparrow to tell him that the proposed attack by 6 Mountain Division scheduled to be launched in the next few hours would not go in that night. Sparrow responded immediately, saying 'From Tiger. Have understood that the task accepted by 6 Mountain Division now not tonight. This action fraught with grave consequences, not only liable to lose substantial gains but also possible to lose mechanised armour equipment. Whole day was there to liaise and reconnaissance. More we delay the worse it will be, will explain later under what stress, strain and risk the gains were achieved. Even now recommend it should be done.'[25]

The timing and wording of this signal underlines the prevailing confusion that existed, and continued to exist even when the post-war reports were written. First, Sparrow's contention that Korla had the 'whole day...to liaise and reconnaissance' confirms that the change of roles had been indicated by Dunn at Maharajke on 16 September and not 17 September as has been contended by Shergill in *The Monsoon War,* co-authored by him and Amarinder Singh. Second, 1 Armoured Division's plan on 16 September was actually based on the optimistic assumption that the defences of Chawinda were indeed lightly held, so once Jassoran was captured, all 8 Garhwal Rifles had to do was wheel to their left, go over the railway line again, and take Chawinda. That had been wishful thinking, leading instead to the ad hoc advance towards Butur Dograndi which achieved nothing, instead resulting in 8 Garhwal Rifles and 17 Poona Horse suffering needless casualties that included both their commanding officers.

The meeting between the two GOCs, Sparrow and Korla, could not have happened before 1700 hours. Amazingly, even before any decision had been taken, K. K. Singh had issued the order from HQ 1 Armoured Brigade in the afternoon that 'Butur Dograndi would be vacated at last light because 6 Mountain Division did not propose to utilize it as a firm base for attack'. The order went on to say the attack that evening (17 September) would be carried out by 43 Lorried Brigade in the Wazirwali–Kalewali–Ballowali area and that one squadron of 17 Poona Horse was to stay on in Jassoran with one company of 9 Dogra and help 6 Mountain Division meet any armoured counter-attack.

Coinciding with the withdrawal to Jassoran on the evening of 17 September, it was later stated that there was a lot of confusion as 35 Infantry Brigade had been moved by 1 Armoured Brigade from Gadgor to Phillora, only to realize there had been a 'misunderstanding'. By the time 35 Infantry Brigade was sent back to Gadgor, valuable time had been lost and the planned attack on the night of 17/18 was postponed.

This was pure hogwash and the myth perpetuated then continued to hold sway even later. Korla simply was not in a position to launch any attack because 1 Armoured Division had stirred up a hornets' nest by going into Jassoran and then Butur Dograndi. So long as the armour was in the area, there was no way Jassoran could be used as a FUP to launch any attack on Chawinda.

Whether Korla's meeting with Sparrow at Papin, the TAC HQ of 1 Armoured Division, was an acrimonious affair or not is irrelevant. What is perhaps more to the point is that either Harbakhsh Singh had no idea what was going on in 1 Corps or, after having been sidelined by Chaudhuri in the planning stages of the operations in the Rachna Doab, he simply did not care. If on the night of 14/15 September it had become obvious that Chawinda had to be captured by 'an infantry division', Sparrow and maybe even Dunn should have been removed from command by the army commander. Harbakhsh's own comments (in *War Despatches*) on Sparrow's performance on 8/9 September and then again on 11 September are extremely critical of the higher leadership.

Worse, even in the Khem Karan Sector, Harbakhsh had demonstrated a naïve approach. An army commander trying to fight a tactical battle where no one down the chain of command had the nerve to challenge him had resulted not only in severe casualties but in handing the advantage to Pakistan. Korla having to drive to HQ 1 Armoured Division and 'explain his position to him (Sparrow)' had created a situation which was absurd. Harbakhsh keeps talking of the failure of higher command—in this case, the finger should be pointing squarely at himself. *He was the army commander.*

As already discussed, Sparrow's southern thrust over the railway line had taken away whatever chance 6 Mountain Division had of achieving any surprise by assaulting along the Jassoran axis. Sparrow not only wanted Korla to launch the attack that night, but was also saying it was not feasible for him to keep the armour deployed south of the embankment in case there was a postponement. Again, it has been implied that Korla wanted to change his attack plans, but the fact is he still wanted his two brigades to go in to Chawinda, keeping the railway line as the dividing boundary. Korla wanted the armour to keep a low profile around Jassoran so the area did not continue to attract Pakistani attention. The two generals parted and the attack on Chawinda was rescheduled for the night of 18/19 September.

Not only were Harbakhsh Singh and Dunn proving to be rudderless commanders, they seemed to have no real desire to push 26 Infantry Division out of its comfort zone either. Thapan's formation, also known as the Tiger Division,[26] was the most stable and therefore potent weapon available in 1 Corps' armoury. The division had been leaning on Sialkot ever since its 162 and 168 Infantry Brigades had crossed the IB on the night of 7/8 September. The two brigades had been expanding their respective bridgeheads and had warded off all Pakistani counter-attacks fairly comfortably. On 12 September 52 Mountain Brigade under Brigadier Rocky Hira had been moved from the Rajouri based 25 Infantry Division. Ever since, plans were being made to expand the area under 26 Infantry Division's control. On the night of 17/18 September, 52 Mountain Brigade was tasked with capturing Tilakpur and Mahadipur and the high features contiguous to these villages. The objectives, situated about 3,000 metres southwest of Sialkot, could pose a threat to the city. In preliminary actions, 5/11 GR commanded by Lieutenant Colonel (later Lieutenant General) Sushil Kumar had to clear Nandpur, Malane, and Dhure, villages to the north of 162 Infantry Brigade's Suchetgarh area. 10 Mahar, a new raising with mixed troops, commanded by Lieutenant Colonel Russi Hormusji Bajina was to capture Mahadipur while 1 Madras commanded by Lieutenant Colonel C. P. Menon was to capture Tilakpur.

In a strange move, at the last minute, HQ 1 Corps decided to postpone the attack to 18/19 September to coincide with the attack on Chawinda.

2ND BATTLE OF CHAWINDA

Sparrow's final understanding with Korla on the evening of 17 September was that since the attack was being put on hold, 1 Armoured Brigade would pull back from the area south of the railway embankment except for Jassoran which would continue to be held *at any cost*. However, after an uneventful night other than routine shelling, daylight found Alpha Squadron 4 Hodson's Horse deployed from the West Hazri Nullah to Alhar while Charlie Squadron formed a screen behind Wazirwali holding the area between Alhar and Basran and Bravo Squadron was at Manga.

Realizing that the Indians had vacated the area, the Pakistanis occupied it up to the Badiana–Chawinda Road but other than a half-hearted attempt to advance towards the bridge on the West Hasri which attracted immediate tank and artillery fire from the Indians, they were quite content to hold ground. 17 Poona Horse was also in the Alhar–Chak Dea Singh area till 0900 hours, after which it was pulled further back to Kotli Jandran, which was adjacent to Phillora. By then it had dawned on HQ 35 Brigade that Jassoran had also been vacated during the night.

Cariappa and Kolra had a hurried consultation and Sparrow was asked to reoccupy Jassoran, which was to be the firm base for 35 Infantry Brigade's assault on Chawinda later that night. Sparrow therefore ordered K. K. Singh to reoccupy Jassoran, but KK said it would not be possible to recapture Jassoran at such short notice. Sparrow, however, promised Korla that he would position his tanks at Jassoran by first light 19 September.

The clock was ticking for Korla—another postponement was definitely out of the question. H-hour for the assault was 0100 hours and with daylight hours dwindling, Korla decided to assign the capture of Jassoran to 20 Rajput. An incredulous HQ 35 Brigade protested and Cariappa pointed out that the Rajputs were an integral part of the attack plan and not a reserve battalion. As per the brigade's plan, 20 Rajput was phase two of the attack, having been allotted the vital task of capturing Milestone 5 on the Chawinda–Pasrur Road extending up to the railway line, after which it was to mop up Chawinda town on the premise that its flanks were secure with the presence of armour.

Korla could have considered using a battalion from 99 Mountain Brigade for the capture of Jassoran, which was the reserve meant for unforeseen contingencies such as this. However, HQ 6 Mountain Division issued the orders for 20 Rajput to occupy and hold Jassoran as a firm base. Cariappa had no choice but to give the onerous task of phase two to 6 Maratha LI.

At 1140 hrs, for a change, it was the Indian artillery guns that started pounding the defensive ring around Chawinda. At the stroke of midnight, to the south across the railway embankment, Alpha Company 20 Rajput commanded by Major (later Colonel; my father's younger brother) Vijay Dhruv Verma on the left and Bravo Company under Harish Swami on the right started to advance along the track running north to south from the direction of Alhar. Delta Company under Major R. C. Jetly was bringing up the rear. During the day, Pattons belonging to 19 Lancers had moved up to Jassoran but they had withdrawn to harbour at last light, after which they were relieved by two companies of 3 FF who had moved in from their position on the bend in the railway line.

The leading platoon of Pakistan's Delta Company 3 FF saw Harish Swami's assaulting troops when they were nearly on top of their hastily prepared trenches. Shouting out their war cry, 20 Rajput surged forward. After a forty-five-minute engagement, Alpha Company 3 FF led by Major Qalander Shah and Delta Company 3 FF, wilting under the Rajput onslaught, fell back in a disorganized state towards the railway bend.

Around the time Jassoran was captured by 20 Rajput, things were going terribly wrong for its sister battalion, 14 Rajput. Pakistani artillery, taking their cue from the Indian pre-bombardment, had begun shelling the entire area, extending from Jassoran to Wazirwali. H-hour for the main attack on Chawinda was 0100 hours, barely fifteen minutes away. The four battalions waiting to advance from north to south were 14 Rajput, commanded by Lieutenant Colonel Rawat, at the extreme left near Wazirwali; 4 JAK Rif in line with Chak Dea Singh; 5 JAK Rif under Major Suraj Singh; and 6 MLI commanded by Lieutenant Colonel Manohar in the gap between Jassoran and the railway embankment.

Alpha Company 5 Jat and Charlie Squadron 2 Lancers were holding ground at Wazirwali. At 0045 hours, the Jats came under fire. 14 Rajput, disoriented in the dark, had missed their line of advance and wandered slightly to the north. As shots rang out in the dark, the familiar Rajput battle cry of 'Bol Bajrang Bali Ki Jai' was clearly heard by Major M. P. Singh, the company commander. He immediately stood up on a tank to order the firing to stop when he was hit on the head and killed outright. 5 Jat began to return fire. Major R. Sharma also realized what had happened and tried to stop the firing but he was wounded as well. 5 Jat, taken completely by surprise, abandoned their positions. 14 Rajput, equally stunned by the unexpected opposition enroute to their objective, dispersed in confusion. Next morning 5 Jat reoccupied their positions—14 Rajput was still out in the blue.

The two companies of 4 JAK Rif found themselves closing in on the Chawinda defences manned by 14 Baluch, but the volume of fire combined with the artillery barrage broke up their advance. For all practical purposes, 58 Infantry Brigade was out of the equation.

On the southern side of the railway line, the Indian artillery guns had been pounding away, forcing Bravo and Charlie Companies of 3 FF to abandon their defences and withdraw towards the Chawinda Railway Station. 5 JAK Rif, advancing along the railway line, was up against Delta Company of 3 FF, whose extreme right platoon had closed ranks with 14 Baluch. Illumination ammunition had lit up the night sky and the two JAK Rif battalions were taking severe casualties, but pushing forward nevertheless.

5 JAK Rif had come up against 3 FF earlier at Chobara and Gadgor and on both occasions had come out on top. The ferociousness of the attack unsettled 3 FF, who started leaving their positions and fled in disorder to the south towards the gun positions, where they were stopped by the gunners. Alpha Company 5 JAK Rif under Second Lieutenant Ravinder Singh Samiyal[27] had overrun the Pakistani MMG dugouts that had been abandoned seconds earlier. Jumping into the pit, Samiyal swung the captured MMG around and caught some of the fleeing Pakistanis.

6 MLI was being led by the CO, Mathew Manohar. With him were Delta Company under Major Tendulkar and Alpha Company was being led by Major Ratnachalam. The usually devastating Pakistani artillery now had to fight for its survival. In keeping with the prevailing confusion in the higher headquarters on

the Indian side, neither 73 Composite Battery or 20 Locating Regiment that had arrived in the sector almost twenty-four hours earlier had been brought into play—which meant Indian guns could not fire at the Pakistani gun positions with any accuracy. The four attacking companies—two each from 5 JAK LI and 6 MLI—had taken on four well dug-in Pakistani companies supported by massive firepower and overcome them. The Pakistanis later described the attack by 5 JAK Rif and 6 MLI as one of the most determined infantry charges made by the Indians.

Phase one of the attack was the capture of Chawinda Railway Station and, after some hard fighting, it was in Indian hands. Manohar came on the VHF radio set and gave the code word 'Abhimanyu' to HQ 35 Infantry Brigade followed by a message: 'Heading for Phase 2'.

There was an ominous silence on the wireless after this message was transmitted. An artillery shell explosion nearby had hit the wireless set which was with Second Lieutenant L. K. Nadgir, the IO, thereby rendering it useless. Pakistani artillery was not only engaging the troops around the Chawinda Railway Station, they continued to relentlessly target the follow-up companies who were not able to advance. Apart from the shelling, small arms fire from three different directions—elements of 3 FF, 14 Baluch, and 2 Punjab—was making it extremely difficult for the Marathas, who now had to advance further south to execute phase two which was the capture of Milestone 5.

Between 6 MLI and the Pakistani gun position was Delta Company of Pakistan's 2 Punjab. All of a sudden, two Pakistani Pattons appeared along the railway line and started firing at the railway station. The tanks had returned from the workshop after repairs that evening and had been parked there for the night. The two Pattons moved onto the railway line and engaged the Marathas with machine guns and their main guns at point-blank range, greatly aided by infrared night vision devices.

'Manohar Mathew was bellowing for a rocket launcher. Suddenly someone must have thrust it in his hands for he fired at one of the Pattons but the shot missed. While the tank crews seemed to hesitate, unsure of where the shot had come from, we could see Mathew brace himself to fire again.'[28] The 3.5-inch rocket launcher, notorious for failing when it was most needed, misfired yet again.

In the meantime, 14 Baluch had fallen back to protect the Pakistani gun positions. Yet 6 MLI pressed forward. Casualties were mounting, men were wounded and dying while others including Major Ratnachalam and Captain (later Brigadier) Pritam Singh Virk were overpowered in the hand-to-hand fighting and taken prisoner. 'We had no heavy weapons, and we kept looking over our shoulders for help—any help. Even our guns were not able to support us anymore for their range did not extend beyond the immediate area of the railway station.'[29] The sky was beginning to turn grey when 6 MLI was told to break contact and pull back.

Dropping down from the railway embankment into the sugarcane fields adjacent to Butur Dograndi, the survivors and the walking wounded started the three to four kilometre walk back towards Jassoran. Manohar's luck finally ran out at this point and he was killed. Captain (later Lieutenant General) Harsh Chaitanya Gangoli, shot through the arm, had used his field dressing to bandage the wound but he was bleeding profusely. Lieutenant Nadgir offered to use his field dressing: 'You take it—I'm lucky I'm alive,' he said. Just a few minutes later, Nadgir was killed by an exploding shell.

Earlier, when Gangoli had emptied his pouch to get to the field dressing, a letter from his fiancé, Sujata, had fallen out. It was later found by Major (later Lieutenant General) Javed Ashraf Qazi, an artillery officer.[30] The letter was used by Pakistan Radio to broadcast fake news that Gangoli was dead. Years later, when they were both brigadiers, Gangoli requested Qazi through a mutual acquaintance to return the letter to him. Qazi refused, claiming the letter as his war trophy.

JASSORAN (19 SEPTEMBER)

At first light, around the time 6 MLI was ordered to break contact with the Pakistanis, Bravo and Charlie Squadrons of 4 Hodson's Horse were sallying forth across the railway embankment towards Sodreke and Jassoran. Both the armoured squadrons had a company each from 9 Dogra with them. Even though 4 Hodson's Horse had only lost two tanks to enemy action, the regiment had been deployed ever since 8 September, as a result of which Bhupinder Singh's Bravo Squadron started the day with just eight tanks, while Captain Rajpal Singh, who was commanding Charlie Squadron now, had just seven serviceable tanks instead of around sixteen or eighteen.

Almost two companies of 5 JAK Rif and 6 MLI were still holding the Chawinda Railway Station and were now stranded, unable to pull back without covering fire from the Centurions. The arrival of Charlie Squadron 4 Hodson's Horse at Jassoran shortly after daybreak allowed HQ 35 Infantry Brigade some relief, for they were in danger of being run over. Pakistan's 19 Lancers had debouched from the Chawinda–Badiana Road and while Bravo Squadron advanced towards Jassoran from the direction of Butur Dograndi, its Alpha Squadron closed in from the direction of Mundeke Berian towards Sodreke.

Though outnumbered by the Pattons, Rajpal Singh deployed his seven tanks at Jassoran facing Butur Dograndi in an effort to keep the Pakistanis at bay. In the meantime, a Bird Dog had also taken to the skies and it started directing the Pakistani guns, which started shelling both Jassoran and the area towards the Chawinda Railway Station. At 1000 hours, HQ 35 Brigade, having realized its two companies inside Chawinda could not hold out much longer against tanks and infantry firing at them from surrounding buildings, requested 1 Armoured Brigade for help to extricate their men. With Bhupinder's Bravo Squadron heavily engaged in Sodreke, and 17 Poona Horse having been pulled back, Madan Bakshi ordered Rajpal to move some of his tanks towards Chawinda.

The moment the tanks tried to reposition themselves, their flanks were exposed, and three tanks, including that of Second Lieutenant H. S. Mann were hit. However, the tanks succeeded in engaging the Pakistanis long enough to allow the remaining elements of 5 JAK Rif and 6 MLI to pull back to Jassoran. Some of the serious casualties were loaded onto a Centurion and it exited the area, leaving three tanks to face the Pattons for the next five hours. By 1500 hours, 35 Infantry Brigade had evacuated its casualties and withdrawn from Jassoran under covering fire provided by the three remaining tanks of Charlie Squadron. Rajpal Singh then withdrew under covering fire by 17 Poona Horse which had moved up to the railway embankment to cover 4 Hodson Horse's withdrawal. The CO of 20 Rajput, Kanwar, had also been hit by a splinter and had been evacuated with the withdrawing tanks. All this while, HQ 35 Infantry Brigade was frantically trying to get through to HQ 6 Mountain Division so that the Rajputs could also pull out with the armour. The orders did not come. This left 20 Rajput standing at Jassoran under the second-in-command, Major J. C. Verma.

The Pakistani 19 Lancers, having been kept at bay through the day, soon realized the Indian armour had pulled out from Jassoran. On the western flank, Bhupinder's Bravo Squadron had been locked in a grim struggle with two squadrons of 19 Lancers who were deployed around Sodreke, trying to get to the railway line. In the morning, after crossing the railway line, the Centurions had fought their way to Sodreke where it was apparent that the Pakistanis had deployed half a dozen RCLs and Cobra missile units (in addition to the tanks) in the area east of Peloke and Lalewali. Having reached Sodreke, Bhupinder's squadron fought off a counter-attack by the 19 Lancer Pattons. By the afternoon, five tanks were lost and a sixth had broken down, leaving Bhupinder with just two operational tanks. Initially one troop of Alpha Squadron was sent to reinforce Bravo Squadron, but shortly thereafter Madan Bakshi ordered the rest of Alpha Squadron to also move up to the area east of Lalewali.

Earlier in the morning, Bhupinder's tank had been hit by a Patton and caught fire. However, the crew had succeeded in putting out the flames and the squadron commander's Centurion tank had continued to fight on through what was perhaps the most gruelling and hard fought day in the Sialkot Sector. In the evening, Bhupinder was just southeast of Alhar when he was hit by a Cobra missile. This time the flames were an inferno, and though Bhupinder was severely burnt, he pulled out two of his crew. The driver could not bail out and was burnt alive in his seat. Bhupinder was evacuated to the hospital in Delhi but died on 3 October.

Just around the time Bhupinder's tank was hit, Subir Mathur (who was with Bhupinder) had his own run-in with the enemy: 'one Pakistani infantry man climbed on my tank thinking it to be a Patton, but as soon as he realised that it was not so, he ran away to save his skin. He was purposely not fired on by my gunner who told me he did not find it correct to fire on a soldier who is lost in battle.'[31]

That night, only Subir Mathur's Centurion made it back to harbour at Chahr after his lone tank had continued to hold up 19 Lancers till last light. On 19 September, 4 Hodson's Horse, despite their depleted strength, had performed magnificently. Not only had they stopped the Pakistanis from getting to the railway line from Sodreke, Charlie Squadron had held out long enough to let 35 Infantry Brigade pull back from a hopeless position in Chawinda Railway Station and then from Jassoran. In pure numerical terms, six Pattons and three RCLs had been destroyed by Bhupinder's squadron, which had lost seven of its eight Centurions.

Fortunately, the communication line between Jassoran and the Alhar Railway Station had survived. At 1600 hours, Major J. C. Verma told HQ 35 Infantry Brigade over the radio that the situation was becoming untenable. The Pattons of 19 Lancers were deploying with 19 FF for an attack on Jassoran. Pakistani artillery fire nearly doubled in its intensity as the Pakistani plan was to secure the entire area south of the railway line and then attack Alhar from the west.

'The division HQ, although through, continued to be unresponsive. I wanted them to give orders to withdraw from Jassoran and hold Alhar's well dug-in, well-prepared position that I had personally reconnoitred and 20 Rajput were holding prior to moving to Jassoran. Alhar–Chak Dea Singh complex was a firm base as a firm base ought to be. Jassoran on the other hand was a pathetic pretence and a poor substitute for a firm base.'[32] Once again, casualties were mounting when HQ 6 Mountain Division finally ordered 20 Rajput to pull back. The wounded Kanwar, by then at the brigade command post in Alhar, told J. C. Verma to take the battalion's layout group and reposition the battalion east of the railway line Chawinda–Sialkot.

Verma replied that some other officer would move with the layout group, after which the companies would withdraw, covering each other. He said on the radio that he would be the last man to withdraw from Jassoran. True to his word, he was the last man standing in Jassoran when he was killed by a direct hit of a tank shell.

20 Rajput fell back to the Gil–Chhal area. All three battalions under 35 Infantry Brigade had lost their commanding officers by then. The command of the battalion passed on to Vijay Dhruv Verma, who quickly reorganized the battalion for the re-occupation of Alhar village. The Pakistani tanks had come right up to the railway embankment and all the Centurions had withdrawn towards Manga. The Pakistani artillery continued to shell the area relentlessly, but by last light, 20 Rajput had dug in to the west of Alhar. Battalion support weapons, mainly RCLs and MMGs, were positioned to cover possible approaches for further Pakistani attacks.

5 Rajputana Rifles commanded by Lieutenant Colonel H. R. Mehandroo, a part of 99 Mountain Brigade, was deployed south of Libbe with a company at Khanawali later that evening. 14 Rajput, after the fiasco with 5 Jat, had regrouped under its second-in-command, Major (later Colonel) Jagat Singh,[33] and it was

deployed on the railway line at the Alhar Railway Station at 2300 hours. The next morning, 5 Raj Rif was placed under command of 35 infantry Brigade whose HQ remained at Manga.

As darkness set in and the last of the few Alouette III helicopters allotted to the sector lifted off with the casualties that could not be evacuated by road, two things stood out. First, the Indian artillery guns, especially 166 Field Regiment under the command of Lieutenant Colonel Rajeshwar Singh, despite its comparative limitations, had helped breach the defences of Chawinda, which was no mean feat. The Pakistani artillery units, using their radar locating systems, had engaged the Indian gun positions as well, whereas in the general confusion that seemed to prevail on the Indian side, the Indians had failed to do so. Second, the Pakistani gunners, seemingly with a supply of almost unlimited ammunition, had fought an outstanding battle through the day.

The assault on Chawinda failed not because of the troops but because of the lack of cohesion at the senior command level. The constant chipping and chopping of formations, the underestimation of Pakistani strength, the lack of coordination with the IAF, and the lack of common sense let down the fighting formations. At the ground level, there were many unsung heroes who were unfortunately never recognized. Among them were the supporting arms who pushed the ammunition and supplies forward, the sappers and the signal detachments that kept the lines of communication open, and, most of all, the medics from the Army Medical Corps who moved with the troops and but for 'their dedication and presence in the thick of enemy shelling, our losses in lives would have been high and morale of the living heavily shattered. The Assistant Director Medical Sciences (ADMS) of 6 Mountain Division went from trench to trench with his team, looking for the wounded and getting them evacuated. No measure of appreciation and gratitude can suffice for their devotion and professionalism.'[34]

52 MOUNTAIN BRIGADE (19 SEPTEMBER)

HQ 1 Corps had postponed the attack by Rocky Hira's 52 Mountain Brigade on Mahadipur and Tilakpur by twenty-four hours to the night of 18/19 September, ostensibly to coincide with the assault on Chawinda. Major General Thapan's brief to Hira was that he should secure the northwestern flank of 26 Infantry Division, which after some initial gains had been engaged in fighting off multiple virulent counter offensives by the Pakistanis. Sushil Kumar's 5/11 GR had created a firm base at Nandpur for the attack by Bajina's 10 Mahar on Mahadipur and another one at Malane to launch Menon's 1 Madras on Tilakpur. Dhure had also been cleared by the Gorkhas to facilitate the advance of Bravo Squadron 18 Cavalry from Chhange under the command of Major (later Lieutenant Colonel) Jai Dev Singh Khera who was to cut off the Chaprar–Sialkot road at Milestone 8 at first light on 19 September. The artillery support was limited—a medium regiment less two batteries commanded by Lieutenant Colonel Keith Shortland with a stipulated niggardly eight rounds per gun per day; one battery of 3.7-inch howitzers commanded by Major Fernandes and one battery of a light regiment under Major S. Singh.

Hira had moved his tactical HQ to a pre-selected site. Shortland had also coordinated the artillery fireplan to be effective once surprise was lost. GOC 26 Infantry Division visited the brigade in the morning. Thapan, after approving the plan for the attack, wished both the battalions good luck.

1 Madras and 10 Mahar launched their attacks at 2330 hours on 18 September. Despite the brigade being unfamiliar with the area, all preliminary actions that are so essential prior to an attack had been religiously put in place, unlike at Chawinda. According to the intelligence provided by 5/11 GR, both villages were devoid of troops. The high ground proximate to the two villages was also expected to be unoccupied, except for a thin screen and standing patrols functioning more in the role of observation posts. Bearing this in mind, very aware that the assaulting troops were hampered by the restricted allotment of artillery ammunition, Rocky Hira had decided to put in a silent attack. The two battalions passed through their FUPs and occupied their respective objectives, brushing aside minor opposition. As soon as green Very lights arched upwards, 5/11 GR took on the role of being the brigade reserve while Charlie Squadron 18 Cavalry under Major (later Lieutenant Colonel) A. K. Poplai positioned itself to blunt the expected counter-attacks.

The success signal galvanized into action those waiting to move forward the defence stores. However, even before the stores could be put to use, the Pakistani artillery let loose with all the guns at their disposal and pounded the two occupied positions. The bombardment was so severe that the reverberations could be felt even at the brigade location, about 2,000 meters to the rear. The troops used every brief lull in the shelling to dig down as fast as they could, utilizing whatever local material they could lay their hands on, even before the defence stores could be allotted. The fleeing villagers had left behind charpoys, which the troops used for overhead protection against the shelling that continued throughout the night. After a while it seemed the Pakistanis were focussing a lot more on 1 Madras at Tilakpur. Their position, unfortunately, was devoid of any natural cover.

At 0430 hours, Alpha Squadron 18 Cavalry set out from Chhange with its six serviceable up-gunned Sherman Vs with the 75 mm gun as their main armament and reached the Chaprar–Sialkot road in an hour-and-a-half. The leading tank, as it crossed the tarmac of the road, went over an anti-tank mine and had its track blown off. Second Lieutenant (later Lieutenant Colonel) Balbir Sahrawat, the troop leader, then ordered a second tank to approach the road to see if there were any other mines. Even as the second tank came up, there was another deafening blast and its track too was ripped apart. The road which led to the village of Gulbahar Nikki was not only extensively mined, the village was defended by Charlie Squadron of Pakistan's 31 TDU.

Not surprisingly, a Bird Dog had taken off from Sialkot and the pilot had the run of the skies from where he could direct the artillery fire 'with impunity as there was no way that we could pose a threat to him with the weapons at our disposal. There were howls from the battalion commanders for air support and they may as well have asked for the moon. There was nothing else to do but bunker down and hope for the best.'[35]

Seeing the stranded tanks to the south of Tilakpur, the Air OP shifted its attention to the tanks, which came under fire from the Pakistani guns. Major Khera's tank was the third to be disabled, a shell breaking its track, damaging its engine, and destroying the wireless system. Anti-tank weapons belonging to 2 Baluch started firing at the tanks and the remaining three Shermans were also immobilized.

As the day progressed, the tanks, though unable to move, continued to fight on. Naib Risaldar Aleem Khan, watching the RCL guns break cover to fire at the tanks, realized the Pakistanis had a predictable shoot and scoot tactic. He started anticipating their movements and destroyed five RCL jeeps with the main gun. Finally, his luck ran out and a RCL hit his gun barrel, putting it out of action. Towards last light, with the Pakistani infantry closing in, Khera and Sahrawat marshalled the crew and hunkered down for the night.

Back in the 18 Cavalry RHQ, Hari Singh asked Captain Inder Lal Grover to go look for Khera. Taking Captain (later Brigadier) Ambika Prasad Bhargava with him, he set off for the neighbouring 7 Jat location. Jasbir Singh was Khera's course mate from IMA and the two officers spent an anxious night worrying about the missing tank men. Grover and Bharghava located the party a short distance from the tanks. Loath to abandon the tanks, they then made their way back to RHQ through the 1 Madras positions.

During the day, Hira had apprised Thapan of the situation in his brigade and discussed the attrition that 52 Mountain Brigade was being subjected to. Hira desperately requested GOC 26 Infantry Division for some means to neutralize enemy artillery, as they were 'at the moment enjoying a duck shoot'. Thapan commiserated with Hira but said that he had no way of sending him support as all the available air effort and the bulk of the artillery resources were engaged in other sectors more crucial to the overall strategic plan.

Despite being subject to incessant shelling by medium and heavy guns through the day, both 1 Madras and 10 Mahar were in high spirits. For the Pakistanis, the loss of both Tilakpur and Mahadipur was a cause for concern as these two villages dominated the Sialkot–Chaprar axis. Opposite 52 Mountain Brigade, deployed on the western side of the road, were the Delta Companies of 13 FF (R&S) and 9 Baluch, a part of 104 Brigade that was a part of Pakistan's 15 Division that was headquartered in Sialkot. A few probing attacks supported by Chaffees had resulted in Poplai's Shermans moving up to support the infantry which was enough of a deterrent for the Pakistanis, who again seemed reluctant to close in against dug-in Indian troops.

After last light, 1 Madras and 10 Mahar moved forward, expanding their area further to the west by capturing Kanpur and Palaura Wada. However, this was short-lived for, by the evening, the Pakistanis had counter-attacked and pushed the Indians back to their positions at Tilakpur and Mahadipur. At daybreak on 21 September, a major counter-attack against 1 Madras was launched but was fought off. Once the attack fizzled out, the Bird Dog was back in the sky above and the usual bombardment began. This time, however, there was a difference, as the fire was directed almost entirely against 1 Madras. The Air OP pilot made some desultory passes over the rest of the brigade's positions, but ignored 10 Mahar's positions around Mahadipur.

Towards last light on 21 September, Menon reported a build-up of the enemy ahead of 1 Madras's defences but the Pakistanis mounted an attack which was beaten back quite easily. Hira thought that it was a simulated attack, perhaps to draw the brigade's attention away from the direction of the actual thrust so that the reserves would be committed prematurely. When Bajina was asked about the state of affairs in his defended area, he confidently said there was nothing to report. Hira warned him to expect an attack that very night. At around 0200 hours on 22 September, all hell broke loose. There were reports from both battalions of large-scale counter-attacks by enemy infantry supported by armour. Bajina and Menon both got on the wireless asking for artillery support. The brigade did not have enough medium artillery to render support to the entire frontage, plus there was a restricted allotment of ammunition. Shortland was in constant contact with his FOOs, each one of whom expressed greater priority for support to his area. Shortland asked Hira to indicate whose demands were most pressing.

Since 10 Mahar was paid scant attention and the earlier attack on 1 Madras was probably a feint, it was apparent that the Pakistanis were trying to deceive Hira as to their main point of attack. From where the brigade commander was, he hollered to Shortland to switch all guns to support 10 Mahar without regard for any ammunition restriction. Hira also warned Poplai and 5/11 GR to be prepared to be committed at a moment's notice. 'Menon soon thereafter stopped clamouring and I realized that I had taken the right decision.'[36]

The Pakistanis withdrew at first light. Both 1 Madras and 10 Mahar had fought a superb defensive battle. Immediately after the fighting ended at around 0800 hours, Hira first visited '1 Madras and found that the battalion was in high spirits. They proudly claimed that they had given the enemy a bloody nose and had not lost an inch of territory. They had however, suffered heavy casualties. Moving to 10 Mahar, I was met by Bajina and Major Dua, his second in command. ... The area was strewn with the bodies of enemy troops, some bayoneted, others shot from point blank range. The air was heavy with the acrid smell of cordite and the sticky sweet smell of blood. The body of the leading enemy company commander was lying atop a bunker. A section of prisoners had also been taken. 10 Mahar had fought a splendid action. Finding the battalion HQ and the depth Companies intact, I went to both the forward Companies. The defences of both had been breached by enemy armour and infantry estimated to be a battalion (4 and 9 Baluch) plus in strength. I observed that a large number of enemy troops were killed ahead of the defences.'[37]

Poplai's squadron had also excelled itself, somewhat avenging the loss of Khera's six tanks earlier. Naib Risaldar Umed Singh had destroyed three Chaffees from 31 TDU, while Daffadar Rajesh Singh had accounted for another, before his own tank had taken a direct hit, killing him on the spot. His gunner Sowar Sukh Ram had been pulled out by 10 Mahar and placed under a culvert with the battalion's other wounded. Sukh Ram died in hospital a few days later.

After this, the situation in the 26 Infantry Division sector stabilized with the three brigades holding the Nandpur–Mahadipur–Tilakpur–Chhange–Khane Chak–Niwe Wains–Salia–Kurar–Tau–Khokar–Dhesian–Kalarwanda–Angraspur line. As a last act of defiance, the PAF sent four F-86 Sabres to attack the 52 Brigade's gun position, which had played a major role in breaking up the Pakistani attack earlier in the morning.

Later in the day, a temporary truce was agreed upon in Mahadipur to enable the Pakistanis to evacuate their casualties and take away their dead. Though no exact body count was taken, it was estimated that over 200 men had been killed or seriously wounded. The Pakistani collection party commander paid handsome tribute to the efficiency of our artillery and mortar shelling, notably that of the light battery and he wished his compliments to be conveyed to the battery commander.

Unfortunately, given the fact that the priorities of HQ Western Army Command seemed to have shifted to areas further south, the three days of fighting in the extreme northern flank of 1 Corps' area of responsibility became a mere footnote in the history of the 1965 war.

While the bodies were being collected by the Pakistanis, Hira was asked to attend a meeting at HQ 19 Infantry Brigade. Present there were the army and corps commanders, Harbakhsh Singh and Dunn along with Thapan. The mood was upbeat and there was talk of an imminent ceasefire. After the 'good shows' and some self-congratulatory backslapping, Hira was told he would be moving with his brigade to the 25 Infantry Division sector for some pressing tasks in the next few hours. The brigade commander managed to speak to Dunn 'questioning the priority of this decision'. 52 Mountain Brigade's battalions had recently fought an action and were not even able to complete evacuation of their casualties or perform the last rites for their dead. Each had about 100 killed and wounded. Moreover, they had fought nonstop for the past three or four days and were in dire need of some rest. The response he got from Dunn was 'now, Rocky, be a good chap. You know the 25 Divisional Sector well and you are just the man for the job.'[38]

ALHAR RAILWAY STATION (20–23 SEPTEMBER)
Back in the Manga–Alhar area, 20 September had been a tense day for all the troops holding ground. HQ 1 Armoured Division had given its formations and regiments a general order for refitting and recoupment, though 17 Poona Horse was asked to cover the area from Hasri to Wazirwali, relieving 4 Hodson's Horse. Alhar Railway Station came in for heavy shelling and Pakistani armour—most likely, 19 Lancers—put in a few probe attacks. 14 Rajput and 5 Raj Rif holding the railway embankment held firm, while Alpha and Bravo Squadrons of 17 Poona Horse moved forward on the Manga and West Alhar axis and destroyed two Pattons each. This proved enough of a deterrent and the Pakistanis withdrew from the area, though the intensity of the shelling intensified. Another probing attack from the western side of Chawinda aimed at Wazirwali was blunted by 2 Lancers and 5 Jat. An air attack at 1400 hours by the PAF damaged two jeeps, weapons, and the wireless communication system of the Jats. Though the Pakistanis could be seen preparing for an attack in the Jalalpur Mahr area, artillery fire could not be called owing to the loss of communication with the guns. Havildar Sunda Ram, the battalion's mortar forward controller, brought very effective fire support, breaking up the attack even before it could be mounted.

In the evening of 20 September, a coordination meeting was held by Dunn, attended by all the divisional commanders. It was decided that 1 Armoured Brigade would remain in the Rurki Kalan area and though 17 Poona Horse would retain its present disposition during the night of 20/21 September, it would be relieved by 4 Hodson's Horse less one squadron at 0530 hours. 43 Lorried Infantry Brigade was also asked to pull back. 4 Madras and 8 Garhwal Rifles were to take over the defences around Khanawali–Wazirwali from 5/9 GR and 5 Jat while 14 Infantry Division was to be at Sabzpir area. Even at this stage, Dunn was still shuffling his troops around and, in some cases, HQ 1 Corps had no idea about the exact location of its formations. The order issued subsequent to the meeting placed 35 Infantry Brigade at Changarian and 5 Raj Rif at the Alhar Railway Station. On the ground it was quite the opposite.

From the deployment of his various formations, it was obvious Dunn had decided to go into a defensive huddle. Harbakhsh Singh, true to character, continued to breathe fire and issued a directive from Western Command: 'It is appreciated that despite the apparent desire for peace, enemy forces might put in a series of strong offensive actions in a last minute bid to save face and strengthen their subsequent bargaining capability.'[39]

At first light on 21 September, 17 Poona Horse was relieved by 4 Hodson's Horse less a squadron and withdrew to Ingam for rest and refit. As it had rained heavily the previous evening and the tracks were not fit for vehicles, 5/9 GR and 5 Jat had to walk back to Mastpur and Mallahna, which were on the Zafarwal–Maharajke–Sialkot road that was just inside Pakistan near the IB. Even as these battalions trudged off, they continued to be shelled by the Pakistani guns. An air strike by the PAF wounded Major A. S. Pawar and Sepoy Chander Singh. For 17 Poona Horse, grudgingly given the title 'Fakhr-e-Hind' (the Pride of India) by the Pakistanis, 5 Jat, and 5/11 GR it was the end of the war. Lieutenant Colonel Rishi Raj Singh took over 17 Poona Horse as Adi Tarapore's replacement the next day at Ingam.

Even as the changeover was taking place between 4 Hodson's Horse and 17 Poona Horse in the early morning hours, 16 Cavalry and 62 Cavalry on the western periphery reported a mixed squadron of Pattons and Chaffees in the Chak Lwaranda–Thoda–Chandar area. Alpha Squadron 62 Cavalry and 3 Madras had moved at first light from the Pagowal crossroads towards Khakhanwali. Three Pattons tried to close in from the direction of Chak Lwaranda, resulting in a firefight in which one Patton was hit and abandoned. 62 Cavalry's remarkable run, wherein Sherman IVs were battling superior tanks, had continued. The Patton, loaded to the brim with ammunition, was recovered.

Harbakhsh Singh's reading of the Pakistani mind was proving to be far more perceptive. The Pakistani Army continued to make frantic efforts to recapture lost areas through the day to the deadline for the ceasefire. They incessantly shelled almost all the Indian positions within range of their guns, followed by probing attacks by their armour and infantry. Unfettered control over the entire railway line was their aim and obsession; whereas the defence of Alhar and the railway station became a crucial obligation for the Indian troops. The first assault from the direction of Jassoran probing the defences of 20 Rajput also ran into Alpha Squadron 4 Hodson's Horse who knocked out four Pattons and four RCLs. The hapless 19 Lancers were once again forced to pull back. A second assault preceded by a severe artillery bombardment was met by the Charlie Squadron Centurions. Once again, a Patton was destroyed and the Pakistanis had to withdraw.

Meanwhile, by the evening of 21 September, there had been some major changes on the Pakistani side as formations were shifted around. Even though GHQ was aware of the impending ceasefire, the timing and details of which were yet to be finalized, the plan for Operation Windup was also being worked out. Orders were issued at 1830 hours on 21 September. The attack, to be launched in multiple phases by 6 Armoured Division and 15 Division, was to be supported by Artillery 4 Corps and the PAF and H-hour was fixed at 0430 hours on 22 September. However, later that night, as soon as it became clear that Pakistan was going to accept the UN-sponsored resolution for a ceasefire, the operation was called off. Even then, 15 Division was ordered to go ahead with its attack on Mahadipur against 52 Mountain Brigade.

Later in the morning, Charlie Squadron 4 Horse reported a squadron of tanks in the Fatehpur area just to the south of the Alhar Railway Station. In the ensuing shoot-out, both sides suffered losses. One troop from Bravo Squadron, which was in reserve in the Gil area, was rushed forward to reinforce the Indian side. Yet again, the Pakistanis failed to push the attack through, and withdrew.

Radio intercepts through the day also indicated that Pakistan would launch three attacks on the night of 22–23 September; through Jheje to capture Changarian; through the Alhar Railway Station to capture Alhar from the direction of Chawinda; and one more effort to recapture Wazirwali also through the secure western defences of Chawinda. By the late afternoon, forward observation posts had started reporting that the Pakistanis were preparing for a major counter-offensive. Rajeshwar Singh, the commanding officer of 166 Field Regiment, moved up to HQ 35 Infantry Brigade and discussed the location of the likely Pakistani FUPs.

At 1700 hours, the first of these attacks started to develop when an infantry battalion plus a squadron of tanks in the Jheje–Bharoke area started moving towards the railway crossing opposite 16 Cavalry's area. After laying down a smoke screen, the Pakistanis opened fire, but 16 Cavalry was in a comfortable position not only to counter-engage them with their main guns, they also called in artillery fire. Four Pattons and an equal number of RCL guns could be seen burning while one Centurion caught fire after being hit.

Pakistani artillery had continuously been pounding away at the Indian positions, almost as if they had instructions to use up their ammunition before the ceasefire came into effect. The most desperate of these attempts were the assaults on village Alhar. After last light, the sky was lit up as both sides opened up with a vengeance. Apart from the guns of his own 166 Field Regiment, Rajeshwar Singh had called up every gun in the Corps zone to go after the Pakistani gun positions. While the artillery duel continued, there were persistent calls from HQ 6 Mountain Division enquiring if the Alhar Railway Station was under Indian or Pakistani possession. At 0115 hours, a battalion attack developed and it was fought off by 20 Rajput. Lieutenant Dharamvir Singh and Second Lieutenant Ravikul Mehta were wounded and had to be evacuated along with dozens of others who were hit by splinters. A second attack was again launched at 0210 hours, with much the same result.

Then, at 0330 hours on 23 September, the last of the guns fired, after which all was quiet on the western front. 'A strange silence enveloped the bloody battlefield where men were locked in a life and death struggle only a few minutes ago. The eighteen hectic days of war were over.'[40] Looking out over the top of his trench, Vijay Dhruv Verma from 20 Rajput quietly took off his helmet. A dent marked the spot where a splinter had hit it. Peering into the still night, he wondered how he was still alive. All around him, medics were going from trench to trench looking for the dead and the wounded. Ahead of them, as daylight started to creep in, they could see the bodies of sixty dead strewn around.

Chapter 21

11 CORPS' CURTAIN CALL

KHEM KARAN & DOGRAI (14–23 SEPTEMBER)

After having bulldozed 4 Mountain Division into mounting a premature assault to recapture Khem Karan, Harbakhsh Singh and Dhillon seemed to have run out of ideas. There was a stalemate everywhere on the Lahore front, with the line of contact more or less established. Not only had the Pakistani offensive been blunted in Khem Karan, it was also known that a major quantum of the Pakistani armoured forces had been shifted to the Sialkot Sector to meet the threat of the much hyped Indian 1 Armoured Division which had severely mauled the Pattons on 11 September during the advance to Phillora. Though the town of Khem Karan remained in the possession of Pakistan, Indian troops held the town of Barki and all the way north to the Ravi at DBN, they were leaning on the east bank of the Ichhogil Canal.

The Pakistanis, as was to be expected given the importance of Lahore, had reinforced the GT Road Sector and deployed the bulk of their forces along the west bank of the Ichhogil Canal. Given the amount of heavy and medium artillery at their disposal, they were effectively controlling the approaches to the east bank by fire. Always expecting the Indians to run away at the mere sight of advancing Pakistani armour, they would put in a probing attack every now and then, which would result in a sharp brief encounter, and they would then pull back to the safety of the west bank.

While the Pakistanis judiciously optimized the deployment of their armour between the Bari Doab (Lahore Sector) and the Rachna Doab (Sialkot Sector), the Indians kept deploying their spare regiments around Amritsar to meet an imaginary Pakistani armoured thrust. A week into the conflict, despite the highly publicized slaughter of Pattons in Khem Karan by 4 Mountain Division and 2 (Independent) Armoured Brigade, Dhillon's handling of 11 Corps had been nothing short of a disaster.

The plans for Operation Riddle in the 11 Corps Sector had been drawn up by Generals Chaudhuri, Harbakhsh, and Dhillon, over a considerable period of time, during Operation Ablaze and the period thereafter. Yet, from 6 September when the Indian Army surged across the IB, despite achieving complete surprise, all three divisions—15, 7, and 4—had fared extremely poorly. Battles are won by the side that pays close attention to detail, but despite the long lead-up, even basic issues had not been addressed.

Unfortunately, personalities matter and the Indian leadership's mutual dislike for one another had taken a tremendous toll. Harbakhsh Singh wanted the bulk of the strike force to be concentrated in the Bari Doab, but Chaudhuri not only had other ideas, he cut off Harbakhsh Singh from the planning of 1 Corps' operations altogether as Harbakhsh notes in *War Despatches*. Even during the Goa Operations, Chaudhuri had shown a tendency towards flamboyance with little or no thought given to the details. 'A succession of high positions in his early career had acquainted him with the glamour of decision-making, but not its substance.'[1] The war games held in 11 Corps to plan the operations proved to be 'woolly headed nonsense' as had been repeatedly pointed out by the GOC of 15 Infantry Division. The Intelligence Bureau had, on more than one occasion, clearly told the army that Pakistan had raised a second armoured division by surreptitiously using equipment marked as 'reserve' by the US. Chaudhuri's style of functioning was such that he rarely relied on staff analysis, often saying things off the cuff which then became the official Army HQ line. On the Intelligence front, HQ 11 Corps was not even in a position to provide basic maps to formations when the fighting began.

Dhillon was indeed born under a lucky star. Had Chavan instituted an enquiry into what went wrong in 1962 against the Chinese, it is highly unlikely that he would have been given command of 11 Corps or any formation for that matter. The strategic plan put into place by 11 Corps was to make multiple limited advances in the hope that the Pakistanis would either panic and abandon their defences, or, if they chose to fight, the Indians would manage to sit tight in the areas they had captured and let the Pakistanis wear themselves out in counter-attacks.

Having chosen to fight a war of attrition, Dhillon had actually played into Pakistan's hands; Barki notwithstanding, not a single formation had achieved even its first objective—which was to occupy the eastern bank of the Ichhogil Canal. A war of attrition had proven to be more of an anti-strategy, especially since India neither had the firepower nor the numerical superiority to wear down the Pakistani defences. On the contrary, Pakistan's artillery had until now proven to be their main weapon and the situation was tailor-made for them. Even a week into the war, HQ 11 Corps (for that matter even HQ 1 Corps) had failed to co-ordinate with the air force, which allowed PAF a free hand to attack positions at will. Having committed the forces in a manner that allowed the Pakistanis to seize the initiative, Dhillon's only contribution had been to write panicky letters up the chain of command. Worse, after 4 Mountain Division and 2 Independent Armoured Brigade had pulled the irons out of the fire thanks to their resoluteness in the face of troops equipped with weapon systems that were a generation ahead, Dhillon still did not seem to have a Plan B.

Having committed the troops to what best could be called a timid plan to start with, Dhillon was to compound the problem by overplaying the threat to

Amritsar. Not only had two additional brigades been deployed to 'plug the gap', the ever-increasing armour at his disposal was being aimlessly frittered away. Let us take the case of 1 Skinner's Horse that had reached Amritsar by train on 11 September. The regiment was familiar with the terrain in the area having been deployed south of Amritsar from April to July 1965 as part of Operation Ablaze. It was then moved to Varanasi and placed under HQ Central Command for internal security duties in connection with the Kumbh Mela!

On arrival, HQ 11 Corps placed Alpha Squadron with 96 Infantry Brigade along the east bank of the Ravi from Kakkar to Ranian. Bravo Squadron was attached to 50 (Independent) Parachute Brigade while the rest of 1 Skinner's Horse was deployed along the Pul Distributary for the protection of gun areas in Mode–Sahara. By 14 September, Dhillon had one Centurion Mk IV, one Sherman Mk IV, three Sherman Mk V, one AMX-13, and one PT-76 regiment, all of which were collected in a defensive zone. Most of these regiments were often, at short notice, moved from one point to the other. At no point was any offensive action even contemplated. 'The GOC of 11 Corps paid heed to his fears and continued to sit on a large bulk of armour, denying it to 1 Corps, which could win a strategic victory. The irony is that the headquarters of 11 Corps created one more armour headquarters, "Bharat Force", because it could not control so much armour! This period saw the most unprofessional employment of such a large number of armoured regiments, never as a brigade, never as a regiment, sometimes as a squadron but more often as two troops, one troop and even a single tank!'[2]

The offensive having ground to a halt, the top brass needed something to help turn the tide in their favour. The window of opportunity provided by 3 Jat at Dograi on day one had been squandered, and, in the ensuing battle of attrition where artillery dominated, the initiative had long been handed over to the Pakistanis. Lahore and Sialkot were never seriously considered to be objectives as the Indian Army could not get across the Ichhogil Canal. Asal Uttar had been a defensive battle and Barki had only helped 7 Infantry Division get to the east bank of the canal, their stated objective on day one! Eventually, what saved 11 Corps, and by extension India from humiliation, was the stoic performance of the men and the younger crop of officers. It was their courage and fortitude that would allow a handful of men to fly the tricolour on the west bank of the Ichhogil.

The arrival of Brigadier (later Major General) Niranjan Singh, from Mhow to take over 54 Infantry Brigade on 12 September was to prove to be a watershed event. Brigadier Kalha, who was holding the fort after Maha Singh Rikh had to be evacuated, had earlier that morning given the commanding officer of 3 Jat the much awaited go-ahead to capture Dograi on the night of 14/15 September and had gone back to being the brigadier, artillery 11 Corps. Hardly had the order been given than Pakistani guns carried out an intense bombardment of HQ 54 Infantry Brigade at Santpura and the neighbouring Jat positions for a long time.

Niranjan Singh having stopped at HQ 11 Corps on the way to his new command was taken aback by what he saw. 'These chaps need a bit of sprucing up, he thought, so far from the firing line and some of them looked shell shocked. A staff officer briefed him, things haven't gone too well, setback at Khem Karan, the Pakistanis almost got to Amritsar on 10 September, your brigade is shaky, we might even have to fall back to the Beas.'[3]

A short while later, at Khasa, the brigadier's impression of HQ 15 Infantry Division was equally gloomy. Niranjan Singh 'had to eat his lunch alone at divisional headquarters since no one from among those watching the sky for enemy aircraft would sit with him. The others were somewhere down below in bunkers where he was taken for a briefing. Some mention was made of the Hudiara Drain—a good alternate defensive position. No enthusiasm here for the war, he reflected. Gloomy, gloomy, what a pickle, terrible.'[4]

Reaching Santpura at 1600 hours, the new commander of 54 Infantry Brigade was met by the cherubic (and unshaven) brigade major, Major (later Major General) Benjamin 'Ken' Gonsalves. Despite having been under intense shelling for the better part of the day, Gonsalves was, as usual full of good cheer. 'Retire to Hudiara Drain, rubbish, sir, the BM ejaculated. Yes, we've had a bit of confusion here and there, only natural, still finding out about the war, and about each other, and about the enemy. But none of my brigade headquarters staff has fallen back, so why the Hudiara Drain? By the way, sir, the Jats are attacking Dograi day after tomorrow.'[5]

The first thing the new commander did was to put a hold on the projected date, saying there would be no attack until he knew what they were dealing with. However, having been given the nod to recapture Dograi, the Jats started to prepare for the attack in real earnest. Over the next few days, Niranjan Singh was everywhere, 'poking his nose into even things he had no clue about'.[6] Clambering onto Second Lieutenant Brijendra Singh's well-hidden Sherman, he wanted to know why the armoured corps was not being aggressive. The Pakistani positions were way beyond the effective range of the tank's main gun, and besides, the last thing Brijendra Singh wanted was to give his position away.

However, in the army, second lieutenants do not argue with brigade commanders. The tank fired, where the shell landed was of no consequence. Niranjan Singh was pleased as punch at the show of aggression and off he went. The tanks' carefully chosen position was now useless, so the troop had to look for some other place to deploy. It was much the same story for both 15 Dogra and 13 Punjab who were holding the forward positions against Dograi around Milestone 13. 'They had the Pakistanis in front of them, and Niranjan Singh behind them,' Desmond Hayde recorded. 'You can't have this gap of 2,000 yards between us and the enemy, dash it,' he told them, "Close up, close up."'[7] Finally, the front-line troops had a commander who believed in the dictum 'the enemy is there to be attacked and destroyed'.

OBSESSED WITH KHEM KARAN

After a week of intense fighting, by 13 September, the Kasur/Khem Karan Sector had simmered down considerably. The Pakistanis, determined to hold on to Indian territory captured on the eastern side of the Ichhogil Canal, had five infantry battalions deployed in the area, extending from Sankatra to Mehdipur, backed by a reasonable amount of armour plus the entire artillery component of 11 Division. Following the failed attempt by 2 Mahar to clear out the Pakistanis from Khem Karan village itself, GHQ Pakistan wanted both 10 and 11 Division to capture as much Indian territory as possible.

On the Indian side, Jogi Dhillon was under pressure to deliver, having failed to make inroads into Pakistan in nearly all the divisional sectors under his command. Interestingly, from his actions, it is quite obvious that Dhillon not only had little or no idea of what was happening on the Pakistani side; he also did not seem to have a realistic idea about the use of armour. On the one hand, he and Harbakhsh Singh were convinced on 11 September that Pakistan's back had been broken and they grossly underestimated Pakistani strength at Khem Karan. By the evening of the next day, Dhillon was convinced he was going to be attacked yet again in the same area, and he grossly overestimated the strength of the Pakistanis.

The capture of Barki by 4 Sikh had saved 7 Infantry Division the blushes, but the brigade and divisional leadership had been questionable. At 1415 hours on 16 September, Brigadier Lerb Ferris ordered 19 MLI, commanded by Lieutenant Colonel (later Brigadier) S. D. Parab, to send a company group to capture Manhiala, which was on the boundary between 7 and 15 Infantry Divisions. HQ 65 Infantry Brigade, in keeping with the new trend of underestimating the strength of Pakistanis holding forward positions on the ground, told Parab that at best there was a 'small detachment' holding Manhiala and mopping up was all it would take. It hardly seemed to matter that the village was 10 km to the north of the battalion's defended area, which meant the troops would only get there around last light.

Charlie Company, commanded by Major (later Lieutenant General) Mohammad Ahmed Zaki, though unfamiliar with the terrain, set off immediately, taking a section each of 81 mm mortars and MMGs plus two RCL gun detachments. Their orders were to capture and occupy Manhiala as soon as the Marathas got there. On arrival, they found the village to be much larger than they had been led to believe and besides, they immediately came under artillery and mortar fire from the Ichhogil defences. About 1,500 yards away from the village was a troop of tanks of CIH under Major J. K. Dutt and, in direct support, Charlie Company had a field battery of 66 Field Regiment. Zaki decided to put in an unconventional attack by using all three platoons to represent a larger frontage simulating a two-company attack. The ruse worked and by 0200 hours on 17 September, Manhiala was occupied and the men dug in towards its northwest in a guava grove. The rest of the battalion arrived from Barka Kalan shortly after dawn.

However, the Indian high command was completely obsessed with trying to recover lost ground and recapturing Khem Karan. On the same day, a company of 2 Mahar found itself hopelessly encircled by Pattons in the area of Bhura Karimpur. D. K. Mehta's Charlie Squadron 9 Deccan Horse, reduced to three troops, was immediately asked to rescue the trapped infantry. Realizing the Shermans were unlikely to scatter the Pattons on their own, Narinder Singh Sandhu's Charlie Squadron 3 Cavalry was also scrambled, for the Pakistanis had learnt to be terrified of the Centurions. R. P. 'Joe' Joshi commanding No. 2 Troop, found himself traversing familiar terrain along the Khem Karan Distributary, while Sandhu positioned himself short of the area to coordinate with Arun Vaidya and Mehta.

In a short and swift battle, Joshi's Centurions immediately destroyed a Patton and even took a prisoner. The Pattons quickly started to withdraw, allowing 2 Mahar to hold its position. Prior to last light, Mehta's Shermans replaced the Centurions which pulled back to harbour for the night.

While 2 Mahar was under pressure holding ground in the Bhura Karimpur area, in a bid to divert troops from the Khem Karan area, it was decided to launch yet another attack on Jhaman, the bridge just north of the boundary between 7 Infantry Division and 4 Mountain Division. While still preparing its defences at Manhiala, at 1000 hours, 19 MLI was ordered to move 25 km to the south and be prepared to attack Jhaman the next day. For this task, 19 MLI reverted again to 48 Infantry Brigade, where Brigadier Piara Singh had replaced Shahaney. Two previous attacks to capture the bridge over the Ichhogil Canal had failed—both attacks by 5 Guards, the second supported by 6/8 GR—and Piara Singh was anxious to capture the area northwest of Jhaman by launching a battalion attack. This would allow him to make yet another attempt to dislodge the Pakistanis, who were said to have since strengthened the bridge location.

With 6/8 GR to the southwest of 19 MLI, the daylight assault began at 1530 hours on 18 September. The FUP was 1,500 yards from Jhaman and the Marathas attacked, with Charlie Company on the left, heading for the built-up area to the northwest of the village. Bravo Company under Lieutenant Vasant Chavan was to the right and even though the advancing columns were subjected to heavy artillery, mortar, and MMG fire from the Ichhogil Canal defences, the attack was successful and Jhaman, as well as a few prisoners, was handed over to 6/8 GR. The Marathas had already received orders to move even further south to Rajoke.

Piara Singh was in a hurry, with orders to clear the right flank of 4 Mountain Division. By nightfall, 19 MLI had reached its location next to the Hudiara Drain where it saw for the first time the Soviet-made PT-76 tanks of 7 Cavalry. At 2200 hours, Piara Singh called a meeting with Parab, Zaki, and the commanding officer of 7 Cavalry, Lieutenant Colonel (later Brigadier) Dalip Singh Jind and his squadron commander, Major Hoshang Nanavati.

48 Infantry Brigade had been designated as a task force comprising 19 MLI

and 7 Light Cavalry less one squadron, under the command of Piara Singh. The area west and south of Rajoke extending up to the Sutlej River had been captured by the Pakistanis. The task force was to clear the Pakistanis from the northern part of the area, as part of a second assault to recapture Khem Karan.

Piara Singh, obviously following the Harbakhsh system of calculating enemy strength, decided that the first objective of the task force was Thatti Jaimal Singh, which he believed was being held by a section of Pakistani infantry. The next objective would be Dholan, which had slightly stronger defences. The advance was to commence at 0615 hrs on 19 September.

The lightweight PT-76s were primarily designed for amphibious operations and were totally unsuitable for the terrain around the Rohi Nullah. 7 Light Cavalry was the first Indian armoured regiment to be equipped with these new tanks, which General Chaudhuri had pushed through on the grounds that they were ideal for warfare in the Eastern Theatre of operations. The guns of the tanks had not even been calibrated when they had been ordered to move to the 11 Corps' sector and were inducted into 2 (I) Armoured Brigade. To get to Thatti Jaimal Singh, the task force would have to cross the Rohi Nullah, which would require coordination with 19 MLI. Since the radio sets in the tanks were Russian and the infantry did not have compatible radio sets, Subedar Dadu Patil with a compatible radio set was deputed to ride atop the squadron commander's tank for inter-communications.

Even as the Marathas secured the start point, orders were received to stay put. At 1000 hrs Piara Singh decided that a company of 19 MLI and a squadron of 7 Cavalry would instead attack Chathanwala, which was to the west, inside Pakistan. Delta Company, under Captain Vijay Kumar,[8] and Charlie Squadron 7 Cavalry, led by Major Man Mohan Chopra, set off immediately, without even the time to brief the junior leaders and troops. Not surprisingly, the Pakistanis were waiting in strength, many more in number than had been appreciated, their tanks positioned in hull down position as a part of Chathanwala's defences. The advance to the objective was under constant fire. Captain Vijay Kumar was wounded along with twenty-nine others and his company second-in-command, Subedar K. B. Sawlekar, and two other ranks were killed. Three PT-76 tanks were bogged down and their recovery under intense fire from the Pakistanis was a challenge. A platoon of Bravo Company, under Second Lieutenant F. A. Khan, provided covering fire while 7 Cavalry personnel engaged in the tricky recovery of the stranded tanks. Man Mohan Chopra was also wounded and evacuated, but later succumbed to his injuries.[9]

Clearly, no lessons had been learnt from the overly optimistic first attack on Khem Karan. Even as 19 MLI and 7 Cavalry were battling it out at Chathanwala, Dhillon at his 11 Corps HQ was yet again briefing Harbakhsh Singh on the ground situation in his zone of responsibility. At the same time, in the neighbouring 1

Corps sector, the attack on Chawinda having failed, 1 Armoured Division was in the process of switching from an offensive posture to a defensive one, having already pulled 17 Poona Horse back to the north of the railway embankment. While 1 Corps was desperately asking for reinforcements, Dhillon, with seven mostly idle armoured regiments at his disposal, put out a highly exaggerated appreciation of the Pakistani capabilities.

Dhillon believed Pakistan had its 8 Infantry Division in the Kasur area with 52 Infantry Brigade deployed at Khem Karan.[10] He also placed Pakistan's 1 Armoured Division at Kasur, which suggested that Pakistan was planning a major thrust against 4 Mountain Division, which, if it succeeded, would also completely destabilize and threaten the left flank of 7 Infantry Division. Dhillon proposed to capture Khem Karan with 41 Infantry Brigade Group by 0200 hours on 22 September while 29 Infantry Brigade would eliminate the Pakistani screen position by 0500 hours on the same morning. On the GT Road axis, the corps commander said the Pakistanis would continue with probing raids across the Ichhogil Canal to keep the Indians from reaching the east bank.

Summing up his appreciation, Dhillon said he needed one more infantry division, an additional Centurion regiment, and one more squadron of AMX tanks.

Amazingly, there was no mention of the ongoing engagement at Chathanwala, or of the impending attack on Dograi, or, for that matter, the proposed closing of the gap with the eastern bank of the Ichhogil Canal by 38 Infantry division or 50 (Independent) Parachute Brigade in the GT Road–Amritsar Sector. This was amazing because of all the armoured regiments available to Dhillon, 14 Scinde Horse was perhaps the most unsuited for assaulting Dograi, equipped with the near obsolete Sherman V tanks and having suffered their fair share of losses. Equally surprisingly, Harbakhsh Singh did not contradict his corps commander at any time.

Having failed to make significant inroads at Chathanwala, the pugnacious Piara Singh turned his attention back to Thatti Jaimal Singh. At 0615 hours on 20 September the Marathas launched their fourth successive attack in as many days against yet another completely different objective. The standing sugar cane crop and high sarkanda grass provided the troops and the PT-76s some element of cover. As the assaulting troops of Charlie Company emerged from the sugar cane field, they appeared on the flank of 7 Baluch, surprising the Pakistani platoon and company HQ. Second Lieutenant (later Brigadier) Kuldip Singh Chhokar, recently commissioned into 66 Field Regiment, promptly called in fire on the Pakistani positions.

The Pakistani artillery was quick to respond, subjecting the assaulting Marathas to repeated salvos which were supplemented by mortar and tank fire from nearby Dholan. After severe hand-to-hand fighting, the enemy's company HQ was overrun. At 0915 hours, Thatti Jaimal Singh was captured by the Marathas, the surviving disoriented Pakistani troops running off towards Sankatra further to the south. The success signal was given and follow-up troops were called forward. Seventeen bodies of Pakistani soldiers were recovered along with an observation post officer's marked map, two RCL jeeps with a trailer, and two trucks full of ammunition.

Hardly had the Marathas settled down than a Bird Dog appeared overhead and the Pakistanis opened up once again with artillery fire, the mortars and tanks positioned at Dholan also joining in. Zaki[11] was wounded by tank fire and was subsequently evacuated after handing over charge to the Alpha Company commander, Lieutenant Bikram Singh. In a unique feat in terms of number of casualties, Charlie Company 19 MLI captured a company position of 7 Baluch at a comparatively meagre price of only five killed: one radio operator, Sepoy Timkre, one MMG gunner, Manohar Kalgutkar, and three other ranks.

However, having continuously been in action for four days was beginning to take its toll; 19 MLI had lost over a company in casualties. As a result, Bravo Company of 17 Rajput under Major V. D. Gupte came under command of the task force from 20 September. Thatti Jaimal Singh was then held with Charlie Company on the left, Alpha Company on the right and with the remainder two companies and the additional company of 17 Rajput deployed in depth. Expectedly, the Pakistanis reacted to the loss of Thatti Jaimal Singh like angry hornets, the first counter-attack supported by artillery and armour developing at 1600 hours that very day. It was beaten back and was followed by a second wave at 1700 hours which was also repulsed.

As per their usual tactics, which centred around their artillery, the Pakistani guns were on a rampage intermittently throughout the night of 20/21 September. Three counter-attacks were launched on the following day, but the Pakistanis could not shake off the Marathas, who hung on grimly. The shelling and counter-attacks resulted in a large number of casualties and damage to two tanks of 7 Cavalry. The Maratha RCL guns accounted for three Pakistani tanks as well. One final effort on 22 September, with the prospect of a ceasefire on the cards, was also foiled. Three officers, one JCO, and twenty-nine other ranks were killed in action and three officers, six JCOs, and 105 other ranks wounded. All company commanders were either killed or wounded. The Marathas operated under three superior headquarters, finally ending up under 4 Mountain Division, which had finally launched its second offensive action against Khem Karan.

Despite having accumulated a considerable amount of armour in the 11 Corps area, for the second attempt at recapturing Khem Karan, Dhillon seemed most reluctant to use it. Still persisting with the Harbakhsh Singh mathematics, Khem Karan was appreciated to be at best occupied by an infantry battalion plus a weak squadron of armour, which would have the usual artillery cover. Unable to contradict the projected figures since they were emanating from the army commander himself, GOC 4 Mountain Division, Major General Gurbaksh Singh, had planned to carry out the assault in two phases.

As a part of the regrouping, 7 Mountain Brigade had been taken out of 4

Mountain Division while Brigadier H. C. Gahlaut's 62 Mountain Brigade continued to hold the firm base around Asal Uttar. 9 JAK Rifles was placed directly under the division while 13 Dogra was allotted to 29 Brigade to supplement 2 Madras and 1/5 GR. Also placed under command of 4 Mountain Division was Rajwade's 41 Mountain Brigade, consisting of 15 Kumaon, 1/8 GR, and 3/4 GR.

In Phase 1 of the attack, 41 Mountain Brigade Group with 1/8 GR and 15 Kumaon was to attack the Khem Karan Distributary from the west of the road with Major (later Major General) H. N. 'Harry' Hoon's three troops advancing through Bhura Karimpur in support. Rajwade's task was to then capture and occupy Khem Karan by 0200 hours on 22 September. Pritam Singh's 29 Infantry Brigade Group consisting of 2 Madras and 1/5 GR, with Jimmy Vohra's tanks in support, was to attack and destroy the screen position by 0500 hours. Vohra knew the area well. He also had Naib Risaldar Gajje Singh with him who had gone across the Khem Karan distributary before having to fall back on 12 September.

9 Deccan Horse, severely depleted from the earlier fighting and suffering from a shortage of tanks and crew, had been organized into three combat groups rather than squadrons, each with three troops. With plenty of time and days to plan the offensive, it is perplexing why additional armour was not moved to Khem Karan or even why 3 Cavalry was not brought into play. Majors Vohra, Hoon, and Mehta were given command of Combat Group A, B, and C respectively. The plan to recapture Khem Karan was once again based on too many assumptions. In the presence of Arun Vaidya, Mehta suggested to Gurbaksh Singh that the Pakistani strength was being underestimated. Pulling out his pistol from its holster, the GOC pointed his weapon at the officer and accused him of cowardice. Vaidya just looked at his squadron commander and shrugged.[12]

The entire divisional plan came apart at the seams right from the start. For some reason, 15 Kumaon was not at its FUP and H-hour for 41 Mountain Brigade had to be staggered. One company of 1/8 GR set off at 0030 hours on 22 September but the follow-up companies failed to link up and the attack faltered. Rajwade asked the Gorkhas to firm up and launched 15 Kumaon at 0400 hours, but the Kumaonese too came under very heavy artillery fire and were bogged down. A second attempt to break through an hour later met with a similar fate. It was discovered the vanguard company of 1/8 GR had actually veered off to the west, which caused some of the subsequent confusion.

Meanwhile, Pritam Singh had launched 2 Madras at 0230 hours and the leading companies had captured the bridge over the Khem Karan Distributary by first light. Once again, with daylight, Pakistani FOOs came into their own and brought down intense artillery and small arms fire. Determined to hold off the Indians, Pakistan also launched air strikes against 2 Madras. With its forward position no longer tenable, the battalion was pulled back where it dug in some 1,500 metres north of the distributary with its depth companies.

Harbakhsh Singh, as usual, was scathing in his comments. '41 Infantry Brigade failed in its mission due to lack of determined leadership. The assaulting battalions, 1/8 Gorkha Rifles and 15 Kumaon, did not press home the attack and were easily repulsed. A fresh attack was planned for the night 22nd/23rd September 1965, but the Cease Fire intervened before its execution. The formation's abortive attempt to capture Khem Karan came as an anti-climax to its brilliant performance at Asal Uttar. The plans were generally poor in conception and irresolute in execution.'[13]

[After the war, it would be discovered that there were six (not one) Pakistani infantry battalions holding the Khem Karan pocket, with at least two squadrons of armour, to say nothing of the artillery support available to the defenders.]

While 2 Madras was having to fall back to its new defensive line in Khem Karan, its sister battalion, 9 Madras commanded by Lieutenant Colonel Satyan, was to play out the final chapter to the north as a part of 65 Infantry Brigade in the 7 Infantry Division Sector. After the fall of Barki and the Pakistani withdrawal on 11 September, before 9 Madras and 16 Punjab could consolidate the east bank, the Pakistanis had somewhat shamefacedly returned and occupied some of their abandoned pillboxes. Before the ceasefire came into effect, it was imperative to clear the Pakistanis out of these positions that dominated the eastern bank.

Satyan had three companies available to him and he decided to throw everything into the assault that was scheduled to begin at 0030 hours on 23 September. It was always going to be a daunting proposition as the Pakistani artillery remained a formidable force, and the west bank just 150 feet across the canal was also bristling with support weapons. The moment the Indian artillery opened up on the Pakistani positions on the east bank, the troops on the elevated west bank lit up the sky with flares and the Pakistani guns began their counter-bombardment. Pakistani machine guns on the flanks began hammering out their message of death and it was imperative to silence them if the attack was to be successful.

Sepoys S. Bhaskaran Nair and Narayanan, began to crawl towards either flank. Twenty minutes later, the machine guns fell silent and the leading elements of 9 Madras charged forward, led by young officers in a suicidal dash, yelling the battle cry 'Veer Madrassi, Adi, Kollu, Adi, Kollu' (Brave Madrassi, Strike and Kill, Strike and Kill). The Pakistani defenders fought on grimly for another two hours, but by 0300 hours, the pillboxes had been cleared. 9 Madras had forty-nine killed including a JCO and Bhaskaran Nair, who was posthumously awarded a VrC, while one officer and sixty-four other ranks were wounded. On the Pakistani side, forty-eight bodies were counted the next morning in addition to one officer and ten other ranks being taken prisoner. An estimated eighty men were estimated to have been washed away in the canal. In addition to a large cache of ammunition, the battalion also captured two RCL guns. It's a wonder Satyan survived, for, throughout the fighting, he stood on the bund in full view of the guns across the canal, encouraging his troops.

PLANNING DOGRAI (17/20 SEPTEMBER)

When Niranjan Singh took over 54 Infantry Brigade on 12 September, the Pakistani line of defence was along the east bank of the Ichhogil Canal, with a screen deployed on the Jhuggian–Mana–Lakhanke line. These positions were supported by armour on the flanks, astride the UBDC and the Pul Distributary.

In the absence of detailed planning, assaulting troops have little or no idea whatsoever of what lies ahead of them and things invariably go wrong. Refusing to get hustled either by Jogi Dhillon or Mohinder Singh, the new brigade commander followed the basic principles of war with his three commanding officers—first define the objective, then dominate the no-man's land with aggressive patrolling by the forward battalions, collect information on the enemy's strength and deployment, identify possible areas of surprise and deception, develop tracks and approach lines, finalize administrative details, and, most importantly, familiarize each man in the formation with the task he is expected to perform. What really helps is to let the men see their senior commanders amidst them, for nothing can substitute for personal courage.

On 13 September, Niranjan pushed up a 15 Dogra platoon to Mana, from where it could secure the right flank and dominate the Pul Distributary to the north and Lakhanke to the west. Another Dogra platoon similarly reduced the gap in the Jhuggian front. The platoon at Mana was relieved by a holding platoon from 3 Jat on 14 September, while the Dogras were pushed forward to Lakhanke. 54 Infantry Brigade was a beehive of activity; observation posts were established, including a few on the high electric pylons along GT Road to provide direct observation for FOOs.

Some other patrols brought back information about the mine fields and Pakistani defensive positions. Both 13 Punjab and 15 Dogra were settling down under their new commanding officers, the newly promoted Lieutenant Colonels E. D. H. Nanawati and A. R. Singh. They were eager to redeem their battalion's honour after the earlier debacles. Niranjan Singh, on a visit to the forward trenches, asked the second most senior JCO of 15 Dogra, Subedar Suraj Bhan, if the Pakistanis were bullying the Dogras. One thing led to the other and the conversation ended with the brigade commander challenging the old war horse to get him a prisoner.

Nanawati was angry, 'You are a company commander, Sahib, you can't go chasing after prisoners.' But Suraj Bhan argued about the izzat of the battalion, the regiment, and his family, and added, 'Besides, this is a personal challenge.' 'The brigade commander did not mean it that way,' said Nanawati. But finally he had to agree that Suraj Bhan could go on a patrol to capture a prisoner.'[14]

Off into the inky darkness of the night went Suraj Bhan with 'three strong men', until they came to the banks of the Ichhogil Canal. There they waited, for the wizened old JCO knew that sooner or later, Pakistani listening posts would be heading back to the safety of the west bank. Sure enough, just as the sky was beginning to brighten, two tired and dishevelled soldiers appeared with their rifles slung over their shoulders. An hour later, as Niranjan Singh was waking up, he had two extremely 'friendly and talkative' captives standing before him.

They belonged to 16 Punjab and their company was deployed at Dograi, Jallo, as the Pakistanis called it, extending up to the UBDC. The company was being relieved by 8 Punjab so their entire battalion could concentrate at Dograi. That was being done not because an attack from the 'buzdil' (cowardly) Indians was anticipated, but because they needed to get the officers out of Lahore. They didn't know who was defending the canal line north of Dograi, but added slyly: send us back and we'll find out, then return and tell you.

Mohinder Singh was under pressure from HQ 11 Corps to secure the east bank of the Ichhogil Canal. On 17 September, obsessed with the still functional bridge at Bhasin, HQ 15 Infantry Division had worked out yet another plan to let 38 Infantry Brigade have another go at closing the gap with the canal. However, Niranjan Singh, confident that 54 Infantry Brigade could take Dograi, insisted his brigade be given the job. By then 3 Jat had made quite a name for itself and AIR had already announced the coveted MVC for Desmond Hayde. In addition, nearly the entire population of Amritsar believed the Jats had saved the city from Pakistani armour which would have reached Delhi if not for them. It would have been very hard for anyone not to agree to Niranjan Singh's plan.

The Pakistanis had an almost intuitive sense of timing—no sooner had the decision been taken than they started bombarding the battalion. At 1400 hours, all three commanding officers were called to Niranjan Singh's brigade headquarters. The capture of Dograi was to be a brigade attack to be conducted in two phases—in phase one, 13 Punjab would neutralize the Pakistani defences at Milestone 13, and in phase two, 3 Jat was to take Dograi. 15 Dogra would be held in reserve. Niranjan then asked Hayde when he would be ready. 'Let's make it the night of 21-22 September.'[15]

The brigade's plans for the attack had been finalized by 19 September. The appreciation based on various inputs was that the Pakistanis were occupying Dograi with a battalion, of which two companies were forward, across the canal, while the rest were on the west bank. The Pakistani tank harbour was also reportedly in Dograi astride GT Road, with a fair concentration in the north along the eastern bank of the canal. It was also estimated that mines had been laid north to south 500 yards east of the canal, while the northeast and northwest parts of Dograi were lightly held.

Ever since Brigadier Kalha had initially green-flagged the attack on Dograi, Hayde had his plan ready. While 13 Punjab had the attention of the Pakistanis, 3 Jat would move along the right flank and assault Dograi from the northern side. During the intervening two days, strong fighting patrols would go forward and keep the Pakistanis on their toes by simulating attacks. Jitter parties would also keep the Pakistanis from standing down—apart from familiarizing the officers and men with the terrain, this would also tire the out Pakistanis, who would have been kept awake night after night.

Accordingly, Major Baldev Raj Varma, the battalion's adjutant, was appointed the patrol master and detailed plans for each patrol were drawn up, ensuring there were no accidental clashes. The patrols that had been going into no-man's land regularly from 12 September had been to establish presence and dominate the Pakistanis.

On the night of 18/19 September, the time had come to activate Hayde's plan. Captain Raghbir Singh Sandhu had been eager to get some action, but had been held back by Baldev Varma. Finally, he had his chance. Hayde wanted Sandhu to simulate an attack on the Pakistani company that seemed to be deployed at the aqueduct extending southwards for almost a kilometre. Sandhu was tasked with putting so much fear into the Pakistanis that they wouldn't be able to stick their heads out of their trenches when the real attack went in on the night of 21 September.

At 0200 hours on 19 September, 3 Jat's mortars brought down a rain of concentrated fire on the aqueduct defences. Sandhu had two platoons with him— one from his own Bravo Company and another from Alpha Company under the command of Second Lieutenant Ajit Singh Bali.[16] The two sections of medium machine guns, one on either side of the Pul Distributary, began firing at 0210 hours and continued to fire and move alternatingly towards the aqueduct. The two platoons also got into the act, dashing forward in short bursts, firing their weapons. All this while, Sandhu was striding along on the embankment, clearly visible as Very lights and parachute flares were fired by the Pakistanis.

As per his own plan, the simulated attack was to pull back, but Sandhu continued to stride forward, firing his weapon and repeatedly shouting 'Pritam! Pritam!' Naib Subedar Ram Phal, a former national wrestling champion, had to physically overpower the officer and drag him away from the curving streams of tracer bullets that were coming their way.

Hayde's fearless attitude, almost bordering on the eccentric, had an electrifying effect on not just 3 Jat, but all those around him as well. Running alongside GT Road was a high-tension power line running along 100 feet high pylons. Though his own pioneers had made a machaan (observation post) on top of a pylon in the 3 Jat area, it was too far to afford a bird's-eye view of the Ichhogil Canal. So with Sri Ram Yadav in tow, Hayde went up a pylon in the 15 Dogra area which was just about 800 yards from the Pakistani positions at Milestone 13. Despite it being a bright day, the two officers couldn't see much of the canal, but they certainly were very visible to the Pakistanis who put on a display of airbursts to bring them down. With the artillery failing to hit the elevated targets, F-86 Sabres were scrambled but Hayde was long gone by then.

2ND BATTLE OF DOGRAI—21/22 SEPTEMBER

H-hour for 13 Punjab's assault on the Pakistani positions at Milestone 13 was 2330 hours on 21 September. As the Indian artillery started firing at the Pakistani positions, 3 Jat behind 13 Punjab at Santpura started moving towards its firm base on the Pul Distributary some 4,000 yards away. Alpha Squadron 14 Scinde Horse under Captain Jagtar Singh Sangha was to support 13 Punjab and two troops under Brijendra Singh had already established a fire base[17] south of Jhuggian. The Pakistanis were quick to respond to the artillery fire and retaliated almost instantaneously against all the known Indian defensive positions. Santpura received its usual quota of shelling but, by then, the Jats were well on their way.

The tanks had a limited role to play during the initial assault by 13 Punjab. H-hour was delayed by fifteen minutes after which the Sherman Vs provided secondary fire support on pre-selected targets, allowing 13 Punjab to close the gap with the Pakistani defences. At 0015 hours, Brijendra Singh's two troops withdrew to Dial to replenish for the next phase of the battle, which would be after first light.

13 Punjab, as expected, found the going impossible as the Pakistanis had nearly every frontal approach covered. Due to the volume of fire directed at them, 13 Punjab went to ground, in contact with the enemy, but unable to push forward. Nanawati, who had been hit by a splinter, realized his battalion had barely managed to gain 100 yards. However, 13 Punjab had partly done its job, for the Jats reached their FUP, 2,500 yards northeast of Dograi and north of Lakhanke, by 0100 hours.

Hayde was working on the assumption that the first phase was unlikely to succeed. The FUP received a message from HQ 15 Division that phase one had got bogged down and the initial fire plan by the artillery was going to be repeated. The division then asked Hayde what he planned to do.

'Phase 2, going ahead!' Two platoons of Alpha Company had preceded the rest of the battalion to secure the FUP and the northwestern flank and clear the minefields. At 0150 hours, as the artillery once again opened up on the Pakistanis at Milestone 13 opposite the Punjabis, Delta Company under Major Rishi Vatsa crossed the start line. Hayde's group was next, followed in single file by Sri Ram Yadav's Charlie Company, Raghbir Sandhu's Bravo Company, battalion headquarters, and, finally, Asa Ram Tyagi's remaining platoon, which was then joined by the other two as they went through.

Though the commanding officer was the live-wire, the key word was team work. The orders were simple: every man follow your leader, the sections the section commander, the NCOs the platoon commander, who in turn will follow the company commander.[18] The terrain was known, the objective was clear, and 3 Jat was ready! Compare this to the Rajputs, Jats, and JAK Rif battalions that had been tasked with capturing Chawinda—even the commanding officers did not know what lay beyond the designated FUPs.

RAGHBIR SANDHU'S WHITE PHEETA

The second round of artillery fire had already begun and 13 Punjab's delayed attack meant there was no requirement to worry about absolute silence. The delay actually worked in favour of the Jats as the entire focus of the Pakistani defenders at Milestone 13 was along GT Road, which they took to be the main assault. 13 Punjab's frontal assault was always a hopeless proposition because the defenders could bring concentrated fire on to pre-allotted arcs. Barely able to gain 100 yards, 13 Punjab's assault seemed to have fizzled out and the Pakistanis were satisfied that yet 'another attack by the Indians was beaten back. Because elsewhere than the GT Road the night was silent of small arms fire, they didn't bother to look over their left shoulders'.[19]

Because the FUP was so close to the objective, the buildings of Dograi loomed in front of Delta Company almost immediately—they were lit by the exploding shells and a burning haystack. Initially it seemed the Pakistanis were not there. And Delta Company momentarily halted. They then made their 'way past some empty trenches, then they were in among the narrow roads. Realisation and opening of fire was spontaneously together and above the sound rose the Jat battle cry—"Jat Balwan!" Delta Company disappeared among the buildings, lanes and gullies, some turning right, others turning left and Vatsa with others going straight ahead.'[20]

The element of surprise was gone. Charlie Company was approximately 250 yards short of its objective to the immediate right of Delta Company when the Pakistanis came alive with sustained small arms automatic fire, cutting down the men where they stood. If the attack faltered now, Bravo and Alpha Companies which were on their way and in the open would be massacred as well. It is at moments like this that a lone voice acts as a catalyst, and like so many times in the history of warfare, Subedar Phale Ram's voice rose above the din and called, 'Sab jawan dahine taraf ne mere sath. Charge!' (All jawans, turn to the right with me and charge!)

To a man, the 108 soldiers turned and followed Phale Ram. Now two platoons of 3 Jat and an equal number of Pakistani soldiers were staring death in the face. Hardial Rai and Subedar Jhabu Ram led the two platoons of Charlie Company which fell upon the closer line of bunkers and trenches. Captain Kapil Singh Thapa, commanding the depth platoon of Delta Company, on hearing Phale Ram's call, had also got drawn into the charge and his platoon attacked the Pakistani positions further behind. The sharp vicious fighting saw eighty-one Jat casualties, including Phale Ram, who had taken six bullets from a machine gun burst in his chest and stomach. Yet, even after getting hit, his body was later found on top of the bunkers. When his men found him, they thought he was dead, but somehow the JCO clung on to life and survived.[21]

Charlie Company's third platoon under Ajit Singh Bali went past the frenetic hand-to-hand fight amidst the trenches and into the buildings, which was their objective. This was considered critical, for it denied the Pakistanis a firm base from which to launch a counter-attack. Bravo and Alpha Company had the maximum ground to traverse as their objectives were the other two corners of Dograi.

Sandhu's Bravo Company had been on the heels of Charlie Company ahead of them, but once past the Delta Company objective, they sprinted past a big pond that was on the eastern edge of Dograi. Almost immediately they came under machine-gun fire that took a heavy toll, decimating almost an entire section. Their objective was to get behind the platoon that was guarding the crossing place on the Ichhogil Canal where GT Road crossed it before the bridge had been blown. The Pakistani platoon, belonging to 3 Baluch, had two sections on the southern outskirts of the built-up area facing the UBDC.

Asa Ram Tyagi's Alpha Company was still at the FUP when the firing started. He had under his command an additional platoon made up of the commanding officer's protection detail and the battalion pioneers. However, a machine gun had opened up at random and sprayed the area, unfortunately smashing into the adjutant's thigh and shattering the bone. The RMO, Captain S. G. Timma Reddi, was trying to treat Baldev Varma in the dark. An anti-personnel mine had also gone off, wounding Sepoy Phool Singh, and there was no sign of Naib Subedar Sardara's platoon that was guarding the right flank.

Taking two of the platoons with him, Tyagi raced off after Bravo Company, telling the others to follow with the wounded as soon as Sardara fetched up. By then the Pakistani artillery, alerted by the fighting at Dograi, opened up, with emphasis on the area around the FUP. Luckily, Tyagi had already moved forward, while the remaining troops with the wounded hugged the ground as the shells went over them.

Alpha Company had to traverse open fields a short distance from the outer perimeter of Dograi's buildings. There was a dark patch ahead of Tyagi where Desmond Hayde had warned he might find a Pakistani tank harbour. With the sound of fighting all around him, he knew he had to push his company along. As he was urging his men forward, Tyagi got hit, the stray bullets coming from the fighting between Delta Company and the Pakistanis inside Dograi. Tyagi was pulled to his feet by the men who continued to rush forward with him. Naib Subedar Chhotu Ram heard his company commander calling out to him, 'Saab, tankon ko pahile marna, tankon ko pahile marna hai,' (Sahib, destroy the tanks first, destroy the tanks first).

The Pakistani tank crews, alerted by the firing almost in their midst, had been scrambling towards the tanks when they saw Alpha Company coming at them. A severe hand-to-hand fight developed around the two tanks. Tyagi was shot in the chest by Major Rehmat Khan, who was halfway up towards the turret when he was shot by Sepoy Ram Singh. As Rehmat Khan slid down the turret, Tyagi plunged his bayonet into his stomach; Rehmat fired his pistol twice more into

Tyagi. A Pakistani soldier who was trying to save Rehmat Khan then bayoneted Tyagi in his side. Ram Singh, grappling with another soldier on the ground, shook himself free and killed the Pakistani with a stone. Chhotu Ram, in the meantime, had clambered onto the tank and fired downwards into the dark interior, killing the rest of the crew. Amazingly, despite the punishment meted out to Tyagi, he was still alive, though unconscious.

The Pioneer platoon had caught up with the rest of Alpha Company. All around Dograi there was absolute bedlam with exploding grenades and small arms fire, above which was the sound of machine guns still spewing from within fortified pillboxes across GT Road.

Amidst the chaos of death and destruction, there were moments that are forever etched in the memory of those who were there, and from whose telling those moments become legend. Lance Havildar Randhir Singh from the battalion's pioneer section crawled towards a pillbox with a pole charge while Sepoy Ram Chander approached it from the other side. Both men died, but together with grenades and the pole charge, they succeeded in silencing the Pakistanis.

The sheer audacity of the assault on Dograi had carried the day. By 0330 hours, all four companies had established themselves in the designated four corners of Dograi. Usually, an attacking force pitted against well dug-in and fortified defences has a much larger ratio of casualties. But the Jat and Pakistani casualties were nearly even. Hayde's orders to his men were clear—they were to dig in wherever they were; and anything that moved could only be Pakistani soldiers trapped in the middle of Dograi trying to break out, so if it moved, shoot it! Sporadic incidents continued till dawn with no quarter asked for or given. Apart from Tyagi,[22] who was mortally wounded, Kapil Thapa[23] and the IO, Second Lieutenant Jabar Singh, Baldev Varma, and Hardial Rai[24] were among the 51 killed and 150 wounded.

On the shoulders of Major D. S. Shekhawat lay the onerous responsibility of not only replenishing the battalion's ammunition, but also getting the battalion's anti-tank weapons across terrain where there were no tracks. This entailed taking ten-wheeled vehicles across a heavily mined area which was being shot at by every conceivable weapon that could fire. As per plan, Shekhawat was at Lakhanke with his convoy of vehicles. But the sappers who were to clear a route for him were nowhere to be seen. At 0430 hours he set off impatiently, telling the vehicles to make a beeline towards Dograi. Despite losing three vehicles and a few men to the mines, Shekhawat got the ammunition to Dograi before first light. With him were also Major Pasricha and Captain Hora, the two artillery officers who were the FOOs assigned to be with 3 Jat.

Perhaps still unable to comprehend how Dograi could be occupied while their positions at Milestone 13 were holding out against the Indian attack, the Pakistanis sent a company from 3 Baluch under Major Karim Khan towards the GT Road crossing over the Ichhogil where there was a temporary rope bridge.

This position was being held by Bravo Company 3 Jat, who were subject to twenty minutes of intense artillery fire before the Baluchis appeared. Seeing the tall figure of Karim Khan in a baggy salwar coming at him, Sandhu shouted, 'Yeh mera, yeh mera' (He's mine, he's mine). They fired at each other almost simultaneously. The Pakistani officer sank to the ground and Sandhu, 'shouting, "Hai Pritam, Pritammm," was on him, jabbing, jabbing, jabbing with his bayonet.... Sandhu had seen his uncle Pritam, ruthlessly butchered during Partition disturbances by just such people wearing heavy turbans and baggy trousers. He had seen the rolling head and the sightless eyes of his murdered uncle, which had ever since haunted him, but no longer after this day.'[25]

Meanwhile, just as day was breaking, three Pakistani Shermans were closing in towards Ajit Bali's position from the direction of the canal. Bali got the rocket launcher ready, but when he pulled the trigger, the notorious launcher misfired. The men, huddled behind mud walls were clutching Molotov cocktails and looking at Bali who was frantically trying to load another rocket. The tanks were almost abreast their position when Naik Nahar Singh yelled, 'Malatu phek do' (Throw the Molotovs) and up went the bottles, while some Jats managed to fire their weapons. The startled Pakistani commanders sank into their tanks, slammed down the turret hatches and opened up with everything they had.

Fortunately for Ajit Bali and his men, the tank fire was too high and the Molotov cocktails had set their track rollers on fire. The second time around, the rocket launcher did fire, but the rocket missed its intended target. But for the Pakistani tank crews, the close encounter with the Jats was too much and they pulled out at top speed. Unfortunately, among the Indian casualties was the brave Nahar Singh.

Around the same time back at Dial, Alpha Squadron 14 Scinde Horse had broken harbour and was advancing down the road towards Milestone 13. Niranjan Singh had briefed Sangha that owing to heavy artillery shelling and intense small arms fire, 13 Punjab's attack had stalled. He also informed Sangha that 3 Jat had succeeded in moving up and occupying Dograi. The only way for the squadron to support 3 Jat was for the tanks to overrun the Pakistani positions at Milestone 13 and clear the way to Dograi to evacuate the casualties and reinforce 3 Jat.

Sangha ordered Risaldar Gurdial Singh, the No. 4 Troop Leader to deploy at Lakhanke and counter any armour threat that might develop from the north. Brijendra Singh's No. 1 Troop was to remain in position at Mile 14 and act as a firm base and reserve. The remaining two troops along with the squadron commander were to overrun and clear the built-up area around Milestone 13. Wanting to get into the Pakistani defences while it was still dark, Naib Risaldar Kishan Singh's No. 2 Troop led the way, with Sangha's tank in the middle, followed by Risaldar Kundan Singh's No. 3 Troop.

13 Punjab, having been pinned down for the better part of the night, moved

in for a second assault with 14 Scinde Horse now in the lead. Tanks in a built-up area are not necessarily at an advantage, and the fighting at Milestone 13 was fierce and desperate, with neither side willing to back down. The leading tank, commanded by Daffadar Dharam Singh, caught fire after a direct hit by a STRIM grenade. Dharam Singh was killed instantaneously while his two wounded crew were evacuated, but Sowar Amar Singh succumbed later in hospital.

However, the accurate tank fire on the concrete Pakistani bunkers was beginning to flush out the Pakistanis, who were then mowed down by the Sherman's co-axial machine guns. From the rooftops on the eastern side of Dograi, 3 Jat had a grandstand view of the fighting at Milestone 13. Shekhawat was jumping up and down on a rooftop, 'Saale baithe hain, lao, ek rifle,' (The bastards are sitting there, get me a rifle). While engaging the tanks and 13 Punjab ahead of them, the Pakistanis had no idea Dograi had been captured behind them. When Shekhawat fired, one or two casually looked back to see where the fire was coming from.

3 Jat, by then up to strength with its anti-tank weaponry thanks to Shekhawat, had Lance Naik Sheo Narain firing at the Patton that had been shot up by 3 Cavalry earlier. The tank caught fire yet again and there was another claimant to it—Sheo Narain added his name to the long list of those who claimed it in the GT Road Sector.

14 Scinde Horse had lost three tanks in the engagement, but the onslaught was too much for the Pakistanis, who abandoned the defences at Milestone 13 and made a dash for Dograi, only to be shot down by the Jats. With 13 Punjab having occupied the Pakistani positions at Milestone 13, at 0615 hours, the remaining tanks of 14 Scinde Horse had linked up with the Jats at Dograi. During the advance from Milestone 13 to Dograi, the voice of Kishan Singh was clearly heard on the radio saying he had the commanding officer of 16 Punjab, Lieutenant Colonel Jal Framroze Golewala[26] as his prisoner. The wounded Pakistani officer, whose battalion had 106 killed including three officers, was then handed over to 3 Jat by Kishan Singh. 16 Punjab had fought well under Golewala's command. Though a Parsi, his men considered him to be a bigger Muslim than all of them.

Sangha also ordered Brijendra Singh's troop to move up but his troop ran into a minefield 500 yards short of Dograi from where he could nevertheless engage Pakistani targets effectively. Brijendra Singh's own tank had a broken traverse wheel, which was a common problem with the obsolete Sherman Mk V tanks.

While the Jats were still mopping up the fleeing Pakistanis in and around Dograi, two IAF Mystères came screaming in. Shekhawat's ammunition-loaded trucks were lined up inside Dograi but, fortunately, the pilots were focussed on the two tanks that were in the harbour that had been neutralized by Ajit Tyagi's company earlier that morning. Their rockets missed the tanks but managed to set fire to some other support vehicles that were in the harbour.

The Pakistani commanders finally figured out that the Indians had indeed occupied Dograi and, at 0700 hours, the artillery opened up with all the fury they could muster, firing close concentrations with their heavy guns. The mud walls of most houses crumbled under the onslaught and Delta Company, the worst hit, disintegrated. Pakistani armour had also simultaneously appeared from the direction of the aqueduct, while Pakistani infantry could be seen converging on their concentration area. Rishi Vatsa, trying to steady the men, came out of his trench and was blown to bits. Others, including Havildar Hari Singh, were dismembered by tank fire, and the rest of the surviving men tried to run back towards the security of the more solid buildings inside Dograi.

Pakistani artillery fire, having done its job, eased off, expecting the infantry and the tanks to close in and assault the Indian positions. The 14 Scinde Horse tanks, firing from between Milestone 13 and Dograi were proving to be ineffective because of the tall crops hampering visibility. However, the Pakistani infantry seemed to hesitate, once again showing a reluctance to close in unless the armour first overran the positions. The scattered Jats who had survived the artillery barrage, now began firing at the Pakistanis and still the Pakistani infantry could not find the courage to advance. Subedar Major Pratap Singh now took charge. Yelling at the RCL gun crews, he positioned them as if they were on parade, while the Pakistani tanks crept cautiously forward. At 500 yards he blew a whistle and all four RCLs fired in tandem. There were four hits, and while a couple of tanks were immobilized, the others reversed and left the area at varying speeds. By then the Pakistani soldiers, tired of standing around and being shot at, had also melted away.

The armour cum infantry assault having failed to get the desired traction, the Pakistanis started shelling Dograi again. At 1100 hours, Brigadier Niranjan Singh moved up into the smouldering ruins with two companies from 15 Dogra as reinforcements and to see the objective for himself. Seeing the near complete devastation around him, there was wonder in his voice when he met Hayde, asking him, 'Are you all right?'

THE FINAL COUNTDOWN

For the Pakistanis, the disaster at Dograi was a major loss of face. The only way they could hope to reverse the situation was to get to the Pul Distributary from the north and get behind Lakhanke, from where they could effectively cut the two Indian battalions off. 38 Infantry Brigade, despite repeated attempts to capture Dogaich and Wahgrian, had not been successful, the last attempt being made during the night of 18/19 September when 3 Garhwal Rifles had put in three aborted attacks. For the Pakistanis to get to the Pul Distributary, they would have to first get past 1 Jat that was holding the ground east of Bhasin–Wahgrian.

1 Jat had suffered considerably since 6 September. Harbakhsh Singh having sacked Lieutenant Colonel Balbir Singh the next morning, command of the battalion had passed to Major K. R. Rathor. Even though 3 Garhwal Rifles had

not succeeded in capturing its objective, the gap between the Pakistani defences on the eastern side of the Ichhogil Canal and the Jat positions had come down from 3,000 yards to about 1,000 yards. Constantly under intermittent artillery fire, Rathor had been hit by a splinter in the neck and had to be evacuated along with seven men. Command of the battalion had by default passed to Captain Pokhar Singh, who barely had six years of service.

To the right of the Jats, 1/3 GR under the command of Lieutenant Colonel (later Colonel) Charles V. Campagnac were deployed. Having been on leave in England, he had hounded the Indian Embassy and finally just got back to his battalion, shooing away the officer who had been sent as his replacement. A former national level boxer, Campagnac was rather avuncular and he had been quick to boost Pokhar's morale. 'If you are in trouble, I'll come to your help, and if I am in trouble, you help me.'[27]

The view beyond Bhasin was restricted by buildings, mango groves, standing crop, and clumps of sarkanda grass. At 1300 hours the first Pakistani tank appeared. Followed by others, they started moving along the eastern edge of the canal, having presumably crossed at the aqueduct adjacent to the Ravi. A protective patrol deployed at the Sadhanwala Bridge watched as the tanks turned off the bank of the Ichhogil Canal onto the track heading towards the Pul Distributary. Captain S. S. Kaler, the Bravo Company commander, ordered the platoon to open fire with their small arms at maximum range. The clanging of the bullets on the tank's armour-led to the Pakistanis shutting their hatches and looking around to find out where the fire was coming from. Having got past Bhasin, it was evident that they were not expecting any opposition in this area.

Coming under fire, the leading troop immediately engaged the platoon on the bridge, while the second troop swung to its left to outflank the opposition. In the process, the tanks ran into the left forward defences of 1 Jat. Alpha Company under Second Lieutenant T. S. Bajwa and Delta Company commanded by Second Lieutenant B. P. Singh braced themselves for the assault. Bajwa had scrambled to man a RCL gun, having completed the recoilless gun course where he had got to fire exactly one round of 106 mm shot. Holding his breath, he waited for the leading tank to close the gap, while Pokhar called out encouragement. When he fired, he hit the tank dead in the centre, which was a signal for all the other weapons to engage the Pakistani tanks. Sepoys Mukhtiar Singh and Baldev Singh from Bravo and Charlie Companies manning RCL guns also had direct hits, forcing the Pakistani armour to pull back temporarily.

The Pakistani armour regrouped as more tanks and infantry arrived. Lieutenant V. Sachar, the FOO with 1 Jat kept the Pakistanis engaged while 1/3 GR pushed up its RCL guns on the right flank. The second Pakistani attack came at 1600 hours, which was yet again fought off, with Naik Umed Singh and Sepoy Khem Chand's RCLs accounting for another couple of Shermans. Refusing to yield ground, their fast dwindling ammunition being constantly replenished by the Gorkhas, 1 Jat fought on with whatever they could. While making yet another supply run, Second Lieutenant Manjit Singh Cheema was caught by a machine-gun burst across his forehead killing him instantly. The final fight 'lasted a deafening and frightful 40 minutes before the Pakistanis withdrew, leaving six metal hulks burning on the battlefield, an entire platoon of Jats crushed and smashed to death beneath the tanks among a total of 65 Jat dead and many more wounded and a large number of Gorkha casualties suffered in the cause of the battle-field brotherhood.'[28]

In frustration, the Pakistani artillery opened up, killing Sachar and a few others. In what was a last-ditch effort, a Pakistani Canberra overflew the battalion area and dropped two 750-lb bombs, as a result of which Havildar Naranjan Singh and Sepoy Rameshwar were charred to death.

Back at Dograi, even though attempts by the Pakistanis to outflank 38 Infantry Brigade and get behind Milestone 13 were on, the fighting was continuing. Hayde's priority was to get his large number of wounded evacuated. It would take a T-16 carrier driven by Naik Khema Ram three trips to ferry the wounded back through the mined area between Dograi and Milestone 13. Apart from the mines, Khema Ram also had to run the gauntlet of artillery fire and tank fire from the direction of the two bridges.

The shelling rarely slackened while snipers and Pakistani soldiers had to be systematically flushed out, most of them getting killed in short, sharp exchanges while a few surrendered. After the wounded had been evacuated, 108 prisoners, including Golewala, were marched off under the command of Naib Subedar Brahm Datt. The shoulder flashes of the POWs represented all the units that had fought 3 Jat that fateful morning—16 Punjab, 12 Punjab, 3 Baluch, 18 Baluch, 30 TDU, 23 Cavalry, Artillery, and R&S elements.

There was a brief lull in the shelling, but before anyone could think the fighting was over, four Sabres came in low. Perhaps the volume of fire from the ground discouraged them, for the leader waggled his wings and pulled up, the others following, and then they were gone. On the ground, as all eyes were still looking up, Major Shekhawat found Sepoy Net Ram lying in the open, 'his leg stuck out at right angles from his body. "Ram Ram Sahib," said the wounded Jat.

"Ram Ram Bhaiya," said Shekhawat.

"Sahib, mere ko jara chhaiya mein kardo," (Sahib, move me please into the shade).

Shekhawat having done that, the Jat said, "Abhi aram hai," (Now I am comfortable). A short while later this Jat quietly died.'[29]

After last light, the Pakistanis were yet to give up, even though they were counting down the seconds to the ceasefire. The listening posts of Alpha Company warned of the Pakistanis assembling at their FUP. Shekhawat in turn warned Hora to get the guns to stand by. The listening posts then fired warning Very lights and as flares lit up the night sky, the advancing Pakistani infantry was 300 yards from Lance Naik Banwari Lal and Sepoy Risal Singh's LMGs, placed on the company's flanks. In the carnage that followed, Bravo Company joined in, while Hora's guns targeted the FUP into which the men of 8 Punjab tried to retreat.

The guns fell silent at 0330 hours and daylight would reveal sixty-five Pakistani bodies lying out in the open, the result of the final attack. The Pakistanis removed some of their dead and looked around for the wounded, in the process picking up a Jat soldier who was badly shot, thinking he was one of their own. Islamuddin, the Pakistani Intelligence JCO who had first detected the presence of Indian troops on the morning of 6 September, came to the west bank of the Ichhogil Canal at 1530 hours. In a fitting tribute to 3 Jat, he shouted across, 'Only my old battalion could have done this.'[30]

Chapter 22

THE BARMER SECTOR

OPERATION BARREL

THE FIGHTING IN THE DESERT

Ever since Independence, India's Southern Command had been constantly in the limelight. The first Indian GOC-in-C, Lieutenant General (later General) Rajendrasinhji Jadeja, had assumed command in May 1948, taking over from Lieutenant General Eric Goddard. Rajendrasinhji would remain at the helm of affairs for nearly five years. During his tenure, Southern Command, responsible primarily for the Deccan, Madras, and Bombay presidencies, had been given the responsibility for the conduct of Operation Polo in September 1948. With the nizam, Osman Ali Khan, unable to check the rise of the communist-backed razakars, 1 Armoured Division, at the time the most powerful and perhaps the only mechanized force in the subcontinent, had led the vanguard into Hyderabad. In command of the division was an officer who was not only fated to become the Southern Army commander himself, but would go on to also become the chief of the Indian Army after the Sino–India debacle in 1962. The tall, strapping, smooth-talking, aristocratic Mucchu Chaudhuri would develop quite a fondness for being in the limelight.

Six years later, Chaudhuri was the Southern Army commander, a position from which he expected to retire in four years. With developments against Pakistan in the west and China to the north dominating the headlines, Chaudhuri ruefully had to accept the fact that unlike four of his immediate predecessors, who had all been elevated to the post of army chief (Rajendrasinji, Shrinagesh, Thimayya, and Thapar), Southern Command would not be a springboard for him.

In 1961, the limelight found Chaudhuri once again, when Prime Minister Nehru took the decision to invade Goa. Operation Vijay was entrusted to Chaudhuri. As the chief, Pran Thapar, and the CGS, Bijji Kaul, were away in the UK, Chaudhuri had been the 'officiating chief' and he was in a position to issue certain directives to himself (as the Southern Army commander). In a move that would have far-reaching consequences, after returning to Poona, he inducted Patrick Dunn, who was also on his way home, into his staff; and together they then prepared the initial blueprint for the military operation.

Chaudhuri had prepared a very detailed document that listed all the approaches, roads, side tracks, bridges, ferries, etc., which though impressive to look at, was based on a 'set-piece' approach which had been handed down to the Indian (and Pakistani) armies by British commanders. If followed, it would take days for the army to get to Panjim. Though it was designed to impress Nehru and Defence Minister Krishna Menon, the CGS and his staff would play a major role in reshaping it considerably. As a result, even though Chaudhuri tried his best to accept the Portuguese surrender at Panjim himself (even helicoptering down to get there) he was beaten to it by the Para Brigade.

In 1962, after Chaudhuri was moved to Delhi as the acting chief, one of the first run-ins that he had was with Lieutenant General Moti Sagar, the CGS. The Chinese withdrawal post the ceasefire stipulated that Indian troops could reoccupy their territory in NEFA up to 20 km from the McMahon Line. Chaudhuri had stubbornly overruled the CGS and everyone in Army HQ, insisting that the Indian Army would not even venture into the foothills—though this made no sense in military terms! But under Chaudhuri's style of functioning, he rarely felt the need to pay attention to what in army parlance is referred to as staff work. The CGS, on the other hand, would have a more considered view. It was not surprising, therefore, that Moti Sagar found himself on his way to Poona in May 1965, designated the new Southern Army commander. After him, the post of CGS was done away with!

In 1965, when the action in the Rann of Kutch began, Chaudhuri took charge of affairs himself. Kilo Force was instituted hurriedly and the chief once again turned to Patrick Dunn, who was designated the force commander. During Operation Ablaze, Kilo Force was re-designated as 11 Infantry Division. Major General N. C. Rawlley, who had been the brigade commander at Walong in 1962, was given command while Dunn was promoted and earmarked to take over 1 Corps. Rawlley, socially extremely well-connected in New Delhi (his wife Sita was a golf champion), had been handpicked by Chaudhuri. In keeping with the chief's style of functioning, he was not averse to his handpicked few bypassing the army commanders.[1]

Until then the Rajasthan border was under HQ Delhi and Rajasthan Area that reported to Western Command. With Moti Sagar having moved to Southern Command, the vast expanse of desert south of Ganganagar that runs through the districts of Bikaner, Jaisalmer, and Barmer, was to be Moti Sagar's overall responsibility. Given the lack of roads and the scarcity of water, even maintaining the few border posts on the Indian and Pakistani sides (manned by the Rajasthan Armed Constabulary (RAC) and the Indus Rangers, respectively) was a logistical nightmare. But the story was different in the Barmer Sector, where there was an existing rail and road network. In addition, Barmer also had an airstrip used by the IAF a few kilometres from the station at Uttarlai, though it was not yet a fighter base. The Barmer Sector was henceforth the responsibility of Rawlley's 11 Infantry Division.

Moti Sagar and his commanders had to quickly familiarize themselves with miles and miles of empty desert. The Thar was dotted with sand dunes and some scrub that passed for vegetation. The weather conditions through most of the year were extreme, with freezing cold nights and daytime temperatures that sent the mercury soaring. As in the Bikaner and Jaisalmer Districts, water, as could be expected, was extremely scarce. Apart from the main road that ran along the railway line to the border, there were only trails and tracks that would often get obliterated by the shifting sands, making navigation a tricky business. As a result, should there be any major fighting in the area, it had to be restricted to a very narrow frontage.

Despite the geographical expanse, the Pakistanis had just the one solitary brigade holding the sector that extended south from Sulemanke to the Rann of Kutch. Moti Sagar, going on the information he had, was given to understand that Pakistan's 8 Division, which had come up against the Indians in the Rann of Kutch, was based in Hyderabad (Sindh). This appreciation would prove to be wrong, but at the time, the entire Indian thrust was on how to keep the threat from this division at bay. Accordingly, Rawlley was tasked with tying down the Pakistani forces in Sind. It would appear neither side had a clear understanding of the forces aligned against them, as a result, each assumed the other had greater firepower in terms of men and material.

On 6 September, Rawlley's 11 Infantry Division consisted of the solitary 30 Infantry Brigade, commanded by Brigadier J. Guha. There were three infantry battalions—5 MLI commanded by Lieutenant Colonel Rattan Singh; 3 Guards, commanded by Lieutenant Colonel V. M. Maghe; and 1 Garhwal Rifles commanded by Lieutenant Colonel (later Brigadier) Krishna Prasad Lahiri—and the camel mounted D Squadron of 13 Grenadiers. 3 (I) Armoured Squadron Scinde Horse and 167 Field Regiment were expected to reach Barmer only by the next evening.

Apart from the Attari–Wagah crossing point, the other gateway between the two countries was the Munabao–Khokhropar crossing. The Thar Express used to run on the metre-gauge line that had been built and was run by the Jodhpur Railways. Running parallel to the Barmer–Hyderabad–Karachi railway line, the main road from Barmer terminated at Gadra Road on the Indian side, and on the Pakistan side, at Gadra city. From Gadra Road, the IB turned westwards to Munabao, from where it again turned northwards. Munabao was the transit station on the Indian side, after which the railway entered Sindh at Zero Point, the first Pakistani station being Khokhropar, 7 km from there to the west. There was also a solitary road running south to Bakhasar, after which the Suigam Sector, a part of the Rann of Kutch started.

On the other side, Pakistan's 51 Brigade, commanded by Brigadier Khwaja

Mohammad Azhar, had under it 18 Punjab, 8 FF, 14 Field Regiment, 83 Independent Mortar Battery, a company of Indus Rangers, and three companies of Mujahids. 6 Baluch was briefly on its rolls on the evening of 6 September but it was diverted to Khem Karan the same night. The brigade was concentrated between Naya Chor and Umarkot, and its designated concentration area was at Khokhropar.

On the night of 6 September, timed to coincide with the attack across the IB in Punjab, Guha had been ordered to capture Gadra City. Though the brigade had moved to its concentration area at Gadra Road by late evening, it was decided to postpone the attack by a day, mainly because there was no information available pertaining to the strength of the Pakistanis across the border. Also, in the absence of artillery and armour, Rawlley felt he would be in a fix if the Pakistanis retaliated with tanks. Accordingly, a decision was taken at the last minute to postpone the assault to the next night.

3 Guards stepped across the IB at 0100 hours on 8 September, marking the formal entry of Southern Command into the war. Gadra City, which was connected by an 8 km track to Gadra Road, was flanked by sand dunes to its north, and these were captured by 0230 hours, after which Lahiri's 1 Garhwal went through and launched their attack. Gadra City was defended by a battalion of Indus Rangers, who were well dug-in with supporting MMGs and mortars. However, 1 Garhwal Rifles displayed excellent field tactics to capture Gadra City by 1400 hours. The Indus Rangers, though not as tenacious as the regular Pakistani units, lost eight other ranks and four were captured, while the Garhwalis had an officer and five men wounded. With the fighting coming to an end, one company of 5 MLI set up stops to cut off the Indus Rangers' lines of retreat, in the process capturing another couple of Pakistani rangers. Realizing there were no regular troops holding Gadra City, Guha quickly despatched another MLI company post-haste to Munabao, which was 40 km to the north, to reinforce the RAC post there.

The next morning, PAF F-86 Sabres, presumably having taken off from Badin, strafed the Garhwal positions in Gadra City. Despite their 30 mm canons kicking up a lot of dust, the air attack did not cause much damage. What was amazing was that despite the fiasco on the Ichhogil Canal when the IAF had not been called in despite the proactive stance taken by the PAF two days earlier, the lessons learnt, if any, had not permeated down to Southern Command.

What had spread through the grapevine, though, was the panic caused by the news (fuelled by rumours) of Pakistani airborne troops having been dropped around airfields in North India. As the night progressed, there were multiple reports coming into various army and police HQs of paratroopers having been dropped just about everywhere in the country. According to then Cadet (later Wing Commander) Leslie Raymond Springett, at Jodhpur Air Force Station, the cadets were issued weapons and told to man the airfield's perimeter in the middle of the night, after someone reported strange noises being made by Pakistani paratroopers who had got injured while landing. Sure enough, as they stared into the inky darkness, the cadets too heard the Pakistanis abusing and laughing at them. The cadets let loose and fired at the shadows as 'the Pakistanis', who they thought had gone to ground by then, were peppered with gunfire through the night. At dawn, a terrified donkey, fortunately very much alive and kicking was recovered from the bushes where the rope around his leg had gotten entangled.

It wasn't just greenhorn cadets who were panicking. In Ambala, the air force station commander, Group Captain D. E. Bouche called up the Western Army commander and told Harbakhsh that he had seen paratroopers floating down with his own eyes. That entire night, search parties were organized and every shadow was investigated. In Gujarat, the situation was even more dramatic—as apart from paratroopers, even Pakistani amphibious assault craft were being reported. The first frantic calls were received by the Gujarat Police in Ahmedabad of both paratroopers and sea landings in Jamnagar. The Gujarat home secretary then informed HQ Southern Command that 700 heavily armed paratroopers had dropped 35 km southeast of Jamnagar at Kanalus, and were heading towards the coastal village of Sikka. Soon there were more phone calls, once again saying Sikka was being attacked by seaborne troops.

Not willing to take any chances, Moti Sagar ordered Brigadier Pahalajani, the former commander of 31 Infantry Brigade, to take a TAC HQ with him plus two companies of 3 Punjab and fly from Poona to Jamnagar immediately. However, having landed at Jamnagar early in the morning on 9 September, a relieved Pahilajani found that the hysteria had been systematically orchestrated by Pakistani agents. By the afternoon, calm had been restored and local government officials began to heave a sigh of relief.

Back at Gadara City, even as Pahilajani was landing at Jamnagar, 5 MLI, less the one company that had been despatched to Munabao previously, was ordered to follow the desert track that linked Gadra City with Khokhropar that was believed to be held by a company of Pakistani troops. The desert on the Sindh side of the border was not as stark, and the dunes were covered with scattered bushes, scrub, grass, and shrub-like trees. The area was full of scurrying partridge and quail, but no one was paying attention to them as the Marathas moved forward, supported by two troops of Sherman Vs, 1673 Field Battery, and detachments of sappers, signal personnel, and a solitary ambulance.

It wasn't long before the PAF picked up the column stretched out below and it was attacked twice during the day. Using their 30 mm guns, Sabres also fired rockets that killed three men, including a civilian whose truck carrying ammunition went up in a ball of fire. With the vehicles getting bogged down in the loose sand and with the constant threat of air attacks, the column decided to firm up in an area well short of Khokhropar. This location was marked on the map, and came to be known as Sakarbu.

The PAF dominated the skies, continuing its unchallenged run, as desperate pleas by HQ 11 Infantry Division for air cover went unheeded. Not only Sabres, but Starfighters and Canberra B-57 bombers also put in periodic appearances and targeted Gadra Road and its railway station in particular. A train coming in from Barmer provided a juicy target for the exuberant PAF pilots, who blew up four coaches and damaged the railway track between Gadra Road and Munabo. Railway gangs, realizing that the track had to be repaired for ammunition to reach the troops deployed at Munabo, worked out in the open and some of the brave men were killed. Unfortunately, few were recognized for their valour subsequently, but they had done their duty.

It was obvious to everyone that the Pakistanis would sooner or later move down the railway link and attack Munabo. One company of 3 Guards along with the recently arrived 954 Heavy Mortar Battery were told to get to Munabo to further reinforce the post held by the solitary Maratha company and the RAC personnel. However, Pakistan's air domination, still unchallenged, was such that these troops could only move after nightfall. The damage done by the PAF during the day had been phenomenal. The price for ignoring the IAF during the planning stage—even the basic support infrastructure had not been set up to coordinate between the army and the air force—was taking a heavy toll even in the southern sector.

So far, Rawlley's division, consisting of a solitary brigade, had been kept on a leash by the PAF, and the extensive damage done by interdiction sorties had further upset the communication networks of the Indian Army. By 10 September, the 5 MLI Task Force, still bogged down between Gadra City and Khokhropar, came under intense artillery fire as well. As a result, the decision was taken to backtrack to Gadra City. During this entire time, Brigadier Azhar was repeatedly asking for permission to capture Munabao, but GHQ was hesitant to open another front, especially since the Indians had already been contained by the PAF. However, on 11 September, Azhar's 51 Brigade was green-flagged to launch its assault, but the Indians had already abandoned Munabao the previous night as PAF raids had continued to take a toll on vehicles, both military and civil. The original 5 MLI company, along with the reinforcements from 3 Guards and the mortar battery had returned to Gadra Road while the RAC personnel had taken up a fresh defensive position on the Jaisindhar Ridge just to the southeast of Munabao. By 1100 hours on 11 September, Azhar informed GHQ he had captured the railway station and the small town and that he was digging in. He also asked for anti-aircraft guns to be rushed up as the IAF was eventually expected to get active in the Barmer Sector.

Meanwhile, on the same day, Rawlley had decided to target Dali, which was to the southwest of Gadra City. A company of 1 Garhwal Rifles with a section of camel mounted troops of 13 Grenadiers, supported by detachments of MMG and mortars, trudged across the barren landscape. Short of Dali, they encountered Indus Rangers dug in on the sand dunes, so after disengaging, they made the long walk back to Gadra City.

On 13 September, news came in that the Pakistanis had attacked the RAC post at Panchla, approximately 40 km to the north of Munabao, killed the company commander and had reached Gadra Road–Jaisalmer Road at Sundra. Survivors reaching Girab, which was 50 km further east inside Indian territory, suggested that the Pakistanis were moving swiftly to cut off the Girab–Harsani–Barmer axis as well.[2] To meet any developing threat from that direction, patrolling was intensified around Harsani extending up to Girab.

13 Grenadiers and their camels, not surprisingly, were proving to be a lot more effective than jeeps and tanks. Delta Squadron, accompanied by sappers who were camel mounted and demolition experts set off into Pakistani territory with the intention of targeting the railway line between Khokhropar and Naya Chor. No Pakistanis were encountered, and the raiding column would subsequently blow up a significant stretch of railway tracks southwest of Lapla Khara on the night of 16 September.

Meanwhile, around the IB, the Indians at Gadra City and the Pakistanis at Munabao continued to eye each other warily. The Guardsmen were again ordered to move up on the Gadra Road–Munabao axis to make contact with the Pakistanis but, after noticing considerable activity at Munabao, the company returned to Gadra Road. A camel-borne patrol from 13 Grenadiers had also probed the area to the east of Munabao and reported back saying the RAC were still holding their position on the Jaisindhar Ridge. Guha asked the 5 MLI company to once again reinforce the position the same night, and the next day Maghe was asked to move up with 3 Guards and establish a firm base with the intention of launching a battalion strength attack to capture Munabao on 14 September.

The feedback from Maghe, however, was not encouraging. From his position on the Jaisindhar Ridge, Maghe reported that the Pakistanis were holding Munabao in strength. Dali too was proving to be elusive, as the two columns that set out on 14 and 15 September—the first from Gadra Road that stayed on the Indian side till Sajjan Ka Par and then swung west across the IB towards Jesse Jo Par, and the second, once again on the Gadra City–Dali track—got bogged down in the sand and returned to their respective start points.

At this time, one cannot help but wonder what Rawlley's game plan was. Right at the start, he had advanced and captured Gadra City, which took him off the main Gadra Road–Munabao axis and left the latter vulnerable. As expected, the Pakistanis had come down the rail/road axis and taken Munabao without a fight. All that seemed to be happening after that was a series of probing movements, which was exhausting for the men, camels, and equipment. Having taken Gadra City across the border, Rawlley had taken two-thirds of the force available and tied himself up in knots, where the advance on Khokhropar from the flank got bogged down because of the nature of the terrain and absence of proper roads. Unable to make any progress along both axes (Gadra Road–Munabao and Gadra City–Khokhropar), he decided to turn his attention towards Dali, which actually took him further away from the road/railway line along which any real threat towards Hyderabad could be mounted. Bogged down again on the Gadra city–Dali axis, he tried another route, pulling back across the IB, then tried to get to Dali by the Gadra Road–Sajjan Ka Par–Jesse Jo Par–Dali axis.

Rawlley at this stage seemed to be completely fixated on Dali, which had no great tactical significance. On 15 September, a company of 1 Garhwal Rifles with MMGs and mortars on camels made its way to Jesse Jo Par and established a firm base there with the intention of allowing 5 MLI to go through and launch an attack on Dali, and then launch raids further west towards Khensar. On 16 September, a probing Garhwal patrol towards Dali was ambushed by the Pakistanis, who took four other ranks and three camels prisoner.

The Pakistanis, by taking Panchla, had also created a stir north of Munabao, which allowed them to expand the area of conflict. With the Indians showing no intention of recapturing Munabao, on 17 September the Pakistanis attacked the 3 Guards positions instead. After Sabres had pounded the position, as was their wont, the Pakistanis peppered the defences with concentrated artillery fire. Then two companies of 8 FF launched their attack. The Guardsmen resolutely stuck to their posts, even though seven other ranks were killed and an equal number wounded. The Pakistanis broke contact, leaving behind three dead and two incapacitated soldiers. It was from interrogating the wounded that the information was gathered that the area opposite 11 Infantry Brigade was in fact being held by Pakistan's 51 Brigade.

Meanwhile, while 3 Guards were fighting off the Pakistanis near Munabao, 17 Madras had reached Barmer and the battalion was getting off the train at Uttarlai when Sabres suddenly appeared overhead. The battalion had been in the peace station of Madukkarai in Tamil Nadu, when it was rushed to Ahmedabad at the start of the war. As the train started moving, crates of weapons—the unfamiliar 7.62 SLR (self-loading rifle), light guns, MMGs, and 81 mm mortars—were thrust inside the train with their packing and grease still intact! Having been in a peace station, the soldiers were not accustomed to any of these weapons and they had had no training in handling them. At Ahmedabad, they shifted to the metre gauge, which transported them to Uttarlai, where they disembarked at the railway station. Within minutes, the men were subject to the terrifying ordeal of 30 mm cannon ripping into them.

Even eight days after the fighting had started in the Barmer Sector, there was simply no opposition and the Sabres were ruling the skies. It was a miracle that only two other ranks were killed, though seventeen others were badly wounded in the air attack.

'More than the casualties, it was a terrible blow to the morale of the troops who were not yet battle-ready. The battalion was shattered even before they commenced operation. It was made worse by the rickety civil trucks provided to them to move to the battle zone which was miles away. These vehicles frequently got bogged down in the sandy tracks further exposing the convoy to PAF,' recalls Second Lieutenant M. G. Devasahayam.[3] Placed under command of the newly raised 85 Infantry Brigade being commanded by Brigadier H. N. Sumanwar, 17 Madras was joined by 5 MLI, which was de-linked from 30 Infantry Brigade. Guha's HQ shifted to the northwest of the Lilma Railway Station, while Sumanwar's TAC HQ came up at Gadra Road.

17 Madras had been shaken to the core and the GOC 11 Division 'needed to help the unit recover its equilibrium after the trauma of the air attack. Instead, Rawlley ordered the battalion to be cannibalized. One rifle company and mortar platoon were detached from 17 Madras and attached to a different battalion. Another company was deployed to defend the small border town of Gadra Road. Balance of the battalion formed part of the brigade group and advanced with unaccustomed weapons, alongside unknown troops in unfamiliar terrain'[4] to Dali on the night of 18/19 September.

In many ways, Rawlley was displaying the same characteristics that had come to the fore at Walong, where he had been the brigade commander in 1962. 6 Kumaon had then been marched up and down from Kibithu, exhausting the men even before they could give battle to the Chinese. This time, in the heart of the Thar Desert, as the GOC of 11 Infantry Division, he was doing much the same. Though the reasons for the division of responsibilities may have been required, the lack of attention to detail that Rawlley was displaying time and again would have disastrous consequences.

17 Madras, having reached and concentrated around Dali, was ordered to delink two companies that were to double back to Harsani and Tamlor (on the Gadra Road–Munabao axis). 5 MLI had two companies at Jesse Jo Par, one company was on the Gadra City–Khokhropar axis (at Sakarbu) and the fourth company at Khadin. Both these companies were to relieve 1 Garhwal Rifles by first light on 21 September, the day set for the next advance, this time from Dali to Khensar. Prior to the attack being launched, 30 Infantry Brigade was to be given the operational responsibility for the Munabao–Khokhropar area and 85 Infantry Brigade's AOR was to be Gadra Road–Gadra City–Dali–Khinser sub-sector. The change of command was to be effective at 1200 hrs on 21 September.

On 21 September, at 0600 hrs, two companies from 5 MLI and 17 Madras, under the command of their respective commanding officers—Rattan Singh and Lieutenant Colonel V. Balachandran—along with a troop of Shermans began their advance on Khensar. Pakistan's 18 Punjab had two companies plus a company of Indus Rangers deployed at Naupatia, Dhole Ki Beri, and Khurkhari. With one

Western Sector
(11 & 1 Corps)

Not to scale: This map has been prepared in adherence to the 'Guidelines for acquiring and producing Geospatial Data and Geospatial Data Services including Maps' published vide DST F.No.SM/25/02/2020 (Part-I) dated 15th February, 2021.

The squadron commander's Centurion from 17 Poona Horse goes past the Phillora Police Station; Lt Col M. M. Bakshi, the commandant of 4 Hodson's Horse; Maj Govind Singh and men from Hodson's Horse Bravo Sqn in front of the Phillora Police Station, one of the most photographed locations.

Capt Kinny Khanna and his fellow officers from 4 Hodson Horse atop a destroyed Patton tank that had its turret blown off, a testimony to the Centurion's firepower; 2/Lieutenants A. S. Sihota, Arvind Kumar, Maj V. K. Chawla, Capt R. 'Wendy' Dewan from 16 Cav at Alhar; Capt Ajai Singh, Majors Cheema and Virender Singh, OC B and C Sqns 17 Poona Horse respectively, Brig H. S. Dhillon, Cdr 43 Lorried Inf Bde, Maj Gen M. L. Thapan, GOC of the neighbouring 26 Inf Div and Lt Col Raj Singh, CO 5 Jat at Phillora.

(Above) The terrain beyond the railway line towards Jessoran; *(Below)* Pakistani B Echelon vehicles destroyed in the Jessoran–Dograndi area; an Indian RCL gun (presumably belonging to 8 Garh Rif) in action; an M36B2 Tank Destroyer with two more destroyed Pattons in the background at Libbe; a destroyed M-48 Patton tank, one of the innumerable war trophies that adorned Indian cantonments across the country. The surprise of the war was the performance of 62 Cav's Shermans which were on the right flank of 1 Armd Div.

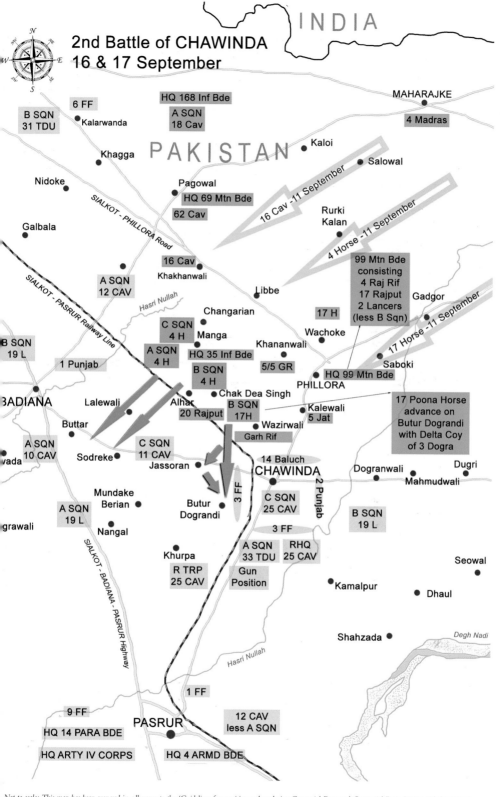

2nd Battle of CHAWINDA
16 & 17 September

INDIA

PAKISTAN

MAHARAJKE

4 Madras

B SQN
31 TDU

6 FF
Kalarwanda

HQ 168 Inf Bde
A SQN
18 Cav

Kaloi

Salowal

Khagga

Nidoke

Galbala

SIALKOT - PHILLORA Road

Pagowal
HQ 69 Mtn Bde
62 Cav

16 Cav -11 September

Rurki
Kalan

4 Horse -11 September

99 Mtn Bde
consisting
4 Raj Rif
17 Rajput
2 Lancers
(less B Sqn)

Gadgor

16 Cav
Khakhanwali

A SQN
12 CAV

SIALKOT - PASRUR Railway Line

Hasri Nullah

Libbe

17 H

17 Horse -11 September

Changarian

Wachoke

C SQN
4 H
Manga

Khananwali

Saboki

B SQN
19 L

A SQN
4 H
HQ 35 Inf Bde

5/5 GR

HQ 99 Mtn Bde

1 Punjab

B SQN
4 H

PHILLORA

BADIANA

Lalewali
Alhar
20 Rajput

Chak Dea Singh
B SQN
17H

Kalewali
5 Jat

17 Poona Horse
advance on
Butur Dograndi
with Delta Coy
of 3 Dogra

Buttar

Wazirwali
Garh Rif

A SQN
10 CAV
vada
Sodreke

C SQN
11 CAV
Jassoran

14 Baluch
CHAWINDA

Dogranwali

Dugri

Mahmudwali

Mundake
Berian

Butur
Dograndi

3 FF

C SQN
25 CAV

2 Punjab

B SQN
19 L

Seowal

A SQN
19 L
grawali
Nangal

3 FF

Dhaul

Khurpa

R TRP
25 CAV

A SQN
33 TDU
Gun
Position

RHQ
25 CAV

Kamalpur

SIALKOT - BADIANA - PASRUR Highway

Shahzada

Degh Nadi

Hasri Nullah

1 FF

9 FF

PASRUR

12 CAV
less A SQN

HQ 14 PARA BDE

HQ ARTY IV CORPS

HQ 4 ARMD BDE

Not to scale: This map has been prepared in adherence to the 'Guidelines for acquiring and producing Geospatial Data and Geospatial Data Services including Maps' published vide DST F.No.SM/25/02/2020 (Part-I) dated 15th February, 2021.

Maj Gen S. K. Korla, GOC 6 Mtn Div, at Gadgor on 11 September; Korla at the Alhar Railway Station, flanked by CO 20 Rajput and the ADMS 6 Mtn Div, Maj Gen M. B. Menon; Alhar had been subject to intense artillery fire; Maj Bhupinder Singh, commanding B Sqn Hodson Horse, was severely wounded and later died in hospital. He was awarded a MVC; Maj Gens Korla, GOC 14 Inf Div Ranjit Singh, and Menon; Lt Col A. M. Manohar, the commanding officer of 6 MLI and his Intelligence Officer, 2/Lt L. K. Nadgir, who were both killed inside Chawinda. Strangely, neither officer was decorated. With the post-war focus being almost entirely on the armoured battle, the role of the infantry battalions at Chawinda was never adequately recognized.

A captured jeep being used by 17 Poona Horse—note the yellow circle painted on the bonnet so that attacking aircraft can identify friend from foe; Lt Col Adi Tarapore, the commanding officer of 17 Poona Horse; Lt Col Jerry E. Jhirad; and Maj Abdul Raffey Khan, the commanding officer and second-in-command of 8 Garh Rif who were all killed in action in and around Butur Dograndi; Maj Gen Korla inspecting a destroyed Pakistani tank. Lt Col Tarapore was awarded the PVC, Jhirad was Mentioned in Despatches, and Raffey Khan got a VrC.

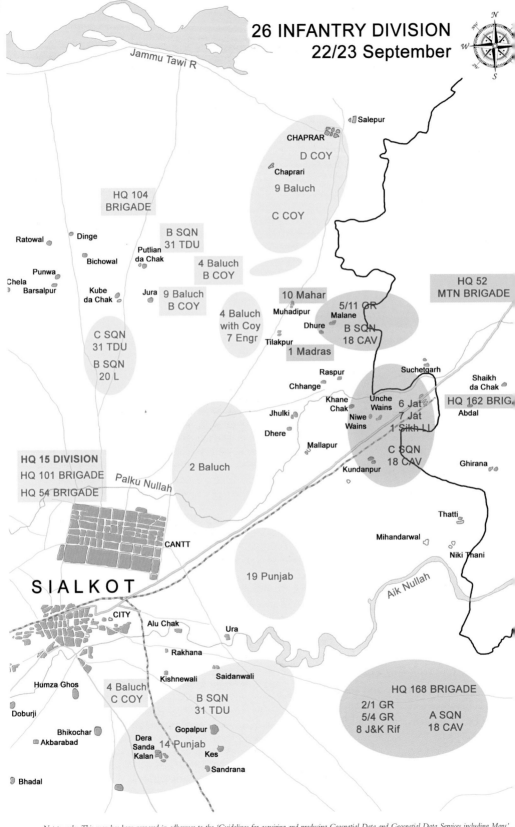

26 INFANTRY DIVISION
22/23 September

Jammu Tawi R

Salepur

CHAPRAR
D COY
Chaprari
9 Baluch
C COY

HQ 104
BRIGADE

Ratowal
Dinge
Punwa
Chela
Barsalpur
Bichowal
Putlian da Chak
Kube da Chak
Jura

B SQN
31 TDU

4 Baluch
B COY

9 Baluch
B COY

4 Baluch
with Coy
7 Engr

10 Mahar
Muhadipur

5/11 GR
Malane
Dhure

HQ 52
MTN BRIGADE

Tilakpur

1 Madras

B SQN
18 CAV

C SQN
31 TDU

B SQN
20 L

Raspur
Chhange

Suchetgarh
Shaikh da Chak

HQ 162 BRIG

Khane Chak
Jhulki
Dhere

Unche Wains
Niwe Wains
Mallapur

6 Jat
7 Jat
1 Sikh LI

Abdal

HQ 15 DIVISION
HQ 101 BRIGADE
HQ 54 BRIGADE

Palku Nullah

2 Baluch

Kundanpur

C SQN
18 CAV

Ghirana

Thatti

CANTT

Mihandarwal

Niki Thani

SIALKOT

19 Punjab

Aik Nullah

CITY
Alu Chak
Ura
Rakhana

Humza Ghos
Doburji

4 Baluch
C COY

Kishnewali
Saidanwali

B SQN
31 TDU

HQ 168 BRIGADE

2/1 GR
5/4 GR
8 J&K Rif

A SQN
18 CAV

Bhikochar
Akbarabad

Gopalpur
Dera Sanda Kalan
Kes

14 Punjab

Sandrana

Bhadal

Not to scale: This map has been prepared in adherence to the 'Guidelines for acquiring and producing Geospatial Data and Geospatial Data Services including Maps' published vide DST F.No.SM/25/02/2020 (Part-I) dated 15th February, 2021.

Lt Col Hari Singh, the commandant of 18 Cav that was the integral armoured regiment with 26 Inf Div; Lt Col R. K. Jasbir Singh, CO 7 Jat, and Lt Col E. W. Carvelho, CO 1 Sikh LI; destroyed Pakistani M-24 Chaffees that were considerably lighter than the Pattons and M36B2 Tank Destroyers; a Pakistani pillbox at Unche Wains, typical of Pakistani defences.

(*Previous page*) Gp Capt Gohain's impression of a Canberra raid. With the IAF's Canberras getting into their stride, the war was entering a critical phase when the COAS informed Prime Minister Shastri that the forces were running out of munitions; Priyanka Joshi's depiction of a pathfinder in action; ground crew loading bombs; A 'tusker' preparing to take off; (*Facing page*) Joshi's depction of the raid on the Badin radar 5 Sqn at Agra, with Wg Cdr P. P. Singh sitting at the center; the workhorses were the three Mystére squadrons, which flew most of the daylight interdiction sorties—Wg Cdr W. M. Goodman, CO 31 Sqn, preparing for a mission.

A Pakistani officer is met by Brig Niranjan Singh after the carnage at Dograi. The remains of 436 Pakistani soldiers were handed over.

(Above) The first flag meeting held after the ceasefire at Butur Dograndi in the presence of UN observers. The destruction caused by Pakistani shelling is visible in the background; The second flag meeting at Alhar Railway Station; (Below) Gen 'Mucchu' Chaudhuri with troops; the COAS and Lt Col Desmond Hayde at the Ichhogil Canal.

(Above) Air Marshal Arjan Singh with his Pakistani counterpart Air Marshal Nur Khan; *(Below)* Lt Gen Bakhtiar Rana receiving Lt Gen Harbakhsh Singh at the UN headquarters in Lahore after the ceasefire. The meeting was to work out the the withdrawl of troops and repatriation of prisoners. The talks were presided over by Brig Gen Tullo Marambio, a special representative of the UN secretary general, U Thant.

(Above) Prime Minister Lal Bahadur Shastri flanked by Pakistan's President Ayub Khan and USSR's Prime Minister Alexei Kosygin in Tashkent. The agreement was signed on 10 January 1966, after which the Indian prime minister passed away in his sleep, having suffered a massive heart attack. *(Below)* India returned the 2,580 sq km of captured territory to Pakistan—4 Hodson's Horse's Centurions deinducting from Pakistan after the Tashkent Agreement.

company of 17 Madras holding the firm base, the remaining three companies attacked and dislodged the Pakistanis from their objectives. By 1130 hrs, 5 MLI had started to dig in on the high ground in the vicinity of Naupatia. Two men had been killed and twenty-nine were wounded; apart from which three officers and 120 men were unaccounted for.

In the middle of the ongoing operation, the reorganization took place, and suddenly all wireless communications between 85 Infantry Brigade and the forward positions around Naupatia, Dali, and even Jesse Jo Par went blank. 85 Infantry Brigade had also moved most of its motorized transport to its Brigade HQ and the bunched-up vehicles were soon targeted by the eagle-eyed PAF which was perennially on the lookout for targets of opportunity. A few hours later, Pakistani artillery started to bracket the Indian positions at Dali and once again the PAF put in air strikes for good measure. Shortly after dark, at 1930 hrs, the Pakistanis put in a swift counter-attack and after an hour of fighting, Dali was back in Pakistani hands. Apart from the one officer and four other ranks who were wounded, three officers and thirty other ranks were missing.

With Dali having fallen behind them, the Pakistanis started encircling the Indian troops at Naupatia. With still no communication from the Brigade HQ, the four companies extricated themselves with some difficulty, 17 Madras losing a company commander—Captain Satyapal—and some ORs in the process. The Pakistanis claimed to have taken 180 prisoners (roughly half the task force that set out from Dali) and captured three Shermans. The remaining troops then skirted past Dali and arrived at Jesse Jo Par where the officers of 5 MLI and 17 Madras desperately tried to bring some order. Some of the 17 Madras troops made their way to Gadra Road, where they were accosted by a furious Rawlley. Looking for an immediate scapegoat for the fiasco, Rawlley gave orders to sack Balachandran,[5] and in fairly colourful language with racist undertones, managed to tell the troops what he thought of them.

With the fiasco on the Dali axis, the Indians were on the back foot. Though the IAF had flown interdiction sorties in the sector, the troops on the ground only knew one thing—if an aircraft appeared above them, it had to be Pakistani. Finally, on 22 September, the IAF came screaming in, and destroyed eight vehicles and damaged a helicopter in and around Khensar. The IAF strikes on the last day before the ceasefire was called only underlined what could have been had the IAF been factored into the initial operational plans!

Based on the reorganization of the two brigades, it finally seemed Rawlley would launch the much awaited counter-attack to clear Munabao that had been under Pakistani occupation ever since the first day of hostilities in the Barmer Sector. On the morning of 22 September, with 1 Garhwal getting to its designated concentration area, Rawlley ordered Guha to capture Munabao the next morning. Though the official version is that orders were countermanded shortly afterwards because the ceasefire was imminent, it is more likely that the Brigade HQ was reacting to a fresh attack launched by the Pakistanis to recapture Sakarbu, the Indian position established inside Pakistan on the Gadra City–Khokhropar axis. With troops that were earmarked for the Munabao attack being rushed to Sakarbu, it seems logical that Rawlley would not want to get involved in a battle where the Pakistanis had almost two weeks to prepare their defences.

However, HQ 30 Infantry Brigade then hurriedly drew up fresh plans for a two-company attack on Maratha Hill and the adjacent sand dunes which were to be captured by 3 Guards and the Garhwalis by 0300 hours. However both these companies lost their way in the dark and at sunrise they were ordered to sit tight where they were. Finally, when the ceasefire was declared, the Pakistani flag still flew over Munabao. On the flip side, India claimed to have captured almost 300-plus sq km of Pakistani territory.

To redress this balance, hardly had the ceasefire been in place for a few hours than regular Pakistani troops accompanied multiple groups of Indus Rangers, mujahids, and dacoits, and went on a village-capturing spree on the Munabao–Jaisalmer axis. Apart from Panchla (which, like Munabao, was never counter-attacked), the Pakistanis extended their area of infiltration to Miajlar, Sato, Chotan, Udisyar, Dedusar, Baori, Kelnor, and others in order to occupy as much Indian territory as possible. Most villages were subsequently cleared by Indian Army units after brief skirmishes, though in the case of Miajlar, it would require the combined force of 1 Garhwal Rifles and 5 MLI to evict the Indus Rangers. It was perhaps the only action after the initial assault on Gadra City where Southern Command troops actually came up trumps.

Rawlley's performance as the GOC 11 Infantry Division unfortunately never came under the scanner. After the debacle at Naupatia and Dali, 17 Madras, having been made the scapegoat, would function for a while without a commanding officer. However, the battalion regrouped splendidly, especially under its new commanding officer, Lieutenant Colonel (later Brigadier) T. Sudarsanam, but the incident would forever remain a black mark on Rawlley's reputation. Unfortunately, the matter did not end there—Rawlley, being Chaudhuri's personal favourite, had to be protected. Subsequently, Brigadier H. N. Sumanwar, the commander of 85 Infantry Brigade, would also find his career abruptly ended a year later, when, without a shred of doubt, the responsibility for the fiasco in the Barmer Sector was Rawlley's, who had dismembered his command by shifting troops around. Covering up for the poor performance of the Indian Army, Chaudhuri later airily claimed that the brief to Southern Command was to create a diversion, which he claimed Rawlley had done splendidly! This was pure rubbish, but then, who was going to point that out?

Chapter 23

ACE IS HIGH
AIR BATTLE III

8–23 SEPTEMBER

After 7 September, the PAF and the IAF had both changed gears. The frenzy of attacks on each other's bases was left once again to the Canberras and, in the case of Pakistan, modified transport aircraft that were used as ad hoc bombers. Though the PAF's losses were much less compared to the IAF, it had suffered because of the blunders made in Pathankot and Kalaikunda. It had lost a higher percentage of its available aircraft so, to conserve its remaining fighters, it concentrated its energies on supporting its ground troops whenever it was called in. The Indians, despite launching their second offensive in the Rachna Doab (Sialkot Sector) seemed at a loss for meaningful targets. 1 Corps, much like 11 Corps two days previously, simply did not ask for meaningful air support, with disastrous consequences.

With India's 1 Corps and the highly rated 1 Armoured Division crossing the start line at first light, it would have been natural for Pathankot to be abuzz with activity on 8 September. On the other hand, given the obsession with secrecy such that army formations had no idea where they were going until they got there, it was hardly surprising that there was no engagement between the PAF and the IAF in the Rachna Doab. The ground liaison officers attached to the IAF base cut sorry figures for they had little or no idea of what was happening. Twenty-two combat air patrols were mounted by the IAF over Pathankot, but other than that, there were no interdiction sorties flown.

Pathankot and Adampur air bases were both anxious about the Pakistani paratroopers that had been dropped in their vicinity. During the early hours of the night, all personnel had been issued weapons and deployed to guard the aircraft pens. To nervous eyes, every waft of breeze that rustles the grass looks like a Pakistani commando, and many a gun blazed away at imaginary targets. Despite being up most of the night, the pilots were raring to get airborne.

Surprisingly, when the orders came for the first strike in the morning, it was a vague order to look for Pakistani tank and troop concentrations around the Mandiala Ridge in the Chhamb Sector. A four-aircraft formation under Squadron Leader Patrick Russel Earle comprising Squadron Leader (later Air Commodore)

Annaswami Sridharan, Flight Lieutenant (later Air Vice Marshal) Ajai Kumar
Brahmawar, and Squadron Leader Raman Kumar 'Uppi' Uppal took off at 1030
hours, flew across the entire 1 Corps frontage, and looked around for Pakistani
tanks in the target area. A Pakistani convoy was spotted and attacked, the pilots
claiming to have destroyed six trucks between them.

32 Squadron also received similar orders—to look for armour and troop
concentrations and it too launched a four-aircraft formation commanded by
Squadron Leader (later Wing Commander) Tej Parkash Singh 'Teja' Gill with
Flying Officer Dara Chinoy, Flight Lieutenant Suresh Vishnu Ratnaparkhi, and
Flying Officer Iqbal Fazal Husain[1]. Fortunately, this time the Mystères found some
tanks in the vicinity of Kalal village. Three tanks and some assorted vehicles were
claimed, after which they set course for Adampur. Shortly thereafter Husain's aircraft,
probably having been hit by ground fire, flamed out in the vicinity of Bhogpur
Sirwal, forcing him to eject. Though this was Indian territory, Husain, by virtue
of his name and religion, was mistaken for a Pakistani pilot and manhandled by
the villagers until a police party rescued him.

The raids in the Akhnoor–Chhamb sector were almost perfunctory in nature.
Precious air effort, risking aircraft and pilots, with no clear-cut objective is almost
criminal. Considering that Chaudhuri's opening of the Lahore and Sialkot Sectors
was to relieve the pressure from the Akhnoor–Chhamb area, more thought needed
to have been given to interdiction strikes to catch the Pakistanis on the move.
That this aspect was altogether ignored is indeed most surprising, and yet typical,
of Chaudhuri's attitude towards the IAF.

Finally, at 1500 hrs, a close air support mission was asked for by 1 Corps,
which reported a convoy of vehicles moving along the Sialkot–Pasrur axis. No. 1
Squadron (Tigers) immediately got airborne with Omi Taneja in the lead and J.
P. Singh as his wingman. They were trailed by Denny Satur and Flight Lieutenant
Dange. However, poor intelligence inputs continued to plague the IAF, for, except
a lone 3-ton vehicle, there was no sign of any activity on the entire road. Satur's
Mystère was not only hit by debris from the exploding 3-tonner, his aircraft also
collected some telephone cables on its wings.

The maximum activity was at Halwara, where the day had started with a B-57
making two strafing passes. Though it failed to do any serious damage, six Hunters
were hit by shrapnel temporarily rendering them unserviceable and ground crews
had to work feverishly to make them air worthy again. Fortunately, late in the
evening on 7 September, two detachments of four Hunters each had arrived in
Halwara from 20 Squadron (Lightnings) which was based in Hindon to augment
27 Squadron (Flaming Arrows) and 7 Squadron (Battle Axes) which together had
lost six aircraft, with two more being damaged on the ground.

Apart from CAPs over Halwara, eighteen Hunter sorties were flown from the
airfield in support of 11 Corps operations, looking for 'targets of opportunity'. At

0730 hrs the first sortie, consisting of two aircraft with two more flying escort, was tasked with attacking Pakistani gun positions and armour on GT Road in the area west of the Ichhogil Canal. The formation met with limited success, engaging some vehicles and armour, but they did not spot any of the gun positions or encounter any Sabres. Flying back over the Ravi, keeping DBN to the north, they did not see any bridging equipment being moved by the Pakistanis in the area. At 1000 hrs, two more aircraft flew an armed reconnaissance in the Kasur–Khem Karan area. Though the Hunters spotted a Bird Dog in the sky directing fire, they did not engage it. Two more aircraft flew a second reconnaissance at 1400 hrs in the Pattakki–Raiwind–Kasur area and reported seeing Indian armour on the move and some Pakistani troops in the area between Dolan and Kasur. Another pair, trailing twenty minutes behind, also flew in the same sector, engaging some tracked vehicles moving in the area between Lullian and Kasur. At 1652 hrs a four-Hunter formation flew to the Narowal–Pasrur area but failed to locate anything of interest.

Finally, at 1812 hrs, 20 Squadron got its debut strike mission in the 1965 war. Four Lightnings got airborne in the fast-fading light for a strike in the Raiwind–Kasur area, after which they were to proceed towards Chandan Singhwala. Armed with sixteen T.10 rockets and carrying a full load of fuel, the formation was being led by Flight Lieutenant (later Group Captain) Chandra Krishna Kumar 'Mini' Menon with Flight Lieutenant (later Squadron Leader) Amarjit Singh Kullar as his wingman, while Squadron Leader Bhupendra Kumar 'Bhup' Bishnoi had Flight Lieutenant D. S. Negi trailing him. If they were to run into Sabres, the formation had instructions to engage them.

Hugging the ground at 100 AGL to escape radar detection, they crossed the IB at 580 knots, after which the Hunters overflew the Ichhogil Canal at Barki. They then banked 30 degrees to the left and approached Raiwind from the north. As they went over the Raiwind Railway Station, a goods train was just steaming in. Apart from military stores, the train also clearly had a tank on one of the wagons that had not been camouflaged. Menon immediately signalled his intention to attack the train.

As the Hunters orbited the station, the Pakistani anti-aircraft gunners held their fire, hoping the Indians would not see the train. To their collective relief, the Hunters flew away, but Menon was only lining up the formation to optimize damage to the train. Pulling up, the four aircraft attacked from the flank. Abreast of the target 'Menon put his Hunter in a shallow dive. The anti-aircraft defences were alerted and ready. Flying through a fusillade of flak, Menon got the locomotive in his sights. He fired his cannons to check his aim and fired a salvo of T.10 rockets.'[2] Between them, they destroyed quite a few coaches of the train.

The elated pilots then saw a concentration of vehicles which they attacked with their cannons before they flew back to Halwara. Two of the Hunters had bullet holes sustained from the ground fire. The next morning, an elated Air Vice Marshal Ramaswami Rajaram,[3] AOC-in-C Western Air Command, sent the senior air staff officer, Air Commodore Gocal to Halwara with the news that the Hunter attack on the train had been a resounding success. Apart from the train itself, seven tanks had been destroyed along with desperately needed fuel and ammunition for the armoured regiments that were trying to push through 4 Mountain Division's defences in Asal Uttar. Subsequently, the vice chief of the IAF, Air Vice Marshal (later Air Chief Marshal) Pratap Chandra Lal elaborated on the implications of the air strike, claiming that according to army intelligence, Pakistani tanks had been reduced to thirty shells per tank and were waiting for replenishments that never came. Post-war Pakistani commentators have also conceded this claim of the IAF, that while most air to ground attacks against Pakistani armour were by and large not very effective, the loss of the train severely impacted their offensive plans in the Kasur–Khem Karan region.

An uneventful night patrol by Dice Dhiman almost came to a tragic end when the anti-aircraft guns in Halwara opened up as the Hunter prepared to land. As the night sky was filled with exploding ack-ack shells, Dhiman had no choice but to abort and fly away. Only when frantic messages had stopped the nervous gunners from firing could Dhiman's aircraft be recovered.

Though most of the Pakistani paratroopers had been rounded up, it was decided not to take a chance and all Mystères from Adampur took off in the evening to harbour at Palam in New Delhi.

During the night, there were two raids on Adampur by B-57s, the second attack materializing at 0300 hours. The ack-acks were blazing away and there was a huge flash indicating that an aircraft had indeed taken a hit. However, since no wreckage could be located later, it's likely that the damaged B-57 managed to fly back to its base in Pakistan.

In New Delhi, the pilots were pleasantly surprised when the air chief dropped by to see them in the evening. Arjan Singh, always a popular figure, congratulated the Mystère pilots. Around this time, the contrail of an unidentified high-flying aircraft became visible. In 1964, India had acquired the VK-750 surface-to-air missiles (codenamed SA-2 Guideline by NATO) from the Soviet Union. These large-sized missiles had stunned the United States by shooting down the hitherto 'invincible' CIA's U2 flown by Francis Gary Powers on 1 May 1960—this had been a defining moment in the history of global aviation. Extremely effective for high-altitude interception but quite useless when it came to engaging low-flying aircraft, a battery had been deployed around Delhi.

As the contrail was identified as being 'hostile', the surface-to-air missile battery launched an SA-2. 'Though the explosion of the missile suggested a direct or a proximity hit, no wreckage was found. No confirmation of Pakistani activity over Delhi on that day has been forthcoming; the incident remains one of the mysteries of the war. No PAF aircraft were lost in the vicinity of Delhi. The only loss of the day was Flight Lieutenant Sadruddin's Sabre,[4] which was shot down by anti-aircraft fire as he crossed over to Pakistani territory after finishing an interdiction mission in the Lahore Sector. He ejected safely and landed behind Pakistani Army lines.[5] He too, like Husain on the Indian side, was beaten up by his own people, until a Pakistani army officer rescued him.

During the day, Pakistani Sabres had attacked Jammu airfield and had been engaged by the anti-aircraft guns. Though one aircraft appeared to be hit, it probably managed to fly back to its own base. In yet another alarming raid, the PAF dropped napalm on a village in the outskirts of Amritsar, causing a large number of civilian casualties. Similarly, there were also civilian casualties in Ferozepur when Sabres appeared over the city.

As the evening progressed, there was still a lot of drama yet to be played out. Though the Mystères had not been used during the day for counter-air missions, at the neighbouring airfield at Agra, Canberras from 35 Squadron had arrived from Poona to join 5 Squadron and the JBCU. Missions were launched targeting Sargodha, Chak Jhumra, Gujrat, and Akwal Dab. With Squadron Leaders Charanjit Singh and (later Wing Commander) Basanta Kumar Sharma in the lead, a seven-aircraft strike against Sargodha was launched in the night, where, despite a virtual umbrella of anti-aircraft fire, bombs hit the runway as well as various installations, including one of the hangers where there was a huge explosion.

Lying in the heart of the Punjab, the airfield at Akwal (Talaganj) was an old airstrip and Indian Intelligence felt it was one of the satellite airfields where the PAF would shelter some of their F-86 Sabres during the night. Leading a strike force of six Canberras, Squadron Leader Chitranjan 'Chinni' Mehta with Flight Lieutenant (later Squadron Leader) Hamir Singh Mangat as his navigator, zeroed in to deliver their bomb loads. A pair of Canberras went for Gujrat to attach the aircraft pens. The second aircraft had a 'hang' and therefore had to return with all twelve 1,000-lb bombs on board. Another pair went to Chak Jhumra and delivered their load of six 1,000-lb bombs. Most aircraft by then had started using Chandigarh as their recovery airfield.

MUCH TOO LITTLE (9 SEPTEMBER)

Even though the Indian offensive had failed to make the anticipated headway, by 9 September the fighting in the Chhamb Sector had been relegated to the back burner; in the Rachna Doab, 26 Infantry Division was leaning on Sialkot but India's 1 Armoured Division had come to a grinding halt after running into a solitary Pakistani armoured regiment and had got into a defensive box; to the south in the Bari Doab, the bridge at DBN had been blown up and to the south, both 15 and 7 Infantry Division were still battling Pakistani screen positions on the east bank of the Ichhogil Canal. 4 Mountain Division, ill-equipped and up against the bulk of the Pakistani armour, had fared even worse, having lost ground at Khem Karan and gone into a defensive posture at Asal Uttar; the area south of the Sutlej, in the Ferozepur axis, the Indians simply had no resources to go on the offensive; the only positive news filtering pertained to the Barmer sector where Gadra City had been taken and troops were expected to move forward to capture Khokhropar.

Considering the ground situation, one would have expected multiple requests from the army for air strikes to soften Pakistani targets opposite them, especially since the entire front was now actively engaged in combat. With the PAF active in most sectors, the Pakistani claim that they had air superiority during these critical days is indeed hard to dispute, though it was more by virtue of the fact that the Indians were not being proactive enough. From Pathankot, the first Mystères to get airborne were on a photo-reconnaissance mission. Squadron Leader Anthony Mousinho was in the lead with Flight Lieutenant Bhupinder Singh bringing up the rear.

Mousinho and Bhupinder Singh couldn't believe their luck when they saw a train below them just south of Lahore, with at least twenty tanks loaded on its wagons. However, they had strict instructions only to photograph targets and not engage them. Unfortunately, when they returned to Pathankot, the film was found to be badly underexposed. Had the two pilots attacked the train and done some damage, combined with the earlier Hunter strike by 20 Squadron, the Pakistanis would have also thought twice before moving their formations around.

31 Squadron launched two more missions during the day. While the first led by Wing Commander Goodman was successful in getting to Kasrur where Pakistani armour could be seen milling around as they attempted to cross the bridge into Khem Karan, his rockets refused to fire. His number two Mike McMahon had aborted at take-off owing to unserviceability of his aircraft. Roundy Raina and Tajinder Sethi making up the reduced three-aircraft formation did fire but the results could not be ascertained. A third strike was also launched by 31 Squadron but problems with three out of the four aircraft meant the mission had to be aborted.

Meanwhile, four Mystères from 3 Squadron led by Squadron Leader Bhagwan Fatehchand Kewalramani with Trilochan Singh as his deputy were tasked to seek out and destroy Pakistani tanks said to be deployed around Phillora.

As they made a quick pass over the area, though the pilots could see tanks below, they had no idea whether they were friend or foe. Three of the aircraft held their fire, but Doraiswamy was quite sure they were Pattons and he fired off an entire salvo of rockets, subsequently claiming one of them as it seemed to blow up. Twenty-seven years later, he described the action, 'I knew it was a Pakistani tank because its gun was pointing east.' 3 Squadron also flew a second mission led by Squadron Leader (later Air Chief Marshal) Swaroop Krishna 'Pandit' Kaul, with Trilochan Singh once again as his number two. This time the Mystères flew further north to Chhamb where they fired at some tanks, claiming two armoured targets.

As most of the Mystères based at Adampur had been moved to Palam the previous evening, there were no offensive missions assigned to the base. It was then left to the three Hunter Squadrons at Halwara to provide some semblance of ground support. In all, four strike missions were launched, the first taking off at 0610 hours to look for targets north-northwest of Kasur. Wing Commander Zachariah with Mini Menon as his number two put in three attacks as there were plenty of tanks milling around in the area, but the other section led by Squadron Leader (later Wing Commander) Avinash Wasudeo Lele with Flying Officer M. V. Singh pulled out of the attack after two runs. The quantum of ground fire from anti-aircraft guns claimed M. V. Singh, who had no option but to eject after his Hunter went out of control. Zachariah's aircraft, though badly damaged, managed to fly back to base. M.V. Singh was badly injured and was immediately taken prisoner by the Pakistan Army. The formation claimed to have destroyed four tanks and about a dozen support vehicles.

A second mission got airborne at 0700 hours but the area around Khem Karan was enveloped in smoke and visibility was extremely poor. The Hunters were being fired at by the heavy 40 mm machine guns mounted on the tanks and three of the four attacking aircraft were hit, though they all successfully returned to Halwara. Two tanks were claimed by the formation.

At 1725 in the evening, a third mission comprising four Hunters got airborne for 'close support and interdiction'. Squadron Leader Bishnoi was accompanied by Flight Lieutenant Gurbux Singh Ahuja as his number two while Flight Lieutenant S. K. Sharma and Flying Officer (later Group Captain) Dilip Kamalakar Parulkar were the second section. They targeted the Kasur Sector once again, and the Hunters, following established practice flew in a broad frontage at 100 feet AGL. They immediately picked up the Pakistani tanks owing to the dust they were kicking up and Bishnoi gave the order to switch the armament to rockets as he pulled up and went in for an attack. The Pakistani tanks, unable to take evasive action at the sudden arrival of the Hunters, fired back defiantly with their mounted anti-aircraft guns. Bishnoi's first salvo of T.10 rockets set three tanks on fire. The other aircraft then lined up and together hit a number of tanks, armoured personnel carriers, and other support vehicles.

Parulkar was number four in the attacking sequence and as he went into a dive, his Hunter was hit. 'The bullet pierced the floor of the cockpit, travelled up and through Parulkar's right arm, through the seat's headrest and finally made a hole in the Plexiglas canopy.' Though his arm was disabled and his flying suit full of blood, the aircraft was still fighting fit and, not wanting the leader to abort the attack, Parulkar continued flying.

Two passes would have been the norm but with so many tanks in the area, Bishnoi's formation put in four passes, using their cannons after their rockets had been expended. On the way back, Parulkar, weak with the loss of blood, finally called the leader and informed him of his condition. Once over Indian territory, Bishnoi gave Parulkar the option of ejecting, but the pilot refused, saying he would bring his aircraft in—a decision that saved his life for, unknown to him, his parachute had been disabled by the damage inflicted by the lone bullet. While the others were getting into position, S. K. Sharma's and Ahuja's Hunters collided. As the pilots and ground crew watched in horror, Ahuja's aircraft flipped over and crashed just outside the Halwara airfield. After landing, Bishnoi's aircraft was found to have sixteen bullet holes while S. K. Sharma and Parulkar found their Hunters too were shot up badly.

The last and final mission for the day was flown by Squadron Leader (later Air Chief Marshal) Nirmal Chandra 'Nimmie' Suri with Flight Lieutenant Herbert Moel David as his wingman. They were tasked with an armed reconnaissance, once again in the Kasur Sector. They claimed that they destroyed two tanks and also fired at some gun positions in the area.

In the Barmer Sector, the advance towards Khokhropar had been severely impacted by Sabres. PAF fighters also kept up a near continuous assault on Gadra Road and Gadra Railway Station. Belatedly, the army at this stage requested for air support, but for the IAF to activate Jodhpur or Uttarlai, which were part of Training Command, at short notice was not possible. Once again, during the planning of operations there had been no thought given to a joint army/air organization to coordinate between Southern Air Command and Western Air Command. Once the PAF appeared unchallenged in the sector, the IAF then nominated Air Commodore Victor Srihari, then the commandant of the Air Force Flying College at Jodhpur, to assume command of air operations in the area. Subsequently, Vampires were clubbed together and designated as 120 Squadron which was commanded by Squadron Leader (later Wing Commander) John Albert Ratnam Balraj. The Vampires carried out a considerable number of reconnaissance sorties.

The main focus of the PAF during that time was 230 SU. Commanded by Wing Commander Krishna Dandapani, the signal unit was the IAF's only eyes in the sector, and the unit's location, close to the IB at Amritsar meant PAF was constantly trying to pinpoint its exact location. Defended by the reasonably effective L-60 AA guns, 'Fish Oil' (as it was called) had first been targeted by a Martin/General Dynamics RB-57F Canberra on 6 September to home onto its location. Flown exclusively by the USAF and NASA, one of these specialized high altitude aircraft was with the Pakistanis and was operating out of Peshawar as a part of 24 Squadron. It was reportedly damaged by anti-aircraft fire and, along with accompanying Sabres, had to abort the mission.

On 7 September a Lockheed T-33 Shooting Star jet trainer had flown over Amritsar and the Pakistanis thought they had a fix on Dandapani's location. On 9 September the first raid materialized at 1815 hours with four F-86 Sabres that came from Sargodha with napalm bombs. This was followed by a second strike at

1850 hours. Despite having zeroed in on the radar's general location, the effective camouflage and intense ack-ack ground fire that damaged a Sabre successfully kept the intruders at bay. Frustrated by their inability to destroy Fish Oil, the Sabres jettisoned their napalm bombs in the countryside, but some fell among villages, killing civilians. Air Marshal Arjan Singh, while talking of the collateral damage caused by the PAF during these two raids, would say later that after this incident he decided not to hold his punches.

Adampur, Pathankot, Jammu, and Halwara were all bombed by B-57 Canberras after dark. Adampur was attacked twice, at 2055 and 2155 hours. The bombs fell close to the airmen's trenches and five airmen from 3 Air Op Flight were killed, a sixth also succumbing to his injuries ten days later. At Halwara the Indian anti-aircraft batteries deployed around the airfield successfully shot down one of the Canberras, the B-57 crashing near the village of Sidhwan Khas in Jalandhar district.

As the night progressed, four separate Canberra missions got airborne from Agra. Wing Commander P. P. Singh led a four-aircraft strike against Dab, Akwal, and Murid airfields; Squadron Leader (later Air Commodore) Ramesh Sakharam Benegal and another Canberra headed for Chak Jhumra; two aircraft flown by Flight Lieutenant (later Squadron Leader) Manmohan 'Shahji' Lowe and Squadron Leader Padmanabha Gautam set course for Gujrat where their combined load of two dozen 1,000-lb bombs decimated the airfield—huge explosions were observed as heavy damage was inflicted; five other aircraft bombed Risalwala and Chak Jhumra airfields.

SIALKOT COMES ALIVE (10 SEPTEMBER)

Reports had come in on the evening of 9 September that the situation in the Khem Karan Sector had stabilized and the immediate threat of a Pakistani offensive towards the Beas Bridge had been blunted. Though there had been sporadic air attacks on the Pakistani armoured units concentrated in the Kasur region, they had been few and far in between. That the IAF played a key role in the battle of Asal Uttar by having blown up the train on 8 September is a known fact, but the lack of visible ground support in the entire 11 Corps sector left the Indian troops bewildered and bitter, especially since PAF Sabres seemed to repeatedly appear in support of its own troops almost at will.

With the situation in the Chhamb and Akhnoor Sectors also under control, the aircraft at Pathankot were finally given the go-ahead to fly in support of 1 Corps in the Sialkot Sector, which allowed the IAF to put in an appearance in the area around Phillora for the first time. The PAF continued with its quest to destroy Fish Oil, which led to vectoring two Gnats onto two intruding Sabres at the start of the day.

A detachment of Gnats from 9 Squadron had landed at Halwara and were on ORP when Fish Oil scrambled Flight Lieutenant Viney Kapila and Squadron

Leader (later Wing Commander) Hari Mohan Singh 'Harry' Chatwal to intercept two Sabres that were heading towards Ferozepur. Flight Lieutenant K. Y. Singh, another respected fighter controller at 230 SU, calmly directed the two Gnats towards the Pakistani planes. As the Gnats closed in, the Sabres either spotted them or were tipped off by Pakistani radar, and they put in a hard turn, one F-86 climbing further up while the second aircraft went down in what looked like an effort to sandwich the Gnats between them.

Kapila latched onto the first Sabre and Chatwal went after the second aircraft. A classic dogfight then ensued as Kapila closed in for the kill. Years later, using his hands to depict the two aircraft, Kapila would describe how he got behind the Pakistani pilot on more than a couple of occasions and with his gunsight on his cockpit and the range down to 150 yards, he pressed the trigger. To his absolute horror, the Gnat's guns jammed and not a single round went off. A disgusted Kapila then broke contact, married up with Chatwal, who had lost contact with his Sabre, and landed back in Halwara. Though his cannons had failed and given the Pakistani pilot a second lease of life, the gun camera had functioned perfectly. The footage would show just how lucky the Pakistani pilot had been.

The bulk of the Adampur Mystères were still at Palam on the morning of 10 September. Ground crews had been working feverishly to make the planes combat-ready so that they could conduct interdiction and ground support sorties and land back at their home base. The first mission to take off was 1 Squadron's four-Mystère formation led by Denny Satur which was to target reported troop concentrations 5 miles southeast of Kasur beyond Ferozepur. Once again Intelligence reports were off the mark, so the aircraft attacked a railway bridge over a canal and some vehicles in its vicinity, after which they landed at Adampur. Following closely on their heels two aircraft flown by Squadron Leader Godfrey Salins and Flight Lieutenant B. S. Raje also attacked the same bridge.

A four-aircraft formation from 32 Squadron led by Teja Gill had been briefed to look for 155 mm guns in the Lahore Sector. Accompanied by Squadron Leader Ravi Kumar, Flight Lieutenant Ratnaparkhi, and Flying Officer Dara Chinoy, the formation took off from Adampur.

Despite a fairly accurate briefing about the suspected location of the guns, the Mystère formation could not initially locate them. They saw a goods train carrying military stores instead and the four aircraft attacked it with their rockets. Even as they pulled out of the attack, they saw the gun positions, but, having expended their rockets, all they could do was return to Adampur. The aircraft were turned around in quick time, not even allowing the pilots time to grab a bite or a drink of water. Airborne again, they were overhead of the gun positions shortly thereafter and Gill led them in the attack. As he came in behind the leader, Chinoy's aircraft was hit by ground fire; with the aircraft in flames, Chinoy had no option but to jettison his canopy and eject.

Landing close to the Pakistani gun position, Chinoy managed to dart into sugarcane fields and evade capture during daylight hours, after which he began the precarious trek back in an easterly direction. Crossing two smaller canals and swimming across the Ichhogil, Chinoy finally ran into an Indian JCO. Having got into the JCO's jeep with another soldier, Chinoy was lucky to survive when the rifle in the vehicle went off accidentally. After proving his identity, he was driven back to Amritsar and was back with the squadron, all set to fly again the next day.

There was considerable excitement in Adampur when Flight Lieutenant Tango Singh was debriefed after a mission north of Lahore where they had been attacking gun positions. Just as he was about to release his rockets, Tango saw a well-camouflaged cluster of tents nearby that seemed to be the headquarters of an army formation. Aborting his attack, Tango came in again and blew up the entire camp. Radio intercepts later in the evening suggested that the Pakistan Army had suffered a major blow, but the identity of the target was not known. It was speculated that a major general had been killed in the attack.

1 Squadron was back in action when the army reported a major concentration of armour in the Lahore sector. At 1500 hours, Omi Taneja led four Mystères with two more aircraft flying as escorts and searched the area but drew a blank, eventually venting their frustration on some vehicles with their front guns. While the Mystères were on their strafing runs, radar warned them of three incoming bogeys. The two escorts were flying at 5,000 feet and failed to spot the Sabres, but Flight Lieutenants Kahai and K. K. Bakshi flying as numbers three and four in the formation saw the F-86s flash past. Jettisoning their drop tanks, the Mystères then made their way back at low level (as per Pakistani records Bakshi's aircraft was fired upon).

Another section, led by Patrick Earle, was launched at 1730 hours with Dange, Handa, and Vinod Kumar Verma. Tasked to take on tanks and vehicles in the Kasur–Khem Karan area, they were also to look for targets on the Khem Karan–Amritsar Road which was under Pakistani control. Down below, the tank battles were raging and the aircraft met with relentless and intense anti-aircraft fire. Amidst the dust and haze, Handa succeeded in making contact with Pakistani armour and dived in for the attack with Verma following him. But both aircraft were too close to the target to engage it successfully, so they pulled up to go around and come in again. Then Earle was hit by ground fire, giving him a fast expanding hole in his fuselage, and forcing him to head for home with Dange, his wingman.

Handa and Verma were coming in for their second run when they spotted what looked like a formation headquarters. Switching targets, they promptly plastered the area, but, as they pulled up, Verma realized his Mystère had been hit and his aircraft was fast developing a hydraulic failure. With Handa shepherding him back to Halwara, Verma was able to land the aircraft, displaying amazing flying skills and a cool head in the midst of a serious crisis.

The IAF was now beginning to get into its stride, launching a fair number of ground attack sorties. However, the aircraft were severely hampered by the absence of FACs and the fact that bomb lines were yet to be clearly established, especially in the Sialkot Sector. According to Air Marshal Bharat Kumar, 3 Squadron flew sixteen strike sorties from Pathankot but these, he records, were not very productive 'due to the fluid nature of the battle going on and close proximity of the troops from both sides'[6]. In addition, 31 Squadron flew seven strike sorties and two reconnaissance missions as well, one of which located Pakistani gun positions in the area but could not engage them due to their limited armament.

Four Mystères from 8 Squadron, which had also returned from Palam in the morning, took off to engage targets in the Lahore Sector. Godfrey Salins had technical problems after take-off and had to return to Pathankot, handing over the lead to Arun Keshav Sapre who, with Flying Officer K. C. Parik and Squadron Leader (later Air Marshal) K. D. K. 'Keith' Lewis proceeded to the target area. Once again the Mystères were engaged by heavy ground fire and though Parik and Lewis both came back with bullet holes in their aircraft, the trio put in five attacks and claimed to have destroyed at least two tanks and half a dozen vehicles.

In a major change of tactics, in the afternoon, Hunters and Gnats from Halwara were to escort two sections of Canberras that would bomb the tank concentrations in the Khem Karan Sector. These were to be the first daylight forays by the Canberras into the tactical area, but no such missions had been practised during peacetime and nor had there been any face-to-face briefings involving the pilots of the Gnats, Hunters, and Canberras. The plan was for the Canberras to come overhead Halwara and the escorting Gnats and Hunters would provide air cover as they took out targets in the Ferozepur area.

However, things were to go drastically wrong. The Canberras had taken off and four Hunters from 7 Squadron were lined up and waiting to take off when the second Canberra had a bird hit, shattering the Plexiglas shield at the bomb aimers station, resulting in the navigator getting a cut above the eye. The pilot immediately radioed, saying he needed to land as his navigator was injured and his air speed indicator was reading zero. The navigator decided to jettison the bombs but, in his panic, forgot to open the bomb doors. The drama continued as the Canberra landed on the wrong runway, tore through the barrier and, finally, with its lethal cargo on board, came to rest in the overshoot area where its wheels sank into the ground.

This fiasco effectively ruled out the first two sections from proceeding further. The third section escorted by Hunters went for Khem Karan and Kasur. While on their bombing run in the area northwest of Khem Karan where they had already destroyed a large number of vehicles, the formation was bounced by three Sabres. The Hunter leader immediately ordered the Canberras to put in a hard turn, following which they dived down to a low level and exited the area. Strangely, the Sabres did not go after the Canberras nor did they take on the Hunters, who escorted the Canberras back to base. The fourth formation flew to the Ferozepur area, escorted by four Gnats. Here too the Canberras were engaged by Sabres, ordered to put in a hard turn by the Gnat leader, who then closed in to take on the F-86s who promptly broke contact.

Flying at number four in the Gnat formation was Squadron Leader (later Group Captain) Kailash Chander Khanna who, during the manoeuvring against the Sabres, found he was nearly out of fuel owing to a malfunction. With Halwara still some distance away, Khanna used his remaining fuel to gain altitude, switched off his engine and glided towards the airfield, switching on his engine when he was at circuit height. Before he could touch down, his engine flamed out but he managed to put the Gnat down safely.

A total of fourteen Canberra sorties were launched that day, of which six aircraft had to return to Agra because of bird hits. Lieutenant General Harbakhsh Singh later sent a congratulatory message saying the enemy had been dealt a crushing blow and that enemy troops were retreating hastily.

The Pakistanis continued to look for Fish Oil but Dandapani's outfit came up with innovative ideas to confuse the attacking aircraft. Squadron Leader Lakhmir Singh, the senior technical officer, placed a charpoy on a turntable to simulate a rotating antenna, and then watched in glee as the Pakistanis went after it, mistaking it for the main radar antenna. There were two raids during the day—the first damaged the spare generator and also the IFF aerial which then had to be repaired and put back on line. The second attack in the afternoon was led by Wing Commander (later Air Chief Marshal) Muhammad Anwar Shamim[7] and though the raid was touted by the PAF to be the most successful against the radar unit, it failed to cause any damage.

In the Sialkot Sector, Sabres almost put paid to GOC 1 Armoured Division, with Sparrow and Brigadier Malhotra having to scramble for cover in the attack that wounded the ADC. Further to the south, in the Rajasthan Sector, the PAF continued to dominate the skies, putting in four raids and slowing down the Indian advance.

11 SEPTEMBER

During the early hours of the night of the 10th, Halwara was bombed eight times by the PAF. A particular B-57 pilot showed great skill. Using all sorts of tactics to confuse the ack-ack guns, this lone B-57 damaged six Hunters, hit a hanger, and killed one of the gunners. This B-57 is believed to have also visited Adampur that night, where he repeated his performance, earning the admiring sobriquet '8-pass Charlie' while in Pathankot, where they were also familiar with his methods, the pilots called him 'Boss Verma'.

Despite all this action, there was a discernible shift in the attitude of the PAF, which was showing signs of running out of steam. The IAF, relatively slower to get off the blocks, was now settling into the war and was increasing its envelope by the day. Despite the fact that the Pakistanis had taken a hammering at Khem Karan and Sparrow's 1 Armoured Division was once again on the move towards Phillora, ground support continued to be a major problem—the requests took a long time to go up the chain of command and had to be prioritized.

Even when aircraft did arrive over the target area, they had a problem distinguishing friend from foe as the FACs either had faulty radio sets or ones that had become unserviceable. The army's communication systems were a perennial issue—battalions were hard pressed to stay in touch with their brigade HQs, let alone talk to and guide incoming aircraft.

The morale was sky-high when AIR announced the first lot of gallantry awards—two of the six MVCs (Wing Commanders P. P. Singh and Jimmy Goodman) and half of the sixteen VRCs (Ghandhi, Neb, Rathore, Cooke, Mamgain, Handa, Jatar, and Tango) were awarded to the IAF. In addition, Squadron Leaders Dahar, Keelor, and Pathania had already been given VrCs on 6 September for shooting down Sabres.

With the resumption of the 1 Corps offensive, Pathankot launched Mystères from 3 and 31 Squadron, which looked for targets in the vicinity of Phillora and Chawinda. Though the IAF claimed as many as eighteen tanks destroyed in that sector, it did not have a major impact on Pakistan's armour. Some airstrikes were also launched in the Sialkot and Zafarwal sectors, but the latter was not heavily defended by Pakistan at that stage.

In the Lahore–Kasur Sector as well, the Indians missed a beat. It should have been obvious to the Indian high command that with the Pakistani offensive having been halted in Khem Karan, Pakistan would try and shift some of its armour northwards to reinforce the Sialkot Sector where they knew India's 1 Armoured Division was deployed. Pakistani railway networks including the railway lines would have been the obvious targets.

The first sortie of the day launched from Adampur by 1 Squadron was indeed tasked to bomb a rail bridge 2 miles east of Kasur after which it was to look for and engage any armour in the area. Red Section, led by Denny Satur, with Brahmawar, J. P., and Uppal, took off with two escorts at 0700 hrs. However, none of the aircraft could release their weapons, as the circuit had been tampered with by a saboteur (who was identified and arrested later that evening). Uppal's Mystère was hit by anti-aircraft fire which resulted in his hydraulic systems packing up. Unable to eject as he did not have sufficient height, he crashed 2 miles east of Kasur. The two escorting aircraft also saw some tanks but once again their weapons did not release.

Two Tigers, Omi Taneja and Kay Kahai, once again got airborne with 1,000-lb bombs when Intelligence sources zeroed in on the location of artillery positions astride a road 2 km southeast of Lahore. Though Omi Taneja's aircraft was damaged by ground fire, Kahai confirmed that his bombing run destroyed the Pakistani positions.

From Pathankot, 8 Squadron too was busy, launching three missions during the day. At first light Godfrey and Sapre engaged some tanks and vehicles in the Lahore Sector. This was followed by another pair, Kashikar and Lewis, who once again scouted around in the same area. Not finding any major targets, they fired at a couple of soft-skinned vehicles that were ferrying troops.

Given the uncertainty of the ground situation in the Phillora area, 1 Corps seemed unwilling to ask for air support. However, finally four Mystères—the by now well-known Black Section comprising of Jatar, Bhatia, Chopra, and Pathania–armed with rockets, were launched. In the vicinity of Chawinda, the formation could see plenty of Pakistani tanks along with other vehicles. Making three passes, the Mystères attacked the spread out targets and returned to Pathankot, where they were quickly refuelled and rearmed. However, the orders were changed and they were told instead to proceed to the Lahore Sector and look for targets of opportunity. The formation was met with a heavy concentration of ground fire, which only allowed them to make a single pass in which one tank and some vehicles were claimed by the IAF.

Two strikes were launched by 32 Squadron. The first four-Mystère armed reconnaissance led by Wing Commander Fernandes flew west of the Ichhogil Canal where they attacked a concentration of vehicles. Two aircraft were hit by ground fire but the damage was not serious. The second mission was specifically tasked to destroy an observation tower in the vicinity of Bedian village which was about 15 nautical miles southeast of Lahore. Squadron Leader Jayawant Singh and his wingman engaged the target that had successfully withstood both tank and RCL fire. The army was particularly pleased with the outcome of the air strike, which only underlined the importance of air support in the entire region.

Halwara had had a relatively uneventful morning. At long last, in the evening, the army reported a concentration of troops and armour in the vicinity of Lulian village and, accordingly, three Hunters took to the air. Flight Lieutenants 'Dan' Nagi and Amarjit Singh Kullar, and (later Air Marshal) K. C. 'Nanda' Cariappa were part of the formation. The low-flying Hunters were once again met with intense ground fire and just south of Khem Karan, Dan's aircraft was hit, forcing him to abandon his attack and head back to Halwara. Kullar and Cariappa lined up the enemy tanks and, after expending their rockets, flew along the Kasur–Lahore railway line, after which they too returned to base. Other strikes had been planned for the area, but these were stood down on the grounds that the situation on the ground had turned for the better and air strikes were not required.

Vampires from the newly constituted 120 Squadron had started carrying out tactical reconnaissance sorties in the Rajasthan Sector. During the day they were active over Gadra, Naya Chor, Khokhropar, and Munabao. According to the IAF, the PAF did not take to the skies in this region, which was interpreted as a sign perhaps that they were beginning to conserve their resources. Fish Oil however, got its daily dose of attention as five Sabres put in an appearance, braved the anti-aircraft fire, and succeeded in disrupting some power supply cables which rendered the radar unit out of action for a few hours.

Pakistani B-57s attacked Pathankot and the C-47 Fairchild Packet that had been damaged earlier was destroyed. Ferozepur also came in for attention, as did Halwara, but there was no damage done by these raids. The PAF for the first time decided to use the C-130 as an improvised bomber, targeting the Kahuta Bridge which had been captured by Major (later Lieutenant Colonel) Megh Singh's Meghdoot Force the previous day. Flying well inside its own territory, the Pakistani crew rolled out the bombs from the open rear ramp, after which the pilot reported an Indian fighter in the area. Taking evasive action, the aircraft returned to its base where it was found to have a bullet hole. Interestingly, there was no IAF interceptor in the vicinity, which suggests that the pilot had mistaken small arms ground fire to be coming from an airborne source.

12–14 SEPTEMBER

Air Marshal Arjan Singh had been pressing Chavan for permission to launch attacks against the airfield at Peshawar, situated near the Khyber Pass. The clearance for this was accorded on 12 September. Earlier in the morning, at 0630 hours, four Mystères from 1 Squadron had taken off from Adampur to launch a counter-air strike against Pasrur from where it was believed the PAF was operating a detachment of F-86 Sabres in support of the ground troops holding ground around Chawinda. Logically, it seemed improbable that the Pakistanis would station aircraft so close to Phillora, where India's 1 Armoured Division had reached in its forward thrust the previous evening. Nevertheless, at 0630 hours, four Mystères from 1 Squadron dutifully got airborne and, not surprisingly, found the airfield deserted with just some light anti-aircraft fire directed at them. The first two Mystères flown by Handa and Flight Lieutenant (later Air Marshal) Prithvi Singh 'Ben' Brar were armed with bombs but they failed to do any damage. Kahai and Vinod Kumar Verma fired their rockets at the runway and succeeded in creating a few craters which rendered it useless for operations. The next mission, flown by the Tigers, launched at 1100 hours, was tasked with destroying a bridge on the Ichhogil Canal. The two aircraft failed to find the target altogether.

Even 8 Squadron had nothing to show for their efforts. A four-aircraft offensive air support mission in the Lahore Sector was assigned targets which the aircraft were unable to locate despite circling the area for a while. Led by Godfrey Salins, Squadron Leaders R. K. 'Gigi' Dhawan and R. N. 'Dogi' Dogra and Flight Lieutenant

N. J. 'Nobby' Misquitta saw some gun positions which they dutifully attacked with their entire complement of rockets. A second mission, this time led by B. I. Singh with Parik, Kashikar, and Lewis, also could not locate the assigned targets in the same area, so they attacked some armoured vehicles and returned to Adampur.

Finally, four days after the launching of the offensive in the Rachna Doab Sector, aircraft from Pathankot were launched for ground support as the fighting around Chawinda began to gain momentum. However, the first strike by 3 Squadron had an inauspicious start as Kaul's aircraft became unserviceable before take-off. Doraiswamy then took the lead, but as they came overhead the target area, Flight Lieutenant Uday Raghunath 'Potty' Potnis was hit by ground fire. With a gaping hole in the wing and fuel streaming out, Potnis' problems kept compounding as he tried to get back to base. Eventually, he was shepherded back by a Gnat.

On the other hand, 31 Squadron was lucky to catch around fifteen tanks on the Chawinda–Phillora road. The four-Mystère formation led by Mousinho with Bal, Raina, and Sethi claimed three positive kills with another one listed as 'probable'. A second four-aircraft strike in the afternoon led by Squadron Leader (later Air Commodore) Surapati 'Bhattu' Bhattacharya also found plenty of tanks milling about in the area. Going after the tanks with Squadron Leader 'Sandy' Sandhu and Flight Lieutenant Andy Sharma, the fourth Mystère in the formation flown by Flying Officer Anukul went after a Bird Dog that was in the area directing artillery fire. Anukul fired his rockets at the Pakistani AOP aircraft, and re-joined the formation which returned to Pathankot. It was later learnt that the Bird Dog had survived, but the pilot had suffered severe burn injuries. The squadron flew eleven more armed reconnaissance sorties in the area.

The Hunters from Halwara concentrated on the Khem Karan–Kasur Sector earlier in the day. Morning visibility being poor, the first two strikes consisting of a pair each on armed reconnaissance missions could not pick up any major activity on the ground but in both cases the Hunters attacked vehicles and goods trains at the Kasur Railway Station.

Major General Sibal's 7 Infantry Division had asked for the bridge over the Ichhogil Canal near Jhaman to be attacked, as the Pakistani defences had been holding out for the last three days against Indian attacks. Accordingly, seven Hunters—three of them in escort roles—led by Rusty Sinha targeted Pakistani positions southeast of Jhaman, strafing Pakistani defences and some armoured vehicles on the Kasur–Lahore Road. A second strike, this time aimed at destroying the bridge on the UBDC on the Lahore–Pasrur road, was launched later in the day with Malik, Suri, Sharma, and Pingale. Owing to the dust thrown up by the exploding bombs, the pilots were unable to make out if the bridge had been destroyed. As they headed back towards Halwara, they saw an F-104 Starfighter but since the Hunters were not capable of engaging the vastly superior enemy aircraft, they stayed clear. On his part, the PAF pilot had seen the Indians, whom he mistook to be two Gnats with two MiG–21s, and he made a treetop level getaway at supersonic speed, barely making it to Risalwala where he landed, desperately short of fuel.

In between the Hunter raids, Squadron Leader (later Wing Commander) Parmarthi 'Prince' Raina and Ben Brar were flying a CAP over Halwara when they were vectored onto four Sabres around 20 km inside Pakistan. The Gnats had approximately two minutes of combat fuel but they engaged the enemy aircraft. Raina's Gnat received seven hits but he managed to disengage successfully and return to base, while Brar's gun camera footage showed his cannon rounds hitting a Sabre although the damage was not sufficient to bring it down. According to Raina's account, there were six Sabres and not just four. The IAF pilots had begun to notice that the PAF was beginning to lose steam, and some of their squadron diaries had noted that as well. The feedback would have almost certainly travelled up the chain of command.

Though reluctant to engage with the IAF in the skies, the PAF's commitment to their ground troops remained steadfast. The Sabres played a significant role in halting the Indian assault when 2 Mahar with tanks from 3 Cavalry and 9 Deccan Horse tried to recapture Khem Karan. Further to the south in the Rajasthan Sector, the IAF flew tactical reconnaissance, Vampire and Harvard sorties over Gadra City, Khokhropar, Gumapur, and Munabao, but neither Starfighters nor Sabres engaged them though they were seen flying in the area. Nor did these aircraft target any ground positions throughout the day.

The PAF continued their war against Fish Oil, however. Though it meant being off the air for a few hours, the radar was shifted shortly after Raina and Brar had tangled with the Sabres. As the equipment was being repositioned, Sabres appeared over the old location, attacking with rockets and guns. At 1130 hours they put in an appearance again, but the barrage of anti-aircraft fire kept them at bay and they went away without discharging their loads. In the evening, three B–57s escorted by four Sabres tried to bomb the radar unit. The bombs however, fell in civilian areas, causing damage to private property. Amritsar ATC confirmed one of the B–57s had been hit by ack–ack and had crashed a few kilometres west of the airfield.

Night raids by the B–57s through the night of 12/13 September continued unabated as the PAF attacked a few additional bases apart from Pathankot and Adampur. Jamnagar was raided four times in which a Hunter trainer and a DC–3 Dakota were damaged inside a hanger, while in Jodhpur the B–57 bombs hit the taxi track and damaged an electrical section. Indian aircraft from Agra staged two strikes—a pair of Canberras bombed Multan for the first time while another two bombed the Nawabshah airfield in Sindh.

Over the Arabian Sea the navy's Fleet Air Arm and the Maritime Wing of the IAF also had a busy day. Two Alizés continued to fly after dark to collect electronic signatures and get a fix on Pakistani radars. During the day, some Indian ships sailed out from Bombay to probe the area to the north while Seahawks from INAS 300 (White Tigers) Squadron were on standby in the event of any Pakistani activity within a range of 150 nautical miles from Jamnagar. Two Seahawks were launched to intercept an unidentified track, but it faded away almost instantly. Two IAF Ouragans (Toofanis), along with Seahawks, also carried out an armed reconnaissance over the sea, as did Liberators and Super Constellations who clocked almost two hundred hours doing maritime reconnaissance flights in the region.

On the morning of 13 September, four Sabres appeared over Pathankot town and pulled up, sending everyone at the air base scrambling for cover. The aircraft attacked Gurdaspur Railway Station instead. Anti-aircraft fire failed to stop the attack and three wagon-tankers of a fuel train were set on fire. Squadron Leader Alauddin Ahmed's aircraft plunged into the ground—either hit by ack-ack or because he flew into some high-tension wires. Even though Ahmed ejected and his chute deployed, he was dead by the time he hit the ground.

Meanwhile, at the railway station, the blazing wagons were endangering all the other trains in their immediate vicinity. With complete disregard to his own safety, Chaman Lal, a fireman at the Gurdaspur station went into the blaze and successfully uncoupled the three tankers, paying for it with his own life. For this selfless act, Chaman Lal was awarded the Ashoka Chakra, the highest gallantry award that could be awarded to a civilian.

Despite the obvious concentration of armour in the Chawinda–Pasrur area, the first strike mission of four Mystères from 31 Squadron was tasked to go to the Chhamb Sector instead and destroy reported artillery positions. With Raina in the lead, McMahon, Bhupinder, and Anukul could not spot the well camouflaged guns. With intense anti-aircraft fire building up, the Mystères returned to Pathankot, with only Anukul having fired off a salvo at what he thought might be a concealed position.

A second mission led by A. S. Chandrashekharan got airborne for an armed reconnaissance in the Pasrur–Satrah–Daska area. Sandhu was the wingman while Flight Lieutenant C. N. Bal and Sethi brought up the rear. Why this area was chosen remains a mystery for it was on the opposite side of the Pasrur–Chawinda axis where the fighting was taking place and served no practical purpose. Nevertheless, not surprisingly, the pilots found no activity in the area but while returning, they found a convoy that included tanks moving on the Mundeke–Sialkot road. They attacked, after which the formation again saw some vehicles close to Pasrur. Coming in to attack again, Sandhu and Bal got hit and Sethi's aircraft was lost. He was declared missing, presumed killed. Sandhu's Mystère was not too badly damaged but Bal was struggling with his aircraft which had a hydraulic failure. Displaying remarkable courage, he managed to belly land at Pathankot and the aircraft was soon brought online again.

Adampur had communication problems on 13 September due to the bombing by B-57s during the early hours of the morning. Apart from the three Mystère squadrons, the Gnat detachment stationed there also saw some action when Squadron Leader (later Air Marshal) Denzil Keelor (Trevor's brother), with Kapila as his wingman, was carrying out a low-level offensive sweep in the Lahore–Kasur Sector. Kapila spotted a PAF Auster and drew Keelor's attention to it, but they decided to leave it alone. The IAF as a rule did not attack aircraft that had little or no fighting capability.[8]

1 Squadron flew two missions that day, the first one in the morning at 0830 hours which was to target an armoured concentration southwest of the Ichhogil Canal headworks. Led by Satur, Brahms, Sridharan, and Dange, the Tigers found a large number of tanks spread out in the area and, between them, claimed three positive and many probable kills. The second strike that got airborne was flown by Omi Taneja with Brar as his wingman. They were tasked with locating a concentration of Pakistani tanks that was reportedly hidden in mango groves near the bridge. Despite searching for a while, the two pilots failed to make any contact and returned to Adampur with all their armament unexpended.

The so-called bridge assigned to 1 Squadron was actually a barrage that supposedly controlled the water level in the Ichhogil Canal which 1 Squadron had failed to find and this had led to some snide comments about navigation by 8 Squadron pilots. So the task was assigned to them and once again Mickey Jatar with his trusted wingman Jimmy Bhatia took to the skies with Flight Lieutenants Chopra and Lal Sadarangani providing top cover. Much to their chagrin, they too could not find the elusive barrage cum bridge despite flying all over the area. Finally, it dawned on Jatar that what Intelligence was reporting as a bridge cum barrage was actually an underground siphon below the Ravi's riverbed. Accordingly, the two aircraft dropped their bombs on the mouth of the canal. There were big splashes as the bombs exploded, but it was hard to accurately assess the damage.

Two armed reconnaissance missions were flown but neither found any worthwhile target. The first was along the Ichhogil Canal and the second mission searched the Lahore–Kasur area. Squadron Leaders R. K. Dhawan and R. L. 'Ravi' Badhwar then dropped their bombs on a secondary target, a bridge.

The final four-Mystère strike with two Gnats providing air cover on the Khem Karan–Kasur road was led by Misquitta. Yet again the quantum of ground fire was daunting, but the Mystères went in and attacked with their rockets. While some tanks were hit and could be seen burning, there were still plenty of targets in the area and the aircraft did a quick circuit and came in again for a second attack. Sadarangani, coming in as number four was hit and, with his aircraft on fire, had to eject. As the aircraft plummeted to the ground, it seemed to the Gnat pilots that Sadarangani had perished with his aircraft, but he had managed to eject. Though Indian troops on the ground also tried to rescue the stricken pilot, the Pakistanis got to him first.

From Adampur, 32 Squadron too put in three strikes, two of which were led by Teja Gill. The first was a four-aircraft sweep 2 miles west of the Ichhogil Canal, resulting in an engagement with Pakistani armour. Resultant ground fire damaged one of the Mystères but the formation returned to base intact. The second mission, again a four-aircraft strike, neutralized some gun positions east of Lahore. A third strike, Flight Lieutenant S. Prakash with Flying Officer Rodrigues as his wingman, also attacked the same gun positions and returned safely to Adampur.

In the morning, two missions were flown by Hunters from Halwara; the first being a two-aircraft armed reconnaissance in the Kasur Sector which located Pakistani armour on the move along the UBDC; these were duly engaged. A second four-Hunter formation with two escorts was launched at 0945 hours to bomb the Raiwind Railway Station. Though plenty of tank tracks could be seen from the air, no armour could be seen on the ground.

Watching the Hunters take off was the detachment of Gnat pilots from 2 Squadron. At 1,000 hours Squadron Leader N. K. Malik and Flight Lieutenant A. C. 'Kakels' Kale were scrambled to intercept a hostile track that seemed to be heading for Amritsar. Over Amritsar, Kale spotted two Sabres and the Gnats turned hard, quickly closing the gap behind them. But unknown to them four more Sabres were on their tail. Kale only realized they were there when one of them fired a burst at him. Breaking off his own attack, Kale put the Gnat into a series of turns and other manoeuvres to shake off his immediate attacker, the aircraft plunging from 20,000 feet to 2,000 feet. At this point, the Sabre's shells hit the Gnat's engine, which flamed out and the attacking Sabre overshot the Gnat, presenting a juicy target.

The Gnats, which had become notorious for their gun stoppages, failed to fire. With no other choice, Kale ejected and was promptly caught by the villagers who were convinced he was a Pakistani paratrooper and proceeded to give him a sound thrashing. When he protested and said he was an IAF pilot and his name was Kale (black in Hindi), the villagers got even more angry because of his fair complexion and the beatings intensified. Soon some troops arrived and rescued him after which he was shifted to Ferozepur hospital where he learnt that Malik had also had a Sabre on his tail, which he had managed to shake off and return to Halwara.

After the interlude by the Gnats, the Hunters continued to look for targets in the Khem Karan–Kasur Sector. On the ground, the battles were being fought at close quarters and in the absence of FACs, it was impossible to differentiate friend from foe. An armed reconnaissance by Squadron Leader Joe Verma with Flight Lieutenant Surendra Nath 'Baby' Sehgal drew a blank though they did pick up some tank tracks; a four-Hunter strike against troops west of Khem Karan, during which Nimmie Suri's aircraft had a flameout in the middle of his attack. He was extremely fortunate that his engine restarted and he could return to Halwara; and, finally a seven-aircraft strike against Raiwind Railway Station led by Ajit Lamba put to flame two goods trains.

In all, the IAF claimed to have destroyed fifteen tanks, damaged another eleven, and also put paid to a large number of other vehicles and a couple of goods trains. By now it was obvious the PAF fleet of Sabres and Starfighters was beginning to feel their losses. Though a much larger number of Indian aircraft had been lost, the rate of attrition was hurting the PAF a lot more.

During the day, Fish Oil was attacked thrice, but once again, 30 SU remained untouched, its radars continuing to scan the skies, much to the mounting frustration of the PAF. Jammu airfield was attacked by four B-57s escorted by four Sabres and an unserviceable DC-3 Dakota parked on the tarmac was destroyed. In the evening four B-57s delivered the PAF's second attack on Srinagar, this time successfully hitting the airfield. Of the sixteen 1,000-lb bombs dropped, four failed to detonate and one exploded on the runway, the shrapnel damaging a UN Caribou and three Mi-4 helicopters. Some buildings in the airport complex were also hit, gutting the armament section that stored most of the arms and ammunition within the airfield.

Adampur was subject to three attacks during which 8-pass Charlie once again displayed his amazing night flying abilities. One of the hangers that had two of 32 Squadron's Mystères, fully armed and fuelled, was hit, gutting the aircraft. In the third raid the bombing claimed the lives of five airmen and damaged some buildings. At the other end of the spectrum, in the Rajasthan Sector, Jodhpur was attacked thrice by a total of eight B-57s. Some buildings and the electrical station were damaged.

IAF Canberras attacked the Sargodha complex, with Wing Commander P. P. Singh and his navigator, Flight Lieutenant (later Squadron Leader) Madan Mohan Maini first doing a reconnaissance cum target indicator run. Coming over Sargodha main at 8,000 feet the target indicator bombs and flares were dropped after which P. P. set course for Agra. Instead of following the usual protocol of descending low while in exit mode, P. P. decided to stay at height. After five minutes the radar started to sound and an incoming blip could be seen. Immediately P. P. put the aircraft in a corkscrew descent and descended to treetop height. Fortunately, once the Canberra went into a dive, the blips faded away. The six Canberras that followed offloaded their bombs on Chhota Sargodha, Sargodha Main, Wegowal, and Risalwala.

THE NIGHT OF THE CANBERRA BOMBERS

Air Marshal Arjan Singh had set his eyes on Peshawar and ever since Defence Minister Chavan had greenlighted the raids, there was a 'spring in the air chief's step!' Located 600 km from the IB, the base was outside the range of Indian fighters. The PAF knew the Canberras would not venture that far as 'any such attack would be suicidal as the attacking aircraft could be intercepted both during ingress and egress'.[9]

Squadron Leader 'Pete' Gautam with the call sign 'Tiger India' was nominated the target indicator aircraft and he had two navigators on board, Squadron Leader R. K. Bansal and Flight Lieutenant (later Squadron Leader) Maini. Eight Canberras (with call signs Victor 1 to 8) as well as a standby aircraft, were to follow. Accordingly, at the stroke of midnight, the first of ten Canberras got airborne from Agra for Chandigarh where the aircraft were refuelled. Victor 1 to Victor 4 were carrying two 4,000-lb bombs while Victor 5 to 8 were loaded with eight 1,000-lb bombs. At 0200 hrs 14 September, they were airborne. Each crew had been allotted their individual targets which included fuel dumps, bomb dumps, the ATC, the headquarters of the PAF, and so on. Maintaining complete radio silence, the Canberras flew at a height of 300 to 500 feet, each navigator ticking off the various check points en route along the desired set course.

Climbing up just as they approached Peshawar, Tiger India found the area below maintaining a complete blackout. However, the navigation had been superb, and the flares were released at the correct time and position, which resulted in the ack-ack guns opening up in unison. This also allowed the crew to pinpoint the exact location of the airfield and the target indicator bombs were dropped. The first fell directly over the aiming point and the other 250 yards away.

Breaking radio silence, Gautam told the incoming Canberras to set their bombing height at 16,000 feet as the ack-ack shells seemed to have a burst height of 14,000 feet. He also transmitted the position of the target indicator bombs in relation to the target, then set a course for Srinagar from where they would then turn and land at Chandigarh.

Victor 5 to 8 aimed their 1,000-lb bombs at the fuel storage tanks and the whole place went up in flames. On the way back, Victor 6 flown by Wing Commander Goodwin had a near miss when a chasing aircraft, undetected by the Canberra's tail radar, fired a missile at him that exploded close to the aircraft just as it was approaching Srinagar. Victor 6 dived down and made a beeline for Chandigarh where it landed with all the other aircraft safely. After a quick refuelling stop, the aircraft once again took off for Agra.

The icing on the cake was a second simultaneous strike on Kohat. Out of an original five Canberras earmarked for the raid, only three could get airborne from Agra. The profile of the attack on Kohat was similar to the Peshawar raid, with Ambala being the staging airfield as against Chandigarh. A total of 12,000 lbs of bombs were dropped at Kohat. After the war, most analysts on both sides agreed that the Peshawar raid by the IAF in the early hours of 14 September was perhaps the most successful air strike of the conflict.

During the rest of the day, most of the attention was on the Sialkot Sector, and though the lack of close air support was being felt by the frontline troops, the higher headquarters at both the corps and command level seemed content with the way things were. In New Delhi, Air Marshal Arjan Singh was pressing Chavan to lift the restriction placed by the government on attacking East Pakistan airfields.

Four strike missions were launched by the Mystères of 3 and 31 Squadron from Pathankot, but, surprisingly only the first one, a four-aircraft formation led by Squadron Leader Pandit Kaul was directed to the Chawinda area. The second formation led by Squadron Leader Kewalramani attacked targets in the Lahore sector, but two out of the four Mystères had technical problems which did not allow them to discharge their weapon loads. Wing Commander Goodman led the first armed reconnaissance from his squadron, also to the Lahore Sector, where they ran into a formation of eight tanks. The squadron diary claims two confirmed kills.

Following much the same pattern were the Adampur Mystères. The Tigers too flew three strike missions, all of which aimed at engaging targets only in the Lahore Sector. Sudarshan Handa, Brar, J. P., and Raje flew the first mission, which targeted a Pakistani gun position west of the Ichhogil Canal near the village of Khagar. Pakistani armour was also seen in the area, and Handa was credited with two kills. Brar also went after a tank and fired his remaining rockets at soft-skinned vehicles, and J. P. and Raje hit the gun positions successfully. The second formation consisted of just Omi Taneja with Brahms as his wingman. They were responding to the developing threat in the area of Bhasin which was east of the Ichhogil Canal. The aircraft requested smoke markers to be laid out as 1 Jat was fighting the advancing Pakistani tanks, but in the heat of the battle, this was not possible. Unable to distinguish friend from foe, the two aircraft strafed a tank and some vehicles on the western bank of the Ichhogil Canal instead. Heavy ground fire from the anti-aircraft guns mounted on the tanks resulted in Brahms's aircraft taking a few hits but he managed to return safely to Adampur.

The third mission was led by Brar with Rajkumar as his wingman, while Squadron Leader Earle and Flight Lieutenant Verma made up the other section. Intelligence had placed a large troop concentration on the Pulkauji Road near Lahore, but by the time the Mystères reached there, the Pakistanis had dispersed or deployed among the groves. Scanning the area, all four aircraft managed to locate targets which they fired on. Earle even located some artillery guns which he destroyed. Verma was hit by ground fire but his luck continued to hold and all four aircraft made it back to base safely.

8 Squadron also launched three strikes in the Lahore Sector—the first a three-Mystère formation consisting of Dhawan, Dogra, and Salins that claimed two tanks and two probables; a second strike was flown by Jatar with Vinod Patney as his wingman. Two Gnats provided them air cover as they were armed with bombs and tasked to destroy a bridge which they hit successfully. The last mission of the day was flown by B. I. Singh with Flight Lieutenant Chopra as his wingman. They too were tasked with bombing a bridge, which they did. However, the bombs were supposed to have a delay mechanism that was not functioning. As a result, B. I. Singh almost became a casualty of his own exploding bombs, a problem which

had almost claimed Vinod Patney earlier on another mission.

Towards the evening, a Starfighter made two high-speed passes over Adampur which indicated that B-57s would almost certainly pay a visit once night set in. All serviceable Mystères from Pathankot and Adampur were therefore ordered to move to Ambala.

The biggest drama however, was to unfold at Halwara which saw a lot of activity involving not just the Gnats and Hunters, but Canberras in their daylight bombing role as well. On a top secret mission, four low-flying Canberras were overhead Halwara early in the morning where they were joined by four Gnats from 2 Squadron. The Gnats, trailing the Canberras, were being led by Wing Commander Bharat Singh, considered to be one of the best when it came to aerial combat. The mission was cloaked in secrecy and the Gnat pilots didn't know where they were going or what the intended target was.

The Canberras were headed for Khem Karan in the hope of catching the Pakistani armour in their overnight harbours. Pulling up sharply to get to their bombing height, the Canberras were surrounded by bursting ack-ack shells. Ignoring the heavy flak, the aircraft dropped their bombs and turned back east towards their home base. The Gnats had climbed up to 10,000 feet or so and were keeping a sharp lookout for Sabres that would almost certainly have been scrambled by then.

The Sabres was already in the vicinity, providing air support to their own ground troops. At first it seemed they had missed seeing the Indians but almost immediately they broke off their own attack and turned towards the four Canberras. Bharat Singh, who had seen the Pakistanis, immediately called out a warning and dived towards the leading Sabre. Realizing he had a Gnat on his tail, the Pakistani pilot displayed excellent flying skill in a desperate bid to get away, but the experienced Bharat Singh was too good for him. The dogfight was witnessed by many on the ground, including the district commissioner of Amritsar, who confirmed that the Pakistani Sabre had crashed within Indian territory and the pilot had been killed.

Tragedy was to strike the Gnats on another mission as well. While escorting a two-Hunter formation that had been launched against troop concentrations 3 miles to the north of Kasur, the four aircraft were returning at high speed at treetop level towards Adampur when N. K. Malik's aircraft experienced a 'trim runaway', a problem that plagued Gnat pilots. With the nose of the aircraft dipping abruptly, even a highly experienced pilot like Malik could do nothing as his aircraft hit the ground 15 km north of Halwara, killing him instantly. Ironically, even on the previous day, a technical problem had robbed Malik of a certain kill.

The Hunters flew three more missions during the day. Zachariah led a four-aircraft formation escorted by two Gnats in the afternoon which blew up a bridge over the UBDC on the Lahore–Kasur road; two Hunters took off at 1415 hrs and attacked a convoy of vehicles in the Lahore–Kasur Sector, in addition to which they also attacked and severely damaged a power house near Lullian village; and finally, in the evening, four Hunters led by Squadron Leader Sinha, armed with 1,000-lb bombs went after a cluster of trees where Pakistani armour was reportedly hidden. Owing to the massive dust and smoke kicked up by the exploding bombs, it was hard to get a damage assessment report. Though two Sabres were sighted by the formation on their way back, in all probability, the Pakistani aircraft failed to sight the low-flying Hunters.

Canberras also attacked the Kasur railway station, dropping sixteen 1,000-lb and four 4,000-lb bombs, severely damaging the marshalling yard and the rolling stock.

As expected, after the bombing of both Peshawar and Kohat, the PAF was thirsting for revenge and struck five Indian airfields. At Jamnagar, they were extremely successful, destroying two Vampires, a DC-3 Dakota, and a Hunter on the ground, a rich haul by any standards. This despite the fact that quite a few of the bombs that were dropped were duds and failed to explode. At Halwara the air defence units were caught napping by the first of two raids as the B-57s were over the airfield with no warning sirens going off. A stick of 500-lb bombs landed near one of the trenches where quite a few airmen had taken shelter, and though they were covered with dust from head to toe, miraculously, there were no casualties. Two Hunters, fully fuelled and armed, that were parked in a hanger were not so lucky, as they were completely gutted and two more were damaged in the second raid later during the early hours of the morning.

At Pathankot too the B-57s succeeded in destroying a DC-3 and flattening out the new ATC building. Jodhpur was also raided, but the real drama was reserved for Adampur where 8-pass Charlie put in an appearance. On its second run, the B-57 was finally hit by anti-aircraft fire, much to the unabashed glee of all in the station. With its right wing on fire, the aircraft jettisoned its bomb load and crashed near the village of Alwalpur, 5 km west of Adampur. The crew, Flight Lieutenant Altaf Sheikh and Flying Officer Choudhary, managed to eject from of the stricken aircraft and initially evaded capture. However, the irate villagers, who had been sleep-deprived because of this particular B-57, were determined to round them up. Choudhary and Sheikh became the first PAF prisoners of war.

15–16 SEPTEMBER

As HQ 1 Corps did not ask for any air strikes in the vicinity of Chawinda, 31 Squadron got to launch only two missions from Pathankot. The first was a four-aircraft formation led by Chandrashekharan, which was told to proceed to the Chhamb Sector where the Pakistanis had deployed some heavy calibre guns. The Mystères could not spot anything as they orbited the area.

Finally, when a request for ground support was received by 4 TAC, it came from the most unexpected quarter—19 Division in Baramulla wanted an enemy position taken out by the IAF. It became evident from maps of the area that neither

Mystères nor Gnats could be used in the deep gorges. Instead, an armed Mi-4 helicopter got airborne from Srinagar and effectively met the army's requirement.

Troops in the Chhamb–Akhnoor sector continued to be pounded by Pakistani heavy calibre guns, which were proving to be a problem. 4 TAC once again ordered a four-aircraft strike against the elusive gun positions but this time 3 Squadron was given the task. As the aircraft came overhead, once again the Pakistanis went to ground, nothing moving to give away their positions. The Mystères continued to orbit the area, scanning every bit of cover for any tell-tale sign. Disappointed, the aircraft returned without having discharged their armament.

Two of the resident squadrons having moved their aircraft to Ambala, all the tasks assigned to Adampur were carried out by 32 Squadron. At least four strike missions were flown during the day, as targets were engaged west of the Ichhogil Canal in the Lahore Sector, near Chawinda and also in the Shakargarh Bulge in the Sialkot Sector and finally in the Chhamb Sector as well.

The third frontline airfield, Halwara, had a quiet morning as there were no calls for air strikes. At 1255 hrs a four-Hunter formation took to the skies on an offensive reconnaissance, shooting up some tanks in 7 Infantry Division's area of operations. Two hours later, as two Hunters got airborne for a CAP, Flight Lieutenant Thapen Kumar 'Chau' Chaudhuri's aircraft suffered a bird hit and started streaming fuel. As Chaudhuri tried to bring the aircraft back for a landing, his number two, noticing that the aircraft was on fire, gave a call for him to eject, but the stricken Hunter continued to hold its course. A second call to eject, however, was heeded and though the aircraft was at low levels, the ejection was successful and the parachute deployed fully. The aircraft however, had crashed just ahead and the parachute drifted into the burning wreckage. Chau was rushed to hospital and later evacuated to base hospital but he succumbed to severe burn injuries later in the day.

In the evening, two Gnats escorted two Hunters that dropped their bombs on an assigned target in the Khem Karan Sector, after which Dhiman and Khullar were asked to destroy a pontoon bridge across the Ichhogil Canal on the Lahore–Attari road. A direct hit on the target demolished it completely.

Accidents and sheer bad luck continued to dog the IAF. At Chandigarh, Squadron Leader (later Group Captain) Narendra Narayan Ubgade's Canberra had a hydraulic failure as he was coming in to land. Unable to lower his undercarriage, Ubgade jettisoned his two external 1,000-lb bombs in a nearby riverbed, but he still had six bombs inside the bomb bay. Landing on its belly, the aircraft came to a halt on one of the two runways. Later in the night, another Canberra accidentally tried to take off from the blocked runway, in the process colliding with and seriously damaging both aircraft. Fortunately, there were no fatal casualties.

Four Canberras attacked Sargodha, while two aircraft bombed Chak Jhumra. The PAF once again put the C-130s in the air with the intention of catching

Indian armour harbouring in the area near Ramgarh in the Sialkot Sector. Two aircraft randomly dropped 18 tons of bombs, but it was a useless exercise for there were neither any troops on the ground nor any tanks. However, the fact that the Pakistanis could fly C-130s at low level at night in the region with impunity underlined the fact that the IAF's Type 76 MiG-21s with night capability were no deterrent for the PAF.

As 16 September dawned, the confusion in the 1 Corps sector continued as 6 Mountain Division was tasked with capturing Chawinda. Even at this stage, it is amazing that neither HQ Western Command nor 1 Corps asked for concentrated bombing of not only Chawinda, but also of all Pakistani positions east of the railway line extending south up to Pasrur.

As it turned out, for the strike formations (which were now operating partly from Ambala) the bulk of the orders were for targets in the Khem Karan and Lahore Sectors. Pathankot, for example, the closest and perhaps the most obvious choice to launch strikes against Chawinda–Pasrur, did not receive a single demand through the day. Nevertheless, 31 Squadron and 3 Squadron between them launched three strikes, but in the absence of any specified targets, all it did was show some air action in the sector.

Along with a major portion of Mystères, Advance HQ had also been shifted to Ambala. Taneja, who was overall in-charge of operations, received his orders and they were almost entirely meant for strikes in 11 Corps' area of operations. 8 Squadron was allotted three strike missions, the first of which was led by Salins. The four-aircraft formation saw some strange tents when it reached the assigned area which it destroyed. The second strike was a three-Mystère formation that was tasked with blowing up a small bridge near the Lahore Sector. The first aircraft scored a direct hit and the mission was accomplished. The third was a two-aircraft strike led by Ravi Badhwar that was assigned a target near the Lahore Cantonment. However, even as the Mystères reached the area, they were ordered to abort and return to Ambala.

1 Squadron was to follow the earlier routine when they had launched from Palam but returned to Adampur after each mission. Accordingly, this time from Ambala, the first strike was a three aircraft mission led by Earle got airborne at 0730 hours and was tasked with attacking Pakistani armour in the Khem Karan–Kasur–Genda Singh Wala axis. Poor visibility combined with no visible activity on the ground meant the entire effort was wasted.

Pakistani armour was reportedly moving on the Lahore–GT and Lahore–Pulkanjri roads. Squadron Leader Sridharan with Philip Rajkumar took off shortly after the first mission but there seemed to be no activity in both the locations. Searching for possible places where tanks could be hidden, the pair were into their third pass when SU 30 warned them of incoming hostile tracks, suggesting the Mystères clear the area and return to Adampur. There was no visual contact with the 'bogeys' and they landed back without having engaged any target.

The two missions having drawn a blank, Taneja was getting frustrated. He started up for a strike mission with Flight Lieutenant Bakshi, but before the aircraft could taxi out, one of the cannons from Bakshi's aircraft went off. The mission had to be aborted. Not to be deterred, Taneja immediately planned a second strike and with Brahms as his number two this time, he got ready to take off again. Unbelievably, Brahms' aircraft, which had been a part of the first strike in the morning, failed to start up. Aborting the mission yet again, Taneja flew instead to Adampur where he quickly had his aircraft turned around. Taneja decided he would do a sweep with Dange as his wingman, and two Gnats were detailed to provide air cover while they searched for targets in the Pasrur Sector.

The Gnats failed to marry up with the two Mystères at the scheduled time; so at 1245 hours Taneja took off without them. Not surprisingly, as the Indians were poised to assault Chawinda, there was plenty of activity on both the Pasrur–Sialkot and Pasrur–Daska roads. With no sign of the PAF, the two Mystères made three passes over the area, shooting up half a dozen soft-skin vehicles as well as a tank. Just as they were leaving the area, the Gnat escort arrived overhead.

While Taneja was taking off from Adampur, four aircraft led by Handa were also roaring into the skies from Ambala at exactly the same time. Philip Rajkumar was the number two while the other section consisted of Kay Kahai and Joe Bakshi. Tasked with destroying gun positions that were said to be deployed near Kin village off Lahore, the formation was supposed to be escorted by two Gnats but, unfortunately, both these aircraft became unserviceable. Using hand signals to communicate, it was decided that Kahai and Bakshi would fly escort and after Handa and Rajkumar had expended their rockets, the roles would be reversed.

The poor visibility of the morning had given way to a bright day and on arrival in the area west of the Ichhogil Canal, the formation could see tanks and vehicles on the move. Quickly diving in to attack, Handa fired his entire salvo at the bunched up tanks. Coming in hard on Handa's heels was Rajkumar but because of the dust kicked up by the earlier salvo, no fresh targets were visible. Handa claimed three tanks and some additional vehicles as most of his T.10s homed in on the targets. Minutes later, after the aircraft had reversed roles, Kahai launched the second attack, in which he too claimed one tank and some soft-skin vehicles. Bakshi coming in behind him, could not see anything to fire at either.

32 Squadron was allotted an armed reconnaissance mission that also took off from Ambala. Ratnaparkhi was in the lead with Dara Chinoy as his wingman. The two Mystères covered a lot of ground, sweeping the area northwest of Lahore, their flightpath along the Nirowal–Gazi Karo–Kalashah and Kaku–Mudrike–Sadhok–Shahdhara Distributary axis. However, no worthwhile targets could be seen from the air and the aircraft returned to Adampur.

8 Squadron were finally allotted two strike missions in the Pasrur Sector.

The first was flown by B. I. Singh with Misquitta as his wingman. The aircraft were armed with two 1,000-lb bombs which were dropped on reported troop concentrations in the heart of the town. With radar control warning of an F-104 Starfighter heading their way, the two Mystères quickly exited the area. The second strike was by Jatar and Bhatia. Intelligence had finally pinpointed the gun positions and the two aircraft had no trouble finding them. As soon as Jatar went in for his attack, radar once again warned of an incoming Starfighter which was around 25 nautical miles from them. Ignoring the threat, Jatar continued the attack. Radar started giving them a real-time countdown. Unfortunately, Bhatia's RT was not receiving the calls so he was oblivious to the unfolding threat. Only when the Starfighter was nearly upon them did Jatar break off, diving down from 2,000 feet to treetop level, a perplexed Bhatia, who still had ammunition left, in tow.

The third mission, Chopi Chopra and Vinod Patney, were assigned gun positions in the Lahore Sector. The two aircraft had no trouble locating the targets after which they headed off to Ambala. Later in the night, at Ambala, two airmen were killed while they were manning the 'goosenecks'—oil cans with a spout on which there is a cloth that burns to light up the runway when aircraft have to be recovered at night and lights are not to be switched on—when an aircraft went off the runway.

Halwara was having a quiet day, as there were no calls for ground support or interdiction sorties. Since 6 September, Hunters in the Western Sector had not been involved in any air combat with the PAF and the impression gaining ground with each passing day was that the Pakistanis had lost their appetite for aerial combat. In the afternoon, Pingale, one of the two pilots who had been shot down during the last engagement, was on the ORP with Flying Officer Farokh Dara 'Bunny' Bunsha when the call to scramble came. Airborne within two minutes, the fighter controller at 30 SU, Flying Officer (later Air Marshal) R. C. Mahadik, gave an initial heading of 345 degrees and asked the two Hunters to climb to 20,000 feet. Pingale was in the lead with Bunsha as his wingman. After a while, they corrected course to 270 degrees and Pingale found a Sabre coming head-on at them but slightly below them.

The Hunters turned and manoeuvred to get behind the Sabre and were closing in when Pingale saw a second Sabre at 4 o'clock, trying to carry out an attack from the flank on the two Hunters. Calling to Bunsha to finish off the Sabre in front, Pingale decided to engage the second aircraft. In the ensuing dogfight, Pingale successfully shot down the second Sabre, but the first one managed to get behind Bunsha, who was very likely killed in the cockpit. Pingale then engaged the surviving Sabre, which almost immediately fled from the scene.

Bunsha's Hunter plunged into the ground 26 miles from Amritsar on the Harike Road and his charred remains were later recovered from the wreckage by the army. The PAF pilot Pingale had shot down had successfully ejected just before his aircraft blew up in mid-air. The captured pilot identified himself as Flying Officer Shaukat Ali,[10] who hailed from East Pakistan. He was extremely miffed with his 'leader' Alam, the 'Pakistani Ace' who had earlier claimed five hunters over Sargodha, now claimed to have shot down both Bunsha and Pingale, taking his tally of kills to a record nine! It's a pity Alam did not actually fight it out with Pingale.

After the first highly successful raid on Peshawar, the Canberra crews were itching to have another coordinated fireworks display. The night of 16/17 September saw a repeat performance. Wing Commander P. P. Singh with Squadron Leader A. S. Ahluwalia and Flight Lieutenant Kumar was Tango India on this occasion, and he was trailed by six Canberras each with an 8000-lb payload. Once again the raid was a success and even though one aircraft had a bird hit, all the aircraft were recovered. Five aircraft led by Squadron Leader Charanjit Singh bombed Sargodha, which was followed with a second raid by five more Canberras. For 16 Squadron, its only earlier mission had been in the Eastern Sector when Peter Wilson had attacked Chittagong. Now Wilson found himself headed for Sargodha from Bareilly with Squadron Leader Shankaran as his sole navigator in the lead aircraft. Approaching Sargodha at 500 feet, Wilson could not spot the runway or the airfield structures in the darkness until the ack-ack opened fire. They released the bombs from that level and the other Canberras released their high-explosive loads from 7,000 feet. Wilson was chased by a F-104 Starfighter but the Canberra, by immediately going to treetop level, shook off the pursuing aircraft. Another Canberra from 16 Squadron was used to pinpoint targets for the fourth raid that was conducted by another three aircraft led by Flight Lieutenant M. M. Lowe with Squadron Leader D. S. Sabhiki as his navigator. They attacked Chak Jhumra and Chiniot which were on the eastern bank of the Chenab in relation to Sargodha Main.

That night there was a solitary raid by B-57s on Halwara, but after having lost 8-pass Charlie, the PAF pilots seemed to have changed their tactics. Previously the aircraft would go into a steep glide and drop their bombs after which they would start to recover well below 4,000 feet. To avoid the ack-ack fire, they now decided to release their loads from 8,000 feet in a shallow dive, which meant they were sacrificing accuracy. The attack on Halwara that night saw this new tactic, where, after dropping their bombs, they cleared the airfield and then dived down to 500 feet to make their getaway. There had also been unconfirmed reports that the Pakistanis were using napalm. Some containers with distinct US markings were recovered from the airfield the next night that had failed to ignite.

4 TAC's use of Mi-4s in an offensive role within J&K continued to pay dividends. The helicopters dropped sixty bombs and fired 702 rounds on raider positions located 8 km east of Rajouri.

17–19 SEPTEMBER

On a day when 6 Mountain Division and 1 Armoured Division were at the receiving end of almost continuous artillery barrages by Pakistani guns in and around Chawinda, it is hard to believe that HQ 1 Corps did not ask for a single air strike. There were very few fighter strikes even in the 11 Corps Sector, where faulty intelligence inputs continued to dog the Indians.

To start with, Pathankot had very poor visibility in the morning. Nevertheless, intelligence sources were insistent that the Pakistanis had deployed one of their mobile radars in the vicinity of the Narowal–Lahore road. The mission was allotted to 31 Squadron and Raina, with Bhupinder Singh as his wingman, was soon over the designated area. The two aircraft searched the entire area and even photographed both sides of the road in detail, but there was no sign of any radar.

Visibility in Adampur that morning had been as bad, despite which a four-aircraft formation from 1 Squadron had got airborne for a strike in the Lahore Sector. Led by Satur, the formation could not see a thing in the designated targeted area, so they headed back to Adampur where visibility was down to less than 1,500 metres. Fortunately, all aircraft were recovered but flying was put on hold till conditions improved. Finally, in the evening three Mystères got airborne, escorted by two Gnats. Raje led the formation that consisted of Brahms and Frisky Verma. Without too much fuss, the formation zeroed in on gun positions in the Lahore Sector that had been identified. During the attack, both Brahms and Verma were hit by ground fire, but other than the tell-tale bullet holes on the forgiving Mystère, the aircraft's flying ability was unhindered.

8 Squadron too were allotted a mission, and this was to be their curtain call of the 1965 War. Salins led the mission in which the lead two aircraft carried 1,000-lb bombs while the following section were armed with rockets. After Salins and Sapre had dropped their bombs on a gun position, Chopra and Patney made four passes and took out individual guns that were spread out in the area. The formation then landed in Ambala.

By then, the PAF was using napalm more and more frequently, dropping it in both the Sialkot and the Rajasthan Sectors. Indian troops were strafed by Sabres near Uttarlai, killing two other ranks and injuring seventeen. B-57s also attacked Sujwan village, killing twenty-five civilians and wounding at least forty. These tactics indicated the growing desperation of the Pakistanis—they were quite willing to use their aircraft to spread terror on the ground rather than go after strategic targets.

Two IAF Canberras bombed Akwal airfield that night while three others attacked the Sargodha bulk petroleum installation.

Even though there was a lot of talk of an impending ceasefire, in the event of the conflict continuing, on 18 September both 8 and 35 Squadrons were ordered by Arjan Singh to withdraw to Gorakhpur.

HQ 1 Corps continued to be most reticent in asking for air strikes in support of its troops embroiled in a slugfest in and around Chawinda. This was extremely surprising since the one demand that did come through resulted in 3 Squadron attacking the Chawinda Railway Station and Rest House, the targets having been clearly marked by the army with coloured smoke. The IAF later claimed that the army had indeed acknowledged the effectiveness of this mission.

Most of the day's drama was reserved for Halwara where, apart from the Hunters, Gnats on detachment remained on ORP and also continued to fly as escorts. During the day, five strike missions were allotted to the Hunters. The first saw Zachariah lead a four-aircraft formation at 0923 hours with four Gnats as escorts to the Kasur Sector. The Hunters were configured with 1,000-lb bombs which they dropped on enemy concentrations, but while they were doing so, they were fired at by ack-ack guns from a distance. Realizing that the fire was coming from a location that had been previously attacked, the second section dropped their bombs on the offending guns.

The second strike took off at 1340 hrs. The four Hunters were being led by Lamba and it had two future air force chiefs—Shashindra Pal Tyagi as number two and Nimmie Suri as number three—with Flight Lieutenant (later Air Vice Marshal) Peter Eric 'Pete' Gaynor bringing up the tail. Since the Hunters were configured with bombs, two Gnats were flying escort. The formation found a vehicular column on the Dastpore–Khem Karan Road heading towards Kasur. The Hunters attacked the enemy concentrations and also strafed a couple of bridges over the Ichhogil Canal near Jhelum town for which Lamba had been given the coordinates. The smoke from the burning vehicles could be seen even from the Khem Karan–Amritsar Road, which was almost 10 km away.

In the evening two more Hunter missions, both consisting of the standard four aircraft, were flown. The first attacked a number of vehicles and troops that were crossing over a bridge near Bassi village while the second strike bombarded troops and gun positions also in the Kasur Sector. Earlier in the late afternoon, a pair of Gnats had taken off from Halwara to escort Canberras who were also bombing targets in the Lahore Sector.

The number of air strikes by Mystères, Hunters, and Canberras in the 11 Corps Sector underlined the fact that though the Indians had been slow to get off the blocks to take advantage of offensive capability of the air force, the army brass had come to realize it could be a major factor in winning battles, if not the war. India's radar coverage, considerably less sophisticated than the US-made radars in use by the Pakistanis, had survived the onslaught by the PAF.

On 18 September, 230 SU picked up the movement of Sabres and the fighter controller, K. Y. Singh had scrambled four Gnats. Trevor Keelor was in the lead while Squadron Leader Kala Sandhu was the sub-section leader. Guided by the cool voice of K. Y. Singh, the formation soon made contact with four Sabres. A dogfight ensued but good tactical flying by the Pakistani pilots ensured they did not get shot down even though Keelor did manage to fire a burst from a head-on position. Finally, the Sabre formation managed to disengage and the Gnats returned to Halwara.

Soon after, they were scrambled again, this time ordered by 311 SU at Patiala. Once again four Gnats screamed into the sky, their initial vector taking them right over Amritsar. This time the leader was Sandhu with Keelor as the sub-section leader. They made contact with four Sabres which were below them. Sandhu promptly led his formation into a dive to engage them. However, as they closed in on the Pakistanis, they realized that there were in fact six Sabres, not four. As the dogfight developed, the Gnats managed to get an edge. The lead pair got behind a section of Sabres, which split immediately. Sandhu followed the leading Sabre but it was obvious the Pakistani pilot knew what he was doing. He tried to shake off Sandhu by carrying out a number of descending spirals and climbing turns and by then the aircraft were down to 3,000 feet. Unable to shake the Gnat off, the Sabre pilot decided to perform the 'vanishing trick' manoeuvre the Sabres were famous for. The pilot went into a vertical dive. 'Sandhu decided to take his chances and stuck to the Sabre's tail. How he recovered from this near suicidal dive simply cannot be explained but when the Sabre recovered from the dive, Sandhu was behind him. At that range, Sandhu needed just a short burst to score his kill.'[11] Having missed out once before owing to gun stoppage, Sandhu finally had his man!

Two B-57s attacked Ambala at 0200 hours on the night of 18/19 September. The airfield, until then a safe haven for aircraft, was packed with Mystères and Hunters and was also the home base for the Gnats. A Vampire belonging to 45 Squadron flown by Flight Lieutenant K. D. Mehta was keeping a lonely vigil, patrolling between Ambala and Palam when the B-57s struck. The majority of the bombs fell outside the airfield and damaged the Sirhind Club, while some hit the military hospital, causing several casualties. Some bombs fell on civilian areas and there were substantial casualties in the Model Town area of Ambala city. The PAF would later sheepishly blame the wild targeting on a faulty automatic bomb release mechanism. Mehta could not get a fix on the B-57s and had no option but to land at Palam.

By the morning of 19 September, it was becoming obvious the PAF was on the back foot and the confidence levels within the IAF were increasing by the day. 3 Squadron launched a four-Mystère strike from Ambala led by Doraiswamy with Flying Officer Prem Ramchandani as his number two and Flight Lieutenant V. R. Nair as the other section leader. They were directed to look for targets in the area around Pasrur. An army convoy was on the move and the Mystères plastered them with rockets in their first pass. With the convoy ablaze, the aircraft turned for Pathankot when they found Pakistani tanks emerging from of their harbour. The only armament available were their 30 mm DEFA guns. Doraiswamy was rolling into the attack when he was hit by ground fire, destroying a part of his instrument panel. Ignoring the damage, he opened fire at one of the tanks which was loaded with barrels of fuel. Both Ramchandani and Nair were also hit as they followed Doraiswamy's lead, but all four aircraft landed back in Pathankot safely.

Three more missions followed from Ambala, two of which were flown by 31 Squadron. The level of activity in the Pasrur–Chawinda Sector was considerable and there were plenty of convoys and troop concentrations to shoot at. As these aircraft were being recovered at Pathankot, the army was reporting a large convoy of vehicles in the Chhamb–Jaurian Sector. 4 TAC reacted instantly and Mystères from 3 Squadron were on their way, but in what had by then become a familiar pattern, there was no sign of the convoy. After searching around for a while, the aircraft attacked some gun positions and some vehicles parked nearby. In all probability, the army's system of reporting up the chain of command was laborious, as a result of which the intelligence was not actionable. The hours wasted chasing after non-targets had been considerable.

Two Canberras escorted by Gnats from Pathankot also went and bombed the gun positions south of Chawinda. The pilots reported considerable damage to the gun positions and fires could be seen raging from a distance.

The targets assigned to 1 and 32 Squadron in the morning were once again all in the 11 Corps area of operations. The first to get airborne was Gill's four-aircraft formation that was being escorted by two Gnats. Armed with T.10 rockets, the formation searched the area west of the Ichhogil Canal between the railway line and the road from Attari to Lahore. Gill spotted a concentration of tanks on the west bank of the canal trying to hide under a cluster of trees. Despite the heavy anti-aircraft fire that came up to meet them, the Mystères made two passes, and Ratnaparkhi, the number four, confirmed targets destroyed and that two of the tanks in that cluster were on fire.

1 Squadron flew the remaining three strike missions in the morning. Handa led the first mission but once again the coordinates of the targets were faulty; Kahai and Raje were airborne almost simultaneously to attack a Bailey bridge on the Ichhogil Canal but the mission had to be aborted as the undercarriage door of Raje's aircraft flew off while en route to the target; a fresh mission was then launched and once again it was Kay Kahai and Raje who had to destroy the bridge. Kahai's bombs delivered in steep glide attack fell short but a second attack with belly rockets resulted in a huge explosion that seemed to seal the fate of the bridge.

Finally, in the evening, 1 Corps asked for a strike against the Pakistani heavy guns that had been playing havoc in the Chawinda area. Accordingly, the formation got airborne with J. P. Singh in the lead with Verma as his wingman. Brahmawar led the other sub-section with Bakshi bringing up the tail. Four Gnats from 9 Squadron, the Wolf Pack, were providing top cover. Keelor was leading the Gnat formation with 'Munna' Rai as his wingman. Viney Kapila was in command of the sub-section, with Flight Lieutenant (later Wing Commander) Vijay Mayadev as his wingman flying in the number four position.

As the Mystères and Gnats were approaching the gun positions at low level, Kapila sighted a formation of four Sabres at 2,000 feet. J. P. Singh decided the Mystères would make a single pass over the gun positions and exit the area. The Sabres, which were from Sargodha's 17 PAF Squadron, were being led by their commanding officer, Squadron Leader Azim Daudpota. The Pakistanis had not seen the Gnats who were in a shallow climbing turn to get into a favourable position behind them, but as Keelor began to manoeuvre to get into a firing position, the Sabres noticed him and went in for a quick defensive break. The Gnats too split up into two sections, Keelor and Rai going after one lot, and Kapila and Mayadev the other.

In the classic low-level dogfight that ensued, the four aircraft got separated. Rai had been asked to head back. 'Our combat was now being fought at 150 to 500 feet above ground level,' Kapila recalled. 'I finally jockeyed myself behind the Sabre at a range of about 150 to 200 yards. I got him flying in my sights and opened up short quarter-second bursts, I had fired three short bursts when I realized I was closing in too fast and needed to do something about it.'

As Kapila repositioned for another attack, Keelor called out, '"Kaps, you've got him! Kaps, he's going down! Kaps, he's hit the ground!" This prompted me to relax my manoeuvre, reverse back and look below me. This was the time I saw the big flash, it was the instant when the Sabre had finally hit the ground and disintegrated, blowing up in a huge ball of fire.'[12]

While Kapila was going after the Sabre, Mayadev was following his leader, keeping his tail clear, and Keelor was still chasing his adversaries. Unfortunately, Mayadev did not see the fourth Sabre who dived in and fired a quick burst which crippled the Gnat. Ejecting instantly, Mayadev got a glimpse of the Sabre whiz past with Keelor now on his tail. Unaware that Mayadev had been shot down, Kapila joined Keelor, acting as his wingman. As the Sabre broke away and tried to escape, Keelor fired a couple of short bursts which hit home and though he was trailing smoke, the aircraft was still flying. Keelor then had to pull out of the attack as his closing speed was too high, allowing Kapila to step up and deliver the coup de grace but once again, incredible as it maybe, his cannons refused to fire.

The Sabre, flown by Flight Lieutenant S. M. Ahmed, crashed just short of the runway at Sargodha and the pilot was extricated from the burning wreck. Kapila had to divert to an alternate airfield as Keelor's aircraft had burst a tire. Gun camera footage later confirmed both Kapila's and Keelor's kills, the latter joining his brother, Trevor, who was credited with a Sabre kill earlier. J. P. too had brought his formation back safely—it had been a satisfying day for the Mystères that had, on 19 September, covered most of the Western Front, hitting targets at

Hussainiwala, Gandasinghwala, Jassoran, and Chhamb. Vampires too had flown on
the day and attacked road and railway communications near Sulemanke, destroying
a few wagons and damaging the railway line.

From Halwara, Hunters were launched against the gun positions south of
Kasur. The first four-aircraft strike escorted by two Gnats was led by Squadron
Leader Rusty Sinha. They bombed the guns and two prominent round bunkers
on either side of the Khem Karan–Kasur Road; a second three-Hunter strike
led by Malik, also escorted by Gnats, took on gun positions to the northeast of
Kasur. This formation also bombed what appeared to be an ammunition depot.

The PAF, with admirable persistence, kept up their attacks on Fish Oil. On
this occasion, the Sabres succeeded in hitting the radar aerial of 230 SU. The
damage was superficial and was set right immediately. The radar unit, however,
was off air for a while as it was decided to shift the location of the antenna unit.
The PAF had expended over twenty sorties and lost four aircraft to achieve this.
However, during the day, the PAF did succeed in attacking the Ferozepur radar,
damaged the garages that housed specialist vehicles and set fire to stored fuel.
B-57s also attacked Jammu airfield after dark and the Jammu radar unit was put
out of commission for a couple of days.

There were by now increasing signs that the PAF pilots were beginning
to lose their cockiness and were getting very uncertain of themselves. Sabres
attacked a convoy on the GT Road, and though the vehicles were stretched out
in a linear configuration below them and with no Indian aircraft scrambled to
distract them, despite making two passes the strike destroyed just the one last
vehicle in the convoy. This was in sharp contrast to their performance earlier
in the same sector.

B-57s continued to be a nuisance, though the number of raids were reduced
considerably. Two attacks were launched against Jamnagar and one of the bombs
hit a refuelling browser killing two airmen. They also launched a strike against
Jodhpur but failed to do any damage.

While Indian pilots had by and large desisted from firing at slow-moving
aircraft incapable of defending themselves against fighters, the PAF showed no
such chivalry. The Gujarat chief minister, Balwantrai Mehta, along with his wife,
three members of his staff, a journalist, and two crew members, was flying in a
Beechcraft aircraft that belonged to Tata Chemicals to Mithapur, a town close to
the India–Pakistan border. Two Sabres intercepted the aircraft which was being
flown by Jehangir Merwan Engineer, a former air force pilot and the elder brother
of the former IAF chief, Aspy Engineer. The Sabres chased the Beechcraft down
and eventually opened fire with their cannons, killing everyone on board. Years
later, a former PAF pilot, haunted by his role in the incident, would write to the
daughter of Engineer and apologize saying that Pakistani radar had mistaken the
plane for a reconnaissance aircraft.

As night fell over the subcontinent, the converted Hercules C-130 bombers once again got airborne and flew two sorties against Indian Army ground positions in the vicinity of Rurki and Pagowal. This had little effect, other than ensuring the troops on the ground kept their heads down. However, at the same time, Sargodha was bombed again by the Tuskers, Wing Commander P. P. Singh with Flight Lieutenant (later Squadron Leader) Pradyot Dastidar and Squadron Leader (later Wing Commander) Satish Nandan Bansal as his navigators in the five-aircraft formation. Earlier, two Canberras configured with rockets and front guns had been launched against Sakesar's high-powered radar whose location had been pinpointed. However, one of the aircraft failed to reach the target while the other, because of haze and poor visibility, did not press home the attack.

THE FINAL COUNTDOWN (20–23 SEPTEMBER)
The aborted strike against Sakesar the previous night meant that the Pakistan's two main radar units had so far escaped being targeted by the IAF. While the radar at Sakesar covered almost the entire network of Indian forward airfields, the unit at Badin could keep a watch over the southernmost airfields in Rajasthan and Gujrat. Though Badin had an airfield, Sabres stationed at nearby Mauripur were earmarked to act as interceptors in the event of an air attack.

Peter Wilson was tasked with taking out Badin. Jaggi Nath's photographs of the Badin radar unit clearly showed that the two main radars—FPS 6 and FPS 20—were housed in mushroom-shaped domes propped up on towers that were 80 feet high. Wilson decided to target the eastern tower that was thought to house the FPS 20 Azimuth radar. Contrary to conventional wisdom which suggested a night or a midday raid, Wilson had decided on an early morning attack. The formation comprised of three pairs of Canberras, each carrying different types of armament. To minimize detection, Wilson also had turned down the suggestion that eight Hunters escort the strike force.

The first two Canberras were flown by Squadron Leader H. B. Singh with Flight Lieutenant (later Squadron Leader) Nammealil Gopalan Bhaskaran as his navigator and Squadron Leader (later Wing Commander) Prithi Pal Singh Madan with Flight Lieutenant (later Air Vice Marshal) Sudheer Rajaram Karkare. These two Canberras were carrying two 4,000-lb bombs which had a fuse set to explode at 3,000 feet. The air burst was expected to maximize the casualties among the anti-aircraft gunners. The next two aircraft were flown by Squadron Leader (later Wing Commander) Rajendra Singh 'Kaddu' Rajput with Flight Lieutenant (later Wing Commander) Baban Vinayakrao Pathak, followed by Flight Lieutenant (later Squadron Leader) Ravindranath Gopalrao Khot accompanied by Flight Lieutenant (later wing commander) Govind Singh Negi who were carrying six 1,000-lb bombs. Coming in at number five was Pete Wilson with Squadron Leader (later Wing Commander) Odayanmadath Shankaran as his navigator, followed by Squadron Leader (later

Wing Commander) Satya Paul 'Tak' Khanna with Flying Officer K. M. Jog as his pathfinder. The last two aircraft were carrying rocket pods under either wing, each loaded with nineteen 68 mm R/P rockets as well as the standard cannons.

Taking off from Agra two minutes apart, the six aircraft climbed to 20,000 feet and maintained that altitude till they reached Nal (Bikaner) and then dropped down to ground level, surfing over the sand dunes. As they approached their target, the first four pulled up sharply to 7,000 feet from where they released their bomb loads. Bhaskaran's bombs fell short, so he immediately called out a correction which helped Karkare, Pathak, and Negi hit their targets with accuracy.

Wilson and Khanna were now screaming in, their aircraft barely 50 feet above the ground. However, Wilson had made a slight error in the final run-up and he failed to align with the towers, which now loomed above the aircraft. Holding his fire, he swung around to make a second pass, this time coming in from the south instead of the east. The ack-ack guns were trying to put up a curtain of fire, but Wilson was so low he that he actually fired his rockets upwards at the radar dome. One of the pods refused to fire, but the nineteen rockets that arched out from the Canberra destroyed the dome. Pulling out, Wilson told Khanna to abort his attack as the job had been done and follow him home. Both aircraft had fuel gauges reading nearly zero when they touched down at Ahmedabad. After refuelling, they stopped over in Delhi for a debrief after which they proceeded to Allahabad. The Badin radar unit was completely destroyed and the air raid was considered the most successful of the entire war.

A four-Mystère mission from 31 Squadron got airborne from Ambala and flew to the Khem Karan/Kasur Sector where they hit a few vehicles, after which the aircraft touched down in Pathankot. Shortly thereafter, four Canberras overflew Pathankot en route to Chawinda. They were joined by four Gnats, led by Johnny Greene. Soon one of the Canberras relayed a message from 230 SU that enemy aircraft in the area were painting on the radar. Ignoring the potential threat, the Canberras kept their rendezvous with the assigned targets, which they bombed in the vicinity of Jassoran. The Gnats in the meantime were looking around but instead of any Sabre or Starfighter, they came across a light aircraft with US markings on it. Greene ordered his formation not to attack it.

Though the weather was beginning to worsen, the Mystères were asked to launch an attack in the vicinity of Jassoran which had been hit by Canberras earlier. Raina led his team of four aircraft who could see the tank columns in disarray owing to the Canberra raid. The Mystères had to choose their targets amidst the dust and smoke. They claimed to have destroyed three tanks, three vehicles, and a signal mast, this despite McMahon's rockets failing to fire.

31 Squadron flew its final mission to the Lahore Sector, this time with Tony Mousinho as the leader and Roundy Raina as his wingman. The four Mystères encountered a train near Lahore. As per the Intelligence inputs, troop trains were

supposed to be running in the area and Mousinho immediately went after the locomotive. Even as he fired at the engine, Tony saw some women jump out and start running away from the train. Raina, who was coming in next, was told to abort his attack.

3 Squadron flew one mission to the Chhamb Sector and nine in the Chawinda-Pasrur area. Most of these strikes were to the south of the railway line, which by then was an identifiable bomb line. Once again, it underlined the lack of foresight on the part of HQ 1 Corps. Had the Pakistani gun positions south and east of Chawinda been targeted by the IAF, even without FACs the aircraft could have played havoc with the Pakistani defences. On 20 September, it was a case of too little too late.

Even on the morning of 21 September, there were no calls for air support in the Chawinda Sector. 1 Squadron flew two four-aircraft missions—the first, led by Denny Satur, went to the Ganda Singh Wala area where it failed to locate any enemy activity; the second was led by Paddy Earle, with Flying Officer V. K. 'Vindi' Chawla as his wingman even though Chawla had to yet to go through two more live-bombing sorties to qualify. Once again the Tigers drew a blank, so on the way back, Chawla was put through the paces, a rare case of a training sortie being flown on the other side of the IB.

At 0620 hrs, the first sign of activity at Halwara was neither Hunters nor Gnats, but two formations of Vampires from No. 45/220 Squadron that were taxiing out on an interdiction mission, loaded with RPGs. The first formation, consisting of four aircraft, was led by Farokh Mehta and had been tasked with attacking Pakistani bunkers and positions near Haveli village. The second formation headed out to the Raiwind area where it was asked to attack vehicles parked under a cluster of trees. Staying at treetop level, the Vampires successfully attacked their targets, then flew back all the way to Palam, only gaining altitude after crossing Sirsa. Interestingly, Vampires from Delhi were scrambled to intercept and identify these aircraft. Why Vampires were being used when Hunters and Mystères were available is puzzling. Perhaps Arjan Singh, keen to let all his combat pilots have at least some operational experience, took the decision.

Since the impression among the pilots was that the PAF was shying away from air-to-air engagements with the IAF, there was a need to lure the Sabres out. There had been a fair amount of talk with regard to this subject even when Air Marshal Arjan Singh had paid a visit to Halwara on 16 September. One of the suggestions was to use Hunters as bait by letting them show up on Pakistani radars. Once Sabres were scrambled to meet them, they planned to ambush them with Gnats that would be part of the same formation.

Unfortunately, this plan had never been practised or, for that matter, even discussed by the two sets of pilots. Nevertheless, with no prior warning, two Hunters and two Gnats were scrambled by 230 SU to put this tactic into practice.

The Hunters were being flown by S. K. Sharma with Squadron Leader Deba Prasad 'Chato' Chatterjee as his wingman while Flight Lieutenants (later Group Captain) Ajoy Kumar 'Muzzy' Majumdar and Kamal 'Kamli' Khanna (later Air Vice Marshal) were flying the Gnats. The fighter controller was the reliable K. Y. Singh, who told the formation to maintain between 12,000 and 15,000 feet and proceed for an offensive sweep towards the Lahore Sector. Unfortunately, K. Y.'s scope was only intermittently picking up the Indian formation, so the pilots were flying blind. After the formation had almost reached Lahore, an uncomfortable Majumdar ordered a turnabout.

Just about then, they made contact with two incoming Sabres, with two more trailing them by a couple of kilometres. Soon the Hunters were embroiled in a dogfight. The two Gnat pilots above them could not tell the Hunters from the Sabres. Khanna who was keeping Majumdar's tail clear describes the first kill; 'Muzzy kept reporting their position and manoeuvred his Gnat to stay on top and control the combat. I was swishing from side to side to clear his tail. While doing so, I could see a tight circular fight between the Hunters and the Sabres....After a few seconds, I saw Muzzy straightening out with a Sabre 300 to 400 yards in front of him. He fired a short burst. The Sabre was hit on the right wing and went out of control. As he passed under Muzzy's aircraft I saw the pilot ejecting.'[13] The pilot, Flight Lieutenant A. H. Malik, landed inside Pakistani lines.

Another Sabre was making a beeline for Majumdar but Khanna forced him to break off his attack, after which the Gnats headed back to Halwara. But both the Hunters were struggling, especially since they were not familiar with the calls being made by Majumdar. Sharma and Chatterjee were shot down. While Sharma ejected near Katron, on the Indian side of the border, Chatterjee's plane crashed inside Pakistan, killing him. According to the Pakistani version, Lahore radar continuously picked up on both the Indian and Pakistani aircraft throughout the engagement, whereas 230 SU's radar failed to function properly, further shortening the odds against the Indians.

In addition, Halwara launched three more strike missions, all of them again in the 11 Corps area of operations. Three Hunters escorted by two Gnats took off for an armed reconnaissance mission and hit a couple of convoys on the Raiwind-Kasur road. Despite meeting heavy anti-aircraft fire, the formation returned to base without any alarms; a second mission led by Squadron Leader (later Wing Commander) George Lawrence 'Dan' Daniel flew to the area around the Sulemanki headworks. The four-aircraft formation destroyed a 50-foot brick tower that was being used by the Pakistani gunners to shell Indian positions. Finally, Rusty Sinha led yet another four Hunters escorted by three Gnats on an armed reconnaissance to the Kasur Sector. The formation attacked the Raiwind railway yard, hitting the loco shed and damaging the power station.

Some of the PAF's tactics had already brought into question the ethics of their attacks—they used napalm in some of the bombing raids near Amritsar and against ground troops; and they had shot down the Gujarat chief minister's civilian aircraft. Though the PAF had brushed it off as the fog of war, eyewitnesses on the ground had reported that the Beechcraft had been chased and when the aircraft tried to land, it had been shot down. By the night of 20/21 September, it was clear that the Pakistanis, by their own admission, were not averse to doing some 'terror bombing'. Plans were being hatched to bomb targets to spread terror, even though the Indians had scrupulously avoided all civilian targets. One of the B-57 pilots of the raid on Ambala that night, Rais Ahmed Rafi (who later became air commodore) wrote: 'Ambala was a heavily defended target. It had anti-aircraft artillery and SAM-II missiles. We had to attack this very important IAF station to keep the enemy defences locked at the rear bases and by spreading fear in the rear, gradually get closer to Delhi. By now we had plans ready for attacking IAF bases in Delhi, Agra and even Bombay.'[14]

The B-57s that came in to attack Ambala knew that their bombs would skip along the ground for up to a mile as they would impact in a horizontal position. This had been discussed in the pre-flight briefings and fuses had been delayed accordingly. Having bombed the Military Hospital just two days before, they still took the call to go ahead with tactics that could have terrible consequences for the civil population that lived near the base. But despite five passes by three B-57s over an airfield that was brimming with aircraft, the PAF failed to damage anything as all the bombs skipped and went flying over the airfield's boundary wall. One of the bombs destroyed Saint Peter's Cathedral that had been in 1857. Even today, it stands in its bombed out state, in mute testimony to Pakistani terror tactics.

B-57s also attacked Halwara, Patiala, and Jammu but failed to cause any serious damage. C-130s were also at it again, trying to drop their bombs on artillery positions near Dograi and Valtoha. These bombs once again failed to have any impact.

On 21 September, the penultimate day of the war, after a peaceful night Pathankot woke up to a rainy morning which temporarily suspended strike missions and CAPs from the base. However, since the bulk of the Mystères had spent the night in Ambala, the first few strikes originated from there. 3 Squadron launched two strikes of four aircraft each into the Chawinda and Najul areas. 31 Squadron's first mission led by Bhupinder Singh took on targets in the Lahore Sector, and though the Gnat detailed to escort the Mystères failed to show up, the strike went through nevertheless and the aircraft landed safely at Pathankot. The second strike, again led by Bhupinder with Vishnu Murti Raina as his wingman, was given definite coordinates of the Pakistani Corps TAC HQ. Taking off with four Gnats as escorts, the formation promptly flew into a dust storm. The Gnats, struggling to maintain visual contact, gave up soon and returned to Pathankot but the two Mystères flew through the storm and found themselves in the area where the Corps HQ was supposed to be. Intelligence inputs had disappointed once again.

After flying in an expanding search pattern for a while, the two aircraft returned with their armament intact. Before the day was out the squadron also flew armed reconnaissance missions in the Chawinda, Lahore, and Kasur Sectors.

Adampur had a relatively quiet day as just the one strike led by Teja Gill was launched, his four-Mystère formation being escorted by four Gnats. With the army unable to push south beyond Chawinda and the Alhar Railway Station, all tanks beyond the embankment were fair game. The four Mystères put in two attacks each, in all claiming the destruction of at least four tanks with their T.10 rockets. The ground fire was intense as the Pakistani tanks used their anti-aircraft guns to create a wall of fire, but fortunately no aircraft went down. After landing in Adampur, it was found that all four aircraft had been hit, with Teja Gill's fuselage in particular being riddled with bullets.

The Hunters at Halwara launched two four-aircraft strikes against heavy and medium artillery guns in the area north of Kasur. The first mission dropped its bombs short of the target area, so they made a second pass with their guns. The second mission struck at gun positions east and northeast of Kasur. The real excitement however, was reserved for later in the day when a planned strike by Canberras against the Sakesar radar unit was to be escorted by four Hunters. Wing Commander George Douglas Clarke, the commanding officer of the Battle Axes, nominated four of his most experienced pilots to undertake the job. However, bad weather forced the cancellation of the strike which was postponed for the next day. However, by then the impending ceasefire had been announced and the strike never materialized.

In the Barmer Sector, the army had been concentrating its forces to capture Dali. With a number of vehicles in the area, they were an easy target for the PAF, especially since there was no effective air cover or a concentration of anti-aircraft guns. But surprisingly, the Sabres only did nominal damage.

Once the weather cleared during the early hours of 22 September, the Canberras were launched for what would be the last bombing raid by the IAF. Seven Canberras drawn from 5 and 35 Squadron got airborne from Agra for Sargodha, but this time the tactics to be followed were different. The pathfinder aircraft was being flown by Flight Lieutenant (later Squadron Leader) Vivian Christopher 'Goody' Goodwin with Squadron Leader (later Air Commodore) Daman Singh Bhandari as his navigator. As part of the six following aircraft, flying at number two was Flight Lieutenant (later Squadron Leader) Manmohan 'Lousy' Lowe who had Flying Officer Kewal Krishan Kapur as his navigator.

Goodwin had one of the most dangerous jobs that night. During peacetime, the IAF had found the blind bombing technique to be a more accurate than visual bombing. This method involved capturing the 'Cat' and 'Mouse' beacons, which could only be done by flying at an altitude of 20,000 feet all the way from Agra to Sargodha. This meant flying a long distance in enemy territory, unarmed, unescorted and, in all probability, showing up bright on enemy radar. Fully aware of the risks involved, Goodwin and Bhandari had volunteered for the job. To make it even more dangerous, after a while, neither 230 SU nor any other Indian radar unit would be able to warn the Canberra of any approaching threat. The other Canberras following would approach at low level as before and pull up just before commencing their bombing runs.

Flying steadily at the designated height, Goodwin's Canberra locked onto the 'Cat' circle but the 'Mouse' beacon failed to lock on. Despite all the risks Goodwin and Bhandari had taken, they now had to fall back on tried and trusted methods. They released the first flares at 12,000 feet but these fell short of the target. Fortunately, Pakistan ack-ack opened up and gave the airfield's position away. Turning around, they dropped the second set of flares on the target area, after which, in a third pass, the TI bombs were dropped. Horror of horrors, the bombs turned out to be duds and failed to explode! A desperate Goodwin came in for yet another pass for he still had four flares. Transmitting the margin of error and informing the incoming aircraft that there was a layer of cloud at 18,000 feet, the lone Canberra set course for Chandigarh.

There was no way interceptors had not been scrambled by this time. So Goodwin climbed into the clouds, weaving this way and that while varying his altitude to avoid a missile lock-on. About 60 miles from the border, just when he thought he had gotten away, he noticed a missile lock on his instrument panel. Putting the Canberra into a steep spiralling dive, Goodwin then saw a yellowish streak in the distance. At 7,000 feet the blip disappeared, but in the process the navigational aid had stopped working. So they were flying entirely by guesswork, until finally Indian ack-acks opened up, allowing Bhandari to get a fix on their position.

By 0415 hrs Lowe was over the target, maintaining a steady course at 14,000 feet, with Kapur lying on his belly in the nose. A few seconds after Kapur called 'bombs gone' Lowe flipped the switch to close the bomb doors and started to turn right. At this point his Canberra was directly above the airfield which had lit up with exploding ack-ack shells. Just then there was a loud thud that indicated the aircraft had taken a hit, but since it continued to fly normally, Lowe dived down to 500 feet and set course for Chandigarh. However, a glance at his instrument panel indicated that one of his fuel tanks had been ruptured and the only way to get back was to climb to 8,000 feet and land at a secondary airfield.

Just then, he noticed an enemy aircraft closing in on the Canberra. Instead of diving down to treetop level Lowe kept climbing, putting in a few sharp turns to throw off any interceptors. At 18,000 feet, Kapur decided to slide down into the nose again to check his position when the Canberra got hit by a missile. Both the engines of the stricken aircraft instantly flamed out.

Sakesar radar had guided Wing Commander Jamal Ahmed Khan's Starfighter close to the Canberra after which the fighter's own radar had kicked in. After getting the distinctive audio tone that indicates a 'lock-on', the Starfighter had launched a Sidewinder. Khan had until then not seen the Canberra and his first visual contact was when the missile hit the right engine. He now stared in awe as the Canberra rolled lazily to its right, with flames shooting off its wings and fuselage. He caught a brief glimpse again as the light from the flames reflected off some clouds, briefly illuminating the Canberra.

Lowe banged with his boot on the floor signalling Kapur to bail-out from the navigator's hatch, and then he himself ejected. The stricken aircraft hit the ground below in a ball of flame. Lowe was taken POW, while Kapur's charred remains were found by the Pakistani Army inside the wreckage. This was the only Canberra that failed to return during the entire war.

That night B-57s raided Jodhpur and Adampur four times and there was a single raid on Patiala. There was no damage to any aircraft or equipment.

The final day of the 1965 war dawned on 22 September. Ferocious fighting was going on at Dograi as 3 Jat set for itself the onerous task of capturing the objective it had taken on day one of the Lahore offensive. In a bid to support our troops, 3 Squadron was asked to launch a four-aircraft strike against Dograi in the morning. Taking off from Ambala, the formation was led by Doraiswamy who had Flying Officer Prem Ramchandani as his wingman while Flight Lieutenant Jal Mistry and Flying Officer Bohman Irani formed the second section. Unaware that the town had already been captured by the Jats, these Mystères appeared suddenly and attacked the Indian troops who were facing westwards, waiting for the Pakistanis to counter-attack.

In the chaos that followed, Ramchandani's aircraft was hit and he had to eject over terrain held by Indian troops. However, even as the parachute drifted down, Ramchandani continued to come under fire and was fatally hit in the stomach.

31 Squadron too had launched a four-Mystère strike from Ambala, the formation looking to engage targets of opportunity on the Pakistani side facing Dograi on GT Road. These aircraft did not find any identifiable targets and, being close to the outskirts of Lahore, it was imperative no civilian targets be engaged. This formation also landed back in Pathankot shortly after Doraiswamy's remaining three Mystères had landed.

From Pathankot, the last effective strike of the war was launched in the Chhamb Sector. This was followed by Gnats taking off to rendezvous with five Canberras that were on their way to bomb the Chawinda Railway Station and damage the railway line on either side of the town. One Canberra was hit by the intense ack-ack that came up to greet the bombers but the aircraft managed to fly back.

The last and final mission from Pathankot was to be a three-aircraft strike led by Sandy Sandhu. However, shortly after take-off, Sandhu's aircraft developed technical snags and he had to be escorted back. The time of the ceasefire was now known and it was feared that Pakistan might launch a last-ditch effort against Indian positions in the Sialkot Sector. Gnat and Mystère pilots were strapped up in their cockpits, waiting to take-off should the call for air support materialize. Eventually, the Mystère pilots were asked to stand down while the Gnats continued to remain on stand-by.

Neither 1 nor 32 Squadron were called upon to launch any sorties from either Ambala or Adampur. However, Halwara continued to be in the thick of the action, as the ground fighting picked up after the ceasefire time was announced, both sides trying to gain as much territory as possible. The first mission of four Hunters took off at 0620 hours and went after armoured columns southwest of Khem Karan. Making five to six passes, the Hunters accounted for a fair number of vehicles and also claimed a few tanks.

Four Gnats had also taken off for an independent sweep of the same area when the Hunters had got airborne. They had made visual contact with four Sabres but were not in a position to take them on. The Sabres too did not close the gap.

As the first formation had seen a great number of tanks, a second mission was launched against the same area. Two out of the four aircraft had technical problems, as a result of which K. C. Cariappa took off with Flight Lieutenant Sehgal as his wingman. The Pakistanis, still disoriented from the first attack, received a few more salvos of rockets from the attacking pair after which they turned to fly back. They then spotted another troop concentration and decided to attack them with their cannons. Cariappa's Hunter got hit almost instantly, and was burning furiously within seconds. Sehgal called out, 'Cary, you are on fire. Eject.'[15] At first, Cariappa did not seem to hear him, but on the third eject call, he ejected from the burning Hunter which exploded into a huge fireball a few seconds later. Nanda was captured by Pakistani ground troops, the seventh and last IAF POW.

At 1615 hrs, four Hunters again struck vehicles in the area between Dograi and Lahore. By then almost all aircraft had been ferried to Ambala and just four Hunters were left in Halwara. At 1830 hrs, Clarke with Lamba as his wingman and Rusty Sinha and Dhiman as his number three and four headed westwards towards Bhasin. The Hunter pilots noticed heavy shelling on both sides of the border and the entire place seemed to be enveloped in huge clouds of black smoke. In the last act of the war by the IAF, the four Hunters dropped their 1,000-lb HE bombs on the assigned target before turning around and setting course for Ambala. The IAF's 1965 war with Pakistan was over.

On the last day of the war, the PAF inflicted the maximum number of civilian casualties. It had been active in the Khem Karan region during the day. In a last-ditch effort to neutralize Fish Oil, two B-57s with two Sabres approached Amritsar at 1615 hours. In what at best can be described as another attempt at terror bombing, the B-57s dropped their loads in the Cherta area and killed at least fifty-three civilians and injured many more. Similarly, even though the ceasefire was hours away, C-130s again tried to do some blind bombing, dropping some 30 tons of bombs, which proved to be as ineffective as before. Finally, as the clocks wound down towards the ceasefire hour, the B-57s put in four raids over Jodhpur, their bombs hitting the civil jail and locomotive sheds killing thirty-five civilians. It was a sad end to an otherwise commendable performance by the PAF.

THE AFTERMATH

CHAUDHURI'S BIGGEST BLUNDER

According to official Indian figures, the total number of casualties during the conflict that began with the Rann of Kutch and culminated with the subsequent ceasefire violations that continued until February 1966 was 12,714, out of which 2,763 were killed, 8,444 wounded, and 1,507 missing. Of these, an estimated 2,000 casualties took place after the ceasefire, something that raised questions about the effectiveness of the UN as an effective global peacekeeping body. Pakistan's official figure was never released but the Karachi-based *Dawn* newspaper quoted a senior Pakistani official in December 1965, who admitted to having lost 1,033 men in all. Pakistan also claimed, perhaps mainly to save face with its own people, that it had captured over 2,500 sq km of Indian territory. Neutral observers more or less agreed with the Indian casualty figures and, in the case of Pakistan, estimated at least 5,000 plus deaths. Chavan in the Rajya Sabha had estimated the total Pakistani fatalities at 5,800.

Considering the propaganda blitz in Pakistan both during and after the war, it would not be surprising if the regular Pakistani thought that India had been obliterated! To keep the public perception alive that the Indians had been walloped and each Pakistani soldier was equal to ten Hindus, Pakistan indulged in some deft footwork. In the Chhamb–Jaurian Sector for example, using an old photograph of bunched up AMX-13 tanks, Pakistan claimed it had decimated 20 Lancers; whereas in reality, the one lone squadron of light tanks had held up two regiments of the far superior Pattons. At the time, strangely, no one in Pakistan wondered if that had indeed been the case, why Operation Grand Slam failed to get to Akhnoor. In the case of the air force, where the Pakistanis had indeed destroyed almost three times the number of Indian aircraft, the perception war reached far greater heights. Squadron Leader Alam's claim of having shot down nine Hunters being the icing on the cake!

The obsession with 'who won the war' almost as if it's a cricket match has continued for more than half a century. Semantics apart, it is pretty obvious that all of Pakistan's initial aggressive moves, starting with the Rann of Kutch to Operation Gibraltar and Operation Grand Slam were successfully checkmated by the Indians, which was extremely creditable because the timing, quantum of force, and the terrain was always of Pakistan's choosing. The lessons in each case were fairly obvious, but the shrill propaganda drowned out any possibility of a sensible critical analysis at the time. The over-reliance on armour and the infantry's hesitation to close the gap, obvious even in the brief skirmish in the Rann, time and again came back to haunt the Pakistani high command.

In offense, the Indians were stymied by a different factor—the Pakistani artillery was in a league of its own altogether. While all the pre-war hype centred around the F-104s and F-86 Sabres, and, of course, the 'invincible' Pattons, the real backbone of the Pakistan Army was its heavy, medium, and light guns with seemingly unlimited ammunition, that played havoc with Indian advances in all the 7 and 15 Infantry and 4 Mountain Division sectors. The seemingly unlimited amount of ammunition, combined with the fact that the PAF was fully committed to ground support and was always on call, played a major role in the final outcome in almost all battles. Whichever way one chooses to look at it, the coordination required between the Indian Army and the IAF simply did not exist.

General Chaudhuri, by virtue of being the army chief since November 1962, had become the single point of contact between the political leadership and the armed forces. With Defence Minister Chavan focussed on protecting Prime Minister Jawaharlal Nehru from being criticized for his handling of the 1962 fiasco, nothing had changed in the higher direction of war. Not only had no one been brought to book, most of those who had made glaring blunders were in critical positions, having since been promoted. Nehru, after the Chinese debacle, had continued the policy of keeping the military isolated from governance, as a result of which Chaudhuri emerged as the last and final word on politico-military issues. Though Air Marshal Arjan Singh was quite a favourite of Chavan's, the government also treated the IAF and the navy as an extension of the army. After Prime Minister Nehru's death, Lal Bahadur Shastri took over but he was careful not to change anything. Having made himself the most important cog with his pushy personality, Chaudhuri was 'still the high flyer trapezing from swing to swing', in the process bypassing the Chiefs of Staff Committee, the JPC (Joint Parliamentary Committee), and the JIC (Joint Intelligence Committee) and 'decided to act entirely on his own'.[1]

The disdain Chaudhuri had for the other two services was clear in his handling of affairs. Air Marshal P. C. Lal, who was at the helm of the IAF six years later, said later that one had to only listen to Chaudhuri's comments to realize that he treated the whole business of fighting Pakistan or China as 'his personal affair, or at any rate that of the Army's alone, with the Air Force a passive spectator and the navy out of it altogether'.[2] Chaudhuri also had much the same attitude when it came to dealing with his own headquarters, having contrived to even do away with the post of the chief of the general staff (CGS). None of the grandiose plans discussed during Operation Ablaze were ever committed to paper, and even the personal staff officers were more often than not kept in the dark. Those who were present at those meetings, as was the case with Jogi Dhillon, did little by way of assimilating local intelligence. Ground level planning and logistics seemed to have little meaning, as did intelligence reports that Pakistan had in fact raised a second armoured division.

S. P. Verma, who had taken over as director of Intelligence Bureau from the infamous B. N. Mullik had, shortly before the fighting spread to the Punjab, warned Chaudhuri (and the army) in a detailed assessment that Pakistan had indeed surreptitiously used equipment earmarked as 'reserve' by the US administration and was planning to launch a major offensive in the Punjab plains.[3] Chaudhuri, who stuck to his position that the Pakistanis only had the one division which was deployed in the Sialkot Sector, refused to pay heed to the warning. Having then moved India's 1 Armoured Division to the north, he created a huge gap in India's defences. Pakistan launching its armoured assault regardless of India's advance in the Khem Karan Sector on 7 September confirmed that Verma's appreciation of the situation had been correct. In what was close to blind panic, Chaudhuri then wanted to fall back on the Beas and abandon the Amritsar region, in what would have been a virtual re-run of the situation that developed in Tezpur and Assam after the fall of Bomdila in 1962.

With pressure building from all sides to cease hostilities, Shastri turned to his chief on 20 September and asked him if the army could achieve a decisive victory over the Pakistanis should the war be prolonged. Chaudhuri, without any recourse to the actual dynamics of battle logistics, advised the prime minister that the army was coming to the end of its ammunition stocks and that it would not be possible to fight on any more. 'I heard about the conversation between the prime minister and the army chief from the previous home secretary,' Ram D. Pradhan would tell me half a century later. 'We were all quite dumbstruck, for we knew even at my level that we had expended less than 20 per cent of our ammunition stocks.'[4] (The real figure as revealed in post-war studies was close to 14 per cent. The Pakistanis, at the time, had expended 80 per cent of their stocks.)

'The PAF had run out of steam, the Pakistani artillery was close to running out of ammunition, the war of attrition needed to give way to some bold moves, which the Pakistan Army would have been hard-pressed to contain. The IAF had absorbed the frenzy of attacks and just when we felt we held all the cards, though we were aware of it at the time, the army chief pulled the carpet from under our feet,' says a bitter Philip Rajkumar.[5] There were a few problems. Non-intensive sectors had had more ammunition trains clogging the marshalling yards, while others closer to the fighting were clamouring for more. It is highly unlikely that the army chief was not aware of this critical factor. 'There were echoes here of 1962. Chaudhuri had probably not fully recovered from the shock of the near disaster at Khem Karan and was unwilling to take any risks. An easy option had been suggested by the prime minister, and he jumped at it. Instead of victory, the war ended in a stalemate that enabled both sides to claim victory.'[6]

The ceasefire that came into effect on 23 September suited Pakistan on another level. While the guns fell silent, it could almost immediately regroup its forces and start probing into areas where it felt its forces could occupy maximum territory. The region immediately to the north of the Barmer Sector was a case in point where the Indus Rangers, combined with irregular forces including dacoits, began to occupy undefended villages. At the other end of the spectrum, in the 25 Infantry Division Sector, Pakistani commanders refused to vacate a dominating feature called Chhu-i-Nar on the Mendhar Ridge. The area in question was about 700 yards in length and was a major infiltration route and supply dump for the raiding columns. It was also an excellent point of observation of all Indian positions along the LOC extending from Bhimber Gali to Mendhar. With the infiltration routes in Gurez, Tithwal, and the Haji Pir area under Indian control, this was perhaps the last option for Pakistan to recover surviving elements of the raiding columns still trapped inside Indian territory.

Ever since Pakistani artillery had opened up in support of the infiltrating raider columns as a part of Operation Gibraltar, the near pinpoint accuracy of their guns suggested they had an observation post somewhere in the Chhu-i-Nar area. A 2 Dogra patrol had, in the second week of August, confirmed that the Pakistanis were holding the post in strength, and hence the name 'Op Hill' was given to the location. In less than a fortnight since the ceasefire, 2 Garhwal Rifles, commanded by Lieutenant Colonel Ujagar Singh, was asked to launch a battalion strength attack and capture Op Hill and other related features around it. Though the Garhwalis successfully reached their objectives, surprisingly, no support troops had been earmarked for the operation, and they could not hold the objective in the face of Pakistani counter-attacks, and were withdrawn by first light on 7 October. The Garhwali lost two officers including the Alpha Company commander, Captain Satish Khera, and Lieutenant Bhim Sain, one JCO, Subedar Govind Singh Gariya, and nineteen other ranks, while four officers, three JCOs, and sixty-eight men were wounded.

It now seemed to Major General Amreek Singh that the Pakistanis were determined to hold Chhu-i-Nar with Op Hill and the surrounding features at all costs. Brigadier (later Major General) B. S. Ahluwalia's 120 Infantry Brigade, a newly raised formation, was given the task of clearing them out. It was estimated that two Pakistani companies were holding the feature, and the main obstacle would be the minefields. In an operational plan fraught with risk, it was decided to launch the attack at night. On the night of 2 November, 5 Sikh LI, commanded by Lieutenant Colonel (later Brigadier) Sant Singh, and 2 Dogra, without a commanding officer, led the attack in phase one of what was to be yet another bloody battle. 7 Sikh, commanded by Lieutenant Colonel Bhagat Singh Sadhu was the third battalion that advanced on the same objective in phase two, while elements of 2 Garhwal and 11 Kumaon were also involved as stops, which would allow them to mop up any retreating Pakistanis.

Despite the ridiculous planning at the brigade and divisional level, the units were outstanding, the men getting to their objectives despite scores being ripped apart by the mines that covered all approaches. Just how difficult the situation was can best be understood from Sant Singh's description of the attack: 'Late Naik Darshan Singh when told by one of his men, "*ustad minefield aa gaya*" (sir, we have entered the minefield), his reply was classic, and his courage infectious…"let us die and clear the way for others to succeed." He then entered the mine field, had his left foot blown off by a mine, then continuing to crawl forward he cut the encompassing wire with a wire cutter, and continued his crawl forward. His left forearm was severed by another mine going off. He then crawled up to a BMG bunker, took out a grenade, pulled the pin with his teeth, and silenced it. His entire section was killed with him.'[7] In the pitch dark (the moon was in its first quarter during that period), there is little doubt that almost all units also suffered badly from friendly fire apart from the mines. The brigade losses were terrible—three officers, four JCOs, and 114 other ranks killed; five officers, ten JCOs, and 317 other ranks wounded. 2 Dogra, 5 Sikh LI, 7 Sikh, 23 Mountain, and 169 Field Regiment were later awarded the Battle Honour for Op Hill.

The fighting at Op Hill was, in a way, a microcosm of the war. Indian generals, in the actual conduct of operations, repeatedly bungled, often resorting to tactics that bordered on the bizarre. Time and again, it was left to the junior commanders and the men under their command to retrieve the situation. Almost all officers in the higher echelons of command were guilty of passing the buck and sacking those under their command for lapses they were guilty of. The case of Niranjan Prasad perhaps best illustrates this point—a former RIAF officer, he had been the forward air controller on various occasions in his career, and he knew the importance of coordinating with the air force. During Operation Ablaze while Generals Chaudhuri, Harbakhsh, and Dhillon played out their war games, he repeatedly pointed out this lacuna which would result in a situation where the high command would fail to harness the operational potential of maximum strategic effect. He was repeatedly snubbed, and subsequently humiliated, by the very men who had failed him. 'As it was, what saved us in the Punjab was the high performance of our men and, most particularly, of our young officers. It was their courage and fortitude that turned a timid and sterile plan in our favour.' It was a different matter that having opted for a war of attrition, when we did have the advantage in logistics, 'the advantage was mindlessly thrown away by an impetuous and unthinking Army Chief.'[8]

In the post-war drum beating and chest thumping, a picture was painted about the brilliant handling of the forces by the Indian leadership. Perhaps that was the need of the time, for it helped put balm on the scars of 1962, but we must face the reality. Recent comments by the newly created chief of defence staff, General Bipin Rawat, on the IAF being a supporting arm of the army, if reported correctly, indicate that not much has changed. Fortunately, the rank and file did not know of the 'bungling and faintheartedness at the top'.[9] There was much to build on, which the army and the air force did, which then paid dividends six years later in the Bangladesh war of liberation. Half the battle, as we are repeatedly told in every profession, is won in the head!

THE LITTLE BIG MAN

Prime Minister Shastri had proven himself to be a man of rare courage and fortitude. He had not only stood up to Pakistan's President Field Marshal Ayub Khan, he had walked the talk by giving the army the freedom to do what few leaders globally have done—take the fight to the enemy on grounds of their own choosing. However, for the little big man there was another, more complex hill to climb. The focus was now on the post-war talks, and the resolutions that would determine the next steps. The Soviets had offered to host a summit between the leaders of both countries in Tashkent, an offer which Shastri had accepted on 22 September, while Pakistan did not immediately commit itself. Until then, both sides remained in occupation of the territory they had captured, with sporadic bursts of localized fighting in some sectors.

Pakistan's entire case rested on the single-point agenda of 'Kashmir'. Having plunged his country into a war with India by launching Operation Gibraltar, Ayub (and Bhutto) needed some concessions to save face with their own people.

The British had taken it upon themselves to broker a ceasefire under the aegis of the UN in May when the initial clashes had occurred in the Rann of Kutch. However, British diplomats seemed to treat the 'Kashmir Issue' as some sort of an unfinished agenda, and Harold Wilson had lost credibility in Indian eyes when his government did not come forward and condemn Pakistan for its aggression when it launched Operation Gibraltar. Nevertheless, on 19 October the British High Commissioner, John Freeman, had met with Shastri and the message was crystal clear—India was not willing to make any concessions whatsoever on Kashmir, even if it had been willing to consider them earlier. Wilson told Ayub that Britain would no longer be able to treat the Kashmir issue as a Commonwealth problem. In any case, the British were fast losing their prominence and dominance in matters of world affairs by then and it suited them to pass the buck on to the Americans. With President Lyndon Johnson and the US administration making no bones about the fact that Pakistan had violated their understanding that American weapons would not be used against India, Pakistan found itself in a position where it had to accept the Soviet prime minister Alexei Kosygin's offer to meet with the Indians in Tashkent in the first week of January 1966. The US was also very unhappy with the growing nexus between China and Pakistan, for it was no secret among intelligence circles that it was indeed Chairman Mao who had egged Bhutto into putting Operation Gibraltar into place. Pakistan's willingness to act as China's cat's paw was becoming a matter of concern, and would also impact the Tashkent Agreement.

On 3 January 1966, the Indian and Pakistani delegations arrived in Tashkent within two hours of each other. Accompanying Shastri were, among others, Defence Minister Chavan and Foreign Minister Swaran Singh; Ayub was accompanied by the mercurial Foreign Minister Bhutto, Foreign Secretary Aziz Ahmed, and other senior cabinet ministers. Over the next week, the two sides were engaged in a series of meetings. Kosygin somehow hammered out an agreement, which, until the very end, seemed to be a non-starter. With Pakistan repeatedly harping on Kashmir, and the Indians refusing to compromise on that score, the first breakthrough came when Shastri discussed with Chavan and Swaran Singh the implications of withdrawing to the pre-5 August positions all along the front, including from the Haji Pir, Tithwal, and Gurez Sectors. Both the ministers felt that, in the larger interest of global peace, India could do so provided the resolution did not say anything about Kashmir. This was communicated to Kosygin by Shastri on the evening of 5 January.

Kosygin, who had staked his all to hammer out an agreement, gratefully accepted Shastri's offer, but he still had to deal with Bhutto. While Ayub Khan would discuss the larger issues and play the good cop, the hardliners were Bhutto and Aziz Ahmed.

The two sides finally agreed to sign the Tashkent Agreement on 10 January 1966. Clause (ii) stated: 'The Prime Minister of India and the President of Pakistan have agreed that all armed personnel of the two countries shall be withdrawn not later than 24 February, 1966, to the positions they held prior to 5 August, 1965, and both sides shall observe the ceasefire terms on the ceasefire line.' Apart from a brief mention in clause (i) that Jammu and Kashmir was discussed, Kashmir did not find any further place in the agreement.

'Though the agreement was being viewed as a diplomatic victory for India and the Soviets, the prime minister was visibly very distraught. He knew by signing away the hard-fought victories in Haji Pir and other areas, the door had been left ajar for Pakistan to...once again resort to infiltration tactics.'[10] The sort of man on whom the decision weighed heavy, the Indian prime minister had a massive heart attack in the early hours of the morning on 11 January. Shastri's unexpected and sad end brought to a close yet another tumultuous and tragic chapter in the saga of India–Pakistan relations. Sadly, within six years, they would clash yet again.

ACKNOWLEDGEMENTS

In the larger context of the war, it was perhaps a non-event. But I remember the jeep with a trailer, my father arriving in the middle of the night, smelling as fathers do, a mixture of canvas and leather mixed with cordite. The church in Ambala had been bombed just around the time he passed it, and it was burning furiously. 23 Infantry Division was on the move, on its way to the Sialkot Sector and 18 Rajput was on its way to the war. He had to leave at dawn, so he had barely two hours and his over-riding concern was for the two men and the driver who were with him. And then it was time to go...and even as a five-year old who had dug his own trench, I knew the gravity of the situation as he said goodbye.

We were the lucky ones, for he came back, the ceasefire having been declared shortly after the battalion had deployed. And through him and so many others who survived, one constantly imbibed the stories and the memories of what had happened. Somehow, like the church in Ambala, those fires continued to burn. Today, many of those who contributed to this book are no more with us. One was fortunate to spend time with the likes of Brigadier Desmond Hayde while he was in R&R, going over every minute detail of the Battle of Dograi; so many–Lieutenant General Eric Vas, Air Vice Marshal C. S. Doraiswami, Air Marshal Viney Kapila, Squadron Leader Trevor Keelor, Lieutenant General Ranjit Singh Dyal, Marshal of the Air Force Arjan Singh, Colonel Mustasad Ahmad, Brigadier D. P. Nayar, and others, their voices echo in the narrative, for all that they said stays in one's head. This book is for all of them.

In acknowledging all those without whose inspiration, encouragement and persistence this book would not have been written, first and foremost is my publisher, David Davidar who first broached the subject of doing a series and then showed infinite patience as I went into freeze frame while I recovered from the emotional ordeal of having written *1962: The War That Wasn't*. After extending the 'final' deadlines repeatedly, I managed to get myself back on track. Even then, it has taken the better part of five years to complete this book. The large multitude of people whom I leaned on is endless, as not only did I ask them to cast their minds back half a century, I also made them search for photographs and paintings that helped complete the story. I can but only mention a few names here, but my grateful thanks to all the others who also spared their time.

Brigadier Amar Jit Singh Behl and Brigadier Dinesh Mathur, both of whom had been young second lieutenants with 17 Para Field in the Rann of Kutch;

Brigadier D. P. Nayar and Colonel Ranbir Singh of 4 Rajput for sharing the details pertaining to Black Rocks and Pt 13620 in Kargil; Colonel Dilip Sopori, Major General Jai Menon, his brother Sunil Menon, for helping recreate the capture of Kala Pahar; Brigadier Jasbir Singh who so generously sent me the material pertaining to 4 Kumaon at Trehgam during Operation Gibraltar; Lieutenant General Arjun Ray who shared his own experience pertaining to the fighting at Naugam; Rahul Roy for sharing details of his father's experiences, Major Bhaskar Roy, MVC; Brigadier Khutub A. Hai (3 Cavalry) and Major General D. K. Mehta (9 Deccan Horse) for details pertaining to the fighting at Khem Karan; Major Brijendra Singh (14 Scinde Horse) for sharing his notes on Dograi; Colonels Vivek Khare and K. K. Sharma, as well as Lieutenant Colonel Deepak Ahuja for details pertaining to actions fought by the Mahar battalions; Nadir Billimoria (5 Gorkha Rifles); Colonel Kehar Singh (Jat); Major General Baldev Raj Verma and former DIG, BSF, Hardyal Singh Rai, both of whom were wounded during the epic Battle of Dograi for their inputs; Lieutenant General Rajiv Sirohi and Brigadier Praveen Airie (Grenadiers); Brigadier Hukum Bainsla (3rd Gorkhas); Lieutenant General Rakesh Loomba (1 Skinner's Horse); Brigadier V. Mahalingam and Major M. G. Devasahayam (Madras); Lieutenant Generals Narendra Singh, H. C. Gangoli and P. J. S. Pannu (MLI); Major General Som Jhingon and Brigadier J. S. Bhullar (8 Garhwal Rifles); Colonel Vijay Dhruv Verma (20 Rajput); Colonel A. J. Arul Raj for the use of his paintings (Haji Pir and Khem Karan); Colonel N. N. Bhatia who made sure every action of the Kumaon Regiment got its due; and Parveen Dyal for looking for Major Dyal's photographs. I am also grateful to Lieutenant General T. S. 'Maun' Shergill for generously sharing images and information whenever I asked for it.

I am particularly grateful to my classmate, Major General Jagatbir Singh who himself commanded 1 Armoured Division for always being at hand whenever I needed something; and also Brigadier A. P. Bhargava, who is my father's course mate—both of them being from 18 Cavalry. Lieutenant Generals Sanjiv Langer (62 Cavalry) and Rakesh Loomba (Skinner's and Deccan Horse) were my 'go to' persons every time I needed to understand armour terms or tactics, and they would cheerfully take my calls even late at night; Major General Sanjay Bhanot for organizing a special trip to the Rann of Kutch so one could study the ground where the initial fighting had taken place; Brigadier M. Sri Kumar (Sikh Regimental Centre) and all the commanding officers of various units and regiments for their unstinted help.

Air Marshal Philip Rajkumar for sharing his notes and fielding my questions at the oddest times of day; Air Marshal Bharat Kumar for sharing his detailed research papers; Flight Lieutenant Alfred Cooke for giving me a second-by-second account of his epic dogfight over Kalaikunda; my good friend P. V. S. Jagan Mohan and the Bharat Rakshak team for providing even the tiniest of details; Wing Commander

Jag Mohan Nath who not only graced the book release of *1962: The War That Wasn't* in Bombay, but alos spared time to go over the minutest details of his sorties over Tibet and West Pakistan—he also sent me some excellent photographs which lay bare the stark reality of the complete non-coordination between the army and the IAF; Air Marshal Nanda Cariappa, the last Indian pilot to bail out over Pakistan and be captured; Air Chief Marshal N. C. Suri who has been more than a mentor on so many occasions; Group Captain Deb Gohain for sharing his wonderful paintings which help bring the aerial war alive; Squadron Leader Sameer Joshi for sending me the paintings done by Mrs Priyanka Joshi which were used to illustrate his own book; also a special thanks to Kapil Chandini whose enthusiastic behind the scenes work is a real boon.

My special thanks to Lieutenant General A. S. Bhinder, GOC-in-C SW Command and Air Marshal Vikram Singh, SASO WAC, who were most helpful in sourcing photographs that were otherwise blanks in the visual narrative. To Colonel Mayank Prabhas, I am specially indebted for diligently following up on leads. I am also grateful to many others—Anjali Nayar (4 Rajput at Kargil), Bhrigubir Singh and Colonel Gautam Jha (7 Jat at Unche Wains), Marilyn Dyer (Siri Force), the two brothers—Vijay and Group Captain Sanjay Dandapani (with whom I flew a MiG 27 sortie in 1992) and and the commandants of various armoured regiments who were, without exception, most helpful.

R. D. Pradhan, former private secretary to Y. B. Chavan and later the governor of Arunachal for his insights at the political level; Colonel B. R. S. Dahiya for double checking details with all his Pakistani counterparts and invariably confusing the 'hell out of me'; Lieutenant General Israr Ghumman (Pakistan's 28 Cavalry) and Major Agha Amin who is a leading military historian in Pakistan; Kirat Dhillon and Colonel Surjit Singh Dhillon (MLI); Joginder Negi of the Delhi Gymkhana Club library; the families of the late Major General Yashwant Deva (Signals) and Lieutenant General R. D. Hira for access to their papers; Lieutenant General Deepak Samanwar, Colonel Pinka Virk, Major Moshe Kohli, Anil Soni, Sunil Kashikar, and Aditya Singh Deora for sharing details pertaining to their fathers (and grandfathers). I was also fortunate to spend time with Lieutenant General Konsam Himalay Singh when he was commanding 25 Infantry Division in Rajouri and had access to the excellent divisional museum, from where some of the portraits have been sourced.

I'd like to thank my editor at Aleph, Pujitha Krishnan, for her tremendous patience. There were times when neither of us could remember which chapter preceded which, but we eventually managed to give it some shape. This is the third book we have worked on together and despite the magnitude and canvas of the war, the edit was almost a painless experience. I'd also like to thank Bena Sareen for designing not just this cover, but also the one for the earlier 1962 book.

Finally, I want to thank my mother, Mrs Usha Verma, who kept pushing me to finish the book even though she couldn't quite understand why I wanted to write about it 'after all these years'. Tragically, she was a victim of the dreaded second wave of Covid-19, which claimed her along with hundreds of other veterans, many of whom had fought in the 1965 war.

Shiv Kunal Verma
July 2021, Bandrol, Kullu

NOTES

These are some of the abbreviations that appear in the book

AGL	above ground level
AOR	area of responsibility
BGS	brigadier general staff
CAP	combat air patrol
CAS	chief of air staff
CGS	chief of the general staff (today called vice chief of army staff)
CO	commanding officer
COAS	chief of army staff
DMO	director, Military Operations (now called DGMO)
FF	Frontier Force
FOO	forward observation officer
FUP	forming-up point
GOC	general officer commanding
GPO	gun position officer
GR	Gorkha Rifles
GSO	general staff officer
IB	International Boundary
IO	intelligence officer
JCO	junior commissioned officer (naib subedar, subedar, subedar major)
LI	Light Infantry
MLI	Maratha Light Infantry
MMG	medium machine gun
MVC	Maha Vir Chakra
NCO	non-commissioned officer (lance naik, naik, havildar)
OP	observation post
ORBAT	Order of Battle, the hierarchical command structure of an army formation
PVC	Param Vir Chakra
R&S	Recce and Support
RCL	recoilless (anti-tank direct firing weapons)
RMO	regimental medical officer
RT	radio transmitter
SSG	Special Services Group
SU	signal unit
TAC HQ	Tactical Headquarters
VrC	Vir Chakra

PROLOGUE: FIGHTING FROM THE ROPES

1   Alfred Cooke, interview with author, Gurgaon, 2015.

2   In the immediate aftermath of the sortie, Cooke didn't remember anything. In 1992, while researching *Salt of the Earth*, Cooke's epic battle seemed to have been wiped off the historical records of the IAF as well. Even Arjan Singh didn't want to talk about Kalaikunda, perhaps too embarrassed by the Pakistani raids to want to dwell on it. None of the squadron histories mentioned it. In 2000, while shooting *Akaash Yodha*, P. V. S. Jagan Mohan and Kapil Chandni from Bharat Rakshak were part of my crew and flew around with me on the last leg of the shoot. Mohan as well as Samir Chopra did yeoman service by digging out Alfred Cooke's epic air battle.

CHAPTER 1: HANDS ON THE TILLER

1   In conversation with the author, Bombay, 20 and 21 June 2016.

2   Paul M. McGarr, 'India's Rasputin? VK Krishna Menon and Anglo-American Misperceptions of Indian Foreign Policy Making, 1947-1964', *Diplomacy & Statecraft*, Vol. 22, No. 2, 239–260, 9 June 2011, p. 254.

3   R. D. Pradhan, *Debacle to Resurgence: Y. B. Chavan, Defence Minister (1962-66)*, New Delhi: Atlantic Publishers and Distributors, 2017, p. 9.

4   Ibid., p. 11.

5   Ibid., p. 34.

6   Ibid., p. 13.

7   Ibid., p. 316.

8   Ibid.

9   See Shiv Kunal Verma, *1962: The War That Wasn't*, New Delhi: Aleph Book Company, 2016, p. 371.

10   Pradhan, *Debacle to Resurgence*, p. 15.

11   Ibid., p. 19.

12   Ibid.

13   Ibid., p. 107; interview with H. C. Sarin in 1992.

14   B. K. Narayan, *General J. N. Chaudhuri: An Autobiography, as narrated to B. K. Narayan*, New Delhi: Vikas, 1978, p. 69.

15   Brigadier Chaudhuri was the last officer to hold this post. After this, Operations and Intelligence were bifurcated and placed under the charge of Brigadier Sam Manekshaw (DMO) and Brigadier Chand Narayan Das (DMI).

16   My paternal grandfather, Narendra Singh Verma, who was from the Central Provinces and Berar Cadre, would then administer Hyderabad.

17   General officer commanding-in-chief.

18   D. K. Palit, *War in High Himalaya: The Indian Army in Crises: 1962*, South Asia Books, 1992, p. 115.

19   Interview with H. C. Sarin, 1992.

20   Palit, *War in High Himalaya*, p. 115.

21   Ram D. Pradhan, in conversation with the author, Bombay, 20 and 21 June 2016.

22   Palit, *War in High Himalaya*, p. 115.

23   Ibid., p. 351.

24   Hanadi Falki, *Field Marshal Sam Manekshaw*, New Delhi: Prabhat Prakashan, 2017.

25   As stated by Mullik in a conversation with the DMO. Palit, *War in High Himalaya*, p. 367.

26   As noted in Chavan's diary, Pradhan, *Debacle to Resurgence*.

27   Narayan, *General J. N. Chaudhuri*, p. 178.

CHAPTER 2: THE FAULT LINES

1   Brigadier Desmond Hayde, *Battle of Dograi*, Dehradun: Nataraj Publishers, 1984, p. 30.
2   Lieutenant General Eric A. Vas, *Without Baggage: A Personal Account of the Jammu & Kashmir Operations 1947-49*, Dehradun: Nataraj Publishers, 1987, p. 23.
3   Planks of wood supplied by the forest department through auctions.
4   Hayde, *Battle of Dograi*, p. 31.
5   The Lieutenant General Kalwant Singh Committee had submitted its report that same year, stating categorically that an India–China clash was very much a possibility in the next nine years. For more on this, see Verma, *1962: The War That Wasn't*.
6   Hayde, *Battle of Dograi*, p. 32.
7   Ibid.
8   Hayde, *Battle of Dograi*, p. 36.
9   Diary of Admiral William Davis, p. 787.
10 Saroja Sundararajan, *Kashmir Crisis: Unholy Anglo-Pak Nexus*, New Delhi: Kalpaz Publications, 2010, p. 287.
11 Philip Ziegler, *Mountbatten: The Official Biography*, London: Guild Publishing, 1985, p. 601.
12 Palit, *War in High Himalaya*, p. 370.
13 Ibid., p. 371.
14 Ibid., p. 393.
15 Roedad Khan (ed.), *The British Papers: Secret and Confidential: India–Pakistan–Bangladesh*, quoted in A. G. Noorani, 'Our secrets in British archives', *Frontline*, 15–28 February 2003.
16 Palit, *War in High Himalaya*, p. 394.
17 Ibid.
18 Mark O'Neill, 'Panchen Lama led life of suffering with one bright spot—a happy marriage', *South China Morning Post*, 18 May 2008.
19 Claude Arpi in conversation with the author, Pondicherry, 2017.

CHAPTER 3: THE EYES OF AYUB

1   McGarr, 'India's Rasputin?', p. 254.
2   Winston Churchill, *India: Early Speeches,* New York: Rosetta Books, 2013.
3   John Barnes and David Nicholson (eds.), *The Leo Amery Diaries,* London: Hutchinson, 1980, vol. II, p. 833.
4   Ibid.
5   'Jinnah Papers: Documenting Partition', *The Tribune*, 16 August 1998.
6   In conversation with the author, Bombay, 20 and 21 June 2016.
7   'New Moves Pressed to Settle Kashmir; Nehru and Ayub Welcome Abdullah's Attempt to Act As a Mediator in Long Standing Dispute', *New York Times*, 24 May 1964.

CHAPTER 4: SLIPPING AND SLIDING

1   E. H. Aitken, *Gazetteer of the Province of Sindh*, Karachi 1907, pp. 4–5.
2   Major General A. H. E. Michigan, *Right of the Line: The Grenadiers—A Historical Record*, Grenadiers Association, 1995, p. 24.
3   B. C. Chakravorty, *History of the Indo-Pak Conflict, 1965*, New Delhi: Ministry of Defense, 1992, p. 18.
4   R. D. Palsokar, *Regimental history of the Grenadiers*, Jabalpur: Grenadier Regimental Centre 1980.
5   Was the army chief between 1957 and 1961.
6   Aitken, *Gazetteer of the Province of Sindh*.
7   Farooq Bajwa, *From Kutch to Tashkent: The Indo-Pakistan War of 1965*, London: Hurst & Company, 2013, p. 68.

8   Later general. Was later the army chief between 1986 and 1988.

9   Description of ground conditions on the Indian side from interview with Brigadier (then Captain) Amar Jit Behl from 17 Para Field, Chandigarh, 21 October 2017.

10   Later as the Western Army commander in 1984 he rushed in to assault the Golden Temple in Amritsar in June 1984 when the then COAS, General A. S. Vaidya and the DGMO were advising Prime Minister Indira Gandhi not to do so. In 1987, as the COAS, he deployed the Indian Army in Sri Lanka as the IPKF. When hostilities broke out with the LTTE, most Indian units had virtually no ammunition.

11   Captain Amarinder Singh and Lieutenant General Tajinder Shergill, *The Monsoon War—Young Officers Reminisce: 1965 India-Pakistan War*, New Delhi: Roli Books, 2015, p. 20.

12   The navy and the air force had kept the royal prefix (His Majesty's) even after Independence. It was finally dropped on 26 January 1950 when India proclaimed herself as a republic.

13   Major S. Ahmad as quoted in Chakravorty, *History of the Indo-Pak Conflict, 1965*, chapter 10.

14   INS *Vikrant* went into dry dock shortly after this exercise where she sat out the rest of the 1965 war, as did most of the navy.

15   Havildar Gopinath Bhingardive was awarded the Vir Chakra for his role in the fighting.

16   Perhaps the only instance in the history of warfare where a small paramilitary force was attacked by an entire brigade of regular army with fire support.

17   The 106 mm recoilless gun is capable of firing either from the ground or from jeeps. These were generally used by the infantry as anti-tank weapons.

18   Order of Battle, or, in simple terms, the hierarchical command structure of an army formation.

19   He went on to command 1 Corps later in the year.

20   *Salt of the Earth* was a historical film that was shot by the author in 1992. Part of the enactment was to show the IAF's Vampire sorties over the Rann of Kutch. Tanks moving in the semi-caked salt plains had also been filmed as part of the film.

21   Interview with Air Chief Marshal (later Marshal of the air force) Arjan Singh in 1991 for the historical film on the IAF, *Salt of the Earth*.

22   Airborne Observation Post. These are fixed wing aircraft which are used by the artillery to help direct fire.

23   Interview with Air Chief Marshal Arjan Singh in 1991 for *Salt of the Earth*.

24   P. V. S. Jagan Mohan and Samir Chopra, *The India-Pakistan Air War of 1965*, New Delhi: Manohar, 2005, p. 62.

25   Interview with Brigadier (then Captain) Amar Jit Behl, Chandigarh, 21 October 2017.

26   Ibid.

CHAPTER 5: ENTER THE PATTONS

1   He later rose to the rank of major general and was killed in Jammu and Kashmir in 1971. To date, he is the most senior Pakistani officer to have been killed in action.

2   Pakistan's third highest award for bravery, on a par with India's Vir Chakra.

3   Pakistan's fifth highest gallantry award.

4   The observation post that controls artillery fire from the front positions.

5   The flight commander of the Air OP squadron that operated from Bhuj and Khavda, Mathur was decorated with an MVC. The Pakistani aircraft that operated in support of their artillery were called 'bird dogs'.

6   Indian records say one man was killed, six were wounded, and five went missing. The Pakistanis claim over forty casualties plus four POWs.

7   Conversation with Brigadier (then Second Lieutenant) Dinesh Mathur, Gurgaon, 5 November 2018.

8   Interview with Air Chief Marshal Arjan Singh for the film *Salt of the Earth*, 1992.

9   Conversation with Brigadier Dinesh Mathur, Gurgaon, 5 November 2018.

10   Utpal Barbara quoted in Air Marshal Bharat Kumar, *The Duels of the Himalayan Eagle: The First Indo-Pak Air War (1-22 September 1965)*, Gurgaon: IMR Media Pvt Ltd, 2015.

11   Flying Officer Utpal Barbara was awarded the Vir Chakra. In addition to the mission on 26 April, the then CO of 101 FR Squadron, Squadron Leader V. Krishnamurthy had flown two previous missions on 22 and 23 April with Barbara in the right-hand seat. However, on those occasions, they had not found any tanks in the area.

12   Kumar, *The Duels of the Himalayan Eagle*, p. 19.

13   Mohan and Chopra, *The India-Pakistan Air War of 1965*, p. 64.

14   Chakravorty, *History of the Indo-Pak Conflict, 1965*, p. 42.

15   Interview with Brigadier Amar Jit Behl, Chandigarh, 21 October 2017.

16   Pradhan, *Debacle to Resurgence*, p. 225.

17   Ian Talbot, *The History of British Diplomacy in Pakistan*, Routledge, 2020.

18   Shruti Pandalai, 'Recounting 1965: War, Diplomacy and Great Games in the Subcontinent, interview with Ambassador Rasgotra', *Journal of Defence Studies*, Jul–Sep 2015.

19   Talbot, *History of British Diplomacy in Pakistan*.

20   In February 1966, the tribunal in an interim judgement upheld most of India's claims. On 19 February 1968, in its final verdict, the tribunal surprisingly gave both Kanjarkot and Chhad Bet, an area of 828 square miles, to Pakistan. India retained Biar Bet, Pt 84, and Sardar Post.

CHAPTER 6: OPERATION ABLAZE

1   Pradhan, *Debacle to Resurgence*. p. 317.

2   Major General Lachhman Singh Lehl, *Missed Opportunities: Indo-Pak War 1965,* Dehradun: Natraj Publishers, 1997, p. 125

3   Major General Gurcharan Singh Sandhu, *The Indian Armour: History of the Indian Armoured Corps Till 1940*, New Delhi:Vision Books, 1987, p. 337.

4   Sandhu, *The Indian Armour*, pp. 337–38.

5   Lehl, *Missed Opportunities,* p. 189.

6   Ibid., p. 190.

7   Ibid.

8   General Mohammad Musa, *My Version, India-Pakistan War 1965*, Lahore: Wajidalis Limited, 1983, p. 20.

9   Lehl, *Missed Opportunities*, p. 245.

10   Mrs P. C. Lal in conversation with the author.

11   Lehl, *Missed Opportunities*, p. 101.

12   Pradhan, *Debacle to Resurgence*, p. 112.

13   Interview with Arjan Singh.

14   Lehl, *Missed Opportunities*, p. 102.

15   Musa, *My Version*.

CHAPTER 7: PRELUDE TO WAR: KARGIL

1   Palit, *War in High* Himalaya, p. 260.

2   Ibid.

3   Pradhan, *Debacle to Resurgence*, p. 318.

4   Brigadier D. P. Nayar in interview with author, Gurgaon, 9 January 2019.

5   Later Major General. A rare case where he started his career as a sapper, then transferred to the Jat Regiment, and then to the artillery. He had raised 85 Light Regiment.

6   Note sent to CLAWS by Brigadier D. P. Nayar and interview with author.

7   Though in Chakravorty's *History of the Indo-Pak War 1965*, 17 Punjab is supposed to have been part of the Brigade Group, this was not the case. The Punjabis moved in later to relieve 4 Rajput.

8   Warnings about Pakistani movement in the area were often based on the Urdu newspapers
     published in Kashmir.
9   This refers to the location and the height marked on the map. Most unnamed peaks in the
     Himalayas are referred to by this method by the army.
10   Chakravorty, *History of the Indo-Pak Conflict, 1965*, p. 48.
11   Colonel (then Captain) Ranbir Singh in interview with author, Chandigarh, 30 May 2019.
12   Havildar Girdhari Lal was posthumously awarded a VrC.
13   Major Baljit Singh Randhawa was posthumously awarded the MVC. Captain Ranbir Singh was
     also awarded a VrC.
14   Second Lieutenant (later Lieutenant) Vijay Kumar Aggarwal, was shot in the thigh but he
     continued to move forward.
15   Second Lieutenant Bhagrawat Singh was later killed in the Uri Sector in September.
16   The barrel, the tripod, and the base plate together weighed 147 kg; each mortar shell weighed 9
     kg. It had a range of about 220 meters.
17   Rinchin had fought the Pakistanis in 1948, when he was awarded an MVC and given the rank of
     a JCO. In 1962 he was involved in the fighting with the Chinese and he was awarded the Shaurya
     Chakra. In 1965 he was a captain, and in 1971 he was a colonel when he won an MVC yet again.
18   This was done in August 1965. Unfortunately, the Ladakh Scouts were not used in the subsequent
     fighting in any meaningful manner.
19   From the personal notes of Major (later Major General) Manjapura Chandra Shekar Menon.
20   Chakravorty, *History of the Indo-Pak Conflict, 1965*, p. 35.
21   As a brigadier, Rawlley had been in command of the Wallong Sector (see Verma, *1962: The War
     That Wasn't*).
22   Chakravorty, *History of the Indo-Pak Conflict, 1965*, p. 37.
23   Altaf Gauhar, *Ayub Khan: Pakistan's First Military Ruler*, Karachi: OUP, 1997, p. 214.
24   Brigadier D. P. Nayar in conversation with author, Gurgaon, 9 January 2019.
25   Lehl, *Missed Opportunities*, pp. 192–93.
26   Pushpindar Singh, Ravi Rikhye, and Peter Steinemann, *Fiza'ya: Psyche of the Pakistan Air Force*,
     New Delhi: The Society for Aerospace Studies, 1991, p. 45.
27   Singh, Rikhye, and Steinemann, *Fiza'ya*, p. 44.
28   Musa, *My Version*, p. 8.
29   Ibid.

CHAPTER 8: OPERATION GIBRALTAR

1   Musa, *My Version*, p. 9.
2   Major General Aboobaker Osman Mitha, *Unlikely Beginnings: A Soldier's Life*, Karachi: OUP, 2003.
3   Sultan M. Ali's interview with Colonel Syed Ghaffar Mehdi, 'Operation Gibraltar–An Unmitigated
     Disaster?' *Criterion Quarterly, Vol. 7, No. 1*, 21 March 2012.
4   Ibid.
5   Musa, *My Version*, p. 35.
6   Gohar Ayub Khan, *Glimpses into the Corridors of Power*, London: OUP, 2007, p. 102.
7   Dennis Kux, *The United States and Pakistan, 1947-2000: Disenchanted Allies*, Washington DC,
     Wilson Center Press, 2001, p. 159.
8   Ibid.
9   Khan, *Glimpses into the Corridors of Power*, p. 102.
10   Andrew Small, *The China-Pakistan Axis: Asia's New Geopolitics*, London, Vintage Books, 2015.
11   Musa, *My Version*, p. 27.
12   Ibid., p. 10.
13   This was the official history published by the Ministry of Defence, Government of India.

14 Lieutenant General Harbakhsh Singh, *War Despatches: Indo-Pak Conflict 1965*, New Delhi: Lancer Publishers, 2013, p. 9.

15 Chakravorty, *History of the Indo-Pak Conflict,* 1965, p. 60.

16 Brian Cloughley, *A History of the Pakistan Army: Wars and Insurrections*, Karachi: OUP, 1999, p. 68.

17 Named after Salahuddin, the great sultan of Egypt and Syria who fought a combined army of many European kings during the Third Crusade.

18 Sterling machine gun, an iconic British weapon that fired 9 mm rounds and had a range of approximately 200 metres.

19 The term came into being much later.

20 Signed on behalf of India by Azim Hussain, secretary in the Ministry of External Affairs and on behalf of Pakistan by Arshad Hussain, Pakistan high commissioner (ambassador).

21 Major (Dr) K. Brahma Singh, *History of Jammu and Kashmir Rifles 1820-1956: The State Force Background*, New Delhi: Lancer, 1991.

22 Recommendation for Award for Kashmir Singh Katoch IC 83 (National Archives, Kew).

23 HQ 10 Division was being set up in Bangalore at the time. 191 Brigade was directly under 15 Corps HQ.

24 Harbakhsh Singh, *War Despatches*, p. 27.

25 Ibid., pp. 7–8.

26 Pradhan, in conversation with the author, Bombay, 20 and 21 June 2016.

27 The branch that is in charge of all postings.

28 Wing Commander D. J. S. Kler in interview with author, 5 January 2019.

29 Captain Chander Narain Singh was awarded a Maha Vir Chakra posthumously.

30 He was later lieutenant general. At that stage in his career, he had been Mentioned in Despatches in Burma and won a VrC during the J&K Ops in 1948.

31 This proved to be a major area of infiltration. Subsequently 6 Dogra liquidated twenty-three infiltrators (including one officer) from this region and captured six Pakistanis including a JCO.

32 The rank of jemadar was still in use. After the 1965 war, it was changed in both the Pakistan and Indian armies to naib subedar.

33 He went on to command 19 Division.

34 Ten of those killed were from 4 Kumaon, while Sapper Chander Singh from the 40 Field Company Engineers had been attached to the battalion.

35 Naik Ram Kumar was posthumously awarded the Vir Chakra.

36 Brigadier Jasbir Singh, *Combat Diary: An Illustrated History of Operations Conducted by 4th Battalion, The Kumaon Regiment—1788 to 1974,* New Delhi: Lancer Publishers, 2010, pp. 198–99.

37 Chakravorty, *History of the Indo-Pak Conflict, 1965*, p. 65.

38 Pradhan in conversation with the author, Bombay, 20 and 21 June 2016.

39 Letter to the author, April 2020.

40 Lieutenant Colonel Mustasad Ahmad, *Living up to Heritage: The Rajputs 1947 to 1970*, New Delhi: Lancer Publishers, 1997.

41 Ibid.

42 The STRIM 40 was an anti-personnel rifle grenade manufactured in Belgium.

43 Lieutenant Colonel Gautam Sharma, *History of the Jat Regiment, Volume III,* Bareilly: Allied Publishers, 1979, p. 119.

CHAPTER 9: BATTLEGROUND KASHMIR

1 Singh and Shergill, *The Monsoon War*, p. 44.

2 Part of 25 Division, the 'All India Brigade' had all three battalions under the command of Indian officers: L. P. Sen, who was Bakshi's CO, K. S. Thimayya, and S. P. P. Thorat.

3 He was later lieutenant governor of the Andaman and Nicobar Islands.

4   Lehl, *Missed Opportunities*, p. 141.

5   Lieutenant Colonel Rohit Agarwal, *Brave Men of War, Tales of Valour 1965*, New Delhi: Bloomsbury, 2015.

6   Ibid.

7   Ibid.

8   The captain had done the Rangers Course at Fort Benning in the United States and was a designated commando.

9   Singh and Shergill, *The Monsoon War*, p. 68.

10   Ajaz Ashraf, 'No one has cared to inform us about the '65 war celebrations: Wounded war veteran', *Scroll.in*, 24 August 2015.

11   Later lieutenant colonel, considered to be the father of the Para Commandos in India.

12   Lehl, *Missed Opportunities*, p. 149.

13   Thirty years later, while making a film on post-Independent history of the Indian Army, the author had stood at exactly the same place on Pt 405. A platoon of BSF troops which was to play the part of the enemy on Raja and Rani failed to show up. After some unofficial parleys, the author and the post commander walked into no-man's land and met the Pakistani JCO, with whom the author struck a deal. For three bottles of XXX Rum (having started by offering just the one) which was the standard Indian Army issue, a platoon of Pakistani troops played their own part in the filming the next morning. They certainly seemed to enjoy themselves, going up and down the hill for a few retakes as well.

14   Major G. C. Verma, who was educated at the RIMC, Naik Prem Singh, and Sepoy Sukh Ram were awarded VrCs while Captain Bawa and Subedar Bansi Lal were posthumously awarded Sena Medals.

15   Musa, *My Version*, pp. 38–39.

16   The battalion had been nearly wiped out in NEFA when the PLA had ambushed the CO, Lieutenant Colonel Brahmanand Avasthy, and his men at the Lagyala Gompa after the ceasefire had been declared. (See Verma, *1962: The War That Wasn't*, p. 393.)

CHAPTER 10: OPERATION GRAND SLAM

1   Personal notes of Colonel K. P. P. Nair.

2   Ibid.

3   Ibid.

4   Ibid.

5   Ibid.

6   Ahmad, *Living up to Heritage*, p. 291.

7   Ibid., p. 292.

8   Ibid.

9   Ibid.

10   A troop of AMX-13 tanks belonging to 20 Lancers had been airlifted to Chushul by AN-12 aircraft (see Verma, *1962: The War That Wasn't*).

11   Singh and Shergill, *The Monsoon War*, p. 94.

12   Notes shared by Rahul Roy via email.

13   Ibid.

14   Lieutenant General Mahmud Ahmed, *Illusion of Victory: A Military History of the Indo-Pak War-1965*, Karachi: Lexicon Publishers, 2002.

15   As described by Rahul Roy in a blog on the 50th anniversary of the battle.

16   C. P. Srivastava, *Lal Bahadur Shastri: A Life of Truth in Politics*, New Delhi: OUP, 2004, p. 224.

17   Air Marshal Bharat Kumar says it was a scheduled halt as Srinagar did not have refuelling capability.

18   Kumar says the army chief definitely did not discuss Chhamb or mention it at all in his

conversation with the pilots in the crew room, for when the order came from Delhi to launch the aircraft, some officers had gone off to their rooms.

19 Chavan's diary as narrated by Pradhan.

20 He was killed in 1968 in a MiG-21 crash.

21 Mohan and Chopra, *The India-Pakistan Air War of 1965*, p. 70.

22 Air Marshal Arjan Singh, interview with author, 1991, for *Salt of the Earth*.

23 Mohan and Chopra, *The India-Pakistan Air War of 1965*, p. 73.

24 Air Vice Marshal C. S. Doraiswami, interview with author, 1992.

25 He was the eighteenth COAS.

26 Rahul Roy interview with author.

27 The location of Brigade HQ as given to Lieutenant Colonel Mustasad Ahmad, CO 6 Rajput, when he enquired where he should meet the brigade commander.

28 Ahmad, Living up to Heritage.

29 Musa, *My Version*, p. 86.

30 The CO of 161 Field Regiment was subsequently court-martialled and GOC 10 Infantry Division was removed from command.

CHAPTER 11: SABRE SLAYERS

1 Conversation with Air Vice Marshal Doraiswamy, 1992.

2 Trevor Keelor retired as a Squadron Leader; Kala Sandhu became a Wing Commander and was commanding 23 Squadron in Pathankot in December 1971. He was killed in a dusk/night flying accident in a Gnat just before the war.

3 Krishnaswamy went on to become an Air Chief Marshal and was the nineteenth CAS. Gill was dismissed from service as a Flight Lieutenant.

4 Mohan and Chopra, *The India-Pakistan Air War of 1965*, p. 79.

5 As narrated to Air Marshal Bharat Kumar.

6 Kumar, *The Duels of the Himalayan Eagle*.

7 Interview with Squadron Leader Trevor Keelor in 1992 for the film *Salt of the Earth*.

8 The PAF's official history makes no mention of this encounter with 23 Squadron on 3 September. That the PAF ran into the Gnats on that day is evident from a comment that the small Gnats are difficult to spot. According to John F. Fricker, the Sabre hit by Trevor Keelor was severely damaged but was safely flown back to base by Flight Lieutenant Yusuf Khan.

9 Mohan and Chopra, *The India-Pakistan Air War of 1965*, p. 80. Pathania's used this term every time he described the aerial engagement to the author. (Motherless, as in a bastard turn, so perhaps his way of getting past the sensors.)

10 Mohan and Chopra, *The India-Pakistan Air War of 1965*, p. 84.

11 Deliberately damaging it so the enemy cannot use it in good order.

12 Kumar, *The Duels of the Himalayan Eagle*, p. 88.

13 Interview with Mally Wollen Goa, 2005; also Mohan and Chopra, *The India-Pakistan Air War of 1965*, p. 86.

14 John Fricker, *Battle for Pakistan: The Air War of 1965*, Littlehampton: Littlehampton Book Services, 1979.

15 Ibid.

16 Wing Commander J. M. Nath in conversation with the author, Bombay, March 2016. Jaggi Nath was a guest speaker during the launch of *1962: The War That Wasn't*.

17 Was part of the first batch of IAF pilots sent to Lugovaya in late 1962 to convert to MiG-21s.

18 Nath in conversation with the author Bombay, March 2016.

19 Harbakhsh Singh, *War Despatches*, p. 171.

20 Mohan and Chopra, *The India-Pakistan Air War of 1965*.

21   Ibid.

22   Harbakhsh Singh, *War Despatches*, p. 171.

23   Ibid.

24   Kumar, *The Duels of the Himalayan Eagle*, p. 96.

CHAPTER 12: ICHHOGIL CANAL: 11 CORPS (PART I)

1   Pradhan, *Debacle to Resurgence*, pp. 236–37.

2   Ibid., p. 238.

3   Narayan, *General J. N. Chaudhuri*, p. 192.

4   Lehl, *Missed Opportunities*, p. 194.

5   Air Marshal Asghar Khan, *The First Round: Indo-Pakistan War 1965*, New Delhi: Vikas Publishing House, 1979.

6   Lehl, *Missed Opportunities*, p. 199.

7   Musa, *My Version*.

8   He graduated from IMA, Dehradun, in June 1939. Six years after the 1965 war, as the chief of staff of the army, he and General Yahya Khan were blamed for the military debacle against India.

9   He was commissioned from the IMA into 1 Punjab. Commanded Pakistan's 10 Corps from where he retired. He later served as Pakistan's ambassador to Libya and Philippines.

10   Commissioned from the IMA into the Baluch Regiment, he retired as a brigadier despite being awarded the Hilal-i-Jur'at.

11   See Verma, *1962: The War That Wasn't*.

12   Lehl, *Missed Opportunities*, p. 201.

13   As a lieutenant colonel he was commanding 2 Rajput at Nam Ka Chu on 20 October 1962. Grievously wounded, he had spent seven months in a POW Camp in Tibet before being repatriated to India. See Verma, *1962: The War That Wasn't*.

14   Pradhan, *Debacle to Resurgence*, p. 240. Italics added.

15   Ibid., p. 241, italics added.

16   Ibid., italics added.

17   Hayde in conversation with the author.

18   Hayde, *Battle of Dograi*, p. 50.

19   Ibid.

20   For this conversation, see Hayde, *Battle of Dograi*, p. 48.

21   Ibid., p. 56.

22   Khazan Singh was in hospital recovering from jaundice when the battalion got its orders to move. He 'escaped' from hospital to join the unit just in time to march with it. He was declared a deserter by the doctors who had no idea where he was.

23   Hayde, *Battle of Dograi*, p. 61.

24   Ibid., p. 62.

25   Ibid., p. 63.

26   Ibid., pp. 63–64.

27   Ibid., p. 64.

28   Singh and Shergill, *The Monsoon War*, p. 147.

29   Hayde, *Battle of Dograi*, p. 71.

30   Ibid.

31   Ibid., p. 72.

32   In a TV interview.

33   Hayde, *Battle of Dograi*, p. 78.

34   Killed in action; was awarded the Sena Medal posthumously.

35   Hayde, *Battle of Dograi*, p. 83. Also in conversation with Major Brijender Singh, 19 April 2019.

36   Hayde, *Battle of Dograi*, p. 86.

37   Ibid.

38   Conversation with Major Brijendra Singh, 19 April 2019.

39   Hayde, *Battle of Dograi*, p. 86.

40   Kumar, *The Duels of the Himalayan Eagle*, p. 101.

41   Sharma, *History of the Jat Regiment*, p. 130.

42   He was severely wounded and evacuated to Ferozepur Military Hospital where he died on 12 September. He was awarded a posthumous VrC.

43   Singh and Shergill, *The Monsoon* War, p. 171.

44   He was awarded a VrC for this action.

45   He would go on to command 17 Rajput.

46   Brigadier Darshan Khullar, *Themes of Glory: Indian Artillery in War*, New Delhi: Om Publications, 2017.

47   General K. V. Krishna Rao, *Prepare or Perish: A Study of National Security*, New Delhi: Lancer Publishers, 1991, p. 132.

48   Lehl, *Missed Opportunities*, p. 222.

49   The agreement entitled 'Agreed decisions and procedures to end disputes and incidents along the Indo–West Pakistan border areas', 11 January 1960.

50   Lieutenant General Jogi Dhillon subsequently recommended Chhajju Ram for a VrC.

51   Harbakhsh Singh, *War Despatches*.

52   Thakur Govid Singh was also the first commandant of the President's Bodyguard. ·

53   Bhupinder Singh, *1965 War: Role of Tanks in India-Pakistan War*, New Delhi: B. C. Publishers, 1982.

54   Harbakhsh Singh, *War Despatches*, p. 112.

CHAPTER 13: PUNCH & COUNTER PUNCH: AIR BATTLE PART II (6 SEPTEMBER)

1   Singh and Shergill, *The Monsoon* War, p. 151.

2   Ibid., p. 152.

3   Ibid.

4   Ibid.

5   Harbakhsh Singh, *War Despatches*, p. 92.

6   Lehl, *Missed Opportunities*, p. 208.

7   Ibid.

8   Harbakhsh Singh, *War Despatches*, p. 92.

9   Pradhan, *Debacle to Resurgence*, p. 249.

10   The actual code name is not known.

11   Ahmed, *Illusion of Victory*.

12   Lieutenant General S. L. Menezes, *Fidelity and Honour: The Indian Army from the Seventeenth to the Twenty-first Century*, New Delhi: Penguin Viking, 1993, pp. 496–97.

13   Musa, *My Version,* p. 42.

14   Lehl, *Missed* Opportunities, p. 208.

15   Harbakhsh Singh, *War Despatches*, p. xx.

16   In an interview with the author in connection with the IAF film, *Salt of the Earth.* He did not elaborate and it was not clear if this was part of the Rann of Kutch discussions or a separate agreement with either Asghar Khan or Nur Khan.

17   3 Squadron Cobra's diary as quoted in Kumar, *The Duels of the Himalayan Eagle*, p. 114.

18   Air Marshal Pingale in Kumar, *The Duels of the Himalayan Eagle*, p. 118.

19   Pradhan, *Debacle to Resurgence*.

20   Later air chief marshal, the fourteenth chief of the IAF.

21   Air Chief Marshal Tipnis in Kumar, *The Duels of the Himalayan Eagle*, p. 130.

22   Kumar, *The Duels of the Himalayan Eagle*, p. 154. Also in interview with A. V. M. Dahiya, Gurgaon, 4 May 2019.

23   Mohan and Chopra, *The India-Pakistan Air War of 1965*, p. 127.

CHAPTER 14: THE PUNJAB PLAINS: 11 CORPS (PART II)

1   Harbakhsh Singh, *In the Line of Duty*, available here: http://www.indiandefencereview.com/ spotlights/the-1965-war-with-pakistan-i/4/

2   Harbakhsh Singh, *War Despatches*, p. 92.

3   Lehl, *Missed Opportunities*, p. 212.

4   Singh and Shergill, *The Monsoon War*, p. 153.

5   War Diary of Major General Mohinder Singh as quoted in Singh and Shergill, *The Monsoon* War, p. 153.

6   Singh and Shergill, *The Monsoon* War, p. 204.

7   Interview with Major (later Major General) D. K. Mehta.

8   Ibid.

9   Musa, *My Version*, p. 54.

10   Interview with Major General D. K. Mehta.

11   Harbakhsh Singh, *War Despatches*.

12   Singh and Shergill, *The Monsoon War*, p. 203.

13   Harbakhsh Singh, *War Despatches*, pp. 101–02

14   Ibid., p. 103.

15   Singh and Shergill, *The Monsoon War*, p. 260.

16   Brigadier Khutub A. Hai, *The Patton Wreckers, An Account of the Actions of 3 Cavalry in the Battle of Asal Uttar—September 1965*, New Delhi: Times Group Books, 2015, p. 35.

17   Daffadar Wasan Singh quoted in Hai, *The Patton Wreckers*, p. 36.

18   Acting Lance Daffadar quoted in Ibid.

19   Hai, *The Patton Wreckers*, p. 36.

20   Musa, *My Version*.

CHAPTER 15: RETRIBUTION: IAF ON 7 SEPT

1   He was later air chief marshal, the thirteenth air chief.

2   Mohan and Chopra, *The India-Pakistan Air War of 1965*, p. 163.

3   Available at: http://www.defencejournal.com/2002/june/hero.htm

4   Mohan and Chopra, *The India-Pakistan Air War of 1965*, p. 179.

5   Air Marshal G. C. S. Rajwar in Kumar, *The Duels of the Himalayan Eagle*, p. 258.

6   Air Marshal Philip Rajkumar's personal notes.

7   KIA (killed in action) in 1971.

8   Kumar, *The Duels of the Himalayan Eagle*, p. 145.

9   Interview with Philip Rajkumar.

10   Ibid.

11   Mohan and Chopra, *The India-Pakistan Air War of 1965*, p. 148.

CHAPTER 16: THE SIALKOT SECTOR: 1 CORPS (PART I)

1   Lehl, *Missed Opportunities*, p. 248.

2   Ibid., p. 247.

3   Ibid., p. 251.

4   Musa, *My Version*, p. 65.

5   Ibid., p. 66.
6   Lehl, *Missed Opportunities*, p. 256.
7   Ahmed in an *Illusion of Victory* says he was not a havildar but a Sepoy Fida Hussain.
8   Major N. S. Cheema, *History of 17 Horse during the 1965 Indo-Pak War* (unpublished).
9   Ahmed, *Illusion of Victory*.
10 Lehl, Missed Opportunities, p. 263.
11 Singh and Shergill, *The Monsoon War*, p. 303.
12 From the Princely state of Jamnagar, Major Sheikh had been the ADC to General Chaudhuri.
13 Singh and Shergill, *The Monsoon War*, p. 308.
14 Major Mohammad Ali Raas Sheikh died shortly thereafter. He was posthumously awarded the Vir Chakra.
15 Singh and Shergill, *The Monsoon War*, p. 308.
16 Ibid., p. 310.
17 Dhaliwal was awarded the Vir Chakra for his fortitude and courage in rescuing his crew from a burning tank.
18 *Indomitable Irregulars, Hodson's Horse (4th Horse)*, as narrated by Second Lieutenant Sodhi.
19 *History of the 17th Poona Horse*, Poona Horse Regimental Officers Association.
20 Harbakhsh Singh, *War Despatches*, p. 143.
21 Ibid.
22 Harbakhsh Singh, *War Despatches*.

CHAPTER 17: A GRAVEYARD FOR PATTONS: 11 CORPS (PART III)

1   Lehl, *Missed Opportunities*, p. 268.
2   Gul Hassan Khan, *Memoirs of Lt. Gen. Gul Hassan Khan*, Karachi: OUP, 1993, p. 204.
3   Singh and Shergill, *The Monsoon War*, p. 172.
4   Harbakhsh Singh, *War Despatches*.
5   Singh and Shergill, *The Monsoon War*.
6   Hayde, *Battle of Dograi*, p. 114.
7   Hai in conversation with the author.
8   Ibid., p. 118.
8   Pradhan, *Debacle to Resurgence*, p. 256.
9   In a meeting with the author in Mumbai.
10 Pradhan, *Debacle to Resurgence*, p. 261; According to Captain Amarinder Singh, the call from General Chaudhuri came at 0230 hours in the morning of 10 September.
11 Hai, *The Patton Wreckers*, pp. 46–47.
12 Conversation with Brigadier Vijay Kumar Vaid, 13 April 2020.
13 Hai, *The Patton Wreckers*, pp. 46–48.
14 Ibid.
15 Ibid.
16 Hayde, *Battle of Dograi*.
17 Ibid., p. 122.
18 Ibid., p. 123.
19 Ibid., p. 124.
20 Major Sam Doctor was my father's course mate. In 1976, his wife, Beroze, visited us in Wellington. All that had been recovered of Sam from the charred tank later was his belt.
21 Hayde, *Battle of Dograi*, p. 128.
22 As narrated by Hayde, in conversation with the author.
23 Hayde, *Battle of Dograi*, p. 132.
24 Later KIA.

25   Colonel Surinder Sagar Duggal, 'The Capture of Barki', *Salute Magazine*, 30 October 2015.
26   Ibid.
27   Singh and Shergill, *The Monsoon War*, p. 177.
28   Pradhan, *Debacle to Resurgence*, p. 261.

CHAPTER 18: A BUFFALO IN A WALLOW: 1 CORPS (PART II)
1   Singh and Shergill, *The Monsoon War*, pp. 321–22.
2   Later general, the thirteenth army chief.
3   Ibid., p. 328.
4   Later general, he became the sixth chief of the Indian Army.
5   Lehl, *Missed Opportunities*, p. 266.
6   Later lieutenant general and governor of Assam
7   Singh and Shergill, *The Monsoon War*, p. 345.
8   Lehl, *Missed Opportunities*, p. 266.
9   Joined the BSF after the war; retired as a commandant.
10   Singh and Shergill, *The Monsoon War*, p. 345.
11   Later lieutenant general; governor of East Pakistan, then ambassador to the United States and finally foreign minister.
12   Lehl, *Missed Opportunities,* p. 312.
13   Singh and Shergill, *The Monsoon War*, p. 349.
14   Brigadier (Dr) S. P. Sinha, *History of the 9th Gorkha Rifles*, p. 158.
15   Singh and Shergill, *The Monsoon War*, p. 349.
16   Singh and Shergill, *The Monsoon War*, p. 354.
17   Chakravorty, *History of the Indo-Pak Conflict, 1965*, p. 207.
18   Singh and Shergill, *The Monsoon War*, pp. 354–58.
19   Lehl, *Missed Opportunities*, p. 314.
20   Harbakhsh Singh, *War Despatches*, p. 147.
21   Lieutenant General Mahmud Ahmed quoted in Singh and Shergill, *The Monsoon War*, p. 360.
22   Chakravorty, *History of the Indo-Pak Conflict*, p. 210.
23   Harbakhsh Singh, *War Despatches*, p. 149.
24   Lehl, *Missed Opportunities*, p. 318.
25   Singh and Shergill, *The Monsoon War*, p. 361.
26   Was killed the next day at Kalarwanda posthumously awarded the Vir Chakra.

CHAPTER 19: A VICTORY BUNGLED: 11 CORPS
(PART IV) 11 TO 13 SEPTEMBER
1   Hai, *The Patton Wreckers*, p. 59.
2   Lehl, *Missed Opportunities*, p. 296.
3   Brigadier Khutub Hai in conversation with the author, June 2018.
4   Hai, *The Patton Wreckers*, p. 63.
5   Lehl, *Missed Opportunities*, pp. 296–97.
6   Harbakhsh Singh, *War Despatches*, p. 109.
7   Ibid.
8   Singh and Shergill, *The Monsoon War*, p. 233.
9   Ibid.
10   Hai, *The Patton Wreckers*, p. 69.
11   Lehl, *Missed Opportunities*, pp. 302–303.
12   Ibid.
13   Ibid., p. 302.

14   Singh and Shergill, *The Monsoon War*, p. 233.
15   Harbakhsh Singh, *War Despatches*, p. 149.
16   Ibid., p. 116.
17   Pradhan, *Debacle to Resurgence*, p. 264.
18   Anant Singh as the second in command of 1 Sikh had been captured at Se La by the Chinese in November 1962. As luck would have it, Lieutenant General Harbakhsh Singh had been the 4 Corps commander for the five crucial days when Se La was chosen as the next line of defence after the fall of Tawang.

CHAPTER 20: THE SLUGFEST AT CHAWINDA: RACHNA DOAB (14–23 SEPTEMBER)

1   See p. 149.
2   Pradhan, in conversation with the author, Bombay, 20 and 21 June 2016.
3   Pradhan, *Debacle to Resurgence*, p. 304.
4   Lehl, *Missed Opportunities*, pp. 326–27.
5   Harbakhsh Singh, *War Despatches*.
6   Lehl, *Missed Opportunities*, pp. 325–26.
7   He had also played a key role in the Battle of Chhamb. Was decorated with the Hilal-i-Jur'at for his role in Chawinda.
8   Lehl, *Missed Opportunities*, p. 326.
9   Major General Yashwant Deva, *Saga of Grit and Cold Courage: Tribute to the Fighters of 35 Infantry Brigade in 1965 War: First Hand Account*, New Delhi:Vij Books, 2015, p. 22.
10   Singh and Shergill, *The Monsoon War*, p. 381.
11   Lieutenant Colonel Jhirad was Mentioned in Despatches.
12   Advance dressing station, casualties are brought here first.
13   Brigadier J. S. Bhullar's account of the Battle of Chawinda.
14   Ibid.
15   Ibid.
16   Ibid.
17   Lieutenant Colonel Adi Tarapore was awarded the PVC.
18   As per HQ 1 Armoured Brigade: 'As both Chawinda and Badiana had been isolated and cut off from three sides and as both had also been invested from the rear by 1 Armoured Brigade, particularly on 16 and 17 September, it was possible to capture easily both these objectives by an infantry assault. These objectives were thinly held by enemy infantry, possibly not more than two companies in each place. The armoured brigade was precluded from assaulting these objectives, as both were built up areas.'
19   Deva, *Saga of Grit*, p. 22.
20   Brigadier J. S. Bhullar's account of the Battle of Chawinda.
21   Ibid.
22   Major Abdul Rafey Khan was awarded the VrC.
23   Shergill says the meeting that was held at Maharajke where 6 Mountain Division was given the task of assaulting Chawinda was held on 17 September and not on the previous day.
24   Harbakhsh Singh, *War Despatches*, p. 154
25   Singh and Shergill, *The Monsoon War*, p. 389.
26   The division had been commanded by Field Marshal Manekshaw and later by my father, Major General Ashok Kalyan Verma.
27   Lieutenant Ravinder Singh Samiyal was awarded a VrC for this action.
28   Lieutenant General H. C. Gangoli, in telephonic conversation with the author, August 2019.
29   Ibid.

30   He was the head of the notorious Pakistani ISI between 1993 and 1995.

31   *Indomitable Irregulars, Hodson's Horse (4th Horse)*, 1922–2010.

32   Personal notes of Major General Yashwant Deva.

33   His son, General Vijay Kumar Singh, would be commissioned into 2 Rajput and go on to become the COAS.

34   Personal notes of Major General Yashwant Deva.

35   Personal notes of Lieutenant General R. D. Hira.

36   Ibid.

37   Ibid.

38   Ibid.

39   Harbakhsh Singh, *War Despatches*.

40   Personal notes of Major General Yashwant Deva.

CHAPTER 21: 11 CORPS' CURTAIN CALL

1   Palit, *War in High Himalaya*, p. 115.

2   Singh and Shergill, *The Monsoon War*, pp. 239–40.

3   Hayde, *Battle of Dograi*, p. 141.

4   Ibid.

5   Ibid.

6   Conversation with Major Brijendra Singh, August 2019.

7   Hayde, *Battle of Dograi*, p. 146.

8   He was awarded a VrC.

9   He was posthumously awarded a VrC.

10   Chakravarty, *History of the Indo-Pak Conflict*

11   Major Zaki was awarded a VrC. He was the author's neighbour in DSSC, Wellington. He was from the RIMC and his father was a brigadier in the nizam of Hyderabad's cavalry.

12   D. K. Mehta in conversation with author, 15 Aug 2018

13   Harbakhsh Singh, *War Despatches*, p. 121.

14   Hayde, *Battle of Dograi*, p. 148.

15   Ibid., p. 166.

16   He later joined the BSF.

17   From where they can fire in support.

18   Hayde, *Battle of Dograi*

19   Ibid., pp. 186–87.

20   Ibid., p. 187.

21   Subedar Phale Ram was awarded a VrC.

22   Major Asa Ram Tyagi was awarded a posthumous MVC.

23   Captain Kapil Singh Thapa was awarded a posthumous MVC.

24   Captain Hardial Singh Rai was awarded a Sena Medal.

25   Hayde, *Battle of Dograi*, pp. 205–206.

26   Was awarded the SJ. 16 Punjab was given the nom de guerre Ghazian-e-Dograi.

27   Ahmad, *Living up to Heritage*

28   Hayde, *Battle of Dograi*, p. 218.

29   Ibid., p. 222.

30   Hayde, in conversation with the author.

CHAPTER 22: THE BARMER SECTOR: OPERATION BARREL

1   For more on this, see Verma, *1962: The War That Wasn't*.

2   A 13 Grenadiers camel patrol was despatched immediately to see what was happening on this axis,

as the RAC post at Panchla was still under the operational control of the Delhi and Rajasthan Area HQ. The column would report back two days later saying that a platoon of Indus Rangers and some armed civilians were occupying Panchla, in what was obviously a spoiling action to divert attention from the Munabao area.

3   He was later major and then joined the IAS; in conversation with the author, June 2021.

4   Major M. G. Devasahayam in conversation with the author, June 2021.

5   Another victim of the debacle at Naupatia and Dali was Brigadier H. N. Sumanwar, the commander of 85 Infantry Brigade. As noted, Rawlley, a personal favourite of General Chaudhuri, was the one responsible for this debacle.

CHAPTER 23: ACE IS HIGH: AIR BATTLE III

1   He was killed in a crash in 1966 after the war.

2   Singh and Shergill, *The Monsoon War*, p. 209.

3   Was promoted to air marshal after the war.

4   Sadruddin Mohammad Hossain, later air vice marshal; 5th chief of the Bangladesh Air Force.

5   Singh and Shergill, *The Monsoon War*, pp. 211–12.

6   Kumar in conversation with the author, 2020.

7   He served as the PAF's chief for seven years.

8   Bird Dogs often benefitted from this chivalry. Directing artillery fire against Indian ground positions, they were perhaps responsible for more casualties than the entire PAF put together.

9   Kumar, *The Duels of the Himalayan Eagle*, p. 203.

10 He was later in the Bangladesh Air Force.

11 Kumar, *The Duels of the Himalayan Eagle*, p. 222.

12 Flight Lieutenant Viney Kapila in conversation with author.

13 Kumar, *The Duels of the Himalayan Eagle*.

14 Ibid., p. 238.

15 Air Marshal Cariappa in conversation with the author, 5 October 2019.

EPILOGUE: THE AFTERMATH

1   Palit, *War in the High Himalaya*, p. 424.

2   Conversation with Mrs P. C. Lal, February 1992; she was the wife of Air Marshal P. C. Lal, who authored *My Years with the IAF*. Mrs Lal completed the manuscript after the air chief's demise.

3   Palit, *War in the High Himalaya*.

4   In conversation with the author, Bombay, 20 and 21 June 2016.

5   Interview with Rajkumar, 22 July 2021.

6   Palit, *War in the High Himalaya*, p. 427.

7   Singh and Shergill, *The Monsoon* War, p. 87.

8   Palit, *War in the High Himalaya*, p. 428.

9   Palit, *War in High Himalaya*, pp. 428–429.

10 Pradhan, in conversation with the author, Bombay, 20 and 21 June 2016.

BIBLIOGRAPHY

Agarwal, Lieutenant Colonel Rohit, *Brave Men of War, Tales of Valour 1965*, Bloomsbury, New Delhi 2015.

Ahmad, Lieutenant General Mahmud, *Illusions of Victory: A Military History of the Indo-Pak War 1965*, Lexicon Publishers, Karachi 2002.

Ahmad, Lieutenant Colonel Mustasad, *Living up to Hertitage, The Rajputs 1947 to 1970*, Lancer Publishers, New Delhi 1997.

Ahmed, Brigadier Gulzar, *Pakistan Meets India's Challenge*, Al Mukhtar Publishers, Rawalpindi 1967.

Bajwa, Farooq, *From Kutch to Tashkent: The Indo-Pakistan War of 1965*, Hurst & Company, London 2013.

Cheema, Brigadier Amar, *The Crimson Chinar: The Kashmir Conflict: A Politico Military Perspective*, Lancer Publishers, New Delhi, 2015.

Cloughley, Brian, *A History of the Pakistan Army, Wars and Insurrections*, Oxford University Press, Karachi 1999.

Hai, Brigadier Khutub A., *The Patton Wreckers, An Account of the Actions of 3 Cavalry in the Battle of Asal Uttar – September 1965, Times Group Books*, New Delhi 2015.

Hayde, Brigadier Desmond E., *The Battle of Dograi*, Natraj Publishers, Dehradun, 1984.

Jagan Mohan, P.V. S & Chopra, Samir, *The India-Pakistan Air War of 1965*, Manohar, New Delhi 2005.

Khan, Field Marshal Mohammad Ayub, *Friends Not Masters*, Oxford University Press, London 1967.

Kumar, Air Marshal Bharat, *The Duels of the Himalayan Eagle, The First Indo-Pak Air War (1-22 September 1965)*, IMR Media Pvt Ltd, Gurgaon 2015.

Lamb, Alastair, *Incomplete Partition: The Genesis of the Kashmir Dispute 1947-1948*, Oxford University Press, Karachi 1997.

Lehl, Major General Lachhman Singh, *Missed Opportunities: Indo-Pak War 1965*, Natraj Publishers, Dehradun 1997.

Michigan, Major General AHE, *Right of the Line: The Grenadiers – A Historical Record*, Grenadiers Association 1995.

Mitha, Major General Aboobaker Osman, *Unlikely Beginnings: A Soldier's Life*, Oxford University, Karachi 2003.

Musa, General Mohammad, *Jawan to General: Recollections of a Pakistani Soldier*, ABC Publishing House, New Delhi 1985.

_____, *My Version: India-Pakistan War 1965*, Wajidalis Limited, Lahore 1983.

Nawaz, Shauja, *Crossed Swords: Pakistan, It's Army and Wars Within*, Oxford University Press, Karachi 2009.

Palit, Major General D. K., *War in High Himalaya: The Indian Army in Crisis, 1962*, C. Hurst & Co. Publishers, London 1991.

Pradhan, R. D, *Debacle to Resurgence, Y. B. Chavan, Defence Minister (1962-66)*, Atlantic, New Delhi 2013.

Praval, Major K. C., *Indian Army After Independence*, Lancer International, New Delhi 1990.

Riza, Major General Shaukat, *The Pakistan Army War 1965*, Services Book Club, Lahore 1984.

Sharma, Lieutenant Colonel Gautam, *History of the Jat Regiment, Volume III*, Allied Publishers Pvt Ltd., Bareilly, 1979.

Sharma, Surya Prakash, *Territorial Acquisition, Disputes, and International Law*, Martinus Nijhoff Publishers, The Hague 1997.

Singh, Captain Amarinder & Shergill, Lieutenant General Tajindar, *The Monsoon War — Young Officers Reminisce: 1965 India-Pakistan War*, Roli Books, 2015.

Singh, Brigadier Jasbir, *Combat Diary: An Illustrated history of operations conducted by 4th Battalion, The Kumaon Regiment — 1788 to 1974*, Lancer Publishers, New Delhi 2010.

Singh, Major General Joginder, *Behind the Scenes, An Analysis of India's Military Operations 1947-1965*, Lancer, New Delhi 1993.

Singh, Pushpindar, Rikhye, Ravi & Steinemann, Peter, *Fiza'ya: Psyche of the Pakistan Air Force*, The Society for Aerospace Studies, New Delhi 1991.

Singh, Rear Admiral Satyindra, *Blueprint to Bluewater, The Indian Navy 1951-65*, Naval HQ, New Delhi.

Singh, Major General V. K., *Leadership in the Indian Army, Biographies of Twelve Soldiers*, Sage Publications, New Delhi 2005.

Vas, Lieutenant General E. A., *Without Baggage: A personal account of the Jammu & Kashmir Operations 1947-49*, Natraj Publishers, Dehradun 1987.

Ziegler, Philip, *Mountbatten: The Official Biography*, Guild Publishing, London 1985.

INDEX

- the geography & topography of the war
- the opposing commanders on both sides
- identifies the brigades & divisions in each sector

- the background: India - China war
- US arming of Pakistan + China's support of Pakistan

- key battles; description of hand to hand fighting

- includes photos of key pol. & mil. leaders

- includes maps explaining operations

- friendly fire incidents - air attacks against India's own ground force by Vampires (planes)

- tank battles
- air combat dog fights

- Indiv. air squadrons
- tank battalions